The Handbook of Gestalt Therapy

COMMENTARY

"This handbook answers many important questions about Gestalt therapy. The historical and cultural background of the movement is included as well as a detailed theoretical statement, various ways to use the Gestalt process, and a comparative view of different therapists' work."

Cindy Sheldon
Co-founder, Gestalt Institute of San Francisco

"The publication of this handbook is an important event for a body of knowledge because it indicates a new maturity. Thus the appearance of *The Handbook of Gestalt Therapy* is to be greeted with enthusiasm by those who have been interested in and followed the development of the subject. This handbook should be especially useful to those seeking to learn about Gestalt therapy for the first time."

Arnold R. Beisser, M.D.
Los Angeles, CA

"The whole Gestalt movement has suffered because of the tendency on the part of many of its leading developers and practitioners to publish their thoughts and experiences. In view of this, a book which offered a coherent explanation of the basic principles of Gestalt would be most welcome. This handbook does that and much, much more."

Mental Health

The
Handbook of
Gestalt
Therapy

Chris Hatcher and Philip Himelstein
Editors

New York • Jason Aronson • London

New Printing 1983

ISBN: 0-87668-683-8

Library of Congress Catalog Number: 84-45112

Manufactured in the United States of America.

About The Editors

Chris Hatcher received his Ph.D. in clinical psychology from the University of Georgia. His principal area of professional activity has been applied clinical/community teaching to psychologists, psychiatrists, and social workers. Currently, Dr. Hatcher is Assistant Clinical Professor of Psychology, Langley Porter Institute, University of California, San Francisco. Previously, he was Director of Intern Training, Psychology Service, Beaumont Medical Center, El Paso, Texas, held Adjunct Professor appointments in both the Department of Psychology and the Department of Educational Psychology and Guidance, University of Texas at El Paso. He trained in Gestalt Therapy with John Enright and Larry Bloomberg in San Francisco, and is particularly interested in Gestalt applications to families and other living groups. He is the author of numerous professional papers, journal articles, and mental health training films, and is a training consultant to family and child agencies in the United States and Mexico.

Philip Himelstein earned his Ph.D. in clinical psychology at the University of Texas in 1955. He has worked in a variety of clinical settings and has taught at the University of Arkansas, New Mexico State University, and the University of Texas at El Paso. He attended the winter residential training program of the Gestalt Therapy Institute of Los Angeles and has conducted numerous Gestalt Therapy workshops. He has the Diplomate in Clinical Psychology from the American Board of Professional Psychology and is the author of more than thirty articles and chapters in professional journals and books.

Introduction

Contemporary psychotherapists are moving toward greater emphasis on emotional experience and on body awareness. At the same time, there is a deemphasis of historical material as the significant item to be sought after in therapeutic sessions. One of the major therapies in this contemporary mold is Gestalt Therapy. Known only to relatively few individuals two decades ago, it is now well established both as a major affiliation of psychotherapists and as a style of personal growth. Gestalt-oriented ideas and techniques have found wide acceptance, not only among therapists, but also with many others seeking greater awareness of their emotions and behavior.

Unlike many other psychotherapists (psychoanalytic, client-centered, rational emotive, and so on), the founder of the movement, Fritz Perls, did not present a fully developed theory and therapeutic method. Most of Perls' ideas are now known to us as the result of transcripts of recordings of his demonstrations made to his followers. One disadvantage of this source of material is that it does not reflect the nonverbal cues and other more subtle factors in the speaker's style. Further, the speaker may alter his demonstration in a way that he might not if committing his thoughts to writing. In any event, Perls' informal remarks have become his legacy to his followers—to be accepted verbatim by some, and to be discussed and modified by others. Even Perls' books have been more of an outline of an area of exploration.

At least in part due to these factors, new developments and growth in Gestalt Therapy have continued at a rapid pace. Unfortunately, with few exceptions, Gestalt therapists have not appeared to be concerned with publishing their new developments and ideas. Much of the exciting and illuminating material on Gestalt Therapy has remained unpublished, circulated by hand as mimeographed handouts at workshops or conventions, or as taped demonstrations. Other significant work has reached the printed stage, but received only limited, local distribution. An important exception to the above trend was the publication of the now classic *Gestalt Therapy Now* by Fagan and Shepherd (1970). The popularity of this book has been dramatic evidence of the demand for Gestalt Therapy material.

The present volume was designed by the editors in response to numerous requests by colleagues, students, and others for an up-to-date examination of the movement of Gestalt Therapy. The goal has been to combine outstanding original contributions with the very best of previously published material which received limited distribution. While the editors believe that Gestalt Therapy can only be "learned" by experiencing it as a participant, we do feel that there is value in having available under one cover the current status of Gestalt theory, techniques, and resources so that it does not become a mysterious and esoteric approach understood only by a limited number.

There are four major sections within this volume: The Contributions of Frederick S. Perls, Contemporary Theory, Techniques, and Perspectives and Resources. Each section is designed to contain both introductory material and, more significantly, a broad perspective on each topic area.

Our first part, the Contributions of Frederick S. Perls, consists of selections from three of Fritz's works. The first selection is drawn from *Gestalt Therapy Verbatim* (Perls, 1969), which was constructed from tape recordings made during Perls' workshops at Esalen Institute, California, and printed with little or no editing. For the new reader, it provides Perls' best introduction to his theories of human behavior change. The second selection is an invitation to experiment with Gestalt exercises on different states of awareness and perception. This material is from an early work, *Gestalt Therapy: Excitement and Growth in the Human Personality*, which Perls coauthored with Ralph E. Hefferline and Paul Goodman. The reader who performs these self-experiments as he proceeds will gain the most from this chapter. But what of Perls, the man? Our third chapter in this section is designed to provide a glimpse of exactly that. It is drawn from *In and Out of the Garbage Pail* (Perls, 1964), a partly autobiographical book written in a "stream of consciousness" style. In this selection, Perls writes Gestalt, rather than writing about Gestalt.

The contemporary theory part opens with remarkably clear, lucid, reviews of the basic foundations and principles of Gestalt Therapy by Gary Yontef, and by James Simkin. These provide the reader with a more concise and integrated theoretical position than is, perhaps, available in the original Perls material. This is followed by Jerry Kogan's fascinating analysis of the European, Jewish, and American origins of Gestalt Therapy. Kogan examines areas which he feels influenced Perls and his work, making a case for their inclusion in any examination of Gestalt Therapy. This section is completed with a personal view of future theoretical developments in "Gestalt Therapy and Beyond," by Eric Marcus.

A major section of the text is devoted to techniques, beginning with "The Ground Rules of Gestalt Therapy," by Jerry Greenwald. "Ground rules" are defined as an invitation to the person to accept a certain attitude in working with the therapist. While recognizing that there are no musts or shoulds in Gestalt Therapy, Greenwald accepts that there are some patterns which can indeed be viewed as ground rules.

Perhaps no one has written as definitively about Gestalt techniques as Claudio Naranjo. In "Expressive Techniques," Naranjo skillfully weaves dreams, illustrations of patient work, and comment into meaningful reading for all students of Gestalt Therapy.

Eric Manus, Ed Hackerson, and Rohe Eshbaugh then follow with the difficult task of providing for review verbatim examples of their therapeutic work, accompanied by their own observations and feelings on the events that occurred during the session.

Many individuals have failed to say goodbye and finish a relationship that terminated in death, divorce, ending a love affair, or in some other way. In "Saying Goodbye in Gestalt Therapy," Stephan Tobin presents techniques for dealing with this hanging-on reaction which inhibits the emotions triggered by the loss and attempts to keep the missing person present in fantasy.

Gestalt Therapy has sometimes been characterized as dealing with intrapersonal events, rather than interpersonal events. Within this framework, "Let the Little Child Talk," by Ben Finney, demonstrates a technique of talking directly to the individual's inner child, the part of the personality which was developed in childhood and continues to influence the adult's behavior and feelings. Such a procedure provides a vehicle for the inner child to express important feelings and to recall "forgotten" events and attitudes of childhood.

"Say It Again" by Ben Finney is a deceptively simply procedure involving sentence repetition. Finney sees intellectual abstractions and verbal complexity as maneuvers to avoid feelings which are best expressed in direct, short, and childlike phrases. Repetition forces simplicity of language structure and blocks one of the ways of keeping an emotional distance from sensitive feelings. Liberal excerpts from therapy assist the reader in understanding his approach.

John Enright has found "You're projecting!" to be a frequent comment in therapy and encounter groups. In "Thou Art That," Enright describes a method of harnessing this basic process, instead of wasting energy opposing or criticizing it. The individual is encouraged to pick out an object in the room and identify with it, making statements as though he were the object. As might be expected, the individual projects his own characteristics upon the selected object, thereby providing important material for awareness and growth.

Form, figure, pattern, structure, and configuration are all possible English translations of the German word *Gestalt*. Janie Rhyne finds this to be the first of many shared areas between the art experience and Gestalt philosophy. Her "Gestalt Approach to Experience, Art, and Art Therapy" shows the way we perceive visually in the art process to be directly related to how we think and feel. The different uses of lines, shapes, colors, structure, and so on provide a unique pathway to self-awareness.

Dreams have always held a certain fascination for psychotherapists, and the student of Gestalt Therapy and process is no exception. Gestalt work, however, encourages the active exploration of dream-fantasy experience. Jack Downing presents one such study in "The Gallant State Trooper" and augments this example with his own feelings and reactions as a therapist.

Recently, the idea that a negative effect may result from an encounter or workshop has been receiving more discussion. Yet there has been little identification of whatever it is that characterizes positive or negative process in the group. Gestalt therapist Jerry Greenwald addresses this in "The Art of Emotional Nourishment: Nourishing and Toxic Encounter Groups." The reader will be particularly interested in Greenwald's perception of leaders, participants, anger, manipulations, catharsis, and therapeutic responsibility.

Muriel Schiffman presents a challenging concept in "Techniques of Gestalt Self-Therapy," which has the individual do all the work himself; he is completely responsible for getting the most out of the experience. Three procedures, accompanied by examples, are dealt with: exploring a known fantasy, playing out all the parts of a recurrent or disturbing behavior, and playing out an imaginary encounter with a person who has aroused an uncomfortable emotional reaction.

The late 1960s and the 1970s have brought a significantly increased awareness of the problems resulting from culturally defined role limitations placed upon women. In "Women in Therapy—A Gestalt Therapist's View," Miriam Polster describes a familiar picture: women who feel trapped in a cycle of activity and demand which keeps them busy but leaves them unsatisfied and unfulfilled. This is followed by an analysis of the ways in which a woman may avoid awareness of this conflict, and by Miriam Polster's approach through Gestalt Therapy to more direct self-confrontation and growth.

Stan Herman has been a pioneer in the application of Gestalt principles to organizational development. In "A Gestalt Orientation to Organization Development," this approach is differentiated from others in its emphasis on developing self-supports for individuals, rather than environmental (team or group) supports. Herman, drawing upon extensive field experience, believes that the most effective manager (and employee) is one who can experience and be what he is now, not one who tries to conform to a prescribed model of management. This position is developed more fully for the reader in "The Shadow of Organization Development." In this chapter, Herman views the shadow as those aspects of the organizational process which are not yet accepted or integrated. The act of denying or disowning this ties up important energy sources and restricts the effectiveness of organizational activity. This material will be of special interest to individuals who have wished to go beyond the therapy setting and explore Gestalt applications to living-working groups.

In continuing our examination of the integration of Gestalt with other therapies. Allen Darbonne contributes an original work on the blending of Gestalt, bioenergetics, and rolfing, and Bob Goulding discusses the use of Gestalt Therapy and Transactional Analysis in working through different types of impasses.

Although the Gestalt process involves both verbal and physical feedback systems, therapists have relied primarily upon the individual's own phenomenological report. "Biofeedback and Gestalt Therapy," by Chris Hatcher, Marjorie Toomim, and Hershel Toomim, first discusses the additional role of feedback that is physiological in report, and then presents clinical advances in the use of biofeedback in Gestalt Therapy.

Joen Fagan is a major figure in Gestalt Therapy training. Her two offerings, "Critical Incidents in the Empty Chair" and "Three Sessions with Iris," will be quickly recognized by the advanced reader as a skilled and experienced Gestalt teacher at work.

The perspectives and resources section opens with Irma Lee Shepherd's "Limitations and Cautions in the Gestalt Approach," a rare and candid assessment of a topic which any therapy handbook must address. Next, Jerry Kogan provides personal interviews with James Simkin and John Enright. In a wide-ranging format, first-generation Gestalt therapists Simkin and Enright comment on the movement itself, their personal experiences, and their view of the field in the future. This is followed by a candid presentation by Stephen A. Appelbaum entitled "The Psychoanalyst Looks at Gestalt Therapy." Appelbaum successfully avoids becoming wrapped up in the caricatures of the uptight, rigid, materialistic psychoanalyst and the sloppy, childlike, fuzzy-minded Gestalt therapist. Instead, he examines each technique's approach to interpretation, determinism, the here and now, the body change, resistance, and several other major areas. While all readers may not find themselves in perfect agreement with Dr. Appelbaum's conclusions, they are certain to be stimulated and challenged by his work. And finally, for the individual who wishes to further explore the growing world of Gestalt therapy, "Gestalt Therapy Resources" by Jerry Kogan and Philip Himelstein offers the most comprehensive available listing of films, tapes, books, articles, and training institutes.

Contents

Part III:
TECHNIQUES

Part IV:
PERSPECTIVES AND RESOURCES

The
Handbook of
Gestalt
Therapy

Part I

THE CONTRIBUTIONS
OF
FREDERICK S. PERLS

CHAPTER 1

GESTALT THERAPY VERBATIM: INTRODUCTION

FREDERICK S. PERLS, M.D., Ph.D.

Frederick S. Perls was the originator of Gestalt Therapy. He was awarded the M.D. from Frederick Wilhelm University in Berlin, Germany, in 1921. Perls' psychoanalytic training took place at the Psychoanalytic Institutes of Berlin, Vienna, and Frankfurt. He practiced in Amsterdam and South Africa before coming to the United States in 1946. From 1946 until 1970, while developing Gestalt Therapy, he worked in New York, Miami, Los Angeles, Cleveland, San Francisco, Esalen, and finally in Vancouver B.C. He died in 1970.

Reprinted from **Gestalt Therapy Verbatim**, pp. 5-76, by Frederick S. Perls © 1969, Real People Press.

1

I would like to start out with very simple ideas which, as always, are difficult to grasp because they are so simple. I would like to start out with the question of control. There are two kinds of control: One is the control that comes from outside—I am being controlled by others, by orders, by the environment, and so on—and the other is the control that is built in, in every organism—my own nature.

What is an organism? We call an organism any living being, any living being that has organs, has an organization, that is self-regulating within itself. An organism is not independent from its environment. Every organism needs an environment to exchange essential substances, and so on. We need the physical environment to exchange air, food, etc.; we need the social environment to exchange friendship, love, anger. But within the organism there is a system of unbelievable subtlety—every cell of the millions of cells which we *are*, has built-in messages that it sends to the total organism, and the total organism then takes care of the needs of the cells and whatever must be done for different parts of the organism.

Now, what is first to be considered is that the organism always works as a whole. We *have* not a liver or a heart. We *are* liver and heart and brain and so on, and even this is wrong. We are not a summation of parts, but a *coordination*—a very subtle coordination of all these different bits that go into the making of the organism. The old philosophy always thought that the world consisted of the sum of particles. You know yourself it's not true. We consist originally out of one cell. This cell differentiates into several cells, and they differentiate into other organs that have special functions which are diversified and yet needed for each other.

So we come to the definition of health. Health is an appropriate balance of the coordination of all of what we *are*. You notice that I emphasized a few times the word *are*, because the very moment we say we *have* an organism or we *have* the body, we introduce a split —as if there's an *I* that is in possession of the body or the organism. We *are* a body, we *are* somebody—"I *am* somebody," "I *am* no-body." So it's the question of *being* rather than *having*. This is why we call our approach the existential approach: We exist *as* an organism—as an organism like a clam, like an animal, and so on, and we relate to the external world just like any other organism of nature. Kurt Goldstein first introduced the concept of the *organism as a whole*, and broke with the tradition in medicine that we *have* a liver, that we have a this/that, that all these organs can be studied separately. He got pretty close to the actuality, but the actuality is what is called the ecological aspect. You cannot even separate the organism and the environment. A plant taken out of its environment can't survive, and neither can a human being if you take him out of his environment, deprive him of oxygen and food, and so on. So we have to consider always the segment of the world in which we live as part of ourselves. Wherever we go, we take a kind of world with us.

Now if this is so, then we begin slowly to understand that people and organisms *can* communicate with each other, and we call it the *Mitwelt*—the common world which you have and the other person has. You speak a certain language, you have certain attitudes, certain behavior, and the two worlds somewhere overlap. And in this overlapping area, communication is possible. You notice if people meet, they begin the gambit of meetings—one says "How are you?" "It's nice weather," and the other answers something else. So they go into the search for the common interest, or the common world, where they have a possible interest, communication, and togetherness, where we get suddenly from the *I* and *You* to the *We*. So there is a new phenomenon coming, the *We* which is different from the I and You. The *We* doesn't exist, but consists out of I *and* You, is an everchanging boundary where two people meet. And when we meet there, then I change and you change, through the process of encountering each other, except—and we have to talk a lot about this—except if the two people have *character*. Once you have a *character*, you have developed a rigid system. Your behavior become petrified, predictable, and you lose your ability to cope freely with the world with all your resources. You are predetermined just to cope with events in one way, namely as your character prescribes it to be. So it seems a paradox when I say that the richest person, the most productive, creative person, is a person who has *no* character. In our society, we *demand* a person to have a character, and especially a *good* character, because then you are predictable, and you can be pigeonholed, and so on.

Now, let's talk a bit more about the relationship of the organism to its environment, and here we introduce the notion of the *ego boundary*. A boundary defines a thing. Now a thing has its boundaries, is defined by its boundaries in relation to the environment. In itself a thing occupies a certain amount of space. Maybe not much. Maybe it wants to be bigger, or wants to be smaller—maybe it's not satisfied with its size. We introduce now a new concept again, the wish to change based upon the phenomenon of dissatisfaction. Every time you want to change yourself, or you want to change the environment, the basis always is *dis*satisfaction.

The boundary between organism and environment is more or less experienced by us as what is inside the skin and what is outside the skin, but this is very loosely defined. For instance, the very moment we breathe, is the air that comes in still part of the outside world, or is it already our own? If we eat food, we ingest it, but can still vomit it up, so where is the place where the self begins, and the otherness of the environment ends? So the ego boundary is not a *fixed* thing. If it is fixed, then it again becomes character, or an armor, like in the turtle. The turtle has a very fixed boundary in this respect. Our skin is somewhat less fixed, and breathes, touches, and so on. The ego boundary is of great, great importance. The phenomenon of the ego boundary is very peculiar. Basically, we call the ego boundary the differentiation between the self and the otherness, and in Gestalt Therapy we write the self with a capital S, as if the self would be something precious, something extraordinarily valuable. They go at the discovery of the self like a treasure-digging. The self means nothing but this thing as it is defined by *otherness*. "I do it myself" means that nobody else is doing it, it is this organism that does it.

Now the two phenomena of the ego boundary are *identification* and *alienation*. I identify with my movement: I say that *I* move my arm. When I see *you* sit there in a certain posture, I don't say, "*I* sit there," I say, "*You* sit there." I differentiate between the experience here and the experience there, and this identification experience has several aspects. The *I* seems to be more precious than the otherness. If I identify with, let's say, my profession, then this identification may become so strong that if my profession is then taken away, I feel I don't exist any more, so I might just as well commit suicide. In 1929, you remember how many people committed suicide because they were so identified with their money that life wasn't worth living any more when they lost it.

We are easily identified with our families. If a member of our family is slighted, then we feel the same is done to us. You identify with your friends. The members of the 146th infantry regiment feel themselves to be better than the members of the 147th regiment, and the members of the 147th regiment feel themselves superior to the members of the 146th. So, inside the ego boundary, there is generally cohesion, love, cooperation; outside the ego boundary there is suspicion, strangeness, unfamiliarity.

Now this boundary can be very fluid, like nowadays in battles— the boundary stretches as far, let's say, as your air power goes. This is how far the security, familiarity, wholeness, extends. And there is the strangeness, the enemy who is outside the boundary, and whenever there is a boundary question, there is a conflict going on. If we take likeness for granted, then we wouldn't be aware of the existence of the boundary. If we take the unlikeness very much for granted, then we come to the problem of hostility, of rejection—pushing away. "Keep out of my boundaries," "Keep out of my house," "Keep out of my family," "Keep out of my thoughts." So you see already the polarity of attraction and rejection—of appetite and disgust. There is always a polarity going on, and outside is strangeness, and wrong. Inside is good, outside is bad. The own God is the right God. The other God is the strange God. My political conviction is sacred, is mine; the other political conviction is bad. If a state is at war, its own soldiers are angels, and the enemy are all devils. Our own soldiers take care of the poor families; the enemy rapes them. So the whole idea of good and bad, right and wrong, is always a matter of boundary, of which side of the fence I am on.

So I want to give you a couple of minutes now for time to digest, and to make comments, and see how far we have come. You have to let me in a bit into your private world, or you have to come out of your private world into that environment which includes this platform.

Question: When a person's in love, his own boundary expands to include the you, or the other, that was previously outside himself.

Fritz: Yah. The ego boundary becomes an us boundary: I and you are separate against the whole world and, in a moment of ecstasy of love, the world disappears.

Question: If two people are in love, do they accept—would they accept each other so completely that their ego boundaries would expand to include other persons completely, or would it just include the person they had contact with?

Fritz: Well, this is a very interesting, relevant question. And the misunderstanding of this leads to many tragedies and catastrophes. We don't usually love a *person*. That's very, very rare. We love a certain *property* in that person, which is either identical with our behavior or supplementing our behavior, usually something that is a supplement to us. We think we are in love with the total person, and actually we are disgusted with other aspects of this person. So when the other contacts come up, when this person behaves in a way that creates disgust in us, then again we don't say, "*This* of you is disgusting, though this other part is lovable." We say, "*You* are disgusting—get out of my life."

Question: But Fritz, doesn't this apply to an individual also? Do we include all of ourselves in our ego boundaries? Aren't there things in us that we refuse to include in our ego boundaries?

Fritz: Well, we are going to talk about that when we come to the *inner split*, the fragmentation of the personality. The very moment you say, "*I* accept something in myself," you split yourself up into *I* and *myself*. Right now, I am talking about more or less the total encounter of an organism, and I am not talking about pathology. Basically there are very few among us that are whole persons.

Question: How about the reverse situation, hate or intense anger? Does that then have a tendency to shrink ego boundaries so that a person's hate toward another person can absorb their whole life?

Fritz: No. Hate is a function of kicking somebody out of the boundary for something. The term we use in existential psychiatry is *alienation*, disowning. We disown a person, and if this person's existence constitutes a threat to us, we want to annihilate this person. But it is definitely an *ex*clusion from our boundary, from ourselves.

Question: Well, I understand that. What I'm trying to understand is what that kind of intense situation—intense involvement in that kind of situation—does in terms of ego boundaries. Does it tend to make them smaller, or make them more rigid?

Fritz: Well, definitely, it does make them more rigid. Let me postpone these questions until we come to talk about projections. This is a special case in pathology, the fact that in the last instance we only love ourselves and hate ourselves. Whether we find this loved or hated thing in ourselves or outside has to do with breaks in the boundary.

Question: Fritz, you mentioned the polarity of attraction and disgust, yet it's possible to feel both of these things toward the same person which, as far as I can understand it, creates a conflict.

Fritz: This is exactly what I am talking about. You are not attracted to a person; you are not disgusted with a person. If you look closer, you are attracted to a certain behavior or part of that person, and disgusted with a certain other behavior or part of that person, and if you find, by chance, both the beloved and the hated thing—we call it a thing, of course—in the same person, you're in a quandary. It is much easier to be disgusted with one person and to love another. At one time you find you hate this person and another time you love the person, but if both love and hate come together, then you get confused. This has a lot to do with the basic law that the gestalt is always so formed that only one figure, one item, can become foreground—that we can think, basically, of only one thing at a time, and as soon as two opposites or two different figures want to take charge of this organism, we get confused, we get split and fragmented.

I can already see where the whole trend of the question goes. You are already coming to the point where you begin to understand what happens is pathology. If some of our thoughts, feelings, are unacceptable to us, we want to disown them. *Me wanting* to kill you? So we disown the killing thought and say, "That's not me—that's a *compulsion*," or we remove the killing, or we repress and become blind to that. There are many of these kinds of ways to remain intact, but always only at the cost of disowning many, many valuable parts of ourselves. The fact that we live only on such a small percentage of our potential is due to the fact that we're not willing—or society or whatever you want to call it is not willing—to accept myself, yourself, as the organism which you are by birth, constitution, and so on. You do not allow yourself—or you are not allowed—to be totally yourself. So your ego boundary shrinks more and more. Your power, your energy, becomes smaller and smaller. Your ability to cope with the world becomes less and less—and more and more rigid, more and more allowed only to cope as your character, as your preconceived pattern, prescribes it.

Question: Is there some kind of a fluctuation in this ego boundary that might be determined by a cyclic rhythm? The way that a flower will open and close—open—close—

Fritz: Yah. *Very* much.

Question: Does the word *uptight* mean shrink?

Fritz: No. This means *compression.*

Question: What about the opposite in the drug experience, where the ego boundary—

Fritz: —Where you lose your ego boundary.

Question: Would this be an explosion in terms of your theory?

Fritz: Expansion, not explosion. Explosion is quite different. The ego boundary is a completely natural phenomenom. Now I give you some examples about the ego boundary, something we are more or less all concerned with. This boundary, this identification/alienation boundary, which I rather call the ego boundary, applies to every situation in life. Now let's assume you are in favor of the freedom movement, of acceptance of the Negro as a human being like yourself. So you identify with him. So where is the boundary? The boundary disappears between you and the Negro. But immediately a new boundary is created—now the enemy is not the Negro, but the non-freedom fighter; *they* are the bastards, the bad guys.

So you create a new boundary, and I believe there is no chance of ever living without a boundary—there is always, "I am on the right side of the fence, and you are on the wrong side," or *we* are, if you have the clique formation. You notice any society or any community will quickly form its own boundaries, cliques—the Millers are always better than the Meyers, and the Meyers are better than the Millers. And the closer the boundary defenses, the greater the chance of wars or hostility. You find wars always start on the boundary—boundary clashes. The Indians and the Chinese have a much greater chance of fighting each other than the Indians and the Finns. Because there is no boundary between the Indians and the Finns, except if now a new kind of boundary is created— let's say an ideological boundary. We are all Communists, we are right. We are all Free Enterprisers, we are right. So you are the bad guys—no, *you* are the bad guys. So we seldom look for the common denominator, what we have in common, but we look for where we are different, so that we can hate and kill each other.

Question: Do you think that it is possible to become so integrated that a person could become objective, and not become involved in anything?

Fritz: I personally believe that objectivity does not exist. The objectivity of science is also just a matter of mutual agreement. A certain number of persons observe the same phenomena and they speak about an objective criterion. Yet it was from the scientific side where the first proof of subjectivity came. This was from Einstein. Einstein realized that all the phenomena in the universe cannot possibly be objective, because the observer and the speed within its nervous system has to be included in the calculation of that phenomenon outside. If you have perspective, and can see a larger outlook, you seem to be more fair, objective, balanced. But even there, it's you as the subject who sees it. We have not much idea what the universe looks like. We have only a certain amount of organs—eyes, ears, touch, and the elongation of these organs—the telescope and electrical computers. But what do we know about other organisms, what kind of organs they have, what kind of world they have? We take for granted the elegance of the human being, that our world—how *we* see the universe—is the only right one.

Question: Fritz, let me go back to the ego boundary again because when you're experiencing yourself, when you're experiencing an expanded state, then the feeling of separation seems to disintegrate or melt. And at that point it seems that you are totally absorbed in the process of what's going on. At that point, it seems there are no ego boundaries at all, except a reflection of the process of what's going on. Now I don't understand that in relation to your concept of ego boundary.

Fritz: Yah. This is more or less the next theme I wanted to come to. There is a kind of integration—I know that's not quite correctly formulated—of the subjective and the objective. That is the word *awareness*. Awareness is always the subjective experience. I cannot possibly be aware of what you are aware of. The Zen idea of absolute awareness, in my opinion, is nonsense. Absolute awareness cannot possibly exist because as far as *I* know, awareness always has content. One is always aware of *something*. If I say I feel nothing, I'm at least aware of the *nothingness*, which if you examine it still further has a very positive character like numbness, or coldness, or a gap, and when you speak about the psychedelic experience, there is an awareness, but there is also the awareness of *something*.

So, let's now go a step further and look at the relationship of the world and the self. What makes us interested in the world? What is our need to realize that there is a world? How come I cannot function, cannot live just as a kind of autistic organism, completely self-contained? Now, a thing, like this ashtray, is not a type of relating organism. This ashtray needs very little to exist. First, temperature.

If you put this ashtray in a temperature of 4,000°, this is not an environment in which it will retain its identity. It needs a certain amount of gravity. If it would be subjected to a pressure of, let's say, 40,000 pounds, it would break into pieces. But we can, for practical purposes, say that this thing is self-contained. It doesn't need any exchange with the environment. It exists to be used by us as a receptacle of cigarettes, to be cleaned, to be sold, to be thrown away, to be used as a missile if you want to hurt somebody, and so on. But in itself it is not a living organism.

A living organism is an organism which consists of thousands and thousands of processes that require interchange with other media outside the boundary of the organism. There are processes here in the ashtray, too. There are electronic processes, atomic processes, but for our purpose, these processes are not visible, not relevant to its existence for us here. But in a living organism, the ego boundary has to be negotiated by us because there is something outside that is needed. There is food outside: I want this food; I want to make it mine, *like me*. So, I have to like this food. If I don't like it, if it is un-like me, I wouldn't touch it, I leave it outside the boundary. So something has to happen to get through the boundary and this is what we call *contact*. We touch, we get in contact, we stretch our boundary out to the thing in question. If we are rigid and can't move, then it remains there. When we live, we spend energies, we need energies to maintain this machine. This process of exchange is called the metabolism. Both the metabolism of the exchange of our organism with the environment, and the metabolism within our organism, is going on continually, day and night.

Now what are the laws of this metabolism? They are very strict laws. Let's assume that I walk through the desert, and it's very hot. I lose, let's say, eight ounces of fluid. Now how do I know that I lost this? First, through self-awareness of the phenomenon, in this case called "thirst." Second, suddenly in this undifferentiated general world something emerges as a gestalt, as a foreground, namely, let's say, a well with water, or a pump—or anything that would have plus eight ounces. This minus eight ounces of our organism and the plus eight ounces in the world can balance each other. The very moment this eight ounces goes into the system, we get a plus/minus water which brings balance. We come to rest as the situation is finished, the gestalt is closed. The urge that drives us to do something, to walk so and so many miles to get to that place, has fulfilled its purpose.

This situation is now closed and the next unfinished situation can take its place, which means our life is basically practically nothing but an infinite number of unfinished situations—incomplete gestalts. No sooner have we finished one situation than another comes up.

I have often been called the founder of Gestalt Therapy. That's crap. If you call me the finder or re-finder of Gestalt Therapy, okeh. Gestalt is as ancient and old as the world itself. The world, and especially every organism, maintains itself, and the only law which is constant is the forming of gestalts—wholes, completeness. A gestalt is an organic function. A gestalt is an ultimate experiential unit. As soon as you break up a gestalt, it is not a gestalt any more. Take an example from chemistry. You know that water has a certain property. It consists of H_2O. So if you disturb the gestalt of water, split it up into two H's and one O, it's not water any more. It is oxygen and hydrogen, and if you are thirsty you can breathe as much hydrogen and as much oxygen as you want, it won't quench your thirst. So the gestalt is the experienced phenomenon. If you analyze, if you cut it further up, it becomes something else. You might call it a unit, like, say, volts in electricity, or ergs in mechanics and so on.

Gestalt Therapy is one of the—I think right now it is one of three types of existential therapy: Frankl's Logotherapy, the Daseins Therapy of Binswanger, and Gestalt Therapy. What is important is that Gestalt Therapy is the first existential philosophy that stands on its own feet. I distinguish three types of philosophy. One is the "aboutism." We talk about it and talk about it, and nothing is accomplished. In scientific explanation, you usually go around and around and never touch the heart of the matter. The second philosophy I would call the "shouldism." Moralism. You should be this, you should change yourself, you should not do this—a hundred thousand commands, but no consideration is given to what degree the person who "should" do this can actually comply. And furthermore, most people expect that the magic formula, just to use the sounds, "You should do this," might have an actual effect upon reality.

The third philosophy I call existentialism. Existentialism wants to do away with concepts, and to work on the awareness principle, on phenomenology. The setback with the present existentialist philosophies is that they need their support from somewhere else. If you look at the existentialists, they say that they are non-conceptual, but if you look at the people, they all borrow concepts from other sources. Buber from Judaism, Tillich from Protestantism, Sartre from Socialism, Heidegger from language, Binswanger from psychoanalysis, and so on. Gestalt Therapy is a philosophy that tries to be in harmony, in alignment with everything else, with medicine, with science, with the universe, with what *is*. Gestalt Therapy has its support in its own formation because the gestalt formation, the emergence of the needs, is a primary biological phenomenon.

So we are doing away with the whole instinct theory and simply consider the organism as a system that is in balance and that has to function properly. Any imbalance is experienced as a need to correct this imbalance. Now, practically, we have hundreds of unfinished situations in us. How come that we are not completely confused and want to go out in all directions? And that's another law which I have discovered, that from the survival point of view, the most urgent situation becomes the controller, the director, and takes over. The most urgent situation emerges, and in any case of emergency, you realize that this has to take precedent over any other activity. If there would be suddenly a fire here, the fire would be more important than our talks. If you rush and rush, and run from the fire, suddenly you will be out of breath, your oxygen supply is more important than the fire. You stop and take a breath because this is now the most important thing.

So, we come now to the most important, interesting phenomenon in all pathology: self-regulation versus external regulation. The anarchy which is usually feared by the controllers is not an anarchy which is without meaning. On the contrary, it means the organism is left alone to take care of itself, without being meddled with from outside. And I belive that this is the great thing to understand: *that awareness per se—by and of itself—can be curative.* Because with full awareness you become aware of this organismic self-regulation, you can let the organism take over without interfering, without interrupting; we can rely on the wisdom of the organism. And the contrast to this is the whole pathology of self-manipulation, environmental control, and so on, that interferes with this subtle organismic self-control.

Our manipulation of ourselves is usually dignified by the word *conscience*. In ancient times, conscience was thought to be a God-made institution. Even Immanuel Kant thought that the conscience was equivalent to the eternal star, as one of the two absolutes. Then Freud came and he showed that the conscience is nothing but a fantasy, an introjection, a continuation of what he believed was the parents. I believe it's a projection *onto* the parents, but never mind. Some think it is an introjection, an institution called the superego, that wants to take over control. Now if this were so, then how come the analysis of the superego is not successful? How come that this program does not work? "The road to hell is paved with good intentions" is verified again and again. Any intention toward change will achieve the opposite. You all know this. The New Year's resolutions, the desperation of trying to be different, the attempt to control yourself. All this always comes to nought, or in extreme cases the person is apparently successful, up to the point where the nervous breakdown occurs. The final way out.

Now if we are willing to stay in the center of our world, and not have the center either in our computer or somewhere else, but really in the center, then we are ambidextrous—then we see the two poles of every event. We see that light cannot exist without non-light. If there is sameness, you can't be aware any more. If there is always light, you don't experience light any more. You have to have the rhythm of light and darkness. Right doesn't exist without left. If there is a *superego*, there must also be an *infra*ego. Again, Freud did half the job. He saw the topdog, the superego, but he left out the underdog which is just as much a personality as the topdog. And if we go one step farther and examine the two clowns, as I call them, that perform the self-torture game on the stage of our fantasy, then we usually find the two characters like this:

The topdog usually is righteous and authoritarian; he knows best. He is sometimes right, but always righteous. The topdog is a bully, and works with "You should" and "You should not." The topdog manipulates with demands and threats of catastrophe, such as, "If you don't, then—you won't be loved, you won't get to heaven, you will die," and so on.

The underdog, manipulates with being defensive, apologetic, wheedling, playing the cry-baby, and such. The underdog has no power. The underdog is the Mickey Mouse. The topdog is the Super Mouse. And the underdog works like this: "Mañana." "I try my best." "Look, I try again and again; I can't help it if I fail." "I can't help it if I forgot your birthday." "I have such good intentions." So you see the underdog is cunning, and usually gets the better of the topdog because the underdog is not as primitive as the topdog. So the topdog and underdog strive for control. Like every parent and child, they strive with each other for control. The person is fragmented into controller and controlled. This inner conflict, the struggle between the topdog and the underdog, is never complete, because topdog as well as underdog fight for their lives.

This is the basis for the famous self-torture game. We usually take for granted that the topdog is right, and in many cases the topdog makes impossible perfectionistic demands. So if you are cursed with perfectionism, then you are absolutely sunk. This ideal is a yardstick which always gives you the opportunity to browbeat yourself, to berate yourself and others. Since this ideal is an impossibility, you can never live up to it. The perfectionist is not in love with his wife. He is in love with his ideal, and he demands from his wife that she should fit in this Procrustes bed of his expectations, and he blames her if she does not fit. What this ideal exactly is, he would not reveal. Now and then there might be some stated characteristics, but the essence of the ideal is that it is impossible, unobtainable, just a good opportunity to control, to swing the whip. The other day I had a talk with a friend of mine and I told her, "Please get this into your nut: mistakes are no sins," and she wasn't half as relieved as I thought she would be. Then I realized, if mistakes are not a sin any more, how can she castigate others who make mistakes? So it always works both ways; if you carry this ideal, this perfectionistic ideal around with yourself, you have a wonderful tool to play the beloved game of the neurotic, the self-torture game. There is no end to the self-torture, to the self-nagging, self-castigating. It hides under the mask of "self-improvement." It never works.

If the person tries to meet the topdog's demands of perfectionism, the result is a "nervous breakdown," or flight into insanity. This is one of the tools of the underdog. Once we recognize the structure of our behavior, which in the case of self-improvement is the split between the topdog and the underdog, and if we understand how, by listening, we can bring about a reconciliation of these two fighting clowns, then we realize that *we cannot deliberately bring about changes in ourselves or in others*. This is a very decisive point: Many people dedicate their lives to actualize a concept of what they *should* be like, rather than to actualize *themselves*. This difference between *self*-actualizing and self-*image* actualizing is *very* important. Most people only live for their image. Where some people have a self, most people have a void, because they are so busy protecting themselves as this or that. This is again the curse of the ideal. The curse that you should not be what you are.

Every external control, even *internalized* external control—"you should"—interferes with the healthy working of the organism. There is only one thing that should control: the *situation*. If you understand the situation which you are in, and let the situation which you are in control your actions, then you learn how to cope with life. Now you know this from certain situations, like driving a car. You don't drive a car according to a program, like, "I want to drive 65 miles per hour." You drive according to the situation. You drive a different speed at night, you drive a different speed when there is traffic there, you drive differently when you are tired. You listen to the situation. The less confident we are in ourselves, the less we are in touch with ourselves and the world, the more we want control.

Question: I've been wondering about Joe Kamiya's brainwave test and the question of self-control. If he puts himself in a calm state when he experiences irritation, would this be avoidance?

Fritz: Avoidance of what?

Question: The cause of the irritation, that he is leaving by putting himself in a calm state of mind. I suppose it depends on what causes the irritation that is alleviated.

Fritz: Well, I partly don't follow you, partly don't know if your report is correct, and I don't know enough of it from the little I have understood. It seems that the alpha waves are identical with organismic self-regulation, the organism taking over and acting spontaneously instead of acting on control. I think he describes that as long as he tries to control something, the alpha waves are not there. But I don't like to talk about it because I have no experiences with this set-up yet. I hope to get to see it. I think it is for once a gadget that seems to be very interesting and possibly productive.

Question: I can see now, on the level of organismic functions, such a thing as this water loss and the need to fill this loss—this process of allowing the organism to function by itself will work. But then you get to the level of relationships, what happens? Then it seems as if there is necessity for discrimination in what's foreground and what's not.

Fritz: Can you give us an example?

Question: Say I'm in a situation in which there are four or five emergencies occurring, what I consider to be emergencies, in which I should be taking some part and doing something. Then comes what I call discrimination, in that one or the other of these is more important than the rest of them. And it's just that it's not as easy for me to see how the organism makes a decision like that, as how it makes a decision that it needs water.

Fritz: Yah. The organism does not *make decisions*. Decision is a man-made institution. The organism works always on the basis of *preference*.

Question: I thought you said it was the feeling of need.

Fritz: Well, the need is the primary thing. If you had no needs, you wouldn't do a thing. If you had no need for oxygen, you wouldn't breathe.

Question: Well, I guess I—what I mean is, the most pressing need is the one that you go to.

Fritz: Yah. The most pressing need. And if you talk about five emergencies, I would say none of them are emergencies, because if one was really an emergency, it would *emerge*, and there would be no decision or computing done. This emergency would take over. Our relationship to this emergency, to the world, is the same as, for instance, in painting. You've got a white figure. Then you make certain blots on this canvas, and then suddenly comes a moment of re-centering. Suddenly the *canvas* makes demands, and you become the servant. It is as if you said, "What does this thing want?" "Where does it want to have some red?" Where does it want to be balanced?" Except you don't ask questions, you just respond.

Now the next thing that I want to talk about is the differentiation between *end-gain* and *means-whereby*. The end-gain is always fixed by a need. The free choice is in the means-whereby. Let's say that I have to send a message to New York. That is the thing that is fixed, the *end-gain*. The *means-whereby* to send the message, the medium, is of secondary importance—whether you send it by wire, by mouth, by letter, by telepathy if you believe in it. So in spite of McLuhan's thesis "The medium is the message," I still say that the end-gain is the primary thing. Now, for instance, in sex, the end-gain is the orgasm. The means-whereby can be a hundred different possibilities and as a matter of fact, the recognition of this by Medard Boss, the Swiss psychiatrist, is how he cured homosexuality. By having the patient *fully* accept homosexuality as one of the means to get to the organismic satisfaction, the end-gain, in this case the orgasm, he then had the possibility of changing the means-whereby. All perversions are variations of the means-whereby, and the same applies to any of the basic needs. If you want to eat, the end-gain is to get enough calories into your system. The means-whereby differ from very primitive, eating some popcorn or whatever, to the discriminating experience of the gourmet. The more you realize this, the more you begin to select the means, come to select all the social needs, which are the means to the organismic ends.

This type of organismic self-regulation is very important in therapy, because the emergent, unfinished situations will come to the surface. We don't have to dig; it's all there. And you might look upon this like this: that from within, some figure emerges, comes to the surface, and then goes into the outside world, reaches out for what we want, and comes back, assimilates and receives. Something else comes out, and again the same process repeats itself.

The most peculiar things happen. Let's say, you suddenly see a woman licking calcium from the wall—licking the plaster from the wall. It's a crazy thing. Then it turns out that she is pregnant and needs calcium for the bones of her baby, but she doesn't know that. Or she sleeps through the noises of the Beatles, and then her child just whimpers a little bit and suddenly she wakes up, because this is the emergency. This is what she is geared for. So she can withdraw from the loudest noise, because this is not gestalt-motivated. But the whimper is there, so the whimper emerges and becomes the attraction. This is again the wisdom of the organism. The organism knows all. We know very little.

Question: You said the organism knows all, and we know very little. How is it possible to get the two together? I guess there aren't two of them.

Fritz: They are often split up. They can be together. If you have these two together, you would be at least a genius, because then you might have perspective, sensitivity, and the ability to fit things together at the same time.

Question: Would you then class experiences that are sometimes called "instinctive" or "intuitive" as integrated experiences?

Fritz: Yah. Intuition is the intelligence of the organism. Intelligence is the whole, and intellect is the whore of intelligence—the computer, the fitting game: If this is so, then this is so—all this figuring out by which many people replace *seeing and hearing what's going on.* Because if you are busy with your computer, your energy goes into your thinking, and you don't see and hear any more.

Question: This is a contradictory question because I am asking you to use words. Could you explain the difference between words and experiences? (Fritz leaves the podium, goes to the woman who asked the question, puts his hands on her shoulders, kisses her. Laughter.) O.K.! That'll do it!

Fritz: I experience a dismissing pat from you. (Fritz pats himself lightly on the shoulder as he returns to the podium.)

Question: You were talking about self-control or inner control, versus external control. I'm not sure that I understood you. I feel sometimes that external control is fantasy—that you are actually doing it yourself.

Fritz: Yah, that's true. That's what I call self-manipulation or self-torture. Now this organismic self-regulation I am talking about is not a matter of fantasy, except if the object in question is not there. Then you have a fantasy, which so to say guides you until the real object appears, and then the fantasy of the object and the real object melt together. Then you don't need the fantasy any more.

I am not yet talking about the fantasy life as such, as rehearsal and so on. This is quite a different story. I am talking about the ability of the organism to take care of itself without external interference—without momma telling us, "It's good for your health," "I know what's best for you," and all that.

Question: I have a question. You talked about control. If what you said is so, that the organism can take care of itself once the integration is complete and self-regulation is available for the total organism, then control no longer becomes a factor—externally or internally; it's something that *is*, and is in operation.

Fritz: That's right, and then the essence of control is that you begin to control the means-whereby to get satisfaction. The usual procedure is that you don't get satisfaction, you merely get exhaustion.

Question: I can recognize that what you say is true, that if I keep on computing, I'll stop seeing and hearing. And yet the problem comes with me all the time how, when I have many many things to accomplish in the day—

Fritz: Wait a moment. We have to distinguish—do you have to accomplish them as an organismic need or as part of the social role you play?

Question: As part of the social role.

Fritz: That's a different story. I am talking about the organism *per se*. I am not talking about ourselves as social beings. I don't talk about the *pseudo*-existence, but of the basic natural existence, the foundation of our being. What you are talking about is the role-playing which might be a *means-whereby* to earn a living, which is a *means-whereby* to get your basic needs satisfied—give you food, etc.

Question: And yet—I know there's something sick about this at the beginning of each day, computing, thinking, planning, scheduling my day, planning that at this hour I'm going to do this and at another hour, that. And I do this all during the day. And I know that it cuts out just seeing and hearing, and yet if I go around just staying with the seeing and the hearing, then certain other things don't get done and I get completely confused.

Fritz: That's right. This is the experience that comes out of the clash between our social existence and our biological existence— confusion.

Question: Well, you're leaving me in that confusion, then.

Fritz: Yah. That's what I'm talking about. *Awareness per se.* If you become aware each time that you are entering a state of confusion, this is the therapeutic thing. And again, nature takes over. If you understand this, and stay with confusion, *confusion will sort itself out by itself.* If you *try* to sort it out, *compute* how to do it, if you ask me for a *prescription* how to do it, you only add more confusion to your productions.

2

I want to talk now about maturation. And in order to understand maturation, we have to talk about learning. To me, learning is *discovery.* I learn something from this experience. There is another idea of learning which is the drill, the routine, the repetition, which is an artifact produced in the person which makes a person an automaton —until he discovers the *meaning* of the drill. For instance, you learn to play the piano. First you start with the drill. And then comes a closure, then comes the discovery: Ahah! I got it! This is it! Then you have to learn how to use this technique.

There is another kind of learning which is the feeding information into your computer, so you accumulate knowledge, and as you know, knowledge begets more knowledge until you want to fly to the moon. This knowledge, this secondary information, might be useful whenever you have lost your senses. As long as you have your senses, as long as you can see and hear, and realize what's going on, then you *understand.* If you learn concepts, if you work for information, then you don't understand. You only *explain.* And it is not easy to understand the difference between explanatoriness and understanding, just as often it is not easy to understand the difference between the heart and the brain, between feeling and thinking.

Most people take explaining as being identical with understanding. There is a great difference. Like now, I can explain a lot to you. I can give you a lot of sentences that help you to build an intellectual model of *how* we function. Maybe some of you feel the coincidence of these sentences and explanations with your real life, and this would mean understanding.

Right now I can only hypnotize you, persuade you, make you believe that I'm right. You don't know. I'm just preaching something.

You wouldn't learn from my words. Learning is discovery. There is no other means of effective learning. You can tell the child a thousand times, "The stove is hot." It doesn't help. The child has to discover it for himself. And I hope I can assist you in learning, in discovering something about yourself.

Now what are you supposed to learn here? We have a very specific aim in Gestalt Therapy, and this is the same aim that exists at least *verbally* in other forms of therapy, in other forms of discovering life. The aim is to mature, to grow up. I would like some audience participation already about maturation. What is your opinion? What is a mature person? Can we start here?

A: I know the answer already, Fritz.

Fritz: Yah. You know the printed answer, according to the gospel of St. Gestalt. What is *your* definition of the mature person?

A: Well, I have had some introduction to Gestalt and maybe this influences me, but I think the mature person is the person who is—

Fritz: Well, if you want to give *my* formulation, I don't want it, because this would be again only information, and not understanding.

A: I was going to say the integrated person is the person who is aware of his various component parts and has put them together into a unified functional whole.

Fritz: And this would be a mature person?

A: He has a minimum of parts of himself of which he is completely unconscious or unaware. There is always a residual—we never get completely aware, or completely conscious.

Fritz: In other words, for you the mature person is the *complete* person.

A: Yes.

Fritz: (to another person) Could I have *your* definition, please?

B: I was thinking of a person who knows himself and accepts himself—all the things he likes about himself and the things he doesn't like about himself—who is aware of his many potentialities and seeks to develop them as much as possible—knows what he wants.

Fritz: You certainly have described some important characteristics of the mature person, but this might also apply to a child, wouldn't you say?

B: To me—sometimes children in my opinion are often more mature than adults.

Fritz: Thank you! Often children are more mature than adults. You notice here we have a different equation, or rather a different formulation. We have not the equation: adult equals a mature person. As a matter of fact, the adult is very seldom a mature person. An adult is in my opinion a person who plays a *role* of an adult, and the more he plays the role, the more immature he often is. (To another person) What would be *your* formulation?

C: The first thought that came to me was that the mature person is someone who wonders from time to time what a mature person is, and who every once in a while has an experience which makes him feel: "Oh! So *this* could be part of maturity! I never realized that before."

Fritz: What would be *your* formulation?

D: A person who is aware of himself and others, and also aware that he is incomplete and has some—an awareness of where he is incomplete.

Fritz: Well, I would rather formulate this as the matur*ing* person. He is aware of his incompleteness. So: so far we would say, from these remarks, that what we want to do is to facilitate the completion of our personality. Is this acceptable to everybody?

Question: What do you mean by completion?—or incomplete?

Fritz: Yah. These terms were brought out here. Could you answer this, please? What do you mean by complete or incomplete?

A: I used it to begin with, and I feel this is a goal to strive for that is never achieved. No one ever achieves it. It is always a becoming, a growing. But, relatively, the complete person is the one who is most aware of his component parts, most accepting of them, and has achieved an integration—a continuing integrating process.

Fritz: Now the idea of the incomplete person was first brought about by Nietzsche, and very soon afterwards by Freud. Freud's formulation is a little bit different. He says a certain part of one's personality is repressed, is in the unconscious. But when he speaks about the unconscious, he just means that not all of our potential is available. His idea is that there is a barrier between the person and the unconscious, the unavailable potential, and if we lift the barrier we can again be totally ourselves. The idea is basically correct, and every type of psychotherapy is more or less interested in enriching the personality, in liberating what is usually called the repressed and inhibited parts of the personality.

E: Fritz, I have the thought that "maturity" in Spanish is *maduro* which means "ripe." I wanted to make this contribution.

Fritz: Thank you. This is exactly what I also want to completely agree with. In any plant, any animal, ripening and maturing are identical. You don't find any animal—except the domesticated animal who is already infected by mankind—no natural animal and no plant exists that will prevent its own growing. So the question is, how do we prevent ourselves from maturing? What prevents us from ripening? The word *neurosis* is very bad. I use it, too, but actually it should be called *growth disorder*. So in other words, the whole neurosis question shifts more and more from the medical to the educational field. I see more and more the so-called "neurosis" as a disturbance in development. Freud assumed there is such thing as "maturity," which means a state from which you don't develop any further, you can only regress. We ask the question, what prevents—or how do you prevent yourself from growing, from going further ahead?

So let's look upon maturing once more. My formulation is that *maturing is the transcendence from environmental support to self-support.* Look upon the inborn baby. It gets all its support from the mother—oxygen, food, warmth, everything. As soon as the baby is born, it has already to do its own breathing. And then we find often the first symptom of what plays a very decisive part in Gestalt Therapy. We find the *impasse.* Please note the word. The *impasse* is the crucial point in therapy, the crucial point in growth. The impasse is called by the Russians "the sick point," a point which the Russians never managed to lick and which other types of psychotherapy so far have not succeeded in licking. The impasse is the position where environmental support or obsolete inner support is not forthcoming any more, and authentic self-support has not yet been achieved. The baby cannot breathe by itself. It doesn't get the oxygen supply through the placenta any more. We can't say that the baby has a choice, because there is no deliberate attempt of thinking out what to do, but the baby either has to die or to learn to breathe. There might be some environmental support forthcoming—being slapped, or oxygen might be supplied. The "blue baby" is the prototype of the impasse which we find in every neurosis.

Now, the baby begins to grow up. It still has to be carried. After awhile it learns to give some kind of communication—first crying, then it learns to speak, learns to crawl, to walk, and so, step by step, it mobilizes more and more of its potential, its inner resources. He discovers—or learns—more and more to make use of his muscles, his senses, his wits, and so on. So, from this I make the definition that the process of maturation is the transformation from environmental support to self-support, and the aim of therapy is to make the patient *not* depend upon others, but to make the patient discover from the very first moment that he can do many things, *much* more than he thinks he can do.

The average person of our time, believe it or not, lives only 5 percent to 15 percent of his potential at the highest. A person who has even 25 percent of his potential available is already considered to be a genius. So 85 percent to 95 percent of our potential is lost, is unused, is not at our disposal. Sounds tragic, doesn't it? And the reason for this is very simple: we live in cliches. We live in patterned behavior. We are playing the same roles over and over again. So if you find out how you prevent yourself from growing, from using your potential, you have a way of increasing this, making life richer, making you more and more capable of mobilizing yourself. And our potential is based upon a very peculiar attitude: to live and review every second afresh.

The "trouble" with people who are capable of reviewing every second what the situation is like, is that we are not predictable. The role of the good citizen requires that he be predictable, because our hankering for security, for not taking risks, our fear to be authentic, our fear to stand on our own feet, especially on our own intelligence —this fear is just horrifying. So what do we do? *We adjust*, and in most kinds of therapy you find that adjustment to society is the high goal. If you don't adjust, you are either a criminal, or psychopath, or loony, or beatnik or something like that. Anyhow, you are undesirable and have to be thrown out of the boundary of that society.

Most other therapies try to adjust the person to society. This was maybe not too bad in previous years, when society was relatively stable, but now with the rapid changes going on, it is getting more and more difficult to adjust to society. Also, more and more people are not willing to adjust to society—they think that this society stinks, or have other objections. I consider that the basic personality in our time is a neurotic personality. This is a preconceived idea of mine, because I believe we are living in an insane society and that you only have the choice either to participate in this collective psychosis or to take risks and become healthy and perhaps also crucified.

If you are centered in yourself, then you don't adjust any more— then, whatever happens becomes a passing parade and you assimilate, you understand, you are relaxed to whatever happens. In this happening, the symptom of anxiety is very very important, because the more the society changes, the more it produces anxiety. Now the psychiatrist is very afraid of anxiety. I am not. My definition of anxiety is the gap between the now and the later. Whenever you leave the sure basis of the now and become preoccupied with the future, you experience anxiety. And if the future represents a performance, then this anxiety is nothing but stage fright. You are full of catastrophic expectations of the bad things that will happen, or anastrophic expectations about the wonderful things that will happen. And we fill this gap between the now and the later—with insurance policies, planning, fixed jobs, and so on. In other words, we are not willing to see the fertile void, the possibility of the future—we have no future if we fill this void, we only have sameness.

But how can you have sameness in this rapid-changing world? So of course anybody who wants to hold onto the status quo will get more and more panicky and afraid. Usually, the anxiety is not so deeply existential. It is just concerned with the role we want to play, it's just stage fright. "Will my role come off?" "Will I be called a good boy?" "Will I get my approval?" "Will I get applause, or will I get rotten eggs?" So that's not an existential choice, just a choice of inconvenience. But to *realize* that it's just an inconvenience, that it's not a catastrophe, but just an unpleasantness, is part of coming into your own, part of waking up.

So we come to our basic conflict and the basic conflict is this: Every individual, every plant, every animal has only one inborn goal—to actualize itself as it is. A rose is a rose is a rose. A rose is not intent to actualize itself as a kangaroo. An elephant is not intent to actualize itself as a bird. In nature—except for the human being—constitution, and healthiness, potential growth, is all one unified *something*.

The same applies to the multi-organism, or society, which consists of many people. A state, a society, consists of many thousands of cells which have to be organized either by external control or inner control, and each society tends to actualize itself as this or that specific society. The Russian society actualizes itself as what it is, the American society, the German society, the Congo tribes—they all actualize themselves, they change. And there is always a law in history: Any society that has outstretched itself and has lost its ability to survive, disappears. Cultures come—and go. And when a society is in clash with the universe, once a society transgresses the laws of nature, it loses its survival value, too. So, as soon as we leave the basis of nature—the universe and *its* laws—and become artifacts either as individuals or as society, then we lose our *raison d'etre*. We lose the possibility of existence.

So where do we find ourselves? We find ourselves on the one hand as individuals who want to actualize themselves; we find ourselves also embedded in this society, in our case the progressive American society, and this society might make demands different from the individual demands. So there is the basic clash. Now this individual society is represented in our development by our parents, nurses, teachers, and so forth. Rather than to facilitate the development of authentic growth, they often intrude into the natural development.

They work with two tools to falsify our existence. One tool is the stick, which then is encountered again in therapy as the *catastrophic expectation*. The catastrophic expectation sounds like this: "If I take the risk, I will not be loved any more. I will be lonely. I'll die." That's the stick. And then there is the hypnosis. Right now, I am hypnotizing you. I am hypnotizing you into believing what I say. I don't give you the chance to digest, to assimilate, to taste what I say. You hear from my voice that I try to cast a spell on you, to slip my "wisdom" into your guts until you either assimilate it or puke, or feed it into your computer and say: "That's an interesting concept." Normally, as you know if you are students, you are only allowed to puke on the examination paper. You swallow all the information and you puke it up and you are free again and you have got a degree. Sometimes, though, I must say, in the process you might have learned something, either discovered something of value, or some experience about your teachers, or about your friends, but the basic dead information is not easy to assimilate.

Now let's go back to the maturation process. In the process of growing up, there are two choices. The child either grows up and learns to overcome frustration, or it is spoiled. It might be spoiled by the parents answering all the questions, rightly or wrongly. It might be spoiled so that as soon as it wants something, it gets it—because the child "should have everything because papa never had it," or because the parents don't know how to frustrate children—don't know how to use frustration. You will probably be amazed that I am using the word *frustration* so positively. Without frustration there is no need, no reason to mobilize your resources, to discover that you might be able to do something on your own, and in order not to be frustrated, which is a pretty painful experience, the child learns to manipulate the environment.

Now, any time the child, in his development, is prevented from growth by the adult world, any time the child is being spoiled by not being given enough frustration, the child is stuck. So instead of using his potential to grow he now uses his potential to control the adults, to control the world. Instead of mobilizing his own resources, he creates dependencies. He invests his energy in manipulating the environment for support. He controls the adults by starting to manipulate them, by discerning their weak spots. As the child begins to develop the means of manipulation, he acquires what is called character. The more character a person has, the less potential he has. That sounds paradoxical, but a character is a person that is predictable, that has only a number of fixed responses, or as T. S. Eliot said in *The Cocktail Party*, "you are nothing but a set of obsolete responses."

Now what are the character features which the child develops? How does he control the world? How does he manipulate his environment? He demands directional support. "What shall I do?" "Mommy, I don't know what to do." He plays the role of cry-baby, if he doesn't get what he wants. For instance, there is a little girl here, about three years old. She always puts on the same performance with me. She always cries when I look at her. So today I was very careful *not* to look at her, and she stopped crying and then she started to look for me. Only three years, and already she is such a good ham. She knows how to torture her mother. Or, the child butters up the other person's self-esteem, so that the other will feel good and he will give him something in return. For instance, one of the worst diagnoses is if I encounter a "good boy." There is always a spiteful brat there, in the good boy. But by pretending to comply, at least on the surface, he bribes the adult. Or he plays stupid and demands intellectual support—asks questions, for instance, which is the typical symptom of stupidity. As Albert Einstein once said to me: "Two things are infinite: the universe and human stupidity." But what is much more widespread than the *actual* stupidity is the *playing* stupid, turning off your ear, not listening, not seeing. Also very important is playing helpless. "I can't help myself. Poor me. You have to help me. You are so wise, you have so many resources, I'm sure you can help me." Each time you play helpless you create a dependency, you play a dependency game. In other words, we make ourselves slaves. Especially, if this dependency is a dependency of our self-esteem. If you need encouragement, praise, pats on the back from everybody, then you make everybody your judge.

If you don't have your loving at your disposal, and project the love, then you want to *be* loved, you do all kinds of things to make yourself lovable. If you disown yourself, you always become the target, you become dependent. What a dependency if you want everybody to love you! A person doesn't mean a thing and yet suddenly you set out and want to make a good impression on this person, want them to love you. It's always the image; you want to play the concept that you are lovable. If you feel comfortable in yourself, you don't love yourself and you don't hate yourself, you just live. I must admit, especially in the United States, loving for many people entails a risk. Many people look upon a person who loves as a sucker. They want to make people love *them*, so that they can exploit them.

If you look a bit into your existence, you will realize that the gratification of the needs of purely biological being—hunger, sex, survival, shelter, breathing—plays only a minor part in our preoccupations, especially in a country like this where we are so spoiled. We don't know what it means to be hungry, and anyone who wants to have sex can have sex plentifully, anyone who wants to breathe can breathe—the air is tax free. For the rest, we play games. We play games quite extensively, openly, and to a much greater extent, privately. When we think, we mostly talk to others in fantasy. We plan for the roles we want to play. We have to organize *in order to* do what we want to do, for the means-whereby.

Now it might sound a bit peculiar that I disesteem thinking, making it just a part of role-playing. Sometimes, we might communicate when we talk, but most times we hypnotize. We hypnotize each other; we hypnotize ourselves that we are right. We play "Madison Avenue" to convince other people or ourselves of our value. And this takes up so much of our energy that sometimes if you are unsure about the role you are playing, you wouldn't dare say a word, a sentence, without having rehearsed it again and again until it fits the occasion. Now if you are not sure of the role you want to play, and you are called away from your private stage to the public stage, then like every good actor, you experience stage fright. Your excitement is already mounting, you want to play a role, but you don't quite dare, so you hold back, and restrict your breathing, so the heart pumps up more blood because the higher metabolism has to be satisfied. And then, once you are on stage and play the role, the excitement flows into your performance. If not, your performance would be rigid and dead.

It is the repetition of this activity which then becomes a habit, the same action that grows easier and easier—a character, a fixed role. So you understand now, I hope, that playing a role, and manipulating the environment are identical. This is the way we falsify, and very often you read in literature about the mask we are wearing, and about the transparent self that should be there.

This manipulation of the environment by playing certain roles is the characteristic of the neurotic—is the characteristic of our remaining immature. So you must already get an idea how much of our energy goes into manipulating the world instead of using this energy creatively for our own development. And especially, this applies to asking questions. You know the proverb, "One fool can ask more questions than a thousand wise men can answer." All the answers are given. Most questions are simply inventions to torture ourselves and other people. The way to develop our own intelligence is by changing every question into a statement. If you change your question into a statement, the background out of which the question arose opens up, and the possibilities are found by the questioner himself.

You see I am already running dry. Lecturing is a drag, I tell you that. Well, most professors take the way out by using a very somniferous, broken voice, so you fall asleep and don't listen, and so you don't ask embarrassing questions.

Question: I have a question. Could you give me some examples of how to turn questions into statements?

Fritz: You have just asked me a question. Can you turn this question into a statement?

Question: It would be nice to hear some examples of how to turn a question into a statement.

Fritz: "It would be nice." But I'm *not* nice. Actually, what's behind all this is the only means of true communication, which is the imperative. What you really want to say is, "Fritz, *tell me* how one does this"—make a demand on me. And the question mark is the hook of a demand. Every time you refuse to answer a question, you help the other person to develop his own resources. Learning is nothing but discovery that something is possible. To teach means to show a person that something is possible.

What we are after is the maturation of the person, removing the blocks that prevent a person from standing on his own feet. We try to help him make the transition from environmental support to self-support. And basically we do it by finding the impasse. The impasse occurs originally when a child cannot get the support from the environment, but cannot yet provide its own support. At that moment of impasse, the child starts to mobilize the environment by playing phony roles, playing stupid, playing helpless, playing weak, flattering, and all the roles that we use in order to manipulate our environment.

Now any therapist who wants to be *helpful* is doomed right from the beginning. The patient will do anything to make the therapist feel inadequate, because he has to have his compensation for needing him. So the patient asks the therapist for more and more help, he drives the therapist more and more into the corner, until he either succeeds in driving the therapist crazy—which is another means of manipulation—or if the therapist doesn't oblige, at least to make him feel inadequate. He will suck the therapist more and more into his neurosis, and there will be no end to therapy.

So how do we proceed in Gestalt Therapy? We have a very simple means to get the patient to find out what his own missing potential is. Namely, the patient uses me, the therapist, as a projection screen, and he expects of me exactly what he can't mobilize in himself. And in this process, we make the peculiar discovery that no one of us is complete, that every one of us has holes in his personality. Wilson Van Dusen discovered this first in the schizophrenic, but I believe that every one of us has holes. Where something should be, there is nothing. Many people have no soul. Others have no genitals. Some have no heart; all their energy goes into computing, thinking. Others have no legs to stand on. Many people have no eyes. They project the eyes, and the eyes are to quite an extent in the outside world and they always live as if they are being looked at. A person feels that the eyes of the world are upon him. He becomes a mirror-person who always wants to know how he looks to others. He gives up his eyes and asks the world to do his seeing for him. Instead of being critical, he projects the criticism and feels criticized and feels on stage. Self-consciousness is the mildest form of paranoia. Most of us have no ears. People expect the ears to be outside and they talk and expect someone to listen. But who listens? If people would listen, we would have peace.

Now the most important missing part is a center. Without a center, everything goes on in the periphery and there is no place from which to work, from which to cope with the world. Without a center, you are not alert. I don't know how many of you have seen the film *The Seven Samurai*—a Japanese film, in which one of the warriors is so alert that anyone approaching him, or doing anything even at a distance, he is already sensing it. He is so much centered that anything that happens is immediately registered. This achieving the center, being grounded in one's self, is about the highest state a human being can achieve.

Now these missing holes are always visible. They are always there *in the patient's projection onto the therapist*—that the therapist is supposed to have all the properties which are missing in this person. So, first the therapist provides the person with the opportunity to discover what he needs—the missing parts that he has alienated and given up to the world. Then the therapist must provide the opportunity, the situation in which the person can grow. And the means is that we frustrate the patient in such a way that he is forced to develop his own potential. We apply enough skillful frustration so that the patient is forced to find his own way, discover his own possibilities, his own potential, and discover that *what he expects from the therapist, he can do just as well himself.*

Everything the person disowns can be recovered, and the means of this recovery is understanding, playing, becoming these disowned parts. And by letting him play and discover that he already has all this (which he thinks only others can give him) we increase his potential. We more and more put him on his own feet, give him more and more power in himself, more and more ability to experience, until he is capable of really being himself and coping with the world. He cannot learn this through teaching, conditioning, getting information or making up programs or plans. He has to discover that all this energy that goes into manipulation can be resolved and used, and that he can learn to actualize himself, his potential—instead of trying to actualize a concept, an image of what he wants to be, thereby suppressing a lot of his potential and adding, on the other side, another piece of phony living, pretending to be something he is not. We grow up completely out of balance if the support that we get from our constitution is missing. But the person has to discover this by seeing for himself, by listening for himself, by uncovering what is there, by grasping for himself, by becoming ambidextrous instead of closed, and so on. And the main thing is the listening. To listen, to understand, to be open, is one and the same. Some of you might know Herman Hesse's book, *Siddartha*, where the hero finds the final solution to his life by becoming a ferryman on a river, and he learns to listen. His ears tell him so much more than the Buddha or any of the great wise men can ever teach him.

So what we are trying to do in therapy is step-by-step to *re-own* the disowned parts of the personality until the person becomes strong enough to facilitate his own growth, to learn to understand where are the holes, what are the symptoms of the holes. And the symptoms of the holes are always indicated by one word: *avoidance.* We become phobic, we run away. We might change therapists, we might change marriage partners, but the ability to stay with what we are avoiding is not easy, and for this you need somebody else to become aware of what you are avoiding, because you are not aware, and as a matter of fact, a very interesting phenomenon occurs here. When you get close to the impasse, to the point where you just cannot believe that you might be able to survive, then the whirl starts. You get desperate, confused. Suddenly, you don't understand *any*thing any more, and here the symptom of the neurotic becomes very clear. The neurotic is a person who does not see the obvious. You see this always in the group. Something is obvious to everybody else, but the person in question doesn't see the obvious; he doesn't see the pimples on his nose. And this is what we are again and again trying to do, to frustrate the person until he is face to face with his blocks, with his inhibitions, with his way of avoiding having eyes, having ears, having muscles, having authority, having security in himself.

So we are always trying to get to the impasse, and find the point where you believe you have no chance of survival because you don't find the means in yourself. When we find the place where the person is stuck, we come to the surprising discovery that this impasse is mostly merely a matter of fantasy. It doesn't exist in reality. A person only *believes* he has not his resources at his disposal. He only prevents himself from using his resources by conjuring up a lot of catastrophic expectations. He expects something bad in the future. "People won't like me." "I might do something foolish." "If I would do this, I wouldn't be loved any more, I would die," and so on. We have all these catastrophic fantasies by which we prevent ourselves from living, from *being*. We are continually projecting threatening fantasies onto the world, and these fantasies prevent us from taking the reasonable risks which are part and parcel of growing and living.

Nobody really wants to get through the impasse that will grant this development. We'd rather maintain the status quo: rather keep in the status quo of a mediocre marriage, mediocre mentality, mediocre aliveness, than to go through that impasse. Very few people go into therapy to be cured, but rather to improve their neurosis. We'd rather manipulate others for support than learn to stand on our own feet and to wipe our own ass. And in order to manipulate the others we become control-mad, power-mad—using all kinds of tricks. I gave you a few examples already—playing helpless, playing stupid, playing the tough guy, and so on. And the most interesting thing about the control-mad people is that they always end up *being controlled*. They build up, for instance, a time schedule that then takes over control, and they have to be at every place at a specific time from then on. So the control-mad person is the first one to lose his freedom. Instead of being in control, he has to strain and push all the time.

Because of this control-madness, no bad marriage can be cured because the people do not want to get through the impasse, they do not want to realize how they are stuck. I could give you an idea how they are stuck. In the bad marriage, husband and wife are not in love with their spouse. They are in love with an image, a fantasy, with an ideal of what the spouse should be like. And then, rather than taking responsibility for their own expectations, all they do is play the blaming game. "You should be different from what you are. You don't fill the bill." So the bill is always right, but the real person is wrong. The same applies to the inner conflict, and to the relationship of therapist and patient: you change spouses, you change therapists, you change the content of your inner conflicts, but you usually maintain the status quo.

Now if we understand the impasse correctly, we wake up, we have a satori. I can't give you a prescription because everybody tries to get out of the impasse without going through it; everybody tries to tear their chains, and this is never successful. It's the awareness, the full experience, the awareness of *how* you are stuck, that makes you recover, and realize the whole thing is just a nightmare, not a real thing, not reality. The satori comes when you realize, for instance, that you are in love with a fantasy and you realize that you are not in communication with your spouse.

The insanity is that we take the fantasy for real. In the impasse, you have always a piece of insanity. In the impasse, nobody can convince you that what you are expecting is a fantasy. You take for real what is merely an ideal, a fantasy. The crazy person says, "I am Abraham Lincoln," and the neurotic says, "I wish I were Abraham Lincoln," and the healthy persons say, "I am I, and you are you."

3

Now let me tell of a dilemma which is not easy to understand. It's like a *koan*—those Zen questions which seem to be insoluble. The *koan* is: *Nothing exists except the here and now*. The *now* is the present, is the phenomenon, is what you are aware of, is that moment in which you carry your so-called memories and your so-called anticipations with you. Whether you remember or anticipate, you do it *now*. The past is no more. The future is not yet. When I say, "I was," that's not now, that's the past. When I say, "I want to," that's the future, it's not yet. Nothing can possibly exist except the now. Some people then make a program out of this. They make a demand, "You *should* live in the here and now." And I say it's *not possible* to live in the here and now, and yet, nothing exists except the here and now.

How do we resolve this dilemma? What is buried in the word *now*? How come it takes years and years to understand a simple word like the word *now*? If I play a phonograph record, the sound of the record appears when the record and the needle touch each other, where they make contact. There is no sound of the before, there is no sound of the afterwards. If I stop the phonograph record, then the needle is still in contact with the record, but there is no music, because there is the *absolute* now. If you would blot out the past, or the anticipation of themes three minutes from now, you could not understand listening to that record you are now playing. But if you blot out the now, nothing will come through. So again, whether we remember or whether we anticipate, we do it *here and now*.

Maybe if I say the *now* is not the scale but the point of suspense, it's a zero point, it is a nothingness, and that is the *now*. The very moment I feel that I experience something and I talk about it, I pay attention to it, that moment is already gone. So what's the use of talking about the *now*? It has many uses, very many uses.

Let's talk first about the past. *Now*, I am pulling memories out of my drawer and possibly believe that these memories are identical with my history. That's never true, because a memory is an abstraction. Right now, you experience something. You experience me, you experience your thoughts, you experience your posture perhaps, but you can't experience *everything*. You always abstract the relevant gestalt from the total context. Now if you take these abstractions and file them away, then you call them memories. If these memories are unpleasant, especially if they are unpleasant to our self-esteem, we change them. As Nietzsche said: "Memory and Pride were fighting. Memory said, 'It was like this' and Pride said, 'It couldn't have been like this'—and Memory gives in." You all know how much you are lying. You all know how much you are deceiving yourselves, how many of your memories are exaggerations and projections, how many of your memories are patched up and distorted.

The past is past. And yet—in the now, in our being, we carry much of the past with us. But we carry much of the past with us only as far as we have unfinished situations. What happened in the past is either assimilated and has become a part of us, or we carry around an unfinished situation, an incomplete gestalt. Let me give you as an example, the most famous of the unfinished situations is the fact that we have not forgiven our parents. As you know, parents are never right. They are either too large or too small, too smart or too dumb. If they are stern, they should be soft, and so on. But when do you find parents who are all right? You can always blame the parents if you want to play the blaming game, and make the parents responsible for all your problems. Until you are willing to let go of your parents, you continue to conceive of yourself as a child. But to get closure and let go of the parents and say, "I am a big girl, now," is a different story. This is part of therapy—to let go of parents, and especially to forgive one's parents, which is the hardest thing for most people to do.

The great error of psychoanalysis is in assuming that the memory is reality. All the so-called *traumata*, which are supposed to be the root of the neurosis, are an invention of the patient to save his self-esteem. None of these traumata has ever been proved to exist. I haven't seen a single case of infantile trauma that wasn't a falsification. They are all lies to be hung onto in order to justify one's unwillingness to grow. To mature means to take responsibility for your life, to be on your own. Psychoanalysis fosters the infantile state by considering that the past is responsible for the illness. The patient isn't responsible—no, the trauma is responsible, or the Oedipus complex is responsible, and so on. I suggest that you read a beautiful little pocketbook called *I Never Promised You a Rose Garden*, by Hannah Green. There you see a typical example, how that girl invented this childhood trauma, to have her *raison d'etre*, her basis to fight the world, her justification for her craziness, her illness. We have got such an idea about the importance of this invented memory, where the whole illness is supposed to be based on this memory. No wonder that all the wild goose chase of the psychoanalyst to find out *why* I am now like this can never come to an end, can never prove a real opening up of the person himself.

Freud devoted his whole life to prove to himself and to others that sex is not bad, and he had to prove this scientifically. In his time, the scientific approach was that of causality, that the trouble was *caused* by something in the past, like a billiard cue pushing a billiard ball, and the cue then is the cause of the rolling of the ball. In the meantime, our scientific attitude has changed. We don't look to the world any more in terms of cause and effect: We look upon the world as a continuous ongoing process. We are back to Heraclitus, to the pre-Socratic idea that everything is in a flux. We never step into the same river twice. In other words, we have made—in science, but unfortunately not yet in psychiatry—the transition from linear causality to thinking of process, from the *why* to the *how*.

If you ask *how*, you look at the structure, you see what's going on now, a deeper understanding of the process. The *how* is all we need to understand how we or the world functions. The *how* gives us perspective, orientation. The *how* shows that one of the basic laws, the identity of structure and function, is valid. If we change the structure, the function changes. If we change the function, the structure changes.

I know you want to ask *why*, like every child, like every immature person asks *why*, to get rationalization or explanation. But the *why* at best leads to clever explanation, but never to an understanding. *Why* and *because* are dirty words in Gestalt Therapy. They lead only rationalization, and belong to the second class of verbiage production. I distinguish three classes of verbiage production: chickenshit —this is "good morning," "how are you," and so on; bullshit—this is "because," rationalization, excuses; and elephantshit—this is when you talk about philosophy, existential Gestalt Therapy, etc.—what I am doing now. The *why* gives only unending inquiries into the cause of the cause of the cause of the cause of the cause of the cause. And as Freud has already observed, every event is *over*-determined, has *many* causes; all kinds of things come together in order to create the specific moment that is the *now*. Many factors come together to create this specific unique person which is *I*. Nobody can at any given moment be different from what he is at this moment, including all the wishes and prayers that he should be different. We are what we are.

These are the two legs upon which Gestalt Therapy walks: *now* and *how*. The essence of the theory of Gestalt Therapy is in the understanding of these two words. *Now* covers all that exists. The past is no more, the future is not yet. *Now* includes the balance of being here, is experiencing, involvement, phenomenon, awareness. *How* covers everything that is structure, behavior, all that is actually going on—the ongoing process. All the rest is irrelevant—computing, apprehending, and so on.

Everything is grounded in *awareness*. *Awareness* is the only basis of knowledge, communication, and so on. In communication, you have to understand that you want to make the other person *aware of something*: aware of yourself, aware of what's to be noticed in the other person, etc. And in order to communicate, we have to make sure that we are *senders*, which means that the message which we send can be understood; and also to make sure that we are *receivers* —that we are willing to listen to the message from the other person. It is very rare that people can talk *and* listen. Very few people can listen without talking. Most people can talk without listening. And if you're busy talking you have no time to listen. The integration of talking and listening is a really rare thing. Most people don't listen and give an honest response, but just put the other person off with a question. Instead of listening and answering, immediately comes a counter-attack, a question or something that diverts, deflects, dodges. We are going to talk a lot about blocks in sending messages, in giving yourself, in making others aware of yourself, and in the same way, of being willing to be open to the other person—to be receivers. Without communication, there cannot be contact. There will be only isolation and boredom.

So I would like to reinforce what I just said, and I would like you to pair up, and to talk to each other for five minutes about your actual present awareness of yourself now and your awareness of the other. Always underline the *how*—*how* do you behave *now*, *how* do you sit, *how* do you talk, all the details of what goes on *now*. *How* does he sit, *how* does he look . . .

So how about the future? We don't know anything about the future. If we all had crystal balls, even then we wouldn't experience the future. We would experience a *vision* of the future. And all this is taking place here and now. We imagine, we anticipate the future because we don't want to have a future. So the most important existential saying is, we don't want to have a future, we are afraid of the future. We fill in the gap where there should be a future with insurance policies, status quo, sameness, *anything* so as not to experience the possibility of openness towards the future.

We also cannot stand the nothingness, the openness, of the past. We are not willing to have the idea of eternity—"It has always been" —so we have to fill it in with the story of creation. Time has started somehow. People ask, "When did time begin?" The same applies to the future. It seems incredible that we could live without goals, without worrying about the future, that we could be open and ready for what might come. No; we have to make sure that we have no future, that the status quo should remain, even be a little bit better. But we mustn't take risks, we mustn't be open to the future. Something could happen that would be new and exciting, and contributing to our growth. It's too dangerous to take the growth risk. We would rather walk this earth as half-corpses than live dangerously, and realize that this living dangerously is much safer than this insurance-life of safety and not taking risks, which most of us decide to do.

What is this funny thing, risk-taking? Has anybody a definition for risk-taking? What's involved in risk-taking?

A: Getting hurt.

B: Taking a dare.

C: Going too far.

D: A hazardous attempt.

E: Inviting danger.

Now you notice, you all see the catastrophic expectation, the negative side. You don't see the possible gain. If there was only the negative side, you just would avoid it, wouldn't you? Risk-taking is a suspense between catastrophic and anastrophic expectations. You have to see *both* sides of the picture. You might gain, and you might lose.

One of the most important moments in my life was after I had escaped Germany and there was a position as a training analyst available in South Africa, and Ernest Jones wanted to know who wanted to go. There were four of us: three wanted guarantees. I said I take a risk. All the other three were caught by the Nazis. I took a risk and I'm still alive.

An absolutely healthy person is completely in touch with himself and with reality. The crazy person, the psychotic, is more or less completely *out* of touch with both, but mostly with *either* himself *or* the world. We are in between being psychotic and being healthy, and this is based upon the fact that we have *two* levels of existence. One is reality, the actual, realistic level, that we are in touch with whatever goes on now, in touch with our feelings, in touch with our senses. Reality is awareness of ongoing experience, actual touching, seeing, moving, doing. The other level we don't have a good word for, so I choose the Indian word *maya*. *Maya* means something like illusion, or fantasy, or philosophically speaking, the *as if* of Vaihinger. *Maya* is a kind of dream, a kind of trance. Very often this fantasy, this *maya,* is called the mind, but if you look a bit closer, what you call "mind" is fantasy. It's the rehearsal stage. Freud once said: *"Denken ist prober arbeit"*—thinking is rehearsing, trying out. Unfortunately, Freud never followed up this discovery because it would be inconsistent with his genetic approach. If he had accepted this statement of his, "Thinking is rehearsing," he would have realized how our fantasy activity is turned toward the future, because we rehearse for the future.

We live on two levels—the public level which is our *doing*, which is observable, verifiable; and the private stage, the thinking stage, the rehearsing stage, on which we prepare for the future roles we want to play. Thinking is a private stage, where you try out. You talk to some person unknown, you talk to yourself, you prepare for an important event, you talk to the beloved before your appointment or disappointment, whatever you expect it to be. For instance, if I were to ask, "Who wants to come up here to work?" you probably would quickly start to rehearse. "What shall I do there?" and so on. And of course probably you will get stage fright, because you leave the secure reality of the now and jump into the future. Psychiatry makes a big fuss out of the symptom *anxiety*, and we live in an age of anxiety, but anxiety is nothing but the tension from the *now* to the *then*. There are few people who can stand this tension, so they have to fill the gap with rehearsing, planning, "making sure," making sure that they don't have a future. They try to hold onto the sameness, and this of course will prevent any possibility of growth or spontaneity.

Question: Of course the past sets up anxiety too, doesn't it?

Fritz: No. The past sets up—or let's say is still present with unfinished situations, regrets and things like this. If you feel anxiety about what you have done, it's not anxiety about what you have done, but anxiety about what will be the punishment to come in the future.

Freud once said the person who is free from anxiety and guilt is healthy. I spoke about anxiety already. I didn't speak about guilt. Now, in the Freudian system, the guilt is very complicated. In Gestalt Therapy, the guilt thing is much simpler. We see guilt as projected *resentment*. Whenever you feel guilty, find out what you resent, and the guilt will vanish and you will try to make the other person feel guilty.

Anything unexpressed which wants to be expressed can make you feel uncomfortable. And one of the most common unexpressed experiences is the resentment. This is the unfinished situation *par excellence*. If you are resentful, you're stuck; you neither can move forward and have it out, express your anger, change the world so that you'll get satisfaction, nor can you let go and forget whatever disturbs you. Resentment is the psychological equivalent of the hanging-on bite—the tight jaw. The hanging-on bite can neither let go, nor bite through and chew up—whichever is required. In resentment you can neither let go and forget, and let this incident or person recede in the background, nor can you actively tackle it. The expression of resentment is one of the most important ways to help you to make your life a little bit more easy. Now I want you all to do the following collective experiment:

I want each one of you to do this. First you evoke a person like father or husband, call the person by name—whoever it is and just say briefly, "Clara, I resent—" Try to get the person to hear you, as if there was really communication and you felt this. So try to speak to the person, and establish in these communications that this person should listen to you. Just become aware of how difficult it is to mobilize your fantasy. Express your resentment—kind of present it right into his or her face. Try to realize at the same time that you don't dare, really, to express your anger, nor would you be generous enough to let go, to be forgiving. Okeh, go ahead . . .

There is another great advantage to using resentment in therapy, in growth. Behind every resentment there are demands. So now I want all of you to talk directly to the same person as before, and express the demands behind the resentments. The demand is the only real form of communication. Get your demands into the open. Do this also as self-expression: formulate your demands in the form of an imperative, a command. I guess you know enough of English grammar to know what an imperative is. The imperative is like "Shut up!" "Go to hell!" "Do this!" . . .

Now go back to the resentments you expressed toward the person. Remember *exactly* what you resented. Scratch out the word *resent* and say *appreciate*. Appreciate what you resented before. Then go on to tell this person what else you appreciate in them. Again try to get the feeling that you actually communicate with them . . .

You see, if there were no appreciations, you wouldn't be stuck with this person and you could just forget him. There is always the other side. For instance, my appreciation of Hitler: If Hitler had not come to power, I probably would have been dead by now as a good psychoanalyst who lives on eight patients for the rest of his life.

If you have any difficulties in communication with somebody, look for your resentments. Resentments are among the worst possible unfinished situations—unfinished gestalts. If you resent, you can neither let go nor have it out. Resentment is an emotion of central importance. The resentment is the most important expression of an impasse—of being stuck. If you feel resentment, be able to express your resentment. A resentment unexpressed often is experienced as, or changes into, feelings of guilt. Whenever you feel guilty, find out what you are resenting and express it and make your demands explicit. This alone will help a lot.

Awareness covers, so to speak, three layers or three zones: awareness of the *self*, awareness of the *world*, and awareness of what's between—the intermediate zone of fantasy that prevents a person from being in touch with either himself or the world. This is Freud's great discovery—that there is something between you and the world. There are so many processes going on in one's fantasies. A complex is what he calls it, or a prejudice. If you have prejudices, then your relationship to the world is very much disturbed and destroyed. If you want to approach a person with a prejudice, you can't get to the person. You always will contact only the prejudice, the fixed idea. so Freud's idea that the intermediate zone, the DMZ, this no-man's land between you and the world should be eliminated, emptied out, brainwashed or whatever you want to call it, was perfectly right. The only trouble is that Freud stayed in that zone and analyzed this intermediate thing. He didn't consider the self-awareness or world-awareness; he didn't consider what we can do to be in touch again.

This loss of contact with our authentic self, and loss of contact with the world, is due to this intermediate zone, the big area of *maya* that we carry with us. That is, there is a big area of fantasy activity that takes up so much of our excitement, of our energy, of our life force, that there is very little energy left to be in touch with reality. Now, if we want to make a person whole, we have first to understand what is merely fantasy and irrationality, and we have to discover where one is in touch, and with what. And very often if we work, and we empty out this middle zone of fantasy, this *maya*, then there is the experience of *satori*, of waking up. Suddenly the world is *there*. You wake up from a trance like you wake up from a dream. You're all there again. And the aim in therapy, the growth aim, is to lose more and more of your "mind" and come more to your *senses*. To be more and more in touch, to be in touch with yourself and in touch with the world, instead of only in touch with the fantasies, prejudices, apprehensions, and so on.

If a person confuses *maya* and reality, if he takes fantasy for reality, then he is neurotic or even psychotic. I give you an extreme case of psychosis, the schizophrenic who imagines the doctor is after him, so he decides to beat him to the punch and shoot the doctor, without checking up on reality. On the other hand, there is another possibility. Instead of being divided between *maya* and reality, we can integrate these two, and if *maya* and reality are integrated, we call it art. Great art is real, and great art is at the same time an illusion.

Fantasy can be creative, but it's creative only if you have the fantasy, whatever it is, in the *now*. In the *now*, you use what is available, and you are bound to be creative. Just watch children in their play. What's available is usable and then something happens, something comes out of the being in touch with what is *here* and *now*.

There is only one way to bring about this state of healthy spontaneity, to save the genuineness of the human being. Or, to talk in trite religious terms, there is only one way to regain our soul, or in American terms, to revive the American corpse and bring him back to life. The paradox is that in order to get this spontaneity, we need, like in Zen, an utmost discipline. The discipline is simply to understand the words *now* and *how*, and to bracket off and put aside anything that is not contained in the words *now* and *how*.

Now what's the technique we are using in Gestalt Therapy? The technique is to establish a *continuum of awareness*. This continuum of awareness is required so that the organism can work on the healthy gestalt principle: that the most important unfinished situation will always emerge and can be dealt with. If we prevent ourselves from achieving this gestalt formation, we function badly and we carry hundreds and thousands of unfinished situations with us, that always demand completion.

This continuum of awareness seems to be very simple, just to be aware from second to second what's going on. Unless we are asleep, we are always aware of something. However, as soon as this awareness becomes unpleasant, most people will interrupt it. Then suddenly they start intellectualizing, bullshitting, the flight into the past, the flight into expectations, good intentions, or schizophrenically using free associations, jumping like a grasshopper from experience to experience, and none of these experiences are ever *experienced*, but just a kind of a flash, which leaves all the available material unassimilated and unused.

Now how do we proceed in Gestalt Therapy? What is nowdays quite fashionable was very much pooh-poohed when I started this idea of *everything is awareness*. The purely verbal approach, the Freudian approach in which I was brought up, barks up the wrong tree. Freud's idea was that by certain procedure called free-association, you can liberate the disowned part of the personality and put it at the disposal of the person and then the person will develop what he called a strong ego. What Freud called association, I call *dis*sociation, schizophrenic dissociation to avoid the experience. It's a computer game, an interpretation-computer game, which is exactly an avoidance of the experience of what *is*. You can talk 'til doomsday, you can chase your childhood memories to doomsday, but nothing will change. You can associate—or dissociate—a hundred things to one event, but you can only experience one reality.

So, in contrast to Freud, who placed the greatest emphasis on re-sistances, I have placed the greatest emphasis on *phobic attitude, avoidance, flight from*. Maybe some of you know that Freud's illness was that he suffered from an immense number of phobias, and as he had this illness, of course he had to avoid coping with avoidance. His phobic attitude was tremendous. He couldn't look at a patient—couldn't face having an encounter with the patient—so he had him lie on a couch, and Freud's symptom became the trademark of psycho-analysis. He couldn't go into the open to be photographed, and so on. But usually, if you come to think of it, most of us would rather avoid unpleasant situations and we mobilize all the armor, masks, and so on, a procedure which is usually known as the "repression." So, I try to find out from the patient what he *avoids*.

The enemy of development is this pain phobia—the unwillingness to do a tiny bit of suffering. You see, pain is a signal of nature. The painful leg, the painful feeling, cries out, "Pay attention to me—if you don't pay attention, things will get worse." The broken leg cries, "Don't walk so much. Keep still." We use this fact in Gestalt Therapy by understanding that the awareness continuum is being interrupted—that you become phobic—as soon as you begin to feel something unpleasant. When you begin to feel uncomfortable, you take away your attention.

So the therapeutic agent, the means of development, is to integrate *Attention* and *awareness*. Often psychology doesn't differentiate be-tween awareness and attention. Attention is a deliberate way of listening to the emerging foreground figure, which in this case is something unpleasant. So what I do as therapist is to work as a cata-lyst both ways: provide situations in which a person can experience this being stuck—the unpleasantness—and I frustrate his avoidances still further, until he is willing to mobilize his own resources.

Authenticity, maturity, responsibility for one's actions and life, response-ability, and living in the now, having the creativeness of the now available, is all one and the same thing. Only in the now are you in touch with what's going on. If the now becomes painful, most people are ready to throw the now overboard and avoid the painful situation. Most people can't even suffer themselves. So in therapy the person might simply become phobic and run away or he might play games which will lead our effort *ad absurdum*—like making a fool out of the situation or playing the bear-trapper game. You pro-bably know the bear-trappers. The bear-trappers suck you in and give you the come-on, and when you're sucked in, down comes the hatchet and you stand there with a bloody nose, head, or whatever.

And if you are fool enough to ram your head against the wall until you begin to bleed and be exasperated, then the bear-trapper enjoys himself and enjoys the control he has over you, to render you inadequately impotent, and he enjoys his victorious self which does a lot for his feeble self-esteem. Or you have the Mona Lisa smiler. The smile and smile, and all the time think, "You're such a fool." And nothing penetrates. Or you have the drive-us-crazy, whose only interest in life is to drive themselves or their spouse or their environment crazy and then fish in troubled waters.

But with these exceptions, anyone who has a little bit of goodwill will benefit from the Gestalt approach because the simplicity of the Gestalt approach is that we pay attention to the obvious, to the utmost surface. We don't delve into a region which we don't know anything about, into the so-called "unconscious." I don't believe in repressions. The whole theory of repression is a fallacy. We can't repress a need. We have only repressed certain expressions of these needs. We have blocked one side, and then the self-expression comes out somewhere else, in our movements, in our posture, and most of all in our voice. A good therapist doesn't listen to the content of the bullshit the patient produces, but to the sound, to the music, to the hesitations. Verbal communication is usually a lie. The real communication is beyond words. There is a *very* good book available, *The Voice of Neurosis*, by Paul Moses, a psychologist from San Fransisco who died recently. He could give you a diagnosis from the voice that is better than the Rorschach test.

So don't listen to the words, just listen to what the voice tells you, what the movements tell you, what the posture tells you, what the image tells you. If you have ears, then you know all about the other person. You don't have to listen to *what* the person says: listen to the sounds. *Per sona*—"through sound." The sounds tell you everything. Everything a person wants to express is all there—not in words. What we say is mostly either lies or bullshit. But the voice is there, the gesture, the posture, the facial expression, the psychosomatic language. It's all there if you learn to more or less let the content of the sentences play the second violin only. And if you don't make the mistake of mixing up sentences and reality, and if you use your eyes and ears, then you see that everyone expresses himself in one way or another. If you have eyes and ears, the world is open. Nobody can have any secrets because the neurotic only fools himself, nobody else —except for awhile, maybe, if he is a good actor.

In most psychiatry, the sound of the voice is not noticed, only the verbal contact is abstracted from the total personality. Movements like—you see how much this young man here expresses in his leaning forward—the total personality as it expresses itself with movements, with posture, with sound, with pictures—there is so much invaluable material here, that we don't have to do anything else except get to the obvious, to the outermost surface, and feed this back, so as to bring this into the patient's awareness. *Feedback* was Carl Rogers' introduction into psychiatry. Again, he only mostly feeds back the sentences, but there is so much more to be fed back—something you might not be aware of, and here the attention and awareness of the therapist might be useful. So we have it rather easy compared with the psychoanalysts, because we see the whole being of a person right in front of us, and this is because Gestalt Therapy uses eyes and ears and the therapist stays absolutely in the now. He avoids interpretation, verbiage production, and all other types of mind-fucking. But mind-fucking is mind-fucking. It is also a symptom which might cover something else. But what is there is there. Gestalt Therapy is being in touch with the obvious.

4

Now let me tell you something about how I see the structure of a neurosis. Of course I don't know what the theory will be next because I'm always developing and simplifying what I'm doing more and more. I now see the neurosis as consisting of five layers.

The first layer is the cliche layer. If you meet somebody you exchange cliches—"Good morning," handshake, and all of the meaningless *tokens* of meeting.

Now behind the cliches, you find the second layer, what I call the Eric Berne or Sigmund Freud layer—the layer where we play games and roles—the very important person, the bully, the cry-baby, the nice little girl, the good boy—whatever roles we choose to play. So those are the superficial, social, *as-if* layers. We pretend to be better, tougher, weaker, more polite, etc., than we really feel. This is essentially where the psychoanalysts stay. They treat *playing* the child as a reality and call it infantilism and try to get all the details of this child-playing.

Now, this synthetic layer has to be first worked through. I call it the synthetic layer because it fits very nicely into the dialectical thinking. If we translate the dialectic—thesis, antithesis, synthesis— into *existence*, we can say: *existence*, *anti*-existence, and *synthetic* existence. Most of our life is a synthetic existence, a compromise between the anti-existence and existence. For instance, today I had the luck to meet somebody who has not this phony layer, who is an honest person, and relatively direct. But most of us put on a show which we are *not*, for which we don't have our support, our strength, our genuine desire, our genuine talents.

Now if we work through the role-playing layer, if we take away the roles, what do experience then? Then we experience the *anti-existence*, we experience the nothingness, emptiness. This is the *impasse* that I talked about earlier, the feeling of being stuck and lost. The impasse is marked by a phobic attitude—avoidance. We are phobic, we avoid suffering, especially the suffering of frustration. We are spoiled, and we don't want to go through the hellgates of suffering: We stay immature, we go on manipulating the world, rather than to suffer the pains of growing up. This is the story. We rather suffer being self-conscious, being looked *upon*, than to realize our blindness and get our eyes again. And this is the great difficulty I see in self-therapy. There are *many* things one can do on one's own, do one's own therapy, but when one comes to the difficult parts, especially to the impasse, you become phobic, you get into a whirl, into a merry-go-round, and you are not willing to go through the pain of the impasse.

Behind the impasse lies a very interesting layer, the *death* layer or *implosive* layer. This fourth layer appears either as death or as fear of death. The death layer has nothing to do with Freud's death instinct. It only appears as death because of the paralysis of opposing forces. It is a kind of catatonic paralysis: we pull ourselves together, we contract and compress ourselves, we *implode*. Once we really get in contact with this deadness of the implosive layer, then something very interesting happens.

The *implosion* becomes *explosion*. The death layer comes to life, and this explosion is the link-up with the authentic person who is capable of experiencing and expressing his emotions. There are four basic kinds of explosions from the death layer. There is the explosion of genuine *grief* if we work through a loss or death that has not been assimilated. There is the explosion into *orgasm* in sexually blocked people. There is the explosion into *anger*, and also the explosion into *joy, laughter, joi de vivre*. These explosions connect with the authentic personality, with the true self.

Now, don't be frightened by the word *explosion*. Many of you drive a motor car. There are hundreds of explosions per minute, in the cylinder. This is different from the violent explosion of the catatonic—that would be like an explosion in a gas tank. Also a single explosion doesn't mean a thing. The so-called break-throughs of the Reichian therapy, and all that, are as little useful as the insight in psychoanalysis. Things still have to work through.

As you know, most of our role-playing is designed to use up a lot of this energy for controlling just those explosions. The death layer, the fear of death, is that if we explode, then we believe we can't survive any more—then we will die, we'll be persecuted, we'll be punished, we won't be loved any more and so on. So the whole rehearsal and self-torture game continues; we hold ourselves back and control ourselves.

Let me give you an example. There was once a girl, a woman, who had lost her child not too long ago, and she couldn't quite get in touch with the world. And we worked a bit, and we found she was holding onto the coffin. She realized she did not want to let go of this coffin. Now you understand, as long as she is not willing to face this hole, this emptiness, this nothingness, she couldn't come back to life, to the others. So much love is bound up here, in this coffin, that she rather invests her life in this fantasy of having some kind of a child, even if it's a dead child. When she can face her nothingness and experience her grief, she can come back to life and get in touch with the world.

The whole philosophy of nothingness is very fascinating. In our culture "nothingness" has a different meaning than it has in the Eastern religions. When we say "nothingness," there is a void, an emptiness, something deathlike. When the Eastern person says "nothingness," he calls it *no thingness*—there are no *things* there. There is only process, happening. Nothingness doesn't exist for us, in the strictest sense, because nothingness is based on awareness of nothingness, so there is the awareness of nothingness, so there is something there. And we find when we accept and *enter* this nothingness, the void, then the desert starts to bloom. The empty void becomes alive, is being filled. The sterile void becomes the fertile void. I am getting more and more right on the point of writing quite a bit about the philosophy of nothing. I feel this way, as if I am nothing, just function. "I've got plenty of nothing." *Nothing* equals *real*.

Question: Fritz, when I was exploding, outside, you seemed cutting down on me, with being sort of witty, by using your wit on me, and it seems to me that this is what I do—that I explode, that I let myself go, and that you were sort of poking fun at me.

Fritz: Oh, yes. You didn't realize what I did. Yesterday we started out with your being afraid. You let out a lot of passionate energy this morning, and I put more and more obstacles in your way so you would become hotter, more convincing. Do you see what I did for you? (Fritz laughs).

Question: Well, I misinterpreted it—I—

Fritz: Of course. If you had known, it wouldn't have worked. I saw you begin to enjoy yourself so much, in your heightened color, and your saving the world. It was *beautiful.*

Question: Where does all this energy in the implosive layer come from?

Fritz: (He makes hooks of the fingers of each hand, then hooks his hands together and pulls) Did you see what I did? Did you see how much energy I spent doing nothing, just pulling myself with equal strength? Where does the energy come from? By not allowing the excitement to get to our senses and muscles. The excitement goes instead of this into our fantasy life, into the fantasy life which we take for real. You might believe, "I can't possibly do this. I am helpless. I need my wife to comfort me," and you are not willing to wake up and see that you might be able to produce your own comfort, and even comfort other people.

Our life energy goes only into those parts of our personality with which we identify. In our own time, many people identify mostly with their computer. They think. Some people talk about the greatness of the homo sapiens, the computer bit, as if our intellect has leadership over the human animal, a notion which has gone out of fashion with Freud. Today we are talking about an integration of the social being and the animal being. Without the support of our vitality, of our physical existence, the intellect remains merely mindfucking.

Most people play two kinds of intellectual games. The one game is the comparing game, the "more than" game—my car is bigger than yours, my house is better than yours, and so on and so on. Now the other game which is of the utmost importance is the fitting game. You know the fitting game in many respects. If you want to play a certain role—let's say you want to go to a party, you want to be the belle of the ball, so you have to put on the costume for this role. You go to a first-class tailor and you play the fitting game. This costume fits me, the tailor has to make the costume to fit me, I have to get accessories that fit the costume, and so on. Now this fitting game can be played in two directions. One direction is, we look upon reality and see where does this reality fit into my theories, my hypotheses, my fantasies *about* what reality is like. Or you can work from the opposite direction. You have faith in a certain concept, you have faith in a certain school, either the psychological school, the Freudian school, or the conditioning school. Now you see how to fit reality into that model. It's just like Procrustes, who had to fit all people into the same size bed. If they are too long, he cut off their legs; if they were too short, he stretched them until they fit the bed. This is the fitting game.

A theory, a concept, is an abstraction, is an aspect of any event. If you take this desk, from this desk you can abstract the form, you can abstract the substance, you can abstract the color, you can abstract its monetary value. You can't add the abstractions together to make a whole, because the whole exists in the first place, and the abstractions are then done by us, from whatever context we need these abstractions.

Now in regard to psychology, I like to point out some of the abstractions you can make from Gestalt Therapy. One is the behavioristic. What we do: we observe the identity of structure and function in the people, organism, and so on, which we encounter. The great thing about the behaviorists is that they actually work in the here and now. They look, they observe what's going on. If we could deduct from the present-day American psychologists their compulsion to condition, and just keep them as observers: If they could realize that the changes which are required are *not* to be obtained by conditioning, that conditioning always produces artifacts, and that the real changes are occurring by themselves in a different way, then I think we could do much toward a reconciliation of the behaviorists and the experientialists.

The experientialists, the clinical psychologists, have one great advantage over the behaviorists. They do not see the human organism as a mechanical something that is just functioning. They see that in the center of life is the means of communication, namely, awareness. Now you call awareness "consciousness," or sensitivity, or just awareness of something. I believe that matter has—besides extension, duration, etc.—also *awareness*. Of course we are not capable yet of measuring the infinitely small quantities of awareness in, let's say, this desk here, but we know that every animal, every plant, has awareness, or you might call it tropism, sensitivity, protoplasmatic sensitivity or whatever you want to, but the awareness is there. Otherwise they could not react to sunlight, or to give you another example: If you have a plant, and you put some fertilizer in one place, the plant will grow roots toward this fertilizer. If you now dig out the fertilizer and move it somewhere else, then the plant will grow roots in that direction.

So, what I want to point out is, in Gestalt Therapy we start with *what is*, and see which abstraction, which context, which situation is there to be found and relate the figure, the foreground experience, to the background, to the content, to the perspective, to the situation, and they together form the gestalt. Meaning is the relationship of the foreground figure to its background. If you use the word *king*, you have to have a background to understand the meaning of the word *king*, whether it's the King of England, the king of a chess game, the chicken a la king—nothing has a meaning without its context. Meaning doesn't exist. It is always created ad hoc.

We have two systems with which to relate to the world. One is called the sensoric system, the other is the motoric system. Now unfortunately the behaviorists, with their idiotic reflex-arc bit, have messed the whole thing up. The sensoric system is for orientation, the sense of touching, where we get in touch with the world. We also have the motoric system with which to cope, the system of action through which we do something with the world. And a really healthy, complete person has to have both a good orientation and ability to act. Now you sometimes get the extreme missing of one side or another, as in the extreme cases of schizophrenia. The extreme cases of schizophrenia are the completely withdrawn persons who lack action, and the paranoic types who lack sensitivity. So if there is no balance between sensing and doing, then you are out of gear.

Many people rather hang on with their attention to exhaust the situation that doesn't nourish. This hanging onto the world, this location, this over-extended contact, is as pathological as the complete withdrawal—the ivory tower or the catatonic stupor. In both cases, contact and withdrawal does not flow—the rhythm is interrupted.

The sickness, playing sick, which is a large part of this getting crazy, is nothing but the quest for environmental support. If you are sick in bed, somebody is coming and cares for you, brings you your food, your warmth, you don't have to go out and make a living, so there is the complete regression. But the regression is not, as Freud thought, a purely pathological phenomenon. Regression means a withdrawal to a position where you can provide your own support, where you feel secure. We are going to work quite a bit with deliberate regression here, deliberate withdrawal, to find out what is the situation in which you feel comfortable, in contrast to the situation you cannot cope with. You find out, what *are* you in touch with, if you cannot be in touch with the world and with your environment.

So let's do another experiment, which might be quite helpful to you. If you're confused or bored or somehow stuck, try the following experiment: Shuttle between *here* and *there*. I want you all to do this now. Close your eyes and go away in your imagination, from here to any place you like . . .

Now the next step is to come back to the *here* experience, the here and now . . . And now compare the two situations. Most likely the *there* situation was preferable to the *here* situation. . . And now close your eyes again. Go away again, wherever you'd like to go. And notice any change. . .

Now again come back to the here and now, and again compare the two situations. Has any change taken place? . . . And now go away again—continue to do this on your own until you really feel comfortable in the present situation, until you come to your senses, and you begin to see and hear and be here in this world; until you really begin to exist. . . Is anybody willing to talk about this experience of shuttling?

P: Initially I went away to a friend's house, it was very nice. I came back. The second time I went to a river-mountain retreat that I go to, and it also was extremely nice. Then I came back. I'm here now, and I realize that working in the future for me is unnecessary. It's more important for me now to be here. The future will take care of itself.

Q: I climbed a mountain with someone with whom I was very much giving and loving and receiving this feeling, and when I came back I still wasn't satisfied because this was not complete in my life. So I will tend to look for that closure.

R: I alternated between three places that are favorite places of nature for me, and I was there alone. And each time I came back, I felt more calm.

S: Fritz, I'm struck by the fact that when I go away, I'm more alive than when I'm right here. I don't operate with as much emotion or as much vitality here—my physical body is much less moved, is much less in reality, than when I go away.

Fritz: You didn't manage to bring any of the vitality back to the here and now?

S: Yes. But not as much. There was still a discrepancy between them.

Fritz: There is still a reservoir left untapped.

T: I feel the same thing that I felt when I go back to my living room at home. Ah, the first time I went back I didn't feel very much, and I came back here and I felt a certain tension. And when I went back the second time, it was the same, and I came back here and I felt more tension. And I went back and I could feel the same tension in my living room as I feel here.

U: I went to a desert island, which was something I escaped to in my dreams as a child. And I appreciated the freedom that I had there. One thing I would do was have no clothes on and be able to swim nude in very clear water. And I appreciated that but at the same time I—I realized, or I think I felt more that I needed people. I'm more aware of my need for people than I was. Ah, I think I brought back some of the—the desire to be free when I came back here. Then the next place I went was on a hike with my husband up Mount Tamalpais—this was when we were courting. And the feelings that go along with that are that he loved me more then than he does now, and there was a great euphoria about our relationship. I brought some of that back with me too, but then I wanted to return to that, which I did. And we were again hiking up Mount Tamalpais, but then I began to appreciate the fact that I wasn't—that he was carrying part of—part of me in the relationship and I think I bring back that awareness now too, to the present situation—both the joy and the realization that I have to carry myself along.

Fritz: Well, I think a number of you experienced quite a bit of integration of these two opposites, *there* and *now*. If you do this with any uncomfortable situation, you can really pinpoint what's missing in this here-and-now situation. Very often the *there* gives you a cue for what's missing in the now, what's different in the now. So, whenever you get bored or tense, always withdraw—especially the therapists among you. If you fall asleep when the patient doesn't bring any interesting things, it saves *your* strength, and the patient will either wake you up or come back with some more interesting material. And if not, you at least have time for a snooze.

Withdraw to a situation from which you get support, and then come back with that regained strength to reality. You know Hercules is the famous symbol of self-control. You know, that obsessional character who cleaned out the Augean stables and so on. Now the most important story may be of Hercules' attempt to kill Antaeus. As soon as Antaeus touched the ground, he regained his strength, and that's what happens in the withdrawal. Of course the optimum withdrawal is the withdrawal into your body. Get in touch with yourself. Turn your attention to your physical existence. Mobilize your inner resources. Even if you get in touch with your fantasy of being on an island or in a warm bathtub, or to any unfinished situation, this will give you a lot of support when you return to reality.

Now normally the *elan vital*, the life force, energizes by sensing, by listening, by scouting, by describing the world—how is the world there. Now this life force apparently first mobilizes the center—*if* you have a center. And the center of the personality is what used to be called the soul: the emotions, the feelings, the spirit. Emotions are not a nuisance to be discharged. The emotions are the most important motors of our behavior: emotion in the widest sense—whatever you feel—the waiting, the joy, the hunger. Now these emotions, or this basic energy, this life force is apparently differentiated in the organism by what I would like to call the hormonic differentiation. This basic excitement is differentiated, let's say by the adrenal glands, into anger and fear: by the sex glands into libido. It might, in case of adjustment to a loss, be turned into grief. Then this emotional excitement mobilizes the muscles, the motoric system. Every emotion, then, expresses itself in the muscular system. You can't imagine anger without muscular movement. You can't imagine joy, which is more or less identical with dancing, without muscular movement. In grief there is sobbing and crying, and in sex there are also certain movements, as you all know. And these muscles are used to move about, to take from the world, to touch the world, to be in contact, to be in touch.

Any disturbance of this excitement metabolism will diminish your vitality. If these excitements cannot be transformed into their specific activities but are stagnated, then we have the state called anxiety, which is a tremendous excitement held up, bottled up. *Angoustia* is the Latin word for narrowness. You narrow the chest, to go through the narrow path; the heart speeds up in order to supply the oxygen needed for the excitement, and so on. If excitement cannot flow into activity through the motoric system, then we try to desensitize the sensoric system to reduce this excitement. So we find all kinds of desensitization: frigidity, blocking of the ears, and so on—all these holes in the personality that I talked about earlier.

So, if we are so disturbed in our metabolism, and have no center from which we can live, we have to do something, we want to do something to collect again the wellspring, the foundation of our being. Now there is not such a thing as total integration. Integration is never completed; maturation is never completed. It's an ongoing process for ever and ever. You can't say, "Now I've eaten a steak and now I am satisfied; now I'm no more hungry," and for the rest of your life there is no more hunger. There's always something to be integrated; always something to be learned. There's always a possibility for yourself and for your life. Of course, taking responsibility for your life and being rich in experience and ability is identical. And this is what I hope to do here in this short seminar—to make you understand how much you gain by taking responsibility for every emotion, every movement you make, every thought you have—and shed responsibility for *anybody* else. The world is not there for your expectation, nor do you have to live for the expectation of the world. We touch each other by honestly being what we are, not by intentionally *making* contact.

Responsibility, in one context, is the idea of obligation. If I take responsibility for somebody else, I feel omnipotent: I have to interfere with his life. All it means is, I have a duty—I believe I have the duty to support this person. But responsibility can also be spelled *response-ability*: the ability to respond, to have thoughts, reactions, emotions in a certain situation. Now, this responsibility, the ability to *be* what one *is*, is expressed through the word *I*. Many agree with Federn, a friend of Freud, who maintained that the ego is a substance, and I maintain that the ego, the *I*, is merely a symbol of identification. If I say that I am hungry now, and in an hour's time I say I am not hungry, this is not a contradiction. It is not a lie, because in between I have eaten lunch. I identify with my state right now, and I identify with my state afterward.

Responsibility means simply to be willing to say "I am I" and "I am what I am—I'm Popeye, the sailor man." It's not easy to let go of the fantasy or concept of being a child in need, the child that wants to be loved, the child that is afraid to be rejected, but all those events are those for which we are not taking responsibility. Just as I said in regard to self-consciousness, we are not willing to take the responsibility that we are critical, so we project criticism onto others. We don't want to take the responsibility for being discriminating, so we project it outside and then we live in eternal demands to be accepted, or the fear of being rejected. And one of the most important responsibilities—this is a *very* important transition—is to take responsibility for our projections, re-identify with these projections, and become what we project.

The difference between Gestalt Therapy and most other types of psychotherapy is essentially that we do *not* analyze. We *integrate*. The old mistake of mixing up understanding and explanatoriness is what we hope to avoid. If we explain, interpret, this might be a very interesting intellectual game, but it's a dummy activity, and a dummy activity is worse than doing nothing. If you do nothing, at least you *know* you do nothing. If you engage in a dummy activity you just invest time and energy in unproductive work and possibly get more and more conditioned to doing these futile activities—wasting your time, and if anything getting deeper into the morass of the neurosis.

It would be wonderful if we could be so wise and intelligent that our rationality could domineer our biological life. And this polarity of mind vs. body is not the only polarity. There are other things to the human being than these two instruments. This identification with the intellect, with explanations, leaves out the total organism, leaves out the body. You *use* your body instead of *being* some-body. And the more all the thinking goes into the computing, into manipulation, the less energy is left for the total self. Since you have bracketed off your body, the result is that you feel like being nobody, because you have no body. There's no body in your life. No wonder so many people, if they are out of the routine of their daily work, get their "Sunday neurosis" when they are really faced with their boredom and the emptiness of their lives.

Gestalt Therapy is an existential approach, which means we are not just occupied with dealing with symptoms or character structure, but with the total existence of a person. This existence, and the problems of existence, in my opinion are mostly very clearly indicated in dreams.

Freud once called the dream the *Via Regia*, the royal road to the unconscious. And I believe it is really the royal road to integration. I never know what the "unconscious" is, but we know that the dream definitely is the most spontaneous expression of the existence of the human being. There's nothing else as spontaneous as the dream. The most absurd dream doesn't disturb us as being absurd at the time: We feel it is the real thing. Whatever you do otherwise in life, you will have some kind of control or deliberate interference. Not so with the dream. Every dream is an art work, more than a novel. a bizarre drama. Whether or not it's *good* art is another story, but there is always lots of movement, fights, encounters, all kinds of things in it. Now if my contention is correct, which I believe of course it is, all the different parts of the dream are fragments of our personalities. Since our aim is to make everyone of us a wholesome person, which means a unified person, without conflicts, what we have to do is put the different fragments of the dream together. We have to *re-own* these projected, fragmented parts of our personality, and *re-own* the hidden potential that appears in the dream.

Because of the phobic attitude, the avoidance of awareness, much material that is our own, that is part of ourselves, has been dissociated, alienated, disowned, thrown out. The rest of our potential is not available to us. But I believe most of it *is* available, but as projections. I suggest we start with the impossible assumption that whatever we believe we see in another person or in the world is nothing but a projection. Might be far out, but it's just unbelievable how much we project, and how blind and deaf we are to what is really going on. So, the re-owning of our senses and the understanding of projections will go hand in hand. The difference between reality and fantasy, between observation and imagination—this differentiation will take quite a bit of doing.

We can reassimilate, we can take back our projections, by projecting ourselves completely into that other thing or person. What is pathological is always the *part*-projection. *Total* projection is called artistic experience, and this total projection is an identification with that thing in question. I give you an idea, for instance. In Zen, you are not allowed to paint a single branch until you have become that branch.

So, I want to start out with a simple experiment to produce magic, to transform ourselves—metamorphose ourselves into something we are apparently not, to learn to identify with something we are not. Let's start with something very simple. Will you all observe me. I'm going to make some faces and expressions and I want you, without words or sounds, to copy my expressions and see whether you can really feel that you become me and my expressions. Now watch this. Go along with it. The main thing is the facial expression. . .

Now I tell you how I did it. I imagined a situation and went into that situation, and I had the impression—I think most of you got quite a bit of the feeling of identification, not so much thinking, just simply following.

Now let's take another step. You come up here and talk to me— just say anything. (As a person speaks, Fritz imitates his words, voice inflection, and facial expressions.) Pair up and do this, and again try to really get the feel of being this other person. . .

Now I want each one of you to transform yourself into something a little bit more different. Say, transform yourself into a road. . .

Now transform yourself into a motorcar. . .

Now transform yourself into a six-month old baby. . .

Now transform yourself into the mother of that baby. . .

Now transform yourself into that same baby again. . .

Now the same mother. . .

Now the same baby. . .

Now be two years of age. . .

Now transform yourself into your present age, the age you are. . .

Can everyone perform that miracle?

Now, I want to show you how to use this identification technique with dreams. This is quite different from what the psychoanalysts do. What's usually done with a dream is to cut it to pieces, and follow up by association what it means, and interpret it. Now we might possibly get some integration by this procedure, but I don't quite believe it, because in most cases this is merely an intellectual game. Many of you may have been brainwashed by psychoanalysis, but if you want to get something real from a dream, do *not* interpret. Do *not* play intellectual insight games or associate or dissociate freely or unfreely to them.

In Gestalt Therapy we don't interpret dreams. We do something much more interesting with them. Instead of analyzing and further cutting up the dream, we want to bring it back to life. And the way to bring it back to life is to re-live the dream as if it were happening now. Instead of telling the dream as if it were a story in the past, act it out in the present, so that it becomes a part of yourself, so that you are really involved.

If you understand what you can do with dreams, you can do a tremendous lot for yourself on your own. Just take any old dream or dream fragment, it doesn't matter. As long as a dream is remembered, it is still alive and available, and it still contains an unfinished, unassimilated situation. When we are working on dreams, we usually take only a small little bit from the dream, because you can get so much from even a little bit.

So if you want to work on your own, I suggest you write the dream down and make a list of *all* the details in the dream. Get every person, every thing, every mood, and then work on these to *become* each one of them. Ham it up, and really transform yourself into each of the different items. Really *become* that thing—whatever it is in a dream—*become* it. Use your magic. Turn into that ugly frog or whatever is there—the dead thing, the live thing, the demon—and stop thinking. Lose your mind and come to your senses. Every little bit is a piece of the jigsaw puzzle, which together will make up a much larger whole—a much stronger, happier, more completely *real* personality.

Next, take each one of these different items, characters, and parts, and let them have encounters between them. Write a script. By "write a script," I mean have a dialogue between the two opposing parts and you will find—especially if you get the correct opposites— that they always start out fighting each other. All the different parts —any part in the dream is yourself, is a projection of yourself, and if there are inconsistent sides, contradictory sides, and you use them to fight each other, you have the eternal conflict game, the self-torture game. As the process of encounter goes on, there is a mutual learning until we come to an understanding, and an appreciation of differences, until we come to a oneness and integration of the two opposing forces. Then the civil war is finished, and your energies are ready for your struggles with the world.

Each little bit of work you do will mean a bit of assimilation of something. In principle, you can get through the whole cure—let's call it cure or maturation—if you did this with every single thing in one dream. Everything is there. In different forms the dreams change, but when you start like this, you'll find more dreams will come and the existential message will become clearer and clearer.

So I would like from now on to put the accent on dreamwork. We find all we need in the dream, or in the perimeter of the dream, the environment of the dream. The existential difficulty, the missing part of the personality, they are all there. It's a kind of central attack right into the midst of your non-existence.

The dream is an excellent opportunity to find the holes in the personality. They come out as voids, as blank spaces, and when you get into the vicinity of these holes, you get confused or nervous. There is a dreadful experience, the expectation, "If I approach this, there will be catastrophe. I will be *nothing*." I have already talked a bit about the philosophy of nothingness. This is the impasse, where you avoid, where you become phobic. You suddenly get sleepy or remember something very important you have to do. So if you work on dreams it is better if you do it with someone else who can point out where you avoid. Understanding the dream means realizing when you are avoiding the obvious. The only danger is that this other person might come too quickly to the rescue and tell you what is going on in you, instead of giving yourself the chance of discovering yourself.

And if you understand the meaning of each time you identify with some bit of a dream, each time you translate an *it* into an *I*, you increase in vitality and in your potential. Like a debt collector you have your money invested all over the place, so take it back. And on the other hand, begin to understand the dummy activities where you waste your energies like, let's say, when you're bored. Instead of saying, "I'm bored," and find out what you're actually interested in, you suffer and stay with what is boring to you. You torture yourself with staying there, and at the same time, whenever you torture yourself you torture your environment. You become a gloom-caster. If you *enjoy* the gloom-casting, if you *accept* it, that's fine, because then the whole thing becomes a positive experience. Then you take responsibility for what you're doing. If you enjoy self-torture, fine. But there's always the question of accepting or not accepting, and accepting is not just tolerating. Accepting is getting a present, a gift. The balance is always gratefulness for what *is*. If it's too little, you feel resentful; it it's too much, you feel guilty. But if you get the balance, you grow in gratefulness. If you make a sacrifice, you feel resentful; if you give a present, you give something surplus and you feel fine. It's a closure—completion of a gestalt.

Question: We practice, in living with each other, what some people would call the amenities. Could you draw a line between taking responsibility and practicing the amenities?

Fritz: Yah. You take responsibility for playing a phony role. You play polite to keep the other person happy.

Any time you use the words *now* and *how*, and become aware of this, you grow. Each time you use the question *why*, you diminish in stature. You bother yourself with false, unnecessary information. You only feed the computer, the intellect. And the intellect is the whore of intelligence. It's a drag on your life.

So the simple fact is that against the—excuse this expression—evil of self-alienation, self-impoverishment, there's only the remedy of re-integrating, taking back what is rightfully yours. Each time you change an *it* or a *noun* into an *I* or a *verb* you get, let's say, a ten-thousandth of your potential back, and it will accumulate. Each time you can integrate something it gives you a better platform, where again you can facilitate your development, your integration.

Don't try to make a perfectionist program out of it, that you *should* chew up every bit of what you're eating, that you *should* make a pause between the different bites so that you can complete one situation before you start the other; to change *every* noun and *it* into an *I*. Don't torture yourself with these demands, but realize this is the basis of our existence and discover that this is how it is. It is how it should be and it should be how it is.

CHAPTER 2

GESTALT THERAPY: RETROFLECTION, INTRO-JECTION, AND PROJECTION

FREDERICK S. PERLS, M.D., Ph.D.

Manipulating the Self

THE MODIFIED SITUATION

All experiments thus far have been concerned with becoming aware of processes which are basic to the integrated functioning of the human organism. They apply to everyone. Now we come to experiments dealing with processes which occur chronically only when the organism is malfunctioning. They are "abnormal." It is their prevalence in a person's behavior that justifies calling him "neurotic" or "psychotic." However, granted certain kinds of upbringing and certain life-situations (which, in varying degree, have been encountered by every one of us) they are *inevitable*.

This is not equivalent to saying that since they are so common, we need not be concerned about them. Those writers of abnormal psychology textbooks who draw a sharp line between "normal" and "abnormal"—they are virtually extinct at last—reveal themselves to be confluent with "the authorities," whose concept of "normal" is so impoverished as to be synonymous with "conspicuously respectable."

There is now nearly universal agreement that every person in our society has his "neurotic trends," "unresolved conflicts," or "areas of maladjustment." Where the informed disagree is not with respect to the ubiquity of neurosis but in regard to what should or can be done about it. The orthodox Freudian, following hard upon what the master set down in *Civilization and Its Discontents*, resigns himself to repression as the price we must pay for civilization. Others, more optimistic as regards the long-view, can, nevertheless, foresee nothing more hopeful than many generations of slow amelioration. Because of the lack of widely available therapeutic techniques and anything more than drop-in-the-bucket methods of social prophylaxis, they use pussyfooting manners of speech for fear of being, as they think, unduly alarmist and upsetting. Were a tested remedy at hand which could be applied wholesale, we may be sure that they would more frankly publicize the epidemic status of the disease.

Still others, with Messianic fervor—and this present work will not fail to be classified as such—bring forth from time to time some simple nostrum and say, "Do this, and the world is saved!"

A major problem for all forms of psychotherapy is to *motivate the patient to do what needs to be done.* He must return to "unfinished business" which he left unfinished in the past because it was so painful that he had to flee. Now, if he is encouraged to go back and finish it, it is still painful; it reactivates his misery, and from the short-run view, it is still to be avoided. How can he be kept at the task—ultimately, how can he keep himself at the task—when there is such a quantity of unpleasantness to live through?

To this question no positive answer exists today for most persons. An unknown number, perhaps a majority, believe they would have no troubles if the world would just treat them right. A smaller contingent does have, at least at times, a vague recognition that they themselves are responsible for the ills that beset them, at any rate in part, but they lack techniques for coping with them other than the old threadbare resolutions "to do better," or moral maxims. Or they displace problems from their true arena to a spurious one which allows a great show of busyness and suffices, at least, to let off steam. A very small number take their troubles to an "expert," hopeful that some magic formula will be uttered and their personal devils exorcised.

Of those who start treatment most do not continue. Their cases are not discharged by the therapist but are self-terminated. Many, when magic is not forthcoming from one therapist, try another, then another, and another. Among myriad ways of expressing dissatisfaction with one's doctor a very common one is to the effect: "He doesn't understand my case." Perhaps he does not, and there may be merit in shifting. But most patients, perhaps all, wish in some degree to prescribe to the therapist how he shall cure them—and this prescription does not include that they shall suffer in the process!

For surgical and pharmacological forms of medical treatment the patient can be perfectly passive, and it is better if he is. He may receive an anesthetic and wake up with the operation over. The notion that treatment should be administered to a passive patient generalizes to notions of how it ought to be possible to cure a neurosis. The latter, however, is not "organic" but "functional." While the patient is not so naive as to suppose there can literally be surgical removal of his symptoms, he is likely to feel that little more should be necessary on his own part than to bring the body. Once he presents himself, the doctor—perhaps with the aid of hypnosis—ought to be able to fix him up.

Since it is, nevertheless, the patient himself who must change his own behavior and thus effect his own cure, all methods of psychotherapy give rise to what, in professional jargon, are called "disappointment reactions." These usually stem from realizing after a time that the therapist actually expects one to do hard work and undergo pain. As a matter of fact, without being fully aware of it, one may have sought out the therapist in the hope of acquiring exactly the opposite, namely, a better way of escaping work and avoiding pain. To discover that therapy involves concentrated doses of what one sought to be relieved of seems as absurd as to take the ailment and apply it as treatment.

In the fortunate case what happens is that, before the patient develops a disappointment reaction strong enough to make him terminate treatment, he learns that the hard work is not mere drudgery. However far removed it may at first seem from what he thinks is urgent and therefore the place to start, he gradually gains orientation and perspective. He comes to see particular symptoms as merely surface manifestations of a more general and complicated system of malfunctioning which underlies and supports them. Though now, in a way, the job looks bigger and will obviously take longer than originally supposed, it does begin to make sense.

Likewise, with respect to the pain involved, he comes to see that this is not pointless, needless pain. He begins to appreciate the rough-hewn wisdom of the advice to get back on a horse, when thrown, and successfully ride him off. The patient's situation is different in that he has, perhaps, avoided his particular horse for a long time; years, perhaps, or even most of a lifetime. Nevertheless, if healthy functioning requires that he learn to ride and manage a certain kind of horse that has thrown him in the past, the only way he can possibly do this is to make approaches to the horse and then, sooner or later, get into the saddle.

Although the therapist keeps leading the patient back to that which he wishes to avoid, he usually is milder and more considerate with him than the patient himself or than his friends and relatives. Their attitude is one of demanding that he snap out of it, stop pampering himself, and take the hurdle, whatever it is, in a blind, compulsive rush. The therapist, on the contrary, is at least as much interested in the avoidance itself as in what is avoided. Whatever the superficial appearances, where there is the tendency to avoid something, this tendency exists for good and sufficient reasons. The job is to explore and become fully aware of these grounds for avoidance. This is called "analyzing the resistance." How the patient experiences and verbalizes these grounds will change, perhaps dramatically, as therapy progresses. With the change, not just in how he talks but in how he feels himself and experiences his problems, he can make further and further "approaches" as he feels the initiative and strength to do so until he settles his neurotic difficulties once and for all.

The strategy of motivating the patient to continue therapy is usually not particularly taxed at the very beginning. There is at that time the so-called "honeymoon period," when what is uppermost is the satisfaction of having made a start after an interval of vacillation, the opinion that one's therapist is wonderful, the conviction that one will be the brightest, the fastest-moving, in short, the most remarkable patient he has ever had, and that one will now blossom forth as that radiant, inimitable personality that one has always felt himself potentially to be.

It is when the "honeymoon" is over that the motivation problem becomes critical. One has worked so hard, been so cooperative, been the model patient, and yet—well, there is so little to show for it! The glamor is gone, and the road still stretches far ahead. In Freudian analysis this is likely to be the time of "negative transference." The therapist, who at first seemed so all-knowing and all-powerful, has revealed his feet of clay. All he knows is more of the same, and the same is getting tiresome. In fortunate cases such discontent with one's doctor breaks into the open as reproaches, disparagement, or even wrathful denunciation. When this occurs, it usually clears the air, and the case may then settle down for the long haul. If it does not—if the patient is "too polite," "too considerate," "too understanding" to attack the therapist outright—the case is likely to clog up with unexpressed resentment and be terminated by the patient.

For the most part, the patient's progress in therapy is not aided and abetted by the persons he sees in everyday life. He may, of course, be fortunate enough to have friends and acquaintances who have themselves benefited from therapy, in which event it is not so difficult for him to maintain belief in the value of continuing. If, on the other hand, he lives with relatives who construe his action as a reflection on the wholesomeness of the family relationships, who view it as "weakness" to be treated for something "mental," or who, to the extent that he progresses, find it less and less easy to domineer, exploit, overprotect, or otherwise be in neurotic confluence with him, he will have to struggle against veiled or open pressures to make him cease and desist from this "foolishness." Many patients succumb to such emotional blackmail levied upon them by "normal" associates.

As the effectiveness of psychotherapy has come to be more generally recognized, this situation has improved somewhat. Nevertheless, even though one may have a verbal understanding of what is involved in psychotherapy and a naturalistic conception of its rationale so that one does not boggle over giving it lip-service at a distance, when it comes close enough to interfere with one's own life— for instance, through changes forced in one's relationship to a friend or relative who is in therapy or through the heightened "temptation" to try it out oneself—then, to the extent that one is neurotic, one *must* fight it—*for it is aggressive toward the neurotic way of life!* The neurotic's resistance to psychotherapy, whether he is actually a patient or simply someone entertaining an opinion on the subject, constitutes his counter-aggression against psychotherapy. He feels threatened by it. And, *as a neurotic*, so he is! What could be more natural—and, with certain qualifications, healthy—than that he should fight back?

All that has been remarked above has centered around formal psychotherapy—that is, the situation where therapist and patient confront each other face-to-face. Now how does the matter stand with respect to your continuing to do the work involved in these experiments? They provide you with instructions whereby, if fully followed through, the crux of what goes on in formal therapy may be reenacted by the single person. But it is difficult to keep going!

Perhaps already, in the foregoing work on orienting the self, you have uncovered strong resistances against continuing. You are certain to encounter stronger objections to doing experiments still to come, for they involve going a step further and taking decisive action in your life-situation.

As you have found out already, this work leads you to the discovery that the human organism functions in a manner which is at odds with conventionally held notions about human nature. These traditionally established opinions, however, have been so deeply trained into all of us and have been so invested with feelings of moral rightness that their modification—even when our own first-hand experience confronts us with this necessity—seems wrong and worthy of condemnation.

There will be times in the work to come when, if you let it break through, your anger will flare against us for intimating that you possess feelings and entertain fantasies which, by your lifelong standards of what is proper, will seem despicable. At such moments you will be tempted to cast aside these experiments in disgust—and should you actually do so, certainly no-one could say that it was not your privilege. On the other hand, if your occasional assumption that we are "dangerous crackpots" does not lead you to such a summary breaking off of our relationship, we are certain that you will sooner or later arrive at a more positive evaluation, for you will have acquired new values without the loss of any of the old ones which were of any real importance to you.

During your moments of wrath against us it would be best if you could express it to us face to face. Since that is not practicable, the next best thing will be for you to fire it off to us in written form via our publisher. If "too polite" for that, then write the letter anyhow, even if you then consign it to your wastebasket. Whatever you do, try to get it off your chest!

We are personally responsible for whatever discomfort you experience in doing these experiments in the sense that, in recommending them to you, we commit an aggressive act aimed at your present status quo and whatever complacency it affords. That we act "with the best of intentions" or "for your own good" is beside the point. A certain highway is said to be paved with good intentions, and your life has been cluttered with meddlers who claimed to act for your own good.

In the experiments to come we shall make use of a formulation of behavior which, briefly stated, is as follows: various excitements, colored with pleasure, aggression or pain, energize the organism to make contacts and creative adjustments in its environment. It is by feeling and contact that the organism grows and expands its boundaries. Every neurotic mechanism is an interruption of some kind of excitement—a prevention of its further development. As explained previously, anxiety is the consequence of such interruption. Rather than risk the new, unknown contact, the neurotic withdraws into a contactless (unaware) confluence with his "safe" habitual functioning.

Three important mechanisms with which we shall work are retroflection, introjection and projection. These could be considered as defining three different types of "neurotic character," since they have their beginning in different life experiences and are rooted in different physiological functions. However, even if one of these mechanisms should predominate in us over the others, we all use every one of them. Since our approach is an all-round one, you need not, hypochondriacally, ask yourself whether you are a typical "retroflector," "introjector," or "projector" for, by proceeding with *all* the abstract possibilities of environment, sensation, body, feeling, speech, and the various characteristic resistances, you will, regardless of what your particular "diagnosis" may be, develop areas of integrated functioning that will then facilitate still further integration.

Retroflection

To retroflect means literally "to turn sharply back against." When a person retroflects behavior, he does to himself what originally he did or tried to do to other persons or objects. He stops directing various energies outward in attempts to manipulate and bring about changes in the environment that will satisfy his needs; instead, he redirects activity inward and *substitutes himself in place of the environment* as the target of behavior. To the extent that he does this, he splits his personality into "doer" and "done to."

Why did he not persist as he started—that is, directing outward toward the environment? Because he met what was for him at that time insuperable opposition. The environment—mostly other persons—proved hostile to his efforts to satisfy his needs. They frustrated and punished him. In such an unequal contest—he was a child—he was sure to lose. Consequently, to avoid the pain and danger entailed in renewed attempts, he gave up. The environment, being stronger, won out and enforced its wishes at the expense of his.

However, as has been demonstrated repeatedly in recent years by a number of experiments, punishment has the effect, not of annihilating the need to behave in the way that met with punishment, but of teaching the organism to *hold back* the punishable responses. The impulse or the wish remains as strong as ever and, since this is not satisfied, it is constantly organizing the motor apparatus—its posture, pattern of muscular tonus, and incipient movements—in the direction of overt expression. Since this is what brings punishment, the organism behaves toward its own impulse as did the environment—that is, it acts to suppress it. Its energy is thus divided. Part of it still strains toward its original and never satisfied aims; the other part has been retroflected to hold this outgoing part in check. The holding back is achieved by tensing muscles which are antagonistic to those which would be involved in expressing the punishable impulse. At this stage two parts of the personality struggling in diametrically opposite directions are in a clinch. What started as conflict between organism and environment has come to be an "inner conflict" between one part of the personality and another part—between one kind of behavior and its opposite.

Do not jump to the conclusion that we imply that it would be fine if we could all without further ado "release our inhibitions." In some situations holding back is necessary, even life-saving—for instance, holding back inhaling while under water. The important question is whether or not the person has *rational grounds* for presently choking off behavior in given circumstances. While crossing a street it certainly is to his advantage if he quells any urge to contest the right-of-way with an oncoming truck. In social situations it is usually advantageous to suppress a tendency to go off half-cocked. (But if fully cocked, aimed and ready, it may be quite a different matter!)

When retroflection is under aware control—that is, when a person in a current situation suppresses particular responses which, if expressed, would be to his disadvantage—no-one can contest the soundness of such behavior. It is only when the retroflection is habitual, chronic, out of control, that it is pathological; for then it is not something done temporarily, perhaps as an emergency measure or to await a more suitable occasion, but is a deadlock perpetuated in the personality. Furthermore, since this stabilized battle-line does not change, it ceases to attract attention. We "forget" it is there. This is *repression*—and neurosis.

If it were true that the social environment remained adamant and uncompromising—if it were just as dangerous and punishable to express certain impulses now as it was when we were children—then repression ("forgotten" retroflection) would be efficient and desirable. But the situation has changed! We are not children. We are bigger, stronger, and we have "rights" which are denied children. In these drastically changed circumstances it is worth having another try at getting what we need from the environment!

When we suppress behavior, we are aware both of what we are suppressing and the fact that we are suppressing; in repression, on the contrary, we have lost awareness both of what is repressed and the process by which we do the repressing. Psychoanalysis has stressed recovery of awareness of what is repressed—that is, the blocked impulse. We, on the other hand, emphasize recovery of awareness of the blocking, the feeling that one is doing it and *how* one is doing it. Once a person discovers his retroflecting action and regains control of it, the blocked impulse will be recovered automatically. No longer held in, it will simply come out. The great advantage of dealing with the retroflecting part of the personality—the active repressing agent—is that this is within fairly easy reach of awareness, can be directly experienced, and does not depend upon guessed-at interpretations.

Theoretically, the treatment of retroflection is simple: merely reverse the direction of the retroflecting act from inward to outward. Upon doing so, the organism's energies, formerly divided, now once more join forces and discharge themselves toward the environment. The impulse which had been blocked is given the chance at last to express and complete itself and is satisfied. Then, as is the case when any genuine need of the organism is fulfilled, there can be rest, assimilation and growth. In practice, however, the undoing of a retroflection is not so straightforward. Every part of the personality comes to its defense as if to head off catastrophe. The person is overcome with embarrassment, fear, guilt and resentment. The attempt to reverse the self-aggression, to differentiate the clinch of the two parts of the personality, is responded to as if it were an attack on his body, his "nature," on his very life. As the clinched parts begin to loosen and come apart, the person experiences unbearable excitement, for the relief of which he may have to go temporarily into his clinch again. These are unaccustomed feelings which are being resurrected and he has to make approaches to them and gradually learn to tolerate and use them. At first he becomes anxious and would rather retreat into his deadened state of unawareness.

A main reason for the fear and guilt in reversing retroflections is that most retroflected impulses are aggressions, from the mildest to the cruelest, from persuasion to torture. To let these loose even into awareness is terrifying. But aggression, in the broad sense of its clinical usage, is indispensable to happiness and creativity. Furthermore, reversing the retroflection does not manufacture aggression that was not already there. It was there—but applied against the self instead of against the environment! We are not denying that aggression may be pathologically misused against objects and other persons, just as it is pathologically misused when directed steadfastly against the self. But until one can become aware of what one's aggressive impulses are and learn to put them to constructive use, they are *certain* to be misused! As a matter of fact, it is the act of repressing them—the setting up and maintenance of the grim clinch of the musculature—that makes these aggressions seem so wasteful, "anti-

social," and intolerable. Once they are allowed to develop spontaneously in the context of the total personality, rather than being
squeezed and suffocated in the remorseless clinch of retroflection,
one puts quite a different and more favorable evaluation upon his
aggressions.

What is also feared in releasing a blocked impulse is that one will
then be completely frustrated—for retroflection does give at least
partial satisfaction. A religious man, for instance, unable to vent his
wrath on the Lord for his disappointments, beats his own breast and
tears his own hair. Such self-aggression, obviously a retroflection,
nevertheless *is* aggression and it *does* give some satisfaction to the
retroflecting part of the personality. It is aggression that is crude,
primitive, undifferentiated—a retroflected childish temper-tantrum
—but the part of the personality that is attacked is always there and
available for attack. Self-aggression can always be sure of its victim!

To reverse such a retroflection in one fell swoop would mean that
the person would then attack others in ways just as ineffectual and
archaic. He would rouse the same overwhelming counteraggression
that led him to retroflect in the first place. It is some realization
of this which makes even the imagined reversal of retroflections
productive of so much fear. What is overlooked is that the change
can be made in easy stages which gradually transform the whole
situation as they proceed. One can, to start with, discover and
accept the fact that he does "take it out on himself." He can become
aware of the emotions of the retroflecting part of his personality—
notably, the grim joy taken in administering punishment to himself.
This, when he achieves it, represents considerable progress, for vindictiveness is so socially disesteemed as to be most difficult to acknowledge and accept even when supposedly one spares others and
directs it solely against oneself. Only when accepted—that is, when
it is reckoned with as an existing, dynamic component of one's functioning personality—does one reach the possibility of modifying,
differentiating, redirecting it into healthy expression. As one's orientation in the environment improves, as one's awareness of what one
genuinely wants to do becomes clearer, as one makes approaches
which are limited tryouts to see what will happen, gradually one's
techniques for expression of previously blocked impulses develop
also. They lose their primitive, terrifying aspect as one differentiates
them and gives them a chance to catch up with the more grown-up
parts of the personality. Aggression will then still be aggression, but
it will have been put to useful tasks and will no longer be blindly destructive of self and others. It will be expended as the situation

demands, and not accumulated until one feels that he sits precariously atop a seething volcano.

Thus far we have spoken only of behavior which the person was unsuccessful in directing toward others and which he consequently retroflected against himself. Retroflections also include what one *wanted from* others but was unsuccessful in obtaining, with the outcome that now, for want of anyone else to do it, one gives it to himself. This may be attention, love, pity, punishment, almost anything! A great deal of what originally was done for one by others—notably, by his parents—he takes over and does for himself as he grows up. This, of course, is healthy, provided it does not include trying to gratify for oneself what are genuinely *interpersonal* needs.

This kind of retroflection combines the absurd and the pathetic. For instance, the story is told of a college student who, though living in a dormitory, was unable to make contact with his fellows. From outside the window of his lonely room he would frequently hear the occupants of adjacent quarters being summoned forth to join their friends. One night he was discovered standing beneath his own window repeatedly calling his own name.

Let us take a look at some typical retroflections. There are those that are simple linguistic reflexives. When we use such verbal expressions as "I ask myself" or "I say to myself," what is involved? In previous experiments we have often suggested: "Ask yourself . . ." Doesn't this seem logically peculiar? If you don't know something, why ask yourself, and, if you do know it, why tell it to yourself? Such ways of talking (and we employ them all the time) simply take it for granted that the personality is divided into two parts, as if two persons lived within the same skin and could hold conversations with each other. Do you regard this as a mere peculiarity of our language, or can you get the feeling that this quite common manner of speaking stems from being a person divided and having parts functionally in opposition to each other?

Try to get a clear understanding that when you "ask yourself" something, this is retroflected questioning. You don't know the answer or you wouldn't have to ask. Who in the environment does know or, so you feel, ought to know? If you can specify such a person, can you then be aware of wanting to ask your question, not of yourself, but of that person? What keeps you from doing so? Is it shyness, fear of a rebuff, reluctance to admit your ignorance?

When you "consult yourself" about something, can you be aware of your motive? Many are possible. It may be a game, a teasing, the administering of consolation, or the making of a reproach. Whatever it may be, for whom are you substituting yourself?

Consider self-reproach. Here you will find no true feeling of guilt, but the mere pretense of guilt. Reverse the reproach by finding that Person X among those you know at whom you are really leveling your reproach. Whom do you want to nag? Whom do you want to reform? In whom do you want to rouse the guilt that you are *pretending* to produce in yourself?

At this stage the important thing is not for you to attempt the full undoing of the retroflection by immediately rushing out and confronting Person X with whatever you hold against him. You have not yet explored and accepted enough of yourself nor examined the interpersonal situation sufficiently. Let the detailed content of any particular problem go for the moment and content yourself with trying to realize the *form* of your behavior as a retroflector. Gradually you will begin to see the role you also play in your interpersonal relations. You will start to see yourself as others see you. If you are forever making demands on yourself, you also, explicitly or implicitly, make demands on others—and this is how you appear to them. If you feel angry with yourself, you will feel angry even with the fly on the wall. If you nag yourself, you may be perfectly sure that there are others, too, whom you nag.

A person who retroflects aggression takes this attitude: "If I'm mean to myself, it doesn't hurt anybody else, does it?" It wouldn't, if his retroflection were complete and if he lived in a capsule, isolated from others. Neither is true. He lives with others, and much of his behavior—of the same general type as that which he retroflects—escapes retroflection. For instance, specific aggressions which have not been specifically punished and turned inward do find their mark in the environment. He is not aware of these, for his self-concept excludes "hurting others." Since he makes his attacks on others in a random, unconsidered way, rationalizing his motives, such actions, just as much as his retroflected aggressions, will be crude, primitive, and relatively ineffectual. Self-aggression can be more easily accepted as genuine aggression—one feels less guilt for hurting himself than for hurting someone else—but aggression toward others exists also in one who retroflects, and it must in the end be made aware and accepted before it can be developed into aggression which is rational and healthy rather than irrational and neurotic.

When a retroflection has been truly realized, reversed, and allowed spontaneously to develop with its proper objects, the meaning of what was retroflected always undergoes changes—for instance, *re*proach turns into *ap*proach. In the long run any interpersonal contact is better than retroflection. We do not mean by interpersonal contact "mixing with people," "being with others," or "going out more"—for such activity, while masquerading as "social contact," may be nothing more than contactless confluence. Making genuine contact sometimes involves what conventionally would be regarded as breaking or avoiding contact. For instance, suppose someone invites you to a gathering in which you haven't the slightest interest. You would greatly prefer to spend the time otherwise. But if you frankly say so, the common view would have it that you are declining "social contact." This is "bad," for we are taught early and late that some special virtue is inherent in gregariousness, even when it consists of nothing more than meaningless, insincere, time-wasting chitchat. But we say, "Yes, I'd be delighted," instead of, "No, thank you, I'd rather not." Thus we avoid breaking confluence with prevailing stereotypes of what constitute good manners. But we must then be *rude to ourselves* and treat with high-handed disregard otherwise possible activities which *are* matters of spontaneous interest and concern for us. When we say, "Yes, I'll come," and thus commit ourselves to what we do not wish to do, we are, in effect, saying "No" to alternative ways of spending the time which are of more importance to us. By preening ourselves on having a "positive personality"—being yes-man for every Tom, Dick or Harry—we retroflect the negative and say "No" to ourselves.

Let us look again at the nature of the retroflecting process. In deliberate suppression one identifies oneself with both the suppressed and the suppressing behavior. As a very simple example, consider the suppression of urination. Suppose one feels the urge to void his bladder at a time and place which is inappropriate. He simply contracts the urethral sphincter to offset the contraction of the distended bladder. This is a temporary retroflection. He has no intention whatever of making it permanent, and he does not disown—alienate or reject from his personality—either side of the conflict. As soon as convenient he reverses the retroflection. This consists, obviously, of merely relaxing the sphincter and allowing the bladder to press forth its contents. The need is satisfied and both tensions released. Persons differ, of course, with respect to how much tension of this sort they will endure before seeking relief. If their attitude toward eliminative functions is that they are "not nice," they may be too embarrassed to excuse themselves from a social group.

In contrast to a simple suppression like this, where both contenders in the conflict are aware and accepted by the "I" as belonging to it—"I want to relieve myself, but I prefer to wait"—one may identify with and accept as his own only one side of the conflict. In forced concentration, as noted in a previous experiment, one identifies himself with the taskmaster who insists that he do whatever the job consists of. He dis-identifies with—alienates and disowns—those counter-interests which he calls distractions. In terms of the structure of the conflict this is similar to the simple suppression cited above; the difference is in the attitude adopted toward one side of the conflict. Although various needs are pitted against each other and working at cross-purposes, the "I" is not split in this situation because it refuses to include in itself (refuses to identify itself with) those background needs which run counter to the task. Not much gets accomplished; it frequently would clear the ground if the "I" could identify with the more urgent of these "distracters," give them priority, get them out of the way, and then come back to the task. However that may be, what we are trying to point out here is that in the type of retroflection which constitutes fighting the "distracters" in forced concentration, the "I" feels itself to exist only in the efforts to get the task done.

Sometimes in retroflections the "I" plays both parts—it is identified with both the active, retroflecting part of the personality, and also the passive part which is the object of the retroflection. This is especially true in self-pity and self-punishment. Before discussing these further, suppose you examine instances of self-pity or self-punishment in your own life and find out what answers you can obtain to the following questions:

Whom do you want to pity? Whom do you want to pity you?
Whom do you want to punish? Whom do you want to punish you?

"Pity," "sympathy," and "compassion" are grossly synonymous, and all are in good standing as "virtuous" words. They have shades of meaning, however, which, while subtle from the linguistic standpoint, are profoundly significant from the psychological. The dictionary distinguishes them as follows: "Pity is feeling for another's suffering or distress, and sometimes regards its object as not only suffering, but *weak or inferior*. Sympathy is fellow-feeling with others, esp. in their grief or affliction; the word implies *a certain degree of equality* in situation, circumstances, etc. Compassion is deep tenderness for another, esp. under severe or inevitable suffering or misfortune" (Italics ours). These words, all expressive of attitudes toward the sufferings of others, are graded in terms of the amount of actual participation in, or closeness to, or identification with, such sufferings. Pity is the most remote, and we contend that most of what passes muster as pity is actually *disguised gloating*. Tennyson speaks of "scornful pity," and most of us have heard the recipient of pity shout, "I don't want your damned pity!" Such pity is condescension. We apply it to those who are in such a low estate that they are not or have ceased to be our own serious rivals. They are "out of the running." By pitying them we emphasize the discrepancy between their lot and ours. Such attitude, we believe motivates much so-called charity.

When concern for the sufferings of others is genuine and not a mask for stand-offish, jubilant self-congratulation, it entails the urge to help in a practical fashion and to assume responsibility for changing the situation. In such cases we are more likely to speak of sympathy or compassion, an entering into and an active participation in the sufferer's situation. These attitudes enmesh themselves with the actuality and are too engaged in it for the luxury of sentimental tears. Tearful pity is mostly a masochistic enjoyment of the misery.

When this is retroflected we have the situation of self-pity. A part of oneself is now the object, but the pitying attitude is still one of scornful, aloof condescension. If the split in the "I" (the division into pitier and pitied) can be healed, the stand-offish enjoyment of the punishment being administered changes into the active urge to help, whether the object of succor be someone else or *neglected portions of oneself*. This new orientation leads to the task of manipulating the environment to bring about appropriate changes.

The *desirability* of self-control in our society goes unquestioned; on the other hand, there is little *rational consideration* of what it involves. This whole program of experiments attempts to develop self-control, but on a much broader and more comprehensive basis —in fact, on quite a different basis—from what is envisioned in the usual, naive, frantic seeking after it. When a person demands, "How can I make myself do what I ought to do?" this can be translated into, "How can I make myself do what a strong part of me doesn't want to do?" In other words, how can one part of the personality establish an ironclad dictatorship over another part? The wish to do this, together with more or less successful attempts to bring it about, is characteristic of compulsion neurosis.

The person who treats himself in this fashion is a domineering bully. If he can and dares to behave like this with others, he may sometimes be an efficient organizer; but where he must accept direction from others or from himself he becomes passively or actively resistant. Usually, therefore, the compulsive accomplishes very little. He spends his time preparing, deciding, making sure, but he makes little headway in the execution of what he has so laboriously planned. What happens within his own behavior is similar to what occurs in a shop or office where the boss is a slave-driver; the "slaves," by slow-downs, errors, sickness, and the myriad other techniques of sabotage, wreck his best efforts to coerce them. In the compulsive, the "I" identifies with rigid objectives and tries to ram them through; the unconsulted other parts of the personality, whose interests are disregarded, retaliate with fatigue, excuses, promises, irrelevant difficulties. In the compulsive, the "ruler" and the "ruled" are thus in a continuous clinch.

Although few of us would be diagnosed as compulsive neurotics, all of us have some degree of compulsiveness, for it is the outstanding neurotic symptom of our times. To the extent that we do, it will color most of our behavior. If the doing of these experiments is taken as an example, it is undoubtedly true that at times they feel like an onerous task imposed from outside and the issue is merely to get through them as expeditiously as possible. You respond with irritation, annoyance, or rage if all does not go according to the cut-and-dried order of your preconceptions. To wait for spontaneous developments is the last thing that the slave-driver in you will tolerate.

Reverse a situation in which you compel yourself. How would you set about compelling others to perform the task for you? Would you try to manipulate the environment with magic words? Would you bully, command, bribe, threaten, reward?

On the other hand, how do you react to your own compelling? Do you turn a deaf ear? Do you make promises you do not mean to keep? Do you respond with guilt and pay the debt with self-contempt and despair?

When you try to force yourself to do what you yourself do not want to do, you work against powerful resistances. The prospect of reaching your goal brightens if, instead of compelling yourself, you clear the ground of whatever obstacles you can find standing in your way (or of yourself standing in your own way). This is the great principle of the Tao-philosophers: make a void, so that nature can develop there; or, as they also express it, *stand out of the way*.

What obstacles, for instance, can you find to doing these experiments? If you say, "I must do them," who is supplying the "must"?

You, apparently, for you are not compelled from outside. What if you didn't do them? No blow would fall. Your life would continue in its customary pattern uninterrupted. Suppose you say, "I want to do them but some part of me objects." What is the objection? Waste of time? Are you equally severe toward other ways of wasting time? If you saved the time that you spend on these experiments, would you have some urgent, "important" task to which you are sure that you would then devote the time?

Suppose you object to the lack of a guarantee that these experiments are going to "do you some good." Are you able to get such a guarantee on other things that you do?

Whatever your objections, don't blame yourself for them. Blame whomever or whatever you think is responsible for the way you feel. After discharging some of this aggression that you have been turning against yourself, you may respond to the situation quite differently.

Another extremely important retroflection to consider is self-contempt, feelings of inferiority—everything that Harry Stack Sullivan called the weak self-system and considered the essence of neurosis. As he put it, when one's relations with oneself are disturbed, all interpersonal relations are likewise disturbed. One is on chronically bad terms with himself when he has the habit of forever taking stock of himself, evaluating himself, and, on the basis of comparative judgments, dwelling all the time on the discrepancy between his actual performances and those which would meet his high-flown specifications. If he reverses the retroflection, he will let up on himself and then start evaluating the persons in his environment. Once he ventures to do this, he will soon come to regard such verbal evaluations, whether applied to others or himself, as of secondary importance. He will realize that his retroflected evaluations were merely a mechanism for dwelling on himself. When he directs the same kind of elaborate evaluating to others, he may soon see the futility of it and stop. Then he will notice persons with simple awareness of what they are and what they do, and will learn either how to manipulate them in a genuinely satisfying way or to adjust himself to them.

What do you doubt about yourself? Mistrust? Deprecate? Can you reverse these attitudes? Who is the Person X whom you doubt? Who makes you suspicious? Whom do you wish to pooh-pooh and take down a peg? Can you feel your inferiority as concealed arrogance? Can you undo self-effacement and recognize it as the retroflected wits to wipe out Person X?

Still another important type of retroflection is introspection. When you introspect, *you peer at yourself*. This form of retroflection is so universal in our culture that much of the psychological literature simply takes it for granted that any attempt to increase self-awareness must of necessity consist of introspection. While this, definitely, is not the case, it probably is true that anyone who does these experiments will *start* by introspecting. The observer is split off from the part observed, and not until this split is healed will a person fully realize that self-awareness which is not introspected can exist. We previously likened genuine awareness to the glow produced within a burning coal by its own combustion, and introspection to turning the beam of a flashlight on an object and peering at its surface by means of the reflected rays.

Examine your procedure when you introspect. What is your aim? Are you searching for a secret? Ferreting out a memory? Hoping for (or fearing) a surprise? *Do you watch yourself with the sharp eye of a stern parent to make sure you don't get into mischief?* Are you trying to find something that will fit a theory—for instance, the theory developed in these pages? Or, on the other hand, are you seeing to it that such corroboratory events do not take place? Then try directing these attitudes toward persons in the environment. Is there someone whose "insides" you would like to search? Is there someone on whom you would like to keep a strict eye? Who is it that you feel bears watching?

Apart from the aim of your introspecting, what is your manner? Do you dig? Are you the brutal police officer who pounds on the door and bellows, "Open up there"? Are you timid or furtive with yourself—that is, do you sneak your glances? Do you stare at yourself unseeingly? Do you conjure up events simply to fulfill your expectations? Do you falsify them by way of exaggeration? Or do you soft-pedal them? Do you abstract only what coincides with your immediate aims? In short, notice *how* your "I" is functioning. This is far more important than the specific content.

The extreme case of introspection is hypochondria—the search for symptoms of illness. Reverse this and search for symptoms in others. You may be an inhibited physician or nurse. What is the aim of such searching? Is it sexual? Have you ever been told that masturbation produces a tell-tale appearance of the eyes? Have you searched your own eyes or those of others for such a symptom? Do you introspect you body for signs that punishment has started for your "sins"?

A few students, in reporting their reactions to this experiment, expressed indignation over what they took to be its "insulting insinuations" and launched themselves upon a defense of the "goodness" of their personal motives.

You assume that all of us have an innate desire to pity or punish someone, and likewise to be pitied or punished. I must reject such a position as utterly preposterous.

When I pity someone, I vehemently deny that there is any disguised gloating in it.

You certainly talk as if you regarded us as a bunch of "abnormals." Or is it that you're "abnormal" yourself?

You make it sound as if I ought to hold myself responsible for the situation I'm in. That may hold for some, but not for me. You just don't know how I've been treated!

Some of the statements you make seem to me quite unnecessarily harsh.

Most reports, on the other hand, indicated attempts to grapple frankly with whatever was turned up.

I don't want ordinary kinds of pity, but I want people to pity me when I've made some important sacrifice.

I have had to acknowledge that what I took to be my kindhearted pity for my step-sister does involve a considerable amount of secret gloating.

My pity goes to those who, as you say, are "out of the running."

I have discovered that I actually want to punish my girl. This bothers me, because I really love her. Fortunately, it's not all the time, but just when I'm blue and down in the dumps.

I couldn't believe that the wish to punish or be punished applied to me. But then I thought of the dreams I'm forever having of punishing someone, usually female, and doing it in a rather violent way. When I was younger the dreams were of someone punishing me physically. I enjoyed it. My parents didn't punish me physically, but by the threat of withdrawing their love. This would go on for quite a while, and I thought how much better I would like it if they actually beat me and got it over with.

Rather than cite short comments from a number of students on the various other parts of the experiment, we give the following rather extended quotation from a single report:

> While there is no-one I would constantly want to shower with pity, there are times when I would like to pity my sister, for I feel she has embarked on an undesirable marriage. But when I see her and have to realize that she is very happy, I know my pity is misplaced . . . I am very happy, for I am deeply in love with my fiance. I am very fond of his parents, and they've been wonderful to me.
>
> At times I would like to punish my father for venting his anger on my mother. If I had to choose someone to punish me, it would be my mother. She is so lenient and good-hearted that the punishment would not be severe. I would like to avoid punishment by my fiance, because he is so stubborn that the punishment, though it would probably be nothing more than prolonged silence or absence would be worse than any sort of fast, violent punishment.
>
> When I try to compel myself, I make promises to myself. I promise that I'll never let my affairs get into such a mess ever again where I have to put myself under pressure. I also promise that, after doing a certain amount of work, I'll give myself the chance to relax. This works pretty well when the relaxation period doesn't go on and on, as it does tend to do.
>
> . . . What I doubt most about myself, and this doesn't recur too frequently, is whether I'm entirely ready for marriage. I still have a wonderful, romantic picture of marriage which doesn't include washing dirty socks and economizing on the groceries. I doubt whether my sister, although she is married, is ready for that. She doesn't have her own apartment yet, and hasn't been faced with these things.
>
> . . . The terms you use are particularly strong. There is no one I would like to "wipe out." If my sister were Person X, I certainly would have no wish to destroy her. Before she got married our relationship was a particularly close one, but I can't say I am jealous of her husband for separating us. . . For the first time I've become really antagonistic toward you. Something inside me seems to be

asking, 'What are they driving at; what are they trying to find out?' It is almost as if you had me backed against a wall with a strong spotlight on me. There is a certain anxiety; it is as if some cobwebs were being pushed aside, but I can't identify what is beyond. I only know that it is disturbing.

. . . When I introspect, it is as if I were waiting for something to turn up—something that is elusive. I'm not sure if it is pleasant, but I think not, for it makes me slightly anxious. . . If there is one person who bears watching, that is my fiance's mother. She is a wonderful person, and has been more generous and gracious to me than most future mothers-in-law would be, but there are times when I am with her when I fear that she will come to dominate me as completely as she does her husband and daughter. My fiance, fortunately, has gone through the period of revolt and been almost completely successful in getting out from under her thumb.

. . . When introspecting, I first stare at myself, unseeingly. Then, almost furtively, I try to sneak glances. . . If the events I hit upon are distasteful, I tend to soft-pedal them, or they become blocked out by other thoughts.

The symptom for which I found myself searching was a sexual one. It probably can be traced to a particularly disgusting French film of which I saw only the smallest part. I suddenly got the idea that women who had had intercourse sat with their legs spread, rather than crossing them at the knees. I looked for this in my sister when she came to visit us. The symptom was there. It has been three weeks since I saw the picture, but it still, from time to time, comes into my mind.

Experiment 2:   MOBILIZING THE MUSCLES

In this experiment we come to grips with the mechanics of retroflection. When your approaches to objects and persons in the environment are frustrated or evaluated as too dangerous to continue, so that you turn your aggressions inward against yourself, the muscular motions by which you do this may retain their form or be modified to conform to the substitute objects. If with your fingernails you scratch your own flesh, this is precisely what, without the retroflection, you would do to someone else. On the other hand, when you control an urge to pound someone with your fist by contracting the antagonistic muscles and thus immobilizing your arm and shoulder, the retroflection does not consist of pounding yourself; it is, instead, a statically maintained counteraction. It is a doing of one thing and also its opposite at the same time in such fashion as to achieve a net effect of zero. So long as the conflict endures, the use of the arm for other purposes is impaired, energies are squandered, and the state of affairs is the same as the military situation of a stabilized battleline. Here the battleline is within the personality.

Retroflections are manipulations of your own body and impulses as substitutes for other persons and objects. Such self-manipulation is unquestionably useful and healthy when it constitutes withholding, biding your time, adjusting yourself to the surroundings, in situations where you need to exercise prudence, caution, selectivity, in the service of your own over-all best interests. The neurotic abuse is when you have once and for all *censored* a part of yourself, throttled and silenced it, so that it may no longer lift its voice in your aware personality. But no matter how squeezed, choked off, clamped down upon this censored part may be, it still exerts its pressure. The struggle goes on. You have simply lost awareness of it. The end-result of such censoring, whether recognized or not, is invariably a more or less serious psychosomatic dysfunction: impairment of powers of orientation or manipulation, ache, weakness, or even degeneration of tissues.

Consider how ineffectual is retroflection in the following example. A patient undergoing treatment may display an extraordinary frequency and amount of weeping, perhaps several outbursts in a single session. The crying occurs whenever one might expect the patient to come forth with a reproach or some other kind of attack. What happens is this: the patient feels like attacking, but, not daring to, retroflects the attack against himself, feels hurt, and bursts into tears as if to say, "See how harmless and how abused I am." The original aim, of course, is to make Person X, perhaps the therapist, cry. When this cannot be achieved, the crying spells and the chronic resentment persist until the aggression can be reorganized and turned outward.

Other cases may have frequent headaches which are, as the Freudians would say, "converted" crying. Here the mystery of the "conversion-process" is readily solved when one recognizes that the headaches, like most other psychosomatic symptoms, are retroflected motor activity. They are produced by *muscular tensing against a swelling impulse*.

If you open a water tap slightly and attempt with a finger to hold back the water against the pressure in the pipe, you find this increasingly difficult. There is a strict analogy between this and many internal conflicts where you squeeze or hold back an urge to defecate, to have an erection or to become tumescent, to vomit or belch, etc. If you clench your fist hard, after a while it will ache from cramp. The "psychogenic" headache—or, as it used to be well-called, the "functional" headache—is the same type of phenomenon. In a given instance, you start to cry, but then you control the impulse by squeezing your own head so as not to be a sissy or to give others the satisfaction of seeing they have made you cry. You would like to squeeze the life out of Person X who has so upset you, but you retroflect the squeezing and use it to hold back your crying. Your headache is nothing but your experience of the muscular straining. If you detense the muscles, you will start to cry and, simultaneously, the headache will disappear. (Not all headaches, of course, are produced in this way; also, crying may be inhibited by tensions other than those in the head—for example, by tightening the diaphragm against the clonic movements of sobbing.)

We repeat once more our opposition to premature relaxation. Suppose you manage to relax the muscles of your neck, brow, and eyes and burst out crying. This by no means solves the original conflict. It merely by-passes it. An important part of the symptom—namely, the tendency to aggressive squeezing—goes unanalyzed. When someone has hurt you, there is the wish to retaliate by hurting him. This tendency gets some expression—you do some hurting—even if it is but the retroflected squeezing which makes you the victim of your own aggression as well as of that of the other person. If, instead of reversing the retroflection, you simply give up the retroflecting behavior—in this case, your self-squeezing—you can succeed only by somehow also getting rid of your proneness to be hurt. This requires a technique more serious than retroflection, namely, desensitization. Not wanting to hurt depends on not being hurt, which depends on ceasing to respond emotionally to the environment. This process can go as far as depersonalization. Admittedly, one may be *hyper*sensitive and "have one's feelings hurt" by almost everything; one has, correspondingly, a heightened urge to "hurt back." The solution for this condition is reorganization of the personality, not further disorganization in the form of going numb. *The healthy organism, when genuinely attacked, fights back in a way and to a degree appropriate to the situation.*

Furthermore, when muscles are willfully relaxed, they are less at your disposal even for behavior not involved in the conflict. You lose agility, grace, and mobility of feature. This accounts for the relaxed facelessness of some "analyzed" persons. They have "mastered" their problems by becoming aloof—too aloof to be fully human.

In the healthy organism the muscles are neither cramped nor relaxed (flaccid), but in middle tone, ready for the execution of movements which maintain balanced posture, provide locomotion, or manipulate objects. In beginning the motor-muscular work of this experiment, do not relax. Later we shall amend this by saying do not relax until you can cope with the excitement which will thereby be released. If relaxation occurs prematurely and you are surprised and frightened by unblocked excitement, you will clamp against it harder than ever and experience great anxiety. With correct concentration, however, on the motor manipulation of yourself, slowly and methodically adjusting to pressures as you feel yourself exerting them, the loosening of tension will often take place as a matter of course.

From the beginning be prepared for sudden urges to break out in rage, to cry, vomit, urinate, behave sexually, etc. But such urges as you experience at the start will come from near the surface of awareness and you will be quite able to cope with them. Nevertheless, to spare yourself possible embarrassment, it is advisable at first to perform the muscular experiments in solitude. Furthermore, if you are prone to anxiety attacks, before attempting intensive muscular concentration, work through what you are going to do by internally verbalizing it.

While lying down, but not deliberately relaxing, get the feel of your body. Notice where you have an ache—headache, backache, writer's cramp, belly-cramp, vaginism, etc. Realize where you are tense. Do not "give in" to the tension, nor do anything about it. Become aware of the tensions in your eyes, neck, around the mouth. Let your attention wander systematically (without making a fetish of system) through your legs, lower trunk, arms, chest, neck, head. Should you find that you are lying in a crooked position, adjust it accordingly. Do not move jerkily, but let the self-sense develop softly. Notice the tendency of your organism to regulate itself—the tendency to pull back into a better position in one place, to stretch out in another.

Do not fool yourself that you are feeling your body when you are merely visualizing or theorizing it. If prone to the latter, you are working with a concept of yourself, not yourself. But this concept is imposed by your "I" and its resistances; it is not self-regulating and spontaneous. It does not come from the felt-awareness of the organism. By waiting, refusing to be put off by visualizations and theories, can you get the glow of awareness which arises directly from the parts attended to?

As you proceed, consider what objections you may have to each particular bit of self-awareness. Do you despise physical functioning? Are you ashamed of being a body? Do you regard defecation as a painful, dirty duty? Are you frightened by a tendency to clench your fist? Do you fear that you will strike a blow? Or that you will be struck? Does the feeling in your throat disturb you? Are you afraid to shout?

In parts of your body where it has been difficult for you to get any feeling at all, what you are likely to experience first as feeling is restored as a sharp pain, a painful numbness, a cramp. When such pangs occur, concentrate on them.

(It goes without saying that we are dealing here with functional or "psychogenic" pains, not those resulting from "physical" lesions or infections. Try not to be hypochondriacal, but, if doubtful, consult a doctor. Get one, if possible, who has an understanding of functional symptoms.)

An extremely useful method of grasping the meaning of particular aches or tensions is to call up appropriate expressions of popular speech. These invariably contain long-tested wisdom. For instance:

I am stiff-necked; am I stubborn? I have a pain in the neck; what gives me a pain in the neck? I stretch my head high; am I haughty? I stick my chin out; am I leading with it? My brows arch; am I supercilious? I have a catch in my throat; do I want to cry? I am whistling in the dark; am I afraid of something? My flesh creeps; am I horrified? My brows beetle; am I full of rage? I feel swollen; am I ready to burst with anger? My throat is tight; is there something I can't swallow? My middle feels queasy; what can't I stomach?

Now, assuming that you have begun to rediscover your bodily existence, your tensions, and their characterological and interpersonal significance, we must take the next step. What you have been doing—searching and softly adjusting so as to orient yourself further —must now give way to the other functions which are latent in contracted muscle. With orientation we must begin to integrate overt expression, to change the muscular contractions into controllable behaviors available for manipulation of the environment.

The next step in solving the problem of chronic muscular tensions —and of every other psychosomatic symptom—is to develop adequate contact with the symptom and accept it as your own. The notion of accepting the symptom—precisely what you feel you want to be rid of—always sounds preposterous. So let us try, even at the risk of unnecessary repetitiousness, to get this perfectly clear. You may ask, "If I have a symptom that is painful or some characteristic that is undesirable, should I not try to get rid of it?" The answer is, "Certainly!" The issue then is reduced to the selection of a means which will work and the abandonment of any means which superficially looks as if it ought to work—but actually doesn't. The direct means of condemning the symptom, of regarding it as something which has been imposed upon you, of appealing to others for help in making it disappear, will not work. The only way that will work is an indirect one: become vividly aware of the symptom, accept both sides of the conflict as *you*—this means to re-identify yourself with parts of your personality from which you have dis-identified yourself—and then discover means by which both sides of the conflict, perhaps in modified form, can be expressed and satisfied. Thus, for your headache it is better to take responsibility than aspirin. The drug temporarily dulls the pain, but it does not solve the problem. Only you can do this.

Pain, disgust, repulsion, are all disagreeable, but they are functions of the organism. Their occurrence is not accidental. They are nature's way of calling attention to what needs attention. You must, where necessary, learn to face pain and to suffer, in order to destroy and assimilate the pathological material contained in the symptom. Reintegration of dissociated parts always involves conflict, destroying and suffering. If, for instance, you are on guard against some "infantile" behavior, you must, nevertheless, learn to accept it as yours in order to give it a chance to grow up and find its proper place in the general integration of your personality. *If not allowed to claim attention and do its work, whatever this may be, it cannot be altered. Given attention and allowed to interact with the rest of your behavior, it is sure to develop and change.*

To gain confidence in this hard task, start with "mistakes" that you are prone to. In playing a piece of music perhaps you keep making the same mistake. If so, instead of being upset about it and trying to block it out, become curious and repeat it deliberately to find out what it means. Possibly your "mistake" is a natural fingering of a passage and the "correct" fingering quite wrong.

Repeated mistakes or acts of clumsiness are often retroflected annoyance. If someone has annoyed or upset you, instead of striking back at him, you upset the next glass of water and upset yourself still further.

For a while allow your pronouncements of moral judgment on yourself to remain in abeyance. Give yourself a chance. When the impulses which you customarily alienate on moral grounds can learn to speak in their own voices, you frequently will find that you change your evaluations of the right and wrong of the matter. Do not, at least, be any more harshly critical of yourself than you are of others. After all, you are a person, too!

Soon you will discover that facing neurotic pain or some "immoral" tendency is not as bad as you feared. When you have acquired the technique for dissolving the pain and reintegrating the "immorality," you will realize that you are freer, more interested, more energetic.

Apply to a headache or some other symptom the method of concentration-experiment. Give it your attention, and let its figure/ground spontaneously form. If you can accept the pain, it serves as a motivating interest; it is a concernful sensation. The important thing in dissolving the pain is to wait for development. Permit this to occur of itself, without interference or preconceived ideas. If you make contact, you will get a clearer figure and be able to dissolve the painful conflict. For a considerable period after you have started work on this technique the changes that occur may be so subtle—especially if you are expecting heavy drama from the outset—that you lose patience.

The pain will shift about, expand or contract, alter in intensity, transform itself in quality and kind. Try to feel the shape, size and direction of particular muscles which you contract. Be on the alert for any trembling, itching, "electricity," shivering—in short for any signs of biological excitement. Such excitement-sensations, vegetative and muscular, may come in waves or be constant, may swell or subside. When an itch develops, see if you can keep it from prematurely scratching or rubbing it away; concentrate on it and wait for it to develop further. Allow the excitement to come to the foreground. Correctly carried through, this procedure should leave you with a sense of well-being. The same technique is applicable not only to psychosomatic aches and pains, but to fatigue depressions, unspecified excitements, and attacks of anxiety.

In the performance of these experiments you are likely to suffer anxiety, which we have seen to be a self-regulating attempt to counteract faulty breathing during mounting excitement. Whether anxiety is present or not, practice the following respiratory experiment:

Exhale thoroughly, four or five times. Then breathe softly, making sure of the exhalation, but without forcing. Can you feel the stream of air in your throat, in your mouth, in your head? Allow the air to blow from your mouth and feel the stream of it with your hand. Do you keep your chest expanded even when no air is coming in? Do you hold in your stomach during inhalation? Can you feel the inhalation softly down to the pit of the stomach and the pelvis? Can you feel your ribs expand on your sides and back? Notice the tautness of your throat; of your jaws; the closure of the nose. Pay attention especially to the tightness of the midriff (diaphragm). Concentrate on these tensions and allow developments.

In your daily activity, especially in the moments of interest—in your work, when near someone sexually desirable, during an absorbing artistic experience, while confronted by an important problem—notice how you tend to hold your breath instead of breathing more deeply as the situation biologically requires. What are you restraining by holding back your breath? Crying out? Shrieking? Running away? Punching? Vomiting? Deflation? Weeping?

At the time of writing their reports on this experiment students varied tremendously in the amount of progress they had been able to make on this passage of the work—from virtually none to important unblockings of excitement. We repeat that there is no standard timetable for assimilation of the concepts introduced here, and it is certainly not to your discredit if at this stage the procedure is, so far as you are concerned, a "bust."

There is nothing that puts me to sleep more quickly than trying to do these exercises. This applies whether I intended to go to sleep or not.

If we say that this person "flees into sleep," it is without any moralistic implication that he ought not to. This is simply the way he functions at present. Structured as he is, he prefers to avoid his problems rather than to solve them. He can continue to exercise this preference so long as he subscribes to one or both of the following propositions: (1) the problems do not exist; (2) the problems are inevitable and cannot be solved.

In permitting one's attention to wander over the body noticing tensions, twitchings, pains, etc., I can report success, if success is to be measured in terms of finding that I do have these physical sensations. It is no great trick to focus attention on parts of the body and experience them. But may not the very focusing of attention, where the result has been foretold by the authors, be responsible for getting such results? How far would one have to go in getting uncomfortable physical sensations before either the help of a doctor was needed or the person worked himself into the position of the hypochondriac? I can't help but be dubious of the theory that every twinge in a tense muscle is associated with some long forgotten experience.

This man still insists on separating his "body" and "mind" so that "never the twain shall meet." For him the sensations are "physical sensations" which are natural to "parts of the body" and which anyone may have for the looking. But in the next breath they owe their existence to our having predicted that they will be found if looked for, that is, they are due to suggestion. At this point he apparently becomes quite able to resist "our influence," for he balks at the theory that the tensions have meanings as conflicts which can be discovered and worked through. Instead, he sees the more unfavorable outcome of having to get a doctor. To do what? Restore inattentiveness to the "body"? Unsuggest what was suggested? Prescribe aspirin in lieu of his previous painkiller, inattentiveness? Tell him to forget it —or, as is actually the case, tell him that it is psychosomatic?

The last sentence quoted above may be an example of misstating an argument to make it easier to dispose of. Muscles may be painful for a number of reasons, including ordinary fatigue, inflammation, or various dietary deficiencies. We are concerned here not with such instances but with chronic contractions which one may, if attentive, notice time and time again in the absence of the usual explanatory factors. It is these which, if developed and analyzed, *may* lead to remembrance of situations in which they were learned as a means of squelching conflict. But such recapture of memories, if and when it occurs, is incidental, a mere by-product of discovering and expressing the conflict's component tensions.

I did not have a headache to experiment on, so I had to use a "barked shin" and its resulting pain.

While concentration on actually injured parts of the body does increase blood circulation and in this way promote recovery, this has no pertinence to the purpose of the experiment.

I had no measure of success whatsoever. I followed through all the directions, but was unable to achieve anything more than a feeling of wasting my time and futility.

. . . This experiment has produced an interesting block. If, while lying down, I feel an ache or itch and concentrate on it, it disappears rather than comes to the foreground, and another in a totally different part of the body begins to distract my attention.

I'm getting *awfully* tired of this whole over-rated rigmarole. I am not upset by any of my urges, and am completely aware of all of them. I have no desire to vomit, to go on a rape rampage, or to commit suicide. I am ashamed of nothing—absolutely nothing—about myself. I am not afraid of my desire to murder people. I am not afraid to holler good and loud, but out of consideration for the neighbors I try not to. I alienate no impulse on moral grounds. I am doubtless a psychopathic personality. I have stolen cars, taken dope, and lived with women. Try to prove it!

The tensions I feel around my shoulders, neck, and at times my legs, are due to the fact that I am worried and nervous of late. I feel all tightened up inside and this seems to manifest itself in the parts of my body just mentioned.

The next quotation is from a student who, at the time of writing her report, had permitted considerable development, but was still confused on what to express and how to express it:

I have great resistance to putting my actual feelings on paper. Let me say that, whereas previously I regarded your statements as very confused, now they seem much clearer and I'm aware that it was I who was confused. Until now I've refused to face the responsibility of awareness—and I'm not really reconciled to it yet. But I realize that I must bring back many suppressed conflicts and either try to live with them or resolve them. I've gone back to the beginning experiments again and now, with reduced resistance so far as *they* are concerned, find them easy. However, when I attempt these present ones I'm afflicted with a nervous irritation which seems to start in my legs and spread slowly through my whole body, so that I scratch and seem to want to tear myself apart. In fact, even as I type this it begins again. I'm banging at the keys as if the aggression and irritation aroused by the experiments could be dissipated by the noise of the machine. Suddenly I have a pain in my left arm which seems to be in the bone. The whole lower part of my left arm is stiff. My right arm is unaffected. I've been trying to remember when the nervous reaction of scratching began.

I can't keep thinking about the scratching, but start to think about crying instead. So I'll say something about that. I come from a family in which any display of emotion, especially of this sort, is frowned upon. At the moment I'm in conflict with my parents, and it is something that produces a guilt conflict, as I feel I'm in the wrong for making them suffer needlessly. I refuse to go home. When I'm there I feel materially very secure, but suffocated in every other direction by their only half-concealed distaste for my ideas and way of life. I have received a letter from them that makes me want to cry. When I got it and read it, or whenever I think about it, I get a lump in my throat, a tightening behind the eyeballs and a tenseness throughout my body. This is repeated now as I report it. But I won't allow myself the luxury of crying about it. What strikes me as peculiar is that I cry easily over a film, book, play, or work of art, but in my own personal relationships it is a privilege that so far I will not allow myself.

Now I am aware that suddenly I feel very aggressive, as if I want to do something violent, and the way I'm pounding the typewriter is in keeping with this feeling. The pain has come back to my left arm.

In regard to inner thinking I'm aware that the odd words, disjointed phrases "in my head" have begun to crystallize. My thoughts seem to be about conflict, about compromise, and about the facades behind which I've hidden myself, a different one for every group I'm in. In one life one plays many roles. Which is the true one that represents the self? The awareness which has shaken me the most is the size of my resistances and their strength.

This person certainly has "unfinished business" with her parents. What, for example, does one owe to parents who will not accept one as he is? How can one make them "come to realize"? What life shall one live—what he chooses or what is chosen for him? Or something in between? This person will have to discover that, of the various roles she plays, there is not a "true one which represents the self." Instead, a part of her self is invested in and finds expression in each of the roles. The problem is to integrate them so that all of her self comes together and lives her life continuously.

The following excerpt is not very specific about the content of the conflict discovered and developed, but we include it because of the partial discharge attained and the consequent differentiation of the primitive impulse:

While trying to be aware of my body certain feelings do arise; certain people are involved in the potential fulfillment of the aroused feeling; and certain embarrassments follow inevitably. I'm really seriously angry at the authors, for what has turned up was, to say the least, somewhat unorthodox and shocking with no chance whatsoever of fulfillment. All that has happened is that I've become aware of a certain function or desire and have become just as aware that its fulfillment is out of the question. I realize that the desire was there before, because I just lay on the bed and suddenly this thing popped into my mind, full-blown, completely developed in all its various details. The whole scenario was complete from beginning to end. I don't think it grew during the short time of the experiment. It probably was there latently all the time, but till now, at least, I was unaware of it. It has merely brought about a state of active, constant self-vituperative frustration. How can I release this by socking a pillow or screaming? There's only one way of getting rid of this. That's by doing it—and I can't! (The report was interrupted at this point and not resumed until several days later.)

Upon rereading the foregoing part of this I was tempted to destroy it and start all over. But I include it because of what I consider a rather curious aftermath. The sudden awareness of the cause of my bodily tension and the discovery of an unfulfillable need had actually made me so angry that I lost sight of what I now believe was important. Since starting on this report again a little while ago, I deliberately tried to imagine the whole sequence being acted out, although I knew it could never actually happen. I suddenly found myself blushing to the roots of my hair, not because it was the *forbidden act*, but because it was so silly! What a ridiculous way of trying to 'wreak vengeance.' I sincerely think that if the opportunity were now offered to do what I thought I couldn't, that now I wouldn't simply because it's so silly and ineffectual. There are other much more adequate ways of dealing with the situation. And now so many of my attitudes and poses in regard to X become meaningless.

What is important in the present context is that the primitive retroflected aggression and the act which it prevented did not for their relief require that the repressed wish be literally carried out against Person X. Once in awareness and fantasied with embarrassment, the primitive aggression underwent differentiation into "other much more adequate ways of dealing with the situation." *It was the repression itself which kept the aggression primitive and incapable of discharge.*

In the following example a symptom of the alimentary tract was subjected to concentration:

For some months—in fact, on and off for a year—I have been suffering from diarrhoea, which, since there has been no physical basis found for it, was probably psychosomatic. During my awareness experiments I concentrated on the stomach and solar-plexus muscles to see if I could become aware of tensions there that might be causing this. I found many tensions in that region, and spent a good deal of time and several sessions isolating and testing them. Since then my diarrhoea has completely vanished. It is too soon to say whether it has gone for good, but, since I have changed neither my diet or anything else in my life-situation, it seems encouraging.

As a final example, we quote some effects obtained by a student which ordinarily require much more prolonged work with these techniques:

I relaxed on the bed, getting the "feel" of my body. After a short while I was in full contact with it, and felt around in first one part and then another. Then I breathed deeply, exhaling completely. Excitement kept starting forward. I'd feel a little surge of it, and then it would recede. That happened several times, and I realized that I was preventing my breath from coming faster. So I deliberately started *panting*—and there came the excitement! It *surged* all through me. It was as though my hands and feet were strapped down while tremendous bolts of electricity were being shot into me. My body strained upward, this way and that, twisting and turning with the force of the current— pelvis, shoulders, back, legs, head. *All of me* moved circularly and in every way. My body was as hot as fire; I actually *burned*, and my hands and feet felt as though they were blazing. The perspiration poured off me, tears streamed down my face, my breath came in huge gasps, and I was saying, 'Ohh . . . Ohh . . . Ohh . . .' I don't know just how long this lasted, but it was for at least several minutes. After it was over (that most intense part) I looked at my hands to see if they were scorched. I wouldn't have been surprised to find that they were. Little chills went through me for about another half hour, and *I felt very alive and strong*!

There is a place in the back of my head that has to be relaxed before I can experience all the excitement. Work on that spot *and* the diaphragm resulted in my being able to have the above experience. By relaxing that little spot in the back of my head I can have little chills run up and down my spine any time.

The word *softly*, which appeared twice in the instructions, was of great importance to me in performing this experiment.

Although I don't know what's around the next bend in the road so far as these experiments are concerned, I'm damn-well going to find out. So far it has just been the "honeymoon phase" that you spoke of in the introduction. Maybe it will be over for me with the next experiment, but I shall continue to *try*.

Experiment 3:   EXECUTING THE RE-VERSED ACT

This is the third and final experiment on retroflection, for which the preceding two were preparation. In them, when you discovered and muscularly explored some retroflecting activity, we suggested merely that you reverse it in fantasy or imagination. The crucial stage, of course, is to reverse it in overt action directed outward upon the environment, for only in this way can your "inner conflicts" be changed back into strivings to obtain what you need in contact with people and objects in the "outer world."

You are not ready for this—and it would be premature to attempt it—unless you have, by concentrating on the muscular clinch, succeeded in loosening it somewhat and differentiating it into component parts. Assuming that you have, next comes the work of making approaches to overt reversal of the retroflected activity. As an example, suppose that you have been choking yourself to prevent screaming and that now, finally, you can feel in your throat the impulse to scream and in your fingers the impulse to choke. However bizarre this may sound if you have not yet become aware of this or a comparable conflict, we mean it literally—not just as a figurative way of speaking. If you do feel something of the sort, what to do about it?

Certainly it would be no solution to rush up to someone and, while screaming at the top of your voice, throttle him! The two parts of the conflict do have this meaning—the wish to scream and the wish to choke—but they are primitive and undifferentiated, and it is precisely their static clinch in your musculature that has kept them so. If you do not become paralyzed by the "silliness" of it, you can now give *some* overt expression to both sides in a way that is perfectly safe. You can choke a pillow! Dig your fingers into it as if it were a throat. Shake it as a mastiff shakes a rat. Show it no mercy! While doing this, fiercely absorbed in squeezing the life out of your enemy, you will also sooner or later find yourself vocalizing—grunting, growling, talking, shouting. This part will come sooner if you can perform the experiment beyond the earshot of others, but once you get into it fully, you are unlikely to care what the neighbors think.

Before such an occurrence you might feel that you want to scream, to pound, to squeeze, but that you "couldn't possibly do it if you tried." The muscular ties holding the appropriate activity in confluence may be so subtle that even with the best concentration they are not loosened in their last details. Various approaches to expressing the impulse, such as the kind suggested above, may be made abortively without having the behavior come to life and be meaningful. It remains dead, a deliberate bit of play-acting. If you persist, however, extending the variations, going along with and falling into whatever absurdities, antics, posturings suggest themselves, eventually the deliberateness will change suddenly to spontaneity; you will become strongly excited, and the behavior will become a genuine expression of what was previously blocked. At this moment what was before impossible for you will now, paradoxically, become possible and be done.

Mere physical execution of what you are aware of wanting to do, be it yelling, punching, choking, or whatever, will be useless unless accompanied by a growing awareness of the meaning of the act, by recognition of its particular role in your own interpersonal situation —at whom you want to scream, whom or what you want to pound —and by the executive sense that *it is you* who are doing it and are responsible for it. Otherwise, the action is a bluff and a mere forcing. If you bully yourself into doing something on the ground that it is what you are "supposed" to do to fulfill the experiment, you will rasp your throat, strain your muscles, wrack yourself with new false excitements, but you will not achieve the integration you are seeking.

Here the truth of the unitary conception of the organism—unitary functioning of the body, feeling, and environment—may dramatically be demonstrated. For if your orientation, your feeling, and your overt actions come together spontaneously and with the proper timing, you will suddenly find that you understand, feel and can act with an unexpected new self-awareness and clarity; you will spontaneously recover a lost memory, recognize what your true intention is in some present relationship, see clearly what is the next thing for you to do, and so on. It is because of the importance of parallel development of all factors involved that we have been reiterating: use an all-round approach—fantasy, analysis of the interpersonal situation, verbal or semantic analysis, emotional training, body-expression; do not prematurely relax and thus by-pass some of the factors; do not force yourself or impose preconceptions, but allow for spontaneous developments.

When expression is overt, there normally is a release of pent-up energy—for instance, the seeming lethargy of depression will, if unblocked, be replaced by what it concealed and held in check: raging or the clonic movements of sobbing. When fears or social pressures remain so great that such expression cannot break through, the miniature and wholly inadequate motions of "thinking" are substituted for them—in this instance a kind of subvocal whining. The big movements which would suffice to discharge the energy are in a clinch with self-controlling tensions in the diaphragm, throat and head. Since the only way to release the energy is to express it and since the self-controlling "I" has no intention whatever of letting this particular impulse find appropriate outlet, the clinch does not change; without change it does not hold attention but becomes "forgotten"—an isolated, unaware conflict in the organism. If the cramped muscles give rise to psychosomatic pains, the "I" does not understand and accept these as consequences of its unrelenting self-control, but regards them as imposed upon it from "outside" and feels victimized. The energy of the organism cannot flow.

On the other hand, if you concentrate on a headache and permit development, you may sooner or later become aware that the headache is produced by muscular squeezing of your head. You may realize, further, that you are sad—in fact, that you want very much to cry. Unless you are alone, you may be unable to loosen the muscles and let go. To make it easier, retire to a place where you can have privacy. Even there, if you are a man, it may be difficult to let yourself weep, for you probably have been brought up on the fiction that "big boys don't cry." (Experiments to follow on "introjection" and "projection" will assist in overcoming this antibiological prejudice.)

When you discover an impulse to do something which cannot reasonably in its primitive form find a direct expression, try above all not to turn it back against yourself; turn it, instead, against any kind of object that is convenient. Don't throttle yourself again, but throttle a pillow, meanwhile allowing the fantasy to develop of whom you really want to choke. Squeeze an orange instead of your own eyeballs. Punch a bag. Wrestle for sport. Kick a box. Allow your head to shake from side to side and shout "No!" At first you will do such things rather lamely, but after a while, if you are convinced that they are not "silly"—that they are, instead, safe first approaches to what you will later be able to do on a less primitive basis —you will permit yourself to express with full emotional force all the kicking, pounding and screaming of a child's tantrum. Despite conventional notions to the contrary, this is the healthy device by which the organism exteriorizes frustrated aggressions.

Symptoms may often be more deeply concealed than indicated in our discussion so far. If the pain of a particular conflict has been too much to bear, you may have desensitized its context, and so developed blind-spots (scotomata). In that case, you may find during body-concentration, not aches and pains, but sensations of numbness, fogginess, nothingness. If so, then concentrate on these until you have them as a veil or blanket that you can lift, or as a fog that you can blow away.

In theory, male and female sexual frigidity are merely such blind spots and are curable by correct concentration. In practice, though, most cases of this sort have extremely complicated resistances. The chief muscular block in frigidity is the stifling of the pelvis, mainly in the small of the back and in the groin. This frequently is linked up with incorrect masturbation. And, since masturbation is a sexual kind of retroflection, normal or neurotic depending on the context, let us discuss it briefly.

Up to a generation ago masturbation was considered extremely sinful and harmful. Now it is approved of in many circles, even encouraged by "progressive parents," though often with great embarrassment on their part. Both attitudes—the condemnation and the approval—are over-simplifications. Whether masturbation is healthy or harmful depends on the urge which it expresses, the accompanying attitude, and the method employed.

It has been said that it is the guilt and remorse which constitute the damage that can be done by masturbation, and this is correct;

without these feelings a person suffers no injury. But there is a general misconception on this point. The guilt does not so much concern the act itself as the fantasies which accompany it—for instance, sadism, watching for someone to surprise and punish one, ambitious self-glorification, etc. Since healthy masturbation expresses an outgoing drive—is a substitute for intercourse—the healthy masturbation fantasy would be that of approaching and having intercourse with a beloved person. Where masturbation gives rise to guilt, the problem is to notice the guilt-producing fantasy and to deal with it separately from the sexual act.

The second point of danger in masturbation is the lack of pelvic activity. The act becomes one in which the hands are the active, aggressive partner to intercourse, while the genitals are merely raped. A man, lying on his back, conceives a passive-feminine fantasy. Or, in the absence of spontaneously developing sexual excitement, the situation becomes a struggle, a striving for victory—the hands try to rape while the genitals resist and defy the rapist. The pelvis, meanwhile, does not move in orgastic waves and jerks, but is immobilized, tense and rigid. No satisfactory orgasm results, the artificially stimulated excitement is inadequately discharged, and there ensues fatigue and the need to try again.

Masturbation, furthermore, is often an attempt to live out tensions not sexual at all—for instance, non-sexual loneliness, depression, annoyance. Or, on the other hand, it is sometimes a non-sexual expression of general defiance and rebellion.

In healthy masturbation, as in healthy intercourse, the lead has to come from the pelvis or—what corresponds to this—genuine sexual need. If the small of the back is rigidly tensed and if the legs are pulled up into the trunk, on orgastic movements are possible. The sexual act, to give satisfaction, requires that one surrender to the sensations. If one "thinks" during intercourse, has fantasies which are not an integral part of what one is doing, avoids bestowing attention on one's partner, or omits to feel one's own pleasure, one cannot hope for the profound relief of consummated sexual expression.

Let us return now to the more general problem of the systematic undoing of retroflections. By concentrating on localized muscle-cramps or areas of numbness as you permit developments to occur, you will release a certain amount of energy that was previously bound up and unavailable. But after a time you will find that you cannot make further progress without giving attention to functional relationships among the larger divisions of the body. The felt-contact between one part and another must be reestablished before reintegration can be achieved. These parts are not detached from each other, of course, since they all go with you when you walk down the street; but still it is necessary to explore and feel vividly the structural and functional connection of upper with lower body, head with torso, torso with legs, right half with left half. As you do this work, you will be fascinated by the novel and yet obvious relationships that will assert themselves. You will comprehend at first hand what is meant by the Freudian notion of "displacement upward" —for instance, that repressed sexual and anal functions appear on an inadequate substitute basis in speech and thought, or the converse, that oral blocks repeat themselves in anal tensions. This presents no mystery, for, since the system is functioning as a whole, when one end of a large sub-system like the alimentary tract is disturbed, the other parts adjust progressively to compensate or at least to maintain a functioning, though less efficient, unity.

Detailed interrelatedness of various parts of the body vary with each personality. By now you should be able to discover and work out the special features of your own particular mode of functioning. For further discussion here, let us restrict ourselves to a few remarks on balance and on the relation that exists between left and right.

When muscular action is retroflected, it is obvious that posture must be deformed in every kind of way. For instance, if you hold your pelvis rigid, there can be no flexible base for any movement of the upper torso, arms and head. Attempts to recover correct posture and grace by "setting up exercises" will prove fruitless unless there is also a loosening of the rigidity. Mothers produce nothing but exasperation in their children by constant admonitions to "stand up straight," "throw back your shoulders," or "hold your head up." The "bad" posture feels "right" and will continue to as long as certain parts are held in a vise-like grip and not allowed spontaneous movement. For proper posture the head, unconstrained by taut neck muscles, must balance freely on the torso; and the upper torso, without any pushed-out chest or pulled-in back, must ride easily on the pelvis. These body-segments have been likened to three pyramids, each resting on its point, so that it can pivot readily in any direction.

Conflict between head and trunk often expresses itself elsewhere as a struggle between right and left hands. When the head, for instance, is moral and "right," the person is stiff-necked—afraid of losing his precarious balance. In this case the neck serves, not as a bridge between head and trunk, but as a barrier—literally, a muscular bottleneck—between the "higher" and the "lower" functions of the personality. The shoulders, afraid to expand and work or fight, are held contracted. The lower body is well "under control." Ambidextrous cooperation is lacking. One hand tends to hold down and nullify the activity of the other, and the same is true for the legs. In sitting, balance is precarious; the upper carriage bears down on one buttock like a crushing piece of lead.

By concentrating on right/left differences you can regain much of the subtle balance required for adequate posture and locomotion. Lie on your back on the floor. Work first on the hollow small of the back and the arch of the neck. Although neither of these spots would remain up in the air as you lie there were your posture correct, do not try to relax or to force the vertebrae to flatten. Bring your knees up and spread them slightly apart, resting the bottoms of your feet on the floor. This will ease the tension along your spine, but you can still notice the rigidity of your back, and the short, pulled-in feeling of your legs. Allow any spontaneous adjustments that may occur in the direction of a more comfortable position. Compare every part of your anatomy on the right side with the left. You will observe many discrepancies in what should be bilateral symmetry. Your feeling that you are lying "all crooked" expresses, though in an exaggerated way, what is actually the case. Following the organism's own pressures as you notice them, softly correct your position—very, very slowly, without jerky movements. Compare your right and left eyes, shoulders, feet, arms, hands.

Throughout this work keep the knees somewhat apart, arms loose and uncrossed. Notice the tendency to bring them together. Consider what this tendency may mean. Do you want to protect your genitals? Do you feel too much exposed and defenseless to the world if you lie open in this manner? What will attack you? Do you want to hang on to yourself for fear that otherwise you will fall to pieces? Is your right/left discrepancy expressive of a wish to hang on to Person X with one hand and to push him away with the other? To go somewhere and not to go, at the same time? As you try to adjust your position, how are you doing it? Are you squirming, wriggling? Are you in a trap?

A highly important connection and discrepancy is between the front of the body and the back. For instance, while to all appearances your gaze is directed ahead, it may be that you are more concerned with what lies behind, in which case you can never see where you are. What unknown thing do you fear from behind? Or what are you hoping will overtake and assault you? If you tend to stumble and fall down easily, concentration on this discrepancy between front and back will prove useful.

As you allow muscular developments to take place, at times you may experience a vague, but fairly strong, urge to perform some particular type of movement. It may be, for instance, a kind of reaching out. If so, go along with it by experimentally reaching out. Should the feeling intensify, then reach out, not just with your hands, but with your arms, and, if it is the natural continuation of what you are doing, with your whole body. For whom are you reaching? Your mother? An absent beloved? At some stage does the reaching out begin to push away? If so, then push. Push against something solid like the wall. Do it with a force adjusted to the strength of your feeling.

Similarly, suppose you feel your lips tighten and your head draw away. Then let your head move from side to side and say, "No!" Can you say it firmly and loudly, or does your voice break? Do you plead? Or, quite the opposite, does your refusal develop into a general sense of defiance and rebelliousness with pounding, kicking, and screaming? What does it mean?

In performing such mimetic movements, nothing is gained by forcing. It then becomes mere play-acting and throws you off the track. Your sense of what to express and act out must grow out of the exploration and development of feelings and their significance. If the movements are the right ones and properly timed, they will crystallize your feelings and clarify meanings in your interpersonal relations.

In quoting reactions to this experiment, we begin as usual with some of the more antagonistic ones.

I'm a creature of habit and quite comfortable with my present posture. I'm not going to lie on the floor and do gyrations. I don't go reaching out for mother or an absent beloved, push things away, plead, kick, scream, or bellow "No!"

I don't have aggressive drives. When younger I was temperamental, aggressive and self-righteous. It was quite a struggle learning to control these things during the past ten years, but *I did it!* It's really not that I now control my temper; the truth is that I don't have a temper any more. What I hoped to get out of these experiments and have completely failed to get is, not an invitation to develop a temper again, but rather to learn how to be self-assured. *That's* my problem! Where are the experiments that deal with that?

When I'm aware of an itch, I scratch it. If I'm uncomfortable, I change my position. Going around asking, "Do you feel something?" isn't going to make me a happier or better-adjusted person.

What's all this stuff about wanting to protect myself from things that *obviously aren't there*? This is all getting farther and farther out into left field.

The frank discussion of sexual fornication and masturbation shocked me. At the risk of sounding like a prude, which I'm not, I may say that this shock has prevented me from doing this whole experiment.

The assumptions in this experiment are utterly ridiculous. I fear nothing in back of me! After reading this kind of stuff, I begin wondering about the authors. The more I wonder, the more I think that the only benefit I'm getting out of these experiments is typing experience.

We now sample reports from those who describe more positive results:

When I inhale, my stomach seems to move naturally, but my jaws are extremely tight, as is my throat and the rest of my face. I experience this as restrained shouting. I had a chance to make sure of this when my father was dressing me down over something where I felt positive I was right. I got this very same choked up feeling, but I couldn't let very much come out even when he demanded what was "eating me." The way it felt to me then was that *I mustn't hurt his feelings*. But that's precisely what I know I did do by sulking and moping around afterward. Next time I'm going to spare myself this pain—and spare him my sulking—by speaking my piece.

Last week when I came home late from a party I had a terrific headache. Instead of taking aspirin, I tried, as you suggested, to take responsibility for it. I lay there quite a while, exploring my forehead from the inside, and gradually it seemed that the pain, which I had supposed was a general one, was actually centered in two, distinct points, one over each eye. It then became clear that it wasn't just a pain, but very definitely a muscular ache. After concentrating for a while on the muscles around my eyes, without trying in any way to relax them, all of a sudden, with no effort on my part, they relaxed, and the pain was gone! It was a wonderful sensation of relief, and, naturaly, I fell asleep almost immediately. It wasn't until next morning that I wondered what the meaning of the ache had been, but by that time I guess it was too late to do anything about becoming aware of that.

The first tension I felt was this tenseness in the diaphragm, and in a heightened state of awareness I felt a subtle urge to vomit. As the awareness increased, I felt several convulsive heaves in the diaphragm region, but these, never too severe, stopped in a short while, and the whole area seemed relaxed. Throughout the whole period of nausea (actually it wasn't nausea in the usual sense) I tried to let my feelings come out, and almost spontaneously I felt my hands clench. The shaking of my head as if to say "no" quite vehemently also came quite easily, and before I knew it I was saying the word "no" out loud —and saying it quite loudly and with much emotion. I followed through with the experiment to the point of strangling a pillow, and it was while doing this that I saw some visual images which were exceedingly interesting and revealing to me. I don't feel that they should be described here, for they were of a rather intimate personal nature. The diaphragm tensions can't be found now, and I have hopes that they won't return with any degree of severity.

There was no one in the house for once and wouldn't be for a while, so I decided to do this experiment in the living room, since by pushing the table aside I would have considerable room for movement. At first, when I stretched out on the floor, I was completely dressed. This hampered me. It was the first time I really could go all out on a manipulation experiment and know I wouldn't be bothered, so I threw a blanket on the floor, drew the blinds, and stripped.

I was more successful in body awareness than I had ever been. I was excited, and my breathing was rapid. I concentrated on it until, though it was still rapid, it was slowly enough to permit full breathing. I tried to verbalize my various feelings—the throb of my chest, shoulders, and upper arms, and it was while I was working on these sensations I realized I was developing an erection. Involuntarily I tried to check this, and then I got an ache in my back. This was very interesting to me, because that particular ache is an old acquaintance, and now I'm beginning to put two and two together.

. . . My spine was extremely tight. Neither the small of my back nor the arch of my neck touched the floor. When I drew my legs up I felt somehow uncomfortable. The base of my spine pressed into the floor and it was quite an effort to put my feet down squarely. My legs felt very tense.

When I began to compare the two sides of my body, I found the right side far more relaxed than the left. My right shoulder was slightly raised and most of my weight was on my left shoulder and left buttock. I had the distinct feeling that my pelvic arch was raised up. As I explored various muscle groups I suddenly had a terrific urge to stretch. I raised my arms high and stretched my shoulder muscles. I then spontaneously "bridged," as do wrestlers, raising my whole body and suspending myself on my feet and neck. When I lay back I felt relaxed and strangely relieved. My spine wasn't so tight and the small of my back was much closer to the floor, although both my neck and back were still "held high" . . . Although the meanings of all this don't come through very clearly, I can feel that they are starting to emerge, and in a general sense I don't feel nearly so confused as I did.

While lying on my bed and trying this experiment I became aware of feeling ashamed of my genitals. I wished to get up and cover myself, but continued to lie there to see what might develop. The desire to cover myself with my hand became very strong, and I remembered my mother telling me that "nice girls never expose themselves." I was brought up in a family which put tremendous weight on moral virtue. Emotions, particularly those related to sexual adjustment, were suppressed in strong verbal warnings and lectures.

In doing this experiment I realized my natural desires and at the same time I felt the fears and warnings that had been implanted in me in childhood. I realize I have a great deal of reappraising and working out to do before I can finally come to terms with myself. There is a great deal of unfinished business in my life, but I'm getting clearer on ways and means of going about the job, and already I feel I've made a good start.

Before doing this particular experiment I felt I had already gained some insight about the matter, but to discover how opposed forces act upon the body was something quite amazing to me. Until recently I was unable to experience anger, no matter what the circumstances. Instead, I felt hurt. I would become nervous and later develop a splitting headache.

As I was lying on the floor with knees brought up and my feet flat, I became aware that my right arm was limp at my side and that my left arm was curved away from the body with fist tightly clenched. To me the right side represents the meek and non-aggressive tendencies in me, and the left side repressed aggressive tendencies. It is amazing to me, but not amusing, that although one might repress aggression, it inevitably comes to the surface in another form.

I used to be very sarcastic, but eventually denied myself even this more or less subtle way of striking. I believe that when I gave this up I became unable to be aware of anger. This awareness has come back with the doing of these experiments, but I'm still unable to do much about it overtly. It somehow feels cruel and unjustified to attack anyone for any cause whatever. I know, though, that I actually want to do this and that in certain situations it is not only justified but necessary. I'm making some progress in that direction, but I've got an awful lot of retroflecting to undo and I'm trying to resign myself to its taking quite a while.

I started shadow-boxing and allowed different people to wander in and out of my fantasies. Finally Sir X arrived. At this point I stopped throwing punches at my imaginary adversary and let go with my right foot. Immediately I felt a cramp in my shin. It surprised me considerably, not so much the cramp, as the thought of kicking someone. I had always abhorred such action and considered it impossible for me even to comprehend. Yet here I was attempting to stomp Mr. X's face! Since the experiment stopped at this point, naturally the cramp in my shin subsided. However, as I'm typing this I can feel tensions in my shin developing again!

I now ask myself whether this is an example of retroflected behavior. Does it mean that I've been kicking myself all these years when I wanted to kick someone else? As yet there is no clear answer to these questions, but I shall pursue them again soon.

Because of its fine attention to detail we quote the following report at some length:

As time went by I found that I could do the motor-muscular experiments for greater and greater stretches, and also that there was a quicker and more complete awareness of internal activities and tensions in each succeeding attempt. The first time I tried it, I got no results for some time. Then I became aware of my heart-beat, and then the results of my heart-beat, namely, circulation through my limbs, and the throbbing of the blood-vessels. Then I lost my gestalt and fell asleep.

The second experiment started negatively. Suddenly I became aware that I was introspecting—doing nothing but stare internally in an attempt to force results. The moment I stopped this the results were instantaneous. I took no notes during the experiment, so I cannot report all the sensations I felt. I can only say, as I report those that I do recall, that they were multitudinous and came so fast that I could not have reported them without interfering fatally with the flow of awareness. First I felt the circulatory awareness I had felt the first time. On this occasion, however, I maintained the gestalt, and soon was rewarded with definite motor-muscular awareness. There were all sorts of twinges, electric currents, and, especially, little internal jumps in the extremities. There seemed little or no anxiety, except for a continued over-eagerness, which I noted as part of a compulsive drive toward premature success. At one time I almost fell asleep again, but as I reestablished the figure-ground, I felt a fine feeling of having overcome this resistance to awareness.

Then I felt a severe pain in the stomach muscles, almost as if someone had kicked me in the solar-plexus. As I tried to concentrate on it, however, it disappeared. Then I felt a severe pain in my upper arm. This remained and intensified as I concentrated on it for about five minutes. It moved slightly, and alternately faded and increased in strength. I now tried to make free-associations with my life-situation to observe whether any connection could be made with this pain. I honestly do not remember what my train of thought was at this time, but some-

thing came to the surface which seemed to cause the pain to explode like an internal mushroom bomb. I can describe my feelings by saying that I felt as if I were about to have an orgasm in
the area of the arm. This feeling mounted to almost unbearable
tension and then faded without resolution, leaving me feeling
very much as if an expected orgasm had not taken place. However, when I ceased the experiment I felt well, rather than having the typical unpleasant after-effect of an incomplete orgasm;
I did, however, have the feeling that something terrific had almost occurred. I must now report further that, as I typed this
report, memory of the experiment returned spontaneously in
greater detail than I would have imagined possible, and suddenly I felt the same pain in the same region of the arm. It is there
right now. This interests me, but also alarms me somewhat.

I interrupted my report at this time to concentrate on the repeated pain in my arm. Internal awareness came at once, and
the pain remained present. Suddenly it spread out over my entire body and I began to tremble with fear (literally), an emotion
which both surprised and disgusted me. As I did this, I felt that
I wanted to stretch my arms out to someone—my mother.
Simultaneously an incident came to my mind of when I had
done just that. It occurred when I was four years old. I was
traveling with my parents, and had taken an intense dislike to
the manager of our hotel. I did something or other that was
naughty, and my mother said that if I didn't behave she would
go off and leave me behind with the hotel-manager, who was
present at the time.

I started to cry and ran to my mother with my arms outstretched. She consoled me, and assured me that she was joking,
while the manager laughed at me and called me a "mama's
baby." All this may be cooked up, and I wouldn't blame you
for being sceptical. I am myself. However, to the best of my
knowledge, I hadn't thought of this incident since the time it
occurred, and now I remember it as clearly as if it had happened
yesterday. The pain in my arm still persists, but it seems to be
less acute and to cover a wider area.

In my next muscle-tension experiment, awareness came a
little more slowly than the previous time, possibly due to anxieties that had been aroused by the results of the previous one.
It took about fifteen minutes for strong awareness to form, and
this time it was in the area of the face. I first noticed a tendency
of the muscles at the corner of my mouth to twitch upward in

what I imagined was an attempt to smile. Ten minutes approximately passed before I realized that this upward twitch was not a smile, but actually part of the facial movement of a crying-spell. I thereupon proceeded to cry! This I hadn't indulged in since a small child. Embarrassment at my own behavior interfered with developments at this point. I could not associate my action with anything in my life situation, except possibly the death of my mother two years ago, on which occasion I had been unable to cry although I wished to. I did become aware, however, that the pressure of my lower lip against my upper and the tension across my forehead—two tensions which I reported previously—existed to prevent my crying. After the experiment I felt fine and extremely happy to have made this outgoing action available to myself.

Introjection

Experiment 1: INTROJECTING AND EATING

In dealing with introjects we again make use of the same techniques of concentration and development which were applied to retroflections, but there is a crucial difference in procedure. In retroflections both the retroflected act and the behavior which it holds in check are parts of one's personality, and what must be done is, first, to accept and identify with both parts, and, second, to find a new integration in which both parts obtain overt expression. An introject, on the other hand, consists of material—a way of acting, feeling, evaluating—which you have taken into your system of behavior, but which you have not assimilated in such fashion as to make it a genuine part of your organism. You took it in on the basis of a forced acceptance, a forced (and therefore pseudo) identification, so that, even though you will now resist its dislodgment as if it were something precious, it is actually a foreign body.

Both as an organism and as a personality one grows by assimilating new material. To compare the acquisition of habits, attitudes, beliefs, or ideals to the process of taking physical food into the organism strikes one at first as merely a crude analogy, but the more one examines the detailed sequence of each, the more one realizes their functional identity.

Physical food, properly digested and assimilated, becomes part of the organism; but food which "rests heavy on the stomach" is an introject. You are aware of it and want to throw it up. If you do so, you get it "out of your system." Suppose, instead, you suppress your discomfort, nausea and tendency to spew it forth. Then you "keep it down" and either succeed finally in painfully digesting it or else it poisons you.

When it is not physical food but concepts, "facts," or standards of behavior, the situation is the same. A theory which you have mastered—digested in detail so that you have made it yours—can be used flexibly and efficiently because it has become "second nature" to you. But some "lesson" which you have swallowed whole without comprehension—for example, "on authority"—and which you now use "as if" it were your own, is an introject. Though you have suppressed your initial bewilderment over what was forced into you, you cannot really use such foreign knowledge and, to the extent that you have cluttered your personality with gulped-down morsels of this and that, you have impaired your ability to think and act on your own.

On this point we differ with Freud. He held that some introjections are healthy; for instance, the models and imitations by which the developing personality of the child is formed—especially the introjection of the loving parents. But in this he was obviously failing to make the distinction between introjection and assimilation. What is assimilated is not taken in as a whole, but is first destroyed (destructured) completely and transformed—and absorbed *selectively* according to the need of the organism. Whatever the child gets from his *loving* parents he assimilates, for it is fitting and appropriate to his own needs as he grows. It is the *hateful* parents who have to be introjected, taken down whole, although they are contrary to the needs of the organism. Accompanying this is the starving of the child's proper needs and his repressing of rebellion and disgust. The "I" which is composed of introjects does not function spontaneously, for it is made up of concepts about the self—duties, standards, and views of "human nature" imposed from the outside.

If you can realize the necessity for an aggressive, destructive, and reconstructive attitude toward any experience that you are really to make your own, you can then appreciate the need mentioned previously to evaluate aggressions highly and not to dub them glibly "anti-social"—on the basis of an introject. As commonly used, "social" often means being willing to introject norms, codes and institutions which are foreign to man's healthy interests and needs, and in the process to lose genuine community and the ability to experience joy.

To eliminate introjects from your personality the problem is not, as it was with retroflections, to accept and integrate dissociated parts of yourself. Rather, it is to become aware of what is not truly yours, to acquire a selective and critical attitude toward what is offered you, and, above all, to develop the ability to "bite off" and "chew" experience so as to extract its healthy nourishment.

To clarify further the process of introjection, let us review the earliest years of life. The foetus is in complete confluence with the mother, who provides oxygen, food, and environment. After birth the infant must get his own air and begin to differentiate the sensory environment, but his food, although now only intermittently available, still comes fully prepared for digestion. All that is required of him is to suck and swallow. Such fluid intake is equivalent to total introjection, for the material is swallowed whole. But this is appropriate to the pre-dental, suckling stage.

In the next stages of oral development, biting and chewing, the infant becomes more active with respect to his food. He selects and appropriates and changes in some degree what the environment offers. With the growth of incisors he is for a period in transition from suckling to "biteling." He makes the discrimination that the nipple is not to be bitten while he sucks from it, but for the rest of his diet he bites off bits of other still partially prepared food. With the eruption of molars, he reaches the chewing stage, which is of paramount importance because it allows for complete destroying of the food. Instead of accepting what is given and uncritically introjecting it, the "chewing" works over what is provided by the environment so as to insure his assimilation of it. It is on the basis of such competence, combined with almost complete development of sensory discrimination and perception of objects, that the child begins to speak and brings to a head the process of forming his "I."

The process of weaning—of "making" the child give up its suckling—is always regarded as difficult and traumatic. But it is very likely that, *if there has been no previous starvation and failure of affection* (that is, no accumulation thus far of interruptions, distortions, or unfinished aspects of the earlier stages), the child will be ready and eager to exercise his newly developed powers and to leave behind the introjective confluence. It was the tragic fact that this normal sequence almost never takes place in our society—that there is, therefore, imperfect biting off and chewing from the beginning —that led Freud and others to conceive as normal "partial introjection," the gulping down of poorly chewed morsels of one kind or another.

With biting, chewing, and the very important functions of locomotion and ability to approach, the child has the chief types of aggression available to him and under his control for his own growth. These, obviously, are not "antisocial," although they are the very antithesis of passive confluence. But if these biological activities are not used in the service of the growth-functions—as initiative, selection, overcoming of obstacles, seizing upon and destroying in order to assimilate—*then* the surplus energy finds discharge as displaced aggressions—domination, irritability, sadism, lust for power, suicide, murder, and their mass-equivalent, war! The organism does not develop in continuous creative adjustment with its environment —so that the "I" is a system of executive functions concerned with orientation and manipulation. Instead, it is saddled with an "I" which is a thrown-together collection of unassimilated introjects— traits and qualities taken over from "the authorities," which he cannot stomach, relations which he did not bite off and chew, knowledge he doesn't understand, sucking fixations he cannot dissolve, disgust he cannot release.

When, by reversing retroflections, an amount of aggressive energy is detached from the self as victim, it may be usefully reemployed for biting through and chewing physical food and its psychological counterpart: problems that must be faced, fixations that must be dissolved, concepts of the "I" which must be destroyed. That is what is attempted in the following experiments, but just as in working with muscular contractions, you must go slowly and not force yourself or you are sure to be disappointed and discouraged. The main resistances of which you will become aware will be impatience and greed, which are emotions perfectly normal to the gulping stage, but not to the more mature, differentiated stage of selection, biting off, and ruminating. Be content at first with the development of awareness. You will have accomplished much when, by concentrating on your mode of eating, you learn to distinguish between liquid food which may appropriately be drunk and solid food which *cannot* be handled adequately by drinking it down.

Concentrate on your eating without reading or "thinking." Simply address yourself to your food. Meals have for us become social occasions for the most part. The primitive goes off by himself to eat. Follow his example to this extent: set aside one meal a day to eat in solitude, and learn how to eat it. This may take about two months, but, after all, you will have acquired a new taste, a new source of enjoyment, and you will not relapse. If you are impatient, this will seem too long. You will want magical effects, quick results without effort. For you to get rid of your introjects, you yourself must do the destroying and the reintegrating.

Notice your resistances to addressing the food. Do you taste the first few bites and then fall into a trance of "thinking," daydreaming, wanting to talk—meantime losing contact with the taste? Do you bite off your food by clean, efficient action of the front teeth? In other words, do you bite through on a meat sandwich held in your hands, or do you close your jaws part way and then tear off a hunk? Do you ever use your molars up to the point of complete destruction of the food, that is, liquefaction? Just notice whatever it is you do, without deliberately changing anything. Many changes will occur spontaneously if you keep in contact with your food.

As you eat with awareness, do you feel greed? Impatience? Disgust? Do you blame the hurry and bustle of modern life for your gulping of meals? Is it different when you have leisure? Do you avoid food that is flat and tasteless, or do you just down it without demurring? Do you experience a "symphony" of flavors and textures in your food, or have you so desensitized your palate that it all tastes pretty much alike?

When it is not a matter of physical but of "mental" food, how does the matter stand? Consider the same questions with regard, for instance, to your intake from the printed page. Do you skip over hard paragraphs or do you work them through? Is your taste for the sweet and easy alone—light fiction or "feature" stories—which you can gulp down without active response? Or do you compel yourself to partake only of "heavy" literature, though you get little pleasure for your effort?

What about your visual intake at the movies? Do you fall into a kind of trance and drink in the scenes? Study this as an instance of confluence.

In the same context let us consider alcoholism, which, although complicated and with many ramifications (including somatic changes), is particularly anchored in oral under-development. No cure can have lasting effect or be more than a suppression unless the alcoholic ("adult" suckling) progresses to the stage of biting and chewing. Fundamentally, the drinker wants to drink his environment in—to get easy and total confluence without the excitement (which to him is a painful effort) of contacting, destroying and assimilating. He is a bottle-baby, a gulper, reluctant to take solid food and chew it. This applies to the steak on his platter and to the larger problems of his life-situation. He wants his solutions in liquid form, prepared, so that he need but drink them down.

Socially, he wants to enter into immediate confluence without preparatory contact with the other person. His acquaintance of the moment becomes a pal to whom he will "pour out his heart." He by-passes those parts of his personality which would exercise discrimination; and then, on the basis of these supposedly deep and sincere but actually most superficial social contacts, he comes forth with impatient, extravagant demands.

Just as uncritically, he takes in social reproaches and accepts them as coming from himself, for he has a strong self-aggressive conscience. He may silence it by drowning it in alcohol, but when he awakes, its vindictiveness is redoubled. Since his aggression is not used in attacking his physical food or his problems, the surplus which is not invested in his conscience often turns outward in surly, irrelevant fights.

Drinking is the adequate way of appropriating fluids, and inebriation's easy sociability is warming and pleasurable. But these are only phases of experience, not the whole of it, and when they continually occupy the foreground as imperious needs, the possibility of other kinds and levels of experience is ruled out.

A similar mechanism manifests itself in sexual promiscuity. The demand here is for immediate terminal satisfaction, without preliminary contact and development of the relationship. Since he is cold and the victim of tactile starvation, the promiscuous person seeks crude tactile proximity of the skin-surface as his final sexual aim. While there are, of course, other complicating factors, what again is outstanding is impatience and greed.

For the most part, our views on introjection arouse nearly unanimous disagreement on first encounter. We cite a few comments from students:

> I cherish the illusion—which you will no doubt diagnose as neurotic—that being a human being implies more respect for the grandeur of the soul than to address myself to food.

> I don't see how changing your eating habits is supposed to aid your ability to reject introjected ideas. I just don't see it. Even if early eating habits are connected with all this, simply changing your present habits isn't going to suddenly enable you to see that Freud's concept of introjection is wrong while this one may be partially correct. Why can't we work on something that will actually be of use rather than all this junk?

> The whole business of the parallel between forcible intake of food and forcible intake of behavior is tenuous, especially when

carried past just being a figurative way of speaking. The organism does not vomit out behavior, nor does it bite and chew experience. True, complex behavior may be introjected but to me this has little to do with the eating functions, certainly when infancy is past. I have disregarded the eating experiments as I think they are useless, *a priori*, and I won't even give them the limited attention I've paid the other experiments—that is, doing them for the sake of curiosity. In the author's own terms, I refuse to introject what they have to say about introjection.

I'm no more impressed or moved to action by this drill than I have been by the others. Although much has been learned in the process of reading it, namely, an acute sense of awareness of one's thoughts, motives, habits, etc., with possible permanent benefits derived therefrom, I still fail to comprehend the essential thought behind this mass of verbal confusion. I assume that the dominating thought is to make the individual more cognizant of various processes within himself, and therefore expel many undesirable factors present in his thoughts and actions. As previously stated, though, I feel that the authors assume too much insight on the part of the student, and I feel further that the drills involve too much preoccupation with self—a decidedly dangerous thing if devoid of trained guidance.

In all of the above excerpts there is the customary modern emphasis on verbal evidence and verbal proof. As a matter of fact, there are a number of "objective" experimental findings which could be brought to bear in this connection, perhaps sufficient to oblige the above-quoted students to give intellectual assent to the theory presented here; however, what we seek is not verbal agreement but the dynamic effects that you may obtain by directly discovering and proving the points in your own nonverbal functioning.

Several persons, apparently unable to reject the theory without more ado, rejected it temporarily by postponing its nonverbal testing:

I question this whole thing on the—Oh, how the hell *can* there be a functional identity of any such sort? I'm going to put this whole thing off until I go home this summer and work on it then.

Whatever doubts they had about the theory, most students took an experimental attitude toward the examination of their eating processes and reported various discoveries about their usual modes of ingestion:

> After concentrating on my eating I found that I didn't know how to eat, but bolted my food gluttonously. I can't stop eating with a great rush even where there's no reason to hurry. I find that I use my molars scarcely at all.

The problem of keeping a presentable silhouette dominated many reports.

> I would try on a dress that looked beautiful in Vogue or Harper's Bazaar. What I saw in the mirror didn't look like my long, willowy, blonde ideal. I would get sore and disgusted at myself and swear to go on a diet. Then I would get to feeling so sorry for myself that I would sit down and eat some candy or a piece of cake.

We quote in detail an account of attempting to chew some food to the point of liquefaction:

> Since I'm quite well known in the family as a food-gulper and a "reading-when-eating" type, I looked forward to the eating experiments with interest. They have worked, but for fear they might work too well, I've stopped before going too far.
> First, I noted how I took the food, and wasn't too surprised to find that I'm a "partial-biter, tear-the-rest-off" sort of operator. It was fairly easy to slow down enough to bite through my food as completely as I could before starting to chew. But since I rarely eat without reading, simply this concentration on biting off instead of tearing off sent me into daydreaming. I just sat there dumb, unaware of what I was doing and not thinking anything —so that literally before I knew it the food was down.
> As to whether I ever liquefy my food the answer emphatically is no (probably a reaction against my father who is an ardent Fletcherizer, although he doesn't actually count, and thus is the slowest eater I've ever seen). I tried to chew and chew until the food was about as liquid as I could stand it and noted two reactions:
> First, my tongue started to ache toward the back. What usually takes place is that after I have food in my mouth nothing happens until the food is on the way down the esophagus—that is,

I'm not aware of swallowing, gulping, breathing or anything else. What happened, now that I tried to masticate completely, was that I found myself running out of air. My tongue started to ache uncomfortably. I seemed to be holding my breath. So I had to push the food to the sides of my mouth, make the gulping motions (although I wasn't swallowing anything), and then take a deep breath before going on. After these setting-up exercises I would have to bring back the food from wherever it had scattered in the sides of my mouth and then go to work on the messy left-overs of that last bite.

This description is particularly detailed and, to me, nauseating, because that's how I felt after a couple of bites—nauseated. The food began to taste terrible and I now found myself deliberately avoiding trying to taste or even feel (in a sensory fashion) what was going on in my mouth. I usually don't taste or feel what's going on there anyhow, but this experiment did bring back a lot of taste, etc., so that now to get rid of the unpleasantness aroused by it I had to try to "desensitize myself."

What I meant above when I wrote that I stopped the above experiment before going too far is that I was feeling so disgusted with what was going on in my mouth that I felt a very strong tendency to vomit. Immediately I switched over into daydream or stupor, telling myself, "Now let's not spoil a whole meal by getting sick; after all, there's a limit." So I stopped. Now this is obviously a resistance, but that's what I did twice.

A student who feels that he has good eating habits mentions the following:

As a child these good eating habits were not present. I was an extremely poor eater and probably introjected most of what I ate, attempting to think or talk about anything to keep from becoming aware of what I was eating. The change occurred somewhere between my tenth and thirteenth year. The major event in my life during this period was when my father remarried and we finally moved away from my uncle's home where we had been living.

A number of students made comments such as the following:

I am utterly amazed at how closely my ways of dealing with problems, with reading matter, with movies, etc., parallel my ways of dealing with food.

Experiment 2:   DISLODGING AND DIGESTING

Introjection is characterized by a particular constellation of emotions and behavioral tendencies: impatience and greed; disgust and its negation through loss of taste and appetite; fixation, with its desperate hanging on and clinging to what has ceased to be nourishing. Let us examine these in detail.

Infants and children are said to be impatient and greedy. But these terms, appropriate as applied to adults who are underdeveloped, are *mis*applied to children. A baby, when hungry, wants the breast. If he does not get it right away, he squalls. Impatiently? No, for this is all that he *can* do in the direction of satisfying his need. This is not something to be corrected but rather to be *grown out of.* Impatience has no meaning apart from its opposite, patience. Adults have had a chance to differentiate these behaviors by acquiring the working-through techniques which, when applied, constitute patience. The child has not.

If he has a loving mother, his "hunger-cry" is to her an adequate and unresented signal. Given the breast, he eagerly and immediately swallows down the milk. Greedily? No, for liquid food requires no delay before ingestion. The behavior of the child is mistakenly called impatience and greed when obviously it is aggression that is fully adequate in the child's mother-confluent situation. Only when the primitive aggression does not, as the child gets older, differentiate into techniques for tackling and working through obstacles are we entitled to speak of impatience and greed. Although equipped with the apparatus and the opportunity for taking care of himself, such an "old child"—still wielding his aggression in its original, primitive form—insists that it be done *for* him and done at once!

If you investigate your own impatience, you will be able to confirm this. You will realize that it is a primitive aggression—a crude, angry reaction to frustration. To say, "I am impatient with you" is equivalent to, "I am annoyed with you because you do not come across with what I want right now, and I don't want to have to put out the additional effort (destruction of obstacles) to get you to come across."

In babies and cubs we can easily observe the further differentiation of aggression at the biting stage. They like to try out this new ability by sinking their teeth into whatever is bitable. The mouth too, becomes an organ of manipulation. Subsequently, the hands take over the early exploratory function of the mouth and then its manipulating. As more and more discrimination and working over of food is

required, the mouth specializes correspondingly in testing and destroying.

Parental interference comes seriously into the picture at the biting
stage. On the one hand, biting is punished as cruel and naughty, and,
on the other, food that the child does not want or does not want *at
the time* is forced into him. His tendency under these circumstances
to make a barrier of his teeth to the unwanted food is forcibly van-
quished. Denied adequate expression, the child's oral aggression
must be displaced. Part of it is retroflected to suppress the punishable
food-rejecting. Part of it turns against persons. This comprises the
so-called "cannibalism" of those who want "to eat you up."

In order to get down and keep down the unwanted food the child
has to repress his disgust. Furthermore, spontaneous use of his teeth
has been denied him; he was punished for his "cruel and naughty"
biting and also for clamping his teeth against the unwanted food.
Only the behavior of the suckling—which he *was* in the process of
outgrowing—is fully safe. His development out of this stage has been
interfered with, and, because of the maiming of his "biteling" behavior, he retains in some degree or relapses into the "impatience and
greed" of the suckling. Only liquid food still tastes good, but this is
never enough to gratify hunger.

Because of "scheduled feedings" and other "scientific" practices
applied to you as an infant, the blocking of oral aggression as described above is probably in some degree present in your own case.
This condition is the basic prerequisite for tendencies to introject—
to swallow down whole what does not belong in your organism. We
shall, therefore, attack the problem at the source, namely, the
process of eating. The solution involves remobilization of disgust,
which is not pleasant and will rouse strong resistances. For once,
therefore, in stating the following motor experiment, we do not
propose it as something to try out in a spontaneous fashion to see
what happens, but we appeal to your courage and charge you with it
as a task.

During each and every meal, take one bite—remember, just
one, single bite!—and liquefy the food completely by chewing. Do
not let one morsel escape destruction, but seek it out with your
tongue and bring it into position for further chewing. When you
are satisfied that the food has been fully liquefied, drink it down.

In performing this task you will "forget yourself" in the middle of
the operation and swallow. You will become inattentive. You will

have no time. On occasion you will feel that you have "spoiled the taste" of something good. When you encounter disgust, you will be sorry you ever started the experiment. But sooner or later a welcome by-product of the experiment will be that you get much more taste and nourishment out of your mouthful than you would have imagined possible, and with this you will begin to have an increased feeling of yourself as an active agent.

The task is restricted to a single bite per meal, for this, no matter how simple it may sound, will be hard to do. It requires the re-marshalling of an enormous amount of energy. The chewing as such is not what you are after but rather *the attitude of destroying and assimilating real material.* Avoid any obsessional practice such as counting your jaw-movements (Fletcherism), for this only distracts your attention.

As the functional counterpart of the task of chewing up a single bit of food, give yourself the same training in the intellectual sphere. For example, take a single difficult sentence in a book that is "tough meat," and analyze it, that is, take it apart thoroughly. Get the precise connotation of each word. For the sentence as a whole decide on its clarity or vagueness, its truth or falsity. Make it your own, or else make clear to yourself what part of it you don't understand. Perhaps you have not failed to comprehend, but instead the sentence is incomprehensible. Decide this for yourself.

Another profitable experiment, one which makes full use of the functional identity between eating physical food and "stomaching" some interpersonal situation is the following: When in an impatient mood—angry, upset, resentful—and thus inclined to gulp, apply the aggression in a deliberate attack on some physical food. Take an apple or a tough heel of bread and wreak your vengeance on it. In accordance with your mood, chew as impatiently, hastily, viciously, cruelly as you can. But bite and chew—do not gulp!

The neurotic's condemnation of aggression has two exceptions. The first is when the aggression is retroflected and he then drives or punishes himself, and the second is when the aggression is invested in conscience and moral judgment and is then directed against both himself and others. If he will use some of the aggression dentally— that is, in the biological aggression of the teeth—he will correspondingly let up in his attacks on himself and others, and, what is more important, he will learn to recognize aggressiveness as *a healthy function which prevents introjection.* He will learn to reject what is indigestible in his physical or psychological system and to bite off and chew what is potentially digestible and nourishing if adequately destroyed and assimilated. And, with respect to the introjects he now has, he will learn to bring them up and get rid of them or else, at last, to chew them properly as preparation for genuine digestion.

Disgust as a word comes from the prefix *dis-*, meaning "without," and *gustus*, meaning "relish." This understates what we experience as disgust. When disgusted we have nausea, the physical sensations that go with reverse peristalsis in the alimentary tract. This changed direction of the gastric and esophageal contractions is, of course, designed to regurgitate and thus make possible the elimination or the further chewing, as in ruminants like the cow, of indigestible or improperly masticated food.

The same process occurs in the organism when the environment presents objects or situations which could not possibly be mistaken for physical food but which can be termed instead "perceptual food." We retch even at the sight of a decomposed horse. You may "feel your gorge rise" slightly at mere reading of these words, and you certainly would if we elaborated further on the possibilities of taking the dead horse as food. In other words, the organism reacts to certain objects and situations—and we cannot impress this upon you too strongly—*as if they had been taken into the alimentary tract!*

Our language is full of expressions which reflect the psychosomatic identity of disgust produced by physical food and by what is indigestible only in the psychological sense. Consider, for instance, "You make me sick," "I gag over having to do this," "The sight was nauseating." It would be easy to think up another series of verbalisms about belching, that relatively milder but omnipresent indicator of bad digestion.

Disgust is the desire to bring up, to vomit forth, to reject material which is disagreeable to the organism. One "gets the stuff down" only by numbing and putting out of commission the healthy organism's natural means of discrimination, smelling, tasting, and so on. In such an event it is crucial at least that one feel the disgust later on, and thus be enabled to "get the stuff back up." Since introjects have been gulped down precisely in this manner, their elimination from your system requires that you remobilize disgust.

Neurotics talk much of being rejected. This is, for the most part, a projection onto others of their own rejecting (as we shall consider further in the next experiment). What they refuse to feel is their latent disgust with what they have incorporated in their own personalities. If they did, they would have to vomit up and reject many of their "loved" identifications—which were unpalatable and hateful at the time when swallowed down. Or else they would have to go through the laborious process of bringing them up, working them through, and then at last assimilating them.

Forced feeding, forced education, forced morality, forced identifications with parents and siblings, result in literally thousands of unassimilated odds and ends lodged in the psychosomatic organism as introjects. They are both undigested and, as they stand, indigestible. And men and women, long accustomed to being resigned to "the way things are," continue to hold their noses, desensitize their palates, and swallow down still more.

In psychoanalytical practice a patient may lie down and bring up verbally all the undigested material accumulated since his last session. This furnishes relief, for he has performed the psychological counterpart of vomiting. But the therapeutic effect of this as such is nil, for he will introject again. At the moment of taking it in he does not feel disgust for what later he will disgorge. If he did, he would reject it *then* and not save it for his treatment hour. He has not learned to chew up and work through what is nourishing and necessary. He will drink down his analyst's words, too, as something new with which to identify, rather than mulling them over and assimilating them. He expects his therapist to do the work of interpretation for him, and he will later spew out these very interpretations to his bored friends. Otherwise, "intellectually accepting" the interpretation—without conflict, suffering, and disgust—he merely imposes on himself a new burden, a further complication of his concept of himself.

Orthodox psychoanalysis makes the error of not regarding all introjects as "unfinished business" to be worked through and assimilated; consequently, it accepts as normal much in the present-life attitude which is not actually the patient's own and not spontaneous. If, instead of limiting themselves to working through merely the dreams and more spectacular symptoms, analysts would concentrate on *every* aspect of behavior, they would find that the introjected "I" is not the healthy "I." The latter is completely dynamic, consisting entirely of functions and shifting boundaries between what is accepted and what is rejected.

When one looks upon the introject as an item of "unfinished business," its genesis is readily traced to a situation of interrupted excitement. Every introject is the precipitate of a conflict given up before it was resolved. One of the contestants—usually an impulse to act in a given manner—has left the field; replacing it, so as to constitute some kind of integration (though a false and inorganic one) is *the corresponding wish of the coercing authority.* The self has been conquered. In giving up, it settles for a secondary integrity—a means of surviving, though beaten—*by identifying with the conqueror and turning against itself.* It takes over the coercer's role of conquering itself, retroflecting the hostility previously directed outward against the coercer. This is the situation usually referred to by the conventional term "self-control." Here, although actually defeated, the victim is encouraged by the victorious coercer to perpetuate his defeat by forever rejoicing in the deluded notion that *he* was the victor!

Though admittedly unpleasant, there is no other way to discover what in you is not part of yourself except by remobilizing disgust and the accompanying urge to reject. If you wish to unburden yourself of those foreign bodies in your personality which are introjects, you must, in addition to the chewing experiments, intensify awareness of taste, find the spots where you are "taste-blind," and resensitize them. Become aware of changes in taste during mastication, differences in structure, consistency, temperature. In doing this, you are sure to revive disgust. Then, as with any other painful experience that is your own, you must confront this too, become aware of it, and accept it. When, finally, there comes the urge to vomit, do so. You will feel it as terrible and painful only because of your resistances to it. A small child vomits with perfect ease and in a strong orgastic stream; immediately afterward he is quite happy again, rid of the foreign matter that was bothering him.

"Fixations" form another most important part of the introjective constellation. They are the tendencies to static clinging and suckling when the situation has progressed to the point where active biting through and chewing are required. To be fixated is to be confluent with the situation of sucking, of skin-proximity, of holding on to, of dreamy recollection, etc. In our view a fixation does not result from a particular traumatic interpersonal or Oedipal experience, but is the work of a character-structure, a rigid pattern repeated continuously in the life of the neurotic. You may recognize the fixated, confluent type by his clenched jaw, his indistinct voice, and his laziness in chewing.

He hangs on "doggedly." He will not let go, but he cannot—and this is the decisive point—bite the piece off. He hangs on to exhausted relationships from which neither he nor his partner are any longer getting any profit. He hangs on to outworn customs, to memories, to grudges. He will not finish what is unfinished and try a new adventure. Where there is risk, he visualizes only the possible losses and never the compensating gains. His aggression, confined to holding his jaws locked—as if trying to bite himself—can be employed to destroy neither the object on which he is fixated nor such new obstacles as may present themselves. He is squeamish about hurting and—projecting his unacknowledged wish to hurt—fearful of being hurt.

Castration-fear has as a major component the clinging fear to hurt or be hurt, and the *vagina dentata*, a frequent fantasy of castration-anxiety, is the man's own unfinished bite projected into the woman. Little can be accomplished in working on castration-fantasies until dental aggression has been remobilized; but once this natural destructiveness has been reintegrated into the personality, not only the fear of damage to the penis but also the fear of other damages—to honor, property, eyesight, etc.—are reduced to proper size.

Here is a simple technique for starting to mobilize the fixed jaw. If you notice that your teeth are frequently clenched or that you are in a state of grim determination, instead of working with ease and interest, make your lower and upper teeth touch each other lightly. Keep them neither clamped nor apart. Concentrate and await developments. Sooner or later your teeth may begin to chatter, as if with cold. Allow this to spread, if it will, into a general shivering excitement all through your muscles. Try to let go until you are shivering and shaking all over.

If you succeed in this experiment, use the opportunity to try to increase the looseness and amplitude of your jaw. Touch your teeth together in various positions—incisors, front molars, back molars—and meantime press your fingers against the sides of your head where the jaws meet the ears. When you find painful spots of tension, use these as foci of concentration. Likewise, if you achieve general trembling in this or other experiments, use it to try to experience a complete giving up of all rigidity—to the point of dizziness or collapse of tension.

Try the alternative of clamping your teeth hard in any position —the situation of biting through. This will create a painful tension in the jaws that will spread to the gums, mouth, throat and eyes. Concentrate on the pattern of tension, and then, as suddenly as you can, let go with your jaws.

To mobilize your stiff mouth, open it wide in talking and bite through your words. Spit them out like bullets from a machine-gun.

The "hanging-on bite" is not restricted to the jaws, but spreads to the throat and chest, impeding breathing and aggravating anxiety. It spreads also to the eyes, bringing about a fixed stare and preventing a "piercing" glance. If your states of anxiety tend to come when you are speaking—for example, in public, or even in a small group—you will benefit by considering the following: speaking is organized exhaling. Inhalation takes in oxygen for metabolism; exhalation produces the voice. (See how difficult it is to speak while inhaling.) When excited, you increase the speed of your speech (impatience and greed manifested not on the intake but this time on the output side) but do not inhale sufficiently, and breathing thus becomes difficult.

An experiment simple in structure yet exceedingly difficult to perform will remedy this, besides being an excellent means of making you feel your non-verbal existence in relation to your verbalizing. It coordinates breathing and thinking (subvocal speaking). You have already done it in part in your earlier work on internal silence. Talk in fantasy, silently and subvocally, but with a particular audience, perhaps a single person. Attend to your "talking" and your breathing. Try to have no words in your throat ("mind") during the inhalation; but let out your thoughts and hold your breath at the same time. Notice how often you hold your breath.

You will perceive, again, how much of your thinking is a one-sided interpersonal relationship, not a give and take; you are always lecturing, commenting, judging, or pleading, inquiring, etc. Seek for the rhythm of speaking and listening, give and take, exhaling and inhaling. (Though insufficient alone, this coordination of breathing and thinking is the chief basic therapy for stammering.)

The introjection experiments call forth more violent protests than any others in the series.

The authors carry this chewing and food consciousness a little too far and insist upon it *ad nauseam*. That we eat the way we do is usually recognized by us, but surely there must be an easier way to point this out.

Your statments are nothing but organized irrationality.

If you are literally inviting us to chew a piece of food until it disgusts us so much that we throw up, then this is the most stupid business I've ever encountered. I do agree that we often do feel like throwing up for many causes, and perhaps we would feel better if we did throw up; however, like anything else it could get to be a habit and then we'd be in quite a fix.

Eating is eating and that's all. Following your suggestion, I took a bite and chewed and chewed it until I was tired and couldn't chew any more. Then I swallowed. Okay, that's it. I didn't feel nauseous. I don't see how anyone can go into such detail about vomiting. What is there to vomit about? It's *food*! They eat it every day. And then, suddenly, after reading your experiment, they eat it again and vomit. They're certainly open to suggestion!

The statement just above came from one of the very few students who expressed any astonishment that food, when chewed thoroughly, should arouse disgust in anyone. Most persons simply took it for granted that masticating to the point of liquefaction would produce nausea, and, furthermore, that *it would continue to do so permanently*! But why should it? As well stated above, "What is there to vomit about? It's *food*!

If there is nothing intrinsically disgusting about *this particular bite of food*—in other words, if it is *good food* and *you are hungry*—then, if thorough chewing of it arouses nausea, *you must be making a mistake*! You must be tapping some *repressed disgust*, which was aroused but not expressed on past occasions. When obliged to down something unpalatable, your method was to inhibit chewing and desensitize yourself to the eating process. You behave now as if you *still* have to do this—and do it with respect to *all* food.

Actually, you are now in a position to be discriminating. You need no longer be, as one student put it, "the good child who eats everything." What disgusts you, you can reject; what you find nutritious and appetizing, you can consume with gusto. But *only after* you have remobilized and *e*xpressed the *re*pressed disgust!

Let us go over this again. Disgust is a *natural barrier* possessed by every healthy organism. It is a defense against taking into the organism what does not belong there—what is indigestible or foreign to its nature. However, by dint of great effort, parents and other authorities can get the child to *de*mobilize disgust—that is, attack and put out of commission its own defenses against what is unwholesome. The child's original ability—which has been experimentally demonstrated over and over again—to pick a balanced diet appropriate to its needs is overthrown by an arbitrary scheduling of officially designated "correct" foods in "correct" amounts at "correct" times. The child eventually "adjusts" to this by gulping down whatever is given with just as little contact with it as possible. Once the natural defenses of the organism have been breached, it is then comparatively easy to get the child to gulp down all sorts of unnatural and arbitrary "mental food" and thus "preserve society" for still another generation.

The healthy organism's way of eating—or, in its broader meaning, its way of selecting and assimilating from its environment what is needed for its own sustenance and growth—cannot, unfortunately, be restored over night. Full remobilization of disgust for what *is* disgusting calls a halt to further introjecting, but it does not forthwith cause to be spewed forth what has already been introjected and now "lies heavy in the mental stomach." This takes time and a transitional period of more or less frequent or chronic nausea.

Persons differ widely in their attitude toward vomiting. For some it comes relatively easily and brings profound relief. Others have highly organized defenses against it.

> I have not been able to mobilize the feelings of disgust spoken of, probably because of tremendous fear of vomiting. I do not remember the origin of this fear, but I can remember that as a very young child I struggled for hours in order to prevent vomiting. Whether or not this was connected with forced feeding I don't know, but my mother still does talk about how, when I was little, she had to force food into me, mouthful after mouthful.

> In doing the experiment I did feel disgust and the desire to regurgitate. But that is as far as I went, for I have always been averse to vomiting. When I have known that it would be good for me and have tried it, the effort has almost seemed too great. Attempts to force vomiting by the finger-in-the-throat technique always produce a pain in my chest, which is my reason for suppressing the desire to complete the act.

> I can vomit easily. As a child, when I had an upset stomach, my parents sent me to the bathroom with instructions on how

to vomit. The result is that, for me, this is perfectly natural and a tremendously relieving process.

When I gulp down my food, I have, pretty soon afterward, a pressure in my stomach or, more often, higher up in my esophagus. It feels as if something is stuck there and can't move forward or backward. This is the very same feeling I had when, as a child, I was late for school. On those occasions I often vomited on my way to school.

Mealtime was the occasion, when I was a child, that my father chose to play the heavy-parent and lay down the law. Sometimes it took my appetite so that I couldn't eat a bite, and I remember several instances in which I had to excuse myself from the table and go vomit.

The remobilization of disgust in connection with eating may bring to the surface a number of past experiences for reconsideration.

Perhaps it was just some kind of generalization, but the results I got in the eating experiments started me to thinking about a lot of things in my life. My father kept coming to mind. He is a very domineering man, one who wants to keep his children from growing up. I think that playing parent is for him his life-work to a much greater extent than his profession, and from *this* I don't think he ever intends to retire. Many of the ideas that he's crammed down my throat I think I'm starting to "vomit up." They flood into my mind, and I analyze them in terms of present-day social and moral views. It is perfectly amazing to see how many things I've taken for granted as being my views, when it's perfectly obvious now that they're his. They don't fit into my life, and already I feel a tremendous relief in sloughing off some of them. They have made my life so needlessly complicated.

One student reported in great detail the bringing up and freeing himself from "introjected blame" in connection with the accidental death, when he was a child, of a sibling. The process of ejecting the introject began with burning sensations in the stomach. These began after he had been performing the eating experiments for a short period.

Another student reported the onset of burning sensations in the stomach almost from the start of these experiments, but it was not until the work with introjects that the following events developed:

In connection with wondering what introjects I might have lodged in me as foreign bodies, I went back to the work on confluence where we considered traits, speech, dress, etc., and from whom we had imitated them. I became aware of thinking about the problem of tolerance. Then came: "How I hate her!" The words "I" and "her" were emphasized—really emphasized, with fists clenched, biceps contracted, lips compressed, teeth clamped together, eyebrows knit, temples pulsating, ears straining backward, and the entire body pressing hard against the ground and bench (this experiment was conducted in the park). Simultaneously—and this is what I considered important—the tension of the stomach and previously mild burning sensation increased to such an extent that I was sick. Then came the words "Aunt Agnes!"—and all the tensions, burnings, pressures and pulsations vanished. The only symptom that lingered on—and then only for a few minutes—was the sour oral taste. "Aunt Agnes" was a masculine, domineering, authoritarian woman who was temporarily put in charge of me when I was three.

Prior to the start of the awareness experiments and throughout the span of my remembered life, I would fall asleep readily and rarely had dreams. Just before the confluence experiment, however, I began to have nightmares, and I had them every night. As soon as I spewed up this "hateful introject," the nightmares disappeared and my sleep has been untroubled since.

Projection

A projection is a trait, attitude, feeling, or bit of behavior which actually belongs to your own personality but is not experienced as such; instead, it is attributed to objects or persons in the environment and then experienced as directed *toward* you by them instead of the other way around. The projector, unaware, for instance, that he is rejecting others, believes that they are rejecting him; or, unaware of his tendencies to approach others sexually, feels that they make sexual approaches to him.

This mechanism, like retroflection and introjection, functions to interrupt mounting excitement of a kind and degree with which the person cannot cope. It seems to require the following: (1) that you be aware of the nature of the impulse involved; but (2) that you interrupt the aggressive approach to the environment which would be necessary for its adequate expression; with the result (3) that you exclude it from the outgoing activities of your "I"; nevertheless, since you are aware that it *does* exist, then (4) it *must* come from outside—notably from a person or persons in your environment; and (5) it seems *forcibly* directed toward you because your "I," without realizing it, *is* forcibly interrupting your own outwardly directed impulse.

A transparent example of the projection mechanism is given by the inhibited woman who is forever complaining that men are making improper advances to her.

For projections to occur, retroflections and confluences also are necessary, just as they are in introjection; and, in general, as we have said before, the neurotic mechanisms are all functionally related to one another and interlocking. In retroflections both components of the conflict inhere in the personality, but, because of their clinch, the person in effect loses part of his environment, for before his outgoing impulse can come to grips with objects or persons, he intercepts it with his retroflecting behavior.

In projections one is aware of the impulse and of the environmental object, but he does not identify with and carry through his aggressive approach—and thereby loses the sense that *he* is feeling the impulse. Instead, he stands stock still and, without realizing it, waits for his problem to be solved for him outside.

These mechanisms constitute neurosis only when inappropriate and chronic; all of them are useful and healthy when employed temporarily in particular circumstances. Retroflection is healthy behavior when it constitutes holding back for the sake of caution in a situation of genuine danger. Introjection of the dull and unimportant material of a required school course may be healthy when one has the chance to spew it forth and relieve himself of it on the final examination. Examples of healthy temporary projection are the activities of planning and anticipating. In them one "feels oneself" in a future situation—projects oneself into the environment—and then, when one follows through, in a practical way, *integrates oneself with the project*. Likewise, in certain kinds of sympathy one feels oneself into the other person and solves one's own problem by solving his. Imaginative artists alleviate their problems by projecting into their work. When a child at a very early age projects his teddy-bear out of the crib to the floor, this may mean that he himself wants to be there. What makes all these mechanisms unhealthy, of course, is the structural fixing on some impossible or non-existent object, the loss of awareness, the existence of isolated confluences, and the consequent blocking of integration.

The fear of rejection is crucial with every neurotic, so we can profitably begin our experimentation with this. The picture of being rejected—first by his parents and now by his friends—is one that the neurotic goes to great lengths to establish and maintain. While such claims may have substance, the opposite is also certainly true—that the neurotic rejects others for not living up to some fantastic ideal or standard which he imposes on them. Once he has projected his rejecting onto the other person, he can, without feeling any responsibility for the situation, regard himself as the passive object of all kinds of unwarranted hardship, unkind treatment, or even victimization.

In your own case, by whom did you or do you feel rejected? Your mother, father, sister, brother? Do you bear them a grudge for it? On what grounds do you reject them? How do they fail to measure up?

Now call up in fantasy some acquaintance. Do you like or dislike this Person X? Do you like or dislike this or that trait or action? Visualize him and speak to him or her aloud. Tell him that you accept this mannerism or characteristic, won't have any more of that one, can't stand it when he does this, etc. Repeat the experiment many times. Do you talk stiltedly? Lamely? Self-consciously? Do you feel what you say? Does anxiety develop? Do you feel guilty, afraid that you might spoil the relationship irrevocably by your frankness? *Assure yourself of the difference between fantasy and material reality, for this is just what the projector confuses.* Now comes the decisive situation: Do you feel that it is you who are rejecting on the very same grounds on which you believe yourself rejected? Do you feel that people "high hat" you? If so, can you be aware of instances in which you do or would like to "high hat" others? Do you reject in yourself the very things you think others reject you for? If you are skinny, fat, have buck teeth—or whatever it is about yourself that you don't like— do you feel that others are as scornful of these shortcomings as you are yourself? Also, can you notice yourself attributing things unwanted in yourself to others? If you take unfair advantage of someone, do you say, "He was just about ready to do it to me"?

It is not always easy to discriminate between what is genuinely observed and what is imagination. Error speedily dissolves when it produces a clear contradiction of some sort; projected behavior is then recognized as crazy, hallucinatory, and you say, "I don't know how I ever could have thought of that." But, for the most part, the projector can find "proofs" that the imagined is the observed. Such rationalizations and justifications are always available to the person who wishes to find them. In the subtleties and many-sided aspects of most situations the projector (up to the stage of true paranoia) can fasten onto a true detail, perhaps some genuine but insignificant grievance, and then exaggerate and embroider it fantastically. Thus he does his damage—or, in his language, *is* damaged.

A person's unfelt need to reject Person X will lead to finding something in his own behavior which he thinks accounts for but does not justify X in rejecting him. If X were operating on the basis which the projector supposes and would actually reject him, then the projector's purpose would be accomplished—namely, it would bring about their separation, which is precisely what the projector wants without being aware of it.

Suppose one has an appointment with Person X and he is late in arriving. If, without further evidence, one jumps to the conclusion that this is a sign of contempt, then one is rejecting one's own contemptuousness.

In everyday life the common case of paranoic projection is, of course, the jealous husband and wife. If you are prone to such jealousies and are continually suspecting and "proving" infidelity, see whether you yourself are not repressing the wish to be unfaithful in the very way that you attribute to your spouse. Apply the suspect details to yourself as clues—that is, *you* would go about it in just that way, make the clandestine phone-calls, etc.

A second important source of paranoic jealousy is also a projection. The jealous partner represses his (or her) own homosexual impulse, and therefore imagines that the partner loves another man or another woman—and calls up images of them together. The epithets he then directs at the fancied lovers are the very ones that he would apply to his own taboo impulse.

In all these cases the degree of evidence or contradiction is unimportant. If one is a jealous husband or a touchy mother-in-law, it does no good to be proved wrong, for the same situation will repeat itself with other flimsy evidence. The projector clings to his passive-suffering role and avoids going outward.

An extremely important and dangerous class of projections is prejudice: race-prejudice, class-prejudice, snobbery, anti-semitism, misogyny, etc. In every such case, along with other factors, the following projection is operating: to the vilified groups are attributed traits which really belong to the prejudiced person, but which he represses from awareness. Hating and refusing to come to terms with his own "bestiality" (which is often, when it appears in proper context, nothing but a useful drive of the organism), he feels and "proves" that the despised race or group is "bestial."

Consult your own views on such matters as candidly as possible and see how many of them are prejudices. A useful sign is that particular salient "confirming" instances loom in your mind. These individual cases, of course, are quite irrelevant in issues which involve masses of people and which can be intelligently considered only in terms of cold statistics. When you notice such striking confirming instances of any pet idea of yours, look to see if you do not yourself possess the trait.

Contrary to the view that this attitude of the passive-suffering projector belongs only to the masochistic and passive-feminine types, we believe it typical of modern dissociated man. It is imbedded in our language, our world-attitude, our institutions. The prevention of outgoing motion and initiative, the social derogation of aggressive drives, and the epidemic disease of self-control and self-conquest have led to a language in which the self seldom does or expresses anything; instead, "it" happens. These restrictive measures have also lead to a view of the world as completely neutral and "objective" and unrelated to our concerns; and to institutions that take over our functions, that are to "blame" because they "control" us, and that wreak on us the hostility which we so carefully refrain from wielding ourselves—as if men did not themselves lend to institutions whatever force they have!

In such a world of projections a man, instead of raging, is "possessed" by a temper that he cannot "control." Instead of thinking, a thought "occurs" to him. He is "haunted by" a problem. His troubles "worry" him—when, indeed, he is worrying himself and anybody else he can.

Alienated from his own impulses, yet unable to obliterate the feelings and acts to which they give rise, man makes "things" out of his own behavior. Since he then does not experience it as himself-in-action, he can disclaim responsibility for it, try to forget or hide it, or project it and suffer it as coming from the outside. He does not dream or wish, but the dream "comes to him." He does not shine in glory, but abstract glory becomes a thing to die for. He does not progress and want to progress, but Progress, with a capital P, becomes his fetish.

When the early psychoanalysts introduced the concept of the Id or It as the source of drives and dreams, they were expressing this powerful truth: personality is not restricted to the narrow sphere of the "I" and its "sensible" self-controlled little thoughts and plans; these other drives and dreams are not idle shadows but real facts of the personality. But, having achieved this insight, orthodox analysis did not sufficiently insist on the next step—to loosen and enlarge the habits of the "I" and change it from a fixed form into a system of shifting processes, so that it can feel the Id-facts as its own facts, use its hallucinations (as a child does in play), and wield its drives for creative adjustment.

A careful criticism of our habitual language points the way to such a loosening and adjustment. Let us reverse the process of alienation, self-conquest, and projection by reversing the "it" language. The aim is to come to realize again that you are creative in your environment and are responsible for your reality—not to blame, but responsible in the sense that it is you who lets it stand or changes it.

Examine your verbal expressions. Translate, as if they were in a foreign language, those sentences in which "it" is subject and you are object into sentences in which "I" is the subject. For instance, "It occurred to me that I had an appointment" translates into "I remembered that I had an appointment." Furthermore, setting yourself in the center of sentences that concern you, look for concealed indefinite expressions. Often, for instance, "I must do this" means either "I want to do this" or "I don't want to do it and won't, and meantime I am making excuses" or "I am keeping from doing something else." Also, recast sentences in which you are meaningfully an object into sentences expressing the fact that although you are object, you are experiencing something. For instance, change, "He hits me" into "He hits me and I am being hit"; "He tells me" into "He says something to me and I listen to it."

Attend to the detailed content of your "it" expressions; translate the verbal structure into visual fantasy. If you say, "A thought struck me," just where and how did it strike? Did it use a weapon? Whom did you want to strike at the time? If you say, "My heart aches," are you aching for something with all your heart? If you say, "I have a headache," are you contracting your muscles so that you hurt your head—or even in order to hurt your head?

Listen to and translate other people's language in the same way. This will reveal to you a good deal about their interpersonal relationships. Eventually you will understand that, as in art, although the content of what is said is important, it is much more the structure, the syntax, the style, that reveals character and underlying motivation.

Some reactions to this experiment are as follows:

. . . You must think we have the intelligence of a child!

The last part of this experiment amounts to a gross dabbling in semantics. Translating "it" phrases is about as constructive in psychological terms as doing a crossword puzzle.

People have told me that I say "I" too much, and in writing letters I've had to search around for substitutes so as not to seem egotistical.

I don't believe that the amount of projecting that most people do is more than healthy. From reading these instruction sheets I get the impression that the authors regard the whole world as filled with paranoids. It seems to me this indicates some projection on the part of the authors!

I was amazed to discover how often I used the impersonal form of speech. "It occurs to me . . .," "It happened that . . .," etc., all seem to be very common and I use them quite extensively. As I try consciously to change the syntax of my speech, I can feel a heightened awareness of the immediate environment and how I am responsible for it. I can make a great deal of sense out of this—I almost said, "It makes a great deal of sense." I shall keep this up, for I find it most important.

I have a friend whom I tend to criticize because she spends so little time on her school work. Just before exams she crams, but the rest of the time she uses for going out and having fun. She does it quite openly, and doesn't seem ashamed. I, on the other hand, stay home with a book open in my hand. What I've just realized is that this is just a pretense of studying, and I might better spend my time doing what she does!

Changing "it" into "I" has been quite an eye-opener for me. When I've dropped something, I've caught myself explaining, "It dropped out of my hand," or when I've missed my train because I dawdled around, I've complained, "It went off and left me." Just the same, some of these home-truths are pretty hard to take!

When I take unfair advantage of someone, I don't say, "He was just about to do it to me." Instead, I say, "He was a fool not to do it first."

I feel rejecting toward my sister because she treats my father like a bum. What I've just found out, though, is that I'm condemning her for expressing something that I hold back. Actually, I'm pretty sore that he hasn't done more for us. He's one of those persons with no other ambition than just to be able to scrape by.

The other day I felt that my father was rejecting me by siding with my brother on an issue. Recalling this experiment, I examined my own attitude. Much to my surprise I found that I was the one who was really rejecting the help and advice they both were trying to give me.

Experiment 2:   ASSIMILATING PROJECTIONS

In the moving picture theatre it is obvious to everyone except small children that the pictures do not emanate from the screen but are reflections of light-patterns cast upon it by the projector. What can appear on the screen, which is simply a blank surface, is strictly contingent on what is on the film in the machine. On the other hand, when a person projects parts of his personality, it ordinarily is not upon a blank surface but upon a screen—another person, object, situation—which *already possesses in its own right* some degree of what is projected upon it. We project onto persons who are "appropriate screen"—that is, who manifest enough of a particular trait or attitude to make it easy for us to justify loading them with our share of it as well.

Abstractions, concepts, theories can also serve as projection-screens. A remarkable case of this occurs in the current terminology of psychotherapy. The system of muscular contractions by which the neurotic attacks and squeezes his spontaneous impulses is called (by Wilhelm Reich) his "character-armor." This gives it the status of an "objective" barrier that must somehow be attacked and broken through. Actually it is the person's own aggression turned against himself. Instead of regarding this armor as a dumb object, a shell or rigid crust to be crushed, surely the appropriate therapeutic technique is to interpret it as misdirected activities of the person himself. On such a basis he will become able to say, "I have a backache and a stiff stomach—that is, I contract my back till it hurts and I am cutting off indecent movements of the pelvis and suppressing evil desires." If this is pursued, he will then say, "I hate sex and my sexual desires," and *then* it will be possible to work on the person's false identification with the social taboo and try to dissolve what he has introjected. In other words, in such a case we must first undo the projection ("I am suffering from my armor"), then the retroflection ("I stifle my pelvis"), and then the introjection ("I hate sex").

No doubt the most important abstract projection-screen is conscience or moral law. It is abstract in the sense that the dictates of conscience are verbalized as "Society demands" or "Morality requires," when actually it is the person himself demanding or requiring *in the name of society or morality!* Conscience is always aggressive in its manifestations, for, like any screen, it reflects back to us what we project upon it. In this connection consider the following obvious facts: it is not those who live most "cleanly," with unbending rectitude, with continuous attention to the rules, who have the lightest consciences. Far from it! Their consciences are forever hounding and upbraiding them.

Is it their demanding consciences that make them restrict themselves and walk the tight-rope of propriety? In your own case consider some escapade in which you succeeded and had a good time. Under those circumstances your conscience gave you little trouble; but if you failed, got caught, or were disappointed, then you felt guilty and your conscience told you you should not have done it. Logically we must say that it is the person's anger against the frustrating obstacles—which anger, however, he cannot vent nor even feel *as such* because of his identification with (introjection of) the social standards—that now he projects into his conscience. Then he suffers under its lash.

It is not the introjected standard that gives strength to the conscience; it merely provides the nucleus—the appropriate screen upon which the person may project aggression. This is shown by the fact that conscience is always more demanding than the taboos and sometimes makes demands that are even unheard of socially. *The strength of conscience is the strength of one's own reactive anger!*

Perfectionism is another projection-screen. This is based on the so-called ego-ideal (as distinct from super-ego or conscience). While conscience serves, as we have said, as a projection screen for aggressions and cruel demands that the person dissociates from himself, the ego-ideal receives by projection his dissociated love and admiration. Such dissociated love is often homosexual; and homosexual love can frequently be analyzed as a still earlier projection of a more primary self-love—which was a retroflection that one was punished for or "shamed out of."

To dissolve irrational conscience you must take two steps: First, translate from "My conscience or morality demands . . ." to "I demand from myself . . ."; that is, change the projection to a retroflection. Second, reverse this in both directions to "I demand from X" and "X (e.g., society) demands from me." You must differentiate the actual compulsion of society from both your private demands and your introjections. In your conscience are you nagging, threatening, blackmailing, casting sad, reproachful glances? If you concentrate on these fantasies you will find how much of your moral duty is your own masked attack, how much consists of particular introjected influences, and how much *is* rational.

Do not be afraid that by dissolving conscience you will become a criminal or an impulsive psychopath. You will be surprised, when you allow organic self-regulation to develop and your outgoing drives to contact other persons, how the principles that *you* ought to live by will seem to emerge from your very bones and will be *obviously appropriate* for living out regardless of the social situation you are in.

Delinquency is to a large extent a matter of inaccurate orientation, a misunderstanding of the person's role in society. As Socrates said long ago, evil is simply error. Pathological delinquency is frequently characterized by an over-stern conscience. As with self-control, so with conscience; too much self-control leads to nervous breakdowns; too much conscience to moral breakdowns. Submission to conscience is identification with rigid principles that do not work and are always lacking in charity. Organic function and self-awareness mean appreciation of concrete situations. Conscience imposes a duty and accomplishes very little work; aware function is interested, attracted, and gets the job done.

When you come to the second step of dissolving conscience, namely, reversing what you demand from yourself to a demand on X, you will experience the greatest reluctance, for accepting your conscience as part of yourself means admitting to powerful dictatorial desires and demands on other people—to be *their* conscience! You can, of course, become a moralist and try to make us all suffer; or let us hope you will restrict yourself to fantasy, and there work out your lust to be our ruler and our judge until you have developed a more integrated orientation and contact with the world. It will change your notions of conscience when you realize how the same intolerance that was invested in your conscience now shows up in your own cravings.

The projector throws outward his unwanted feelings, but he does not get rid of them. *The only way actually to get rid of an "unwanted feeling" is to accept it, express it and thus discharge it.* Projections are still bound to the person, just as repressed material is still "in" the person. The projector is connected with his projected omnipotence by awe, with his projected aggression by fear. Thus, it is not possible for the prejudiced person to rid himself of his "bestiality" simply by projecting it onto the vilified group; he must also become an anti-semite, an anti-vivisectionist, or what not, and ruin his life with such idiocies. The distinction between a prejudice and some simple, foolish notion that one is too lazy or unconcerned to correct can be made in terms of whether you can let the matter go. If you cannot—if it is an imminent, haunting danger—then you have a prejudice.

In dreams, projection of aggression becomes nightmares. Dreams with projected dental aggression, where you are threatened by crocodiles, dogs, the *vagina dentata*, are typical for introjectors. In attempting to interpret a dream, at the beginning, at least, regard all persons in it and all the features of it as projections—that is, as parts of your own personality. After all, you are the maker of the dream, and whatever you put into it must be what is in you and therefore available for constructing the dream.

Just as with dreams, many "memories" are projections of the present situation. This frequently occurs in psychoanalysis with respect to childhood memories. The transference (emotional relation to the analyst) is construed as the reliving of the childhood events, when the simple facts of the analytic situation are sufficient to account for whatever happens, without reference to the past at all. For example, the patient, angry with his analyst in the present situation, does not express his anger openly, but brings up memories of the times when his father "mistreated" him in similar ways. To assimilate such projections it is not necessary to go roundabout through the long memories when the relevant events happen under one's nose. Whether the patient says, "You are bored," or "You think such and such of me," or "You want to be rid of me," the projection is obvious.

Your "reality" (what to you is the real world) is playing either of two functions: it is either the concernful environment of your needs and is known by sharp, interesting figures against empty grounds, or it is a screen for your projections. If the latter, you will attempt to make the projections conform with observation—you will always be seeking proofs, making mountains out of molehills, or otherwise distorting your perspective.

Instead, do the following: go through a period in which you say to everything, *Tat Twam Asi*—*that otherness is myself!* And do the same on any subsequent occasion when you feel a violent reaction, particularly of fear or passive helplessness. Be on the watch for projected initiative, rejection, admiration, aggression. Think yourself into the shoes of the aggressor, admirer, rejecter, foolhardy one. More often than not, the reversal will click.

Some reactions to this experiment are as follows:

The instructions to "think yourself into the shoes of the agres-
sor, admirer, et al. and more often than not the reversal will
click" is the perfect final note for you to end on. It really caps
the climax of absurdity!

I believe it will be a very long time before I can accept responsibility for all my projections, for I've scattered the parts of my
personality pretty widely. But I'm going to continue to put myself into all my various shoes, for, as nearly as I can judge at
this time, all the shoes do fit!

I tried the Tat Twam Asi experiment and discovered that I
have an over-stern conscience. In time I hope to reduce it sub-
stantially, but I can see that it's going to take time.

Just as taking responsibility for one's behavior doesn't necessarily mean taking blame for it, I suppose it's just as unwarranted to take the credit for it. So long, though, as I continue
to think in moralistic terms, I'm finding it exhilarating and releasing to take credit for what I do and to give credit to others
for their actions. More and more I am noticing that when I or
the people I know suffer a defeat, it almost always can be recognized to be, at least in part, an "inside job."

I "dissolved" some irrational conscience that I've had as far
back as I can remember. I've always felt that I must complete
any job I start and, further than that, I must complete it in a
given measure of time (in one day, for instance). In some specific instances I've recently stated it as "My conscience demands
that I finish the job today even though I have plenty of time
later." My foolishness became perfectly clear, though, when I
carried it on to, "Society demands from me that I complete this
job today," for it was obvious that society was doing no such
thing. Without any fireworks of an emotional sort this has made
a radical change in my attitude toward my work. When I start a
job-now it's without the hopped-up melodramatics (the-die-is-
case-and-there's-no-turning-back sort of feeling) but instead I
realize there's plenty of time and if anything more important
should come up before I get this job finished, I can give it priority without the world's coming to an end. When I look back at
the way I was operating, I wonder, "How stupid can you get?"

You'll probably diagnose this with some fancy name, but I intend to get it off my chest just the same. In your attempt to induce a "permissive" atmosphere, you bend too far the other way. With a casualness that can't be casual, you tell us how to masturbate, vomit, and choke pillows. You are moralistic all the way through, although not in the ordinary way. You are trying to get us to introject your views in place of the ones we now have. Do you go to sleep at night happy in the thought that at this very minute countless people are vomiting up their insides for you?

I had trouble at first getting the hang of what was involved in putting myself in the shoes of all these other people who seemed so different from me. I wasn't aware of projecting and the whole thing fell flat. Then I figured that maybe I could sneak up on it by trying first to notice when I thought other people were projecting. Boy, what a revelation! I experienced what away back you called the "aha! phenomenon." The time when it hit me right between the eyes was at a committee meeting to select candidates for election to a club that I belong to. Whenever a particular name came up and somebody wanted to give it a thumbs-down, he had to state his reasons. Well, the reasons he would give for disliking the candidate and not wanting him in the club would amount to a listing of *his own worst faults*! After seeing this sort of thing happen I sure got the point about trying on the other fellow's shoes and checking on whether they fit. Sad to say, they do!

CHAPTER 3

LIVING GESTALT: A SELECTION FROM *IN AND OUT OF THE GARBAGE PAIL*

FREDERICK S. PERLS, M.D., Ph.D.

I feel rather desperate about this manuscript. I've got a view, looking at a tapestry, nearly completely woven, yet unable to bring across the total picture, the total gestalt. Explanations don't help much towards understanding. I can't give it to you; you may take what I offer, but do I know your appetites?

When I could write in verse I knew you would enjoy swimming with the flow: I knew I would communicate something, a mood, a thrust, even a bit of a dance of words.

I am still stuck and determined to get through this impasse. I am too easily inclined to give up and let go. But to force myself to do something against my inclination likewise does not work out. Thus, suspended between the Scylla of phobia, avoidance, flight, and the Charybdis of chore, strain and effort, what is one to do?

I would not be a phenomenologist if I could not see the obvious, namely the experience of being bogged down. I would not be a Gestaltist if I could not enter the experience of being bogged down with confidence that some figure will emerge from the chaotic background.

And lo! the theme emerges. Organismic self-control versus dictatorial control, authentic control versus authoritarian control. The dynamic of gestalt formation versus the superimposition of manufactured goals. Dominance of life versus the whip of moral prejudices, concerted powerful flow of organismic involvement versus the drag of *shouldism*. I am returning to the human split: the animal versus the social, the spontaneous versus the deliberate.

What kind of built-in self-control does the organism have; what kind of self-regulation enables the organism, those millions of cells, to cooperate harmoniously? Up to the mechanical age the dichotomy of the organism was perfect. Man was split up into a body and a soul. The soul had a separate existence, often immortal, often entering and taking charge of other bodies via rebirth. With the biological realization that what we call life is the specific function of any organism and that we classify any object without that function as dead, as a thing, some theoretical shifts occurred. Thus dichotomy was not eliminated, but shifted to a somewhat different one, very much in vogue with scientists and lay people alike, the dichotomy of mind and body. The function of the body is being explained by a number of partly contradictory theories: from the penny-in-the-slot machine-like mechanical reflex-arc (the stimulus-reflex bit) to a multitude of biochemical reactions, to a number of mysterious elements which manage the regulation, maintenance, and purposiveness of life. The absoluteness of stimulus-response theory has been debunked by Kurt Goldstein. The chemical aspect is one of several possible abstractions, very interesting and important, but so far not capable of accounting for the instinct theory.

Something is wrong with the instinct theory, otherwise we wouldn't have many authors differing on the numbers and importance of various "instincts."

I am slipping again. Instead of writing down my thoughts and experiences, I behave as if I want to write another textbook and sort out, reformulate, clarify an issue. Actually I wrote about the instinct issue in 1942. My present confusion comes from hesitating about whether or not I can claim originality for my "no-instinct" theory, as if this mattered a damn.

I called the book I wrote in 1942 *Ego, Hunger and Aggression*, a really clumsy title. At that time I wanted to learn typewriting. After a few days of exercising I got bored. So I decided, similarly to this present book, to write whatever wanted to be written. In about two months the whole book was finished and without much editing soon published in Durban, South Africa.

I had come to South Africa in 1934. The arrival of Hitler and my flight to Holland in 1933 had interrupted my training as a psychoanalyst. My analyst at that time was Wilhelm Reich and my supervisors were Otto Fenichel and Karen Horney. From Fenichel I got confusion; from Reich, brazenness; from Horney, human involvement without terminology. In Amsterdam, Holland, I had some more supervision from Karl Landanner, another refugee who had been my wife's psychoanalyst in Frankfurt, Germany. He was a man of considerable warmth who did his best to make the Freudian system more understandable. At least he did not do what I had seen Fenichel and others do: perform an intellectual juggling performance with "latent negative counter-transference," "infantile-libidinal sublimation," etc., a performance which usually made me dizzy and which I could never repeat. No wonder that Fenichel often got impatient with me.

One could not imagine a greater contrast in fortune between our life in Amsterdam and a year later in Johannesburg, South Africa.

In April 1933, I had crossed the German-Dutch border with 100 marks (25 dollars) hidden in my cigarette lighter. In Amsterdam I lived together with quite a number of other refugees in a house provided by the Jewish community.

We were packed rather tightly together. The atmosphere, of course, was subdued. Many had left close relatives behind in Germany. Though the deportations were not yet in full swing, we felt the danger strongly. Like most of the refugees who had left Germany that early, we were sensitive to the war and concentration camp preparations.

Although Lore and our first child had found a home with her parents, I was unsure how safe they were as I was on the Nazi blacklist. They came to Holland a few months later. We found a small attic apartment where we lived for another few months in utter misery.

In the meantime, I tried to make the best out of our charity life, with two people I still hold in my memory.

One was an actor, a real ham. Nothing outstanding about him except for a real skill. He could fart a whole melody. I admired his ability and asked him once for a repeat performance. Then he confessed that he had to tank himself up the day before by eating beans or cabbage.

The other was a young married woman, rather erratic and hysterical. I was one of her two lovers for a while. I would not mention her if it were not for the one time in my life when I really became superstitious and believed in something supernatural—in the power of a "mi-no-ga-me."

My minogame was a Japanese bronze about ten inches long, something between a lizard and a dragon. It was given to me in Berlin not long before Hitler came to power. It was given to me by a famous movie director as a token of appreciation and with the assurance that it was a luck-bringing symbol.

I was skeptical. It had not brought him luck.

It certainly did not bring me luck. Soon I had to flee Germany. The life in Holland was difficult, especially after my family came over and we lived in that icy apartment in below-freezing weather. We had no work permission. The valuable furniture we finally managed to get out arrived in an open boxcar, badly damaged by rain. The money we got for the furniture and for my library did not last long. Lore had an abortion and subsequent depression. In addition to all this, the young woman I mentioned before started to make trouble.

Then I decided to tempt the gods. I was convinced by then that the minogame was the bringer of ill luck. I gave it to the trouble maker and, coincidence or not, her rich husband threw her out and she had plenty of other troubles in addition.

At the same time, our situation changed completely. It was as if a curse had been lifted.

Ernest Jones, Freud's friend and biographer, did a magnificent job for the persecuted Jewish psychoanalysts. He had a request for a training analyst in Johannesburg, South Africa. I got this position. I did not ask for any guarantees. Not only did I want to get away from the desperate situation in Amsterdam, I also foresaw the future. I told my friends: "The greatest war of all times is coming. You just can't put enough distance between yourself and Europe."

At that time they thought me mad, but later they complimented me on my foresight.

Another obstacle, L200 guarantee for the immigration, was quickly and miraculously cleared. Soon we got a loan that covered both that and the cost of the voyage.

The last obstacle was the language barrier. Besides Latin, Greek, and French, I had studied some English in school. I loved French and was quite proficient, but I never took to English. Now I had to learn it, and quick. I used a four-pronged attack: During the three-week voyage on the *Balmoral Castle*, I read any easy and exciting story I could get hold of, such as mysteries. I read on, without bothering about details, guessing from the context what was going on. I also studied grammar and vocabulary through the Langenscheidt self-teaching method. I also overcame my embarrassment and involved crew and passengers in conversation. Later on, I went to the movies and sat through the same picture several times. I have never lost my German accent, which embarrassed me for a long time, but I never bothered to take lessons in diction. Later on, in America, I was often confused by the difference in American and English diction. As they announced in Paris shops: "English spoken, American understood."

We were made very welcome. I established a practice, and founded the South Africa Institute for Psychoanalysis. Within a year's time, we built and owned the first Bauhaus-style house in a posh neighborhood, with tennis court and swimming pool, a nurse (we had another child), a housekeeper, and two native servants.

For the next years, I could indulge in a lot of hobbies: tennis and table tennis. I got my pilot's license. My friends enjoyed going flying with me, though Lore never trusted me with it. My greatest joy was to be alone in the plane, to switch off the engine, and go gliding down in that magnificent silence and aloneness.

We also had a very large ice-skating rink. How I loved dancing on ice. The wide sweeping movements, the grace and balance cannot be matched by anything. I even won a medal in a competition.

Excursions to the ocean, swimming in the warm waves of the Indian ocean, wild animals galore to be watched, movie-making on a modest scale, directing plays (I had studied under Max Reinhardt) and getting the most out of amateurs, visiting witch doctors, making some inventions, learning to play the viola, building up a valuable stamp collection, having a few very satisfactory and some not so satisfactory love affairs, forming some warm and lasting friendships.

What a difference from our previous life. I had always made enough money to get by and was always engaged in many ways, but never like this. This was an explosion into activity and making and spending of money. Lore used to call me a mixture of a prophet and a bum. There certainly was now a danger of losing both.

I was caught in the rigidity of the psychoanalytic taboos: the exact 50 minute hour, no physical eye and social contact, no personal involvement (counter-transference!). I was caught by all the trimmings of a square, respectable citizen: family, house, servants, making more money than I needed. I was caught in the dichotomy of work and play: Monday to Friday versus the weekend. I just extricated myself through my spite and rebelliousness from becoming a computing corpse like most of the orthodox analysts I knew.

The first break came in 1936, a year of great expectations and great disappointments. I was scheduled to give a paper in Czechoslovakia at the International Psychoanalytic Congress. I wanted to impress with my flying and with a Freud-transcending paper.

I intended to fly, by myself, the 4,000 miles across Africa in my own plane: the first flying analyst. I found a second-hand Gypsy

Moth that would make 100 miles an hour. The price was *L*200 but someone got in and outbid me. So this was out and I had to take a boat.

The paper I presented was on "oral resistances," still written in Freudian terms. The paper found deep disapproval. The verdict, "All resistances are anal," left me dumbfounded. I wanted to contribute to psychoanalytic theory, but I did not realize, at that time, how revolutionary that paper was and how much it would shake and even make invalid some basic foundations of the Master's theory.

Many friends criticized me for my polemic relationship to Freud. "You have so much to say; your position is securely grounded in reality. What is this continuous aggressiveness against Freud? Leave him alone and just do your thing."

I can't do this. Freud, his theories, his influence are much too important for me. My admiration, bewilderment, and vindictiveness are very strong. I am deeply moved by his suffering and courage. I am deeply awed by how much, practically all alone, he achieved with the inadequate mental tools of association-psychology and mechanistically-oriented philosophy. I am deeply grateful for how much I developed through standing up against him.

Sometimes one comes across a statement which, with a shock of recognition, illuminates the darkness of ignorance with a brilliant flash. I had such a "peak" experience as a teenager. Schiller, a much underestimated friend and contemporary of Goethe, wrote:

> Und so lange nicht Philosophy
> Die Welt zusammen haelt,
> Erhaelt Sie das Getriebe
> Durch Hunger und durch Liebe.

(Until the day when philosophy will rule the world, it is being regulated by hunger and love.)

Freud wrote in the same attitude later: "We are being lived by the forces within ourselves." But then he made an unforgivable blunder in order to save his libido-oriented system. To him the mouth of a new-born had an energy not yet differentiated into a libidinal zone and its functions for food intake. Practically, he dropped the second function and took up a position in opposition to Marx. Marx put sustenance down as man's main drive; Freud brought libido into the foreground. It is not a question of either/or, but of both. For the survival of the individual, sustenance is the important function, for the survival of the species, sex. But is it not artificial to prefer one to the other? Can the species survive without the sustenance of the individual, and would the individual exist without its parents' sex?

All this is so obvious. I am rather embarrassed to mention it at all. And I would not talk about it if it were not for the implications that it harbors for the Marxist as well as the Freudian philosophy.

Wilhelm Reich had tried to combine the two. He made the mistake of attempting to get the two *Weltanschauungen* to relate to each other on a high level of abstraction instead of on the gut level. The result was rejection and name-calling. The Communists rejected him because he was an analyst, and the analysts rejected him because he was a Communist. Instead of a chair with a broader base, he found himself falling between two chairs. He got into trouble through relating two systems before relating his own subsistence and his own sex. He was, so to say, punished for violating some basic laws of general semantics—Korsybski vindicated.

Topdog: Stop talking about Reich. Follow your intentions and stick to your theme, the oral resistances.

Underdog: Shut up. I told you a few times, this is my book, my confessions, my ruminations, my need to clarify what is obscure to me.

Topdog: Look! Your readers will see you as a senile, loquacious rambler.

Underdog: So, we are back again to my *self* versus my *image*. If a reader wants to look over my shoulder, he is welcome, even invited to peep. What's more, I have been more than once prodded to write my memories.

Topdog: Fritz, you are getting defensive.

Underdog: And you are wasting too much of my and the reader's time. So sit still and bide your time and let me keep *you* waiting. Let me be just as I am, and stop your chronic barking.

Topdog: O.K., but I'll be back again when you will least expect me and you *need* guidance from your brain: "Computer, please, direct me."

At present I don't want to think,
I want to be indulging,
A memory in which I see
A pompous figure bulging.
I will return to sex and food
To make your knowledge richer
Right now I feel emerging mood
Of sadness for a teacher.

To understand my appreciation for Reich better we have to go back to my analyst before him, a Hungarian with the name of Harnick. I wish that I could, in some way, describe the state of stupidity and moral cowardice to which this so-called treatment reduced me. Maybe it was not meant to be a treatment. It was, possibly, a didactic analysis to prepare for me the status of an accredited psychoanalyst. But then this was never made clear. All that was stated was: "The therapist had to be free from complexes, anxiety and guilt." Later I heard a rumor that he died in a mental institution. How much psychoanalysis had helped, I could not say.

He believed in passive analysis. This contradictory term means that I went for eighteen months, five times a week, to lie on his couch without being analyzed. In Germany one took a handshake for granted: he would shake my hand neither on arrival nor on departure. Five minutes before the end of the hour he would scratch the floor with his foot to indicate that my allotted time would soon be up.

The most he would speak was about one sentence per week. One of his statements in the beginning was that I appeared to him to be a ladies' man. From then on, the path was given. I filled the void of my couch life with amorous stories to build up the Casanova image he had of me. In order to keep up I had to engage in more and more, mostly phony, adventures. After a year or so I wanted to get away from him. I was too much of a moral coward to come right out with it. After my failure in my analysis with Clara Happel, what would my chances be to ever become an analyst?

At that time Lore pressed for marriage. I knew I was not the marrying type. I was not madly in love with her, but we had many interests in common and often had a good time. When I spoke to Harnick about it he pulled the typical psychoanalytic gimmick: "You are not allowed to make an important decision during your analysis. If you marry, I'll break up your analysis." Being too cowardly to discontinue my couch life on my own responsibility, I put the responsibility on him and exchanged psychoanalysis for marriage.

But I was not ready to give up on psychoanalysis. Always haunted by the fixed idea that it was myself who was too stupid or disturbed, I was determined to lick the problem. In my dispair I consulted Karen Horney, one of the few people I really trusted. Her verdict was: "The only analyst that I think could get through to you would be Wilhelm Reich." Thus started the pilgrimage to Wilhelm Reich's couch.

Well, the next year was a completely different story. Reich was vital, alive, rebellious. He was eager to discuss any situation, especially political and sexual ones, yet of course he still analyzed and played the usual genetic tracing games. But with him the importance of facts begins to fade. The interest in attitudes moved more into the foreground. His book *Character Analysis* was a major contribution.

In his seminars I met some lovely people who later on turned out to be good therapists, such as Helmuth Kaiser. Then Hitler struck. Reich, too, had to get out in a hurry. He went to Norway. From then on he seems to have become quite peculiar. Except for having his book translated by one of my South Africa students, Sylvia Beerman, I lost touch with him until I saw him again during the Psychoanalytic Congress in 1936. He was the third disappointment. He sat apart from us and hardly recognized me. He sat there for long intervals, staring and brooding.

Again I lost touch with him until ten years later when I visited him shortly after I came to the States. Then I really got a fright. He was blown up like an immense bullfrog, his facial eczema had become more intense. His voice boomed at me pompously, asking me incredulously: "You have not heard of my discovery, the orgone?" So I inquired. This is what I found:

His first discovery, the muscular armor, was an important step beyond Freud. It brought the abstract notion of resistance down to earth. Resistances now became total organismic functions, and the anal, resistance, the tight ass, had to give up its monopoly on resistances.

Another step forward from the couch life was the fact that the therapist now actually got into touch with the patient. The "body" came into its own rights.

Later on, when I worked with some patients who had been treated by Reichians, I usually found some paranoid symptoms, though not severe, and easily coped with. Then I had another look at the armor theory, and I realized that the idea of the armor itself was a paranoid form. It supposes an attack from, and defense against, the environment. The muscular armor actually has the function of a strait-jacket, a safeguard against explosions from *within*. The muscles have assumed an *implosive* function.

My second objection to the armor theory is that it reinforces the Aristotelian-Freudian defecation theory: "Emotions are a nuisance. A catharsis is required to rid the system of these disturbers of the peace."

Nature is not so wasteful as to create emotions as a nuisance. Without emotions we are dead, bored, uninvolved machines.

The third objection is that these breakthroughs externalize, dis-own, and project material that could be assimilated and become part of the self. They promote the formation of paranoid features. In other words, the materials that come out in these breakthroughs are still experienced as foreign bodies. All that has been changed is the locale. The chance of growth and becoming more whole-some has been missed.

However, compared with the importance of having made a tre-mendous step toward a holistic approach, these objections of mine do not amount to too much.

Not so with the invention of the orgone, an invention of Reich's fantasy which by then had gone astray.

I can understand what happened. Having made a verifiable reality out of the notion of resistance, he had to do the same with Freud's main term, libido.

Now resistances do exist, there is no doubt about it, but libido was and is a hypothesized energy, invented by Freud to explain his model of man. Reich hypnotized himself and his patients into the belief of the existence of the orgone as the typical and visible equivalent of libido.

I investigated the function of the orgone-box with a number of owners and invariably found a fallacy: a suggestibility that could be directed in any way I wanted. Reich died in prison rather than give up his fixed ideas. The *enfant terrible* of the Vienna Institute turned out to be a genius, only to eclipse himself as a "mad scientist."

To write about the fourth disappointment, my meeting with Freud, is more difficult. No, this is not true. I anticipated that it would be more difficult, because in my exhibitionistic period I was often vague about it and pretended that I knew more of Freud than was actually the case. The fact is that, except for S. Friedlander and

K. Goldstein, my meetings with such famous people as Einstein, Jung, Adler, Jan Smuts, Marlene Dietrich and Freud were casual encounters, mostly resulting in nothing but providing some material for boasting and indirectly impressing my audience with my own importance—glamor often overshadowing vision and judgment.

I spent one afternoon with Albert Einstein: unpretentiousness, warmth, some false political predictions. I soon lost my self-consciousness, a rare treat for me at that time. I still love to quote a statement of his: "Two things are infinite, the universe and human stupidity, and I am not yet completely sure about the universe."

My meeting with Sigmund Freud, in contrast, turned out to be 1936 disappointment number four.

I had been in Vienna before. I went there in 1927 upon a suggestion from Clara Happel. I had been with her in analysis in Frankfurt for about a year. One day, to my surprise, she declared that my analysis was finished. I should go to Vienna to do control work.

I was glad, but skeptical. I didn't feel finished and the fact that the verdict coincided with the time when my money ran out did not contribute any conviction.

I had met Lore that year. Apparently, at the University, I appeared to her and some of the other girls as a marriageable bachelor. It was time to escape the tentacles of the threatening marriage octopus. It never dawned on me that Lore would catch up with me wherever I went.

Vienna, city of my dreams—or shall we say, city of my nightmares?

I went to Vienna with no money; I had no resources and did not earn much. When I had money, I liked to spend it, and when I had none, I could get by with next to nothing. Clara Happel, I am grateful to say, had not cured me of my restless gypsy nature. I took a cheap furnished room in the *Eisengasse*, only to abandon it very quickly for two reasons.

One, as the story goes, was a dead cockroach in my bed, a fact that would not have bothered me *per se*. But the dozens of relatives that came to express their sorrow! No, no, no.

And then, the verdict of my landlady who said:

"No lady visitors after 10 o'clock."

"Why just 10 o'clock?"

"Well, before 10 o'clock something might happen. After 10 something is bound to happen!"

There was no argument against this type of reasoning. Freud had a name for it: *Suppen Knodellogik—Matzohball* logic.

I found Vienna rather depressing.

In Berlin I had many friends and much excitement. We fools believed we could build a new world without wars. In Frankfurt I felt a belonging—not completely, more fringelike—to the existential, Gestalt group which had a center there. The psychoanalysis with Happel was more a "must," a fixed idea, a compulsive regularity, with some—but not many—experiences.

In Vienna, psychoanalysis was the center for me. I fell superficially in love with a beautiful young doctor in training. She was like the whole Freudian clique, beset with taboos. It was as if all the Viennese hypocritical Catholics had invaded the "Jewish science" practitioners.

It is difficult for me to write about that year in Vienna. Before this, I wrote the last fifteen pages without effort, between seminar hours. I finally got so excited about writing that "it" seemed to have taken me over. I see that I spoke several times about a center—I don't know, should I spell it center or centre? Both seem to fit. So far, the last week of writing seems to form my center, the excitement shifting from movie and tape-making to self-expression. Writing in verse has disappeared. Ha! Not true, not completely. Here is an interesting contradiction: my contempt for poetry is vanishing. I experience Esalen, this beautiful place of ours and my seminarians (I have a four-week-long workshop going) poetically. I don't have that feeling for my present biographical spell. Last week I wrote a poem for the girls in the reception office and I don't consider this to be poetic. I have, now and then, in my fantasy, a poem forming on death versus dying. This would be a theme worthy of poetry. Yet the line I wrote for the girls, who are always inundated by visitors with endless questions, were fun to write. We even used those lines for the "Fritz" film which Larry Booth is making. What's more, I was pleased to hear the replay: Good enunciation and feeling. Not too much of my heavy Berlin accent.

You want to hear that poem?

"Of course!"

Well, if you insist, I will gladly comply.

The Devil's Game

There is a place like Eden
Where you have miscellaneous
Enjoyments like the maiden,
The baths, the sun and wisdom groups
It's truly Esaleneous.

A devil comes along and prays:
"I also want employment.
I wrote some lovely torture plays
To foster my enjoyment.

"Some silly questions which I ask
Will set you quick a-cringy
If you consider this your task
To answer, not too stingy."

An angel sounds a silver bell:
"Oh God, don't be so furious,
The devil really means so well!
He merely is . . . just curious."

I hope you like it as much as I do.

Well, this showing off did not help. I am still reluctant to go back to Vienna, 1927. What makes me so phobic about Vienna? Anything special that I am ashamed of? I went to Vienna a few times in the last 10 years. I enjoy the opera, the theatre, the cafes, the food.

The fog begins to lift. In spite of their reputation, *die Wiener Maderln*, the Viennese maidens, did not attract me especially. Never did I have an affair in Vienna. There was very little in between the extremes of bourgeois Puritanism and prostitution there. The free and easy entering into a sexual relationship I knew so well from Berlin and Frankfurt was missing.

I took an assistantship at the mental hospital where Wagner-Jauregg, famous for his malaria treatment for cerebral syphilis, and Paul Schilder were my bosses. Schilder was bright and had quite a good understanding of the structure/function/relationships of the organism. I did not feel comfortable sitting through his lectures. His falsetto voice and disturbed movements made me cringe. Yet there was something lovable and honest about him. Another psycho-analyst who left an impression on me was Paul Federn, especially a sentence of his during a lecture. Imagine a very dignified patriarchal figure saying: *"Man kann gar nicht genug vogeln."* (You just can't fuck enough.) This was in an atmosphere where usually only mind-fucking was esteemed.

When I met him later in New York, we had many discussions about the nature of the ego. He saw the ego as a reality; I have the position that the "I" is merely an identification symbol. What this means I am not willing to discuss right now.

My supervisors were Helene Deutsch and Hirschman, a warm easy-going man. When I asked him once what he thought about the different para-Freudian schools that were developing, his answer was: "They all make money."

Helen Deutsch, on the other hand, seemed to me very beautiful and cold. Once I gave her a present and instead of a "thank you" I got an interpretation in return.

The Master was there, somewhere in the background. To meet him would have been too presumptuous. I had not yet earned such a privilege.

In 1936 I though I had. Was I not the mainspring for the creation of one of his institutes and did I not come 4,000 miles to attend his congress? (I am itching to write *His* congress.)

I made an appointment, was received by an elderly woman (I believe his sister) and waited. Then a door opened about 2½ feet wide and there he was, before my eyes. It seemed strange that he would not leave the door frame, but at that time I knew nothing about his phobias.

"I came from South Africa to give a paper and to see you."

"Well, and when are you going back?" he said. I don't remember the rest of the (perhaps four-minute long) conversation. I was shocked and disappointed.

One of his sons was delegated to take me to dinner. We had my favorite dish, roast goose.

I had expected a quick "hurt" reaction, but I was merely numbed. Then, slowly, the stock phrases came; "I'll show you—you can't do this to me. This is what I get for my loyalty in my discussions with Kurt Goldstein."

Even in the last few years, with a much more balanced mind, this remains one of the four main unfinished situations of my life. I cannot hold a tune very well, though I am getting better. I never made a parachute jump. I never went skin diving (though I discovered a school in Monterey and may still learn to do it). And last, but not least, to have a man-to-man encounter with Freud and to show him the mistakes he made.

This great need came out as a surprise during a kind of clowning session with a trainee recently. That session was, like hundreds of them, videotaped and, like some, transcribed into a 16mm film.

My break with the Freudians came a few years later, but the ghost was never completely laid.

Rest in peace, Freud, you stubborn saint-devil-genius.

This is the story of my *four* disappointments in the year of our Lord 1936.

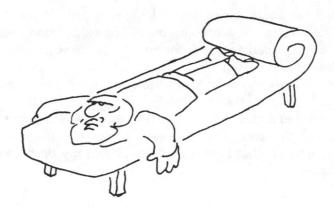

The 1936 trip to Europe was by no means all disappointment, and not everybody turned against me, but only very few were with me. I felt approval, for instance, from Ernest Jones, my sponsor for South Africa. He even seemed enthusiastic about some remarks I contributed to a discussion of anxiety.

After the congress, we spent a few days in the Hungarian mountains. He remarked during a chess game, "How can a person be so patient?" I hugged that compliment to my slightly caved-in bosom.

I don't remember how I got back to Johannesburg. Probably by boat, as in that corner of the world the airlines were not yet well-established. My self-esteem was bruised and I felt free at the same time. Between my poles of worthlessness and arrogance, something like a center of confidence was often there, but unacknowledged. Mostly I took it for granted that I knew what I wanted. I was shaken when I was taken by surprise by some awe-inspiring divine-like device that made me humble and small. It could be the emperor or

it could be a Freud; a great actress did it, or an inspiring thought; a heroic action, a daring crime, or a language I don't understand makes me pray with admiration.

On my trip out, the passengers—all strangers and remaining strangers for three weeks—made me the sports treasurer. The last day of the voyage, they feted me with "Auld Lang Syne." I had done nothing to deserve it. I was moved to the core, ran into my cabin and cried my heart out. A lonely gypsy bemoaning his lack of belonging?

It's beautiful to see how this writing helps. I had tried to make psychoanalysis my spiritual home, my religion. My reluctance, then, to go along with the Goldstein approach was not a loyalty to Freud, but my fear of being once more without spiritual support.

We are witnessing a disintegration of organized religion in the States. The church as a community center, the priest as the spiritual leader and *Seelsorger* (carer for the souls) are losing their significance. A desperate attempt to salvage God is under way. Many denominations, smoothing out differences that previously were fuel for intense hatred, are calling for inter-denominational understanding. "Ministers of the world, unite!" "Unite to deny Nietzsche's verdict that God is dead!" Many ministers begin to rely on psychotherapy more than on prayers.

As a child, I witnessed a similar disintegration of the Jewish religion. My mother's parents obeyed the orthodox customs. Here was a family with strange and often warm and beautiful events. My parents, especially my father, were "assimilated" Jews. That is, he compromised between being ashamed of his background and holding onto some of the customs—going to temple on the high holidays, in case there was a God somewhere around. I could not go along with this hypocrisy, and rather early declared myself an atheist. Neither science nor nature, philosophy nor Marxism could fill the void of a spiritual home. Today I know that I expected psychoanalysis to do this for me.

After 1936, I had tried to re-orient myself. The damned-up and unexpressed doubts about the Freudian system spread and engulfed me. I became a skeptic, nearly a nihilist—a negator of everything. Buddhism—Zen—a religion without a God? True, I accepted then much of Zen, in a cold, intellectual way.

Then the enlightenment came: No more spiritual, moral, financial support from any source! All religions were man-made crudities, all philosophies were man-made intellectual fitting games. I had to take all responsibility for my existence myself.

I had trapped myself. Through being preoccupied with psychoanalysis in Frankfurt, I remained uninvolved with the existentialists there: Buber, Tillich, Scheler. This much had penetrated: existential philosophy demands taking responsibility for one's existence. But which of the existential schools has the Truth with a capital T?

Skeptically, I searched further and this is where I stand now. In spite of all the anti-conceptual and pro-phenomenological bias, no existential philosophy stands on its own legs. I am not even talking about the typical American existentialist who preaches and bullshits about existence but walks the earth as a dead, conceptualizing computer. No, I am talking about the basic existentialists. Is there anyone who does not need external, mostly conceptual support?

What is Tillich without his Protestantism, Buber without his Chassidism, Marcel without Catholicism? Can you imagine Sartre without support from his Communist ideas, Heidegger without support from language, or Binswanger without psychoanalysis?

Is there then no possibility of an ontic orientation where *Dasein* —the fact and means of our existence—manifests itself, understandable without explanatoriness; a way to see the world not through the bias of any concept, but where we understand the bias of conceptualizing; a perspective where we are not satisfied to take an abstraction for a whole picture—where, for instance, the physical aspect is taken as all there is?

There is indeed! Surprisingly enough, it comes from a direction which never claimed the status of a philosophy. It comes from a science which is neatly tucked away in our colleges; it comes from an approach called—Gestalt psychology.

Gestalt! How can I bring home that gestalt is not just another man-made concept? How can I tell that gestalt is—and not only for psychology—something that is inherent in nature?

If, at the time of the gods or the different forms of energies, someone would have come up with the statement that all energies are invested in the smallest indivisible particle—called an atom—he would have been a laughing-stock of the world. Today it is taken for granted that atomic energy is the energy of energies. The atomic bomb sure is a reality.

I can very well understand that you might not follow me in the theory that everything is awareness, but I cannot accept your reluctance about the gestalt idea, and I will patiently describe some aspects of its significance.

But first for station identification: 1926, Frankfurt—Kurt Goldstein, Clara Happel, Lore, and now Professor Gelb, lecturer in Gestalt psychology, a pupil of Wertheimer and Kohler.

I'm playing with the number "6":

1896 My parents move from a Jewish neighborhood into the center of Berlin, into a more fashionable part. I have no memories before that time.

1906 *Bar Mitzvah*, puberty crisis. I am a very bad boy and cause my parents plenty of trouble.

1916 I join the German army.

1926 Frankfurt.

1936 Psychoanalytic Congress.

1946 Immigration to the United States.

1956 Miami, Florida. Involvement with Marty, the most significant woman in my life.

1966 Gestalt Therapy is on the map. I finally find a community, a place of being: Esalen.

I added one more name to the significant people in Frankfurt. Professor Gelb—I have forgotten his Christian name. Of course, I could pick up the telephone and ask Lore, who was involved to the degree of a doctoral dissertation on Farben constancy. No, that's not right—I can't reach her just now. She is in Tampa giving a workshop, probably with the American Academy of Psychotherapists.

Gelb was a rather colorless person, but a good teacher. He is known for his work on brain injuries with Goldstein, especially on the case of Schneider. Their discovery was that a brain injury did not only mean the loss of certain faculties, but that the *total* personality undergoes a change. A regression, a de-differentiation takes place. Most significant, the patient loses the ability to think and understand in abstract terms and language. He acquires the innocence of a small child. For instance, he cannot lie. You ask him to repeat the sentence, "Snow is black," and he would not do it and nothing in the world could make him do it. He would stubbornly stick to the reply, "Snow is white."

My relation to the gestalt psychologists was a peculiar one. I admired a lot of their work, especially the early work of Kurt Lewin. I could not go along when they became logical positivists. I have not read any of their textbooks, only some papers of Lewin, Wertheimer, and Kohler. Most important for me was the idea of the unfinished situation, the incomplete gestalt. The academic Gestaltists of course never accepted me. I certainly was not a pure Gestaltist.

My prominent fantasy was that they were all alchemists looking for gold, for complete verification, and that I was satisfied to use the less impressive but more useful products that fell by the wayside.

A gestalt is an irreducible phenomenon. It is an essence that is there and that disappears if the whole is broken up into its components.

Something very interesting happened just now. I was rehearsing about how to explain this gestalt principle in the example of the water molecule—H_2O and its parts, H and O atoms—when I realized that the formulation as expressed by the Gestaltists cannot possibly be correct. They say that the whole is more than the parts. In other words, something is added to the world simply by a configuration. This would ruin our picture of the energy balance of the universe. *Some*thing would be created out of *no*thing, an idea that would even transcend God's creative power. For it is written that God created the world out of *tohu wawohu*, out of chaos. Shall we then let the Gestaltists attribute to gestalt formation more power than our pious ancestors gave to God?

Before we allow this to happen, let's have another look and, even if this is merely my fantasy, let's try another explanation.

I am neither a chemist nor a physicist, so I might be way off. $2H+O=H_2O$ as a formula, is correct; as a reality, it is false. If you try to mix the two gases oxygen and hydrogen, nothing happens. If you add temperature, they explode, give up their status as atoms, and form the molecular gestalt $H2O$, or water. In this case, the gestalt is dynamically speaking less than the parts, namely minus the heat which is produced. Likewise, to separate the atoms, to break down the gestalt, you have to add electricity, to give the atoms a separate existence. We can draw several conclusions from that. Without the electronic support, and once they have given up their innate heat energy, these atoms lose their independence and have to create an alliance. This integration, alliance, might not be a symptom of strength, but of weakness.

The Gestaltists might disagree: "Look at this motor engine. The whole is more than the parts. Even if you have surplus parts—extra sparkplugs and pistons, etc.—they are nothing compared to the engine." I disagree. I accept the functioning motor as one gestalt, and I accept the unassembled parts as another gestalt—maybe merchandise, or junk, or potential engine—according to the context, the background in which they appear. Certainly not a strong gestalt, except maybe if the parts would be heaped in the middle of a living room.

There exists a most interesting contribution of the Gestaltists to our understanding: the differentiation of the gestalt into figure and background. This contribution relates to semantics, or the meaning of meaning.

Usually, if we think of meaning, we have two opposite opinions —the objective and the subjective. The objective one says a thing or a word *has* one or several meanings which can be nailed down by definition—otherwise dictionaries could not make a living.

The other, the subjective opinion, is the "Alice in Wonderland" one, saying, "A word means just what I meant it to mean." Neither is tenable. A meaning does not exist. A meaning is a creative process, a performance in the here and now. This act of creation can be habitual and so quick that we cannot trace it, or it can require hours of discussion. In every case, a meaning is created by relating a figure, the foreground, to the background against which the figure appears. The background is often called context, connection, or situation. To tear a statement out of its context easily leads to falsehood. In *Ego, Hunger, and Aggression* I wrote extensively about this issue. No clear communication is possible without clear understanding of this figure/background relationship. It is as if you are expected to listen to a radio when the signal (for instance, words) is drowned out by a loud background noise (static).

Perhaps the most interesting and important property of the gestalt is its dynamics—the need of a strong gestalt to come to a closure. Every day we experience this dynamic many times. The best name for the incomplete gestalt is the unfinished situation.

I want to make clear a fallacy of Freud's and to compare this fallacy with the academic and my personal gestalt approach, and to cut through some superficial similarities. In this context, I want to show the therapeutic hopelessness of the Freudian (and every) instinct theory.

Freud observed that some of his patients showed a need to repeat a pattern of experiences over and over again. Some, for instance, sabotaged themselves at the moment of success. He named such an attitude "compulsive repetition." This is certainly a valid observation and an adequate term. Repetitive nightmares and similar gestalten are easily traced in many neuroses. It is doubtful whether we should include in this category the need to go five days a week to the same analyst at the same time to the same place on the same couch, come rain or come sunshine, whether sad or gay, disturbed or calm.

Freud ended up with his theory that life is a conflict between Eros and Thanatos. As each one of us participates in life, he participates, according to this theory, in Thanatos, the death instinct. That means that each one of us suffers from compulsive repetition.

This seems to be a supposition that is rather far stretched.

How does one come from a compulsive repetition to a death instinct? (How does the spinach get on the roof? A cow can't fly!) A simple sleight of hand, Gentlemen! You see, here is the repetition—now this repetition is a habit. A habit deprives you of your freedom to choose. It petrifies your life. Petrification is death. *Voila!* Simple, isn't it? Now watch: this death can be life too. If you turn petrification outward, it is aggression, which is very much alive. I feel like an s.o.b., but someone has to see the emperor's nakedness.

Where is the fallacy? In the assumption that all habits are petrifications. Habits are integrated gestalten and, as such, in principle, are economical devices of nature. As Lore once pointed out to me, "good" habits are life-supportive.

If you learn to type, you will have to orient yourself in the beginning about the location of each letter, then move your finger to that key and depress it with a certain amount of force. Your orientation, as well as your manipulation of the keys, will change from strangeness to familiarity, from an unending stream of discovery and rediscovery to certainty—that is, to knowledge. Less and less time and concentration is required, until this skill becomes automatic, becomes a part of the self, empties out the foreground and makes room for "thinking," undisturbed by the search for the keys. In other words, "good" habits are part of a growth process, the actualization of a potential skill.

Now it is true that once a habit is formed—once a gestalt is established—it is there and becomes a part of the organism. To change a habit involves pulling that habit out of the background again and investing energy (as we saw with H2O) to disintegrate or to reorganize the habit.

Freud slipped up by not recognizing the difference between the pathological compulsive repetition and organismic habit formation.

The compulsive repetition cannot empty out the foreground and be assimilated. On the contrary, it remains a constant source of attention and stress just because the gestalt has no closure, just because the situation remains unfinished, just because the wound will not heal.

The compulsive repetition is not death-directed, but life-directed. It is a repeated attempt to cope with a difficult situation. The repetitions are investments towards the completion of a gestalt in order to free one's energies for growth and development. The unfinished situations are holding up the works; they are blocks in the path of maturation.

One of the simplest examples of the unfinished situation is illness. An illness can be finished by cure, by death, or by organismic transformation.

The fact that illness, a distorted form of life, will disappear with cure or death is obvious. And also that an illness, especially if accompanied by pain, will assume the importance of a chronic figure, unwilling to recede into the background, and still less to be assimilated and to disappear permanently from the foreground. This often changes through *organismic transformation*.

If a person is nearly blind, he will invest much effort to retain or improve on what is left of his eyesight. It remains a continually unfinished situation. He is occupied and preoccupied.

Once he is completely blind, the situation mostly changes in a dramatic way. He has got over the fallacy of hope. He is crippled in the eyes of his fellow man, but he himself becomes a different organism, living in a different *Umwelt* (environment), relying on a different way of orientation. He is now an organism without eyes, as we are organisms with two and not ten legs. His chances of becoming content have greatly improved, cf. Helen Keller, who had several handicaps.

If we are not exercising control, if the organism is not controlled by orders, how are we able to function? How is the cooperation of those millions of cells achieved? How are they able to cope with their sustenance and the other exigencies of life? If we reject even the mind/body dichotomy, what miraculous power makes us tick?

Do we have a built-in dictator who is making the decisions, a council of consensus, a government with executive power? Is there an unconscious, or emotions, or a computing brain, which does the job? Is there a God, a soul permeating the body and taking charge of all its requirements and goals with infinite wisdom?

We don't know! We can only make up fantasies, maps, models, working hypotheses, and check out every second as to their correctness and reliability. And if we know, what good will it do?

No theory is valid if there is one exception to it. If we cheat, conceal evidence, we are not scientists but manipulators, hypnotists, mountebanks, or at least propagandists for the aggrandisement of our self-importance.

Out of the fog of ignorance, are there emerging any building stones for a reliable, complete, applicable, and unified theory of man and his functions?

Some, not too many yet. But enough to give us reliable guidance for our specific purposes.

• I have made awareness the hub of my approach, recognizing that phenomenology is the primary and indispensable step towards knowing all there is to know.

Without awareness there is nothing.

Without awareness there is emptiness.

The average person is wary of nothingness. He feels there is something uncanny about it. To him it seems absurd to turn to it and use it philosophically.

There are many existents: things, beings, chemicals, the universe, newspapers, and so on, indefinitely. We certainly don't see them all as belonging to the same category.

I don't see many categories of nothing, and I believe it is worthwhile, even required for our purpose, to talk about a few of them. As an example, take the story of the creation.

From all we know, time is infinite, without a beginning or an end. We are already learning to count in billions of years. Man found it impossible to tolerate the idea that there is "nothing" in the beginning. So he invented stories about how the world was created, stories that differ with the different cultures and which conveniently leave out the answer to how the creator was created. These stories fill up a nothing which we could call uncanny emptiness, or void.

Sometimes nothingness takes on a desirable aspect, as when it is experienced in the context of pain, distress, or dispair. Shalom, the Hebrew greeting, is peace, absence of conflict. Nirvana is cessation of the trouble of living. Lethe is oblivion, the blotting out of the intolerable.

Sometimes nothingness is the result of destruction, and in psychoanalysis, repression: the annihilation of unwanted things, people, and memories.

Nothingness in the Western sense can also be contrasted with the Eastern idea of *no-thing-ness*. Things don't exist; every event is a process; the thing is merely a transitory form of an eternal process. Among the pre-Socratic philosophers, it was Heraclitus who held the same ideas: *Panta rei*—all is in flux; we never step into the same river twice.

To call a girl empty-headed is an insult for us. With an oriental, it may be a great compliment; her head is not clogged up, it is open.

My first philosophical encounter with nothingness was the naught, in the form of zero. I found it under the name of *creative indifference* through Sigmund Friedlander.

I recognize three gurus in my life. The first one was S. Friedlander, who called himself a Neo-Kantian. I learned from him the meaning of balance, the zero-center of opposites. The second is Selig, our sculptor and architect at the Esalen Institute. I know that he would be very angry if he knew that I am writing about him. This truly is an intrusion into his privacy. *Ecce homo!* Here is truly a *Mensch*, a human being of complete unpretentiousness, humility, wisdom, and know-how. As a city dweller, I had not much contact with nature. To watch him and his involvement and understanding with humans, animals, and plants, to compare his unobtrusiveness and confidence with my excitability and prima-donna-ishness, to feel at last the presence of a man to whom I feel inferior, and finally the feeling of mutual respect and friendship that came about—all of this has helped me to overcome most of my pompousness and phoniness.

My last guru was Mitzie, a beautiful white cat. She taught me the wisdom of the animal.

Twice in my life I have been furious about missing a photographic recording. The first time was when a member of one of my groups had a *deja vu* experience with trance and *petit mal* (a minor epileptic seizure). We had my video recorder going. I was thrilled at the chance of possibly having taken the only videotape recording of that symptom in existence. In spite of my clear marking, "Don't erase," the tape was erased and re-used.

The other event happened with Mitzie. One morning I woke up and I saw my 2½-foot wide sombrero moving next to my bed. I lifted the hat and there was Mitzie, cradling a bird in her front paws. I felt a shock. Three weeks before, I had seen my living room strewn with feathers, a sure sign that Mitzie had caught and eaten a bird. I took the bird away, her eyes sad. The bird was intact and could fly away after ten minutes recovery. How could I assume that Mitzie was merely affectionate? Who has ever heard of a cat cradling a bird? Without my shock, I could have taken a picture and could have shown off such a rare occurrence.

I know how I got Mitzie, I remember the kindly critical eyes of my early encounters with Selig, but Friedlander is rather submerged in a fog. When my mother mentioned one day the food parcels I had sent him, I was surprised. I had totally forgotten. The parcels would belong to the year 1922.

The inflation of the German mark was already increasing in tempo, although it had not yet run away. Food, especially meat was scarce. My ability to see things in perspective was an asset at that time. Just as later on I beat the dangers of the concentration camp and the turmoil of World War II, so I beat inflation.

Jitters about the present dangers of inflation in the States unlock a smile. Inflation! You have no idea what inflation means! If money bears a, let's say, interest of 4%, the law of balance says that the money loses 4% per year of its value, and this is about the degree of your inflation.

Whether the German inflation was manufactured in order to wipe out war debts I could not say, but I suspect it. The fact is that the dollar went from 4 marks quickly to 20, then 100, then 1000 and finally into many 1000's then ran away to millions of marks and ended up with the price of several billions. The value of the mark came very close to "nothing." I have a historical collection of German stamps from the fragmented kingdoms to the empire through the Third Reich until the West Germany/Berlin/East Germany split. The inflation stamps cover several pages of it.

The paper money had to be carried in bags. People rushed to buy something with the money they had earned that day in the evening, because the next morning the value was already halved. Mortgages were not worth the paper they were written on.

Two patients plus my alertness saved this critical situation. One was a banker. I did not know anything about the stock market and its manipulations. One day he suggested I should buy some stock at a price about a hundred times my monthly earning. I told him that he was crazy, but he only smiled: "You can trust me! I will take the risk. You buy the stock now and pay for it in four weeks." So I did, and paid a fifth of its value after a month. I did this once more; then there was no need anymore. The respite came from another source, a patient who was a butcher from Bremerhaven.

Soon after the beginning of World War I the food situation in Germany started to deteriorate. Soon the word *Ersatz* (substitute) got an ominous connotation. After the war and especially during the inflation, the food situation did not improve at all. A rather funny episode might highlight this.

1919. My friend Franz Jonas and I went for a semester to study in Freiburg. One fine day we went hiking and hopefully to secure some food from some farmers. All we got for our day's effort were two eggs. On our way home we got somewhat drunk and gay. Fooling around he slapped the pocket where I had hidden the eggs, since foraging was forbidden. A mess instead of a precious breakfast! A boiled egg for breakfast in Germany is nearly a status symbol.

Enough of free dissociations! Let's return to my savior, the butcher angel, who fell out of the skies of Bremerhaven right into my consulting room—or shall we say larder? He suffered from headaches and wanted, of course, to be cured, as all neurotics maintain. Bremerhaven was an eight-hour train journey away and he came once a week with a big parcel of meat and sausages. I live with my parents and sister Elsie. We never had it so good, as the saying goes. But this was not all. After some weeks he insisted that he felt better, but not cured, and those long train journeys did his head not a bit of good. He had many friends who wanted to consult me and there was no *Nervenarzt* (a kind of neuro-psychiatrist) in Bremerhaven. "I am not interested," I answered, "to be tortured by a joggling railroad coach."

"Well," was his reply, "we could pay you in American dollars." My heart sank. This could not be true. Such miracles just did not exist. But it was true.

What the dollar meant during the galloping inflation is hard to grasp. Just one example instead of many. In 1923 I intended to go to the States. I never had the money to have my M.D. diploma printed, which you were only allowed to do after you had paid for the printing of the dissertation. I rarely was interested in medicine per se, and my dissertation was about a silly theme: *Lipodystrophia adiposo-*

genitalis or something like that, a rare disease where women looked like kangaroos with big masses of fat above the waist and skinny below. I was interested in its publication. I went to the *Castellan*, a kind of university purser, and suggested I would give him a dollar if he would get the printing job done. His eyes shone; he did not believe his ears. "A whole dollar?" He took charge and within a week I had my things printed and signed, and had made him deeply grateful without having to lift a finger. Such was the magic of the dollar in 1923.

By that time I was a rich man. I had accumulated 500 dollars for which I could have bought a few apartment buildings in Berlin. Instead of that I used it for a trip to New York.

Bremerhaven had the reputation of being a suburb of New York. It was the German port for one of the two great transatlantic lines that had big boats like the *Bremen* and *Europa*. The crews were paid in dollars. For several months I went to Bremerhaven every week for two days, had quite a few patients, using at that time mostly hypnoanalysis, and I had lots of fun besides.

Most of the German M.D.'s were uptight and wore masks of utter respectability. I am sure they frowned on me for those trips. I frowned back. They belonged to the stuck-up, stuck-upper-middle-class-bourgeoisie. I and some of my M.D. friends belonged to the Berlin bohemian class that had its hangout in the Cafe of the West and later in the Romanische Cafe.

Many philosophers, writers, painters, political radicals plus a number of hangers-on met there. One of the crowd, of course, was Friedlander, though we met mostly in a painter's studio. Friedlander made his money by writing very humorous stories under the name of Mynona which is anonym spelled backwards. His philosophical work *Creative Indifference* had a tremendous impact on me. As a personality, he was the first man in whose presence I felt humble, bowing in veneration. There was no room for my chronic arrogance.

If I try to rationalize and to sort out what attracted me to Friedlander and his philosophy I experience a whirl of thoughts, feelings and memories. Philosophy was a magic word, something one had to understand to understand oneself and the world, an antidote to my existential confusion and bewilderment. I could always cope with sophistication. The question "How many angels can dance on the point of a needle?" was a cheap cheat, mixing up symbols and things. "What comes first, the chicken or the egg?" not only dismisses the total picture of a continuous process, but specifically leaves out the point of departure, "Which chicken, which egg?" Reich was a typical victim of such messy thinking.

In school we read Sophocles and Plato in the original Greek. I liked the dramatist, but Plato, like so many philosophers, was putting up ideals and demanding ways of behavior which they themselves surely did not follow. I had enough of that hypocrisy through my father who preached one thing and lived another.

As for Socrates, he even surpassed my arrogance by saying: "You all are fools to think that you know something! But I, Socrates, am not a fool. I know that I don't know! This gives me the right to torture you with questions and to show you what a fool you are!" How much glory can you give to the intellect?

The current teaching in psychology was a mixture of physiology and four classes of mind: reason, emotions, willpower, and memory.

I could not even start to mention the one hundred different explanations and purposes that were produced as representing the Truth (with capital T again).

Into this turmoil Friedlander brought a simple way of primary orientation. Whatever is, will differentiate into opposites. If you are caught by one of the opposing forces you are trapped, or at least lopsided. If you stay in the *nothing* of the zero center, you are balanced and in perspective.

Later I realized that this is the Western equivalent of the teaching of Lao-tze.

The orientation of the creative indifference is lucid to me. I have nothing to add to the first chapter of *Ego, Hunger and Aggression*.

Oh boy, am I stuck! That was the only sentence that came. Referring to old stale shit! Pfaw, Fritz, shame on you. One hour ago a session finished heavy, over-therapized. Finally got some resentments out. Black bats leaving the room. Went down to the lodge. They were dancing, turned on, once more over the hump.

Sitting there sad, unresponsive to eye overtures, opening eyes myself, sadness, tiredness, unresponsiveness. It took me sometimes several days to get over a depression. This time I stayed fully with it, resisting the impulse to reach out in false comfort. Today it took only twenty minutes. I am myself again. Pen roving over the paper. It's nearly one o'clock. Last two nights I wrote until three o'clock or so. Up early. Listen to the one o'clock news. We have no FM or TV reception. Only AM with fading and static. At night a classical music program "American Airline" comes through not too badly. We have no newspaper, either. So I listen to one news broadcast if possible.

Once a week catching up with the news through *Newsweek*. This week's excitement: we were in *Life* magazine. Feels funny, as if we were becoming respectable. And I have a bad reputation to maintain!

> Come off it Fritz, stop that ranting,
> Stop that raving.
> Be a writer, give the goods.
> Poetry is good at times, likewise contemplation
> Of your own disturbing moods
> And your own elation.
> Sit you down and tell us how
> Better than a soul, or God
> Can creative nothingness
> Give us understanding.
> Leave that chapter in the bin
> With the other garbage.
> Pick some samples, illustrate
> Give some light to darkness.

Light and darkness—irreconcilable opposites seen from the abstract point of view. How can there be light when there is darkness, the very essence of nothingness? One *excludes* the other.

Now look at that tree in sunlight. You see the shadow? Shadow without light, light without shadow?—Impossible! In this case, light and darkness determine each other; they *include* each other.

Does an open-air movie theatre show a picture during the daytime? To have foreground figures, we need darkness as background.

In order to stay simple, let us stick to a black and white movie. We need the contrast of black and white. We need balanced contrast. Too much contrast and the picture will be hard, too little and it will be flat. Your TV set has adjustments for optimum balance. Again, black and white determine each other. A screen that is completely white *or* black constitutes a *nothing* in regard to its content. The content that is the picture is a differentiation into meaningful black and white dots.

Moving up the ladder, we find Rembrandt, whose juxtaposition of light and darkness is one of the great achievements of art.

Zero is naught, is nothing. A point of indifference, a point from which opposites are born. An indifference that is automatically creative as soon as that differentiation starts. We can randomly select any point at will, and zero-in at that point. If you decide to launch a missile on x/y/z day, you start with a countdown of days, hours, minutes, and seconds, to zero and follow with counting up of seconds, minutes, hours, and days.

A balanced budget is one in which credit and debit add up to zero, whether the budget deals with pennies or millions.

We make a habit of calling the zero point "normal." We then talk about normal temperature, normal bloodcount, etc., *ad infinitum.* Any plus or minus is called abnormal, a sign of malfunctioning— of illness, if the plus or minus is considerable.

In the case of the biological organism, the zero point of normalcy has to be maintained or the organism will stop functioning; the organism will die.

Each cell, each organ, each total organism has a considerable number of normal functions to maintain.

Each cell, each organ, each total organism is busy disposing of any excess (+) and filling up any deficiency (-) in order to maintain the zero point, the point of optimal functioning.

Each cell, each organ, each total organism is in touch with its environment, disposing and replenishing.

Each cell, each organ has an intra-organismic environment (body fluids, nerves, etc.) in which it is embedded. The total organism has the world as environment in which it must maintain the subtle organismic balance.

Any disturbance of the organismic balance constitutes an incomplete gestalt, an unfinished situation forcing the organism to become creative, to find means and ways to restore that balance.

Any deficiency—of calcium, amino acids, oxygen, affection, importance, etc.—produces a need to get those from somewhere. We don't *have* an "instinct" for calcium, amino acids, oxygen, affection, importance, etc., we *create* those thousands of possible "instincts" *ad hoc* whenever a specific balance is disturbed.

Any surplus creates a temporary instinct to get rid of it—carbon dioxide, lactic acid, semen, feces, irritations, resentments, fatigue, etc.—in order to restore the organismic balance.

Each breath replenishes oxygen and disposes of carbon dioxide. Breathing often—lopsidedly—is equated with *in*haling. "Take a breath."

I don't want to wash my hands in a basin half-filled with dirty water. I don't pour fresh water on top of the dirty water. I drain the dirty water first.

To drain the "dirty" air, first *ex*hale! If *in*haling becomes a fetish, you might develop asthma, a desperate attempt of nature to squeeze out used-up air.

I have a number of so-called miraculous cures in my garbage bin. Here is a lulu I can pull out. These types of cures are as little miracles as the fact that you can see a tree which the blind cannot see. It is merely that my intermediate zone is less crowded than the average and that I am capable of seeing the obvious. I need to mention the following case as an example of imbalance.

A violinist was sent to me for a cramp which he developed in his left hand after playing his instrument only fifteen minutes. He had the ambition to be a soloist; he did not have his cramp while he was playing in the orchestra. All neurological investigation proved to be negative. Obviously this was a psychosomatic case and psychoanalysis was indicated.

I have seen many cases of psychoanalysis of long duration. Five to ten years are quite frequent. But he was tops. He had had twenty-seven years of it with six different therapists. Needless to say, all aspects of the Oedipus complex, masturbation, exhibitionism, etc., were gone over again and again.

When he came to me and made a dive for the couch, I stopped him and asked him to bring his violin along.

"What for?"

"I want to see how you manage to produce this cramp."

He brought his violin and played beautifully, standing up. I saw that he got his support from his right leg and that he had his left leg crossed over. After about ten minutes he began to wobble slightly. This wobble increased imperceptibly, and within a few more minutes his fingering slowed down and many notes were inaccurately played. He interrupted: "You see? It's getting difficult. If I force myself to gon on, I get my cramp and I can't play at all."

And you don't get the cramp in the orchestra?

"Never."

Do you sit?

"Of course, but as soloist I have to stand up."

O.K. Now let me massage your hands. Now stand with your feet apart, slightly bent in at your knees. Now start again.

After twenty minutes of perfect playing, tears came to his eyes. He muttered: "I won't believe it, I won't believe it."

By then his hour was over, but I let my next patient wait. This was too important! I wanted to make sure and let him play a few more minutes.

What had happened? We have several polarities which, if not properly balanced, will produce a split and conflict. Most frequent is the right/left dichotomy. Less frequent the front/rear or the upper/under carriage split, first observed by Lore. The part above the waist has essentially contact functions, the lower part supportive functions. Now, my patient had enough support when he was sitting, but standing mostly on his right leg was not enough support for the subtle finger movements of his left hand. As soon as his right leg got tired of carrying the whole load, he began to wobble and he had to regain his balance nearly every second. This imbalance was a strain influencing the upper carriage and especially the left hand. We still had to work some more weeks, not only to wean him from his couch life, but also to soften his "grim determination"—clenched jaws, etc.

I don't know if he ever made it. He played well enough, but I never saw his name announced as one of the star soloists.

At that time, I was already well-established in New York and began to get a name as somebody who was willing and eager to get refractory cases.

Actually, for a while it was touch-and-go if I would stay in the States.

I am at a minor impasse. I feel like writing about my coming to the States, and at the same time, I don't feel too good about it. This shuffling from one context to another begins to feel like a gimmick, like a technique. It is not even counterpoint style, mutually support-ing. But then, who else but me is going to set the rules on what to throw into the garbage and what to pick out? What's more, I am not even writing of what is troubling me at the moment. It is a quarter-past-three in the morning, and I can't sleep. This is a very rare occurrence. Usually I am able to get in touch with and localize any overexcitement. This dissolves and dissipates, and "I" awareness fades, the body awareness diminishes, and then "nothing" until the morning.

Larry Booth has made a film in color, called "Fritz." This film is a poem, a rather exciting portrait of me, though there was some re-mark that my warmth and love is not coming through as in the films dealing with therapy sessions. This would not bother me. What is upsetting is that I am suspicious and irritable about some paranoid attitude of mine. This has become very rare. I feel I am being taken advantage of. Actually and factually, I am justified as far as the agreement and the financial situation is concerned. But I cannot allow myself to be generous and to experience myself as a sucker. I can afford it. I make good money. So what the hell!

I lived through the terrors of Flanders, I lived through plenty of mudslinging, I lived through that time in Holland, and through many other troubles—still I cannot be rational about it. It is still the arrogant self-concept, "You can't do this to me!"

I had a number of paranoid spells, even in situations where I was in the wrong. These spells were very marked and exaggerated after my first few LSD trips. At those times, I lost my perspective and experienced plenty of revenge fantasies. I know this would be the time to talk about psychedelic drugs and my relation to them, but I begin to feel heavy and tired. I have to postpone it. Will this writing bring me sleep?

Part II

CONTEMPORARY THEORY

CHAPTER 4

THEORY OF GESTALT THERAPY

GARY M. YONTEF, Ph.D.

Gary M. Yontef is a clinical psychologist and clinical social worker in private practice with Gestalt Associates in Santa Monica. He is also a training therapist and chairman of the Training Committee of the Gestalt Therapy Institute of Los Angeles and was formerly on the UCLA Psychology Department faculty.

Reprinted by permission from G. M. Yontef, **A Review of the Practice of Gestalt Therapy**, Los Angeles: Trident Shop, California State University, 1969, pp. 2-8.

Gestalt Therapy emphasizes two principles that need integrating if behavioral and experiential psychology are to be meaningfully combined into one system of psychotherapy: "The absolute working in the here and now," and "The full concern with the phenomenon of awareness" (Perls, 1966, p. 2). The Gestalt therapist claims neither to cure nor to condition, but perceives himself as an observer of ongoing behavior and as a guide for the phenomenological learning of the patient. Although a full understanding of the theoretical support for this would entail a detailed examination of the Gestalt therapy theory of psychology, personality and psychopathology, a short detour into this subject will be necessary.

Gestalt Therapy is based on Gestalt theory, a discussion of which is beyond the scope of the present chapter (see Perls, et al., 1951; Wallen, 1957). Gestalt therapists regard motor behavior and the perceptual qualities of the individual's experience as organized by the most relevant organismic need (ibid.). In the normal individual a configuration is formed which has the qualities of a good gestalt, with the organizing figure being the dominant need (Perls, 1947; Perls et al., 1951). The individual meets this need by contacting the environment with some sensori-motor behavior. The contact is organized by the figure of interest against the ground of the organism/environment field (Perls et al., 1951). Note that in Gestalt Therapy both sensing the environment and motor movement in the environment are active, contacting functions.

When a need is met, the gestalt it organized becomes complete, and it no longer exerts an influence—the organism is free to form new gestalten. When this gestalt formation and destruction are blocked or rigidified at any stage, when needs are not recognized and expressed, the flexible harmony and flow of the organism/environment field is disturbed. Unmet needs form incomplete gestalten that clamor for attention and, therefore, interfere with the formation of new gestalten.

At the point where nourishment or toxicity (Greenwald, 1968) is possible, awareness develops. Awareness is always accompanied by gestalt formation (Perls et al., 1951). With awareness the organism can mobilize its aggression so the environmental stimulus can be contacted ("tasted") and rejected or chewed and assimilated. This contact-assimilation process is operated by the natural biological force of aggression. When awareness does not develop (i.e., figure and ground do not form into a clear gestalt) in such a transaction, or when impulses are kept from expression, incomplete gestalten are formed and psychopathology develops (Enright, 1968). This shifting figure/ground of awareness replaces the psychoanalytic concept of the unconscious, the "unconscious" being phenomena in the field which the organism does not contact because of a disturbance in the figure/ground formation or because it is in contact with other phenomena (Polster, 1967; Simkin, 1966).

The point at which this awareness is formed is the point of contact. "Contact, the work that results in assimilation and growth, is the forming of a figure of interest against a ground or context of the organism/environment" (Perls et al., 1951, p. 231). Gestalt Therapy focuses on what and how, and not on content.

By working on the unity and disunity of the structure of the experience here and now, it is possible to remake the dynamic relations of the figure and ground until the contact is heightened, the awareness brightened and the behavior energized, most important of all, the achievement of a strong gestalt is itself the cure, for the figure of contact is not a sign of, but is itself the creative integration of experience (Perls et al., 1951, p. 232).

Awareness is a gestalt property that is creative integration of the problem. Only an aware gestalt ("awareness") leads to change. Mere "awareness" of content without awareness of structure does not relate to an energized organism/environment contact.

Gestalt Therapy starts a process, like a catalyst. The exact reaction is determined by the patient and his environment. The "cure" is not a finished product, but a person who has learned how to develop the awareness he needs to solve his own problems (Perls et al., 1951). The criterion of success is not "social acceptability" or "interpersonal relations" but "the patient's own awareness of heightened vitality and more effective functioning" (ibid., p. 15). The therapist does not tell the patient what he has discovered about the patient, but teaches him how to learn.

Perls calls the system of responses or contacts of the organism with the environment at any moment the self (Perls et al., 1951). The ego is the system of identification and alienation of the organism. In neurosis the ego alienates some of the self processes, i.e., fails to identify with the self as it is. Rather than allow the self to proceed with the organization of responses into new gestalten, the self is crippled. The neurotic loses awareness of (alienates) the sense of "it is I who am thinking, feeling, doing this" (ibid., p. 235). The neurotic is divided, unaware, and self-rejecting.

This division, unawareness, and self-rejection can be maintained only by restricting the organism's experiencing. The naturally functioning organism experiences by feeling, sensing and thinking. When the person rejects one of his modes of experiencing the formation of new gestalten becomes blocked by unmet needs that form incomplete gestalten and, therefore, demand attention. Without experiencing needs and impulses, organismic self-regulation is impaired, and reliance on moralistic external regulation is necessitated (Perls, 1948).

The rejection of modes of experiencing can be traced far back in Western culture. Since Aristotle, Western man has been taught that his rational faculties are acceptable but sensory and affective faculties unacceptable. The human organism has become split into the "I" and the "me." Western man identifies with his reigning sovereign (reason), and has alienated his sensory and affective modalities. However, without balanced organismic experiencing, man cannot be in full contact with nature or in support of himself and, therefore, is impaired in learning from his environmental transactions (Perls, 1966; Simkin, 1966). Western man has been alienated, split, out of harmony with nature (Perls, 1948; Simkin, 1966).

Learning takes place by discovery, by the formation of new gestalten, i.e., insight. As an organism interacts with the environment gestalten are completed, awareness develops, and learning takes place (Simkin, 1966). Perls found his patients suffering from alienation of ego functions and set out to find a therapy that would integrate the split personality so that new gestalten could be formed, the patient could learn, etc. (Perls, 1948). He noticed that patients showed their basically faulty figure/ground formation in their transactions with him. This was the clue for his founding of Gestalt Therapy. A fuller discussion of this can be found in the literature (Perls, 1947, 1948; Perls et al., 1951; Simkin, 1966; Wallen, 1957).

The basic therapeutic dilemma as Perls sees it is that the patient has lost awareness of the processes by which he alienates (remains unaware of) parts of his self-functioning. He found that by using experiments with directed awareness, the patient could learn how he kept from being aware—in a sense Perls taught patients how to learn (Perls et al., 1951).

The therapeutic change process in Gestalt Therapy involves helping the patient rediscover the mechanism which he uses to control his awareness. The directed awareness experiments, the Gestalt Therapy encounter, the group experiments which we shall discuss all have as their goal making the patient aware of the habitual acts he engages in to control his awareness. Without this emphasis the patient might increase his awareness, but only in a limited and circumscribed way. When the patient reexperiences control of awareness control, his development can be self-directive and self-supportive.

The ultimate goal of the treatment can be formulated thus: We have to achieve that amount of integration which facilitates its own development (Perls, 1948, p. 12).

The therapeutic tasks the Gestalt therapist gives the patient are all reports of the patient's awareness. In therapy the patient can gain something different than he gains from experience outside of therapy, i.e., something other than an isolated piece of knowledge, a temporary relationship or catharsis. What therapy can create is a situation wherein the very core of a person's growth problem, restricted awareness, is the focus of attention.

For therapist and patient alike Perls' prescription is "lose your mind and come to your senses." Perls stresses the use of the external senses as well as the internal proprioceptive system of self-awareness. By resensitizing the patient, the patient can become aware once again of the mechanism by which he (ego) rejects awareness and expression of impulses. When the organism once again controls the censor, it can fight the battles of survival with its own sensorimotor behavior, learn and become integrated, that is to say, self-accepting (Simkin, 1966).

When the neurotic—with his split in personality, underuse of affective and sensory modalities, and lack of self-support—attempts to have the therapist solve his life problems, the Gestalt therapist refuses; the Gestalt therapist refuses to allow the patient to thrust the responsibility for his behavior onto him (Enright, 1968). The therapist frustrates the attempt to operate manipulatively in core areas.

In Gestalt Therapy the goal is not to solve the problem (Enright, 1968), for the patient will remain a cripple as long as he manipulates others into doing his problem-solving for him, i.e., as long as he does not use his full sensorimotor equipment. Gestalt Therapy is holistic and sees the human organism as potentially free of internal control hierarchies. The patient-therapist relationship in Gestalt Therapy is also relatively hierarchy-free.

The patient is an active and responsible participant who learns to experiment and observe so as to be able to discover and realize his own goals through his own efforts. The responsibility for the patient's behavior, change in behavior, and the work to achieve such change is left to the patient.

Thus Gestalt Therapy rejects the notion that the therapist must or should assume the role of a conditioner or deconditioner.

> Every patient barks up the wrong tree by expecting that he can achieve maturation through external sources . . . Maturation cannot be done for him, he has to go through the painful process of growing up by himself. We therapists can do *nothing* but provide him the opportunity, by being available as a catalyst and projection screen (Perls, 1966, p. 4).

The role of the Gestalt therapist is that of a participant-observer of here-and-now behavior and catalyst for the phenomenological experimentation of the patient. The patient leans by experimenting in the *"safe emergency* of the therapeutic situation" (Perls, 1966, p. 8). He continues to take the natural consequences of his behavior in and out of therapy.

> The basic assumption of this therapeutic approach is that people can deal adequately with their own life problems if they know what they are, and can bring all their abilities into action to solve them . . .Once in good touch with their real concerns and their real environment, they are on their own (Enright, 1968, p. 7).

Although the therapist in Gestalt Therapy does not focus on mentalistic concepts, or on the past, or on the future, no content is excluded in advance. Past or future material are considered acts in the present (memory, planning, etc.). Nor is Gestalt Therapy static. But the focus is not on finding the "whys" of behavior or "mind" nor is it manipulation of stimulus consequences to bring about a change in behavior. "Contrary to the approaches of some schools which stress 'insight' or learning 'why' we do as we do, Gestalt Therapy stresses learning 'how' and 'what' we do" (Simkin, 1966, p. 4).

In Gestalt Therapy the therapist is not passive, as in older Rogerian therapy, but is quite active. Attending to behavior not mentalisms, to awareness not speculative questions, here-and-now and not there-and-then all necessitate action and assertiveness on the part of the therapist.

The goal in Gestalt Therapy is maturity. Perls defines maturity as "the transition from environmental support to self-support" (1965; also see Simkin, 1966). Self-support implies contact with other people. Continuous contact (confluence) or absence of contact (withdrawal) are contrary to what is implied (Perls, 1947). Self-support refers to self-support in the organism/environment field. Confluence obviously is not self-support. Withdrawal still involves the essence of nonself-support. Critical here is continuous use of the sensorimotor equipment of the organism in transaction with the environment, with awareness (Enright, 1968). Such is self-support, and it leads to integration.

This process is achieved in the natural environment when there is struck "a viable balance of support and frustration." Gestalt therapists attempt to balance support and frustration. Excessive frustration, especially in individual therapy, will result in the patient's "disowning" the therapist. Excessive support encourages the patient to continue to manipulate the environment for that support which the patient erroneously believes he cannot provide for himself. While temporary improvement may result from such supportive treatment, the patient will not be aided in moving beyond the impasse point.

The impasse point is what the Russian literature calls the "sick point." "The existential impasse is a situation in which no environmental support is forthcoming and the patient is, or believes himself to be, incapable of coping with life on his own" (Perls, 1966, p. 6). In order to achieve or maintain support from the environment the patient will engage in a number of maneuvers. Such "manipulations" or "games" are used by the patient to maintain the status quo, to keep control of his environment, to avoid coping with life on his own. When the neurotic patient avoids coping, he avoids the "actual pains" any organism avoids, and, in addition, "the neurotic avoids imaginary hurts, such as unpleasant emotions. He also avoids taking reasonable risks. Both interfere with any chance of maturation" (ibid., p. 7).

Therefore Gestalt Therapy calls the patient's attention to his avoidance of unpleasantness and his phobic behavior is worked through in the course of the therapy.

In summary, the therapist balances frustration and support while maintaining a relationship in the "I and Thou, Here and Now" tradition of Martin Buber. The patient at first works hard at avoiding his actual experience and the consequences of his actual behavior. Because the patient has long since learned and practiced the manipulating of his environment to obtain support and means of avoiding becoming aware of his actual experiences, he is usually quite skilled at this.

He does this by acting helpless and stupid; he wheedles, bribes, and flatters. He *is not* infantile, but plays an infantile and dependent role expecting to control the situation by submissive behavior (Perls, 1965, p. 5).

REFERENCES

Enright, J. *An Introduction to Gestalt Therapy.* Unpublished manuscript, Esalen Institute, California, 1968.
Greenwald, J. "The Art of Emotional Nourishment," unpublished manuscript, 450 N. Bedford Drive, Beverly Hills, California, 1968.
Perls, F. *Ego, Hunger, and Aggression.* Woking, Great Britain: Unwin Bros., 1947.
_____ "Theory and Technique of Personality Integration," *American Journal of Psychotherapy,* 2, (1948), 565-586.
_____ *Gestalt Therapy and Human Potentialities.* Unpublished manuscript, Esalen Institute, California, 1965.
_____ "Workshop Versus Individual Therapy." Paper presented at American Psychological Association, New York City, September, 1966.
_____, R. Hefferline, and P. Goodman. *Gestalt Therapy: Excitement and Growth in the Human Personality.* New York: Julian Press, 1951.
Wallen, R. "Gestalt Psychology and Gestalt Therapy." Paper presented at Ohio Psychological Association Symposium, 1957.
Simkin, J. S. *An Introduction to The Theory of Gestalt Theory.* Cleveland: Gestalt Institute of Cleveland, No. 6, 1966.

CHAPTER 5

THE DEVELOPMENT OF GESTALT THERAPY

JAMES S. SIMKIN, Ph.D.

James S. Simkin is in private practice in Big Sur, California, where he is involved in conducting intensive training workshops for Gestalt therapists. He is recognized as being a leading figure in the continuing development of Gestalt Therapy, and has been a member of Gestalt Therapy Institutes in both New York and Los Angeles.

Reprinted by permission from R.-R. M. Jurjevich, ed., **Direct Psychotherapy: 28 American Originals** (Vol. 1). Coral Gables, Florida: University of Miami Press, 1973, pp. 423-432.

Gestalt is a German word meaning whole or configuration. As one psychological dictionary put it: "an *integration* of members as contrasted with a summation of parts" (Warren, 1934). The term also implies a unique kind of patterning. Gestalt Therapy is a term applied to a unique kind of psychotherapy formulated by Frederick S. Perls and his followers.

Dr. Perls began, as did many of his colleagues in those days, as a psychoanalyst, having first been trained as a physician in post-World War I Germany. In 1926 he worked under Professor Kurt Goldstein at the Frankfurt Neurological Institute where he was first exposed to the tenets of gestalt psychology but, as he puts it, "was still too preoccupied with the orthodox psychoanalytical approach to assimilate more than a fraction of what was offered [to me]" (Perls, 1947, p. 5). Later Dr. Perls was exposed to the theories and practice of Wilhelm Reich and incorporated some of the concepts and techniques of character analysis into his work.

While serving as a captain in the South African Medical Corps, Perls wrote his first manuscript outlining the emerging theory and technique of personality integration (during 1941-1942), which ultimately appeared as a book, *Ego, Hunger and Aggression*, subtitled, *A Revision of Freud's Theory and Method*. The term Gestalt Therapy was first used as the title of a book on Perls' method, written by him with two coauthors, Professor Ralph Hefferline of Columbia University and Dr. Paul Goodman of New York City.

A thumbnail sketch of the aim of psychoanalysis has sometimes been given as Freud's dictum: "Where Id was shall Ego be," or in other words, to replace the instinctual striving with self-control as mediated by the ego. A capsule comment describing Gestalt Therapy

might be Perls': "I and Thou; Here and Now" (with a bow to the late
Professor Buber). In Gestalt Therapy the emphasis is on the present,
ongoing situation—which, of course, involves the interaction of at
least two people (in individual therapy), the patient and the therapist.

According to the theory underlying Gestalt Therapy, man is a
total organism functioning as a whole rather than an entity split into
dichotomies such as mind and body. With the philosophical backing
of the brand of humanism represented by Otto Rank, the organism is
seen as born with the capacity to cope with life rather than (what I
call) the original-sin theory of human development: that the organism must learn to repress or suppress its instinctual (bad) strivings
in order to become "civilized." Recently the emergence of existential
philosophy appears to be so compatible with the development of
Gestalt Therapy that Dr. Wilson Van Dusen (1960) in an article on
"Existential Analytic Psychotherapy" claims that only one psychotherapeutic approach unites the phenomenological approach with
existential theory and that is Gestalt Therapy.

Before examining some of the main concepts of Gestalt Therapy
and describing actual situations that will give the experiential flavor
necessary to an understanding of the approach, I need to do a little
more "talking about" the approach (which is really a taboo approach
to Gestalt Therapy) in order to supply an adequate context or background.

The theoretical model of the psychodynamic schools of personality, chiefly the Freudian school, envisions the personality as an
onion consisting of layers, each time a layer is peeled away there is
still another layer until one finally comes to the core. (Incidentally,
in the process of "analysis" of the onion, very little or nothing may
be left by the time one comes to the core!) I envision the personality
more like a large rubber ball that has only a thick outer layer and is
empty inside. The ball floats or swims in an environment, so that at
any given moment only a certain portion is exposed to the outside
and the rest is submerged in the water. Thus, rather than inventing
an unconscious or preconscious to account for behavior that we are
unaware of, I would suggest that the unaware behavior is a result of
the organism not being in touch with, not sensing, what is out there
because the organism is submerged in its own background (environment) or is in contact with (usually preoccupied with) fantasies.

In his recent paper, "A Review of the Practice of Gestalt Therapy,"
Yontef summarizes the theory of Gestalt Therapy. Organismic needs
lead to sensory motor behavior. Once a configuration is formed

which has the qualities of a good gestalt, the organismic need which has become foreground is met, and a balance or state of satiation or no-need is achieved. "When a need is met, the gestalt organized becomes complete, and it no longer exerts an influence—the organism is free to form new gestalten. When this gestalt formation and destruction are blocked or rigidified at any stage, when needs are not recognized and expressed, the flexible harmony and flow of the organism/environment field is disturbed. Unmet needs form incomplete gestalten that clamor for attention and, therefore, interfere with the formation of new gestalten" (Yontef, 1969, p. 3).

According to Perls, "the most important fact about the figure-background formation is that if a need is genuinely satisfied, the situation changes" (Perls, 1948, p. 571). Thus, in order to bring about change, patients are taught to focus their awareness, which is the primary tool for effecting change in Gestalt Therapy. Frequently, undirected awareness alone is sufficient to ensure change. At other times a person needs to experiment with directing awareness, as in some of the exercises in Perls, Hefferline, and Goodman (1951, pp. 116ff.).

Gestalt Therapy emphasizes organismic self-regulation. The organism, in order to survive, needs to mobilize itself and its environment for support. The means whereby the organism contacts its environment is through the mobilization of aggression. If we successfully survive the attempts of others to civilize or enslave us, we pick and choose what we need from our environment to support ourselves. Picking and choosing, however, is not enough. We need also to chew up and swallow those parts of what is out there that we find edible and to our liking and thus make it (foor or idea or whatever) part of ourselves. What we do not need, we discard either as waste products or garbage, etc. Thus, if we are able to mobilize sufficient aggression to not only pick and choose but also chew up and swallow, we are able to get the support necessary for our survival. It is important to note that the organism itself picks and chooses, chews and swallows, etc., and not the significant other out there who determines for us what is palatable, nourishing, etc.

In Gestalt Therapy the therapist is frequently "active" in attempting to have the patient once again learn to use his sensory-motor equipment. At one time Dr. Perls described the process as a sort of "losing your mind to come to your senses" activity. This phrase means that the patient is taught how to direct his awareness via the resensitization of his primary sensory modalities: to look rather than stare, to listen rather than overhear, or to play deaf and dumb, and the like. Directed awareness experiments help the patient get off what I call the "Why merry-go-round." Many patients trust only their capacity to intellectualize, think, have fantasies. So when they become aware of a bit of their own behavior that is incongruous with their ideal self-image or role, they jump on the "Why merry-go-round" only to repeat the same unacceptable behavior and then again go chasing after reasons and explanations. Frequently, learning *how* by directing his awareness, the patient is able to undo the unacceptable behavior. At least, the patient does not remain an intellectual cripple.

In working with my patients in the "here and now," using the technique of directed awareness—"Where are you now?" or "What are you aware of now?" etc., I have discovered that usually verbal communication is indeed misleading or misdirecting and that body language is not. Thus, both the patient and I take his symptoms seriously in that these symptoms—I call them truth buttons or truth signals—communicate how a patient really feels. If he is in conflict, experimenting with first taking one side of the conflict in fantasy and then the other, he will inevitably bring on the body language, the truth signals, when he takes sides with that aspect of the conflict which is antiself.

Recently a patient was describing a conflict between continuing a project on his own that he had begun with a partner or dropping the project. His truth button was a hard, rocklike feeling in the pit of his stomach. He worked through his conflict by imagining first that he would continue the project without his partner and would see it through the acquiring of property, erecting a building, and manufacturing the article in the new plant. As he fantasied these various steps, he experienced increasing discomfort in his stomach; his "rock" was getting more and more unbearable. He then proceeded to fantasy dropping the project, abandoning the plans that had already been made plus his investment of time and money. At this point, he reported feeling more relaxed and comfortable, especially in the pit of his stomach. Experimenting several times (reversing so that at times he fantasied giving up the project first and at other times continuing the project first) brought the same results. The patient became convinced that he knew via his truth button which was the appropriate decision for him.

Being able to self-validate what is the "correct" solution through one's own body language is a tremendous help in the economy of psychotherapy. Many of the transference, countertransference difficulties can be avoided, as well as the pitfalls of interpretation, through teaching oneself and one's patients how to use their symptoms—how to listen to their own body language (Simkin, 1968, p. 4).

One of man's most basic experiences is excitement. If you become aware of your excitement and attempt to suppress its overt expression, you inevitably will wind up squeezing or tensing yourself. In addition, you will stop breathing. Perls formulated that excitement minus sufficient support of oxygen equals anxiety. And, as we know, anxiety is the experience least tolerated by the human organism.

In all the cases that I have seen so far, people seeking psychotherapy show an imbalance among their three primitive modes of experiencing. Most patients that I see, and this seems to be also true of the bulk of the patients seen by my colleagues, are very dependent on and have overly stressed their development of the intellectual or the "thinking-about" mode of experience. Most of the time, these people are in touch with their thought processes, and their experience is with a fantasy (memory) of the past or a fantasy (wish, prediction) of the future. Infrequently are they able to make contact with their feelings and many are also sensory cripples—not seeing or hearing or tasting, etc.

In the organismically balanced person, there is the capacity to experience intellectually and emotionally and sensorially. The therapeutic task therefore is to help the patient regain the use of his own equipment which has been desensitized at some earlier time and which now desensitized is no longer appropriately at his disposal.

Contrary to the approaches of some schools which stress "insight" or learning "why we behave the way we do," Gestalt Therapy stresses learning "how" and "what" we do. Gestalt therapists are convinced that the only possibility for changing behavior is through an awareness of what we are doing, that is, using our sensory and motor equipment as well as our intellectual equipment and knowing how well we are doing whatever it is we are engaged in.

In Gestalt Therapy we begin with the obvious, with what is ongoing at the moment, recognizing that patients can and do quickly learn to tell us dreams if we stress dreams as the "royal road to the unconscious!" Or, that patients will spend session after session dredging the past (telling us stories about their previous experiences) if we are convinced that cures are dependent on the recall of genetic material. Thus, my question to the patient: "Where are you now?" or "What are you experiencing now?" may lead to the past or a dream, but the patient may just as easily not be in fantasy; he may be experiencing in the "here and now" feelings of expectancy or joy or anger or whatever. He may be concentrating his awareness on sensory experiences, seeing the room we are in or listening to sounds or experiencing his body against the chair he is sitting in or the like.

Many patients are quite startled to discover that they filter every experience through their "thinking machine," that it is almost impossible for them to trust their feelings or senses without first getting approval, so to speak, from their intellect. Frequently, when a patient becomes aware that he is overly dependent on his intellectual equipment, he will try to manipulate me into telling him that he should not be so dependent. He is very fearful of exploring other modes of experience without some support—approval from me—if he cannot experience support within himself. All people need support from within and from without. Each person finds a suitable balance (for him) of self and environmental supports. Most patients have very little or very inadequate self-supports and tend to lean heavily on environmental supports. Then they become very hurt or disappointed or shattered when the other to whom they gave this power (the shifting of self-support to someone out there) fails to live up to their expectations.

During Freud's time, repression appeared to be the most frequently used defense. My own clinical experience leads me to conjecture that projection is now by far the most commonly encountered defense. We project onto another person those attributes or traits that we find unacceptable in ourselves. Then we point our finger at him and castigate him for being whatever it is we do not like in ourselves. This act permits us to maintain a fantasy or fiction of how we imagine we are rather than realizing and accepting how we are. The problem here is the problem of the introject: Swallowing something whole without first adequately chewing it up.

My primary psychotherapeutic task, as I see it, is to help the person I am working with accept himself. My patients say to me, in effect, "I want to change how I am." "I don't like myself when I act this way." "I'm so stupid." Yet, they expect to change how they are, not by fully experiencing their behavior and thus their discomfort, embarrassment, joy, humiliation, excitement, pleasure, shame (feeling) but by judging their behavior as bad, stupid, unacceptable, and the like (intellectual judgments) and thus talking about rather than fully coming in contact with what they do and how they do it. And, paradoxically, these people will be the first to claim the organismic truism that "we learn from experience." They confuse "thinking about" with experiencing.

I trust that if I fully experience what I do and how I behave, I will successfully finish (complete) a particular bit of behavior and learn

from this experience. The crux is how I learn. Do I learn by fully experiencing organismically (sensing and feeling as well as judging), or
must I restrict my experience to "thinking about"? When my patient
says: "I did it again. I got angry at my wife and beat her," my patient
is telling me a story (a memory of an event that has already taken
place). I may ask, "What are you aware of now?" If his response is,
"See how stupid I am; I never learn. I repeat the same idiotic behavior!" I may ask, "In telling me stories?" Once he understands what he
is doing now, telling me a story and thus keeping two situations unfinished—the beating of his wife by recalling the memory of the
event and the using of this memory with me now, playing the good
patient perhaps by telling me how "bad" or "stupid" he is—he has the
possibility of learning how he remains stupid. He can only learn by
being fully aware of what he is experiencing. The other way he is
split into the two (sometimes more) aspects of himself.

Dr. Perls referred to these two selves as the top dog and under-dog
who are constantly carrying on an internal (infernal might be a better
term!) dialogue. "You stupid idiot, why did you beat her again?"
"Gee, I'm sorry, I promise I won't do it again." Or, "How many
times do I have to tell you not to repeat that silly mistake?" "I'm
going to do better next time, I promise." Perls claimed that the
underdog self—the promiser—usually wins: he defeats the top dog
through unkept promises, sabotage, etc. I believe that the underdog
always wins.

The integration of these selves, the full acceptance of how one is
rather than how one should be, leads to the possibility of change. As
long as people persist in remaining split and not fully acknowledging
(taking sides with and experiencing) what and how they are, real
change, I believe, is not possible.

To illustrate, an excerpt from a training film follows:

Jim: What do you experience at this moment?
Colman: A feeling of sadness . . . I don't know why. Because I said
   that they were in, I said I wanted them in.
Jim: Yeah. Colman, would you be willing to say now that you are
   sad.
Colman: I am sad.
Jim: Again.
Colman: I'm sad. I'm sad. And I'm angry.
Jim: Yeah.
Colman: Crazy.
Jim: Okay, add that. "I'm sad, I'm angry, I'm crazy."

Colman: I'm sad, I'm angry, I'm crazy.

Jim: And now?

Colman: Now I feel good again.

Jim: Yeah. Now I think you're beginning to catch on. Anytime that you acknowledge, really go with how you are, you finish . . . let go. You are sad, you are angry, you are crazy, you are happy, and so on. If you stay with . . . all your me's.

Colman: My sad, angry, crazy me.

Jim: Yeah. Okay, I'd like to stop at this point.

This excerpt illustrates how, by Colman being aware (responsible), his sadness changes first to anger and then his anger changes to perplexity and then he experiences the humor of his situation and then feels "good again." Much of the impact of this transaction, however, is not conveyed through the arid medium of the printed word. The best way to fully experience Gestalt Therapy is obviously through the experiential mode.

As Fagan and Shepherd say in their preface: "In Gestalt Therapy, much importance is attached to tone of voice, posture, gestures, facial expression, etc., with much of the import and excitement coming from work with changes in these nonverbal communications. . . . Fortunately the increasing availability of Gestalt films and tapes helps in making the nonverbal communications more accessible" (Fagan and Shepherd, 1970, p. viii). Or, in the words of the late Fritz Perls, "To suffer one's own death and to be reborn is not easy" (Perls, *Gestalt Therapy Verbatim*, 1969).

REFERENCES

Fagan, J. and I. L. Shepherd. *Gestalt Therapy Now*. Palo Alto, Calif.: Science and Behavior Books, 1970.

Kogan, J. *Gestalt Therapy Resources*. San Francisco: Lode Star Press, 1970.

Lederman, J. *Anger and the Rocking Chair: Gestalt Awareness with Children*. New York: McGraw-Hill, 1969.

Perls, F. S. "Theory and Technique of Personality Integration," *American Journal of Psychotherapy*, 2 (1948), 565-586.

―――*Ego, Hunger and Aggression*. London: Allen & Unwin, 1947 (Republished: New York: Random House, 1969).

―――*Gestalt Therapy Verbatim*. Moab, Utah: Real People Press, 1969.

―――*In and Out of the Garbage Pail*. Moab, Utah: Real People Press, 1969 (Bantam edition, 1972).

―――R. F. Hefferline, and P. Goodman. *Gestalt Therapy*. New York: Julian Press, 1951 (Dell edition, 1965).

Perls, L. "Notes on the Psychology of Give and Take." *Complex*, 9 (1953), 24-30.

―――"Two Instances of Gestalt Therapy," *Case Reports in Clinical Psychology*. Brooklyn: Kings County Hospital, 1956.

Polster, E. A. Contemporary Psychotherapy. *Psychotherapy: Theory, Research and Practice*, 3 (1966), 1-6.

Pursglove, P. D. (ed.). *Recognitions in Gestalt Therapy*. New York: Funk and Wagnalls, 1968.

Simkin, J. S. (ed.). *Festschrift for Fritz Perls*. Los Angeles: Author, 1968.

————*Innovations in Gestalt Therapy Techniques.* Unpublished manuscript, 1968.

————Individual Gestalt Therapy: Interview with Dr. Frederick Perls. Audio-tape recording, A.A.P. Tape Library, No. 31. Philadelphia, Pa., 1967.

————*In the Now.* A training film. Beverly Hills, 1969.

————*An Introduction to the Theory of Gestalt Therapy.* Cleveland: Gestalt Institute of Cleveland, No. 6, 1966.

Van Dusen, W. "Existential Analytic Psychotherapy," *American Journal of Psychoanalysis,* 20 (1960), 35-40.

Warren, H. C. *Dictionary of Psychology.* Boston: Houghton Mifflin, 1934.

Yontef, G. M. *A Review of the Practice of Gestalt Therapy.* Los Angeles: Trident Shop, California State College, 1969.

CHAPTER 6

THE GENESIS OF
GESTALT THERAPY

JERRY KOGAN, Ph.D.

Jerry Kogan recently retired from private practice in Berkeley, California, in order to study with the Zen painter and philosopher Rudolph Ray. He teaches at Diablo Valley College, Pleasant Hill, California and is also a member of the training faculty of the San Francisco Gestalt Institute.

This essay is a first attempt at exploring the cultural history of Gestalt Therapy, which was a uniquely European and American synthesis of existentialism and phenomenology developed over a period of forty years by Fritz Perls and Laura Perls.

The perspective of what you are about to read is mainly geographical. As your guide, my intention is to provide you with some sense of the broadest parameters of the terrain, occasionally plumbing the depth of one region or another. The regions of this essay are like the points of the compass to Gestalt Therapy, and in fact describe something of the flow of life—one life in particular, that of Fritz Perls, the co-founder of Gestalt Therapy.

EUROPEAN INFLUENCES

Perls' manuscript *Ego, Hunger and Aggression* completed in 1941-2, was the necessary bridge he created between his past and his present, and offers precise evidence of the formative European influences on Gestalt Therapy. Although it was not until some years later (1950) that the name, character, and form of "Gestalt Therapy" were officially born,[1] Perls' first book crystallized the various influences upon his conceptualizations over the previous two decades of his life. Between the two world wars, Perls' principal teachers were Sigmund Freud,[2] Wilhelm Reich, Sigmund Friedlander, Professor Galb, Kurt Goldstein, and Laura Perls. Of a secondary influence were Karen Horney, Max Wertheimer, Wolfgang Kohler, Kurt Lewin, I. A. Richards, and J. C. Smuts. Collectively, these people and their ideas constitute what I have here identified as the European influences on Gestalt Therapy. The following chart attempts to delineate two relative dimensions in respect to European influences upon Perls: time and importance.

EUROPEAN INFLUENCES ON PERLS

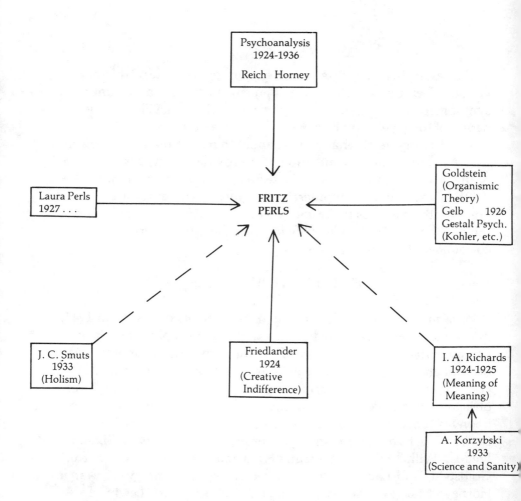

Solid line = primary influence

Broken line = secondary influence

Psychoanalysis provided Perls a theoretical framework for all his subsequent thinking, and was a constant against which he checked out points of similarity and difference. However, psychosexuality, the structure and nature of the unconscious, the tripartite anatomy of personality (id, ego, superego), and the principles of behavior were omitted from Perls' writings. Instead he mainly directed his attention to the etiology of the neurosis, taking a significantly different view from that of classical psychoanalytic theory.

Two conclusions can be drawn from his omissions—that in principle he had no disagreement with the major Freudian postulates, and that his focus was originally less theoretical and more applied and behavioristic. The latter correlates with the concept of the emergent gestalt, with its emphasis on *how* and not *why*, and the here and now. For example, to Perls the neuroses represented "holes" in development; psychodiagnostically, they were manifest as incomplete awareness. Nevertheless, despite such differences, psychoanalytic theory was for Perls the major foundation upon which he built his understanding of human behavior. Not until much later in Perls' life, however, do we see his constructs as something like a life-orienting philosophy rather than psychodynamic system of existential psychotherapy.

It was Karen Horney who directed the young and rebellious Perls to the very rebellious and eccentric Reich. Of her, Perls says (1969b), "from Horney, [I got] human involvement without terminology." Reich, in addition to being Perls' training analyst, introduced him to the idea of body armor [3] in the somatic translation of the neurosis. Perls wrote: "It was W. Reich who first directed my attention to a most important aspect of psychosomatic medicine—to the function of the motoric system as an armor" (1947, p. 5). This "piece of reality [he later noted] gave Freud's resistance notion a body" (1969b). Later it gave Perls some basis for his own theory of the neurosis. In the chart, Reich is placed to the far left, as he was in the psychoanalytic movement.

Professors Gelb and Goldstein were teachers of Perls in 1926, when he worked at the Goldstein Institute for brain-damaged soldiers in Frankfurt, Germany. It was also at this time that Perls became acquainted with the work of the Gestalt laboratory psychologists, particularly Max Wertheimer (to whom *Ego, Hunger and Aggression* is dedicated) and Wolfgang Kohler (and later, in the United States, Kurt Lewin, of whose work Perls spoke highly). As to the Gestalt psychologists, Perls said,

My relation to the Gestalt psychologists was a peculiar one. I admired a lot of their work, especially the early work of Kurt Lewin. I could not go along when they became logical positivists. I have not read any of their textbooks, only some papers of Lewin, Wertheimer, and Kohler. Most important to me was the idea of the unfinished situation, the incomplete gestalt. The academic Gestaltists of course never accepted me. I certainly was not a pure Gestaltist.

My prominent fantasy was that they were all alchemists looking for gold, for complete verification, and that I was satisfied to use the less impressive but more useful products that fell by the wayside (1969b).

Thus, early in Perls' development, practicality and a regard for utility were a part of his emergent needs; both are recurrent themes found among Perls' students. In the structure of the diagram, Goldstein and Gelb are located with the Gestaltists, for indeed both were influenced in their study of brain damage by such Gestalt laboratory concepts as figure/ground, the emergent and ever-changing gestalt, the unfinished gestalt, etc.

Perls credits Goldstein for introducing him to Gestalt psychology, of which Perls had actually read little.

To Professor K. Goldstein, I owe my first acquaintance with Gestalt psychology. Unfortunately, in 1926, when I worked under him at the Frankfurt Neurological Institute, I was still too preoccupied with the orthodox psychoanalytical approach to assimilate more than a fraction of what was offered to me (1947, p. 5).

Goldstein's theory of holism, with its emphasis on figure/ground as a primary organizing function of the organism is a principle cardinal to the practice of Gestalt Therapy. Goldstein's appeal to Perls was strong but not sufficiently spiritual to draw him from the psychoanalytical fold; this Perls accomplished himself much later with his first revisionist formulation, *Ego, Hunger and Aggression* (subtitled *A revision of Freud's Theory and Method*). To this point, psychoanalytic thinking dominated Perls' attention. His introduction to Gestalt concepts, however, provided him significant new ideas, most of which later became central to his therapy.

Several years prior to Perls' work at the Goldstein Institute he was influenced by the ideas of Sigmund Friedlander. Friedlander, a

German philosopher, had a lasting and dynamic impact upon Perls and his Gestalt philosophy. Friedlander's philosophy concerned two cardinal ideas—creative indifference and differential thinking. Differential thinking proposes that:

> . . .every event is related to a zero point from which a differentiation of opposites takes place. These opposites show in their specific context a great affinity to each other. By remaining alert in the center, we can acquire a creative ability of seeing both sides of an occurrence and completing an incomplete half. By avoiding a one-sided outlook we gain a much deeper insight into the structure and function of the organism (Perls, 1947, p. 15).

Differential thinking, then, means *thinking in opposites*, which is a paradoxical rather than a linear cause-effect thinking modality. "Causality," according to Perls, "is a clumsy conception" (ibid., p. 21) and produces the Freudian effect of overdetermination. Differential thinking is more closely related to Eastern thought forms than to Western ontology, which abounds in splits and dichotomies. Friedlander, according to Perls (1969b),

> . . . brought a simple way of primary orientation. Whatever is, will differentiate into opposites. If you are caught by one of the opposing forces you are trapped, or at least lopsided. If you stay in the *nothing* of the zero center, you are balanced and in perspective.

When, according to Perls, thinking in opposites is achieved (differential thinking) then we have full interest "extending toward both sides of the differentiation" (1947, p. 15). This is called "creative indifference."

Friedlander, whom Perls describes as "one of my three gurus," (Perls, 1969b) gave him a connecting link between Gestalt psychology and Zen and the concept of nothingness—and with Perls' own later formulation of figure/ground reversals, and the emergent gestalt. Friedlander's concepts eventually clarified for Perls Goldstein's term "self-actualization" (used also by Maslow thirty years later), which in 1926 meant little or nothing to Perls. In my view, Friedlander's conceptualizations were decisive in Perls' development and were eventually instrumental in his break with psychoanalysis.[4]

Another European influence upon Perls' thinking was the work of the English semanticist, I. A. Richards (*The Meaning of Meaning*,

1923) and, later, A. Korzybski (*Science and Sanity*, 1933). Richards, like Korzybski (and, later, the general semanticists), was concerned with word-object confusion and, more importantly, with the effect of language upon thought and behavior. Many of Perls' ideas are closely related to principles of general semantics, particularly splits and dichotomies and the relationship of the Aristotelian two-value system to both cognition and conation. In the practice of Gestalt Therapy, Perls distinguished between thought and feeling. In this process, he encouraged greater precision of meaning, as, for example, in the use of I/it, me/one. In analyzing Perls' work, similarities between semantic theory and Gestalt Therapy are striking. Given little more than an occasional reference to these semanticists, the importance of semantic theory to the development of Gestalt Therapy is a product of my analysis rather than some clear link of documentation.

Laura Perls was yet another ("European") influence upon Fritz. From the perspective of this analysis, I consider her the co-founder of Gestalt Therapy. Laura and Fritz met in 1926 in Frankfurt, Germany, at a lecture given by Professor Gelb. At the time Laura was a student at the university, where later she received a Ph.D. in psychology. Fritz, perhaps romantically, identified himself as coming from a "lower middle class" Jewish family; Laura's family, in contrast, was affluent, materially and culturally. Laura's family, like Fritz's, was not particularly involved in Jewish life—a fact which seems also characteristic of their life together. A biography of Laura is much needed for future study of Gestalt Therapy.

Laura and Fritz worked closely together until at least the 1950s— a period of perhaps twenty-five years. In fact, when Fritz left South Africa for America with the intention of establishing a home there, Laura assumed his private practice. Durint their years together the content and form of Gestalt Therapy were developing and maturing.

The particular contributions made by Laura Perls are obscured in the available literature on Gestalt Therapy for two important reasons. The first is that although Gestalt Therapy was introduced in America at the New York Gestalt Institute by Fritz and Laura, it was not until Fritz found a home at Esalen Institute at Big Sur, California, where literally thousands came to work and study with him, that Gestalt Therapy was nominally recognized as a new psychotherapy. During this time Fritz became known as the discoverer, the father, of Gestalt Therapy, recognitions he deeply coveted and proudly fostered. Meanwhile, Laura's residence in New York City put her outside the mainstream of the human potential movement, which ostensibly began in California. The second fact accounting for Laura's special contributions being obscured is that she published few of her papers and was consequently known only to a handful of people. Those familiar with the work of Laura and Fritz note interesting differences in their separate practice of Gestalt Therapy. Among these are the dimensions of control and permissiveness. In Laura's work there is a more apparent permissiveness, while in Fritz's work, more apparent control. How these differences have been integrated into Gestalt Therapy and how during their life together their separate ideas were mingled seem questions for further study.

From Fritz, at least this much is clear about Laura's contributions to *Ego, Hunger and Aggression*:

> . . . [I] had much help, stimulation and encouragement from books, friends and teachers; but above all from my wife, Dr. Lore Perls. The discussions I have had with her of the problems brought forward in this book have clarified many issues; and she has made valuable contributions to this work . . . (p. 5).

And in his autobiography, *In and Out of the Garbage Pail*, Fritz discusses some aspects of their initial meeting and life together, and again attributes to Laura specific insights such as the observance of the front/rear or the upper/under carriage splits. Overall, however, Fritz effectively assigns Laura a minor role in the development of Gestalt Therapy.

More may be said about Fritz's European influences by future scholars. In my view, these are the most pertinent. I continue now with the main historical and geographical approach of this essay.

In the early 1930s, prompted by the rise of Hitler to power, Fritz (and Laura) moved to South Africa.[5] Anti-Semitism was on the rise and Perls' survival behavior was alerted. In Germany, Fritz had met or known most of the scholars and psychologists of the day. For him this period of intellectual excitement and creativity was over—there was no more "Vienna Circle," not even figuratively.

According to a resume Fritz prepared in the late 1960s,[6] while in Johannesburg, South Africa, he was a training psychoanalyst from 1934 to 1942;[7] he established the South African Institute for Psychoanalysis in 1935, and was an army psychiatrist from 1924 to 1945. In reflecting on the various people whose work had influenced him, Fritz had often referred to the philosophy of Jan Christian Smuts, whose major work, *Holism and Evolution*, lent further support to Perls' developing ideas. Some years after the appearance of this book, Smuts became Prime Minister of the Union of South Africa.

In 1941-2 Fritz wrote his first book, *Ego, Hunger and Aggression*, a new formulation of orthodox psychoanalytic theory, existentialism, semantics, and Gestalt psychology.[8] This work formed the bridge to Gestalt Therapy. It was a clear break with every traditional clinical model. Perls had made a quantum leap into his own creative maturity.

JEWISH INFLUENCES

Fritz Perls was like a Moses, eschewing false gods, leading the children of Israel out of a wilderness to a promised land. The wilderness was unawareness. The children were his students. The false gods those constructed from abstract philosophic rationalism.

For some, Perls was a prophet, teacher, and guru. To others, he was merely a therapist. Still others saw him with disdain, as a magician, a charlatan, and manipulator of people. And still others saw him as a charlatan, magician, prophet, guru, teacher, *and* manipulator of people. One way or another, everyone with whom he made contact went away affected by the man and his cosmology.

Of the man himself, little has yet been written. Of his books and papers only *In and Out of the Garbage Pail* provides us a clear and direct channel to Perls as he lived and worked. While no biographical descriptions of him have yet been completed by any of his students, these people are sources of much interesting and valuable anecdotal material.[9]

Here Perls' Jewishness is considered and several questions are posed: *What is the nature of Perls' Jewishness?* and, *How has the effect of that Jewishness been manifest in Gestalt Therapy?* Toward some understanding of these questions, Perls himself has provided very little information; as he remarks in his autobiography, *In and Out of the Garbage Pail*,

> My relation to Judaism and the Jews is extremely undefined. I know quite a bit about German, Greek, and Roman history. About the history of—I can't even say my people, so little am I identified with them—the Jewish people, I know next to nothing. The East European Jews with the caftans and payes [long whisker curls] that I saw in my youth were uncanny, frightening, like monks, not belonging to my world. Yet I love Jewish stories and their pregnant wit. Israelis come frequently to my

seminars, and especially if they are Sabra [born in Israel], I am prejudiced in their favor. I have veneration and appreciation for the wholesome Jew who is one with his religion, history, and way of life. Their Zionism makes sense, though I looked and still look upon Zionism as an unrealistic, foolish sentimentality. The majority of Jews did not come to Israel in spirit. They came as refugees from Hitler, and there are many places in the world where Jewish ingenuity could have made deserts bloom more easily, and with less dissemination of hostility. In the balance, however, I bow to you, Israel, and your Makabbi spirit. Even the American anti-Semitism has greatly diminished. To be a Jew no longer disqualifies one automatically from a job for which he is fit. As for the latent American Fascism, the target will be the Negro and the hippie rather than the Jew, and the Negro will not suffer it as submissively, with cowardice, as the European Jew did. He has tasted freedom, and flexes his muscles.

Thus, while Perls was deeply impressed by particular facets of Jewish cultural life, evidently he understood little of the effect of his own Jewishness upon his personality or therapeutic system. What, one may wonder, might account for Perls' "undefined" relation to his own Jewishness? A partial answer to this question is found in Fritz's early life. As a German Jew, particularly a Berlin-born Jew, Fritz Perls was among the most assimilated of European Jewry. These Jews, not unlike American Jews, often identified themselves along national rather than religious and cultural lines. Moreover, as assimilated Jews, their education was only secondarily Hebrew. In addition, from Fritz's own writing, there is little to indicate that his family life provided him much of a source of support for understanding of being a Jew.

In a broader context further insight to the question of how the effect of Perls' Jewishness has been manifest in Gestalt Therapy may be found in a study of a dual trend in Jewish history itself. This dual trend refers to the Talmudic and Kabbalistic traditions, a theme I have more completely developed elsewhere. [10] In Perls' genesis and evolution his Jewishness as reflected in Gestalt Therapy is both Talmudic and Kabbalistic. His concerns for and with spontaneity and creativity are not a concomitant attack upon intellect, although he did aim to "make paper people real people." However, like Buber, Perls may be more clearly identified with the antirational, mystical element of the Jewish faith.

Beyond such broad aspects, Perls did manifest specific characteristics of Jewishness. For example, in his life there is a "wandering

Jew," a "to-the-promised-land" quality, which in the idiom of America is like a Horatio Alger story. In his autobiography, he says of himself,

> . . . from an obscure lower middle class Jewish boy to a mediocre psychoanalyst to the possible creator of a "new" method of treatment and the exponent of a viable philosophy which could do something for mankind (1969b).

Like the millenial wandering Jew, he sought his promised land in Europe, later in South Africa, in world travels (especially to Israel and Japan), in the United States, and then finally in Canada, where, in British Columbia, he created the first Gestalt community—which he considered a kibbutz. Other Jewish aspects of Perls' personality are his humor and depressiveness, his optimism, his longing and searching, and his avowed belief in the authority of each individual, perhaps based on the direct relation each Jew has with God. All these qualities are at once specifically characteristic of Perls, of Gestalt Therapy and of the Jews themselves.

AMERICAN INFLUENCES

Gestalt Therapy, as a major articulated phenomenological-educational philosophy, [11] both received energy from the human potential movement in America and also gave energy and focus to that movement. The period of time considered here roughly corresponds to the years Fritz Perls lived in America—1947 to 1970. Kurt Goldstein emphasized "the inner determinants of behavior and the principle that the organism finds the environment which is most appropriate for self-actualization," although of course the organism "is not immune to the events in the external world" (Hall and Lindzey, 1957, p. 304). Perls was not of course immune to the events of Nazism and world war, but his travels brought him to America, to the West Coast of America, and to Esalen Institute, which turned out to be a most appropriate environment for his own self-actualization, and the first place he found numbers of people who would utilize his concepts.

In America, the human potential movement grew out of what may have been the most dismal decades of national life and culture. To comprehend the form, energy, and direction of this movement, we must briefly explore what is by now a fairly well-documented period of national malaise and indirection. Writers in many fields of inquiry

(Cousins, 1945; Friedenberg, 1963; Goodman, 1956; Larrabee and Meyersohn, 1958; Lewis, 1963; Riesman, Glazer, and Denney, 1950; Rosenberg and White, 1957; Tournier, Frankl, Levinson, Thielicke, Lehmann and Miller, 1966; Wheelis, 1958) have discussed the quality of life during the post-World War II decades; the 1971 film *The Last Picture Show* characterizes the sad ambience of this period.

In *Ego, Hunger and Aggression* Perls discusses the appearance of the visualization of water in the mind of a person whose body is suffering an absence of water (p. 34). Thus, Perls' organismic theory of environmental disturbance leading to felt needs in the organism, which then reaches out to fulfill these needs, may serve as an operating model to explain the paradox of the eruption of the humanistic psychology movement during a period of national life which was so entirely opposed to it.

The Disappearance of Authorities: Values in Conflict

Many writers have chronicled the history of disappearing authorities in our century:

> . . . Some say God died. This much we know: everything that was nailed down suddenly came loose. Chaos was king and the moral world looked like a furniture store after a hurricane. Everywhere the credentials of the authorities were challenged and great impostors were discovered in high circles. The consensus about morals disintegrated in pluralism. The credibility of revelation, and therefore the whole massive structure of organized religion, was gradually eroded away by empirical and pragmatic habits of thought. . . . So what is there left to trust? Perhaps even this story about the death of the authorities is false. There is no way to tell for certain because there are no authorities to tell us. When the gods speak with conflicting voices, or are silent, the men must decide. If authority has collapsed, where is the individual to discover the principles of a style of life which is authentic? Indeed, by what criteria is he to decide what an "authentic" life style is (Keen, 1970, pp. 1-2)?

The conflict of values produced by the absence of trusted authorities has been described by Carl Rogers.

> The world culture, in all its aspects, seems increasingly scientific and relativistic, and the rigid, absolute views on values

which come to us from the past appear anachronistic. Even more important perhaps, is the fact that the modern individual is assailed from every angle by divergent and contradictory value claims. It is no longer possible, as it was in the not too distant historical past, to settle comfortably into one's community and live out one's life without ever examining the nature and the assumptions of that system.

In this situation it is not surprising that value orientations from the past appear to be in a state of disintegration or collapse. Men question whether there are, or can be, any universal values. It is often felt that we may have lost, in our modern world, all possibility of any general or cross-cultural basis for values. One natural result of this uncertainty and confusion is that there is an increasing concern about, interest in, and a searching for, a sound or meaningful value approach which can hold its own in today's world (Rogers and Stevens, 1967, p. 13).

Rapid changes undermined values; an emergent value was speed itself—which conflicted harshly with common sense. Alvin Toffler, in his book *Future Shock* (1970), makes this point, as does C. Marshall Lowe (1969), who observed:

In this century time's flow has become a flood which renders values anachronistic even within the same generation. Some feel socially dispossessed because they have not had time to attain the latest mode of good living before that vision of the American dream is swept into historical oblivion. . . . The good which our society allows its members to achieve is already outmoded, having been replaced by something better which is not yet attainable. The results are chronic frustration and confusion in a search for moral permanence (p. 6).

The collective impact of these forces intensified personal uncertainty for many and produced profound loneliness, while at the same time a national search for immediate, temporal relief ensued. Meanwhile, we depended on a traditional American idea—abundance. Our answer was "more"—more defense, more consumer goods, more, more, more. All of this described the curious paradox of a demand for immediate pleasure and a concomitant sense of continual wanting—a split which manifested itself spiritually as *anomie* and behaviorally as energistic deadness. Our leaders were political, industrial, or militaristic men, whose values characterized state and corporate ideals. These values represented the apotheosis of "the man in the gray flannel suit" and the denouement of the Western humanist heritage. Human values such as decency toward oneself and others, joy, love, human spirituality, community, creativity, and spontaneity suffered; and the apparent health of our people was belied by the decay rising from the urban centers of America, as well as from our militaristic excesses on foreign soil.

The Search for Values in Education

Although traditional values disintegrated and personal anxiety increased, we still nominally proclaimed our traditional social and religious standards. However, as Lowe (1969) observed:

In times past the final good was God, who was quite clearly known. But, first for Nietzsche and now for many others, God is dead. If God is the highest good and He cannot now be known, then the ultimate nature of good and evil is similarly unknown. Man today, left without clear-cut beliefs of what is good and bad, experiences so-called existential anxiety (p. 7).

The private search for meaning and values which could somehow make sense in one's own life experience was frequently unarticulated, but confoundingly real. Lowe (1969), Frankl (1962), Fromm, (1961), and others have shown how the search for personal meaning to life focused in the area of secular pursuits—in work, material possessions, and culture heroes (rock and roll singers, movie stars, athletes).

Values were also being sought in education, which superseded religion as the major culture carrier. Although education had long been seen as a major avenue of social mobility and material improvement, the traditional model of education in America (our democratic professions notwithstanding) was the German one of private, authoritarian training for the elite and vocational training for the rest. The GI Bill and Sputnik changed this, promoting education from a position of being valued by all, but available only to the elite, to one where education became nominally available to all. (Black-white consciousness, women's liberation, and indeed all ethnic consciousness that questioned this assumed availability had not yet been popularly born. The American dream of prosperity and goodness became more generally reachable. "To be educated" meant at least a high school education; in the decade of the 1950's "success" came to mean a college degree.

The 1950s brought theorists of education into endless debate over what the content and form of education should be. Concomitantly, education provided a secular value system which was as bureaucratically clumsy as its religious counterpart. During this same period, the cliches "education for life" and "educating the whole child" were frequently heard; yet (as in every neurotic condition, whether personal or national) little attention was given to the obvious—the clients of education. "Progressive" theorists notwithstanding, the actual experience for many of those being educated was vague, yet rigid, at once boring and alienating. And still, for the college students at least, the college experience remained a delayed four-year hustle to the job market.

All acceptable popular forms of education—including radio, television, and motion pictures (the comic books may have provided for many one of the few forms of escape into creative imagination)—served largely to undermine the phenomena of individual experience. Formal education, particularly public education, was a dismal failure for many people. Challenges to educational anachronisms were few, but glinted with promise of something different, of something better. Paul Goodman, a frequent critic of education, spoke sharply against its rampant absurdities. Goodman and Perls knew each other; they worked closely together in the first years of Perls' life in America. In fact, Perls credits Goodman for being influential in his decision to come to America from South Africa. [12] Goodman, Fritz, and Laura established the first Gestalt Institute in America, in New York City in 1951. Perls recognized that Goodman's work on thesis and antithesis helped crystalize his own work with polarities and was a significant American contribution to Gestalt Therapy. In a letter to me (March 14, 1975) Laura Perls urges,

> "More credit is due to Paul Goodman without whom there would not have been a coherent theory of Gestalt Therapy as conceived in the second part of *Gestalt Therapy: Excitement and Growth in the Human Personality.*"

Developments in Psychotherapy

As the emergence of the human potential movement gave hope for education, so did it for American psychology, particularly clinical psychology. In the post-World War II era, psychology gained attention and value, just as did education. At one time, psychotherapy was the prerogative of only a privileged few Americans. The method most used, psychodynamic psychotherapy, was principally analytical, conducted on a one-to-one basis, and consequently lengthy in duration. It was far too costly for most Americans. Also, the emphasis in American psychology was upon what was wrong with the individual, upon symptomology; it was a psychology of mental illness. Few then would have agreed with Abraham Maslow's belief that "if psychologists study crippled, stunted, neurotic people exclusively they are bound to produce a crippled psychology" (Hall and Lindzey, 1957, p. 327).

In this climate of morbidity Perls continued to develop Gestalt Therapy. While his principal formulations probably were complete by the early 1950s, place and time were not yet congruous for him. Gestalt Therapy was relatively unknown in America until Perls went to Esalen Institute in 1963. Meanwhile, in 1955 Perls traveled around the world, stopping to study at a Zen Buddhist temple in Kyoto, Japan; later, he spent some time in Israel.

Before and after Perls' arrival in America, changes in American psychology and psychotherapy were occurring, however fractionally. Group dynamics and small-group research was an early development. In 1939 Kurt Lewin coined the term "group dynamics." [13] Lewin's work in field theory and its application in group dynamics clearly demonstrated the reciprocal effect of groups and individuals upon behavior. Group dynamics eventually became a major vehicle for the human potential movement, in part by focusing attention away from "sick" behavior of a "patient" viewed individually by a psychiatrist and toward the "normal" and even healthy behavior of people in different group situations.

In my analysis, the group dynamics movement vitally contributed to the eventual form of Gestalt Therapy, and the group workshop form of Gestalt Therapy that Perls eventually favored is in fact an American development. His earliest paper on this subject was "Workshop vs. Individual Therapy," published in 1966.

The richly heuristic work of two important American psychologists, Abraham Maslow and Carl Rogers, was instrumental in creating a climate for a dramatic shift in our view of human illness and potential for health (what we have called the human potential movement). Maslow, it appears to me, was one of the gentle men of American psychology. This gentleness was combined with a talmudic reverence for the spirit of the intellect, both qualities reflected in his concept of self-actualization. His early writings, brought together in *Motivation and Personality* (1954), aligned him with "an organismic, or as he calls it, a holistic-dynamic point of view" (Hall and Lindzey, 1957, p. 325). In my analysis Maslow's need-motivation theory corresponds to and complements Perls' view of unfinished business and Gestalt psychology's concept of closure—that unsatisfied needs demand attention and press forward, consuming both attention and energy until satisfied. This satisfaction may be now or never; however, we remain stuck at one or another level of development accordingly.

Although not providing either a clinical or especially articulated theoretical model, Maslow did much toward giving the study of human potential scientific respectability. If Perls was at the furthest outpost of exploration in his practice of Gestalt Therapy, Maslow provided fuel and nurturance to the whole of the human potential movement, which also partially sustained Gestalt Therapy.

Another major figure is Carl Rogers. His influence was and still is of enormous importance to American education and psychology. Thousands of students in colleges and universities throughout the country became his disciples and their effect seems incalculable. Rogers also stressed self-actualization. "Self-actualization" in one or another form was easily translated into our American ethos and provided a banner for the human potential movement. Rogers' formulations of unconditional positive regard and "feedback" which was "client-centered" can also be observed in the practice of Gestalt Therapy, although the latter is not limited to these formulations. According to Rogers,

> . . . the therapist has been able to enter into an intensely personal and subjective relationship with this client—relating not as a scientist to an object of study, not as a physician expecting to diagnose and cure—but as a person to a person (Hall and Lindzey, 1957, p. 475).

This I understand, is what Buber meant by "I and Thou." Although Gestalt Therapy appears significantly different from Rogers' client-centered therapy in practice, philosophical similarities are apparent. Most important of these is the phenomenological nature of the person—a view held by both Rogers and Perls.

Maslow and Rogers provided American psychology an impetus for change from which Perls distinctly benefited. Perls and his theories appealed to people who had been affected by Maslow and Rogers and their holistic attitude concerning the person.

Perhaps the single most exciting contribution to spurring the human potential movement was the creation of Esalen Institute at

Big Sur, California, by Michael Murphy and Richard Price, in 1961. Although a history of Esalen seems eminently worthwhile, it is beyond the scope of this chapter.[14] This brilliant creation brought together thousands of people from all over the world, from street people to the most eminent men and women of letters and science. By 1965 the institute was *the* major center for humanistic psychology in America and by 1972 literally hundreds of growth centers through the United States and the world were operating on the Esalen model.[15]

Fritz Perls arrived at Esalen in 1963 and made the institute his home and official base of work. During his residence at Esalen of nearly six years, Gestalt Therapy firmly established itself as an articulated statement of Western phenomenology.[16] Contemporaneously, many of the same people involved with Esalen participated in forming the Association for Humanistic Psychology; a list of the organizing members included some of the most notable American psychologists, such as A. H. Maslow, Clark Moustakas, Joe K. Adams, to name but a few. The Association of Humanistic Psychology provided morale and an apparent value system that could coherently address itself to a psychology "that takes account of gaiety, exuberance, love and well-being" (Hall and Lindzey, 1957, p. 325, quoting Maslow). These were the values so conspicuously absent from American life, education, and psychology during the dismal 1950s.

GESTALT THERAPY AFTER PERLS

At his death in 1970, Fritz had many students throughout the United States. His wife, Laura Perls, who was instrumental in the development of Gestalt Therapy, separately continued her work in New York City. I identify the students of Fritz and Laura as the first generation of Gestalt therapists. Those they trained became second-generation Gestalt therapists. Currently a third generation is in training in California and elsewhere. Although no certification in the general public sense is offered by the various training institutes, trainees are usually already certified in a helping profession—education, clinical psychology, psychiatry, social work, and nursing.

One such institute, the San Francisco Gestalt Institute, trains approximately sixty students per year, in a continuous two-year training curriculum. At the San Francisco Institute, half or more of the training therapists are first-generation students of Perls. The other major Gestalt training centers are located in Cleveland, New York and Los Angeles.

Gestalt Therapy is also being practiced by probation officers, social workers, college and high school counselors, nurses, dentists, and many others. Furthermore, many psychotherapists practicing behavior modification, conjoint family therapy, transactional analysis, and various psychoanalytic therapies have found ways of integrating the technology of Gestalt Therapy into their orientations. Gestalt Therapy is more and more evident in many different settings —schools, hospitals, dental, and legal professions. Thus, at the time of Fritz's death, there were thousands of Gestaltists in America.

One fascinating account of the application of Gestalt Therapy to education is given by G. I. Brown in his Ford-Esalen study.[17] Brown offers a guidance system for the education of persons in the twentieth century—a means through which, by attention to total human needs, creative potential may be actualized. Affective education, as he calls it, is concerned with the noncognitive side of learning, the integration of emotions, feelings, interests, values, and character with the more traditional sensibilities. Brown provides a brilliant example of his own integration and application of Gestalt Therapy to education.

Another example is given by Janet Lederman's study.[18] She offers us a poetic account of Gestalt Therapy in the classroom. Of her work, Perls has said,

> In front of our eyes we see a miracle performed. We see what might be potential criminals find their bearings not in unbridled rage but in a center of a budding personality. We see the eyes of children opening to the possibility that they are somebody and not just a cauldron of desperate rage (Lederman, 1969, p. 7).

The model and manner of Fritz Perls have profoundly affected the lives of countless thousands of individuals personally and professionally. In twenty years or less—three generations of Gestalt Therapists, as well as myriad applications of the concepts of Gestalt Therapy, have appeared on the scene. Just as Gestalt Therapy has been applied in many different settings, so also it has drawn upon concepts from diverse sources—European and American, Near Eastern, and Oriental in character and flavor. It was Fritz Perls' genius to have integrated all these into a new gestalt.

NOTES

1. James Simkin, *Interview with Dr. Frederick Perls* (50 min.), American Association of Psychotherapists Tape Library, No. 31, track two.

2. In actuality. Perls *met* Freud only once; he has spoken of this event with considerable disappointment in *In and Out of the Garbage Pail* (1969).

3. For further discussion of Reich's body armor concept, see a brief but clear statement in Freedman and Kaplan, *Comprehensive Textbook of Psychiatry* (Baltimore, 1967), pp. 379-381.

4. For a more detailed exposition of the integration of Friedlander's work into Gestalt Therapy, see G. Kogan, "The History, Philosophy and Practice of Gestalt Therapy: Theory of Human Nature and Conduct in Frederick Perls' Psychology," doctoral dissertation, University of California, Berkeley, 1973.

5. Ernest Jones recommended Perls for the post he assumed in South Africa.

6. This resume is in the possession of Jack Gaines, of Stinson Beach, California; Gaines is preparing a biography of Fritz Perls.

7. Laura Perls in a recent letter (3/14/75) says: "Fritz was a training analyst until '37 or '38 when the International Psychoanalytic Association decided that only analysts who were already training analysts in Europe could train others."

8. Laura apparently was responsible for at least two chapters of *Ego, Hunger and Aggression*, according to Jack Gaines, as well as assisting Fritz throughout the development of the manuscript.

9. My impressions of Perls span a five-year period—the last five years of his life and the first five years of my continuous memory. It was in the summer of 1965 at Esalen that I first made contact with Fritz, and, in fact, Gestalt Therapy. At the time I was participating in a workshop conducted by Dr. Eugene Sagan. One particular evening, his workshop joined one led by Dr. Perls. All the participants and staff of the workshops had arrived; Dr. Perls arrived later. There was some excitement among people present waiting for Dr. Perls. My impression of this scene was that people were behaving rather bizarrely—very impulsively and highly emotionally, in a kind of public display of feeling . . . small groups of people moving together as though in some strange dance, some yelling, others crying . . . I was confused and quite unable to comprehend what I was then experiencing; the more usual ways I had of understanding were inadequate for these experiences. I felt amusement and fright variously.

That first contact with Perls was brief and distant; I made little contact with him. What now impresses me most was my first sight of him: I initially refused to believe this was the man over whom all the fuss was made. He was short, rather plump, very whiskered (all gray), and wearing a fuzzy jump suit of some color I don't now remember. He seemed slightly stern—although looking more like a tired Santa Claus than my psychotherapist expectations, which then ran more toward a younger and more virile-looking hero. When he spoke, his German accented speech almost immediately collapsed my expectations, and then he seemed more a "Freud" image. I was fascinated.

Soon afterward I became a patient in Gestalt Therapy and also began reading *Gestalt Therapy* by Perls, Hefferline, and Goodman, which I thought was terrible. Subsequently, whenever Perls came to San Francisco to give a talk or demonstration, I attended. As my experience with and interest in Gestalt Therapy grew, I collected more information—anecdotes and gossip—about Perls. Occasionally at Esalen, attending workshops, I would attempt to talk with Fritz; my talks with him were more in fantasy than in fact, however, and I would happily settle for merely sitting next to him at a meal in the Esalen dining room or eavesdropping as someone else talked or tried to talk with him. Rarely did I believe I had anything to say to him, which was of course the mechanism by which I inhibited myself. Others I discussed this with indicated they too responded in precisely that way. For these many people, I believe, Perls was experienced as a revered father or guru, distant and powerful. He always seemed a very private person, even lonely. He did not usually encourage conversation but would participate when he was not being "mind-fucked."

In 1967 I participated in a two- or three-month workshop held in Berkeley; Fritz officiated. The group consisted of about seventeen people, meeting on weekends. This was my first work with Perls. What I learned of him during this workshop was that he was tough and loving, tremendously intuitive and creative. Fritz became for me the model of a brilliant teacher and therapist—authentically believable. At times, my "uptightness" with respect to him would evaporate as I allowed myself to contact him through the authenticity of my humor —touching his in the process. At the conclusion of this workshop we celebrated with the favorite "gestalt food"—Chinese. While walking through San Francisco Chinatown to the restaurant Fritz and I exchanged some jokes. They only one I now recall him telling was a corny jingle:

Roses are reddish
Violets are blueish
If it wasn't for Christmas
We'd all be Jewish.

There had obviously been a turn of high energy Jewish jokes. Fritz's Jewishness seemed apparent in his humor. In most of what has been said or written of Perls and Gestalt Therapy, however, no mention has yet been made of his Jewishness or indeed the impact of this Jewishness upon Gestalt Therapy.

10. See G. Kogan, "The History, Philosophy, and Practice of Gestalt Therapy: Theory of Human Nature and Conduct in Frederick Perls' Psychology," doctoral dissertation, University of California, Berkeley, 1973.

11. Gestalt Therapy is one of the three psychiatric schools that have arisen from phenomenology and existentialism, the other two being Frankl's logotherapy and Binswanger's *Daseins Analyse*. Of these, the latter does not and cannot claim to be a therapeutic procedure. Van Dusen, in his discussion of existential analytic therapy, claims, "There is a psychotherapeutic approach which most closely fits the theory. In fact, a close adherence to the theory demands a particular approach. The approach has been called Gestalt Therapy, and considerable credit for it is due to Dr. F. S. Perls. . . ." (Claudio Naranjo, "Contributions of Gestalt Therapy," in *Ways of Growth*, eds. Herbert A. Otto and John Mann, New York: Viking Press, 1968, p. 128, n.).

12. James Simkin, *op. cit.*

13. Phil Bandt, "A Survey of Contemporary Approaches to Group Counseling," Summer, 1970.

14. See *Hot Springs* (1971) by Stuart Miller for a personal account of his experience at Esalen; *Turning On* (1969) by Rasa Gustaitis; and *Please Touch* (1970) by Jane Howard.

15. See the Association for Humanistic Psychology's *Growth Center List*, published April, 1972, 416 Hoffman, San Francisco, California.

16. See again the statement by Naranjo, quoted in footnote 11.

17. *Human Teaching for Human Learning: An Introduction to Confluent Education*, New York: Viking Press (An Esalen Book), 1971.

18. *Anger and the Rocking Chair: Gestalt Awareness with Children*, New York: McGraw-Hill, 1969.

REFERENCES

Bakan, D. *Sigmund Freud and the Jewish Mystical Tradition*. New York: Schocken Books, 1958.
Bandt, Phillip L. *A Survey of Contemporary Approaches to Group Counseling*. Unpublished manuscript, 1968.
Brown, G. I. *Human Teaching for Human Learning: An Introduction to Confluent Education*. New York: Viking Press (An Esalen Book), 1971.
Buber, M. *Paths in Utopia*. Beacon Press, 1949.
Cousins, N. *Modern Man Is Obsolete*. New York: Viking Press, 1945.
Elkin, E. H. "Gestalt Awareness: A Western Way of Being as a New Yoga." Prepared for World Conference on Scientific Yoga, New Delhi, India, December 1970.
Enright, J. B. "An Introduction to Gestalt Therapy." Published as "Introduction to Gestalt Techniques," in J. Fagan and I. Shepherd (eds.), *Gestalt Therapy Now*. Palo Alto, Calif.: Science and Behavior Books, 1970, pp. 107-124.
Fagan, J., and I. Shepherd (eds.). *Gestalt Therapy Now*. Palo Alto, Calif.: Science and Behavior Books, 1970. Also in paperback, New York: Harper and Colophon Books, 1970.
Frankl, V. E. *Man's Search for Meaning: An Introduction to Logotherapy*. Boston: Beacon Press, 1962.
Friedenberg, E. Z. *Coming of Age in America: Growth and Acquiescence*. New York: Random House, 1963.
Fromm, E. *May Man Prevail?* New York: Doubleday, 1961.
Goldstein, K. *The Organism*. New York: American Book, 1939.
Goodman, P. *Growing Up Absurd*. New York: Random House, 1956.
Hall, C., and G. Lindzey. *Theories of Personality*. New York: Wiley, 1957.
Keen, S. *To a Dancing God*. New York: Harper & Row, 1970.
Kogan, G. *Gestalt Therapy Resources*. San Francisco: Lodestar Press, 1970, 1971, and 1972.
————"The History, Philosophy and Practice of Gestalt Therapy: Theory of Human Nature and Conduct in Frederick Perls' Psychology." Doctoral dissertation, University of California, Berkeley, 1973.
Kohler, W. *Gestalt Psychology*. New York: New American Library, 1947.
Korzybski, A. *Science and Sanity: An Introduction to Non-Aristotelian Systems and General Semantics*. Lancaster, Pa.: Science Press Printing, 1933.
Larrabee, E., and R. Meyersohn. *Mass Leisure*. New York: The Free Press, 1958.
Lederman, J. *Anger and the Rocking Chair: Gestalt Awareness with Children*. New York: McGraw-Hill, 1969.
Lewis, A. O., Jr. (ed.). *Of Men and Machines*. New York: Dutton, 1963.
Lowe, C. M. *Value Orientations in Counseling and Psychotherapy: The Meaning of Mental Health*. San Francisco: Chandler Publishing Co., 1969.
Maslow, A. *Motivation and Personality*. New York: Harper & Row, 1954.

Naranjo, C. I. "I and Thou, Here and Now: Contributions of Gestalt Therapy," in H. A. Otto and J. Mann (eds.), *Ways of Growth: Approaches to Expanding Awareness.* New York: Grossman, 1968.

Ogden, C. K., and I. A. Richards. *The Meaning of Meaning.* New York: Harcourt Brace Jovanovich, first-published 1923.

Otto, H. A., and J. Mann (eds.). *Ways of Growth.* New York: Viking Press, 1968.

Perls, F. S. *Ego, Hunger and Aggression.* London: Allen & Unwin, 1947. Also, San Francisco: Orbit Graphic Arts, no date. Also, Big Sur, California: Esalen Institute, 1966. Also, New York: Random House, 1969.

———"Theory and Technique of Personality Integration," *American Journal of Psychotherapy*, 2, (1948), 565-586.

———"The Anthropology of Neurosis," *Complex*, 2 (1950), 19-27.

———"Morality, Ego-Boundary, and Aggression," *Complex*, 9 (1953), 42-51.

———"Gestalt Therapy and Human Potentialities," Esalen Institute, Big Sur, California: paper #1, 1965, and paper #11, 1968. Also, Gestalt Institute of Cleveland, Ohio: paper #3. Also, in H. A. Otto (ed.), *Explorations in Human Potentialities.* Springfield, Ill.: Charles C. Thomas, 1966.

———"Group vs. Individual Therapy," ETC: A Review of General Semantics. 24 (1967), 306-312.

———"Workshop vs. Individual Therapy." Paper presented at the 74th Convention of the American Psychological Association, New York, September, 1966. Also, in *Journal of the Long Island Consultation Center*, 2 (1967), 13-17.

———*Gestalt Therapy Verbatim.* Moab, Utah: Real People Press, 1969a.

———*In and Out of the Garbage Pail.* Moab, Utah: Real People Press, 1969b (Bantam edition, 1972).

———"Gestalt Therapy," in A. Bry (ed.), *Inside Psychotherapy.* New York: Basic Books, 1972, 57-70.

———, R. F. Hefferline, and P. Goodman. *Gestalt Therapy: Excitement and Growth in the Human Personality.* New York: Julian Press, 1951 (Dell edition, 1965).

———"Gestalt Psychotherapy," in W. S. Sahakian (ed.), *Psychotherapy and Counseling.* Rand McNally.

Perls, L. P. "The Psychoanalyst and the Critic," *Complex*, No. 2 (Summer, 1950), 41-47.

———"The Gestalt Approach." Paper presented at the 4th Annual Conference of the American Academy of Psychotherapists, New York, 1959. Also, in J. Barron and R. A. Harper (eds.), *Annals of Psychotherapy*, Vols. 1 and 2, 1961. Adapted as "One Gestalt Therapist's Approach," in J. Fagan and I. Shepherd (eds.), *Gestalt Therapy Now.* Palo Alto, Calif.: Science and Behavior Books, 1970.

———"Notes on the Psychology of Give and Take." *Complex*, 9 (1953), 24-30. Also, in P. D. Pursglove (ed.), *Recognitions in Gestalt Therapy.* New York: Funk and Wagnalls, 1968.

———"Two instances of Gestalt Therapy," *Case Reports in Clinical Psychology.* 3 (1956), 139-146. Also, in P. D. Pursglove (ed.), *Recognitions in Gestalt Therapy.* New York: Funk and Wagnalls, 1968.

———"Some Aspects of Gestalt Therapy." Unpublished manuscript, no date.

Pursglove, P. D. (ed.). *Recognitions in Gestalt Therapy.* New York: Funk and Wagnalls, 1968.

Reich, Wilhelm. *Character Analysis.* 3d. ed. New York: Farrar, Straus and Giroux, 1972.

Riesman, D., N. Glazer, and R. Denney. *The Lonely Crowd.* New Haven: Yale University Press, 1950.

Rogers, C. R., and B. Stevens. *Person to Person: The Problem of Being Human.* Moab, Utah: Real People Press, 1967.

Rosenberg, B., and D. M. White. *Mass Culture: The Popular Arts in America.* New York: The Free Press, 1957.

Ruitenbeek, H. M. *The New Group Therapies.* New York: Avon Discus, 1970.

Schweitzer, F. M. *A History of the Jews.* New York: Macmillan, 1971.

Simkin, J. S. (ed.). *Festschrift for Fritz Perls.* Los Angeles: Author, 1968.

Smuts, J. C. *Holism and Evolution.* New York: Viking Compass, 1961 (first published 1926).

Tofler, A. *Future Shock.* New York: Random House, 1970.

Tournier, P., V. Frankl, H. Levinson, H. Thielicke, P. Lehmann, and S. Miller. *Are You Nobody?* Richmond, Va.: John Knox Press, 1966.

Van Dusen, W. "Existential Analytic Psychotherapy," *American Journal of Psychoanalysis*, 20 (1) (1960), 35-40. Also, in P. D. Pursglove (ed.), *Recognitions in Gestalt Therapy.* New York: Funk and Wagnalls, 1968.

Wheelis, A. *The Quest for Identity.* New York: Norton, 1958.

CHAPTER 7

GESTALT THERAPY AND BEYOND

ERIC MARCUS, M.D.

Eric Marcus is in private practice in Los Angeles, California. He is also an assistant clinical professor of psychiatry at UCLA Medical School and a staff member of the Gestalt Therapy Institute of Los Angeles.

What I want to do in this chapter is inform you about my newer thoughts concerning psychotherapy. I have moved away from Gestalt Therapy as an exclusive modality and have incorporated certain other therapy systems. I came to this position by evolution, by thinking about what was missing in Gestalt Therapy, but I didn't have it jelled until I went to a workshop with a psychologist named Paul Bindrim. I really enjoyed his theoretical presentation of the process of psychotherapy and growth. When I used his scheme, then a variety of approaches such as Gestalt, meditation, and psychedelics seem to fit together.

Bindrim schematizes the personality as a series of concentric circles, the outermost circle representing a person's defenses, including his "character." Not in the sense of having a good or bad character as is the common usage, but character as defined as a fixed way of being, a life-style, a life-script. It is also referred to as "character-armor" or "character defenses."

Underneath this outermost layer are painful and strong emotions. In Gestalt we define four basic emotions, although I really don't think these are necessarily the only basic ones. According to Fritz Perls they are anger, fear, grief, and orgasm. The first three may be expressed in therapy; I don't deal directly with orgasms. This second layer is where, in my opinion, most therapies stop, including Gestalt. Of course many therapies never even reach strong feelings. In contrast, persons such as Janov say that we have "primal" feelings, and people come to him by the thousands, all trying to get down to that level of emotion. Don't forget that "strong" feelings include positive feelings such as joy. Somehow I suspected that the above-described two layers are not an adequate conceptualization of a total being.

Although many people I know are going to "systems" other than psychotherapy, I still had no clear concept as to what was the next level down until I went to Bindrim's lecture. Level three, he calls "aloneness"; getting in touch with actually being totally alone, having no real support in life. No one will live for you; nobody is going to die for you. You're going to do those things really by yourself and neither your parents nor anyone else can really help. This realization is a very frightening gut feeling. Very few therapies touch on this level and there aren't many techniques available. One technique is isolation. The Gestalt Institute of Canada used to have people come up for one month and stay alone in a cabin and get as much therapy as they wanted. While they were not getting therapy, they were to remain alone. Janov's technique is to have people stay a week or two alone in a motel in order to get in touch with aloneness as well as weaken defenses. I think that isolation gets people down quickly to these deeper levels.

At the center of the concentric circles is "love-fusion," the place representing complete centeredness. This, of course, is an ideal or at least a place where we can get to sometimes. Most of us don't have the kind of lifestyle that makes an existence in such a place possible. In Zen philosophy this "place" is called the state of "Zen"; where there is no difference between you and the universe. There are very few people who can reach this level and be able to move in and out of it. And yet people do reach it by a variety of methods. Psychotherapy is perhaps an inefficient way to get there. Some have gotten there with drugs such as LSD. People by the thousands all over the world are meditating; whether it's Yoga, Zen, or Transcendental meditation, they're getting to this level. Many and varied religious groups focus on this level. To be always at this level is, I think, quite unrealistic in our usual Western society; you still have to drive, buy groceries, make phone calls. To love everyone just doesn't work out —you just don't leave your purse lying around—it won't be there in twenty minutes (at least in Los Angeles!).

In terms of the process of psychotherapy, clients can be worked with, either starting at the outermost layer working in toward the center, or starting at the center proceeding outward. An ideal combination is working in both directions with patients. Actually I don't like the term *patient*, and I don't use it, although my training is as an M.D. Using the term "patient" sets up a dichotomy between "patient" and "doctor" and that defines the patient's role. Sick people are called patients. The doctor supposedly is a helper or curer and has some sort of answer. The "patient" comes and takes "treatments" and at the end of the treatment he is "cured." I don't like that as a model for personal growth. My model is an educational model. I consider myself a teacher/tutor and I work with students/trainees. I think it makes more sense.

Certain therapy schools and techniques start at the superficial layer and work inward. For example, psychoanalysis, transactional analysis, Synanon games, encounter groups, and Gestalt all start at the outermost layer and work inward by penetrating defenses. There are other techniques for removing defenses from the inside out. This approach is sometimes much faster, much more effective than spending years trying to "break" defenses from outside in. For example, massage may start at the center. I remember workshops where we used massage and some persons became very upset and dissolved strong defenses. The massage generated feelings of love, security, warmth; and consequently defenses broke (or dissolved). Another way, which is unusual, is the way Bindrim works. He has a group in a body-temperature pool and has them rock and float each other. Usually within a very short time many persons become very emotional.

Another technique (which I don't use) is administering psychedelic drugs. I am learning about the effects of LSD and mescaline from medical students and psychiatric residents that I supervise at UCLA. Most of them have had growth experiences from psychedelic drugs. I expect them to be quite a different breed of psychiatrists than my former classmates. Of course, drug experiences are not integrated experiences—they are momentary flashes of insight. And yet, the persons remember what openness and awareness they felt under these drugs and they can then work toward that goal without drugs. At least the drug experience gave them a taste of something they might have never tasted otherwise. In a way it's as if you've been brought up on McDonald's hamburgers and are quite satisfied with them. You may not even know that such a thing as a steak exists. So, people who take these drugs I think have tasted steak and thereafter want to eat steak again.

Another way is by means of meditation and/or religion; people are really getting to the love-fusion center. Unfortunately, if a person doesn't stay within a particular philosophical system, he may quickly revert to his character defenses. He is only in an open, blissful state within a particular group, reinforced by certain chants, rituals, and so on. It takes many years to achieve and integrate basic personality changes in order to function in a centered way, regardless of environment.

I have been using neo-Reichian and bioenergetic techniques to get persons in touch with strong emotions very quickly. However, sometimes it's almost too fast. People "pass through" character quickly and discharge strong emotions, but they may not integrate well, because as soon as they stop "emoting" they may revert to their character defenses. On the other hand, therapists who never facilitate clients' getting in touch with strong emotions keep therapy at a predominantly intellectual level. I favor a combination of approaches that facilitate powerful emotional expression and integrating the experience by means of Gestalt Therapy.

One of my ways of having persons experience the "love-fusion" level is by means of participating in a warm, loving group. In such a group they are more willing to risk giving up defenses. Their defenses are "melted" rather than "cracked" by means of (attacking) group pressure. I am convinced that defenses are more easily melted by love and affection than "broken" by harsh techniques. For example, many growth experiences occur *outside* the therapeutic setting. Think of your own experiences. How many of your own growth experiences happened in therapy? Remember, also, indelible moments with a good friend, spouse, or teacher. The interaction with a warm, loving person (including a therapist) is the predominant "healing" factor, *not* the theory or technique of the therapist.

Part III

TECHNIQUES

CHAPTER 8

THE GROUND RULES IN GESTALT THERAPY

JERRY A. GREENWALD, Ph.D.

Jerry A. Greenwald is in practice in Los Angeles, California and is also a staff member of the Gestalt Therapy Institute of Los Angeles.

Reprinted by permission from J. Greenwald, "The Ground Rules of Gestalt Therapy," **Journal of Contemporary Psychotherapy**, Vol. 5, No. 1, 1972, pp. 3-120.

The "ground rules" in Gestalt Therapy constitute an invitation to the person, if he is willing, to accept a certain attitude in working with the therapist. They are not intended as *musts* or *shoulds*. Following the ground rules in a mechanical manner, or dutifully playing "good patient," is in itself a negation of the philosophy of Gestalt Therapy. The purpose of the ground rules is to create an atmosphere and attitude toward working in therapy that lead to greater awareness of the reality of oneself and how one interacts with others, and how one functions in the here-and-now. The ground rules are intended to enhance awareness and make obvious what a person does that is his authentic self and what he does that is phony, manipulative, or avoids being his own person. This emphasis on increased awareness is intended to confront the person with the full responsibility for all of his behavior, to increase authentic self-expression and relating, to minimize self-deceptive, evasive, self-frustrating and meaningless behavior.

Much of the work in Gestalt Therapy involves increased awareness of obsolete attitudes and behavior patterns which were learned in the past and which continue despite their frustrating effect on the person's well-being in the present. While he adopted these as the most effective way he could find to cope with conflicts in his past life, he may begin to see that they no longer fit present reality. As he becomes aware of these archaic responses, he may begin to experiment by takings risks in letting go of them and discovering new, more effective attitudes and behavior. The energy that had been diverted into frustrating or non-nourishing activities is then freed and available for more meaningful experiences in the here-and-now.

The goal of Gestalt Therapy is growth. This involves movement away from what a person no longer wants for himself and movement in new directions, or an interest in exploring different behavior patterns and experiences. The growth process *is* awareness and the willingness to experiment with different self-initiated behavior.

In Gestalt Therapy, there is no preconceived concept into which an individual should fit. There are no goals as to how he "should" be, nor is there a fixed concept of what a mature person is like. The emphasis is on growth through self-discovery—becoming aware and experimenting with what fits and what does not fit the unique self of each individual. This respect for the integrity of the individual applies whether the person experiences himself as fully functioning or as confused, bewildered, or baffled about his identity.

Nothing supersedes the self-regulating capabilities of the individual; this basic principle always takes precedence. No one is pressured or coerced to do anything or to participate in any way. Anything the leader suggests or asks of anyone is an invitation. The rule is specifically stated that it is up to each person to say yes or no to any invitation by the leader or any approach from others in the group. The participant is responsible for not allowing others to intrude on him by pressuring him into something he really objects to doing. He is also encouraged not to pressure himself into doing something he really doesn't want to do. This attitude is often stated as follows: "Say what you want to say and don't say anything you don't want to say." Similarly, each participant is asked not to push, urge, or coerce others to work or otherwise participate more actively. All such attempts to be "helpful" are considered to be intrusions on the other, even when motivated by a feeling of caring and well-meant intentions.

There are two methods of working in a Gestalt group. The first involves work between the leader and a single participant within the group setting. When one-to-one work occurs, the rest of the group is usually asked to refrain from interaction until the work is finished. Then the other participants share whatever they wish about what they experienced and how they reacted while the one-to-one work was taking place. This feedback is a source of much group interaction. It becomes apparent that others relate to (identify with) the participant who is working with the therapist and do a great deal of silent self-therapy, becoming aware of unfinished situations or fragmented parts of themselves. Experiencing the work of someone else frequently has the effect of helping other group members to recognize their own frustrating attitudes and behavior patterns.

Often the leader will make an explicit statement to the effect that each participant, *if he is interested*, can relate to anything that is happening when another person in working.

The second method of working in a Gestalt group includes all other interaction within the group. There are definite limitations to what can be considered valuable or meaningful ways of interacting and relating. Intellectualizing, "psychologizing," and advice-giving are considered wastes of time and energy. Any kind of "talking about" which has any flavor of a lecture, a case history or story-telling about oneself or someone else is considered dead material which avoids or dulls awareness and aliveness.

All attempts to fit someone's behavior into a theoretical framework—to analyze or explain it on the basis of psychological theory—are irrelevant. Usually, this becomes an explanation game. It focuses on "why" questions and answers. In Gestalt this process is considered endless and without growth potential. "Why" questions avoid the here-and-now and are "explanation games." In Gestalt Therapy *explanations* are translated to mean *excuses* for not living in the present. Participants are encouraged to make statements in the first person about what they are experiencing and how they are reacting in the here-and-now.

In Gestalt Therapy, the group setting has the advantages of providing an atmosphere of "safe risk-taking" in letting go of obsolete behaviors and experimenting with new ones. The attitude of open self-expression within the group enables the participant to experience honest interaction between himself and others. For each person, there is no substitute for the experience of expressing himself to others and checking out catastrophic fantasies of how people will react if he shows who he really is.

Each participant is encouraged to express himself *primarily* to satisfy his own need for self-expression. Attempts to convince, persuade or "sell" another participant on his own opinion or viewpoint are considered manipulations which detract from authentic relating.

Frequently the leader will suggest group "games" or other procedures. These include exercises for enhancing awareness and focusing on the here-and-now, as well as a number of techniques to encourage authentic interaction and relating within the group.

A meaningful growth-enhancing group atmosphere minimizes interaction which is meaningless, time-wasting, or poisonous. The ground rules restricting behavior are intended to minimize ineffective activities which avoid awareness and aliveness in the here-and-now. Usually the only outright prohibition is against physical violence.

The Continuum of Awareness

Being in touch with one's flow is an essential aspect of the Gestalt method. Participants are encouraged to tune in to what they are experiencing from moment to moment. The emphasis is on nonintellectual awareness as opposed to thoughts and speculations. The person is asked to focus on the sensory data, feelings, emotions, and reactions to experiences from within himself and his environment.

Reality Is

Because the past and future are considered fantasy, to be in touch with reality *is* to be in touch with the here-and-now. This is reflected in the rule that each person is asked to speak in the present tense. Various techniques are used to implement this rule. When a person is in touch with something that happened in his past, he is asked to bring the memory into the present using Gestalt techniques. For example, referring to a childhood episode with a parent, he may be invited by the therapist to put the parent on an empty chair and talk to him as if the episode were happening now and to express the feelings he experiences now. *Any* experience—a past episode, a future fantasy, a dream, etc.—can be brought into the present by various Gestalt methods.

Everything I Say or Do Is Part of Me

Every thought, feeling, verbalization, action, etc., is an expression of the person's identity at the moment. In order to become more aware of his identity, the person is asked to "own" everything he says and does by speaking in the first person singular and avoiding abstractions and impersonal statements. Instead of saying, "There is a funny feeling in my stomach," the person is asked to own the funny feeling by saying, for example, "I feel funny in my stomach."

A person can realistically make only first person singular statements about what *he* experiences or how *he* reacts. A person who becomes restless at the empty verbalizing of another may say in irritation, "You are very boring to us"—he speaks for the whole group. He fantasizes that everyone present is reacting with boredom as he is. People often generalize by using the pronoun "you." A participant will say, "You can't go around telling everyone how you feel." He is asked again to personalize and own his statement by saying *I* instead of *you*. For example, "I am very bored with you," or, "I can't (won't) tell everyone how I feel."

Speaking in the first person singular avoids the endless "talking about" which tends to be impersonal and intellectual. First person statements enhance awareness of the emotional aspect of what is being said.

Meaningful Dialogue

Interaction between participants is also on a first person basis; each person makes statements about himself to the others. Meaningful dialogue involves a sequence of first person singular statements in which what one person says to another is reflected in the response of the other. The result is ongoing feedback, and it is obvious in the responses of both that each person is reacting to the other and really hearing him.

An essential aspect of the "make first person statements" principle is that the person makes his statement *primarily* for the purpose of self-expression. When this is his attitude he sounds as if there is a period at the end of his statement. He feels finished and satisfied. While a person usually wants a favorable response to what he has said, this is the prerogative of the person to whom the statement is made. In authentic dialogue, no one attempts to sell anything to anyone else. To respond as he chooses, or not to respond at all, is respected as being the other person's right.

No Gossiping

The no gossiping rule applies to talking about another person, regardless of whether he is present or not. To enhance feelings of contact and interaction, each person is asked to make statements directly to the other person. For example, instead of saying to the group leader about another patient, "He makes me angry with his intellectualizing," the person is asked to make the statements directly to the participant toward whom he feels angry; i.e., "I am angry at your intellectualizing."

To avoid talking about people who are not present, various role-playing techniques are used so that the absent person may be spoken to as if he were actually present.

Questions

Questions generally are discouraged. They avoid meaningful interaction. Questions frequently ask a person to explain, defend or justify some aspect of himself or of his existence. Questions often are attempts to manipulate other people; they can usually be restated as first person statements. The leader often asks a participant to check with himself to see if there is a statement behind his question. When someone does ask a question of another member, the other person is asked to take the responsibility for deciding whether he wants to respond and *how* he would like to answer. In general, questions are considered to be an evasive way of interacting without revealing anything of oneself to the other.

Relevant Subject Matter

A participant may work on any attitude or behavior pattern relative to his functioning as a human being. These conflicts may concern the person's past, present or future. There is no aspect of behavior which is considered more or less desirable in terms of what the person "should" work on. Rather, each participant decides for himself what he feels is most important of those things he is willing to work with or share in the group.

What and How

The achievement of greater awareness involves getting more in touch with the "whats" and "hows" of behavior. The focus is on *what* a person does and *how* he goes about doing it. *Why* questions are avoided. Gestalt Therapy is noninterpretative and avoids any kind of explanation of behavior. This explanation is usually called the "why merry-go-round"; it is the psychoanalysis game. In Gestalt, explaining why one behaves as he does, even when the explanations are valid, is considered an intellectual exercise which does not lead to behavior change. Furthermore, explanations about oneself or one's behavior serve as excuses for one's frustrations and are considered poisonous. They are often attempts by a person to justify his existence or to defend himself rather than encouragement to change or growth. Such activity enhances stalemated behavior.

Taking Risks

By trusting the self-regulating potentials of the individual, the therapist affirms that he has neither the desire nor the willingness to push or in any other way work at "getting the person to open up." The individual is responsible (and free) for whatever self-expression he decides to initiate. In Gestalt Therapy, "taking a risk" refers to a person's fears—grounded in his past—that if he reveals himself he invites a catastrophic reaction: he will elicit scorn, contempt, rejection, or even annihilation from others. Frustrated self-expression usually reflects a person's fear that he will inevitably experience rejection if he shares his feelings with others. When he is willing to check out his fears and anxieties in the reality of the now, he is open to the possibility that these squeezed-in-parts of himself are acceptable and will not lead to the catastrophes and rejections he anticipates as a result of his past (particularly childhood) experiences.

Can't versus Won't

The "won't" attitude emphasizes the Gestalt philosophy that a person has the potential power (and freedom) within himself to change when he is genuinely interested in doing so. "Can't" means that whatever change the person wants is impossible. This is rarely realistic with respect to a person's attitudes and behavior patterns. *Won't* means, "I don't want to," or "I am not willing to." Often a person is asked to change his statement by using the word *won't* instead of *can't*. This confronts him with taking responsibility for what he is willing or unwilling to do on his own behalf.

Psychological Interpretations

Interpreting behavior is contrary to the Gestalt approach. When a person makes a statement about how he experiences the behavior of another, that is self-expression. When one makes a statement interpreting the *meaning* of another's behavior, that statement implies that the interpreter knows what is motivating the other—which is fantasy. Statements intended to answer a *why* question are often interpretations. Statements by one person about how he is *experiencing* another person reflect *his* observations about how or what the other person is doing.

When a person is interested in self-expression, he is willing to own everything he says. When he is interpreting to another person, his attitude is that he believes his statement fits the other person. The interpreter "puts" his statement on the other person, and in so doing violates the integrity of the other by not allowing him to decide what fits him and what doesn't. When someone is interpreting, his attitude usually has the flavor of manipulation of the other to accept his statements. The more persistent the interpretation, the more obvious the "selling" becomes.

Don't Push

Trust in the self-regulating potentials of the person, a respect for each individual's integrity, and the attitude that each person is responsible for himself are reflected in the ground rule that no one pushes or pressures anyone in a Gestalt group. The leader does not challenge individuals to work nor does he criticize them when they are nonverbal, withdrawn, or appear bored. In stating the ground rules each person may be asked to "mind his own business." If he wishes to express his resentments or irritation at the behavior of another, or his own disappointment that another person is not working, he is asked to do this as an expression of his self at the moment. This is in contrast to expressing oneself for the primary purpose of manipulating the other person into responding in some particular way. All pushing is considered manipulation and violates the integrity of the other by not allowing him to be where he is. Pushing implies a judgmental attitude that the person is failing to do something he *should* do.

Gestalt Games

There are endless variations in the techniques the therapist may use in the working process itself. The "games" constitute invitations by the therapist to a person to say or do something relating to what he is working on at the moment. These procedures are called games because they are initially artificial; that is, the person is asked if he is willing to do something that comes from the therapist rather than from his own spontaneity. He may initially feel the suggestion is pointless or his compliance is phony. This is part of the risk-taking procedure. The meaningfulness of the game to the participant depends upon what he actually does experience for himself as real when he decides to go along with the therapist's suggestion. The purpose of the game is to focus the attention of the person on—and to enhance his awareness of—some aspect of himself or his behavior.

The Hot Seat

When one-to-one work is occurring, and the rest of the group is observing, the person working is described as being "on the hot seat," since he is obviously the center of attention and the focal point of the group.

In front of the hot seat is an empty chair. The person working is often asked to role-play by speaking to a significant person in his life, past or present, as if that person were actually sitting in the empty chair. Usually the person working is asked to be the other person, too. He may be asked to develop a dialogue, writing his own script as he goes along, and actually changing seats each time the person speaking changes. Or, the dialogue may be between parts of himself. For example, in a decision-making conflict he may be asked to have a dialogue with "pro" and "con" occupying the two chairs. Similarly, in working with dreams, he may be asked to be any person or object appearing in his dream and to give each a voice.

Making Rounds

This involves a participant making some kind of contact with the other members of the group. The leader may invite a participant to make a specific statement to each person. The variety of "rounds" is limited only by the ingenuity of the leader. "Making a round" may utilize the Gestalt principle of figure and ground developed into a technique to enhance awareness. By making the same statement to each person, the meaning of that statement can become focused in the center of the person's awareness. For example, a person may feel at ease expressing anger and resentment but be quite unwilling to express warmth and affection. He might be asked to make a round and express his resentments *and* his appreciations to each person in the group.

Dreams

In Gestalt, dreams are a statement of the here-and-now existence of the dreamer. The person is asked to bring the dream into the present by telling it aloud as if he is describing a movie which he can see and the group cannot. Every detail of the dream is part of himself. He is all the people, all the things, all the places, all the actions in his dream. In theory, if he were to work with every aspect of a dream it would be a comprehensive statement of his existence. Because of time limitations, the person is usually asked to focus on one or a few outstanding aspects of the dream. In dream-work technique in Gestalt Therapy, the person is asked to animate his dream: to give voices to the people or objects; to write his own script of monologues, or dialogues between people or objects or any combination of these in his dream. No interpreting of the dream or symbolism is used or recognized as valid.

It does not matter whether the dream occurred recently or years ago. When a person remembers an old dream, he is still holding on to the "unfinished business" of his dream.

The therapeutic value of the dream is based on the increased awareness which comes from owning every aspect of the dream. Fragmented parts of the personality are often revealed by what happens (or by what is avoided) in the dream.

Growth Is a Process of Small Steps

The ongoing process of adjustment and growth involves gaining and assimilating new awareness in small steps. A person is encouraged to stop working when he is in contact with some increased awareness that he is interested in holding on to (assimilating). Or the therapist may state that he would like to stop working at that point.

The Therapist and His Attitude

The therapist rejects any kind of authority position toward the person with whom he is working. The therapist does not attempt to lead, guide, advise, or in other ways take away the other person's responsibility for himself. Rather, his attitude is that each person knows best what he needs for himself and how to get it; even when he is stuck, he is more capable of finding his own solutions than anyone else. The therapist accepts the premise that each person is the center of his own existence and the most important person in the world to himself. This attitude of respect for the integrity and individuality of every human being is essential. The therapist uses the ground rules for the sole purpose of creating an environment in which the philosophy of Gestalt Therapy may most readily evolve into an awareness-increasing, growth-enhancing experience.

A popular statement reflecting the Gestalt philosophy emphasizes the respect of the therapist for the integrity of the individual: "Right now I cannot be any other way than I am right now." For example, if a participant decides to criticize himself for not following the ground rules, this is what *he* needs to do. The therapist is not interested in evaluating or criticizing him for this. The therapist *is* interested in helping the participant become more aware of what he is doing. Respect for the other person means that the therapist recognizes and allows each person to be where he is.

The therapist is explicit in stating that he is available to work if the other person is interested. Nothing is excluded as a potential source of work. This includes any kind of problem or "symptom." The therapist emphasizes that anything he initiates while working with the other person is an invitation or a suggestion, and it is the other person's responsibility to decide whether he is interested in accepting the offer or not.

The therapist seeks to be continuously in touch with his own awareness of how he experiences others and what he observes them doing. He does not respond with his knowledge of psychology; he does not use case history data. He does not make interpretations of the *whys* of behavior. He does not try to *fit* the person into a theoretical orientation. He shares his experiencing and awareness at the moment, and interacts in an "I and thou" dialogue. It is the responsibility of the therapist to work this way. The therapist is an observer, not a mind reader. He *offers* his observations to the participant; he doesn't try to *sell* them. He respects the right of the participant to accept what he experiences as meaningful and to reject what he doesn't want from what the therapist shares with him.

In essence the therapist's attitude is:

I won't help you by trying to gratify your needs or trying to live up to your expectations (whatever your fantasy is of what I *should* be able to do for you). I am not interested in doing this. Whatever your past experiences have been, your behavior in the here-and-now of your life is your responsibility. Your attempts at manipulation of yourself or others lead to further frustration when you fail and to stalemate of your own growth when you succeed. I am interested in helping you become more aware of when you are taking responsibility for yourself and when you are being manipulative. It is my responsibility not to manipulate you even if it brings temporary relief or gratification.

I *am* interested in helping you become more aware of how you cut off your potentials for greater self-reliance. I am interested in working with you in this direction as long as you are interested. This is how I show my caring for you as a person and my respect for your integrity as an individual. It is my responsibility to openly and honestly share with you how I experience you. It is your responsibility to take from me what you decide is valuable, or meaningful, to you. It is also your responsibility to reject what you feel doesn't fit you.

Our goal in working together is to increase your awareness of your needs, behavior patterns and responsiveness to yourself and others. As you become aware of these, it is your decision what, if any, behavior patterns you wish to change and what you wish to keep or develop. The goal is discovering through increased awareness how you hamper your ability to satisfy your needs, grow as a person, and fulfill more of your potentials. From that point you're on your own.

CHAPTER 9

EXPRESSIVE TECHNIQUES

CLAUDIO NARANJO, M.D.

Claudio Naranjo is currently in practice in Kensington, California, and is the publisher of SAT Press. His career has included positions as Fulbright Visiting Scholar at Harvard University and at the University of California, Berkeley, and as a research associate at the Institute of Personality Assessment and Research, University of California, Berkeley.

Reprinted by permission from Claudio Naranjo, **The Techniques of Gestalt Therapy**, Berkeley: SAT Press, 1973, pp. 31-61.

Awareness may be enhanced through suppression or through expression. Opposing an impulse may lead to increased awareness of it, just as we feel the push of a stream more strongly if we resist it with our hand than if not. Also, in suppressing the cliches—conditioned responses, games—that constitute some of our reactions, we become aware of what we are beyond these automatic responses.

Exaggerating the expression of an impulse, however, is an equally effective approach to enhanced awareness. Moreover, suppressive rules may be seen as a means of revealing (just as the suppression of noise reveals the message) an individual's true expression.

We are aware of our "selves" largely through our expression. Our notion of what we are is affected, if not completely determined, by what we fail to do, and what we have done. (Some existentialists would go further, saying that we *are* what we do: there is no essence divorced from our existence.) Yet, even if we are what we do, we only experience as if "through a glass darkly" the concrete actions and physical states that manifest our being.

The place of intensified expression in a discipline in awareness might be compared to what the contrast control does to the vision on a television screen or the volume control to the listening. In this analogy, the pure practice of attention, which is the ever-present background of Gestalt Therapy, would correspond to the action of concentrating upon the screen, and deliberately watching or listening to the show. The suppressive aspect of Gestalt Therapy, on the other hand, might be compared to turning off the light in the room, or closing the windows to eliminate distracting noises from the street.

By means of suppressive requests, the therapist discourages in the patient what he is not; by inviting his expression, he stimulates what he is. When the patient becomes able to express what hitherto was unexpressed, he will not only be revealing himself to another, but to himself, much as the true artist gains self-knowledge through his work. Not only is self-expression a way to self-awareness, but a means to itself: the capacity to express himself, like consciousness, is part of the fully developed person, and therefore an aim of psychotherapy. To express oneself—that is, to translate one's feeling and understanding into action, forms, words—is to *realize* oneself, in the literal sense of making oneself real. Without such realization we are phantoms, and feel the frustration of not being fully alive.

To express (and thus actualize) ourselves would be as natural a process as the germinating of seeds or blooming of flowers, were it not for the fact that early in our lives we experienced friction, anxiety, pain, and learned to manipulate through "strategies" rather than risking openness to the world; and this has served us—to a point. The sum of these strategies, however, in the form of a "character" became, to a greater or lesser extent, an end for itself, an "identity" to which we cling, which we justify, which we promote, while we alienate ourselves from what we truly are, and fail to express our nature.

In behavioristic terms, Gestalt Therapy might be viewed as a program of positive reinforcement of self-expression, coupled with negative reinforcement of manipulation and inauthenticity. Every act of self-expression, in its context, is not only an occasion for self-awareness, but an opening up of an avenue to action—a corrective experience in which the patient learns in some measure that he can be himself without his catastrophic expectations being confirmed; one in which he takes risks in breaking his phobic patterns and learns that to express himself is satisfying and the basis of true contact with others.

A man reported a dream in which he was a bear. Asked to become the bear, he felt at first very inhibited. Urged to imagine himself in this role, and do whatever—as a bear—he felt inclined to do, he started giving "bear hugs" to other group members, tentatively at first, and then with much feeling and delight. At last he exclaimed: "I much prefer to be a bear than myself." Someone else commented: "There is no more effective way of changing behavior than changing behavior."

Expressive techniques in Gestalt Therapy may be regarded as instances of one or the other of three broad principles: the initiation of actions, the completion of actions, the pursuit of directness. Or, in other words: expressing the unexpressed, completing expression, making expression direct. In what follows, I will deal with these three groups of techniques under separate headings.

INITIATING ACTION

Gestalt Therapy sees much of current behavior as phobic: patterned in such a way that all of it may seem fluent and yet true contact is avoided, true expression suppressed. Beyond the almost universal avoidances of pain, of depth in contact and of expression, some of our phobias are individual, and are related to the disowning of specific functions that are part of our potential.

The idea of initiating action or expression has, accordingly, two forms of technical application in Gestalt Therapy: one universal, the other individual. A universal technique is that of *maximizing initiative*, risk-taking and overt expression in word or deed. One of individual application is a "prescription" based upon individual diagnoses, of something in the doing of which the person will be forced to overcome his avoidance.

Maximizing expression: This principle is applied in Gestalt Therapy in various forms. One of them, of indirect relevance, is *the minimization of nonexpressive action*. After cliches and verbiage have been suppressed, all that will remain is the choice between emptiness and expression.

A second technique leading to the maximization of expression is *the providing of unstructured situations*. To the extent that a situation is unstructured, the individual is confronted with his own choices. To the extent that no rules of interaction are laid out, or behavior expected of him, he must determine his own rules, be responsible for his actions. Lack of structure requires of the individual that he be creative rather than a good player of a predetermined game.

Absence of structure is, as are many other aspects of Gestalt Therapy, a component in its basic exercise: the practice of the awareness continuum. Moreover, I believe that only through an appreciation of this aspect of the exercise can the therapist be in a position to respond effectively to the patient.

At every turn of the awareness continuum, the patient is either following or not following the dictates of his desires, impulses, leanings of the moment. Whichever he does, *he* does. He is *choosing*, and one of the functions of the therapist is to make him aware of his decisions, to help him realize that *he* is choosing—i.e., that he is responsible.

Patient: I am holding my jaw very tight. I also feel like clenching my fists . . . and I would like to stamp my feet.
Therapist: And that, you are *not* doing.
Patient: Yes, I am holding back from stamping my feet . . .

To the extent that a person is not integrated, being confronted with his own choices will inevitably expose his inner splits in the form of conflicts:

Patient: I feel like standing up and roaring at all of you!
Therapist: I see that you are not doing that.
Patient: I am afraid that it would be ridiculous.
Therapist: It?
Patient: I would feel ridiculous doing such a thing.
Therapist: So here you are in conflict: to roar or to fear the group's opinion. Let us do some work on this . . . etc.

The conflicts most often manifested during the awareness continuum practice are between the organismic needs, on the one hand, and the social roles of behavior and consideration of other people's reactions. This might be summarized by the dilemma of

> *"whether to belch and bear the shame*
> *or squelch the belch and bear the pain."*

I think it is worth pointing out how important lack of structure is in dealing with such conflicts. In this situation, where the rule is "no rules," the patient cannot fail to acknowledge conflict as *his own*. In other words, the interpretation of conflict as one between self and external world (or social rules) would only be here a disowning of responsibility. The rule being "be yourself," he must meet the challenge of his freedom. This does not necessarily mean that on another occasion in his life he will not meet a conflict from the environment or that he *should* in every situation act upon his desires. That will be a matter of his mature choice. All that lack of structure does is provide an emptiness that he will fill with his expression or, alternatively, with the awareness of his inability to do so, an awareness of his conflicts and their nature.

In the group setting, lack of structure takes on an additional dimension, and the rule of "no rule" may deserve being pointed out explicitly.

I generally make a statement to the effect that our session(s) will be in the nature of exploration into truth—our truth, and we can benefit most by risking not only the verbal exposure of our feelings, but the expression of ourselves in non-verbal actions. What we say or do may turn out to be very relative truth or carry an admixture of self-deception, yet even that we can only find out by sharing and acting upon the extent of truth we are in touch with at the moment. The rule also has exceptions, which will vary with the therapist. One, for instance is that of the suppressive techniques. Another sometimes is a request of not interrupting the therapist's work on a singled-out individual. My own formula is that of *restricting* interruptions to expressions, verbal or other, of intense feeling (no imperatives or comments), and when no single individual is on the "hot seat," maximizing spontaneity.

The other major component in the maximization of expression is a direct prompting to express, in words or actions. This prompting is implied in the description of the basic exercise, again, since the patient is urged to *express* moment after moment what he experiences. Furthermore, verbal expression is often requested by the therapist when the patient fails to do so:

Therapist: What do you experience now?
Patient: I feel angry at Joe's remark.
Therapist: You apparently stopped expressing your experiences at the point of feeling angry.
Patient: Yes, I was also feeling afraid.

In the group setting, verbal expression may be stimulated in various ways. Fritz Perls used to say: "You always have the alternative of interrupting somebody else or interrupting yourself. I want you to interrupt others more than yourself." A useful procedure is to take the time more than once in each session to request from each group member a brief statement of his experience at the moment. This serves as an awakener to feelings or reactions that might otherwise have been bypassed, points out something or somebody deserving attention, and contributes to keeping the channels of communication open.

A technique in which lack of structure and the injunction to express come together, is that of relating to the members of the group one after the other—frequently called "making rounds." This may be done verbally or otherwise, and is most effective, as a rule, as a one-way act of expression, without the expectation of a reaction or the obligation to carry on the exchange. An instruction leading to this may be: "Tell each person something"; or, "Say to each what you want to say"; or "Tell each person here how you feel about him," etc. Or, to emphasize non-verbal expression: "*Do* something to each one of us"; or, "Do to each what you feel prompted to do, acting on your impulse of the moment."

These procedures, as most others in Gestalt Therapy, should not turn into stereotyped forms in which each participant in the group is asked to engage, but are most useful when employed as part of an organic development, and according to the needs of the individual at the time. Their function is mainly that of overcoming the individual's inhibition of expression or lack of expression in the interpersonal domain. The catalytic effect of others is here used as a stimulus to elicit what the continuum of awareness does not spontaneously show.

The active form is valuable in the case of risk-avoiders, with a marked split between verbal-intellectual responses and their emotional-impulsive behavior. In such cases, the prescription of *doing* something may either bring the individual to an impasse or reveal an aspect of himself altogether inaccessible through verbal terms.

Aside from the requests of saying or doing something, whether to other group members or not, there is a form of expression which deserves to be singled out because of the degree it brings together unstructuredness and initiative: unstructured vocalization, or gibberish. Gibberish is one of the few actions that cannot be programmed or rehearsed. Willingness to "speak" gibberish may be seen as a willingness to say the unknown, the unthought. Yet the nature of the task is not only unpatterned, but expressive. Anyone who has experimented with gibberish will know how it reflects, for each one of us, something of our individual style and feelings of the moment. In its lack of structure, there is something predetermined to gibberish: it obediently molds itself to our inner reality, as an artwork.

The technique of requesting expression in gibberish can be valuable, as random actions are, to stimulate initiative and risk-taking in general, but has a more specific use too. Gibberish has the uniqueness—at least for some individuals—of allowing for a spontaneity of expression that their words or other actions would not allow. In this way, the message conveyed through these seemingly meaningless syllables can serve for both cue and seed for self-awareness. Sometimes the person may censor all anger from his statements, voice, and awareness, and yet produce gibberish that he acknowledges as angry beyond a doubt. Or his ordinary voice and stance will become collected while his gibberish will be pleading, and this may inspire further work on his suppressed needfulness. Whatever the patient has said in gibberish he may experiment in saying in words later, and this is most likely to lead to expanded awareness.

Individual Prescriptions. Whatever the basis for the therapist's intuition or perception, it is a fact that he may sometimes see the "holes" in an individual's personality.

> . . . every one of us has holes in his personality. Wilson Van Dusen discovered this first in the schizophrenic, but I believe that every one of us has holes. Where something should be, there is nothing. Many people have no soul. Others have no genitals. Some have no heart; all their energy goes into computing, thinking. Others have no legs to stand on. Many people have no eyes. They project the eyes, and the eyes are to quite an extent in the outside world and they always live as if they are being looked at. . . . Most of us have no ears. People expect the ears to be outside and they talk and expect someone to listen. But who listens? If people would listen, we would have peace (Perls, 1969, p. 39).

He may develop a notion of what the patient is avoiding in his life and behavior, what he is failing to acknowledge, allow or express, and yet is part of himself. In helping him to express the precise aspects of himself that he is suppressing, he is helping him to know himself, to take responsibility for what he is and thus to become whole. The type of intuition or perception referred to above, which in ordinary psychotherapy would originate in interpretation or comment, the Gestalt therapist is most likely to put in the patient's mouth rather than his ear. Perls' formula, "May I feed you a sentence?" has become standard technique, whereby the patient experiments with the possible truth the therapist has seen, making it his own statement about himself. Most often, this action will elicit a sense of either truth or falseness, or another reaction more significant than either intellectual agreement or lack of it.

The therapist's invitation to the patient to do something avoided is generally more effective when this entails actions rather than statements, or if these be words, words that have the value of actions.

Therapist: I see that you avoided looking at her.
Patient: Yes.

Therapist: Experiment with the opposite: look at her directly.

Patient: I do not feel at ease when I do so. I feel I do not want to communicate with her.

Therapist: Tell her.

Patient: I do not feel drawn to. I feel like being far away from you. I would not want to see you at all. (more assertively) I do not like being around you. You are sucking me in all the time with your demands. (loudly) And I hate you!

In this instance, the therapist's role is somewhat that of a midwife helping to bring into expression what otherwise would be left unsaid. In other instances, he may take greater leaps: he may request a complying "good boy" to express anger, he may direct a superman type to ask for help, an arrogant intellectual to repeat "I do not know." In many such instances, he will be acting upon his intuition of the "killer" in the "good boy," the insecurity in the know-it-all, or the superman's need for affection.

At other times, prescriptions such as these may be based upon a formulation other than intuition or perception of cues: the principle of reversal.

One of Perls' original ideas has been the application of the figure-ground distinction to the question of self-perception and personality functioning in general. To the extent of our neurosis, we inflate the magnitude of some of our traits, which we regard as virtues, and we scotomize those that we call vices. Similarly, we filter down our spontaneity, fostering some manifestations, inhibiting others. What if we shift our point of view, and choose to see as figure what we have been regarding as ground? What if we carry out an experiment of living up-side-down in the world for some time? If it happened that we are up-side-down in it now, without knowing it, the experiment may reveal to us a better possibility.

The idea of reversing habitual self-perceptions and actions may take different forms, all of which may be seen as a means of eliciting the expression of what is postponed, bypassed, or suppressed in terms of an incompatible gestalt. The assumption here is that the opposite to the person's attitude is likely to be a part of him too, yet a less developed side of his personality.

The principle of reversal can be applied not only to feelings but also to physical attitudes. Opening up when in a closed posture, breathing deeply as an alternative to a restraint in the intake of air or exhalation, exchanging the motor attitudes of left and right, etc., can eventually lead to the unfolding of unsuspected experiences. The following is an example of this kind:

The therapist notices that while expressing his ongoing experiences the patient often interrupts what he is saying and feeling and in such moment he swallows or sniffs. The therapist suggests that he do the opposite of sniffing and swallowing. The patient engages in a forceful and prolonged exhalation through the nose and mouth, that ends with what he reports as an unfamiliar and surprising feeling: ". . . somewhat as if I were sobbing, but also pushing against a resistance, and my muscles are tense, as when I stretch in yawning; I enjoy this tension when trying to exhale to the very end of my breath, which also feels somehow like an orgasm."

Later, he discovered that he had been living with this feeling for a long time without being aware of it: "It is like wanting to burst, wanting to explode from the inside, tearing down a sort of membrane in which I am wrapped and limited. And I am at the same time this strait jacket and I am squeezing myself."

This short experience was the starting point of a spontaneous development which took place in the coming months. The muscular tension and concomitant feelings were always very much in his awareness from then onward, and he felt more and more inclined to do physical exercise. He then discovered the pleasure of dancing and becoming much freer in his expression, both in movement and general attitude. Finally, he could sense the anger implied in his muscular contractions until he would be aware of it in his reactions to people to a degree he had not been before.

Still another guideline for the initiation of action or expression that has been withheld is the person's own sense of lack of "finishedness," or in Gestalt terminology, lack of closure. Words unsaid and things undone leave a trace in us binding us to the past. A considerable part of our daydreaming and thinking is an attempt to live out in fantasy what we fail to live in reality. Sometimes, as we shall see, the therapist invites the patient to make fantasies more real by acting them out; at other times he merely inquires about his sense of unfinishedness, and invites the patient to carry out what he has postponed or avoided. This idea may apply in different forms: finishing in fantasy an unfinished dream; saying to parents what was not said to them during childhood years; saying goodbye to a divorced spouse or a dead relative. In group therapy it is a common practice to inquire at the end of sessions or days about unfinished situations between group members. Most frequently, "unfinishedness" is created by withholding the expression of appreciation or resentment, and such expression may be required directly as a group exercise.

COMPLETING EXPRESSION

We are always expressing ourselves, to a point. The true novelist will portray the most anonymous character in such a way that the lack of anything special may be revealed as an expression of himself, after all. There are moments when we are all artists, and see the miracle of every individual's uniqueness through his seemingly insignificant actions. Yet just as with awareness, self-expression varies in degree from one person to another. One of the things a Gestalt therapist does is to *intensify* the person's self-expression. This he does, first of all, by recognizing the moments or elements of true expression in an action, and inviting their development.

Therapist: What do you experience now?
Patient: Nothing special.
Therapist: You shrugged your shoulders.
Patient: I guess so.
Therapist: There, you did it again (shrugs shoulders).
Patient: I guess it is a habit.
Therapist: Please do it again.
Patient: (Complies.)
Therapist: Now exaggerate that gesture.
Patient: (Shrugs, grimaces, and makes a rejecting gesture with elbows and hands.) I guess I am saying "don't bug me."—Yeah, leave me alone.

For the sake of clarity, I think we can distinguish at least four types of procedures leading to an intensification of action.

1. Simple repetition
2. Exaggeration and development
3. Explicitation or translation
4. Identification and acting

I will deal with these four in turn.

Simple Repetition. This is a method the purpose of which is to intensify the person's awareness of a given action or statement of his, and may be seen as a step beyond the therapist's action of simply mirroring or reflecting. The example of shrugging shoulders, above, may serve to illustrate the point. Sometimes verbal repetition may have a dramatic effect, in that the person brings himself to see more and more wholeheartedly something that he was minimizing or not weighing fully, or was covering up under a mask.

Patient: (Talking to her mother) I don't want anything from you anymore. I just want you to keep away from us. Don't intrude on us. I am not your daughter anymore. I never was, really. You never understood me. I resent that you never did. I resent you and I hurt because you don't understand me. You don't see me. How I would like you to see me!

Therapist: Repeat that.

Patient: I would like you to see me, Mother. See me. Here I am for you to see. I want you to be able to see me. Don't look away. Don't form theories about me. *This* is me. Take me as I am; no more, no less. Can you *see* me?

Therapist: Can she?

Patient: I think she can (melts into tears).

Sometimes repetition results, not in an intensification of meaning, but if the original statement was contrary to the patient's true self, *increased meaninglessness*, and a reaction against the original statement.

The technique of repetition can be adapted to the group situation by addressing the repetitive statement or action to different members. In these instances there is room for several variations of the exercise:

1. Strict repetition, (for instance, saying "Good-bye" to each).
2. Strict repetition followed by elaboration according to the way the statement applies to the person in question.
3. Repetition of *content*, adapting the *form* of the statement to each person.
4. Repetition of *attitude* with variation in *content*, (i.e., expression of anger in whatever way seems fit according to the individual encountered).

As in the case of other techniques, these cannot be expected to effect miracles by themselves, but afford an occasion for discovery when applied in the right attitude. It is the therapist's role to oversee the procedure and rescue the individual from slipping into a mechanical procedure, a performance or an avoidance. If he is stimulated to remain aware of what he is feeling and doing, something real is likely to happen.

Exaggeration and Development. Exaggeration is one step beyond simple repetition, and frequently takes place spontaneously when a person is asked to do or say something again a number of times. A gesture will become broader or more precise, a statement louder, or more whispering-like: more intensely expressive of whatever its feeling-tone initially was.

When a person is asked to exaggerate and does this a number of times, he may discover something new in his action. Perhaps this is not a completely new quality, but one which lay in his original behavior like an invisible seed, so that only exaggeration could make it obvious.

In the following illustration (which I am reconstructing after several years) Fritz Perls plays the therapist's part and I am the patient:

Therapist: I have brought a gift for you. Here. (Produces a bowl with sand.)
Patient: (Takes the bowl.)
Therapist: Eat it.
Patient: I feel perplexed. I don't know whether you really want me to eat it or whether there is another message that I am not getting.
Therapist: Eat it.
Patient: (Takes a pinch of sand between two fingers and puts it into his mouth.)
Therapist: What do you experience?
Patient: I feel the grains of sand in my mouth and between my teeth and I hear the sound of the grains when I chew them. I notice more saliva coming to my mouth and I feel the desire to get rid of the sand. I start spitting some grains out but they still stick to my tongue. I take my tongue between my fingers to clean it—and now the sand sticks to my fingers. I'm rubbing my fingers with each other—while I continue to spit.
Therapist: Exaggerate that.
Patient: And I rub my hands with one another, and against my pants and keep throwing away sand, throwing it away, away, away! (With broad rejecting movements of arms and hands.) Yes —that is what I feel—I have been swallowing down too much that had nothing to do with me. I'll get rid of you now. Out of me! Thank you very much for your sand!

Exaggeration constitutes a form of development of an action, but development does not always involve exaggeration. Sometimes, if we stay with an action or statement through repetition, emphasis will result in a modification of the said action, in such a way that one movement leads to another, one feeling or thought to a different one. The instruction "develop that" is an invitation to the patient to explore the *trend* of this movement, gesture, posture, vocal sound, or visual image. In this way the urge, only imperfectly expressed in a fleeting action, may reveal itself fully in a sequence which may at times constitute a piece of dance, music, or poetry.

Patient: I don't have any marked feeling. I don't see the point of enumerating my physical sensations . . .

Therapist: Please go on speaking with the same voice but without the words.

Patient: Da da da da da da da da da da da da. (with an expression of hopelessness)

Therapist: Exaggerate that expression in your voice.

Patient: (goes on; this time with more apparent sadness)

Therapist: Still more. Exaggerate it and see what develops.

Patient: (His voice becomes a melody, sad and majestic, and with increasing potency.) This is what I wanted to do all my life! To sing! (tearful) That was truly *me*, more than in all my words! How wonderful! I don't want to stop!! (goes on singing)

Explicitation or Translation. I'm giving the name "explicitation" to one of the most original techniques of Gestalt Therapy, which the therapist generally introduces with statements such as "Give words to your nodding"; "If your tears could speak what would they say?" "What would your left hand say to your right hand?" or "Give a voice to your loneliness." In doing so the patient is being urged to translate into words a piece of non-verbal expression—a gesture, visual image, physical symptom, etc.—and he is thus requested to make explicit a content which was only implicit.

Therapist: What do you have to say to Martha?

Patient: (With a very dead voice.) I don't have much to say to you. I like your expression and what you have said today but I am a little afraid of you. . . .

Therapist: Speak to her in gibberish.

Patient: (Turns very animated while doing so, leans forward, smiles and gesticulates with his hands.)

Therapist: Now translate that into English.

Patient: Martha, you're lovely; I'd like to caress you, kiss you, take care of you. I feel very tender toward you. You are like a beautiful flower and I always like to be near you.

In the process of explicitating the patient must necessarily empathize with that aspect of himself or his perception that he tries to put into words. He must, so to speak, experience the event from the inside rather than as an external onlooker: the result may be surprising when applied to the perception of persons or dream images, both of which are screens for our projection. In these instances the projected phantom may grow and become explicit in its fantastic quality, or, alternatively, a true perception that was covered up by a projection may come to light:

Patient: I hated him, and I still do. He was a dirty old man. He always liked to touch me or kiss me and I was scared of him. . . .

Therapist: Let him speak. Imagine what he would have said if he had been able to talk to you in complete honesty about how he felt.

Patient: He would have said "You're a beautiful little girl. You're so much as a little girl is meant to be: so healthy, so pure! It's like drinking fresh water in the middle of a desert. I feel so lonely and cut off from life, and all my loneliness vanishes when I'm with you."

Therapist: How do you feel about him now?

Patient: I feel compassion. I wish I had not been so mean to him. There was nothing to be scared about.

The process of explicitation leads to the desired end of interpretation through a radically different approach. In the first place, it is not the therapist who tells the patient the supposed "meaning" of his action, gesture, voice; but the patient is urged to *contact* his message for himself. In the second place, there lies the great distance between "thinking about" a piece of behavior or symbol and empathizing with it.

The implicit first step in explicitating is *experiencing* the feeling-content of the action to be explicitated. Secondly, translating that content into the alternative medium of words. This process is similar to that involved in poetry or in the figurative arts. Attempting to draw, for instance, is, above all else, learning how to *see*.

This process of contacting an experience and then exaggerating it in words may be seen as one more instance of exaggeration and development of an expressive act. The difference is that, in explicitation, development does not remain within a single domain of experience (movement, voice, words) but flows from one domain into another.

When a message (hitherto invisible as such) is translated from actions, sounds, or images into words, the process rightly deserves to be called one of explicitation, since ordinarily motor-visual activity is closer to our automatic and unconscious processes, whereas the verbal or conceptual, linked to the "secondary process," are part of our wakeful activity. The process of translation need not be from action to words, however, in order to serve the general aim of amplifying alone:

Therapist: What are you feeling now?

Patient: I feel restless. I am impatient at myself for not coming up with anything important. And I'm very aware of the group as a captive audience.

Therapist: I see that you're stamping your left foot.

Patient: (Exaggerates the movement.) Yes.

Therapist: Now do with your whole body what your foot is doing. (gradually develops movement until he is stomping forcefully with both feet while he slaps his thighs with his palms and bares his teeth)

Therapist: Make some sounds, too.

Patient: Ah! Ah! Ahh!! (forceful exhalations proceeded by glotal stops which turn more and more into laughter)

Therapist: Now *do* something in the same attitude.

Patient: (uncrosses somebody's arms and straightens out his posture) Wake up, man! (walks around stomping his feet and motions with arms and hands as if to indicate standing up) Wake up everybody! Let us get out of this sick, dark place! (opens the door and pushes somebody out of the room) Or *you* get out. I'll clean up this house and throw away all your shit. (drags somebody by the arm) Be clean and joyful or get out of here!

Identification and Acting. Acting is an important part of Gestalt Therapy both in the external sense of going through the motions that fit a given role and in the inner sense of experiencing oneself as another, imagining oneself as possessing the attributes or actions of other beings or things.

In the sense that acting gives motoric expression to an idea, feeling, or image, it may be regarded as one more instance of *translation* from one expressive modality to another. Indeed, it is the converse of explicitation: while in explicitating we give words to our movements, in acting we give movements to a thought. Acting, therefore, may be understood as one more way of *completing* or implementing expression. The private behavior that we call "thinking" might be regarded as incomplete action or symbolic action. In embodying or carrying it into the medium of flesh and bones, we carry out that action to its full expression. The same may be said of anticipation and remembering. What the Gestalt therapist is doing when he asks a patient to act out his memories or expectations is equivalent to asking him to carry out physically an action that he is carrying out, repetitiously sometimes, in fantasy. While doing so the patient may discover that he is hanging on to that particular memory or fantasy as a consequence of its very "unfinishedness"—an urge to take action, chronically prevented and substituted by halfhearted rehearsing.

Aside from the principle of completion there is still another sense in which acting expresses the attitude of Gestalt Therapy. In an inner sense, acting entails a process of identification, of becoming one with the part that we act or recognizing "its" experience as our own. The instructions "*be* him," "*be* your hand," "*be* your voice," etc., are one step beyond the empathy required by explicitation. Between "give a voice to the crybaby in you," and "be the crybaby" there is a difference in the degree of identification with us as actor. The task will probably be harder for the patient when it amounts to identifying with an unpleasant side of himself that he is trying hard to disown. On the other hand, to the extent that he is able to identify with all that he is—good or bad—he will be taking responsibility for himself.

Not only do identification and acting shorten the distance between *I* and its processes, but they are major avenues to awareness. We can know by *being* something or somebody more than by reasoning about it or him. Acting calls for the holistic understanding that is the function of intuition more than of any other single task. What is specific to the Gestalt employment of acting, however, is that the injunction behind every task is a variation upon "be what you are." Scenes and characters are not the gods of a religious ritual or the creations of a classical author, but aspects of our own lives which we might be prone to regard as accidental or trivial, sometimes meaningless: a favorite figure of speech, a gesture, a fantasy.

The main applications of acting in Gestalt Therapy are the enactment of dreams, the acting of anticipations of the future (which lie behind most real-life conflicts), the representation of the past and playing the different parts that are in conflict in personality. With the approach of Gestalt Therapy to dreams, to the past and to the future, I will deal in *The Attitude and Practice of Gestalt Therapy* (work in preparation), so I will only speak here of the enacting of personality traits.

Some of the most dramatic moments in a Gestalt Therapy session are those in which the patient takes sides with the different parts that constitute non-integrated aspects or conflicting sub-selves within his personality: the good boy and the spiteful brat, the bully and the philanthropist, the caring person and the selfish one, the masculine and the feminine, the active and the passive, parent and child, top-dog and underdog and so on.

I think that much of the artistry of the therapist lies in his ability to indicate to the patient the key roles to explore through acting—a matter which requires, like all else in Gestalt Therapy, sensitivity to the moment. The assumption or knowledge that practically everybody wants to feel special, for instance, is not enough for telling a given person "be special" or "act special." In order for such role-playing to be successful the patient must have been coming into contact with this region of his psyche by gradual steps, so that acting "special" crowns an organic development during the session.

Here are some of the cues that may reveal to the therapist the presence of an attitude eligible for enactment:

1. *Psychological symptoms* such as anxiety, guilt, shame. Most instances of anxiety involve either:

A. The imagined judgment or reaction of another (as in stage-fright) who may then be chosen as a subject of role-playing and eventually recognized as one's own attitude toward oneself; or

B. A catastrophic fantasy of the future, which may be similarly acted out: failure, disgrace, death, etc.

In guilt there is always a self-accusation or projected self-accusation that may be likewise dramatized by playing guilty to the fullest measure and then by playing accuser. In both instances other members of the group may be used as targets by seeing them as being judges or underdogs.

In the case of shame or embarrassment the sense of exposure implicit in such feeling also implies an onlooker or a judging witness, the attitudes of whom may be explored by acting him (or her) out.

2. *Conflicts.* Even micro-conflicts such as smiling or not, looking at the therapist or away from him, etc., are usually the expression of a broader split than that which is apparent in the specific action under consideration. By explicitating or exaggerating both alternatives in this conflict—at the moment—the patient is likely to arrive at two broad aspects of his psychological functioning.

3. *Exaggeration and reversal.* The amplification of virtually any feeling or expressive act: gesture, posture, voice inflection, verbal statement—may soon disclose a broad attitude worthy of further exploration by enactment. Once this is defined, the converse attitude may be explored as well.

4. *A discrepancy between verbal and non-verbal expression* may be the avenue of investigation of another split. A patient, for instance, was reporting anxiety and trembling while his voice, posture, and demeanor conveyed great poise and security. I asked him to act overtly afraid and poised, alternatively, matching in either case verbal and non-verbal behavior. In doing this, he soon discovered that he was *always playing* poised, that he did not feel free to show his weakness, and that he had a top-doggish compulsion about being the master of the situation and so forth. In another instance the patient spoke with calm collectedness, reporting pleasant feelings, while at the same time he obviously writhed in his chair and rubbed his sweating hands. An indication similar to the one above, to the effect of *being* anxious and *being* a person who "feels fine" alternatively, revealed to him his own pretense and the fact that not only when asked to play "a cool role" he did so, but always.

5. *Total behavior.* At times the therapist may become aware of a patient's role through the style of his total behavior rather than by any precise cue. To the degree that the game so spotted by him is subtle, he will rely on his intuitive apprehension of the behavioral gestalt. After reflecting his observation (i.e., "You seem to be playing innocent," or "I think you are looking for the limelight") and if his observation is acknowledged by the patient, he may move on to suggest an exaggeration or the acting out of the relevant characteristics.

Minimization. Self-expression is frequently blunted by actions such as minimization, roundaboutness, vagueness, etc., and in such cases an increase in directness will amount to a greater message-to-noise ratio in an individual's communication:

Patient: I feel rather tired and a little bored. Perhaps I am a little irritated at you, too. It might be that I don't enjoy very much being here at the moment . . .

Therapist: I notice that you use many qualifiers: "*rather* tired," "a *little* this or that," *perhaps*, it *might* be . . .

Patient: I think you're right.

Therapist: (ironically) You "*think*," *perhaps* it *might* be true.

Patient: Yes. I use a lot of qualifiers. It is . . . kind of a habit.

Therapist: "Kind of."

Patient: It is a habit.

Therapist: Please tell us again of your feelings, this time omitting perhapses and maybes. Could you repeat what you said a while ago with this change.

Patient: I feel tired. Yes, I do. And I feel irritated and bored. I would like to go to bed rather than being here. No. I do not prefer that: I intensely desire to rest and yet I am interested enough to stay.

A frequent source of minimization is related to the use of the conjunction *but,* and therefore the very occurrence of the word may be taken as a signal. Aside from valid meanings that require the existence of the word in our language, *but* is all to often introduced to disqualify a statement or take away some of its weight or validity. At any rate, *but* is an audible reflection of conflict. "Yes, but . . . ," "I would like to do this, but . . . ," "I like you, but. . . ." By means of this ambiguity the individual avoids taking sides or fully experiencing either half of his statement—each half invalidating the other. Aside from the indications that the therapist may give him at this point to the effect of taking sides with or exaggerating either one of them, he will sometimes discourage the use of the word *but* and sugest, instead, *and.*

Patient: I am holding back from you but I like your peacefulness.

Therapist: Try *and* instead of *but.*

Patient: I'm holding back from you *and* I enjoy your peacefulness. Of course! This is much more true.

It. Another turn of language intimately related to the issue of directness is the use of *it* instead of a specific content.

Patient: He wanted us to do something that I couldn't agree to. And he insisted so much on it that it became the object of endless fights between us . . .

Therapist: Could you tell us what the *it* is?

Patient: (a long pause) He wanted us to take a psychedelic trip.

Frequently the real meaning substituted by *it* is *I,* or *you,* and in this way *it* acts as a buffer to dampen the directness of an encounter:

Patient: My hand is doing this movement . . .

Therapist: Is *it* doing the movement?

Patient: I am moving my hand like this . . . and now the thought comes to me that . . .

Therapist: The thought "comes" to you?
Patient: I have the thought.
Therapist: You *have it?*
Patient: I think. Yes. I think that I use *it* very much, and I am glad that by noticing it I can bring it all back to me.
Therapist: Bring it back?
Patient: *Bring myself back.* I feel thankful for this.
Therapist: This?
Patient: Your idea about the "it."
Therapist: My idea?
Patient: I feel thankful toward you.

Perls first suggested the use of *I* instead of *it* in *Ego, Hunger and Aggression* and he gave much importance to this seemingly trivial detail of language in his work. He says, in the above-mentioned work: "Every time you do apply the proper ego language you express yourself, you assist in the development of your personality." As with many techniques, though, I prefer to regard this particular one as a useful prop, the value of which will be determined by the appropriateness of its use at the moment. I have seen therapists picking at words and accomplishing little, for that was seemingly a wrong choice at the moment. I am personally willing to let many *its* pass when the request of rewording would interrupt a feeling, disrupt concentration on an image, distract the patient from identifying with a dream character, etc.

Avoidance of *I* is not always paralleled by the introduction of *it.* Here are some alternatives:

Patient: We are all feeling nervous and I don't think that we like what is going on.
Other Patient: Speak for yourself.
Patient: Well, I am nervous . . .

In this case, *we* serves as the forest that hides the tree and entails an unwillingness to take responsibility for an experience. Another screen is *one:*

One does not do this easily.
One?
I have trouble expressing myself to all of you.

Impersonal statements are frequent and pass as scientific:

Patient: I see your eyes are looking at me . . . There is perspiration in my hands . . . And there is a quavering in my voice. There is fear . . .

Therapist: Your manner of speech is that of a very detached observer: "there is" or that, never "*I* feel afraid"; or "*my* voice quavers."

Patient: Yes. That is so true. That is what I want most, *to be able to say I.*

Retroflections. One instance of indirectness that is the object of a specific technique in Gestalt Therapy is the undoing of retroflections: the redirecting of an impulse that has been displaced in such a way that, instead of meeting its intended object, it reverts to the agent.

Perls has given the name of *retroflection* to the behavior by which a person "does to himself what he originally did or tried to do to other persons or objects." Instead of directing his energies to actions upon the environment which will satisfy his needs, he "redirects activity inward and *substitutes* himself in place of the environment as the target of behavior." To the extent that he does this, he splits his personality into "doer" and "done to."

Retroflection is a consequence of environmental obstacles to the expression of impulses, which have led to an active holding back on the part of the individual. In holding back, the person does to himself what originally was done to him by environment (he introjects) and uses for this activity the energy of his own impulses (retroflects).

Retroflection, according to Perls, may be quite functional: "Do not jump to the conclusion that we imply that it would be fine if we could all, without further ado, release our inhibitions! In some situations holding back is necessary, even lifesaving—for instance holding back inhaling while under water. The important question is whether or not a person has *rational grounds* for presently choking off behavior in give circumstances."

Many of our retroflections, however, are dysfunctional and unconscious. To Perls *repression* is "forgotten" retroflection.

I think that the concept of retroflection is of particular value to the psychotherapist, for it brings into his attention the *active* aspect of repression and inhibition. As Perls has said, "Psychoanalysis has stressed recovery of awareness of what is repressed—that is, the blocked impulse. We, on the other hand, emphasize recovery of awareness of the blocking, the feeling that one is doing it and *how* one is doing it. Once a person discovers his retroflecting action and regains control of it, the blocked impulse will be recovered automatically . . . The great advantage of dealing with the retroflecting part of the personality—the active repressing agent—is that this is within fairly easy reach of awareness, can be directly experienced, and does not depend upon guessed-at interpretations."

The content of retroflections may vary, and so its outcome: self-hate, self-pity, greedy self-squeezing, and so on. Even introspection is considered by Perls as a retroflective peering at oneself: "This form of retroflection is so universal in our culture that much of the psychological literature simply takes it for granted that any attempt to increase self-awareness must of necessity consist of introspection . . . The observer is split off from the part observed, and not until this split is healed will a person fully realize that self-awareness, which is not introspected, can exist. We previously likened genuine awareness to the glow produced within a burning coal by its own combustion, and introspection to turning the beam of a flashlight on an object and peering at its surface by means of the reflected rays."

I think that by far the most common type of retroflection with which we deal in psychotherapy is the retroflection of aggression. Just as aggression toward others may constitute a projection of aggression toward the self, self-aggression may well constitute a retroflection of an impulse originally directed toward another. In this way, a person may turn resentment into self-accusations and guilt, sarcasm into a feeling of ridicule, hatred into a feeling of having no right to exist, and so on. In general terms, retroflected aggression becomes depression, as psychoanalysis has established long ago.

The possibility that a person's feeling toward himself may constitute a case of retroflection is tested out in Gestalt Therapy, not via interpretation, but through experiment. When a person is directed to do to another what he is doing to himself, he *may* find out that this is what he really wanted to do. If this is so, he will have regained some of his directness of expression.

The prospect of reversing a retroflection frequently meets considerable anxiety, shame or guilt, and when the retroflection is finally undone, this may lead to socially inappropriate or childish behavior. However, this is one of the instances in which acting out may be the quickest road to insight upon the repressed as well as toward a redirecting of impulse. Perls gives us the following example:

> A religious man, for instance, unable to vent his wrath on the Lord for his disappointments, beats his own breast and tears his own hair. Such self-aggression, obviously a retroflection,

nevertheless *is* aggression and it *does* give some satisfaction to the retroflecting part of the personality. It is aggression that is crude, primitive, undifferentiated—a retroflected childish temper tantrum—but the part of the personality that is attacked is always there and available for attack. Self-aggression can always be sure of its victim.

To reverse such a retroflection in one fell swoop would mean that the person would then attack others in ways just as ineffectual and archaic. He would rouse the same overwhelming counteraggression that led him to retroflect in the first place. It is some realization of this which makes even the imagined reversal of retroflections productive of so much fear. What is overlooked is that the change can be made in easy stages which gradually transform the whole situation as they proceed. One can, to start with, discover and accept the fact that he does "take it out on himself." He can become aware of the emotions of the retroflecting part of his personality—notably the grim joy taken in administering punishment to himself. This, when he achieves it, represents considerable progress, for vindictiveness is so socially disesteemed as to be most difficult to acknowledge and accept even when one supposedly spares others and directs it solely against oneself. Only when accepted—that is, when it is reckoned with as an existing, dynamic component of one's functioning personality—does one reach the possibility of modifying, differentiating, redirecting it into healthy expression. As one's orientation in the environment improves, as one's awareness of what one genuinely wants to do becomes clearer, as one makes approaches which are limited tryouts to see what will happen, gradually one's techniques for expression of one's previously blocked impulses develop also. They lose their primitive, terrifying aspect as one differentiates them and gives them a chance to catch up with the more grown-up parts of the personality (Perls, 1951, p. 149-150).

REFERENCES

Perls, F. S., R. F. Hefferline, and P. Goodman. *Gestalt Therapy: Excitement and Growth in the Human Personality.* New York: Julian Press, 1951.

Perls, F. S. *Gestalt Therapy Verbatim.* Moab, Utah: Real People Press, 1969.

CHAPTER 10

CHARACTER ARMOR AND BEING A GOOD BOY: AN INDIVIDUAL GESTALT SESSION

ERIC MARCUS, M.D.

In this selection, a middle portion of a Gestalt workshop session, Eric Marcus employs several Gestalt techniques to good advantage: obtaining a statement from the participant concerning what he would like to work on ("the contract"), staying with a feeling, and finishing the unfinished business. Marcus typically uses the participants in his workshops to play a variety of roles for the member in the hot seat. The feedback and group interaction that typically follows working is omitted here due to transcription difficulties.

Eric: Is there anything in particular that you'd like to avoid? (My question is a very unusual "opener" for a therapy encounter. It is of course more customary to ask what the person would like to work on. In this particular situation I had a hunch that the client was very reluctant to have a Gestalt experience with me.)

Curt: Yes.

Eric: What would you like to avoid?

Curt: Feeling frightened. Making the decision. Taking a stand. To go somewhere.

Eric: Don't change position. Just be aware of your hands.

Curt: Um-hum. I know that my hands are there. They're there purposely.

Eric: Tell us. What's the purpose? I'm curious.

Curt: My feet are cold and I sneeze from cold allergies so I try to keep them warm. No, it's true. That's why I usually wear shoes.

Eric: That's not what Gestalt theory says about all that. That's the way it is.

Curt: I'll have to change doctors then.

Eric: In addition to that, see what else your feet were going to say. But it's too late now, you've let go.

Curt: No, it's just to keep warm, really. My feet are very cold. They always are when I don't have shoes on.

Eric: Does this sentence fit? Right now I have very cold feet.

Curt: Yes, in many ways.

Eric: Try it.

Curt: Right now I have cold feet, I'm scared. I'm very tense. My mouth is dry.

Eric: My guess is that you are prepared, today in your work, to suffer, and feel pain. My hunch is that you are girding and that you have prepared yourself during the week to come here and do that.

Curt: No. I have a fear that . . . something occurred two weeks ago that has never happened in my life . . . to that extent . . . and it frightens me. I was even afraid to talk last week. The word is even blocked out. The suicide heightens it.

Eric: What's the "it"?

Curt: The fear, this great emotional thing that happened two weeks ago. I was unconsolable.

Eric: You keep talking about it but you haven't said what it is.

Curt: Uh. Two weeks ago I was transferred to another assignment. It meant the end of my personal ambition for a higher or an administrative position—the end of a ten-year fight . . . which was my ambition not theirs. And I realized it was coming but I refused to acknowledge it until it occurred.

Eric: Let me ask you, is that situation unfinished for you at this time? (If a situation is unfinished it means that there are unexpressed emotions—either positive or negative—attached. An unresolved conflict or situation will prevent the person from utilizing his full energy. I was attempting to find any connection between his emotional turmoil and unfinished business.)

Curt: No. Well, it's resolved. Yes.

Eric: And what do you want with me in telling the story?

Curt: Well, the same day my wife and I decided—well, should you move out or should I? For all practical purposes I have no other family. I have a brother but he's dead and so am I to him. Everything was gone there was . . . I was going to lose my child . . .

Eric: Again, what do you want to do with that at this time? Let me ask you another question. Is that finished or unfinished? (I still do not have a clear idea as to where to focus my attention. He has thus far presented two very distinct *possible* areas of conflict.)

Curt: It's finished. I'm upswinging but it scared me so much that I don't know if I were to go back to something like that whether I wouldn't give up. It scared me that much.

Eric: Well, what would you like right now?

Curt: Strength, I think. Ah . . . Courage. I gave up, Eric, two weeks ago. I was ready to read the whole world off.

Eric: All of your statements are in the past, Curt.

Curt: Okay.

Eric: And it's sort of an endless recitation of history. I am getting lost as to what you want from me now. Twice I've asked you if something was finished and you said yes, it's finished. I need more of a now type of contract with you.

Curt: (Coughs.) I honestly don't know what . . . I can do or want to do. I feel like a scared little kid.

Eric: Say that again.

Curt: I feel like a scared little kid.

Eric: Are you willing to go with that?

Curt: Yes.

Eric: Close your eyes and be that scared little kid part of you. (Pause) Without words, with just a nod of your head . . . take your time . . . indicate to us when you are in touch . . . when you have something specific, something major. (The client is in touch with a very specific feeling. I am attempting to find out whether he can connect the present feeling with any past "unfinished business.")

Curt: (Nods.)

Eric: What age of a scared little kid are you?

Curt: Ten.

Eric: What's happening?

Curt: I just got beat up for the first time in my life and only time . . . by four or five black kids. I was terrified. I came home . . .

Eric: I come home . . . mention it in the present . . . I am coming home.

Curt: I come home and say, Mom, I just got beat up, I'm scared; I'm hurt.

Eric: What happens next?

Curt: She washed my face and then says you're okay, forget about it, and then leaves.

Eric: What do you feel?

Curt: Alone, like there's no one to protect anybody . . . and I can't trust people. I couldn't trust the guy who beat me up not to do it again, I couldn't trust my mom.

Eric: Feel that . . . see if you can get into the state you were in at that time . . . say something . . . stay at that age and relate at that age and say something to your mother . . . call her or something . . . if you could have done it over again in a different way.

Curt: Hey, Mom, stop cooking and sit down with me . . . talk to me. (A participant takes part of Curt's Mom . . . indicated by Peg when she speaks.)

Peg: Got to cook dinner now, Curt, you're okay.

Curt: I'm not really. Mom, it's important.

Peg: I have to get dinner ready here . . . you're okay now. I washed it off. You got beat up . . .

Curt: I want you to stop that, Mom. Talk to me and sit down. Stop it . . . if you don't stop that, Mom, I'm going to take that and throw it on the damn ground. I mean it.

Peg: Curt, you're kinda upset, you got beat up . . .

Curt: Stop it, now.

Peg: I gotta get dinner ready here.

Curt: I don't give a damn. Stop now, now. (Pause.) You aren't going to stop, are you?

Eric: Make her listen.

Peg: I gotta get the dinner ready and I have a lot of things to take care of, Curt, I don't have time to talk.

Curt: Mom, this is very important. I don't know if I can go back to school tomorrow.

Peg: Oh, Curt, come on . . . You'll be okay tomorrow. I've got to get busy and take care of the house, so why don't you run along and find something to do.

Curt: No. When do I come first instead of last?

Eric: You're getting into your adult life (from the tone of voice) . . . try to stay with your ten-year-old as much as possible.

Curt: I'm important, Mom, you've gotta listen to what I have to say.

Peg: Not right now, Curt, I have to get dinner ready. You're okay, I know you've been beat up, but you'll be okay.

Curt: (Sighs.) I'm not ten anymore. I just want to hurt that old lady.

Eric: Stay with the words "pay attention to me."

Curt: (Coughing.) Mom would you take five minutes and sit down please?

Eric: Pay attention to me.

Curt: Pay attention to me.

Peg: I'm very busy now, Curt.

Curt: I need something now. I don't know if you can give it, but I need it right now.

Eric: Say that again. (Important statements are emphasized by asking the client to repeat them. The client is usually so caught up in his work that statements of particular importance may not be given emphasis; accordingly I ask clients to repeat those statements.)

Curt: I don't know if you can give it, but I need it now.

Peg: I gotta get dinner on the table now, Curt.

Eric: Stay with it. Let yourself experience your power in demanding this.

Curt: Huh. (Sighing.)

Eric: What's happening? (Some cushions are put behind him.)

Curt: I'm starting to sweat . . . Mom, I've never yelled at you.

Peg: I hope you're a good boy, Curt.

Curt: I'm not supposed to. I'm supposed to never yell; I'm supposed to do what I say, but I've got to have you . . . (sigh) . . . Talk to me. It's important.

Peg: Not now, Curt, I'm fixing dinner.

Curt: (Sighs.) What do I have to do for you to hear me? Do you hear me at all? Are you listening?

Peg: You see, right now it's dinner time.

Curt: I can't scream and yell at her.

Eric: Well, lose control.

Curt: My whole story, well, forget it, head stuff.

Eric: Lose control.

Curt: I'd better not. If I do I get clobbered. I've been clobbered.

Peg: Who clobbered you?

Curt: My father. And worse, I followed every order.

Eric: Now is the chance to reverse some of that and experience things that you never dared to experience. (I am now proposing that the client reexperience some original situation in a new way. This is one way of finishing the unfinished business. It is a way of "reprogramming.")

Curt: (Deep sigh.)

Eric: Peg will be your mother and she won't give you the satisfaction of a reply.

Peg: Just be a good boy, Curt, and you'll be okay. I can't talk, son, I'm busy right now.

Curt: (Sighs.)

Eric: What's happening with you now?

Curt: I . . . want to hurt somebody.

Eric: Let the pillow be somebody.

Curt: (Sighs.)

Eric: Take your watch off before you get started.

Peg: Be a good boy, Curt, don't make a lot of trouble.

Curt: I never make trouble.

Peg: That's right, that's my boy. You're my good boy who doesn't make noise. Just don't make trouble and you'll be okay. Take care of yourself.

Curt: (Yells.) Shut up, shut up, shut up.

Peg: Such a good boy, talking to his mother like that . . .

Curt: You don't give a shit about me, you don't give a shit . . . you don't, you don't give one rotten shit about me.

Peg: (Constantly giving good boy conversation in a very low voice.)

Curt: You don't care. My brother doesn't care. My father doesn't care. He's no good. When he dies, I'm going to laugh.

Eric: I'm glad you've calmed down and are going to talk about it instead of . . . I thought for a minute you were going to get upset and do something to the pillow, but I'm glad that you've decided just to calm down instead. We can always talk things out. (I am deliberately employing sarcasm to help Curt become aware of his retreat from allowing his emotions to come out by "getting into his head.")

Peg: Right. As long as everybody is reasonable, in time . . . don't get too upset about things, I hate to see people upset . . .

Curt: We can't talk, goddamnit, we can't talk . . .

Eric: Just watch what you're doing . . . calm down, we can talk, just settle down.

Peg: Keep your voice down.

Curt: (Monotone, constantly, while Eric and Peg are talking.) We can't talk, we can't talk, we can't talk (louder and louder), we can't talk.

Eric: Keep your voice down . . .

Curt: No, no, no, no, no.

Eric: Knock it off, for goodness sake . . .

Curt: Just like those other kids at school . . .

Peg: It's terrible, our son has been such a good boy . . .

Curt: I'm nobody, I'm nothing.

Eric: Keep that up and you'll go to prison . . .

Peg: Settle down, Curt, you're such a good boy . . .

Curt: (Calming down.)

Peg: That's it, just calm down and you'll be okay.

Curt: I can't fight you.

Peg: You won't.

Curt: I won't fight you.

Eric: Are you aware of that distinction?

Curt: Yes.

Eric: I imagine that for most people that you just went underground. And you developed your own style. (By "style" I mean character. The therapeutic task is to facilitate the client in "loosening" his character, i.e., style, and developing more flexibility.)

Curt: I've developed a lousy style. I can't yell.

Peg: Won't.

Curt: I don't yell. I won't get mad.

Eric: Okay. I want you to do one more thing. I'd like you to stay with that sentence, I won't get mad. I want you to say it ten times. Each time you say it I want you to slap the cushion, and look at Mother and tell her, "I won't get mad." (What I'm doing, of course, is to present the client with a paradox. The paradox will increase the psychological pressure within him and hopefully result in a break in his character armor, via allowing himself to get angry.)

Curt: I won't get mad (slap); I won't get mad (continuing with greater force).

Eric: Stay in eye contact, look at Mother.

Curt: I won't get mad (slap, etc., ten times).

Curt: I hate your fucking guts.

Eric: Tell her some sentences beginning with "What I've done with my anger is . . ."

Curt: What I've done with my anger is to hide it, to push it down, to become a freak. What I've done with my anger is made myself afraid to feel. What I've done with my anger is to make me someone I don't want to be. What I've done with my anger is to make me my image of a good guy, and I don't like it and I don't want to live with it. What I've done with my anger is to screw up my whole life and waste good energy on shit.

Eric: Okay, then. Satisfied? Take a look around the group just to reestablish contact.

Curt: I feel for the first time that I've released part of me and I feel good.

Not only has the client been able to release pent-up anger, but the release also begings to loosen his character armor and consequently his need to maintain a "good guy" image.

CHAPTER 11

"HELP ME": SUPPORT AND RESPONSIBILITY IN GESTALT THERAPY

ED HACKERSON, M.A.

Ed Hackerson is in the private practice of marriage, child, and family counseling in El Paso, Texas, and is also a co-director of the Gestalt Therapy Institute of the Southwest. Previously, he has held positions as coordinator of the Adolescent Unit, Big Spring State Hospital, Texas, and as a researcher for the Human Resources Research Organization.

> *"Look at me," he said. "I have no doubts or remorse. Everything I do is my decision and my responsibility."*—Don Juan in *Journey to Ixtlan* by Carlos Castaneda.

The consistent and often obvious thread woven through the following work is the issue of responsibility. I think of the Gestalt concept of the individual's being responsible for his feeling, thinking, and behaving as grounded in the basic assumption that everyone can be self-supporting and need not manipulate others in order to survive. In fact, the manipulation of others is a growth-suppressing and toxic process. Since the individual's everyday manipulations vs. self-support occur in microcosm in the group, this issue can take the form of the individual's self-support vs. the therapist's "helping" in the therapeutic situation. As a Gestalt therapist I want to handle this by structuring a situation in which I frustrate the persons using me for support and stimulate them to experience their own self-support. I see as implicit in my contract as therapist that I will use myself as a tool and provide only enough support to stabilize the person on his feet: he then starts and continues walking. A more classic Gestalt therapist might avoid helping or supporting in any way.

The explicit contracts I make with group members are that there will be no physical violence and that the individual identify when he wants to work, and that he be willing to work. I'm not willing to overextend myself and do the person's work for him. Often, with new people who have difficulty staying in touch with what is in the forefront of their awareness, I will help by structuring the situation.

I do this by having them focus their awareness on the different levels of their experience—feeling, thinking, and doing. In providing structure for the person working, I am careful, for in doing so, I risk losing my personal integrity and becoming confused in the other's reality (or risk their getting lost in mine). I balance this against what I consider my contract to structure the situation and provide the person with the tools necessary for self-change.

In order to use myself effectively as a tool for change and not get lost I must maintain my own balance and self-awareness. Not getting lost in helping and interpreting is difficult, and is especially so for the therapist entering Gestalt from other methodologies. My own getting lost occurs most often when I'm out of balance and fogging myself out, in short, when I lose touch with myself. In such situations I've had training therapists turn to me and say "What do I do next?"; my statement to them is: "Get in touch with yourself." I think that through my awareness of my own here and now I will be able to bring vitality, clarity, and excitement to the therapeutic situation.

In each of the following pieces of work I have to stay in touch with myself, with how much I want each person to "get somewhere," and how I could easily "help"—which produces the opposite effect. Although the first person in the sequence to work (Chris) has had considerable experience, she makes a clear statement, early in her work, that she will use me for support if I'll let her. The second person to work (Ann) has had little Gestalt experience (three group sessions). Both of them tempt me and make available opportunities in which I can take responsibility for them, and in certain instances I do. I would like to be able to say that I do so with awareness each time, only I don't and I hook myself into the game occasionally. These are difficult situations in which to use myself as an effective tool in that they require good judgment, timing, and constant self-awareness. The second piece of work is difficult in that the person working is inexperienced with the Gestalt process and has a difficult time staying with her present experience. Her inexperience and difficulty provide ample opportunity for me to hook myself into helping.

The first two pieces of work are from one group session in which the two worked one after the other. The first woman, Chris, is twenty-three years old and has had considerable experience with Gestalt work. She entered the group motivated by wanting personal growth and thinking that Gestalt provided the process she could use to experience being "her." Shortly after the work presented here, she left the group, indicating that she was in the kind of peace she liked and that she felt no need to continue working.

The second woman, Ann, is a student and came to the group as part of a class assignment to study community facilities. My contract with her, and others in similar situations, is that they come to the group as working participants, not observers. When her class-work terminated, she continued in the group as a regular member and worked with her own personal growth.

The dreamwork, presented last as a counterpoint to the earlier work was done in a Gestalt Institute of the Southwest training workshop by a woman in her thirties who is a therapist and mother. Outwardly she is very self-sufficient and has many talents.

Someone has just finished working and the group is sitting quietly. I want to focus on the now and ask each person to get in touch with his present experience. Quite often, in such a round, an individual will focus on feelings stimulated by the work just completed.

Ed: Let's just go around, summarize what your present experience is . . . in one word, what you're into.
Client 1: I'm comfortable.
Client 2: (Sigh and laughter.)
Client 3: Judging.
Client 4: Thinking.
Client 5: Mixed.
Client 6: Happy.
Ed: Comfortable. Okay, anyone want to work?
Chris: Yes, starting with where I am right now.

Each time someone wants to work with their present, and makes that clear, I become very aware of my own excitement and my eagerness for them to accomplish something. To me, this work is the essence of Gestalt since the focus is on the individual's present and not a "problem." The person is in a position of allowing whatever is of concern to them as an organism to develop. This work requires the person to stay in touch with his present experience and deal with what is in the forefront of awareness.

As a therapist I sometimes scare myself in this situation by wanting something to happen and thinking how I could "help" this person. The paradox of the situation is that if the person does not attend to his awareness I can easily and helpfully supply him with mine. I do this by attending to the situation and my experience and stating what is obvious to me; soon I have the situation structured with experiences or experiments. Thus, in my excitement and eagerness, I can become very directive and/or supportive and eliminate whatever self-support the person might manifest. In my early work I tended to try something, some gimmick, which would produce action. Now, I realize that this is the person's opportunity to find himself—to work with his awareness, take responsibility for his work, and become self-supporting.

Ed: All right, work with your present experience.

My opportunity—I want her to discover herself through the medium of self-awareness. In asking her to work with her own experience I avoid projecting myself into her work.

Chris: Just restless. I feel like I want to be somewhere else, but I don't know where it would be. I feel like out there somewhere is something I could get turned on to and excited about and . . .
Ed: Have an encounter with your "out there somewhere."

I see such entities as "out there somewhere," "confusion," "nothing," etc., as definite resistance and as explicit statements of the person's Here and Now. Therefore, I ask the person to stay with his Here and Now and encounter his resistance as something he is responsible for and with which he can work for change. I think this is an excellent example of the way in which the Gestalt therapist turns resistance into work and takes every possible advantage of the person's present experience.

Chris: Okay. Uh, I want to be out there with you because there is something out there—I am expecting to go out there, and in ten minutes, be or do with you whatever you have to offer. As if I have plans for you out there and I'm waiting for you to get out of here and go out there and do them. If you . . . and, uh, I'm kind of picking and shifting and my mind is just wandering and I'm not here at all. (Laughs a nervous laugh as if she were scared or ashamed.)
Ed: Did I hear a judgment on that? What's going on?

Here she is developing the theme of using someone else for excitement and not using her own resources: someone else has what's necessary. As she approaches this she discontinues the encounter and backs off into awareness of what she is doing. I go with what I hear in her voice, which is almost a mistake, since I can easily project my judgment on her.

Chris: (Looking angry and excited) I don't understand what you're talking about. I was looking at you and waiting for you . . . and I'm not finished with this . . . I didn't have anything else to say so I was looking at you and waiting for you to explain or tell me to do something else . . . waiting for you to guide me.

Ed: Put Ed out there (on the empty pillow).

I don't want to explain or tell her what to do, and since I'm going to get used I will let her do me herself. I want to frustrate her manipulations and structure a situation in which she mobilizes her own self-support. By having her interact with her fantasy of me she can observe *how* she attempts to manipulate. This replacement of "me" is something I use when I want to be helpfully unhelpful. This maneuver sets the stage for her owning her lack of self-direction and again I avoid helping.

Chris: (To empty chair with Ed) I'm unfinished, Ed, and I'm waiting for you to use your expertise to come through with what I'm unfinished with and your face looks blank when I look at you. You're not helping me out any.

Ed: The bastard.

Chris: No, I'm not uptight with you (very nice voice).

Ed: That won't help.

Chris: (Laughs)

Ed: Switch and be Ed . . . (She does and, as Ed, looks at the therapist) . . . You're looking at me? For God's sake! (Raspberry) She's looking at you for help and you're looking at me.

Chris: I'm blanking out. I can't help you. I don't have any answers for you.

Ed: . . .

Chris: Well, I'm trying to think of what Ed would say because I know Ed would say something that would be exactly Ed . . . (laughter) and I'm not coming up with anything.

Ed: You're not going to be able to deal with him.

Chris: (To fantasy Ed) You're no good; you're not helping me out any. Why am I wasting my time with you? You're not any help.

Ed: More.

Chris: You're not any help. You're not helping me out in any way and you're not guiding me in any way and so what am I doing wasting my time here? You're the one with the experience, you're the one who knows what to do, and you're not doing it.

Ed: Put Chris out there and tell her those things. Listen to yourself.

Now she can encounter her own self-frustrating behavior. With a person who is new to the Gestalt process, I use this method as a working introduction to the concept of ownership. She can now play the blaming game with herself.

Chris: (To herself) You're not helping me any and you're the one who knows you and me better than anybody else. And you're not coming up with any answers . . . and you're not doing any good . . . you're not any good because you're not doing anything.

This is an obvious judgment and probably top-dog all the way. I missed it. The developing theme appears to be a judgment on herself for not being self-supporting or "having the goods." I go with the support issue as much out of my involvement as her judging.

Ed: And you?
Chris: Me? Well, I'm depending on *her.*
Ed: So, be her.
Chris: Well, what good will it be in splitting myself up? Oh, I confuse myself when I split myself up (laughs).
Ed: Again.
Chris: I confuse myself when I split myself up ("help me" voice quality).
Ed: (To dependable Chris on empty pillow) She's depending on you now, I just think you really ought to do something . . . hurry. She's probably going under for the third time. Hurry.
Chris: I don't know what to do.
Ed: Tell her.
Chris: I don't know what to do. Quit depending on me. Take care of yourself. And I don't like you throwing all that control on me. If I make a mistake then I'm sunk. You judge me to death.
Ed: So switch. What is your experience over there?
Chris: Excited. Not bad excited, not good excited, just excited.
Ed: How about developing that excitement?

I want her to go with her excitement and see what she discovers about herself. The concept of "developing" in Gestalt is a method whereby the person can focus on an experience or idea. I often have someone develop excitement or movement as a way of contacting their body and the physical aspects of their personal communication.

Chris: Excited and my breathing is kind of not completed—my breathing is fast and shallow. Uh, . . . (sigh) . . . Hm . . . I don't have anything else to say . . .

Ed: Well, you're not helping much.

Chris: No. And I'm not helping it much either. I don't know what she should do. I don't know what to do. I'm not helping you . . .

Ed: (To the group at large) Have we got any helpers? Anybody to help Chris? Help will probably come somehow.

Chris: I don't want any pity or help; I only want someone to tell me if I ask for it.

Ed: Oh, you're damned particular, huh?

Chris: Yeah, and I haven't asked for it.

Ed: You're asking for help.

Chris: I can lean on her all I want.

Ed: Tell her.

Chris: (Angry voice) I can lean on you all I want and I can thrown all kinds of shit on you if I want. Because you're so mean, so, it's okay to pile you with shit (switches seats).

Ed: How about responding to her last statement.

Chris: It's okay to pile me with shit . . . (questioning voice).

Ed: How about me, can I pile you with shit?

She has developed her own split here and I want to test whether her actions are personal or developed from a fantasy of what others feel and think.

Chris: No.

Ed: How about going around and telling everybody, "It's okay if I pile me with shit but you can't. I won't allow you to."

Chris: It's okay if I pile me with shit, but I won't let you dump anything on me. I'm the only person who really cares about myself so I'll take shit from myself but I won't take it from you.

Ed: Say that first part again.

Chris: I'm the only person who cares about me so I'll take shit from myself . . . Hum. I don't like the way that sounds.

Ed: Say that again. To John.

Chris: I'm the only person who cares about myself so I'll take shit from myself. If you don't care about me, you can't give me any shit. Because I won't take it . . . uh . . . you're lucky you don't care about me . . . you're lucky you don't care about me because I'm not going to let you put shit on me.

Ed: How about making that an active process, "You're lucky you don't care about me or I'd give you a bunch of shit."

What stands out for me is her judging/caring process. As she makes a statement to each group member I imagine that she is saying this to herself and about herself. In this framework her statement, ". . . because I'm not going to let you put shit on me . . .," comes out as a projection. This is what she does to others, so I ask her to own the projection and make the caring/shitting process an active one.

Chris: Hmm. Well, okay. You're lucky you don't care about me because I'd give you a bunch of shit. You're lucky you don't care about me, because I'd feel free to put all kinds of shit on you and expect you to take it . . . Yeah, you're in a good place that you don't care about me and you're smart not to care about me. I would expect you to take all the shit I'd give you (excited voice). When I care about people, I give them all kinds of shit (laughter). That's how I show people I care about them.

Ed: I show you I care about you by giving you a bunch of shit.

Chris: I show you I care about you by giving you a bunch of shit. So you're pretty lucky that I don't care about you.

Ed: Say that again.

Chris: So you're pretty lucky I don't care about you.

Ed: Now, I'm hearing a different thing—in the earlier sentences it was—You're pretty lucky you don't care about me or I'd give you a bunch of shit; now it's you're lucky I don't care about you or I'd give you a bunch of shit.

Chris: Well, you're the one who put the switch to it.

Ed: Not the last one. Say it again, "You're lucky I don't care about you . . ."

Chris: You're lucky I don't care about you or I'd give you a bunch of shit. That's what you had me say. No, you don't care about me . . . when did I switch?

Ed: When you got to Gary.

Chris: Yes, well in terms of Don it fits. (Don is her boyfriend.)

Ed: Well, tell it to Don.

Chris: You're lucky I don't care about, wait . . . I bet you're sorry you cared about me because I gave you a bunch of shit. And that's true. I'm sorry I cared about you because I gave you all kinds of shit (crying).

She is getting in touch with her judging and her projections: others don't give her shit; she gives it to them and since she has judged herself, she *is* the shit and she gives herself to them.

Ed: Again.

Chris: (Crying) I'm sorry I cared about you because I gave you all kinds of shit. Like once I start caring I open up and just pour out the piles of shit . . . (pause)

Ed: So, what are you wanting?

Chris: I want, well, I'm wanting to not close off from caring about people because I'm scared now that when I care about someone I'll just lay my shit on them.

Ed: What is your fantasy of what is going to happen then?

Chris: I'll lose them. They won't want to know me anymore . . . and that's true because little by little I have been having layers and layers of walls to keep from caring . . .

Ed: How about describing that process. What I do is . . .

Chris: The walls?

Ed: Yeah.

Chris: What I do is . . .

Ed: What I'm doing is . . . make it in the now.

Chris: What I'm doing is seeing how I lay shit on people I care about and so I get like I don't like losing people because of the shit I hung on them so each time I encounter a person, I, uh, cover myself up with a layer and let less show through so I won't care, so I won't lay any shit on them. And . . . and . . . I'm protecting them. I'm not doing much good for myself, though.

Ed: Try out this sentence . . . you'll learn to care about me, I'll chase you away with enough shit.

Chris: You'll learn to care about me . . . because I'll chase you away with enough shit. Wait, it fit when you said it.

Ed: So change it so it fits.

Chris: . . . Yeah, when you said it it fit and now it doesn't . . .

Ed: What is the meaning to you?

Again I'm going with making an active process of doing to others what she is doing to herself. She's covering herself with shit and it's very difficult for others to relate to such a pile. This is what my tone of voice says, and I get lost in the transcription. She has trouble with this and I think I moved too fast. Since she does continue working with this I ask her to use the statement her way to clarify her thinking.

Chris: Well, I'm saying it, it seems like a paradox and doesn't fit at all. You'll learn to care about me because I'll chase you away. That doesn't fit. The two phrases don't go together at all.

Ed: It was the way I said it but I meant it differently than you're saying it.

Maybe I could title this statement: "What Am I Doing Here?" or "Pitfalls of Interpretation" and get out easily, only I don't and I'm certainly wishing I had kept my mouth shut.

Chris: Oh, say it again?

Ed: What I'm wanting . . . the fantasy I have is, in order to keep people from caring, you will chase them away by piling them with shit. And, if that fits, how about rephrasing so it comes out your way.

Chris: . . .

Ed: I'll keep you from caring. I'll cover you with shit.

I'm really helping here and scaring myself by thinking I've helped too much: now how do I get myself from under all the shit?

Chris: I'll keep you from caring about me by laying all kinds of shit on you. That's the way to make sure you don't care about me, uh, by laying all kinds of shit on you and then that way I don't have to put up any more walls.

Ed: Who are you feeling close to here?

Chris: Willa.

Ed: So tell that to Willa.

Chris: I can keep you from caring about me by giving you all kinds of shit and then that way I don't have to worry about putting up a wall to keep . . . I'm getting really confused.

Ed: Have an encounter with your confusion. Talk to it. Don't worry about making sense . . .

Chris: I keep you from caring about me by giving you all kinds of shit and that way, since you won't care about me I won't have to put up a wall, to keep from caring about you. How can that make sense?

Ed: How about developing a fantasy about this girl who keeps people away . . .

I've gotten into this shit and now I'm confused, which also happens when I'm helping too much. Now I'm in touch with my own confusion and having a fast dialogue in which I get in touch with what I'm doing, which is leading her. What I want now is for her to take responsibility for herself and so I set up a step-by-step structure in which she first deals with her confusion and then steps outside the situation, via fantasy, for a closer look at what's going on here.

Chris: There's this girl and what she does is that she's very afraid of getting hurt, so what she does is lay all kinds of shit on people and that way they're not going to care about her and that way, uh . . . that way she doesn't have to worry about getting hurt because no one cares about her and she doesn't have to care about anybody. And, uh, and, she's not happy, she's really lonely but at least she's not getting hurt. She's protected.

Ed: How about owning not being happy and being lonely?

Chris: I'm not really happy and I'm lonely and I'm not getting hurt because nobody is seeing parts of me that are easily hurt . . . (long pause) . . . well, I . . . (very far away look in her eyes).

Ed: Just stop and close your eyes.

Chris: . . . (long pause)

Ed: Just allow whatever develops to develop.

Chris: . . .

Ed: Anything else?

(The vacuum is loud as hell—may be missing something here.)

This note was put in by the typist during transcription and fits very well. There are several minutes of silence in which Chris is working in her head.

Chris: Yeah, well, I have treasures in me . . . (crying) . . . loving . . . tenderness . . . and caring (still crying) that I've been covering up and not letting them see . . . I'm really puzzled by that because . . . (pause) . . . she's been locked away and I haven't let me out . . . I really am . . . okay.

She discovers she does have the resources and that she is not all shit. What I want is for her to risk showing this part of her to others, in this way she could grow and come out from behind her walls. She is not willing and I will respect her and not push.

Ed: Do you want to stay with that?

Chris: I like what I worked with. I want to stop. . . (long pause)

Ed: How about some statements about where people are, what you're experiencing now, what's happening.

Ann: I'm identifying with Chris. There's a parallel that just happened recently.

Ed: With you?

Ann: Yeah, exactly. And, uh, the only thing is the person is with me and . . . (laughing) the wall I put up; I'm appreciating her piece of work.

One person's work often serves as a trigger for the work of another and the way their lives touch produces intimacy in a Gestalt group. The finished and unfinished business of the present and past thus complement each other.

Ed: Anything else?

Ann: Well, it's a lot easier to be an observer than it is to be a participant and after you've gone through, what, three levels of observing . . . but I'm willing to . . . I want to work.

Ed: Work with where you are, expressing your present experience.

Ann: Well, my hands are getting colder, I guess because . . .

Ed: Without the becauses, express your experience.

Ann: Think of my experience?

Here she is asking me to help and I'm willing to carry her and explain. She has sat through four group sessions and made only short comments; now she is expressing a willingness to work. I want to structure the situation so she changes her behavior and I want to provide her with the tools.

Ed: Yes, what I heard you doing was saying because. Leave all those out, just express your present experience.

Ann: Fearful.

Ed: Okay. Be more fearful, start to express being fearful. (I want her to intensify and express her fear—to uncover herself.)

Ann: I'm afraid of what I'm going to see, or what I'm going to do.

Ed: Uh-huh, keep on going, develop your fantasy of what you're going to say or do. In Gestalt we call these catastrophic fantasies. Now, how do you scare yourself into stopping being what you want, or doing what you want to do? What are your fantasies? These are your fantasies, get in touch with them. What are your fantasies?

Ann: To say something that I might be embarrassed about . . . uh, later.

Ed: What kinds of things could you say? Stay with this . . . are you aware of your posture? The position of the body, don't change that, just stay in contact with what's going on. So, what kinds of things could you say—what sort of dire things are in your fantasy?

Again, I'm helping and crowding many things in here. I'm doing this to establish some structure which I'll use later on in her work—at this point I'm taking care of me more than her. My earlier explaining and describing I also use in establishing the structure of the situation. As a therapist I consider it implicit in the therapeutic contract that I will provide information. Often the information is "helpful" to the client—just as often I'm helping myself. These I consider as the tools necessary for change. With persons having more experience I'm not as free with help.

Ann: Well, if I could say it, then, uh . . . I couldn't say it. Well, I couldn't say anything I really wanted to say because then I'd be embarrassed. I couldn't tell anybody.

Ed: How about making that an act? I'm not going to tell you anything about me. Tell everybody here. I'm not going to tell you anything about me, and . . .

As soon as possible I want to have her take responsibility for her behavior. I do this by having her turn her passive "can't" behavior into a positive act, something she is doing. This process also rearranges the message so that she can contact how she is stopping herself.

Ann: I'm scared and I'm not going to tell you anything about me. I'm scared and I'm not going to tell you anything about me. I'm scared and I'm not going to tell you anything about me.

Ed: Now add something to the end of that. Say that and add something on the end.

Ann: I'm scared and I'm not going to say anything about me . . . you'll remember I'm scared. I'm scared and I'm not going to say anything about me . . .?

Ed: Hear that? (She had made a definite question out of the statement.)

Ann: I'm scared and I'm not going to say anything about me. I wonder what you're going to think? (This is said very directly to a group member.)

Ed: How about changing that to how you're going to judge me?

Ann: I'm scared and I'm not going to say anything about me because you're going to judge me. I'm scared and I'm not going to say anything about me because I feel you're already judging me.

Ed: So, come out here and be the judge. How do you judge?

I move a little too fast here—which soon becomes apparent. I want her to own her judging process and she has not worked through her fear sufficiently to make the judge identification. A better way would be to have her be the person being judged and stay in touch with her experience.

Ann: (In a chair as a judge) I'm scared.
Ed: More.
Ann: I'm afraid.
Ed: Are you switching? What is your experience right now? (This is to clear up my thinking—as a judge she is being afraid.)
Ann: I'm there (points to opposite chair where person being judged sits).
Ed: Okay. Go back over there . . . what is your experience over there?
Ann: I'm more comfortable here (as a person, not a judge). Uh, only I'm sorry, I wanted to go over there (as a judge) and I felt a real panicky thing.
Ed: What is your experience over here again (as a person being judged)?
Ann: A little more relaxed than over there.
Ed: Tell your judge that.
Ann: I'm more relaxed here.
Ed: Make a response as the judge.
Ann: Respond to the judgment (sighs and does not change)?

She is acting very confused and is obviously not in touch with the directions I've given her. My decision at this point is to focus and clarify her feelings in the situation as it has been defined.

Ed: How do you feel about her judging you?
Ann: Really bad.
Ed: Tell her how you are responding. This is what I mean by responding to her judgment. Get in touch with what you're doing. Part of this process is getting to know what you're doing in response to how you define your world. Now, this is your definition (points to judge), and your response to that (points to her). We've talked about that. Now, over her is your fantasy of what the world is all about (points to judge) now the world may not be, it may, I don't know. Okay? So, how are you responding to your setup? Get in touch with that. Not this person, not this fantasy, but how you set the world up here and now.

Ann: (To judge) I'm responding in a very childish way, very inhibited about everything I'm doing because you're always there.
You tell me everything to do and what not to do.

Ed: How are you feeling?

Ann: My poor child.

Ed: How old?

Ann: About seven or eight.

Here I have my "Aha" experience. All this confusion is the past
protruding into the Now. What I want to know is for the past experience to be brought into the Here and Now as a living reality. As she
brings the past to the present she can unscramble her reactions. In
doing this I will ask her to bring to the present the old situation she is
caught up in. I will ask her to focus on her experience as a child and
to describe the situation in the first person, present tense, as if she
were a character in a play or movie. I then work with the situation as
I would a dream or fantasy, asking her to take each part in the unfolding drama. Some therapists would take a psychodrama approach
here and ask various group members to take various parts. In Gestalt
this is considered unnecessary and contaminating since each group
member would bring to the part their own projections and fantasies
of how the person would behave. My approach here will be more
traditional Gestalt and intrapersonal. As the person working plays
the various parts, he is able to "try on" and own various unintegrated parts of himself, to get in touch with the patterns and demands of others he has internalized, and to grow through risking
new ways of being and behaving. I think everyone carries unfinished
business around with him which then colors his perceptions of how
others are feeling, thinking, and behaving. To the extent that the
person reacts to these fantasies, he is living then and there or in his
head rather than with the obvious of the Here and Now. The fantasies are unintegrated, unassimilated parts of the self the person is
responding to, and thus he is responding in an interpersonal situation
to intrapersonal patterns which are outside his awareness.

Ed: Can you be that seven or eight-year-old child?

Ann: I don't know.

Ed: Are you willing?

Ann: All right.

Ed: So talk to your teacher and bring this situation to the Here and
Now.

Ann: . . .

Ed: You're seven or eight years old.

Ann: (As a child) I finished my work, how do you like it? (child-like voice)

Ed: What are you experiencing now? (Asked to provide a focus, she still appears unfocused in the Here and Now.)

Ann: Silly, I don't feel like an eight-year-old child. I'm really getting embarrassed now.

Ed: Tell the teacher that.

Ann: (As a child to teacher) I'm getting really embarrassed now. (She now switches to the teacher's chair.)

Ed: What's your experience as the teacher?

Ann: . . .

Ed: So, what is your name?

Ann: As the teacher?

Ed: Uh-huh. (She can really play dumb—I'm not willing to help this time.)

Ann: I gotta give myself a real name?

Ed: Uh-huh, is this a real teacher?

Ann: Uh-huh.

Ed: So, what's your name? I have a hard enough time with this without you going unidentified. What are you going to do with this young lady?

Ann: (Speaking as a teacher) You're a very messy little girl.

Ed: So how about laying some of those judgments on her.

Ann: You're very messy. You're yelling, and you're getting all dirty. Just look. Your page is a mess, it's got to be erased and it's all over with marks. (She changes places.)

Ed: Do you like this?

Ann: No.

Ed: How about you tell her?

Ann: Mrs. Adams, I didn't do that. I was just having fun out there. If I had a better eraser I wouldn't make such black marks.

Ed: What are you experiencing, talking to your teacher?

Many of my comments during this phase of the work are intended to stimulate her to focus awareness on her Here and Now experience, bring that awareness to the forefront and start communicating more of herself, so that she uses herself to her best advantage. Many new clients often have difficulty dealing with the many different levels—physical, behavioral, feelings, fantasy and imagery, and thinking of their experience. In listening to this tape I decided I had helped too much and was very directive—which I realize is my style.

Ann: What I felt was very gritty and disliking her.

Ed: How about telling her that.

Ann: I don't like you, Mrs. Adams (low voice).

Ed: Again.

Ann: I don't like you, Mrs. Adams (stronger).

Ed: What are you experiencing now?

Ann: I don't feel like, I wish I could be as big as her. I'm feeling mean.

Ed: Tell her that.

Ann: I'm feeling mean, Mrs. Adams, and I'd like to hit you.

Ed: Now, what are you experiencing?

Ann: (sigh) Well, I think I hit her.

Ed: Be her.

Ann: Nasty little girl. Why did you hit me? (laughing) I'm going to tell the principal and you know what she'll say. Go stand outside in the hall.

Ann: ... (pause) ...

Ed: What are you experiencing now?

Ann: Like I'm out in the hall.

Ed: Come back over here. Don't go out in the hall. Continue your confrontation.

I think this is how the situation remains unfinished—she goes out in the hall and there is no resolution. Now we have a situation in which she can resolve the conflict by not avoiding and learn some new ways of being. Inside this nice girl who scares herself with fantasies is probably a nasty kid.

Ann: I'm not going out in the hall and you're not going to make me.

Ed: What are you experiencing now?

Ann: I'm afraid I'm going to go to (?) ... Mrs. Adams I'm sorry.

Ed: What are you experiencing now?

Ann: Fear.

Ed: Stay with the fear. Stay with your feeling. Now what are you experiencing?

I want her to experience herself, her fear, without running away (remember her earlier fear). In this way she is already becoming more self-supportive and a background is established out of which imagery, thinking, and behavior arise.

Ann: The same things.

Ed: What's going on in your head? (I would like her to bring all aspects of her ongoing behavior into the situation.)

Ann: I think I'll go see the principal in her office.
Ed: Uh-huh.
Ann: She's going to tell my parents.
Ed: Then what's going to happen to you?

A leading question—I want her to contact the content of her fantasy and see how she's scaring herself. Then, I'll want her to do something active with her fear and thus begin to deal with herself.

Ann: (Crying) Dad's going to spank me.
Ed: Tell that to your teacher.
Ann: I'm scared, Mrs. Adams. Don't send me to the principal's office.
Ed: Tell her what your fear is.

Making her fear explicit gives her something concrete to work with and enables her to differentiate fact and fantasy.

Ann: They'll tell my Dad and my Dad's going to spank me.
Ed: What are you experiencing?
Ann: Getting spanked by Dad.
Ed: How old are you now?
Ann: Sort of two.
Ed: How old are you really, twenty-two?
Ann: Yeah, twenty-two.

I ask her present age to focus on reality in the Here and Now: she may be feeling and acting like she is two years old—she is really twenty-two. I like to do this to develop the past versus the present polarity. This past/present encounter provides a situation in which she can experience her ability to be self-supporting. I think this is an important step in Gestalt work for the individual and demonstrates several principles: self-support, integration, and personal responsibility in the ownership sense. From her chronological age of twenty-two she can be self-supportive with the eight-year-old and dispel some of the fantasies.

Ed: Be that twenty-two and talk to the two-year-old.
Ann: . . .
Ed: I want you to act like that twenty-two-year-old . . . be a twenty-two-year-old.
Ann: And, what, reassure her and everything?

Ed: Uh-huh. Talk to the eight-year-old. She's scared.

Ann: (As a twenty-two-year-old) I'm not scared. Dad loves you and he only wants you to do good in school.

Ed: Who are you talking to?

Ann: Myself . . . Why don't you talk to Mrs. Adams and tell her how you really feel (said to eight-year-old)?

Ed: Switch to the eight-year-old.

Ann: I don't think Mrs. Adams is going to understand. She's very mean. She won't listen to me.

Ed: Switch and be the twenty-two-year-old.

Ann: Okay. Then go to Mother . . . she's a nun, she should be very interested in you and you might be able to tell her how you feel.

Ed: Switch and be the eight-year-old.

Ann: Well, I don't think I'll go and tell her how I feel. She's very stern. And she's going to tell my dad.

Ed: So, how about becoming a twenty-two-year-old and talk to Mrs. Adams over here.

Ann: Well, Mrs. Adams, you scared me a lot, but you won't scare me anymore. I've got power over you. I'm not defenseless.

Ed: Say that again.

Ann: I've got power over you. I'm not defenseless.

Ed: How do you feel now?

Ann: Really surprised. I didn't think that I could really feel what I just felt, just thinking about it. Uh . . .

Ed: I like you much better as a twenty-two-year-old.

Ann: Yeah, I do too . . . you know I never realized how I was doing that, being a little girl, giving my . . . I'm really strong and capable. I usually get compliments on my work.

Ed: What has stood out for me in our relationship is how I sometimes feel like taking care of you. I see you looking wide-eyed and little-girlish . . . I'm happy with myself that I haven't babied you . . . too often . . .

Ann: I've really been scared a lot here . . . I mean I've scared myself thinking what I'd find out if I worked. Now I'm glad I did . . . I'm stronger than I thought . . . I'm strong and not afraid.

Ed: Okay, uh (long pause) I'm available and, first, I'd like each of you to summarize or state your present experience in one word or phrase . . .

Here I skip "talking about" her experience and I do not ask the group for feedback. I do this when I want the person to have time to assimilate. Other times I will be quite talkative and involve the group in making statements which I then ask them to own in order to discover something of themselves. Ann's work began with her asking me for support, which I gave, and ended with her experiencing self-support. Working in this way—providing support and then withdrawing—is one way I use myself as a tool in the Gestalt process.

DREAMWORK

The following dreamwork is in several ways illustrative of the polarities in my work and of the polarities possible in Gestalt. In the previous work I was supporting/frustrating by giving and withdrawing. In the following, the giving/withdrawing is how the woman frustrates herself and so I stay out of the work and she must apply her own support. This work also has more emphasis on the use of body posture and movement in focusing the person's awareness on their present. I find myself focusing on what stands out for me in my experience and what is obvious to me about the person's behavior. Through this obvious process I find my work often has more emphasis in certain areas than others. In this dreamwork I focus more on imagery and body posture than in the earlier work.

As this work opens, the participants in the workshop have been (contrary to Gestalt principles) talking about what has been happening. Part of the contract I have with the groups is that when I'm available for work we can stop any bullshit and go to work when someone identifies that they want to. We do that here.

Jo: I just remembered a dream I had last week . . . I'd like to work.
Ed: Okay, now I see the dream as being a statement of your present existence or development or frustration and uh, to make this statement explicit you tell the dream as if it's happening, here and now . . . in the present tense.
Jo: I am in the back seat of my mother's car and she is behind the driver's wheel in the front. And I've been asleep and I wake up and we're going backward at a very high rate of speed and it almost develops into a tunnel where we're going so fast that things are just whizzing by, very blurred, and I can feel like about three or four g's, a lot of pressure against the back seat pushing me up against the back seat and we are going backward, completely out of control.
Ed: Would you say that again?

This concept of personal control may be the core of her dreamwork. I ask her to repeat so that she can experience the message.

Jo: Completely out of control and going *backward* (saying this with a big giggle) I am completely out of control and going backward (laughs again).

Ed: So go with being completely out of control and going backward, bring your body into this action.

Jo: (laughs a great deal and falls backward to lie on the floor)

Ed: What are you experiencing as you are completely out of control and going backward?

Jo: Out of control and going backward. I feel like I'm falling.

Ed: Falling . . .

Jo: I am and I find myself catching my breath trying to stop myself from falling. I do not feel the pressure I felt before because it's moving with me . . . I'm just falling . . .

Ed: What is your experience as you fall? (I want her to focus.)

Jo: I . . . feel some tightening in my stomach, trying to stop myself from falling. A feeling of lightness . . . It's both heavy and light . . .

Ed: *I* am both light and heavy.

Jo: I am both light and heavy . . .

Ed: So have an encounter between your light and your heavy.

Jo: I am heavy; I am falling fast. I am out of control and falling faster and faster . . . I'm light and I'm still falling . . . (laughing) I'm a featherweight. (waves hands in air . . .) (laughing) I feel slightly buoyant when I'm a featherweight and when I'm heavy I feel like I'm accelerating; the other one I'm just falling. Yeah, when I'm lightweight I'm just falling. When I'm heavy, I'm falling and accelerating.

Ed: Have these two talk with each other (to focus on integration and polarity).

Jo: We're both falling, aren't we (laughing)?

Ed: Who's that?

Jo: (Still laughing) Both of me is falling from mutual agreement.

Ed: How do you feel in this experience of falling?

Jo: (Sighing) Well, I'm beginning to enjoy myself. Before, I was frightened . . . I'm becoming less frightened of falling (speaking in a very soft voice). The rest of me sits flat on my ass (great deal of laughter).

Ed: So say the whole sentence.

Jo: (Still laughing a great deal) I'm becoming less frightened of falling flat on my ass. That fits, (more laughter) I am . . . (thoughtfully) . . . yeah.

Ed: What is the message?

Jo: I'm afraid of falling on my ass.

Ed: So, let's go with some more of the dream. Are you willing to do that?

She made a connection with part of herself and maybe with how she avoids personal control and responsibility. The rest of the dream will help pull all the pieces together.

Jo: Yeah.

Ed: What stands out for you in the dream?

Jo: What stands out for me?

Ed: Is that the finish of your dream? (I change my direction since I want her to finish and not avoid the end of the dream.)

Jo: Yeah, I woke up. I woke myself up because I became frightened.

Ed: I'd like for you to finish the dream.

Since dreams are a statement of the person's present existence in some form it is essential to examine what is avoided and which situations are left unfinished. An obvious avoidance in this dream is the end and what soon becomes obvious is that the end of the dream involves some unfinished business for Jo.

Jo: . . . I'm finding it difficult to do because all I'm doing is falling backward. Moving backward. It's not really falling now in the dream. It's moving backward, not falling.

Ed: Okay. So be in the dream and you're in the car moving backward out of control.

Jo: My mother's behind the wheel. I am completely unable to do anything about it.

Ed: Uh-huh. What are you wanting?

Jo: I'm aware of what I want to do in the dream. I want to overcome the weight, the g force and get forward. Just put on the brake (laughing). . . . That's the only option I can see . . . okay . . . I'm overcoming the weight, my weight. I can pull myself, pressure myself against the back seat and I'm coming forward. I'm moving my mother out from behind the wheel and I'm climbing over. I get under the wheel and I'm back in control CONTROL! (laughs) I'm CONTROLLING MY WORLD.

Ed: Say that again. (Here she contacts her own control and power.)

Jo: I'm controlling my world (very bright-eyed).

Ed: How about having an encounter with your mother?

Jo: My mother?

Ed: What stands out for me is that you said you moved your mother out from behind the wheel.

Jo: Yes. She won't control.

Ed: Won't control whom?

Jo: Me. The automobile. Yeah, that's me, too.

Ed: Put her over here.

Jo: (giggles and sighs) Move over . . . I find you to be a very neutral object. Move over . . . Huh, you can't control me. I won't let you control me to begin with so move over and let me get behind the brakes (looks up at picture on the wall).

Ed: What are you in touch with?

Jo: When I look up that way?

Ed: Yes.

Jo: The loops. Loopy loops . . . Hum . . . I know what I'll say. Hi, why don't you do that, Mother? Why the hell don't you do that?

Ed: Are you aware of your right hand?

Jo: Yes, scratching my head. Trying to figure out why I haven't done that before (switches seats).

Ed: . . .

Jo: (as mother) Right, I'm trying to figure out why she has not done that before.

Ed: You, as mother, are trying to clear up why she . . .?

Jo: Has not gotten in control of her self before. She should be in control of her life (such a profound top-dog statement).

Ed: How do you feel about the confrontation?

Jo: Right now as mother?

Ed: As mother.

Jo: Oh, shit. I've been trying to get her to get off her ass and control for a long time now (laughing). I feel helpless in the fact that I can see her unable to make decisions for herself.

Ed: Again.

Jo: (as mother) I feel very helpless in the fact that I cannot help her make decisions . . . I would like you to do what I want you to do but I know you won't so you might as well make your own decisions.

Ed: Switch.

Jo: (sighs)

Ed: Do that some more with your hand.

Jo: Passive acceptance. You're right (laughs). I'm accepting her judgment.

Ed: Are you aware of your posture?

Jo: I'm holding myself up.

Ed: Say that again.

Jo: I'm holding myself up (very low voice).

Ed: (Whispering very softly) Again.

Jo: (Louder) I'm holding myself up . . .

Ed: Um-hum.

Jo: I feel a lot of pressure on my arms and a lot of pulling on my back. Here I tighten up.

Ed: Go ahead and pull on yourself there . . . Pull yourself up.

Jo: Up?

Ed: Yeah. Stay with your experience.

Jo: I can't from this position.

Ed: Say that again.

Jo: I can't pull myself up from this position.

Ed: Tell your mother that.

Jo: I can't pull myself up from this position.

Ed: Stay with that. Be back in your dream in the back seat. Tell this to your mother.

Jo: I can't pull myself up from this position (laughing).

Ed: What are you doing? You're laughing . . .

Jo: I want to say help me and I'm too damn proud to do it . . .

Ed: And what is the message?

Jo: The message is she won't help me. Hum . . .

Ed: And your experience?

Jo: Well, uh, I feel hurt . . . I feel hurt knowing she won't help me . . .

Ed: Tell her this. Put it in the context of the dream as if this is reality.

Jo: Uh, I want your help and I won't ask for it (softly). Because I feel you don't want to help . . . I believe you don't want to help (very softly) . . . Sooo. I'll do it myself. I will do it myself. Just . . . I want to say gut forward and from here I can get up (changes her posture to more flexible position).

Ed: How does this fit your existence now?

Jo: . . . Yeah, it pretty well fits it.

Ed: So you're looking up there (looks at her artwork on the wall from earlier Gestalt-artwork).

Jo: No, I'm looking at my blue fish (very tiny voice, a few mutterings). (louder) I think I was in touch with the need for more support which I'm not getting. Hum.

Ed: What are you wanting now?

Jo: I am wanting moral support.

Ed: So tell her.

Jo: I want moral support from you . . . (switches to mother) I'm not going to give it to you (laughs) . . . (soft sigh and moan). I'm not going to give it to you because that's how I can control you.

Ed: That's how you can control?

Jo: (As mother, softly) Um-hum. Yes, that's how I can control her.

Ed: So, what are you in touch with at this moment?

Jo: Uh . . . as mother, I'm a very powerful figure. I am very power-ful. I really don't want her to control herself. I want to control her . . . I want her to do what I want to do . . . what I want her to do with her life . . . I blew my image there.

Ed: You want to control as mother?

Jo: Yes, I do. She's really a screwed-up woman and I could have done much better . . . I tell her to do what she wants to but what I *really* want her to do is what *I* want her to do.

Ed: How do you let her know that?

Jo: By not supporting her (laughs). When she wants to do something else that I don't want her to do (laughs).

Ed: Ha. Ha. Ha.

Jo: Yeah. That's exactly how I control. I don't give her any moral support when she wants to do something that I don't want her to do . . . That's it. If she's going to do it, she's going to do it on her own.

Ed: Tell her.

Jo: If you're going to do it, you're going to do it on your own.

Ed: Switch.

Jo: (As herself, sighs, moans, laughs; changes to old posture) auto-matic back here. Here I am, holding myself up (laughs).

Ed: Can you get up from there?

Jo: No (laughs) . . . (sighs, moans). And here I am pulling on those same goddamn muscles. I have a feeling my migraines are pulling on those muscles.

Ed: When do you get migraines—when you're pulling yourself up?

Jo: Yeah (softly). I never thought about that. When I'm pulling my-self up (crying), right back there (crying).

Ed: Stay there a minute. Stay with yourself there.

Jo: (Soft moan) . . .

Ed: What are you experiencing?

Jo: (Soft laugh) I got a migraine right up here when I woke up this morning.

Ed: How about making up some sentences, "I give myself migraines by . . ."

Jo: I give myself migraines by hanging on and pulling myself up by my elbows. Hold yourself up by your elbows (giggles). That's my message and that's not working (laughing). I give myself a head-ache by trying to pull myself up by my elbows. (laughing) Very uncomfortable.

Ed: Say that again.

Jo: It's very uncomfortable position. Hum (softly). Hum (softer). (starts to change her posture)

Ed: And now what are you experiencing?

Jo: When I changed positions I noticed a release of tension on my back. I notice I can breathe easier!

Ed: And now what are you experiencing?

Jo: As I'm breathing easier, the pressure reduces.

Ed: In terms of yourself before?

Jo: Oh, much more confident.

Ed: So tell your mother that.

Jo: I'm much more confident (laughing). I will make my own decisions and I will do what I want to do. I'm a willful kind, aren't I (laughing again)?

Ed: Do you hear your voice as you say that?

Jo: I'm fully aware of the fact that I'm willful . . .

Ed: So how do you stop yourself?

Jo: From being willful?

Ed: Yes.

Jo: I stop myself by wanting moral support. By wanting support of any kind . . . That's a pitiful thing to do.

Ed: Rephrase that.

Jo: (laughs) That's a difficult thing to do (softly). It's a difficult thing to do to give up one's moral support. I find it difficult to give up my means for moral support.

Ed: Are you willing to give that up?

Jo: I'm not sure I will. I'm not sure I want to (softly). I'm not sure I will. I'm not sure I want to . . . Hum . . . (extremely long pause) I'm experiencing the feeling of not knowing where to go next . . . I'm going to turn the idea over in my mind. Hum (very long pause interspersed with sighs). Might as well give it up because I'm not getting moral support . . . Screw them all, screw the moral support (laughing and crying together). (long pause)

Ed: And what is your experience now?

Jo: Hell of a lot of less pressure.

Ed: How do you experience—how are you experiencing having less pressure on you now?

Jo: How do I experience less pressure on me . . .

Ed: How are you experiencing it right now? Having less pressure on you?

Jo: My face is cooler and I'm feeling more pressure from within. My blood pressure feels good. I'm able to breathe easier . . . lighter quality.

Ed: A lighter quality (laughs). (I'm remembering the early part of the dream).

Jo: Hum . . . But I'm still going backward (laughing). I'm ready to quit now.

Ed: Got what you wanted?

Jo: Yeah.

Ed: I'm wanting to give you a sentence. I want you to say a sentence and you see if it fits . . .

Jo: All right.

Ed: I pressure myself by wanting moral support.

Jo: I pressure myself by wanting moral support . . . Yeah. I do. I really do. When I want moral support, I feel the tension going swoosh, getting tighter.

Ed: (laughing) Okay.

Jo: And the rest of the sentence is . . . and not asking for it.

Ed: Um-hum. So what are you in touch with now?

Jo: I pressure myself for wanting it and not being able to ask for it. That's my game.

Ed: What's that?

Jo: Wanting moral support and not asking for it. I'm tough. I don't need anybody's support (sighs).

Ed: That must be true, seeing as you never give any.

Jo: (laughs) Nyeah . . . I may set myself up not to get any. That moral support comes out when I don't need it. I ask for it, too, sometimes.

Other group member: You don't feel weaker when you do, do you?

Ed: Make a statement out of that.

Jo: I feel like I'm begging when I ask.

Other member: Even when you ask your friends?

Jo: Yes . . .

Ed: What does begging mean?

Jo: I'm humbling myself. I'm prostrating myself (changes to posture of early work). Help me (laughs). That's the way I feel.

Ed: Questions, answers, statements, unfinished business?

I think this work is fairly clear and demonstrates how much a person can do if they are willing to stay with their experience. As therapist I did very little here and she closed many gestalts. I think this happy note of self-support makes a good finish for this work.

CHAPTER 12

FRUSTRATION, FUN, AND FOLLY

ROHE N. ESHBAUGH, Ph.D.

Rohe N. Eshbaugh is in private practice in Las Cruces, New Mexico, and El Paso, Texas. He is also the founder of the Gestalt Institute of the Southwest. He has been a psychologist at Camarillo State Hospital, California, and chief psychologist and director of Youth Services at a New Mexico Mental Health Center.

In psychotherapy, frustration is the blocking of the maladaptive verbal and nonverbal behaviors. The maladaptive behaviors will be in the foreground of the psychotherapeutic encounter, and are present and relevant at the earliest moment of the first session. The persons will "be" their "problem" during the opening encounter. That is, if they are having personal or interpersonal difficulties from being helpless, then helplessness will be presented in their immediate behavior. Confusion, control, and other modes of avoiding self-responsibility or self-support will be apparent to the therapist whose senses are open and whose mind is clear of plans, procedures, and gimmicks. How the therapist behaves will either confront and interfere with the behavior or minimize the maladaptive aspects and reinforce the behavior. Once the maladaptive styles of interacting are interrupted the process of growth, relearning or reparenting can begin. Some therapists will stop at this beginning point, prevent frustration and change, and not get to the point of facilitating the growth which will follow. Frustration of the maladaptive is necessary for the process of psychotherapeutic growth. The "how" of frustration separates the Gestalt therapist from others.

Perls (1969) identifies frustration as an explicit goal of psychotherapy. Other psychotherapeutic schools do not emphasize frustration, per se, but each of the schools of psychotherapy frustrates the maladaptive behaviors by not being socially predictable or socially typical. For example, Albert Ellis (1962) will take over and begin a lecture about the sentences one says to oneself. Mainord (1973) directly attacks the crazy, maladaptive behaviors with a verbal assault. The transactional analyst begins with a lecture on, and aggressive verbal attack of, "games," or immediately confronts the "discount" (Schiff and Schiff, 1971). The client-centered therapist is seen as immediately frustrating through telling the client what he or she just said. Rosen (1953) outcries the crazy. The psychoanalyst tells the person to lie down on the couch while the therapist sits up in a chair.

Each therapeutic school begins with immediate frustration even though it doesn't acknowledge frustration as a key factor in psychotherapy. With the exception of Gestalt Therapy, each of the therapeutic schools is particularly frustrating as a result of its stylized method. Gestalt Therapy is most effectively frustrating through the avoidance of method and emphasis on spontaneity.

The Gestalt therapist frustrates through his spontaneity, and how spontaneous he is will be related to his understanding of the issues of responsibility and authenticity.

"Responsibility" has become a loaded word and a much maligned factor among psychotherapists. For some therapists (e.g., Mowrer, 1964) responsibility implies moral accountability. Others (e.g., Mainord, 1973; Glasser, 1965) tend toward using "responsibility" in the obliging sense, but emphasize responsibility as the consequences of one's actions. There are unpublished therapists and counselors who use "responsibility" as a substitution for "fault." Perls (1969) presents responsibility as an ability—the ability to respond, and as ownership. I am responsible for my thoughts, and my behaviors are mine. You are not able to "make" me feel (emotionally), you are not able to "make" me think (I am, therefore, I think!), you are not able to "make" me behave.

In Gestalt Therapy, this ownership of responsibility is a given—a fact of life. The therapist "owns" his or her thoughts, feelings, and behaviors. The client, patient, or person "owns" the client's thoughts, feelings, and behaviors. The consequences of actions and individual accountability are simply givens—facts of life. Fault-findings and assumptions of obligations are viewed as manipulations or means of self-torture. The Gestalt therapist takes responsibility for him/herself and responds with his/her skills, knowledge, and presence. The therapist knows that the client is responsible and much of the work will involve the client's discovery of the fact. The manipulating client will be immediately frustrated by his or her own attempts to avoid responsibility. If the person is using his potential, skills, or energy to manipulate others into "doing for" them and the other is not manipulated, then the person will immediately experience frustration. This is lawful, predictable behavior and will lead either to a change point or to new avoidance techniques. A key issue is to allow the client to frustrate him/herself with his/her own maladaptive behaviors. The therapist simply is responsible for his/her own presence as an authentic, genuine person with skills for facilitating change.

The authentic therapist is one who offers a present-oriented "I" statement for which he takes total responsibility and ownership. Authenticity may lie in the expression of feelings, thoughts, or behaviors. Therapist's statements such as "*You* make me feel angry," "*You* scare me," "Your parent (ego state) is scaring my child (ego state)," beg the issue of responsibility and skirt authenticity.

Discourses involving "How I used to be," "I did that, too," "I don't feel good about the way my mother treated me either" may be true and genuine statements but avoid the relevance of the immediate interaction (the Now) with the client (the Thou) to whom the therapist is responding. Such discourses also make it difficult to determine who is getting the therapy.

Authentic, I-now statements by the therapist will result in the client's natural frustration of himself. This type of "frustrating behavior" remains true to the basic philosophy of Gestalt Therapy in keeping the responsibilities clear and present-centered and by avoiding the use of techniques and gimmicks for "turning on" or "turning off" the person. The psychotherapeutic process then becomes one of the person's frustrating him/herself to the point of change where the therapist can then respond with his or her skills in facilitating growth, change, adjustment of whatever the person wants.

Some therapists pursue frustration with great vigor and with a variety of ploys and gimmicks to create immediate and high-intensity frustration. The high-intensity frustrator is the cousin of the "chicken soup" helper (Resnick, 1970). Basically, the chicken-souper is intolerant of frustration and becomes quite helpful in "taking care" of the client's frustration by spoon-feeding, reassuring, smoothing over, medicating, hospitalizing or engaging in some other behavior designed to "make" the person feel good. The high-intensity frustrator, however, is not interested in "making" the person feel good, but is committed to "making" the person feel frustrated. The high-intensity frustrator prevents the individual's own natural frustration process. Furthermore, the "energizer" data of Lieberman, Yalom, and Miles (1973) suggest that high-intensity frustration results in a high incidence of emotional casualties.

Frustration of the maladaptive manipulation will eventually lead to a point of fight or flight. In psychotherapy the fight/flight reactions are typically expressed as anger, fear or withdrawal and it is

here that the supportive, facilitating skills are important. The therapist facilitates movement to the change point—the impasse. A characteristic of Gestalt therapists is that the frustration occurs more naturally and is seen much earlier in the therapeutic process. Thus, the
process of change begins earlier.

It is not necessary for the therapist to use any special "techniques"
for frustration. The authentic, non-manipulative presence of the
therapist is enough to create a natural confrontation leading to frustration. The therapist wanting to know what the person is wanting
will frustrate the "take care of me," or "do me" expectations. "I"
statements will avoid "garbage" and focus attention on the Now.

It is also unnecessary for the therapist to maintain an aloof, formal
posture throughout his endeavors. Psychotherapy can be fun as well
as serious. Many therapists become so serious they lose their spontaneity and liveliness, and present instead a dire, monotonous model
for the patient. Other therapists and clients are saved from dull living
and monotonous ruts by the implicit permission to be "you" in Gestalt Therapy.

As I think of the issue of me as frustrator, I have images of my being authentically me and numerous professors, supervisors, administrators, and parent-types hanging their heads in woe from their frustrations in attempting to get me to meet their demands. I am also
aware that this frustration resulted in their expressing anger (or great
patience). Yet, they did not reject me and they have strong positive
feelings for me. I am frustrating when I am not taking things too
seriously, and being playful. I think it is my playfulness that attracts
a spontaneous enjoyment that overrides the serious authority.

The following transcript presents an example of a style of playfulness. Read the transcript through rapidly, and then go back and
analyze it.

The woman had arrived ten minutes early. I had planned on using
that ten minutes for me, and did.

Sue: Second wind for the day, huh?

Rohe: Yes, I took care of me.

Sue: I feel good today. I did what you told me to do. I was totally
aware of everything that I did, thought, and said. Along with it, I
did quite a bit of soul searching.

Rohe: I notice you're looking over there.

Sue: Well, I'm sitting that way; we're sitting that way (small laugh).
Okay (coughs). I did a lot of soul searching, too, and, uh . . .

Rohe: I notice you're looking away again.

Sue: (half-laugh, voice low) I have terrible habits. (louder) I have come to the conclusion that I can answer your "I am" questions a little bit more specifically (voice drops at end).

Rohe: And are you aware of your voice?

Sue: Uh . . .

Rohe: On "a little bit more specifically."

Sue: A little bit more specifically.

Rohe: Ah, your voice changed.

Sue: A little more honestly.

Rohe: You don't sound as tentative as you did when you said it the first time.

Sue: Well, (tentatively) I don't mean to be tentative. I'm pretty sure of the way I feel.

Rohe: (Voice smiling) You're *pretty* sure of the way you feel? Big deal. Let me know when you're sure.

Sue: (Lively voice) All right.

Rohe: All right. Does that mean you will? Oh, okay.

Sue: (Alive voice) Okay?

Rohe: (Brightly) I'm delighted. You look good.

Sue: (Dropped voice) I feel good for a change. Uh, some of the things I'm not too pleased with (self-chastising voice) . . . some of the things I've come up with.

Rohe: (Fliply) Well, good. We can just dwell on them so you can feel lousy.

Sue: (Seriously) No, we can either accept them or figure out a way to change them.

Rohe: (Matter of factly) *We* can! I'm not.

Sue: (Acceptingly) I can (laughs). All right. (strongly) *I* can, then.

Rohe: (Offhandedly and rapidly) Good, congratulations! I am glad to hear you're capable. *Will* you?

Sue: (Surprised). Yeah. (pause) Uh, (good little girl offering with a grin) do you want me to go through the "I am" list like I did the other day?

Rohe: (Mimicking grin and voice) Do you want to go through the "I am" list like you did the other day (chuckles)?

Sue: (Free laugh) Oh, shoot. Um.

Rohe: (Serious voice) No, don't shoot. Tell me whether you want to go through the "I am" list again.

Sue: I don't know why the hell not. I want to know if you *want* to or not.

Rohe: (Don't-give-a-damn voice) Why the hell not.

Sue: (Tentatively) Yeah.

Rohe: (Mimicking her tone) Yeah. How did your voice sound when you said that?

Sue: Eey ah (tentative, why-the-hell-not voice).

Rohe: Eey ah (mimicking).

Sue: Well, just, you know.

Rohe: (Interrupting, quickly) Does your voice say you want to do it or does your voice say you don't want to do it?

Sue: (Over Rohe's words) It takes a lot of time.

Rohe: (Immediately) It takes a lot of time, huh?

Sue: Yeah.

Rohe: It takes a lot of time to do past history stuff, huh?

Sue: (Correcting voice) It's not necessarily past history. There are a lot of things that are a little bit different.

Rohe: (Starting) "A lot of things . . ."

Sue: But I'm feeling totally honest with myself.

Rohe: (Impatiently) I'm feeling teased. I'm ready to say, "I would like you to tell me, blah, blah, blah" (Sue: I-got-caught laugh) and you have not told me whether you want to tell me or not.

Sue: Welllll, (not-I-got-you voice) you're here to listen, aren't you?

Rohe: (Na,-didn't-get-me laugh) Am I? (teasingly)

Sue: (Ignoring, offhandedly) Might as well tell you.

Rohe: (Grinning) Might as well, but you still haven't said whether you want to or not.

Sue: (Big grin) All right, all right, all right. I want to.

Rohe: All right, all right, all right. You want to (chuckling).

Sue: (Big grin) Yeah (laughs).

Rohe: (Big grin) Okay; I'd like to hear.

Sue: Okay (with finality on *kay*). Uh, (seriously) I'm Sue (gives name factually). I'm 31 years old (lightly). I am a (hesitantly) woman, a wife (hopelessly), and a mother (firmly forlorn). I, uh, amnottotallypleasedwithbeingamother. I honestly feel that, uh, I should not have had children (quietly). I don't have the patience (factual), and (sadly) I don't get the enjoyment that I though I would get out of being a mother. (Sad acceptance, voice fades, and then with forced strength) I find that, so far at least, being a mother has brought nothing but work and worry and frustration.

Rohe: Sounds miserable.

Sue: But, uh, I honestly feel that I had both my childrenforthewrongreasons (voice dropped, like confession).

Rohe: (Picking up on "should not" and fatalistic tone) No wonder everybody makes a big deal of motherhood (voice tone emphatic and chastising of the "should"-ers).

Sue: Uh, I think I felt that it was the thing that (pause) I was supposed to do. (Explaining voice) I always loved children but I should have taken a job working with them where I could *get away* (laugh) from them when I wanted to (Presented in a self-chastising, empty voice).

Rohe: (Clearly presented) What I'm really hearing is you've lost your excitement. (softly) You're reporting now. (Then tone rebukes self-chastisement) And your reports are including your shoulds and supposed tos and shoulds and shouldn'ts.

Sue: Well . . . (I-couldn't-help-it tone)

Rohe: You got yourself into the mess following your shoulds.

Sue: Well . . .

Rohe: (Continuing in matter of fact voice) And you're staying in the mess with your shouldn'ts. (Firmly) I think (clarifying ownership).

Sue: (Hesitantly protesting) I love him. I don't want to get rid of him now. (pause, short laugh) Maybe temporarily. (enthusiastically and with enjoyment) There are times when I wish to hell I could pack him off to Timbuktu for a week.

Rohe: (Picking up on wish) So, who do you know in Timbuktu?

Sue: Nobody (laughs).

Rohe: (Focusing on "How" and "Now") Do you have someplace else you could send him?

Sue: Well, (dismissingly) to grandma's or something. The problem is he would be ten times as hard to handle when he got back from grandma's. But, uh . . . (seriously)

Rohe: Okay (acknowledging seriousness). Do you see how you stop yourself from doing something you would like to do. From getting some relief?

Sue: (Yes-but voice) Well, this is the problem, though. You have to, uh, look, at the end results, I think, uh, from past experience the end results would be more problems than learning to cope with what's there. (Rough, tough voice) To accept what's there and learning how to handle it. How to accept it. (Pause; quickly) One thing is to stick him in bed at 7:30 at night and have at least therestoftheeveningtocallmyownevenifallhedoesislaythereandreadorsingorwhateverhewantstodotokeephimselfawake.

Rohe: (Clarifying) That's one thing you *can* do.

Sue: Yeah.

Rohe: (Focusing on now) What are you doing?

Rohe: (Focusing on now) What are you doing?

Sue: Putting him to bed this past week at (half-laugh) 7:00 or 7:30, telling him to get in there and to "shut up" (chuckles). I want some time for myself (grinning). (Pause) Uh, (pause; seriously) you know when I said that I felt that I had my children for the wrong reasons. (Ugly voice) I was raised in a family where you got married and you had children (dismissingly). (Urgently) This was what a woman was supposed to do to be a woman. This is what made a woman a woman or a girl into a woman. Uh, my first child I had, I think, looking back on it, to save my marriage. Because, uh, all he talked about was wanting a family and I guess I felt that if I had his child, things would work out. And, that's another reason probably why I . . . the divorce was over a year and a half going through, because I was thinking in the back of my mind that when he sees the child and realizes that this child is his that things will work out. (Pause, shift to low, accusing voice) That's a pretty stupid reason for having a kid. Uh, with Brian, I had waited for delivery so long, I dearly loved it; I *love* my babies. I *adore* children—when they're somebody else's (short laugh).

Rohe: What is that about? What is the difference? Somebody else's baby and your baby. Develop the contrast.

Sue: When it's someone else's, uh, if you get tired of it or you find yourself too bogged down, you can give it back. Yours, you can't (short laugh). There's nobody to give it to when the going gets rough.

Rohe: How do you tire yourself and bog yourself down?

Sue: Probably by trying so desperately hard to get him to fit into my mold—into what I feel.

Rohe: That's a problem. Do you hear your words? Say it again.

Sue: (Hard voice) I try to get him to fit into my mold. To do what I feel a child should be and what I feel a child should do. Instead of just saying, well, he's a little people, instead of saying he's a person in his own right, and, uh, meeting him halfway once in a while. And, uh, instead of just getting totally (hard pause) fighting with him. That's what I do. I fight with him. And, it's, uh.

Rohe: (Offhandedly curious) What are you fighting about?

Sue: (Big sigh) Everything (short laugh). I fight to get him to eat. I fight to get him to go to bed. I fight to get him to pick up his toys. I fight to get him to take care of his dog.

Rohe: When he does all these things, what do you get?

Sue: (Hard voice) Then at least I feel he's going to grow up healthy and knowing what the hell to do. I . . . I don't know. Maybe I'm doing it all for the wrong reasons.

Rohe: Maybe?

Sue: I keep thinking if . . .

Rohe: Are you?

Sue: (Curiously) That part I'm really not sure about.

Rohe: (Encouragingly) Say that; own that statement. Like own two statements instead of maybe. "I *am* doing things for the wrong reasons" and "I am *not* doing things for the wrong reasons." See which one fits for you now. (voice supportive, accepting, permitting)

Sue: (Softly) I am doing things for the wrong reasons. I am not doing things for the wrong reasons. (Pause, then strongly) I am not doing them for the wrong reasons, for the end result, but I think I am going about trying to achieve that end result wrong! (Pause; hesitantly with light laugh) Do you know what I'm trying to say?

Rohe: (Following her playful lead) I never know what you're trying to say. The only time I *know* is when you tell me what you say.

Sue: I mean, does that sentence make sense.

Rohe: Does that sentence make sense to you?

Sue: (Running over Rohe's words) I mean I have a habit . . . well, it did to me because I know what's going on up here (points to head), but . . .

Rohe: (Interrupting) I don't.

Sue: I'm not sure I'm coming across clear.

Rohe: Do you want to come across clear?

Sue: Well, I can give you an example of what I mean, if that would help.

Rohe: (Interrupting; firmly and impatiently) Do you want to come across clear?

Sue: (Irritated and protesting voice) Yes.

Rohe: All right (gently). I want you to come across clear.

Sue: (Pause) (you-ding-a-ling voice) My reasons behind what I'm doing (pause) are right but it's the way that I'm going *about* it that's wrong. (Pointing or aiming forefinger at Rohe)

Rohe: (Firmly and precisely) I'm aware of your right hand and your finger. Freeze. (Pause; regretfully soft) You didn't freeze.

Sue: (Laughs) Freeze, okay.

Rohe: Put words with your hand and finger.

Sue: (Laughing) Did you understand what I'm trying to say? (Pushing finger toward Rohe)

Rohe: (Correcting) That's a question. Now, continue doing that without words.

Sue: (Laughing and pushing finger) Continue doing it with words?

Rohe: Exaggerate that. (Pause) What are the words that go with that?

Sue: (Laughing, rapidly and almost shouting) Stick my words in there. Emphasize them. Try to push them that way and make them go with words. (Pushing finger toward Rohe)

Rohe: I notice as you say that you're looking at the floor.

Sue: (Coughs, enthusiastic, after-all voice) I told you you've got distracting eyes. I like blue eyes (laughing) and they are distracting, but . . .

Rohe: (Matter of factly, with grin) My eyes are green.

Sue: (Quietly, argumentative) From here they look blue. (defensively) From this angle they look blue.

Rohe: (Emphatically) My eyes are green!

Sue: (Lightly dismissing) Okay, they're green then. (second breath laugh)

Rohe: (Matter of factly) I don't want your . . .

Sue: Okay!

Rohe: I don't need your permission for my eyes to be green.

Sue: (Delightful chuckle)

Rohe: (Chuckling and speaking distinctly) My eyes are green.

Sue: (Get-off-my-back, laughing voice) All right, so they're green. But from here they look blue. That's all I can say.

Rohe: (Ending matter of factly) Will you accept that I have green eyes?

Sue: Since I, I don't know. (laughing) They still look blue. Maybe I'm color-blind.

Rohe: (Permitting, accepting, requesting voice) Tell me you're not going to see me the way I am. Make that statement to me. "I won't see you the way you are."

Sue: I won't see you the way you are.

Sue: (Curiously) How does that fit?

Sue: (Laughing, rolling words) It doesn't. I'm trying to see you the way you are.

Rohe: (Matter of factly, rhetorically) When you're trying, what are you doing?

Sue: What am I doing? (you-ding-a-ling voice) I'm looking.

Rohe: And what are you trying?

Sue: Okay. I'm seeing you the way that *I* see you (shaky). Okay?

Rohe: Not the way I am.

Sue: Maybe (teasingly) I don't know.

Rohe: (Matching her tone) Maybe you don't know?

Sue: (Enjoyable, frustrated, lively) Well, the, the, do you always (laughs) (resigning) . . . Oh, you always confuse me.

Rohe: *I* confuse *you* (matter-of-fact disbelieving).

Sue: Right.

Rohe: (Curiously) How do I do that?

Sue: By changing my train of thought.

Rohe: (Distinctly) *I change* your train of thought.

Sue: (Matter of fact) Well, I'm thinking one way and into one thing and you stop me midstream and everything.

Rohe: (Quickly) How do I do that?

Sue: By stopping things midstream.

Rohe: How do I stop things midstream?

Sue: Okay. (harder voice, frustrated) I'm talking about something and all of a sudden you start talking about my hand and what I was talking about just kind of . . . drifts away while my hand becomes the focal point.

Rohe: (Matter of factly) How would you describe what that is?

Sue: (Laughing) Changing the subject.

Rohe: (Seriously and explaining) The way I describe that is I interrupt what you're talking about.

Sue: (Softly) Okay. (hard voice) You interrupt my talking about one thing.

Rohe: (Directing) Focus on what you're doing now.

Sue: (Frustrated) Right now I'm sitting here wondering where this is all leading (uneasy laugh).

Rohe: (Playful, fatalistic) Who knows?

Sue: That (hesitant laugh) . . . that's the truth. (accepting)

Rohe: (Widening eyes) Down the garden path maybe.

Sue: (Second-breath laugh) Has anybody got a garden? (chuckling and second-breath laugh) Oh, shoot.

Rohe: (Correcting) No, don't shoot.

Sue: (Lightly) Why not?

Rohe: I might get hurt.

Sue: (Laughing) The way I handle a gun, it's quite impossible. Anybody that shoots a mattress. But, uh, maybe I was mad at the bed or something.

Rohe: Stay with the bed, why you're mad about the bedroom.

Sue: (Loudly) It's empty (hysterical laugh).

Rohe: Ha. Ha. Do you hear your laugh?

Sue: (Still laughing, frustrated) Yes. (pause) Well, it ain't always fun to be in an empty bed (frustrated). See. Now, I'm off on tangents. I'm not on what I was going to talk about at all. I wasn't going to talk about that at all.

Rohe: (Interrupting and persistent) Stay with the empty bed.

Sue: Okay. The empty bed is a perfect, uh, lead-in to (pause, drops voice) something else I've realized about myself. It's uh . . .

Rohe: (Playfully suspicious) Hey, it sounds like you're taking me to bed . . . to lead me into something.

Sue: (Laughing) I hadn't thought of that. (second-breath laugh three times, chuckle, then serious) Whoooo. Oh, God. I have had two nights of absolutely no sleep this week and . . .

Rohe: Sounds like you're making an excuse for something there.

Sue: No, I'm silly; I'm giddy.

Rohe: Are you justifying your giddiness because you haven't been to sleep or blah, blah, blah? You're using the bed to justify your giddiness then.

Sue: Nooooo, I can thing of a lot better things to use the bed for besides justifying my giddiness.

Rohe: (Quietly) Likewise.

Sue: (Pause) Like, uh (lightly, hesitantly) sex. Having a good time. Enjoying life. Relaxation. Let's face it, it's a hell of a lot better than the Valium.

Rohe: (Distinctly) I agree.

Sue: But, uh, I still nine times out of ten take a Valium and go to bed . . . by myself. Nine times out of ten. That's a very misleading statement. (Voice drops very low, flat) More like, uh, oh, say four months is 120 days and three months is 90, it's (hey-hey laugh) uh, 210 days, about one out of 210 times.

Rohe: (Reporting) I am bored.

Sue: All right.

Rohe: I wasn't even listening to the last words about whatever you were reciting about numbers.

Sue: Well, I was just trying to calculate for myself what was the proper ratio.

Rohe: (Very flatly) How exciting.

Sue: (Flat) Yeah. Isn't it though.

Rohe: Yeah.

Sue: (Frustrated laugh) All right, so I'm boring. (pulls on hair)

Rohe: (Easily) Pay attention to your right hand and what you're doing to your head.

Sue: (Frustrated; annoyed) I don't know why I do that. It's a habit.

Rohe: I don't care why you . . .

Sue: (Interrupting, exasperated) I do it watching television; I do it reading a book . . .

Rohe: (Talking over her, very distinctly) I don't care about your habits; I don't care about your whys. I do want to say that I did not say you were boring. I said I was bored (chuckles). And whatever you did to change my saying I was bored into your being boring was about the time you started doing that number with your head.

Sue: (Very softly) Oh.

Rohe: (Continuing) My hunch is that whatever thinking you did before that is what you do to pull on yourself.

Sue: My security blanket?

Rohe: Question?

Sue: (Long pause) Maybe it's my security blanket.

Rohe: (Laughing) Maybe.

Sue: (Laughing, frustrated) I don't know.

Rohe: Do you want to know?

Sue: I do it without thinking. Yeah! All right.

Rohe: You want to know.

Sue: All right.

Rohe: I will tell you how to know.

Sue: Okay.

Rohe: As you do that, continue doing it, exaggerate what you're doing; then pay attention to how you're thinking at that moment.

Sue: (Pause) Hurt. (softly) Insecure. (sniff) And, yet I don't, uh, if that's what it is, why do I do it when I'm sitting around reading a book? (pause) Now, see, that's why it doesn't make sense. It doesn't fit into a category. How can you categorize something that you do a dozen times a day?

Rohe: (Exaggerated, controlled patience) Substitute "I" for "it" and "those things."

Sue: I am a habit. (softly) It doesn't make sense.

Rohe: It . . . doesn't make sense.

Sue: I don't make sense.

Rohe: It doesn't fit into a category.

Sue: (Laughing) I don't fit a category.

Rohe: Looks like you enjoy that.

Sue: Why should I fit into a category?

Rohe: Why should you?

Sue: (Softly, disgusted) Because society says you gotta fit in someplace.

Rohe: Who?

Sue: (Loudly) People.

Rohe: Who are they?

Sue: Husbands. (Loud and angry) Parents.

Rohe: Who (louder)?

Sue: Jobs.

Rohe: Who (louder, emphatically)?

Sue: Bosses.

Rohe: Who (very loud)?

Sue: (Pause, then softer voice) Just people that, that, uh . . .

Rohe: Who are they? Sounds like there's a you in there.

Sue: Mother (loud, angry).

Rohe: What does mother say to you?

Sue: You gotta fit. Belong.

Rohe: And what do you say to mother?

Sue: (Laughing) I haven't seen mother in a long time. I don't know what I'd say now.

Rohe: Say that to mother. All right, I'll fit.

Sue: (Disgusted) I'll fit in your mold.

Rohe: What do you hear and what do you experience?

Sue: Exasperation.

Rohe: So put that together and say to your mother, "I exasperate myself by fitting into your mold."

Sue: (Clearly) I exasperate myself by fitting into your mold. (angrily) Because I don't belong in your mold. I'M ME.

(Another ten minutes of dialogue is included without description now that you have the flavor.)

Rohe: You're telling me that.

Sue: I'll tell mother that (laughs). She's in Florida and can't hear me anyway. (Rohe joins in laughter.) She don't listen when I tell her.

Rohe: Do *you*?

Sue: Yeah, I've tried to.

Rohe: Do *you*?

Sue: Yeah, I listen to what I say. Yeah.

Rohe: Do you believe?

Sue: Yeah. More and more I'm believing it.

Rohe: It.

Sue: (Frustrated) Believing me. (laughs) Oh, fudge. (laughs again) Is that better than shoot. Do you like fudge? (giving Rohe a hard time, pointing a finger)

Rohe: Are you aware of your finger?

Sue: Yeah. I'm asking you.

Rohe: Now stay with your hands.

Sue: Does that fit, does that . . .

Rohe: Freeze. Pay attention to your hand.

Sue: (Mumbles)

Rohe: What?

Sue: Does that fit with what . . .

Rohe: (Very distinctly) Stay with your hands.

Sue: My hands asking you.

Rohe: Look at your hands. Stay with the obvious. (Copying hand by squeezing fingers more)

Sue: No, I don't have it like that. I have it like that.

Rohe: You keep moving your finger more and more to the side.

Sue: (Laughing) Okay. (laughs) Bang! You're dead. (laughs again) Ohhhh. That's what I get for taking Valium this morning.

Sue: Well, it gets, it makes me silly.

Rohe: Bullshit!

Sue: It does. I hype up easily, but I had a tension headache and I spent two nights this week.

Rohe: I'm aware that you're not taking responsibility for silliness or whatever it is you're doing. I would like you not to take any more Valium while you're working with me.

Sue: All right. This is the first time.

Rohe: I mean like at night, in the morning, any time.

Sue: Well, like I said, this is the first time I've taken one. But, I've had—to get off the subject for a minute—I've had a, I don't know whether migraines or what, headache starts in the back of your neck type of thing. And I took two Excedrin the other night and I, I don't know, I don't, but I was up pacing the floor all night with my gut killing me and then, uh, I didn't associate it with the Excedrin but then two nights later I took some for a headache and I was up all night then. And, uh.

Rohe: I would like to tell you what to substitute in dealing with your headache.

Sue: What?

Rohe: And then you can decide which way you want to go.

Sue: Okay.

Rohe: You can do the awareness thing you did this past week. Focus your awareness with wherever you are. Go with, the headache is drawing your attention to something going on with you and you're giving yourself a headache. You're doing that. And, then I want you to begin with giving your headache a voice and describe how you are. Stay with, "right now I am a headache and I" whatever fits. "I am a headache." And stay with that.

Sue: Next time I get a headache.

Rohe: Next time you give yourself a headache, you do that.

Sue: I get a headache, I'll try.

Rohe: You don't *get it* and you don't *try.* You give yourself a headache and you do it.

Sue: (Laughing) Well, I'm not going to give myself a headache just to do it. (laughs) If one happens, though, I'll try it.

Rohe: *Happens,* you'll *try* it.

Sue: You . . . oh, come on now.

Rohe: Come on? What do you want?

Sue: (Abruptly) It's like you're making fun of me.

Rohe: I am.

Sue: I know.

Rohe: Now you know reality. So what.

Sue: Oh, where was I?

Rohe: Where are you?

Sue: Here.

Rohe: What are you experiencing?

Sue: (Pause) Uhhhh (pause). Insecurities.

Rohe: Oh.

Sue: (Long pause) The insecurities and sensitivities that I always come up with that always, ah . . .

Rohe: You're talking about. How are you dealing with insecurity right now? You started with the thing about my making fun of you.

Sue: It makes me feel insecure.

Rohe: Who's it?

Sue: Being made fun of.

Rohe: Who is it?

Sue: YOU. Okay.

Rohe: I cannot make you.

Sue: Okay. I feel insecure.

Rohe: How do you do that? You do that with thinking first and then feeling something. What are you thinking to create your insecurity? Start with, I make fun of you, you do what?

Sue: I feel that everything I came here to do and all the things I felt before I came here, uh, (pause) are wrong.

Rohe: What is wrong?

Sue: Uh. (long pause) Is immature.

Rohe: What does *that* mean?

Sue: Childish.

Rohe: What does *that* mean?

Sue: (Long pause, eyes becoming moist; frustrated) I swore at the beginning I wasn't going to do that.

Rohe: What are you not going to do?

Sue: I wasn't going to be supersensitive.

Rohe: How are you?

Sue: I always let things *bother* me.

Rohe: How are you now?

Sue: Weepy.

Rohe: So go with being weepy.

Sue: I don't want to. I'll ruin my makeup. I spent an hour putting it on.

Rohe: Well, you'll learn.

Sue: See, I felt good and now I'm weepy.

Rohe: So?

Sue: I didn't want to feel weepy.

Rohe: Are you aware of how you created your weepiness?

Sue: Yeah.

Rohe: How'd you do it?

Sue: I let every little thing bother me.

Rohe: How do you bother yourself?

Sue: I take every little thing as a personal insult.

Rohe: What does that mean? In five-year-old language, tell me what personal insult means.

Sue: (Crying) I let everything hurt. Being put down. Like I'm not up to what I should be up to. And don't say the shoulds again because I don't know what they mean.

Rohe: Should, should, should, should.

Sue: All right, (pause, calmer) I take everything people say, any people, teachers, doctors, parents, husbands, and I let it hurt.

Rohe: This is (it).

Sue: I let whatever it is hurt.

Rohe: You let.

Sue: Yeah.

Rohe: You let. Try that on for size. "I hurt myself. I cut myself. I put myself down with other people's words."

Sue: I hurt myself. I cut myself. And I put myself down with other people's words.

Rohe: Your voice sounds like you mean that. It sounds like you're doing what I told you to do.

Sue: It's just that, that . . .

Rohe: It's just. I want you to substitute I, me, or myself for all your its.

Sue: (Little girl voice, I told you so tone) I won't make sense if I do that. (laughs) Grammatically, I won't make sense.

Rohe: Promises, promises.

Sue: I guess that I don't understand . . . how you think I'm hurting myself purposely when it angers me so much to be hurt like that, by myself, Rohe.

Rohe: So now I know and you don't know.

Sue: Okay. (frustrated) So, now, how the hell do I get rid of this sensitivity?

Rohe: (Indifferent shrug) Beats me.

Sue: Do I go through the rest of my life being sensitive?

Rohe: Do you want to?

Sue: To a point everybody is sensitive, but . . .

Rohe: (Interrupting) Do you want to?

Sue: NO. I don't want to go through life being *super*sensitive, no.

Rohe: Whatever that means. What is that? Supersensitive. How are you supersensitive?

Sue: By taking what other people say and hurting, by hurting me because of it.

Rohe: Okay. Will you put that together with what you want and don't want?

Sue: I don't want to hurt myself with other people's words.

Rohe: (Simply) Then stop.

Sue: (Pause) Just like that.

Rohe: (Shrugging) If you want.

Sue: (Pause)

Rohe: I notice you're laughing.

Sue: Well, it's kinda par for the course. I come in thinking one way and end up totally confused before it's all over with anyway (laughing).

Rohe: You look delighted. Be aware of your face and your smile. So nice. Your eyes.

Sue: I'm laughing, and giggling, and crying.

Rohe: Well, you cry, I'll laugh.

Sue: (Laughing) Thanks.

Rohe: (Still laughing) You're welcome.

Sue: (laughing)

Rohe: Smart ass.

Sue: (Both still laughing) Right. Every now and then I get one in. Not very often.

Rohe: Ah, be aware of your finger.

Sue: Yeah.

Rohe: And your tears.

Sue: Right.

Rohe: And your laughter.

Sue: Ohhhh (several sounds of pleasure mixed with laughter). You know, trying to keep ahead of you is ridiculous.

Rohe: Yes, I have discovered that myself.

Sue: Okay. I came upon a very good revelation about myself and I haven't had a chance to say it yet. (Pause)

Rohe: Oh, I'm getting teased.

Sue: Okay.

Rohe: (Pleadingly, laughing) Please tell me what the revelation is.

Sue: (Laughing) Oh, come on. (Both laughing heartily) Oh, you think I've been drinking today and I haven't. Honest. I had one Coke today and that's it. Not even a whole one of those. I told you I was in a good mood. A silly mood.

Rohe: Sounds like you're excusing yourself.

Sue: Well, this is supposed to be something serious.

(Both laughing)

Rohe: You're supposed to.

Sue: Huh?

Rohe: I'm glad to discover I'm following one of those "supposed tos" of yours. (Deep, pedantic voice) Supposed to be a serious business. Be miserable.

Sue: You're making a mess of my makeup.

Rohe: *I've* been messing your makeup.

Sue: Yes.

Rohe: (Chagrined) Jesus.

Sue: It's more fun to blame you than me.

Rohe: I believe you.

Sue: Okay. (laughter, then serious) You were talking the other day about my not being able to cope with sex and my being able to turn it off. I think the whole thing in a nutshell, when I really sit down to think about it, is, uh, if I let myself, I could probably (quickly) hop in bed with a dozen men between now and the time Bob comes home and have an absolute ball. But, uh, that could have a very big price, so I feel that I better not do it and that's why I haven't except for one little slip (laughs).

Rohe: (Mimics her laugh)

Sue: That was *fun*. I enjoyed it and there's no sense in saying I didn't.

Rohe: Yeah. One comment on that. I doubt that you would hop into bed with a dozen men. I agree with you that you could mess yourself up with that at this point. That you would probably be doing something destructive to yourself at this point. And that destructiveness is whatever that price was you mentioned.

Sue: Yeah. That and possibly losing my child because of it. And, as much as I think I'd like to get rid of him at times, I don't want to lose him.

Rohe: What I'm aware of is that you're not taking responsibility for any of that. Your not taking responsibility for any of the whole package. It's "if I did, I know I could, and then there will be a price and so I'm not going to let it happen." The whole description was in that you had not made a decision as to whether you are going to or not.

Sue: Well, I'm not going to.

Rohe: Oh.

Sue: Because, uh . . .

Rohe: What are you not going to do?

Sue: I'm not going to hop into bed with a dozen different men.

Rohe: That's twelve. What are you going to do?

Sue: I'm going to try to go back to controlling things.

Rohe: TRY to go back to controlling things. What are you going to do? Eleven?

Sue: No, it's very hard to say never.

Rohe: How about ten then?

Sue: No.

Rohe: Nine?

Sue: (Laughing) No.

Rohe: Eight?

Sue: No.

Rohe: You see the ridiculousness in your statement.

Sue: All right.

Rohe: What are you going to do and what are you not going to do?

Sue: I'm going to try very hard to keep myself from getting into situations that could lead to bed. I cannot, in all honesty, with you or with myself, sit and say that it may not happen again.

Rohe: All I notice is I'm not hearing your words. Like you're vague as if you're explaining something. And what I'm wanting from you is to make a clear statement for today about taking responsibility for whether you go to bed with a dozen men, a half a dozen men, one man, no men, and not through this magical control stuff, you can lose with booze.

Sue: Well . . . (long pause)

Rohe: I'm also willing to accept you're not going to do that—make any agreements or that kind of stuff. Like I'm realizing I'm demanding you make some kind of commitment to me. I don' care. What I'm doing is for you to be clear about what you're wanting and not wanting.

Sue: Oh, I miss sex very much.

Rohe: I know that.

Sue: And, uh (pause), it's hard to sit and say even in the next ten more months I may not change my mind and say to hell with it.

Rohe: I know it's hard.

Sue: So, that's what I said all I can do is—keep myself from situations that could—lead to sex.

Rohe: Okay. What I hear is that is a clear statement for you.

COMMENTS

The voice descriptions are included to present the flavor of the changes, and rapid speaking is indicated by the running together of words. Feedback from fellow therapists have indicated that a significant part of my work is nonverbal and is intimately related to voice tone. I became concerned with how I would look in print without my voice tones, facial expressions, and body movements apparent. I sat down with Patricia Henry, a typist and Gestaltist, to describe the different voice tones, and began to realize that some very heavy work was done during this therapy session!

The *Okays* are shifts in tone. The *O* is said with the same tone quality as whatever preceded, and the *kay* is a distinctively different tone and signals changes in the overall content and affect of the verbal process. The *uhs* precede a ruminating, "ugly mother" type of content. The *wells* are protesting, frustrated responses. The "second breath" laughs are the kind of laugh which the person does quietly and internally with the only noise occurring when there is an intake of breath.

The woman had come to the session with the plan of telling me what a good girl she had been. She had done her homework and had gotten a lot from her homework. I knew she had benefited because of the way she looked and her second comment. I then responded to what she did at the moment.

A major theme in her work has dealt with not taking responsibility for her own behavior or lifestyle. She is struggling with living to please others for their approval of her. Had I been serious, I might have sat down and listened to her "good girl," thus reinforcing her other-supportiveness, her dependence, her transference, her games, or her maladaptive behaviors. As the session closes, she finally makes a statement of ownership and clarity of *her* decision to retain control, and *her* decision not to make changes at this time.

This *style* of frustration, the therapists' spontaneity, is a variable that differentiates Gestalt Therapy from other schools of psychotherapy. The spontaneity is a natural frustration of the avoidance or resistances and occurs from the first moment of the psychotherapeutic encounter. What we want then is beyond frustration. Frustration precedes growth. There will be no effective psychotherapy or growth without frustration.

REFERENCES

Ellis, A. *Reason and Emotion in Psychotherapy*. Secaucus, N.J.: Lyle Stuart, 1962.

Glasser, W. *Reality Therapy*. New York: Harper & Row, 1965.

Lieberman, M. A., I. D. Yalom, and M. B. Miles. *Encounter Groups: First Facts*. New York: Basic Books, 1973.

Mainord, W. A. "Therapy #52—the Truth (Operant Group Psychotherapy)," in R. R. Jurjevich (ed.), *Direct Psychotherapy* (Vol. 1). Coral Gables, Fla.: University of Miami Press, 1973, 757-895.

Mowrer, O. H. *The New Group Therapy*. New York: Van Nostrand Reinhold, 1964.

Perls, F. S. *Gestalt Therapy Verbatim*. Moab, Utah: Real People Press, 1969.

Resnick, R. W. "Chicken Soup Is Poison," *Voices*, 6 (1970), 75-78.

Rosen, J. *Direct Analysis: Selected Papers*. New York: Grune & Stratton, 1953.

Schiff, A. W., and J. L. Schiff. "Passivity," *Transactional Analysis Journal*, 1 (1971), 71-78.

CHAPTER 13

SAYING GOODBYE IN GESTALT THERAPY

STEPHAN A. TOBIN, Ph.D.

Stephan A. Tobin is in private practice in Los Angeles, California, and is also a staff member of the Gestalt Therapy Institute of Los Angeles.

Reprinted by permission from Stephan A. Tobin, "Saying Goodbye in Gestalt Therapy," **Psychotherapy: Theory, Research and Practice**, Vol. 8, No. 2, 1971, pp. 150-155.

I find that most patients have failed to say goodbye and finish some relationship that terminated in death, divorce, ending of a love affair, or in some other way. This "hanging-on" reaction occurs with missing persons who were of strong emotional significance to the patient. The relationship does not have to have been filled with love. In fact, *most* such relationships were characterized by much fighting and resentment rather than by love.

The adaptive reaction to the loss of a loved person is a fairly long period of grief followed by renewed interest in living people and things. The adaptive reaction to the loss of a hated person presumably would be relief. The hanging-on reaction is to inhibit the emotions triggered by the loss and to keep the person present in fantasy.

In this chapter I shall discuss the causes of the hanging-on reaction, the symptomatic results in the hanger-on, Gestalt Therapy techniques I use in working with patients to say goodbye, and a sample of such work.

One cause of the hanging-on reaction is the presence of much unfinished business between the two persons long before the relationship terminates. By "unfinished business" I mean the inhibition of an emotion that was experienced at one or more times during the relationship. A simple example would be the employee who feels angry toward his boss but, because he is frightened of being fired, decides not to express his feelings. Until he expresses his anger in some way, he is left with the physical tension that results from the impasse between the physical excitation of the anger and the inhibiting force that suppresses the emotion. He may try to deal with this unfinished situation in indirect ways, e.g., by having fantasies about telling his boss off or about the death of his boss in an accident, or by taking it out on his wife and children when he goes home that night. No matter what he does, he is tense and anxious and has a nagging feeling of not having done something he should have done. Until he finds some *direct* way of finishing the business of his anger toward his boss, he will be unable to relax or involve himself fully with any person or in any activity. In addition, his relationship with his boss will be strained.

This is, of course, a minor situation that probably wouldn't cause much difficulty. Most of the people I see in therapy have accumulated many unfinished situations of great emotional intensity. For example, one man as a child was continually humiliated and rendered helpless by his father. To express his rage toward his father would have meant his own destruction. Today he continually attempts to finish this situation by provoking authority figures into attacking him and then attacking back. [1]

How do people stop themselves from finishing situations? First, most of them are unaware of their bodies and, since all feelings are located in the body, they are unaware of their feelings. This lack of awareness makes it impossible for them to finish emotional situations. Even if they do become aware of their emotions, they are apt to suppress them; their minds tell them they shouldn't be angry, shouldn't express love, shouldn't feel sad. So they turn off the messages their bodies give them and the emotional excitement then turns into physical pain, tension, and anxiety.

A second way people stop themselves from finishing situations is by placing great value on some of the secondary gains they get from hanging on. If the present is unexciting or if they feel incapable of getting involved with other people, they can relieve their loneliness by thinking about past relationships. While one might imagine that these past situations are pleasurable, more often than not they are negative. Hanging on to resentment, for example, can be used to enable one to feel self-righteous or self-pitying, characterological ways of being many people are willing to settle for. Resentment can also be used as an excuse for not getting close to the object of one's resentment.

For example, a woman in a therapy group talked continually about what an awful mother she had. Whenever anyone else spoke of his mother, she would very dramatically start to recount the "terrible" things her mother had done to her. When I asked her to imagine her mother in the room and to talk to her, she would blame her mother for ruining her life. She would not, of course, ever confront her mother directly with her resentment; her excuse was that she didn't want to hurt her mother and, "It wouldn't do any good anyway." Her real reason for not confronting her was that she didn't really think she had the resources to change her existence and her mother served as a ready excuse for her failures in life. Another benefit of her game was that she could project all her own undesired traits on her mother; when I pointed out that she resembled her description of her mother in many ways, she would shudder and plead with me not to say that because she hated her mother so much.

While her complaints to the group afforded her some expression of resentment, the situation was still incomplete for her. She still harbored resentment and hatred which appeared even when she was not speaking of her mother in her tone of voice, her posture, and her gestures.

Self-righteousness, which is a particularly prevalent side-benefit of hanging-on, is common in those patients who evaluate every conflict between themselves and others in a good-bad, right-wrong fashion. They think that the only way to resolve a conflict is for one person to admit that he is guilty or bad or stupid. Since admitting to these judgments is humiliating and degrading, many people hang on to their resentments hoping that the other will see the light and humiliate himself by admitting he was wrong.

So we see that even before termination of the relationship, there is a great deal of unfinished business. Matters become more complicated when one of the persons leaves and the relationship is ended.

The unfinished business can be between a parent and child, between spouses, between lovers, between friends, or between any other two people who have had an intense, long-standing relationship. There is much unfinished business within the relationship while it lasts; when the relationship ends—through death, divorce, one person moving away from the other, etc.—the relationship itself becomes unfinished. The individual is still carrying around much accumulated unexpressed emotion: old resentments, frustrations, hurts, guilts, and even unexpressed love and appreciation. The presence of these unexpressed emotions makes it difficult for him to finish the relationship simply because the other person is no longer around to hear them. One of the ways it can be done is for the person to express his feelings in fantasy to the one who is gone. I find, however, that few of my patients have done this. There are a number of reasons why they have not.

First of all, some of the ways in which people prevent themselves from finishing things discussed in the previous section are also used to prevent themselves from finishing the relationship and saying goodbye. Many patients have been unaware of what they felt at the end of a relationship. For example, a young man in a workshop I ran was almost completely unaware of the intense guilt and grief he felt about his sick pet cat whom he had had to have destroyed.

People also get much secondary gain from not letting go. The woman who is fearful about attempting new relationships with men can use her attachment to her dead husband as an excuse for not getting involved.

Many Americans have simply lost the ability to let go of dead relationships because of their distaste for intense emotion of any kind, particularly when a death has occurred. The mourning process, which is recognized as natural and necessary in other parts of the world, frequently does not occur in the United States. The Kennedy wives, e.g., were praised for their lack of public emotion after their husbands were assassinated. In contrast, the widow of Tom Mboya, the African politician, was shown in a national magazine attempting to throw herself on her husband's grave.

Another example of this inability to do what is necessary to finish dead relationships is the individual who has been jilted. Instead of venting his feelings of hurt and anger, he is apt to keep them to himself so as not to give his jilter any "satisfaction" for rejecting him. The adaptive reaction to divorce would be for each person to express his lingering resentments and to go his separate way; instead, most divorced people continue hanging-on in a kind of guerrilla war, particularly when complicated alimony and child settlement agreements are legally enforced.

Another reason for my patients' inability to say goodbye is their unwillingness to experience the pain they would feel if they did let go. Probably as a reaction to American Puritanism, which taught people that life was supposed to involve nothing but pain, we have become a nation of people who believe it's wrong to feel any pain at all. As soon as most people feel anxious, they take tranquilizers or smoke pot; as soon as they come into conflict with others, they try to end the conflicts as quickly as possible by either avoiding the others or by trying to overpower or manipulate them and "win." Rather than letting go of dead relationships, most people avoid the emptiness and loneliness by "keeping busy," by finding a new relationship as quickly as possible, or by pretending that the dead person is still around.

Finally, many people avoid saying goodbye because they feel that letting go, particularly of the dead, is a dishonor to them. Most of my patients no longer believe in a life hereafter, and they often feel that the only kind of immortality possible is to be remembered by the living. They don't realize that, had they really had a meaningful relationship with the person when he was still around, had they really said "hello," they would have been continually enriched and changed through the relationship (Friedman, 1970). The lost person then would *really* have become part of the one who is left and live on in a much more meaningful way—as part of that person's being—instead of as an introjected lump of dead matter that comes between the person and his world.

RESULTS OF HANGING-ON

Physical symptoms are one result of hanging-on. Some patients have identified parts of their bodies as representatives of the persons who are gone. Two women I saw in therapy kept their mothers present in the form of ulcers. Another example is a young woman with whom I worked in a weekend workshop who had chronically cold hands, maintained an attitude of contemptuous aloofness toward others, and literally would not touch others. Her mother had died when she was three and she became aware during our work together that her cold hands were both links with her cold, dead mother and also symbolized her mother. When she was able to say goodbye to her mother, her hands suddenly warmed up and she was able to make meaningful contact with others for the first time in her life.

Other people identify their whole beings with dead people and appear to be walking zombies: their voices and faces are expressionless, their movements are controlled and mechanical, and they report feeling physically numb.

Secondly, those who have refused to say goodbye usually exhibit emotional symptoms. For example, those who have identified with dead people are emotionally dead. I am not referring to depressed persons; these people feel neither depression nor anything else. There are also, however, many persons who, because of incompletion of the mourning process, become chronically depressed in an attenuated way. They are gloomy, apathetic, and have little real interest in life. They have been depressed for such a long time that they frequently are even unaware of their depression.

Another emotional result of the hanging-on reaction is a whiny, self-pitying attitude toward oneself, and a blaming, complaining attitude toward the person who has gone. The whiner often uses the lost person as an excuse for his inadequacies: "If my father had loved me more, my life wouldn't be such a mess now." The obverse of the whiner is the person who blames himself rather than the dead person and feels guilty: "If I had been nicer to my father before he died, he would have been happier and I would be better off now. Now there's no way I can make it up to him."

A third symptom is an inability to form close relationships. One who is continually fantasizing about the past, or is having relationships with people who are gone, has little time for those still around. He does not see or hear or feel in the present.

I have found that the more a person is able to finish things in a relationship, the more authentic that relationship is. What happens, however, in most intimate relationships is that, after a while, there are so many unexpressed resentments and disappointments that the people in the relationship cease really seeing or hearing each other or feeling *in the present*. In contrast, those people who can say "goodbye" when they part temporarily are better able to get fully involved with each other in a fresh, meaningful, realistic way when they next meet.

Thus, in a very important sense, saying goodbye to the dead parent or the divorced spouse is an identical process to expressing feelings to another person and to letting him go during a temporary absence.

The first step in helping the patient who is hanging-on to say goodbye is *to make him aware of hanging-on* and of how he is doing this. Usually something the patient says or does in group or individual therapy makes me suspect that he is in conflict about some unfinished business. Sometimes it is a dream in which the dead person appears, sometimes a gesture (e.g., a few patients have looked up when speaking and I found out they were looking up at "heaven"), sometimes the patient appears so lifeless that I have a hunch he has identified with a dead person.

I then ask the patient if he has some unfinished business with someone who is gone and, if the answer is affirmative, I ask him if he wants to say goodbye. Most patients at this point will say that they do; if they openly state they do not wish to let go, I will just work with them long enough to get them aware of their objections to saying goodbye. If they still insist, after finding out their objections, that they don't want to let go and are in no conflict about this, I stop at this point. If a patient does wish to work on saying goodbye, I then proceed to the next stage.

WORKING THROUGH

The second step is, I first take an empty chair and place it in front of the patient and ask him to imagine the dead person sitting in it. I next ask him what he experiences as he imagines the dead person there. Whatever the emotion or thought expressed, I ask the patient to say that directly to the dead person. Frequently, e.g., patients experience resentment at not having been "loved enough," or guilt about not having been kinder to the dead person before he died. After he has said what he wants to, I ask him to switch chairs and become the dead person. Frequently the patient will spontaneously say something; if he does not, I again ask him what he is experiencing, this time as the dead person. When he replies, I ask him to say that to himself sitting in the other chair. The dead person as imagined by the client may feel anger for the lack of kindness in the patient toward himself. The dead person may become defensive at the resentment expressed by the patient, and give excuses for the lack of love. After the dead person has had his say, I ask the patient to switch back to playing himself in the first chair, and he is asked to reply to the fantasied dead one. When the patient gets into the two roles completely, I ask him to let himself switch back and forth as he finds himself changing roles.

In almost every case there is much emotion expressed—anger, hurt, resentment, love, etc. When the patient seems to have no more unfinished business, I ask him if he feels ready to say goodbye. Frequently patients say they are ready to say goodbye but are unable to do so when I ask them to say it directly to the imagined dead love-object. At other times they say goodbye but it just doesn't sound convincing. In either case, I help them to become aware that they are not ready to let the dead go, either because of a fear they won't be able to find living people to relate to, or because they have more unfinished business. I do not push or encourage the patient as long as he is willing to take responsibility for his hanging-on.

If the patient is ready to terminate the relationship, however, there is usually some explosion of emotion. Usually the patient completes the mourning process and cries; occasionally, however, the emotion is one of great relief and joy at the dead weight that has been eliminated. When this kind of work occurs in a group, it tends to be a very moving experience for me and all the other people present. Typically, feelings of greater group closeness, warmth, and a kind of profound, religious love of all of life are expressed by all the people participating as observers of this work.

I have done no systematic study of the follow-up effects, but my impression is that the results are long-lasting: little or no thinking about the dead person, a feeling of more energy, and increased interest in life and other people.

CLINICAL EXAMPLE

The following is a re-creation of some work I did with a woman in a weekend workshop with whom I had had no previous contact. The woman, whom I shall call "Mrs. R.," was a married housewife in her mid-thirties. She spoke in a very mechanical way, sounding like a child who was reciting a poem she had been forced to memorize but didn't understand. In her relationship with her husband and children she played the part of a masochistic martyr, controlling them by showing how much they made her "suffer." Our work on her saying goodbye to her dead mother started during a dream in which her mother appeared. While working on the dream, her voice and demeanor suddenly changed; she began to cry and sounded whiny and complaining. I asked her if she had some unfinished business with her mother, and she said:

Mrs. R: Well . . . if only she had loved me, things would be different. But she didn't and . . . and I've never had any real mother love (crying).
Steve: Put your mother in that chair and say that to her.
Mrs. R: If only she had cared for me, I'd be much better today.
Steve: I want you to say this to her, not to me. Can you imagine her sitting there in front of you?
Mrs. R: Yes, I see her as she looked when she was still alive. Mother, if you had only loved me. Why couldn't you ever tell me you loved me? Why did you always criticize me? (Almost a wail, more tears)
Steve: Now switch over to the other chair and play your mother. (She moves over to the other chair and doesn't say anything.)
Steve: What do you experience as your mother?
Mrs. R: I-I-I don't know . . . I don't know what she would say.
Steve: Of course you don't know. She's not around any more. You're just playing the part of you that is your mother. Just say whatever you experience there.
Mrs. R: Oh, I see. Well, I don't know what to say to her.
Steve: Say that to her.
Mrs. RM: (Mrs. R as mother) I don't know what to say to you. I

never knew what to say to you. I really did love you, you know that. Look at all the things I did for you, and you never appreciated it. (Voice sounds defensive and whiny)

Steve: Now switch back and reply as yourself.

Mrs. RS: (Mrs. R as self): Loved me! All you ever did was criticize me. Nothing I ever did was good enough! (Voice beginning to sound more whiny) When I got married to J. you disapproved, you were always coming over and telling me what I was doing wrong with the kids. Oh, you never came right out and said any thing, but you were always making snide remarks or saying, "Now, dear, wouldn't it be a good idea to put another blanket on the baby." You made my life *miserable*; I was always worrying about your criticizing me. And now I'm having this trouble with J. (Breaks down and starts to cry)

Steve: Did you hear your voice?

Mrs. RS: Yes.

Steve: What did you hear in it?

Mrs. RS: Well, I guess I sounded kind of complaining, like I'm feeling sore—like I'm feeling mad.

Steve: You sounded more like feeling self-pity. Try this on for size: say to your mother, "Look what you've done to me. It's all your fault."

Mrs. RS: Look what you've done. Everything's your fault.

Steve: Now let yourself switch back and forth as you find yourself changing roles.

Mrs. RM: Come one, stop blaming me for everything. You are always complaining about something. If you had been better—if you had been a *decent* daughter, I wouldn't have had to criticize you so much.

Mrs. RS: Oh, oh. (Under her breath) Damn. (She's swinging her right leg slightly.)

Steve: Notice your leg.

Mrs. RS: I-I'm shaking it.

Steve: Exaggerate that, shaking it harder.

Mrs. RS: (Shakes leg harder; it begins to look like a kick)

Steve: Can you imagine doing that to your mother?

Mrs. RS: No, but I-I-I'm sure feeling pissed at her.

Steve: Say this to her.

Mrs. RS: I feel pissed off at you! I hate you!

Steve: Say that louder.

Mrs. RS: I hate you! (Volume higher, but still some holding back)

Steve: Louder!

Mrs. RS: I HATE YOU, YOU GODDAMNED BITCH. (She sticks her leg out and kicks the chair over.)

Steve: Now switch back.

Mrs. RM: (Voice sounds much weaker now) I-I guess I didn't show you much love. I really felt it, but I was unhappy and bitter. You know all I had to go through with your father and brother. You were the only one I could talk to. I'm sorry . . . I wanted you to be happy . . . I wanted so much for you.

Mrs. RS: You sure did! . . . I know you did love me, Mother, I know you were unhappy (voice much softer now, but sounding real, not whiny or mechanical). I guess I did some things that were ba—wrong, too. I was always trying to keep you off my back.

Mrs. RM: Yes, you were pretty sarcastic to me, too. And that hurt.

Mrs. RS: I wish you had told me. I didn't think you were hurt at all.

Mrs. RM: Well, that's all over now.

Mrs. RS: Yeah, it is. I guess there's no use blaming you. You're not around anymore.

Steve: Can you forgive your mother now?

Mrs. RS: Mother, I forgive you . . . I really do forgive you. (Starts crying again, but not in the whiny way of before. She sounds genuinely grieving and cries for a couple of minutes.)

Steve: Now switch back.

Mrs. RM: I forgive you too, dear. You have to go on now. You can't keep blaming me forever. I make my mistakes but you have your own family and you're doing okay.

Steve: Do you feel ready to say goodbye now?

Mrs. RS: Yes. I-I think so (starts to sob). Goodbye, Mother, goodbye. (Breaks down, cries for a few minutes)

Steve: What do you experience now?

Mrs. R: I feel better. I feel . . . kind of relieved, like a weight is off my back. I feel calm.

Steve: Now that you've said goodbye to her, to this dead person, can you go around and say hello to the live people here, to the group?

Mrs. R: Yes, I'd like that.

(She goes around the room, greets people, touches some, embraces others. Many in the group are tearful. When she reaches her husband, she starts crying again, and tells him she loves him, and they embrace.)

NOTES

1. The Freudians have discussed such neurotic behavior and have coined the term "repetition compulsion" to describe it. They have not, however, dealt with the physical changes that take place. In addition, Freudian therapy, with its stress on thinking and its endless why-because games, reinforces hanging on to the past rather than encouraging letting go of it. Behaviorism, on the other hand, while working toward the elimination of outmoded response tendencies, does not give the client tools he can use to prevent future hanging-on reactions.

REFERENCE

Friedman, L. F. Personal communication, 1970.

CHAPTER 14

LET THE LITTLE CHILD TALK

BEN C. FINNEY, Ph.D.

Ben C. Finney is currently professor of psychology at California State University, San Jose, and is also in private practice in San Jose, California.

Reprinted by permission from "Let the Little Child Talk: A New Psycho-therapeutic Technique," **American Journal of Psychotherapy**, Vol. 23, 1969, pp. 230-242.

This is a psychotherapeutic technique which allows the therapist to talk directly to the "inner child" (Finney, 1969), the part of the personality which was developed in childhood and which continues to influence adult behavior and attitudes. It allows the "child" to express strong and important feelings, to recall "forgotten" events and attitudes of childhood, and it allows the "adult" to listen to the opinions and feelings of the "child" and to change these in the light of adult reality and judgment. Memories that have not been thought about for years become vivid realities, attitudes are expressed which are surprising and "unfamiliar" to the "adult self," and emotions are relived and experienced in a way that is cathartic and gives a sense of relief. Childhood attitudes are expressed that are seen as erroneous in the light of the adult viewpoint, and these childhood misconceptions can be corrected by the "adult"; similarly, the "adult" can remind the "child" that the present reality is not as bleak and painful as that of the past, and can "comfort" his "inner child," providing the nurturance that was missing in the past. And it usually provides the "adult" with a much clearer conception of how his "child" influences his current behavior, as well as giving the therapist some insight into the central conflicts and traumas of the past. And, most importantly, it helps the person recognize and value the spontaneity, the creativity, and the directness of awareness of the "child-self," who is in touch with the feelings which are so essential to a full and balanced life. This technique can be used either individually or in a group, and in addition to providing immediate relief or insight, it brings out material or feelings which can be explored and dealt with in the more usual therapeutic manner.

Essentially, this technique consists of asking the client's permission to let the therapist talk directly to his "inner child," to the child that he was when he was five or six, that still exists as one of the "selves" that influences his outlook and who "owns and controls the feelings." The therapist asks the client to close his eyes and to answer spontaneously without censorship, and then questions the client actively as if he were talking to a child living in the "present" that existed when he was five or six. With a little encouragement and exploration of his resistances, the client will usually agree. If at first the client talks with his usual adult vocabulary and sentence structure, he is admonished "I don't want to talk to big John; let little John talk"; the therapist asks simple questions, using simple words and childish phrases, talking about the past as if it were the present. While sometimes it does not work, usually the client will begin to talk in a childish voice, answering "yes" or "no" and adding a few comments, much as a child will respond to questioning. The content of the conversation usually goes directly to important and emotionally intense topics, often with tears and anger.

In introducing this technique to the client, I usually wait until we have gotten acquainted and the client is used to therapy and the therapist. I do not use it frequently or regularly, but more as an occasional change of pace to break through to important feelings. A natural time to introduce it into psychotherapy is when the client has brought out his immediate presenting problems and has worked through some of his feelings and the pace of therapy has begun to slow a bit.

The technique can be used effectively in a group, especially after the group has become cohesive and trusting. With the lights out, I talk to the clients as a "child" one at a time, but different members will talk as a "child," following the themes that other members have brought up. When listening to other members talk, the clients first listen as an "adult," but the feelings tend to draw out their own "child" and when they speak it is as a child.

This technique will be illustrated with a typescript from the fourth interview of a twenty-four-year-old student who had come to the Student Counseling Center for help with anxiety, identity problems, and her relationship with her husband.

Clare had begun the hour by talking about her rivalry with her brother and her relationship with her father, saying that she was "daddy's girl," able to get the affection which her brother could not.

TYPESCRIPT	COMMENTS
Clare: I think part of Dad's problem was Russ. Russ was real late developing physically and he was always the runt of his class. Dad was real bad with him, and Russ had a whole lot of hostility in him and he was too small to take it out on me or the other smaller children. Bullying and things like that. And because of his emotional problems he didn't do well in school, and this was a big area in which Dad felt— you know, emotionally concerned. Disappointed in this area too. So Russ had the worst kind of deal you can get.	Note the length of the sentences and the size of the words; this was spoken in a reasonable and "adult" voice, except for a tearful note at the end.
Therapist: He had a very rough time of it. . . . Seems to me I sense a feeling here someplace. I wonder what that feeling is.	The "child" is crying here. I have heard and decided to see if I can find out what is wrong.
Clare: I think it is maybe because I have a cold. Maybe not . . . I don't know. I sensed that too in my voice. I don't know what they are. I can't pinpoint it.	Big Clare is almost ready to shut her up—but she heard it too.
Therapist: Sounds like sad feelings.	
Clare: I feel sad—I kind of feel like crying. (There followed some exploration about where the feelings were coming from, without results.) I don't know, it just escapes me. I don't feel that way so much anymore.	Big Clare now notices she is sad, but Little Clare has pulled back and isn't crying anymore. Big Clare can't get in touch directly.
Therapist: I have some ways of talking that might possibly help.	

One of the things that sometimes I do . . . to kind of find out what the feelings are . . . is to talk to the little girl in you.

Clare: Oh?

Therapist: There is a little Clare inside. The little girl who is six—five —she is still there. And often it is the little girl who has the feelings.

Clare: Okay.

Therapist: Can I talk to little Clare?

Clare: Sure.

Therapist: What I would like you to do is . . . I'd like Big Clare to stay out. Just as if you brought your little sister in and sat her down. I don't want *you* telling me; I want *her* to talk.

Clare: Okay.

Therapist: And I want you to let out whatever comes out, no matter how foolish it sounds. It might make sense. And if you listen it might make sense to you, too. . . . Will you talk to me? I'd like to talk to you.

Clare: Maybe.

Therapist: Maybe. Would you be afraid to talk to me?

I decided to ask to talk directly to Little Clare: I guessed that if there were feelings they belonged to the "child."
New, but not really new.

She accepts more readily than most clients; she knows that Little Clare is there.

Big Clare is treated like a parent in an interview with parent and child; only the child can talk.

Sometimes the "adult" gets uneasy with what the child says and wants to shut her up. She should just listen. This is in a more gentle and coaxing tone, as with a shy child.

Note that I supply the suggestion; I only ask assent or denial.

Clare: Yeah.

Therapist: Why would you be afraid?

Now I demand a response.

Clare: It might hurt.

This is the child talking! Note the brevity—the condensed and direct meaning. The "adult" would have given longer reasons. The "child" sums up "resistance": "It might hurt!"

Therapist: It might hurt . . . You don't want to get hurt.

Clare: No.

Therapist: Why would it hurt?

I repeat her phrase—to let her know I heard, and follow with an assertion she can agree with.

Clare: I don't know.

Therapist: You don't know. You don't have to talk, you know. But maybe if you did talk you would feel better.

I open up the question of how she might get hurt; she doesn't answer.

I give permission not to talk, with some persuasion. She accepts.

Clare: Okay.

Therapist: Are you sad?

I can tell I have Little Clare talking here; Big Clare would volunteer thoughts and use long words and sentences.

Clare: No.

Therapist: Are you happy?

Clare: No.

The problem now is to find the theme. I start with the feeling I heard. She is not in that mood now, or not ready to say. I try the opposite. No results. Now I have to find a topic to get started on; the most difficult phase.

Therapist: Are you good?

Clare: Yes.

Therapist: How are you good?

She says "Yes"; that's a start! Note I ask "how" not "why"; "how" leads to talk about action.

Clare: . . . I don't do bad things.

Therapist: You don't do bad things. What do you do?

I call for more response from here.

Clare: I play!

Now she talks!

Therapist: You play. What do you play?

I want more specifics.

Clare: Oh . . . horses.

Therapist: Where do you play horses?

I want the scene to become more concrete.

Clare: In the clubhouse in the backyard.

Therapist: In the clubhouse in the backyard. Who do you play with?

Now we are getting into real topics.

Clare: Laura Block and Jane.

(I will not reproduce the rest of this phase of the interview. She talked about her friends, her school teacher who didn't like her, who was mean and grouchy and scared her, and about Russ who is mean to her and is bad and twists her arm. She doesn't like him but she loves him, because he is her brother. She went on to the topic of a playhouse, killing a snake, going to purgatory because she disobeyed her parents, and then she seemed to run down.)

Therapist: Why did big Clare feel like crying?

This is the question which opens up the important area.

Clare: She was sad.

She is sad! We are getting closer!

Therapist: She was sad. Why was Big Clare sad?

Clare: Because of Russ and Daddy!

Therapist: Because of Russ and Daddy? Did that make her sad? (Yeah!) Why did it make her sad?

I repeat—and ask for simple agreement. Then "why" question.

Clare: She felt sorry for Russ.

That's what big Clare said too!

Therapist: She felt sorry for Russ? (Uh-huh!) Did she feel sorry for Daddy?

I guess that she felt sorry for Daddy too. Big Clare said so.

Clare: Uh-huh!

Right! Short words; intense meaning!

Therapist: Why did she feel sorry for them?

A "fishing" question; it isn't clear yet.

Clare: They weren't happy!

Therapist: She didn't like to see them fight! (Uh-huh!) Why didn't she like to see them fight?

I guess that the fighting is the pain. It is. But why?

Clare: BECAUSE DADDY SPANKED RUSS! (Crying with intense, piercing, poignant feeling)

Now all the hurt and pain come out!

Therapist: Because Daddy spanked Russ!

I echo the feeling as best I can, but necessarily in a lower key because I don't hurt like she does.

Clare: AND HE WOULD CRY! (Crying—intensely!)

Therapist: And he would cry!

Note that I do not soothe or try and stop her tears; with tears one pushes

Clare: And I would cry too!

further and harder. She is
less intense here.

Therapist: And you would cry too.
When did you do that?

An "echo" and a query. I
want her to go back to
Russ being spanked.

Clare: When he spanked Russ!

Therapist: Did it make you feel bad
when he spanked Russ?

A question just to get
more response.

Clare: Yes, because he was spanking Russ because Russ was mean to
me.

Aha! And she probably
did something to provoke
Russ, too.

Therapist: He was spanking Russ
because Russ was mean to you.

*Clare: And if I hadn't told on him,
he wouldn't have spanked Russ.*

Identification plus guilt!

Therapist: Did it make you feel bad
when he spanked Russ?

An "echo" just to keep her
talking; she can hear
herself better when I re-
peat it.

Clare: Yes, because he was spanking Russ because of me.

(She continued as a child to say with very immediate feeling that
nobody liked Russ, everybody tried to hurt him and, with intense
pain and tears, that Daddy didn't love Russ and Daddy was a mean
Daddy.)

Therapist: Always mean. That's
why you cry. . . . You cry because
Daddy is mean to Russ. Because
Daddy is a mean Daddy and you
want him to be a good Daddy. . . .
Did this hurt to talk today?

A summary. I note the
time is running out, and
ask her reactions.

Clare: No. It felt good.

Therapist: It felt good to talk today.

Usually these painful sessions leave a sense of relief. It is like doing play

Have you ever told anybody . . . that you feel sorry for Russ?

Clare: No.

Therapist: No, you thought it but you didn't tell anybody.

Clare: I don't know.

Therapist: Well, we have to stop talking now. (Okay.) It is good to talk to you. I'd like to talk to you again. (Okay.) . . . Well, how did it seem?

Clare: It is funny! . . . I'm kind of two people at once and I can't . . . (Laughs) . . . It's very strange.

Therapist: Kind of being yourself and some other self too.

Clare: I can't really understand *that it happened.*

Therapist: Those were real feelings though.

Clare: Sure were! Oh. It's kind of hard to come back.

therapy with a child; expression of the forbidden feelings brings relief, when expressed in the presence of an accepting adult. She didn't get a chance to express these feelings then, but she can now. This is a bit like doing the therapy with the child that should have been done at the time.

The question addressed to the adult Clare was in a different tone of voice. She uses her "adult" voice. There has been the observing adult and the experiencing child. I am bringing her "back" almost too rapidly here; the time pressure isn't giving enough time for her to make the transition gracefully. Note that there is no amnesia for the "child" state, as is sometimes true in hypnotic "age regression."

A few days later she wrote a letter, giving the "adult's" evaluation, and how the experience was used.

Your nutty technique paid off. It started a chain reaction in my mind which I feel has led to some rather important discoveries about myself. I was quite surprised to discover the intense ambivalent feelings I had for Pop. I loved him, because he was good to me and loved me. At the same time, I hated him, and probably didn't even admit it to myself, because (1) kids are supposed to love their parents, and (2) you are expected to love someone who loves you. I also feel guilty because I felt that I had stolen Russ's share of love. I felt that parents should love all of their children the same and Pop obviously loved me more than Russ, so I must have been receiving Russ's share. So I felt guilty toward both Russ and Pop.

I don't ever recall directly expressing my hostility toward Pop. I think I enjoyed it vicariously through Russ. Perhaps that added to my feelings of guilt when he was punished for actually doing what I secretly wanted to do . . .

It occurred to me this morning that this pattern of living vicariously through Russ carried over into my relationship with my husband. The very things which cause tension between us, the qualities in him which I outwardly deplore, are really very attractive to me.

Now, let us see if we can identify what happened and what produced the effects.

First, it is clear that this experience had a constructive and therapeutic effect. She was able to evaluate it as an "adult" and incorporate the emotional meaning, and it stimulated her to see how these old reactions are being repeated in her current relationships. Although she talked about the same topic, Russ and her father, as an "adult" and as a "child," the feelings were markedly different. It might have been possible to have discussed these memories as an "adult," but they would have been muted and distant, and the realization of her anger toward her father would have been diluted.

The "how" and "why" of the therapeutic effect is worth speculation. One possibility is that the technique allowed her defenses against recognizing some of the denied feelings to become lower and she experienced them in a way that could not be denied. Perhaps the pretense of being a "little child" relieved her from the responsibility to have "reasonable feelings." But on the other hand, if I had talked to her as a child, her opinion that she should not hate her father would have tended to have kept her from expressing these. But as an interested adult who wanted her to say her real feelings, I could have gotten her to say them; this is what I did here, but talking to the "Little Clare" who still had these feelings. Until they became "present" they could not be changed in the light of the "adult's" knowledge that it is all right to hate a parent.

But unlike age-regression in hypnosis, where the "adult" consciousness tends to be excluded, her "adult self" was listening—much as if I were to interview the child in the presence of the parent, who can listen and understand and correct misconceptions. The "adult" was observing while the "child" was experiencing, much like the separation of the experiencing and observing ego referred to in psychoanalytic literature.

At the same time, Little Clare was experiencing and expressing honestly her pain and anger at her father and his rejection of her brother in a way that she had not permitted herself as a child; by accepting the adult "superego" view that one should love her father and that if he loved her she should love him, she was denying her accurate perceptions that her father was unfair and mean. The values of recovering the direct and undistorted perceptions of the child has been expressed by Fritz Perls (1951):

> We hav said that the recollection of the old scene is unnecessary; it is at most an important clue to the meaning of the feeling, but even in that way it is dispensable. Does it follow that, as Horney, for instance, maintains, the recovery of child-life does not occupy a privileged positions in psychotherapy? No. For our thought is that the content of the recovered scene is rather unimportant, but that the childish feeling and attitude that lived that scene is of the utmost importance. The childish feelings are important not as a past that must be undone, but as some of the most beautiful powers of adult life that must be recovered; spontaneity, imagination, directness of awareness and manipulation" (p. 297).

Perhaps it is this encouragement of the childish feelings, which really include all the feelings, which contributes to the therapeutic effect of the cathartic emotional expression. The "child" part of the personality becomes accepted as important, not to be changed or "educated," but to be expressed under the guidance and cooperation of the "adult" and "parent" parts of the personality.

Sometimes it almost seems as if the "child" gets the same therapeutic effect in talking to an interested and sympathetic adult as "he" would have if he had been able to talk out these feelings as an actual child.

The refreshing and exhilarating effect of getting in touch with the "child" has been expressed by the written evaluations some of my clients have given after first experiencing "Little Child Talk" in a group:

"In the small group meeting, I thought the meeting was very good. I admit at first I was very skeptical, but after we started I got some good emotional feelings. When I first started to talk it was my older self that talked first. But as we progressed I found my little child doing all the talking. It was very rewarding and helped me greatly."

"I would like first to write about the "Little Kid" experience in the group. The 'after effect' on me was dynamic. I kept thinking about my childhood. Again and again, my mind would vision scenes of my youth. This returning to my childhood was a very pleasant thing for me. I think kids have a fantastic world—they are free with their emotions; therefore it seems, when they're happy, they are very happy. Kids go from tears to laughter in seconds. To return to the child of my past was a wonderful feeling. The greatest thing about the experience you conducted was the lingering; the child stayed awake in me for many hours."

This technique has many similarities to Eric Berne's formulation (1961) although it was developed prior to Berne's publication. Interestingly, Berne himself has developed a technique very similar to "Little Child Talk" which he calls "Regression Analysis." In this technique Berne takes the role of another child and talks to the "child." He reports rather briefly, but apparently gets much of the same kind of response from the "child." He too uses it in groups, and finds it has a very considerable impact upon a group, and can bring about catharsis, emotional closeness, and intensification of exploration.

Fritz Perls, in his Esalen Seminars, uses techniques very similar to Little Child Talk, and often will get the "Child" self to talk or act out his feelings or motivations. He combines it with a wide range of other techniques, including having the person take the part of and speak for parts of his body, feelings, different selves, and characters and scenery in dreams (1951).

S. Shaprio (1962) has developed "Ego Therapy" in which he talks to a number of different "selves" as if he were conducting "family therapy" with them. The "child selves" will appear and interact with "parent selves" and "adult selves"; it differs in that the selves are interacting in the present rather than reliving the past. Ego Therapy brings out the interactions among the "inner family," but does not seem to generate the amount of emotional catharsis that "Little Child Talk" does. I have found them to be supplementary, often shifting from one to another.

In age-regression, as described by Erik Fromm, (1965), it is more as if the "adult" and "parent" had been excluded while the therapist talks to the child, although the patient is encouraged to remember as much as he can in the waking state. Since the "return of the child" is rather like "age-regression" in hypnosis, it is interesting to speculate how similar "Little Child Talk" is to hypnosis.

In "Little Child Talk" there is some sensory restriction as in hypnosis, but on a much more limited basis. There is no attempt to induce monotony, although sometimes the repetition of what the "child" says is a bit like hypnotic "patter." However, there is definitely no attempt to get the patient to give up his "autonomy"; in fact, the permission of the adult is requested and he is assured he will remain in control at all times. There is some indirect suggestion in the therapist's confident assumption that the child will talk, but no attempt at direct command or suggestion. The phenomena seems quite similar to the effects of age-regression, except that there is less "magic" about it and the adult is more in the picture. There does seem to be some alteration in the state of consciousness; clients differentiate between the "child" state and the "adult" state. In the beginning they find themselves talking or listening as the "adult," but soon find themselves reacting and talking in a way that seems different and which can be observed from the outside by the "adult." Clients describe this difference:

"I guess my main reaction to having you talk to the little child in me was astonishment! I didn't think I would be capable of letting myself go that much. When the experiment first started and for about the first 45 minutes I was still a 19-year-old. Mostly I just tried to think back to my childhood but still I thought not as a child but as I am today. However, once you started talking to me directly the little child did the talking. I really surprised myself with some of the answers that were coming out of me. I know that if I had been asked some of those questions as a nineteen-year-old I would have answered them differently. I guess it just goes to show what a high wall people build around their feelings, especially those that hurt."

"I felt that it was a fantastic experience. I will have to admit that when I first heard of the idea I was a little skeptical. I was sure that the participants would have to pretend at least a little. When I tried it myself I found that pretending wasn't necessary. I felt like I was eight years old again. I was letting out emotions that I wanted to let out eleven years ago, but I didn't know how to. The tears I was crying were real tears and the feelings I had were real feelings. At times it seemed that I had no control over what I was saying. The words seemed to be coming out of my mouth without any help. I could listen to myself talking; grown-up Joan was actually listening to Little Joan. That experience I'll never forget, and I'm willing to do it again. I hesitated at first only out of fear but soon I felt myself really involved and that I wanted to share with the others. It almost seemed like a dream. A dream of the past. It was fun looking back observing myself. I should like to do it again. Group therapy can be very interesting and I can see that many of my problems are pretty common."

"After the experience was over I really felt good! I think this experience will help the group as a whole too. Last week we seemed to be able to communicate better, and I think the 'little child experiment' was partially responsible for this. It helped show everybody that they had many problems and experiences that were common to all, and this helped relieve some of the uneasiness that the group had experienced previously."

Since this discussion is concerned with explaining and transmitting this particular technique, I will describe some of the specific aspects which I have found important in using it effectively. This is the style which I have developed in a sort of trial-and-error manner over the last six years; however, some of my colleagues who have used it have found some aspects of my style not congenial for them and have evolved a somewhat different approach. It will take wider usage and more experience to decide which of these are of general value, and which are effective for me mainly because of my personal style of reacting.

1. The client is asked to close his eyes or the room is darkened, so that the impact of the immediate environment is minimized. I usually close my own eyes to heighten the "illusion" that I am talking to a "child" in some "past time."

2. The therapist asks the permission of the "adult" to talk to the child; the implication of taking over control of the "will" of the person is deliberately avoided. The situation is treated much as if the parent and child were both present and the therapist first secures permission of the parents before talking to the child.

3. If the "adult" breaks into the conversation, as indicated by long sentences or large words, the therapist asks him to "stop interrupting" such as he would if a parent tried to answer for a child. This insistence that the "child" has a right to be heard tends to reinforce the view that it is important to listen to the "child's" opinions and thoughts.

4. The therapist's language should be simple and direct, using words that would be understood by a child. Feeling and action words draw out responses from the "child"; long sentences and intellectual

concepts do not. The therapist should let his own "child" guide him; to get a child's answer one should ask a child's question.

5. The words and action should be present tense, and when the client answers in past tense, the therapist should repeat the response in the present tense.

6. Questions and statements about concrete actions and sights often help to draw out the child and bring back memories into vivid reality. For example, "Do you cry? (Yes.) Do you go in your room to cry? (Yes.) Do you put your face in your pillow when you cry? (Yes, and I kick my feet and beat the bed!)" or "Do you have a dog? (Yes.) Do you love him? (Yes.) Do you put your arms around him and hug him? (Yes, and he licks my face and smells good.)" or "Does your mother bake cookies in the kitchen? (Yes.) Does she let you lick the bowl? (Yes.) Do they smell good when they are cooking? (Oh, yes! And she puts them on the refrigerator so I can't get to them till they get cool.)"

7. The therapist tries to build up momentum, by repeating the phrases and amplifying the feeling in the repetition. Often the therapist may repeat the important sentences to summarize and emphasize impact. If a client fails to respond, rather than waiting, he picks up on a phrase where the client did respond and tries to keep the momentum going.

8. The therapist takes a rather active, "leading" role. I will express a series of feelings or events for the client, to which they respond with "uh-huh" or "yes"; if they are reacting emphatically, they will usually come out with a short, emotionally intense statement which expresses the strong feelings and points the way to go. It takes experience and empathy to know what to ask, but the client can be having some very intense experiences with a minimum of words.

9. Often one will find a chain of emotional statements which go in a circle, which expresses the unsolved childhood conflicts. For example, "Why are you unhappy? (Because my father doesn't love me.) Why doesn't you father love you? (Because I cry all the time.) Why do you cry all the time? (Because I'm unhappy!) Why are you unhappy? (Because my father doesn't love me.)" Sometimes if one goes over the chain again and again, a new train will break in, leading to new areas of pain. "Why doesn't your father love you? (Because I cry all the time. He thinks girls cry too much.) Why do girls cry so much? (Because they aren't boys so their father will love them.)"

10. In addition to the cathartic aspect of expressing and accepting the childhood feelings, the childhood misconceptions can be correc-

ted. Sometimes the therapist can explain to the child that his parents did not really desert him when they left him in the hospital, or he did not really cause his parents' divorce. There is a very great difference in impact and effectiveness between explaining directly to the "child" and in talking about a past event with an "adult." Sometimes the therapist can talk with the "adult" about the need of his "child" for love and comfort, and work out ways in which the "adult" can give love and guidance to his "child" who might not have gotten it from his parents.

11. A final variation in technique, which I have only recently begun to explore, is to try and change unpleasant traumatic realities by reliving them in fantasy as if they had occurred the way they should have happened rather than the way they did. For example, after having a girl go over her real experiences of being seduced by her father, I had her relive a scene in which she told her father that it wasn't right and she wished she hadn't done it, and he told her he was sorry and that he also wished he had not done it. These were conversations which she did not have with her father, but which were plausible. These imaginary interactions seemed to shift her feelings toward forgiving her father (and other men) in a way that reliving the actual reality had not done.

"Let the Little Child Talk" is thus a psychotherapeutic technique in which the therapist asks permission of the client to talk to his "inner child" and then proceeds as if he were talking directly to the "child" who existed when the client was five or six years old. With direct questioning in simple words about past events as if they were "here and now," the "child-self" will express feelings and opinions which are often unfamiliar or which have been "forgotten" by the "adult-self." "Letting the Little Child Talk" appears to release emotions which may be contributing to adult and current conflicts, allows for correction of childhood misconceptions, and brings the "adult" more in touch with the strengths and spontaneity of the "child-self."

The typescripts which are presented next illustrate the use of "little child talk" in a group. These typescripts are from the first time I had actually used it in a group; it was for me, as well as for the group members, an "experiment." It turned out to be a very powerful technique, as can be seen from the typescript and from the comments by the students given at the end of the chapter. These groups were part of the Peers (Finney, 1971) and had been meeting twice a week with student leaders.

I have given the typescript verbatim, so that the way in which I present it can be seen, and the way in which it developed during the hour that followed. You will note that after the initial exploration, I ask to talk to Charlotte. Immediately the "child" starts talking; this was unusual, but there was no question that I was talking to the "child" re-experiencing her "childhood." The cues were the short sentences, and the "uh-huhs" that followed when I asked her what she was doing. It was just like talking to a shy child, who will answer an adult, and later spontaneously add comments of his own. As you read this, I think you will get the distinct impression that I am talking to real "personalities," not just "play acting" to pretend being a child. And furthermore, the other "kids" are listening. In the comments written by the students, they describe how they are drawn into expressing their child, and how it just seems to flow out of the mouth of an eighteen-year-old, surprising them by what comes out.

And you will note the experiences come out as viewed by a child. Jack described his grandfather and his reactions; his grandfather looked like him but also like a wax model of him. The theme of death brought out Charlotte's reactions to her cat's death, an important event to a child. And she told how she didn't want her cat anymore because she was ruined and how it made her mad to have the veterinarian try to save her.

Irene talked about her dog, and then her tears began to come, the reaction to seeing her dog bleed to death. You will notice the child-like language, "Nasty old car hit him." I bring in her feelings about God, and she explains she thought God took him away because they spoiled him. Children must have an answer for meaningful events, and she made up one to explain the death of her dog.

Ralph talks about some very meaningful events in his childhood and the pain of being whipped and misunderstood by his father. His comment "They want you to be an adult when you are a little kid" expresses a central problem, and Dave chimes in "Yeah, why can't they let us be little kids." There is sharing and mutual support of the "children"—these are not eighteen-year-olds talking together, they are "kids" talking together.

The catharsis is a healing one, as the students describe in their comments written later. And this technique puts them in touch with the "inner child." Irene writes:

> I really felt like a child. I also had the same expression of feeling in my experiences. For example, when my dog died, I had cried and also been angry at God. One thing that I couldn't under-

stand during the whole experiment was my crying—it just flowed. After the ordeal, I felt great! I felt I had unburdened a lot of feelings. I'm really glad I joined the experiment. I only wish it could have lasted longer.

I am going to let the typescript speak for itself:

Finney: This I'm going to try today is something I've just tried now for the first couple of times here with the groups. I've tried it with Clemintina's and John's group and last week I tried it with the group across the way. . . . And that is what I do is . . . talk to the "little child" in you. Often we get a lot of feelings—memories and feelings flood back which you haven't thought of for a long time. And sometimes it's very helpful to get in touch with those—for yourself. Now, ah, each time it's different, and how it goes we don't know. And sometimes it doesn't go. One of the things that I would like you to do . . . I will be talking along, and if I get to talking to one person I'll stay right with them for a while and then I will stop and let people come in and then I may move over to another—that person and talk with them a bit. And then you may want to talk back and forth a little bit. One of the things that people have found is that . . . at first it is . . . as Claudia said it, it seems like maybe it's sort of play acting, and in a way it is a little bit . . . you are going to have to make believe a little bit. But often you will find that the talking draws you back, and as people have commented who are listening to somebody else, they were the adult, and then when they started talking they pulled back out again. Try as best you can to go in, and don't hold back and think, "I wonder what's going on and what Dr. Finney's thinking," . . . go with it. The important thing is when some feeling or thought pops up, don't push it around as if it doesn't belong here. Say it. . . . Now, just let me check out your feelings. How are you . . . as you just sit here and anticipate this . . . How about you, Irene, as you anticipate what we are going to do . . . what are your feelings?

Irene: I feel that it's going to be another show.

Finney: Another show. Any feeling of any reluctance to get going into it? (No.) You say another show. Have you been involved in anything that seemed to you as sort of a show?

Irene: No, it just seems like it would be a show. That's just what I think about.

Finney: How about you? (Charlotte)

Charlotte: I'm optimistic. I think it will be neat. I don't know. I haven't thought of things from my past . . . feelings I have from my past, and I thought it would be . . . something different.

Finney: And you? (Vicki)

Vicki: Kind of curious as to what it's going to bring out.

Finney: And you, Bob?

Bob: I'm kind of curious too, but it seems kind of scary, I think. The first time I heard it I didn't see how it could work . . . I didn't see how you could go back and be a little kid, but I guess other people have done it.

Finney: But kind of scary.

Bob: I can't picture myself sitting here and being, you know, seven.

Nancy: I was just wanting to know whether I could do it or not. That's the first thing that came into my mind. Maybe I can't go back or something . . . and everybody else can.

Finney: Sort of the feeling that "they did and you'll be sitting on the outside." (Yeah.)

Nancy: I think it would be interesting if I could because I know I have a lot of feelings in there.

Finney: Dave?

Dave: Kind of anxious to see how it's going to turn out. And what it is going to bring out within each one of us. And kind of reluctant to join myself.

Ralph: Looking forward to it. I don't really see how it could work. I can't picture myself talking in the way of a little child. But I'm really interested in seeing how it could work.

Finney: How about you, Fred?

Fred: I'm interested and really curious about how it's going to turn out. But, I sort of feel like it's going to be like . . . in other meetings . . . where I've sort of felt that I just . . . sit here, you know. I don't really say much, you know. I wonder if it's going to be like that. Other people will be talking and here I'll be over here.

Jack: (Graduate student leader) When I've done this . . . I've done this once with Ben, once by myself, and once with a group. And it's really good. Like when I . . . what I do, is try to think of what the feelings were, and . . . as a kid, and what was happening . . . and just like . . . describe what was happening inside of me while I was thinking about it. You know with my twenty-four-year-old mind. And after about twenty minutes or fifteen minutes . . . like my twenty-year-old mind was over here watching what was happening, but it wasn't like it was participating. And I was talking and feeling like I was six and seven and so forth. And it is really, really something else. You have complete control over what is happening, but you want to get stuff out. And it's so good, it really is. It's no big magical thing.

Finney: Okay, let's . . . we don't want to build it up so everybody gets . . . What we are going to do is . . . we are going to turn out the lights and that's going to be a . . . jolt. Because I don't think you have ever been anyplace that's going to be as dark as it's going to be in here. Even at home with the drawn window shades there is some light, but here . . . (laughter). Just to . . . just to check it out . . . is there anybody here who finds now . . . that if they get in the darkness it makes them uncomfortable? (Let me out of here!) Does it make you uncomfortable? (I don't think so.) I'm sure that there are many of you who when you were little kids in the dark you were scared. (Several comments) They don't become accustomed to it much, you know. (Lights out—but some light) Oh, wait a minute. This isn't quite as dark as the other room. Now, what I want you to do is . . . I want you to let your little child talk . . . and . . . just as if you had brought in your twin . . . who was six years old, and your twin was sitting here around the table with us. And if you, . . . if you let me talk to her, then I want you to stay out. If you come in, and I can tell when the adult comes in, I'll tell you to butt out. Because I want her to get a chance to talk. Now . . . Charlotte, you're close. Would you be willing to let me talk to the little girl in you. (Um-hmm.) Okay. What did you call yourself when you were six? (Charlotte.) Charlotte. Will you let me talk to little Charlotte, I'd like to talk to you. Will you talk to me?

Charlotte: Yes.

Finney: Would you be scared to talk to me? (No.) No. Would you like to? (Yes.) What would you like to talk about?

Charlotte: Games.

Finney: Games. What kind of games do you play?

Charlotte: Cars.

Finney: Do you play cars? (Mmm-hmm.) Who do you play cars with?

Charlotte: My friends.

Finney: You play cars with your friends. You like to play cars. (Mmm-hmm.) Where do you play?

Charlotte: In the sand.

Finney: You play in the sand. You play in the sand . . . and you have fun and make little roadways and things like that.

Charlotte: And build houses.

Finney: And build houses. Is that fun? (Hmm-humm.) . . . Do you play in the backyard? (Neighbor's backyard) Neighbor's backyard.

Whose backyard is it? (The Macy's.) The Macy's. Do you go over there a lot? (Uh-mm.) Yes. Have fun? (Yes.) Do you kids ever fight? (Yes.) What do you fight about?

Charlotte: Who gets the best . . . spots.

Finney: Are you able to get along well. (Uh-huh.) It's fun to play with them? (Yes.) Do they ever get mad at you and make you go home? (No.) No. You get along pretty well. (Yes.) How many friends do you have there?

Charlotte: Oh, ten.

Finney: About ten. That's a whole lot of kids. What else do you like to do?

Charlotte: Ride bikes.

Finney: Ride bikes. Where do you ride bikes?

Charlotte: Around the block.

Finney: Around the block. Can you ride a bike? (Uh-huh.) Can you ride it good. (Regular.) . . . Do you have your own bike? (Yes.) Yes. Did you get your bike for Christmas? (Yes.) Can you remember that Christmas? (Yes.) What was it like?

Charlotte: My brother got a bike just like mine. We were both happy.

Finney: Was that a happy Christmas? (Uh-huh.) Did you have a Christmas tree? (Yes!) Yes! Can you see the Christmas tree? (No, just the bikes.) Just the bikes. What color is your bike? (Blue.) What does it look like?

Charlotte: It's a light one. Small.

Finney: I'll bet it's pretty. (Yes.) Did you go out and ride it that morning? (Yes.) The other kids look at it. (Uh-huh.) Were you proud of it? (Yes.) That was fun, wasn't it. (Yes.) Did your brother get a bike that Christmas too. (Yes.) Is he littler than you?

Charlotte: No, he's older.

Finney: Older than you. But you got one just the same kind as he did. (Yes.) That must have been nice. (Uh-huh.) Was yours a girl's bike? (Yes.) His a boy's bike? (Uh-huh.) Did they look just alike, except for being girl's and boy's bikes?

Charlotte: Except that his was a different color.

Finney: Was that a happy Christmas. (Yes.) What else do you remember?

Charlotte: My brother wanted a blue bike like mine. His was red.

Finney: What happened? Did he get mad?

Charlotte: No, he forgot about it. He thought that he should have blue.

Finney? Do you and your brother get along? (Yes.) Do you ever fight? (No.)

Charlotte: We argue, but not fight.

Finney: Anybody else get a bike for Christmas?

Ralph: Yes.

Finney: What was your bike like?

Ralph: It was green. And it had a basket on it.

Finney: Are you proud of it? (Yes.) Could you ride it when you got it? (No.) Did you learn? (Yes.) Did you fall down when you were learning? (Yes, it hurt.) Huh? (It hurt.) It hurt. Did you keep with it? (Yes.) Until you could do it? (Yes.) What else did you get for Christmas.

Ralph: Baseball glove.

Finney: What kind is it? (Real nice.) Real nice. (Yes.) Do you play with it? (Yes.) Who do you play with? (Friends.) Do they think your glove is good? (Yes.) Do they ever want to borrow it? (Yes.) Do you let them? (Yes.) That's sort of fun, isn't it? (Yes.) You had a good Christmas then. (Very good.) Do you like Christmas? (Very much.)

Ralph: I get anxious.

Finney: You get anxious? (Yes.) When do you get anxious?

Ralph: Before Christmas comes.

Finney: Before Christmas comes. Why do you get anxious?

Ralph: Because I like it. You get good things.

Finney: Do you get excited? (Yes.) Do you have a hard time . . . When do you have Christmas . . . Do you have it in the evening or do you have it in the morning? (The morning.) Do you have a hard time going to sleep? (Very much!) Stay awake all night? (Yes.) Wake up really early? (Yes.) Will your folks let you go down as soon as you wake up or do you have to wait? (Wake them up.) How do you wake them up?

Ralph: I yell "It's here! It's here!"

Finney: Do you get to play with your stuff right away as soon as you find it? (Yes.)

Ralph: After I open it.

Finney: That's fun! (Yes.) Anybody else remember Christmas . . .

Jack: Yeah!

Finney: What do you remember?

Jack: Well, I got a bike. And I didn't know how to ride it and . . . my grandfather rode it. It was just a little bike.

Finney: Did that make you mad?

Jack: No, it was funny.

Finney: Funny to see him ride that little bike. (Yeah.)

Jack: He was just a little guy and it was a little kid's bike.

Finney: Was he havin' fun. (Yeah.) Did your folks see him?

Jack: Yeah! We took a picture of him.

Finney: Of him riding your bike. (Yeah.) Did they take a picture of you riding the bike?

Jack: No, I couldn't ride it.

Finney: Oh, you couldn't ride it. (Yeah!) He could ride it though.

Jack: Yeah! He was really funny.

Finney: Do you like your grandfather?

Jack: Yeah! But he died.

Finney: He died! (Yeah.) Did you feel badly when he died?

Jack: I don't know. I don't know what happened.

Finney: He just went away?

Jack: No—they just called up and said that he went away. I don't know what happened.

Finney: They didn't tell you.

Jack: Yeah! They told me about it, but I didn't know what it means.

Finney: What does it mean when a person dies?

Jack: I don't know. Just that he doesn't come around anymore.

Finney: Did you think he was mad and didn't want to come back or . . . What did you think?

Jack: No, I thought he wanted to come back.

Finney: Then why doesn't he get to come back.

Jack: I don't know. It's something . . .

Finney: Did you ever see any animals that died? (Yeah.) What do they look like?

Jack: Oh, they look bad.

Finney: Do they look all rotten?

Jack: No, they just looked . . . like they weren't animals that I knew anymore.

Finney: Do you think your grandfather looked like that when he died?

Jack: Yeah! I saw him.

Finney: You saw him. What did he look like?

Jack: He looked like . . . a model of him.

Finney: Did you go see him in the casket? (Yeah.) He looked like a model . . . he looked like he was made of wax? (Yeah!) Was that your grandfather?

Jack: I didn't—I didn't think so. . . . Well, I knew it was, but . . . it wasn't.

Finney: Did you cry? (No.) Were you scared? (Yeah.) What were you scared about?

Jack: I don't know. Like . . . everybody was so different.

Finney: Were people crying? (Yeah.) Do you know why they cried?

Jack: Well, because they wouldn't see him anymore. And my mom cried because he was her father.

Finney: Was that scary?

Jack: It made me feel bad because I didn't like to see my Mom cry.

Finney: Did you look at your Mom crying? (Yeah.) Were her eyes all red? (Uh-huh.)

Jack: Yeah. And you know, I held her hand and everything.

Finney: When you held her hand, did you say "Mommy, don't cry"? Or did you just hold her hand?

Jack: I asked her why she was crying.

Finney: What did she say?

Jack: She said because her father was gone.

Finney: Anybody else here have anybody die?

Charlotte: My cat died.

Finney: Your what died?

Charlotte: My cat.

Finney: Your cat died. What happened to your cat?

Charlotte: It got ran over.

Finney: Who ran over it.

Charlotte: I don't know. Somebody on the street.

Finney: Did it kill it?

Charlotte: Not right away.

Finney: Did she cry?

Charlotte: No. She just laid there.

Finney: What do you think?

Charlotte: The veterinarian came from across the street, and he said he would try to save her and that made me mad, because . . . she was already ruined. It wasn't the same cat.

Finney: You didn't want her saved when she was that bad.

Charlotte: No. I decided I should take her away and bury her nice.

Finney: Did you feel bad?

Charlotte: I felt strange. Like, I was in the backyard and the cat was out front and . . . It just seemed so strange. It got hit.

Finney: Anybody else feel sad thinking about somebody dying?

Ralph: Yes.

Finney: Yes. What do you think?

Ralph: I think it must be bad that I don't see him again.

Finney: It must be bad—Do you think you're bad that you don't see him anymore?

Ralph: I just get a bad feeling.

Finney: You get a bad feeling. Who don't you see anymore?

Ralph: My grandpa.

Finney: You don't see your grandpa anymore. Do you feel real sad? (Yes.) Yes. What happened to your grandpa?

Ralph: He died of cancer.

Finney: He died of cancer. Is cancer bad? (Yes.) What happened to your grandpa? He died of cancer. What happened?

Ralph: He was put in a hospital and got operated on. Wasn't cured.

Finney: Did you pray for your grandfather to live? (Yes.) Yes. You told God you wanted your grandfather to live and come back, is that right? (Yes.) But, your grandpa died. Why did your grandpa die?

Ralph: He couldn't get cured.

Finney: He couldn't get cured. He has to go away and not come back? (Yes.) Did you see your grandpa at the funeral parlor? (Yes.) What do you think?

Ralph: I didn't think it was real.

Finney: Didn't think it was real. Didn't look like your grandpa? (No.) Is it scary there? (Yes.) What's it like?

Ralph: Like a bad horror movie when you see dead people. You don't know what's going to happen.

Finney: Sort of like a horror movie. (Yes.) And your grandpa is dead. That's sort of scary. (Yes.) You afraid.

Ralph: I stick next to my Mom.

Finney: You hold on to your Mom. (Yes.) Do you go look at the casket?

Ralph: Once or twice.

Finney: Does your Mom cry? (Yes.)

Ralph: Grandma cried too.

Finney: Grandma cries too. You feel sorry for your grandma? (Yes.) You feel sorry for your mother? (Yes.) Do you feel sorry for yourself because you won't have your grandpa around? (Yes.) Do you cry? (No.) Why don't you cry?

Ralph: I don't have that bad a feeling.

Finney: Don't have that bad a feeling. Other people feel but you don't. Maybe you don't know what it means for him to die? (Yes, maybe.) But you feel bad? (Yes.)

Finney: Anybody else have anybody die?

Irene: Yes. My grandpa died.

Finney: Your grandpa died. What happened to your grandpa?

Irene: I don't know. He had a heart attack.

Finney: A heart attack.

Irene: I don't remember anything, except everyone was all in black. I don't like black.

Finney: You don't like what . . .?

Irene: Black.

Finney: Do you feel sad? (No.) What do you feel?

Irene: I didn't know anything that was going on.

Finney: You didn't know anything that was going on. (No.)

Irene: I just remember going to church. Everybody wore black.

Finney: Everyone was wearing black. Why did they wear black?

Irene: 'Cause they were sad.

Finney: 'Cause they were sad. Did you wear black?

Irene: I don't know.

Finney: You don't know. Were you scared in the church?

Irene: No.

Finney: No. What did you think?

Irene: There were so many people there crying.

Finney: So many people crying. Why were they crying?

Irene: They were sad.

Finney: They were sad. Did you see your grandpa? (No.) No. But you remember . . . Did you miss him afterwards? (No.) No. Where is your grandpa now?

Irene: Up in heaven.

Finney: Up in heaven. What's it like up in heaven?

Irene: Must be pretty.

Finney: Must be pretty up there. Are you glad he's up there? (Yes.) Who else is up in heaven?

Irene: My dog.

Finney: Your dog? Is your dog waiting for you up there?

Irene: He bled to death! (tears)

Finney: He bled to death. Did you want to help him? (Uh-huh.) And you couldn't help him? (Uh-huh.) Do you feel sad? (Uh-huh.) Do you miss your dog? (Uh-huh.) Do you love your dog? (Uh-huh.) You miss him and you love him and you feel sad! Did he suffer? (Yes.) And he died! (Uh-huh.) He cried and you couldn't help him! (Uh-huh.) That's sad! Do you feel bad now? (Uh-huh.) You feel sad thinking about your dog! But he's up in heaven! (Uh-huh.) Mmm-hmm. Why did God take your dog?

Irene: Nasty old car hit him!

Finney: Nasty old car hit him. Why did God let a car hit him?

Irene: He wanted to take him away from us?

Finney: He wanted to take him away from you. Why did he want to take him away from you?

Irene: 'Cause we spoiled him.

Finney: You spoiled him. (Uh-huh.) Did God think you spoiled your dog so much that he should take him away? He should take him away from you? You spoil your dog a lot. (Uh-huh.) Why did you spoil your dog?

Irene: 'Cause we loved him.

Finney: You loved him so much. You loved him so much that you spoiled him all the time. (Yes.) Did you feel mad at God for taking your dog away? (Yes.) What did you want to say to God?

Irene: I don't love you anymore. (tears)

Finney: I don't love you anymore! If you take my dog away I won't love you anymore. . . . Did God get mad at you? (I don't know.) You don't know. But you were mad at him! (Uh-huh.) You loved your dog and he took him away. (Yes.) . . . Anybody else want to say anything? . . .

Ralph: I lost my dog.

Finney: You lost your dog. (Yes.) What happened?

Ralph: People next door took him away for killing chickens.

Finney: They took him away. What did they do with him?

Ralph: They must have killed him.

Finney: They took your dog away and killed him? (Yes.) That's terrible! (Yes!) Couldn't you save him?

Ralph: No. I sure cried and wanted him back. They took him to a dog pound.

Finney: They took him away even though you cried! Did you tell them your dog wouldn't kill chickens? That you would keep him from killing chickens?

Ralph: Yes, but they said that I couldn't.

Finney: Couldn't you keep him from killing chickens?

Ralph: I tried but I couldn't.

Finney: Why wouldn't he do what you told him to?

Ralph: He must have been a bad dog, but I loved him.

Finney: He was a bad dog, but you loved him. (Yes!) You love him even though he kills chickens. (Yes.) Did you tell him not to kill chickens?

Ralph: Many times.

Finney: Yes. Why didn't he listen to you?

Ralph: I don't know. I guess he couldn't understand.

Finney: He couldn't understand. Maybe if you'd have been able to get him to understand he wouldn't have killed chickens. (Yes.) (tears) Did you put your arms around him and tell him that if he does it anymore they will kill him and take him away? (Yes.) Did he listen to you?

Ralph: I don't think so. (tears) He just looked at me pitifully.

Finney: He looked at you. Did he look at you when they took him away? (Yes.)

Finney: And you knew what they were going to do?

Ralph: Yes. My Mom told me.

Finney: She told you . . . what they were going to do. (Yes.) And your dog looked at you. (Yes.) What did you say to your dog when he went away?

Ralph: I was crying. I said, "Come back."

Finney: Come back! Come back! . . . Were you mad at the people that took him away? (Yes!) Did you want to kill them? (Yes!) They were taking your dog away and you loved him! (Yes.) They were *cruel!* (Yes.) (tears) They were mean and they were cruel. (Yes.) And your poor little dog didn't know any better than to kill chickens.

Ralph: No! *He was just a little dog!* (tears)

Jack: They can't do that! They can't take him away!

Ralph: They did though! *They took my dog!* They are mean! (tears)

Jack: I don't know why people do that!

Ralph: Just mean people. (tears) The dog didn't know any better.

Irene: My dog did that too. He ate our ducks.

Finney: Did they take your dog away too?

Irene: No. We just didn't have any ducks.

Finney: What did he do?

Irene: We got ducks for Easter and the dog ate them.

Finney: He ate up the ducks. Were you mad at him for eating up the ducks?

Irene: Yes. I loved them.

Finney: People can be mean sometimes, can't they? (Yes.) People don't know how much you love a . . . how much you love a dog and they take him away. . . . What did your mother say to you when they took the dog away?

Ralph: She said it was a mean dog. He should be killed.

Finney: Was he a mean dog? (No!) (tears) No. He wasn't mean. He just liked to kill chickens. That's just what dogs are supposed to do.

Ralph: I guess.

Finney: He didn't understand.

Ralph: He didn't know better.

Dave: Maybe he was hungry.

Ralph: I fed him all the time. . . . He just killed chickens . . . I loved him!

Finney: You really loved him. What did you and your dog do together?

Ralph: We chased balls and played games.

Finney: Did he love you? (Yes.) He loved you a lot! (Yes.) And you loved him a lot too. (Yes.) And they took him away and they killed him. (Yes.) That's terrible! (Yes.) (tears) What did you say to yourself?

Ralph: That I don't like these people and I want my dog back!

Finney: I WANT MY DOG BACK! What else did you say?

Finney: I prayed to Jesus. To bring him back!

Finney: You prayed to Jesus to bring him back. Did Jesus bring him back? (He must have thought he was a bad dog.)

Finney: He thought he was a bad dog! Did you tell Jesus he wasn't a bad dog? (Yes.) Did you get mad at Jesus because he wouldn't bring your dog back? (Yes.) What did you say to Jesus?

Ralph: I said, "Bring him back or I won't believe in you!"

Finney: Bring him back or I won't believe in you! Did that make Jesus mad at you? (I don't know.) (Probably.) Did you stop believing in Jesus? (No.) No. But, you were still mad at him because he let something like that happen. (Yes.) Did you do anything bad so you lost your dog? (Yes.) What did you do bad?

Ralph: I wouldn't mind.

Finney: You wouldn't mind. You're like your dog! You won't mind! (Yes.) He wouldn't mind either. (Yes.) Are they going to take you away if you don't mind?

Ralph: I didn't know.

Finney: Are you scared sometimes that they might take you away if you don't mind?

Ralph: I'm scared I'll get whipped.

Finney: Scared you'll be whipped.

Ralph: I get whipped all the time.

Finney: You get whipped all the time. (Yes.) Why don't you stop doing those things?

Ralph: I try as hard as I can. But, I can't do it!

Finney: Do you keep doing bad things? (Yes.) You don't mind! And then you get whipped. (Yes.) Who whips you?

Ralph: Daddy.

Finney: Daddy. He whips you. What does he whip you with?

Ralph: A belt. And his hands.

Finney: He whips you with his belt and his hands. Does it hurt? (Yes.) It hurts a lot! (Yes.) And you cry! (Yes.) Do you get mad at your daddy? (Yes.) What do you say?

Ralph: I don't talk back or I'll get hit more!

Finney: If you talk back you'll get hit more! (Yes.) Well, why don't you mind?

Ralph: *I try! I try!* (tears) I don't know!

Finney: Are you just bad?

Ralph: I don't think so.

Finney: They why don't you mind? . . . What does your daddy tell you?

Ralph: He tells me that I'm lazy and no good! (tears)

Finney: He says you are a lazy no-good boy. (Yes.) He says that he will whip you if you don't do those things. (Yes.) Then why don't you do them.

Ralph: I don't know. *I try.*

Jack: It's hard! It's hard to do all those things they want you to do.

Ralph: They want you to be an adult when you are a little kid.

Dave: Yeah! Why can't they let us be little kids!

Ralph: We are not big. We're small!

Finney: They just tell you to do those things and you can't remember to do them! (Yes!) (tears) Are you lazy? (NO!)

Ralph: I work hard!

Finney: Does that hurt your feelings when your Daddy calls you lazy? (YES!) What do you want to say?

Ralph: I do hard. I work hard. But he gets mad for talking back! I'm scared of my Dad.

Finney: He's pretty big. (Yes.) Does he yell at you? (Yes.)

Ralph: Mommy sticks up for me though.

Finney: She sticks up for you. (Yes.) She says don't yell at him so much! (Yes.)

Ralph: And he gets mad at her. And they have a big argument.

Finney: They fight over you. (YES!) Does that make you feel bad? (YES!) You don't want them to fight over you. (NO!) But you want your Mommy to stick up for you. (Yes.)

Ralph: I need her!

Finney: You need your Mommy! If your Mom didn't stick up for you could your Dad be too mean? (Yes.) Anybody else have anything to say? . . . Anybody else's Dad yell at them? . . .

The typescript of the hour continues on; this is enough, I believe, to give the reader a sample of what is developed and brought out with this technique. The following day the students wrote their reactions to this "experiment."

Here are their letters:

Ralph: "In the small group meeting Friday, I thought the meeting was very good. I admit at first I was very skeptical, but after we started I got some good emotional feelings. When I first started to talk it was my older self that talked first. But as we progressed I found my little child doing all the talking. It was very rewarding and helped me greatly. I am looking forward to going to the marathon on Saturday."

Irene: "I really enjoyed revealing my 'little child' experiences. Remember what I said before the experiment—that it was going to be a big show? After going through it I don't think that way anymore. In fact, I think it's neat! All the experiences I blurted out are the ones I never think of. I think it was partly the dark room and partly my ability to concentrate that made me able to think in terms of my childhood.

"I really felt like a child. I also had the same expression of feelings in my experiences. For example, when my dog died, I had cried and also been angry at God. One thing that I couldn't understand during the whole experiment was my crying. It seemed that I couldn't control the tears—it just flowed.

"After the ordeal, I felt great! I felt I had unburdened a lot of feelings. I'm really glad I joined the experiment. I only wish it could have lasted longer."

Charlotte: "I would like first to write about last Friday's 'Little Kid' experiment experience in the group. The 'after effect' on me was dynamic. I kept thinking about my childhood. Again and again, my mind would vision scenes of my youth. This returning to my childhood was a very pleasant thing for me. I think kids have a fantastic world—they are free with their emotions; therefore it seems, when they're happy, they're very happy. Kids go from tears to laughter in seconds. To return to the child of my past was a wonderful feeling. The greatest thing about the experience you conducted was the lingering; the child stayed awake in me for many hours.

"It was an enjoyable and worthwhile experience. I would have liked it to evoke something in me that I hadn't seen for a long time. This it did not do. I don't really think my feelings (and fantasies) have changed much from when I was a child. Ever since I was a baby I've always loved and wanted to be cuddled. I still have this need to be hugged. . . . I envied and was awed at both Bob and Irene and Ralph and Dave, because they all had hostile bad feelings that come out from their childhoods. I guess I just like to see emotion—especially that in kids. . . ."

Nancy: "I would first like to comment upon your visit to our small group. I thought your experiment in helping us bring out our little child was very revealing. Unfortunately, for me, I found that I couldn't communicate my thoughts orally—it might have been the presence of the tape recorder—I don't know. I was glad to see some of the other members of the group open up for the first time and express some deep emotional feelings. I now feel much closer to those persons, and I think they feel more like they're a part of the peer group. I was very disappointed in myself for not speaking up and expressing my thoughts. At times I know that I was only an observer."

Bob: "I guess my main reaction to having you talk to the little child in me was astonishment! I didn't think I would be capable of letting myself go that much. When the 'experiment' first started and for about the first forty-five minutes, I was still nineteen-years-old. Mostly I just tried to think back to my childhood but still I thought not as a child but as I am today. However, once you started talking to me directly the little child did the talking. I really surprised myself with some of the answers that were coming out of me. I know that if I had been asked some of those questions as a nineteen-year-old I would have answered them differently. I guess it just goes to show what a high wall people build around their feelings, especially those that hurt.

"I think what I really gained from the experiment was this . . . When I look back I think of how foolish some of what I said must have sounded; ordinarily I would have been afraid to act that way, but I was not the least bit self-conscious while I was speaking. I think this is one of the biggest assets of the group. I know that I can always be myself and say what I feel. I feel completely secure. I know that the other members are not there to judge me or for that matter me them."

Some letters from another group:

Ophelia: "You asked us to write our reactions to the 'little child' experiment. My reaction was probably quite obvious. I felt that it was a fantastic experience. I will have to admit that when I first heard of the idea I was a little skeptical. I was sure that the participants would have to pretend at least a little. When I tried it myself I found that pretending wasn't necessary. I felt like I was eight years old again. I was letting out emotions that I wanted to let out eleven years ago, but I didn't know how to. The tears I was crying were real tears and the feelings I had were real feelings. At times, it seemed that I had no control over what I was saying. The words seemed to be coming out of my mouth without any help. I could listen to myself talking; grown-up Ophelia was actually listening to Little Ophelia.

"My parents started divorce proceedings while I was home for Easter vacation. That day in class was the first day I allowed myself to show any emotion about my family situation since I heard about the divorce.

"Many factors contributed to the success of the experiment, at least in my group. One thing was the lights out. Darkness helped me feel more secure. I could block out the whole world. It was as though only you and I were in the room. Secondly, I think the experiment worked because it was done within the group. I don't think the results would have been so good if the experiment had been performed in just any group of eight people. I can say and do many things when I'm with the group that I can't say and do with other people. Maybe *can't* isn't the right word; perhaps it's just that I try harder when I'm with the group. We all try harder."

Joan: "I would like to make a few comments on the experiment of trying to bring out the child in ourselves. I participated, but wish I had before I did and that more of my Peers should have joined me. That experience I'll never forget, and I'm willing to do it again. I hesitated at first only out of fear but soon I felt myself really involved and that I wanted to share with the others. It almost seemed like a dream. A dream of the past. It was fun looking back observing myself. I should like to do it again. Group therapy can be pretty interesting and I can see that many of my problems are pretty common."

Sharon: "Well, I'm going to write about what happened in our group two weeks ago. That was when you came and talked to the little child in some of us.

"At first I was a bit apprehensive, but I guess everyone was. I didn't object to what you were going to do. I thought that turning the lights out was a good idea. I felt more secure, yet I felt closer to the people in the group.

"When Sharry started talking I sort of felt that it might have been a bit fake, especially when Big Sharry cut in. After a while I started identifying with her, and I was slowly assimilated into the mood of things.

"When Claudia was talking I strongly identified with her. Then, I knew that my little child wanted to talk. Here comes the funny part of it. I felt that I (my little child) should talk about the time just before my parents' divorce. I really was my little child talking and answers and remarks were quite spontaneous.

"I was hardly thinking about what I was saying. When I was talking about my Dad's face and a glass of beer with a copper penny floating around in it, I wasn't in touch with the rest of the group at all. I guess it really was my little child talking.

"After the experience was over I really felt good! I think this experience will help the group as a whole too. Last week we seemed to be able to communicate better, and I think the 'little child experiment' was partially responsible for this. It helped show everybody they had many problems and experiences that were common to all, and this helped relieve some of the uneasiness that the group had experienced previously."

I hope this letters and this typescript give the reader an impression of the power of this technique, and I would hope that it will help you learn how I do it so that you might try it out for yourself with your clients. I would be very interested in hearing from therapists who try it and about how it works out for them.

REFERENCES

Berne, Eric. *Transactional Analysis in Psychotherapy*. New York: Grove Press, 1961.
Finney, B. C. "Let the Little Kid Talk: A New Technique of Psychotherapy." Paper presented to California State Psychological Association, 1960.
————"Let the Little Child Talk: A New Psychotherapeutic Technique." *American Journal of Psychotherapy* 23 (1969), 230-242.
————"The Peer Program: An Experiment in Humanistic Education." Unpublished manuscript, 1971.
Missildine, H. *Your Inner Child of the Past*. New York: Simon & Schuster, 1963.
Perls, F., R. F. Hefferline, and P. Goodman. *Gestalt Therapy: Excitement and Growth in the Human Personality*. New York: Julian Press, 1951.
Shapiro, S. "Ego Therapy in Action: A Case Study." *Psychological Reports*, 11 (1962), 821-831.

CHAPTER 15

SAY IT AGAIN: AN ACTIVE THERAPY TECHNIQUE

BEN C. FINNEY, Ph.D.

Say it again is a powerful, active technique for releasing feelings, bringing out insights, and changing behavior. It's simple to explain to the clients, easy for them to do and usually accepted without resistance. The simplest forms of say it again are *repeating*, in which the client is asked to repeat each sentence several times before going on to the next sentence, and *prompting*, in which the therapist, like the stage prompter, provides "lines" for the client to say. A more complex and powerful variation includes the use of *directions*, where the therapist, like the dramatic director directs the client in how to act and how to express his feelings. It can also be combined with contact comfort, where the therapist provides emotional support by physical touching and holding, but these two different techniques can be used separately.

As I have developed it over a period of several years, Say It Again is both a technique and some theoretical concepts; I shall present the techniques, which can be used with different therapeutic approaches first, and then discuss my theories of what produces therapeutic change.

REPEATING

In repeating, the client is instructed to repeat each sentence he says several times before going on to the next phrase, letting it "echo" and recruit feelings and associations until a new sentence comes to mind. He is also asked to repeat this new sentence several times before saying the next one, which is repeated in turn. He is encouraged to "listen" to what he is saying and to try to feel the emotional impact rather than think about what he is going to say next. When he stops talking because he is blocked or is trying to sort out what he is thinking, he is urged to keep on repeating the last sentence until a new one emerges.

When the client says a sentence, the therapist repeats the sentence and says, "Say that again!" or, "Again!" This example from a typescript will illustrate the technique:

Client: Nobody cares what happens to me.
Therapist: "Nobody cares what happens to me." Say that again!
Client: Nobody cares what happens to me.
Therapist: Again!
Client: Nobody cares what happens to me. Nobody cares what happens to me. Nobody cares whether I can do it or not.
Therapist: Say *that* again! "Nobody cares whether I can do it or not."
Client: Nobody cares whether I can do it or not. Nobody cares whether I can do it or not. Nobody has *ever* cared!
Therapist: Again! "Nobody has *ever* cared." Say that again.

The simple procedure of having a client repeat a sentence over and over rather than immediately moving on to the next sentence has several important effects. Forcing such a novel mode of expression disrupts the habit pattern of talking in a series of sentences and encourages new ways of perceiving. In problem-solving tasks people often fall into familiar and nonadaptive routines; directing them to attend more consciously to their implicit assumptions frees them to view the task differently and to restructure their perceptions. Saying a sentence over and over again with more directed awareness allows for a similar restructuring of thinking. It is difficult to repeat long and complex sentences, and of necessity the phrases are kept short and simple. Intellectual abstractions and verbal complexity are usually maneuvers to avoid feelings which are best expressed in direct, short, and child-like phrases; repetition forces simplicity of language structure and blocks one of the ways of getting emotional distance from sensitive feelings.

In the usual way of talking in therapy the client will often say something that expresses a feeling which has aversive anxiety associated with it. Then he immediately moves on to the next thought without stopping to experience the full impact of what he has said; he avoids anxiety by moving away and prevents the relearning and desensitization from occurring. As he repeats and stays with a sentence, there is more opportunity for the positive aspects of the therapy situation to counter-condition an anxiety response.

Sometimes I will deliberately make a person say a phrase over and over again because I observe twitches and grimaces indicating anxiety and conflict; with repeated exposure to the feeling in the sentence, the twitches subside and he is able to express the feeling directly without conflict. Usually, the next sentence he says will be much closer to the core feeling than if he had gone on immediately without desensitizing the anxiety. One way of judging whether the anxiety has been reduced is to ask him to look directly at me as he says the phrase; if he turns away or blinks, it indicates that there is still residual conflict. This technique of "reading twitches" I learned from Zaslow (1969). The idea of repeating a phrase over and over I learned from observing Perls (1969) in his Dream Work Seminars at Esalen Institute. He asks a person to repeat one sentence again and again, each time louder, to mobilize feelings. Usually he does this with only one sentence, and then goes on to another technique. I tried it and found it effective, and discovered that it could be continued as a separate procedure. Not only does repetition of a sentence tend to counter-condition the anxiety blocking the expression of the emotion, but repeating itself tends to mobilize feelings, especially if the person is instructed to say it with more feeling. In the James-Lange theory of emotion the action of flight tends to produce the emotion of fear; repeating a phrase in an emotional manner tends to reactivate the associated emotions and to generate real physiological emotion. Thus there are two processes operating simultaneously to release emotion—desensitization of the aversive anxiety and mobilization through action.

Preserving emotional momentum is important. I insist that the person keep talking, repeating the last phrase he said if nothing new comes to mind. When a person stops, I will be very insistent that he keep on talking. The following typescript, from a group situation, illustrates the process:

Client: I feel embarrassed today with everybody looking at me. (Stops talking)
Therapist: Say "I feel embarrassed today with everybody looking at me." (Client hesitates, then says it reluctantly)
Client: I feel embarrassed today but I didn't yesterday. . . .
Therapist: Again! Keep your mouth moving! Say that again! "I feel embarrassed today!" (Insistent tone)
Client: I feel embarrassed today because I am the center of attraction.

Therapist: Again! "I feel embarrassed because I am the center of attraction." Again!!

Client: I feel embarrassed because I am the center of attraction. (Again.) I feel embarrassed because I am the center of attraction. I'm afraid I'll cry if I talk today!

Therapist: That is it! Say *that*! "I'm afraid I'll cry if I talk today!" (She continued on, did cry, and got much relief.)

With continuing pressure to repeat the sentences and keep on talking, she was able to express the feeling that was blocking her, and was able to work it through. When a person moves into an area in which anxiety is attached to expression, resistance overwhelms the approach response and the person blocks and stops talking. By insisting that the person keep repeating the last sentence, the motor component is kept in activation, even though no new material is coming out. It is somewhat like a production machine with no product coming out; by keeping the machine running the added effort of restarting the machine is not added to the blockage of output. Also, repeating the old phrase in itself tends to lower the aversive anxiety and it gradually desensitizes. Nudging a person with a *prompt* will also help them to get past the block.

Another way in which I keep the momentum going is for me to repeat over and over and over the last phrase that the client said before he stopped; by continuing talking, I "keep the record playing." This is especially effective if the client is right on the edge of strong feelings and to stop talking would lose momentum which might push them past the impasse. Also, when they are crying so hard that speech is not possible, I keep the level of the feeling up by repeating the last phrase with the same feeling. I can also amplify the feelings that have been expressed by a client by repeating the phrase with more intense emotional expression than he did. By using my voice and expression to intensify feeling, I draw out more emotion from the client. It is somewhat like the effect of an actor projecting emotion, except that in this case the "lines" are the client's own. I think the therapist should be able to express feelings effectively and use this ability to get the client to do likewise; this is of course different from the approach of many therapists who learn to be models of impassive imperturbability. One client commented about this technique:

I think another advantage of the therapist's repeating sentences and being histrionic is that he demonstrates to a reluctant or self-conscious client that he is willing to play this silly and/or embarrassing game and therefore makes it vastly easier for the client to follow suit. If he can shout that loud, so can I. It also demonstrates an acceptance of feelings the client may be a-shamed of—if he doesn't flinch when he says that, maybe it's not so bad after all.

Another commented:

Emphasize the part about the therapist expressing feelings and not being impassive, and emphasize the part about feeling with the client, and your tuning with him and how it helps getting past the blocks.

Another variation is to repeat the phrase in unison with the client, like a choral chant, starting softly but increasing the feeling with each repetition. On occasion I have had the client sing the phrase, like a child singing to himself, which stirs feelings. When a phrase comes up the seems pregnant with meaning and feeling, I will urge its repetition with encouragements like "That's it!" "That's the feeling!" "Feel it! Deeper! More!" communicating my feeling of urgency that they push toward expressing more feelings. By repeating a phrase with slightly different emphasis I can bring out somewhat different meanings and feelings. Here the client is led to look at different feelings implicit in his initial statement.

I try more to feel with the client than to think about his dynamics, and when I am feeling open and in tune I do a much better job than when I am abstracted and not feeling empathetic. Therapy is always very much the product of the personality of the therapist; in this technique the personality of the therapist is even more important than is usual, because he is being so actively involved. One client who has used Say It Again as a therapist commented on this:

My primary problem with Say It Again is that its effective-ness is so much dependent upon my mood and feelings toward the person involved that I sometimes find myself getting jam-med up in the use of it. I've found that I have better results when I don't use a purely Say It Again format, but interject it among other techniques. The real beauty of Say It Again is that it can be picked up at any time during the session when you feel that the person could really move.

Another client-therapist, commenting on an initial draft of this paper, said:

It is my feeling that you should openly state a moderate a-mount of praise of your own sensitivity. I grant that you make the point subtly but it needs emphasis lest some "impassive imperturbable" therapist try it and fail *himself* without recognizing where the failure is.

Here is a typescript example illustrating the effectiveness of these repeating techniques:

Client: The hurt is still way down.
Therapist: "The hurt is still way down. The *hurt* is still way *down!"* (Increased feeling with a shift of emphasis)
Client: The hurt is still way down!!! (Increased feeling) The hurt is still way down!!! *I want to cry that hurt out!*
Therapist: "*I want to cry that hurt out!!!"* (With stronger, poignant feelings)
Client: I want to cry that hurt out!!! *I want to cry that hurt out!*
Therapist: (In unison with client) "*I want to cry that hurt out!"* Go deeper! More feeling!!!
Client: Its been pushed there for so long. Its been pushed there for so long. Its been pushed there for so long—and it makes me all tight! (She stops, just on the edge of tears, her face drawn up, chin quivering.)
Therapist: "It makes me all tight!!! I just *need* to get that hurt out!!! *I want to cry that hurt out!!!"* (She is responding, but still blocked.) I NEED TO GET THAT HURT OUT!! I NEED TO GET THOSE TEARS OUT!!! I NEED TO LET THOSE TEARS OUT!!! I NEED TO CRY THOSE TEARS OUT!!!
Client: (Breaks—with hard sobbing) IT'S SO SCARY! IT'S SO SCARY. I'M AFRAID EVERYTHING BAD WILL COME OUT WITH THOSE TEARS!!!
Therapist: That's the feeling! "*I'm afraid everything bad will come out with those tears!"* Keep going!
Client: I NEED TO FEEL THESE BAD FEELINGS AND FEEL I CAN BE LOVED! (Hard sobbing)
Therapist: That's it! "I NEED TO FEEL THESE BAD FEELINGS AND FEEL I CAN BE LOVED." (Client is sobbing so hard she cannot talk.) "I NEED TO FEEL THESE BAD FEELINGS AND FEEL I CAN BE LOVED. I NEED TO FEEL THESE BAD FEELINGS

AND FEEL I CAN BE LOVED." (The therapist continues to repeat this several times, and then she repeats it with intense feelings—lasting three or four minutes.)

Client: Maybe they are not so bad!

Therapist: "Maybe they are not so bad." (Softly)

(She continues on, in a subdued way for a while, but later moves to new levels of intensity. This illustrates a typical impasse, with a breakthrough, and a shift in feelings after the experience. Experiencing the fear and pain of expression—actually the "Child" talking to "Daddy"—desensitizes this area and allows the loving feelings which have been held back because of the fear of crying and anger to be experienced.)

The effect of the therapist repeating what the client says has some interesting aspects. It allows the client to hear from outside himself what he has said; there is a psychological difference between saying something and hearing it repeated by another person. A similar result is obtained by hearing one's own voice on a tape recorder; it sounds different and one can hear it a little differently. The effect of repeating is much like a Rogerian reflection, except the phrase is in the client's words and has more impact. Incidentally, I usually record the sessions and send the client home with the tape to listen to it; often it helps them get intellectual grasp of the emotional experience which they have had during the session. At one time I actually wrote down the sentences as the client was repeating, and gave them a written copy to keep. This is effective, but a lot of work for the therapist.

I find that there is an interesting effect on me as the therapist in repeating what the client says with his emotional expression. Saying his words with my mouth lets me feel more closely what he is feeling. There is a subtle but important difference in my capacity to tune and feel the feelings when I say "You need to let those tears out" and when I say "I need to let those tears out." It moves me away from thinking about the person to feeling with him. And when I am relating emotionally with him, I am able to feel more sensitively where he is and where the next emotional step will go. When the client senses I am tuning with him and saying and feeling what he said, he feels understood and less vulnerable, better able to face the blocks and reach resolution of the emotional conflict.

There are some variations of the repeating technique which are effective. One is the *split half repeat*, in which the therapist asks the client to repeat just one half of the sentence he had just said; often this will bring out another association or meaning.

Client: I won't forget her as long as I live. I won't forget her as long as I live. I won't forget her as long as I live.

Therapist: Say "As long as I live."

Client: As long as I live. As long as I live. I'm afraid I won't live long. I want to kill myself!

(This split half repeat brought out the suicidal impulses in the phrase "as long as I live." Often a phrase will have several meanings which can be brought out in this way. The effect is a bit like putting the phrase under the microscope to see the fine detail.)

Another variant is *word repeat,* in which the therapist chooses just one word out of the sentence and asks the client to repeat just that word. Usually I choose a word that seems to have feeling attached to it.

Client: I am sorry about all the times I rejected her. I am sorry about all the times I rejected her. I am sorry about all the times I rejected her.

Therapist: Say "Sorry."

Client: Sorry. Sorry. I am a sorry person. I am a worthless person.

(In this phrase "sorry" expressed several feelings—regret and self-rejection; by concentrating on it these implicit feelings were brought out.)

Sentence Completion Repeats are another variant which encourages exploration of causal chains or develops the emotional logic implicit in the situation. The therapist asks the client to say the last sentence he is repeating, but as an incomplete sentence.

Client: I drive people away. I drive people away. I drive people away.

Therapist: Say "I drive people away because . . ." Finish that sentence.

Client: I drive people away because . . . I drive people away because . . . I drive people away because . . . I'm afraid they won't accept me.

Therapist: Say that! That's it! "I drive people away because I'm afraid they won't accept me."

(Other incomplete sentences which could have been offered:

"When I drive people away . . .

"I drive people away by . . .

"If I drive people away . . .)

Another style is to continue this in a continuing series, using the split half technique and taking the last half of each sentence and adding "because"; this tends to develop a causal chain. "I drive people away because I'm afraid they won't accept me. I'm afraid they won't accept me because I'm selfish. I'm selfish because I never had any discipline. I never had any discipline because I never had any parents," etc.

PROMPTING

In *prompting* I offer the client a phrase to say which is not one which he has previously said, but which I feel is close enough to what he is ready to express that he could accept it as *his* feelings. He is asked to repeat it at least once to see if it feels correct; if it does not express his thoughts correctly, he should then change it so that it does. Asking him to say it at least once even though it does not feel right at first hearing has proved to be worthwhile; sometimes the phrase he rejects at first hearing will turn out to be acceptable after he has said it and felt its impact. Clients seem to be able to reject phrases offered by the therapist if they do not feel right; however, I often ask "Is that right?" to remind them that it is their responsibility to decide whether the phrase correctly expresses their thoughts.

One difficulty which sometimes develops is that a passively resistant client will not add phrases of his own but waits for me to offer new sentences; later he may say that he was not feeling the sentences he was repeating and it had minimal emotional impact. When a client begins to depend upon me to offer *prompts* and does not come through with his own sentences, I stop prompting and just repeat until he begins to take more initiative for his own movement. Sometimes I might offer a prompt focusing on the immediate situation, such as "Ben, I don't know what to say. I'm waiting for you to tell me."

The term *prompting* is an allusion to the prompter in the theater who reminds the actors of lines they have forgotten; the therapeutic prompt is designed to provide a nudge to push past the resistance that is holding a thought below the threshold of expression, and to "remind" the client of "forgotten" thoughts or feelings. It is similar to an interpretation, in that the therapist is directing the client's attention to some feeling which he has not been immediately aware of; it differs in that prompting can be used repeatedly to push the client with small nudges, whereas interpretations are used less frequently and usually involve larger steps.

In general the prompt should be very close to the feeling the client is expressing, but it moves a little further in the direction he was going. The gradations between a repeat and a prompt can be very small; a repeat which emphasizes a different word by the way the therapist says it is sort of a prompt. A phrase with amplified feeling is a nudge by the therapist. The therapist may put two sentences together in one prompt which have been said in different contexts by the client, or he may put into words the feelings that the client is expressing in his voice or gestures. In general, the closer the prompt is to the threshold of expression, the better it works; but by repeating small prompts the therapist can influence the rate of progress significantly. In this illustrative example the client is re-experiencing her "Child" and is imagining herself talking to her father; the illustrative prompts move from very small steps to one that was too large and incorrect:

Client: You don't show your love to me! You don't *show* it!!! *You show it to that baby!* (There is increasing anger; then she introduces the baby.)

Therapist: "You show it to that baby and not to me!" Say that! (This prompt involved a very small step; I simply combined "You don't show it to me" and "You show it to that baby.")

Client: You show it to that baby and not to me!!! You show it to that baby and not to meee!!! (Increasing anger) *And it's all gone!*

Therapist: Say, "You took your love away and gave it to that baby!!" (This prompt amplified the feeling "It's all gone" and that the love had been taken away and given to the baby.)

Client: Yes!! You took your love away and gave it to that baby!! *You took your love away and gave it to that baby!!!* (Increasing pain and emotional expression)

Therapist: "You took your love away and gave it to that baby and it *hurts!*" Is that right? (This prompt put in words the hurt she was expressing in her tone; the "check-out" was to encourage her to check and see if this was the correct feeling.)

Client: YES! It *hurts!* You took your love away and it *hurts!* You took your love away and gave it to that baby and it hurts!!!!

Therapist: Say, "If that baby wasn't here maybe you'd love me." (This prompt expresses the emotional feelings I would expect her to have, the familiar childhood wish to get rid of the rival sibling.)

Client: YES! If that baby wasn't here maybe you'd love me! If that baby wasn't here maybe you'd love me. If that baby wasn't here maybe you'd show me you love me.

Therapist: Say, "I hate that baby!" (Here I was making a larger prompt, one my theoretical expectations would lead me toward; it turned out that this was somewhat incorrect, and I would have done better to pick up her last sentence, which brought it back to her father not showing love.)

Client: No, it's funny! I don't think I really hated him. He was my friend. (Her tone changes—a more "adult" tone.)

Therapist: Say it at least once just to see how it sounds. Say "I hate that baby." (I recognized the rejection of the prompt, but I pressed her to repeat it just once, since sometimes saying it will recruit feelings. In the case the "hate" moved her toward finding what she *did* hate.

Client: I hate that baby . . . No . . . I just hated his being a boy.

Therapist: That's it! "I just hated his being a *boy!*" (My repeat emphasized that we had now found what she did hate—and that we were back on the track again.)

Client: I just hated his being a boy. I just hated his being a boy!! If I was a boy my father would love me too!!! (Her increased feelings showed we had found the main emotional current; her last statement showed she was developing the theme constructively. She continued on and found that she had given up trying to be a daughter and had tried to please her father by being sexual.)

A prompt differs from an interpretation in that instead of pointing out to the client what he might be feeling, it asks him to express the feeling as if it were his own. When he has said it with his mouth he has a much more immediate feeling of whether it is correct or not. It is much more involving to say, "I hate my baby brother" than to listen to the therapist say, "Do you think you hated your baby brother" and then to agree or disagree. Also, I always try to phrase the prompt in terms of the present tense; "I hate that baby" rather than "I hated that baby." I want the client to re-experience the feeling as a child rather than recall it as an adult in memory form; for an emotional change to take place the feeling has to be vivid, immediate, and physiological.

Another aspect is that it allows the therapist to be active in working very closely with the client. Psychologically it feels much like working with someone putting together a jig-saw puzzle; instead of sitting back and observing, giving encouragement, and making some general observations about how he is making errors, I actively participate, offering pieces, sharing the good feelings when one fits, and working closely with the client. Some therapists have objected to the extent to which I help, feeling that this deprives the client of his self-reliance and independence and cultivates dependence. My experience is that the client senses that he is being active although helped, and that this is more encouraging than struggling unsuccessfully. One client in a typescript expressed this thought.

Client: I trust this group. I trust this group. I trust each of you.
Therapist: Again.
Client: I trust each of you. I feel like I figured it out by myself, even though I know I didn't, I'd like to think I did. (She is here expressing the feeling that even though she had been aided by the therapist's prompting and the responses of the group, she felt it was her achievement too.)
Therapist: Again. "I feel like I figured it out by myself, even though I know I didn't. I'd like to think I did."
Client: I'd like to think I did. In one day it has helped me to feel things more. In one day it has helped me to feel things more. (Her sense of relief and achievement is genuine; also, the fact that she could accept help and use it constructively was a positive step.)

I view the situation as being similar to an adult or a teacher helping a child learn a new task; too much interference and doing it for the child will not let him learn, but encouraging assistance helps him past the discouraging blocks that might help him to stop in discouragement or bafflement. One of the tasks of adulthood is to learn to ask for and accept help without either clinging dependence or unrealistic independence; the experience of working with a therapist in joint collaboration is a step toward learning this. The answer to whether too much help is being given lies in the responses of the client; if after a prompt he moves on in a constructive way, it has been helpful; if he stops moving, then it was not.

When a therapist is offering prompts he is showing by his responses that he is understanding the client and following his feelings closely; when the client talks and the therapist just listens the client does not have the feedback as to how well the therapist is following, nor does the therapist know how well he is listening. Rogerian reflections of feelings are a similar way of giving feedback and encouragement, but they do not offer so much in terms of active collaboration.

This sense of two people working closely together is an important aspect, especially when there is continual feedback between the two; in Say It Again I am being active and guiding, but I am also being careful not to lead the clients away from their own direction or push them into feelings they are not ready for. Their responses to my prompts let me know how well I am following. The whole combination of touching, saying words together, and offering little nudges in the form of prompts gives a feeling of closeness. A client expressed this feeling:

Client: I have a sense of your leading me to a solution. Those other therapists I had . . . they just let me lie around and struggle . . . like an animal in a cage . . . and not getting any particular help. Just a little verbal encouragement once in a while. (Here she is talking in the more usual way. She had had extended therapy with a psychoanalytically oriented psychiatrist and some marriage counseling, both of which she felt had been helpful.)

Therapist: Say "Ben, I have a feeling you are leading me and you can help me."

Client: I have a feeling you are leading me and you are going to help me. And the way you lead is completely safe.

Therapist: "The way you lead is completely safe."

Client: The way you lead is completely safe and I can accept it. And it usually works through, and I don't know where we are going . . . its kind of like both of us are going in the dark. Except that I feel safe. And that you are helping me go too. And all of a sudden we come out somewhere in the daylight. And it's come true! It's something I've never been able to do and I feel very free doing it, and just to do it and not feel as if I were making myself do it. The angry feelings really came out. (She seemed to want to talk as an "adult" and evaluate the process, so I did not insist that she stay on Say It Again.)

One kind of prompting is aimed at keeping the client expressing his feelings directly toward the person to whom the feelings are directed. Both Perls (1969) and Janov (1970) use this technique, and I, too, have found it very effective. It provides a sense of immediacy to talk *to* the person rather than *about* him. I also try and keep it in present tense, so they are encouraged to go back and experience it as if it were happening "now" in the past. This tends to bring out the "inner child of the past."

Client: My mother said some awful things to me. My mother said some awful things to me.

Therapist: Say "Mother, you said some awful things to me." (I should have phrased it "You say some awful things to me.")

Client: Mother, you said some awful things to me. You really did! You shouldn't have said those things to me. You shouldn't have!

Another variant is to move a statement of feeling about someone in the present back to the past family relationships; often when I hear feelings that sound as if they have old childhood derivatives I will give a prompt which moves them in that direction.

Client: I can't count on anybody to listen to me. I can't count on anybody to listen to me.
Therapist: Try saying that to someone in your family . . . Try "Mother, I can't count on you to listen to me."
Client: Mother, I can't count on you to listen to me. No, it's Dad! Dad, I can't count on you to listen to me. You've *never* listened to me. You *never* listen to me!!! (In this example, a general feeling was directed back to where the feeling originated, and it was experienced in "present time" and vividly. To unlearn a childhood attitude which is intruding into present relationships, the person needs to go back on their "time track" so that unlearning occurs in the "time and place" where it was first learned.)

I use prompts to encourage expression of feelings toward me, on the assumption that the relationship, real and transference, is a powerful force for emotional learning. I provide them with the phrases directed toward me, which offers an implicit encouragement and permission to say their feelings to me. I am interested in bringing out transference feelings in the relationship, which can then be directed toward the person with whom they originated, but also in getting them to experience and learn from a real, close relationship with me as a person rather than a projection screen.

Client: I want them to be, but nobody wants *me* to be *me*! I want them to be, but nobody wants me to be me! Nobody cares about me being me. Not the boys and not my husband!
Therapist: "Not the boys and not my husband." Say, "Ben, it feels like you care about me being me!" (She was holding on to me firmly and her expression indicated warmth; I put into words the feelings I was picking up nonverbally. Also, I wanted to direct her attention to the difference between what she expected and what was happening right now.)
Client: Yes, Ben it feels like you care about me being me. (Said with feeling, but she did not look at me. This indicated some distance; I wanted her to approach me closer emotionally.)

Therapist: Again. Look directly at me and say that. "Ben, it feels like you care about me being me."

Client: (Looks directly and warmly at me) Ben, it feels like you care about me being me. *And it feels so good!!!*

This prompt brought out the warm feelings toward me, which were not being said in words. This experience of feeling and saying the close, warm feelings in the relationship helped desensitize her fears of emotional closeness. Her looking away was a way of expressing the avoidant tendencies; having her say it while looking directly at me was a step toward moving closer emotionally. I find that the fears that block warm, loving feelings are often central in the emotional difficulties, and to push past these with the aid of a *Direction* from the therapist is helpful. I give prompts to bring out all kinds of feelings toward me, including anger, fear, dependency, sex, and love.

I use these kinds of prompts and directions in couple therapy or in a group when we are doing Say It Again. When a person is expressing feelings and becoming more relaxed, I will give a *Prompt* and a *Direction* like, "Look at Paul and say 'Paul, it feels good to share my feelings with you,' " or "Say, 'Paul, I like feeling closer to you and telling you my feelings' and look at him and touch him." In this kind of prompting there is an element of showing the client how to express feeling, a sort of "coaching" him to make a response which will let him experience how it feels to be more open and expressive, and often he will get positive reinforcement from his partner. In a group I give prompts which express interpersonal feelings which a person might not do spontaneously; usually these produce positive feedback from the group. The learning principle operating is that the behavior has to be emitted before it can be reinforced; I guide him to show new and more productive behaviors and these are reinforced, both by his own internal responses and by the other people. As in all prompts, the therapist has to tune finely to find the behavior that is close to the threshold of response, so that it will have an element of genuineness; however, the James-Lange principle that acting produces feeling operates. I find the direction to touch or show warmth is consistently effective in bringing out warm, cohesive feelings between me and the client or within the group.

Prompting in couple therapy—married or "together"—has been especially effective. I have the two talk directly to each other, repeating what they say under my direction. I control who talks and when we shift back and forth; this control tends to keep them out of their usual patterns of "dysfunctional communication." I offer prompts, often feelings they would like to say but which are below the threshold of expression; my prompting gives them sanction to say and feel responsible for what they said. When they do say it in response to a prompt, if they accept the prompt, it becomes "their" statement, especially when they repeat it and experience it. Sometimes we have been able to generate some very deep, extremely intimate interchanges, with tears and affection, in which important changes occur in the relationship, despite the fact that I am controlling and guiding the interaction with the Say It Again structure. One reason this technique seems to work in this setting is that it slows the interaction down so that each can hear what the other is saying; rather than hearing the first sentence and then turning off and going inside their head to phrase a rebuttal, one partner is forced to say his phrase over and over while both of them listen to it, with the listening partner having to wait before he comes back with a response. It gives them both time to assimilate what is being said and there is less tendency for the communication system to become overloaded and confused. Another aspect is that I lead the person who is talking to go inside himself and explore the feelings and the historical "echos" rather than just focusing on the other person's reactions; there is more encouragement to "internalize" and take responsibility for his own feelings rather than focusing on the other person and his responses. By hearing what he is saying himself, he is less prone to project onto the partner; it seems to help them both separate out the "projections" from the real interpersonal interaction.

Similarly, in a group in which there has been an encounter which does not seem to get resolved, I will put one and then the other on Say It Again and try and get them to explore the personal significance of what they have been saying to the other person. Often when one has gotten to old hurts and has expressed them with pain and tears he is able to come back and relate to the other person in a more "real" way; moving from one to the other, with time to really get into their deeper, internal feeling, is especially effective.

A somewhat different style of group Say It Again is effective in getting a beginning group to interact in a "deeper" way. In my college classes of Group Dynamics I rotate among three or four groups who otherwise operate as leaderless groups; they often have difficulty breaking away from the usual superficial group talk. I control the interaction in the Say It Again structure, putting one person "on" and getting him to express some feelings; then I instruct him to ask someone in the group how that person is feeling about what is going on. When the new member is asked and responds, I put him on Say It Again for a while, drawing out his feelings, perhaps having the two interact with each other while repeating and taking prompts and directions from me. Gradually we may go around the whole group in this style, and usually we generate more personal and feeling interaction, and the group gets a feeling of cohesion and accomplishment. While this inhibits spontaneity and deprives them temporarily of the experience of doing it themselves, the advantages outweigh the disadvantages. Sometimes the next meeting on their own is a "let down" by comparison, but frequently they are able to pick up and carry on in a more usual encounter style at a deeper level. Sometimes they have used Say It Again on their own, with effective results.

Another style of group Say It Again which I have recently developed is to focus intensively on one individual at a time rather than encouraging short interactions among the members, either in Say It Again structure or in the more usual encounter style. I ask around the group and we establish which members are really needing attention and which members have not had a turn for a while, setting up tentative priorities. Then one person will volunteer to "go down," meaning that he lies on the floor with his head in my lap, while the other group members cluster around, touching him in a comforting way. The person who is "down" is in an exposed, vulnerable emotional position, and usually we spend a bit of time checking out that the whole group is in tune and that he is feeling safe; if there is another member who is angry at the person "on," we may need to make sure that they can hold their feelings in abeyance for a bit. Then I will have the person "on" go on Say It Again, working toward "high voltage," intense feelings, and with patience and effort we usually get to intense pain, tears, crying, and catharsis. Since the person "on" feels pressure to "produce," we need to give him the feeling that he has all the time he needs, and that if he doesn't get to the feelings it is all right. This feeling that it is his time, and others will wait is important. Usually it takes some time to work past the blocks which are holding back the feelings, and the group waits patiently; when he does get into feelings they may be reacting intensely with their own "echos."

This method of conducting a group tends to minimize the usual "encounter" between members, but the personal sharing of feelings is high. While a person is "on," the other members are not allowed to interpret, attack, give their emotional reactions to what he is doing, or interfere; they are encouraged to offer prompts if they feel they know where the next step is going. Prompts given out of empathic feelings can be helpful and give the member a sense the others are with him; if the other member is reacting to his own pain stirred up by listening to the member "on" but is not aware of his own hurt, the prompts are usually blocking and I will stop them and encourage them to feel their own feelings. While this is somewhat like individual therapy in a group setting, the influence of the group is powerful, and the effect of the feelings of the person "on" has impact on the others. Sometimes the listening members will break into tears or anger with their own pain; frequently another member will put them "down" and on Say It Again while I continue on with the first member. In some intense sessions three or four members may be "discharging" with tears, crying, or shouting. This can be disruptive if the feelings of the different members are out of tune, i.e., one is raging while another is grieving. Sometimes members will simply let themselves feel their pain and go on their own "trip" in their head, but not expressing it openly. This emotional contagion seems to have a positive effect; seeing and hearing other people express strong emotion seems to lower the threshold for "letting go." Despite the noise and activity in a "multiple discharge" session, clients report that they do not feel they are being overwhelmed or out of control. Quite often after a member has had an intense cathartic session, he will be quite relaxed and will shift over to the "parental" role and put the person "on" who has just been helping him. Of course, sometimes in these intense sessions the members are watching me and seeing how I am taking it all; if I am looking pleased and happy with all the turmoil and feelings, they feel reassured. I try and keep some track of what is going on, and if someone gets stuck or it is going badly, I may move over to help. These intense sessions are not the usual occurrence, but are more likely to occur on marathons or week-long training sessions.

The persons about whom I feel concern are those who withdraw. The emotional contagion may threaten a person, and he tries to handle his inner turmoil by distancing mechanisms. Persons who respond by becoming emotionally detached, analytic, or amused often later report bad aftereffects, such as continuing tension. I give permission for a member to leave if he feels it is too disturbing, but in general I encourage him to move in closer, to touch the person "on" and to feel with him. When they let themselves feel, they get release rather than blockage.

I have observed that the professional therapists who have experienced these "high voltage" sessions in training settings are the most prone to retreat into the "therapeutic stance"—becoming analytic and interpretive. It strikes me that much of our professional objectivity is simply defensive—ways of keeping our "crying child" under control. Furthermore, I observe that this kind of objectivity does not lead to more accurate perceptions but rather to projections; the clients who are involved and feeling with the person "on" can offer prompts which are "on target" and helpful but the detached observers are usually "off" in their prompts.

I find that when I am feeling my own feelings—listening to my own "child"—I am intuitive and can be pushy in helpful ways. The key is to recognize when it is my own pain which I am feeling, an then to use it to guide me to feel the client's pain. It is also true that a part of me is evaluating the whole situation and keeping some perspective; it is as if my "child" and "adult" are working together, each contributing something different. If I am out of touch with my own feelings for personal reasons, it is apparent to both myself and the group, and they may comment on it and encourage me to explore the difficulty.

This style of group Say It Again is much like the group sessions described by Janov (1970) although the situation as he describes it has some differences. The group with which I have been doing this regularly has had a lot of experience in the more usual encounter style, and they prefer this new style, although from time to time we go back to encounter style to work on more "here and now" interactions. The disadvantages are that only three or four persons can get "on" in a two and a half hour session, and often members have to wait a couple of sessions to get "on." And the noise of the crying and shouting sometimes disturbs people in other offices.

This is an effective style for marathons, taking one person after another and giving him all that he wants up to two hours. In my last marathon every one of the members was able to break through the impasse into intense feelings and some resolution, and the feeling among the group was very close and warm and elated. However, it was very hard work for me, since I was working all the time and I got very fatigued. One way I handled this was to take a turn "going down," with the group putting me on Say It Again and keeping me there for an hour or so until I had discharged a lot of childhood tears and grief. Following this I felt relaxed and refreshed and was able to continue on as therapist.

This shifting role from therapist to co-member is something which I have explored gradually in small steps over the last few years. I do not have the space to discuss the complexities and advantages of it in this paper, but a member of the group reviewing this paper urged me to emphasize how helpful it was for the members for me to share my pain and feelings. She wrote: "This is so important you show it was helpful to us too. By involving yourself you show us you really care and love and that brings out all the warm loving in us and so we can give to ourselves and others. We unite as a team and become stronger."

DIRECTIONS

An additional technique for increasing involvement in Say It Again is that of *directions*. In this the therapist acts like the stage director who tells the actor not only what to say, but how to say it and how to move and gesture. The therapist may tell the client to say the phrase louder and with more feeling, and he may himself shout it angrily with a fierce expression to show the client how to express it, just as a director shows the actor how to express the feelings. When the client is beginning to experience a breakthrough of feeling, the therapist can increase the momentum by repeating the phrase more vividly and with more pain. This amplification of feeling by dramatic, emotional expression is somewhat akin to the effect on the audience of an actor "projecting" feeling. Interestingly, Gilot (1964, p. 277) describes the "Weepers" in Vallauris, France, who help a dying person relive his life with emotion as a step toward dying happily. They ask the dying person to recall important events, especially painful ones, and then they begin to weep and wail, expressing the pain implicit in the event. The patient is induced to cry too, by their example and emotional contagion, and they carefully cover all the unresolved griefs and pains of his lifetime. When the person has expressed his feelings from his lifetime, he is then ready to die in peace. Not only do they pull for tears, they will also get him to laugh over amusing episodes in his life; since they know him well, having lived in the same village, they usually know the important areas. I have not tried expressing emotion quite so intensely, but I do express a lot of feeling in my prompts. The encouragement a client feels toward expressing feeling when the therapist has expressed it was described earlier.

As Director, the therapist can tell the client to act or talk more assertively, to look directly at the therapist or another member, or to clench his fist, pound a pillow, or touch and hold someone. I use a lot of action during the therapy hour, having a person act out a feeling, move around, cover up their head and crouch in the corner when they are feeling like hiding, etc. These blend into the techniques of Gestalt Therapy and Psychodrama and Pesso's Psychomotor therapy (1969).

CONTACT COMFORT

Contact Comfort is a separate technique from Say It Again but the combination is very powerful. The therapist encourages regressive relaxation by holding and touching the client like a child being comforted, cradling him in his lap, holding his face in his hands, or sometimes just holding his hands warmly. This holding and touching transmits a feeling of warmth and safety which provides a positive, relaxing input which works to extinguish or counter-condition the aversive anxiety associated with the painful memories being experienced. One of the ways in which therapy produces changes is that the client re-experiences painful events in the context of a warmly supportive atmosphere without the primary aversive stimulation being present; by a process of counterconditioning the fear attached to the experience and to the associated cues is gradually reduced.

I will not be able to go into the literature on touching, but the research of Harlow has demonstrated how vital it is in development of sexual, maternal, and social responsiveness. Physical touch and holding is a direct and convincing way of producing the feeling of being protected from fear and harm; it may very well be an instinctive response, and communication by touch probably preceded verbal communication in evolutionary development. Holding, rocking, and comforting is the natural and very effective way of soothing a frightened child and we calm and reassure frightened animals by touch. John Rarey (McCarthy, 1969) was able to turn a wild, vicious horse into a docile, trusting pet in a couple of hours of petting after he had immobilized him, and he demonstrates this in front of large crowds in the 1850s. Children usually get a good deal of contact comfort, although those who do not suffer in their development; with sexual maturation there is usually a sharp decrease in nonsexual contact from family members, and I hear my college students wistfully recalling how deprived they felt with the change—often associating it with "bad" sexuality. But there remains a strong need for nonsexualized contact comfort in the adult; often sexual contact is substituted for the contact comfort which is missing.

Providing contact comfort is a direct way in which a therapist can show care and closeness; in fact the "inner child" seems to regard comforting noises as not "really" caring—he needs to be "shown" that I care. Touching is much more in the therapeutic *Zeitgeist* now, but it was my college students who first showed me the value. In their groups without me as a leader they would comfort the member who cried—in contrast to my groups which sat impassively or talked when a member was in tears and pain. Watching how effective that was I tried it and have found it to be very powerful.

There must be a genuine feeling in the therapist, since touch is a two-way communication and tension, twitches and stiffness are "read" on an emotional level by the client. The person's fear that he is being offered counterfeit or mechanical affection makes him sensitive to any cues that the therapist's feelings and actions are not harmonious. In general I move in small steps, such as holding hands first and explore with the client how he is feeling and what his fears and anxieties are. Since touching in adults is so closely associated with sexual feeling, I watch for fears of sexual advances and I make clear that the expressions of warmth are limited to what would be appropriate in a family. In case the client is feeling intruded upon or fearful, I may back off, but generally I keep pressing for them to accept physical touch and warmth. When the phobic responses to touch are diminished, it provides great support. I find that men are especially responsive to warmth from me when they get past their cultural taboos; generally boys are not given as much contact by their fathers as they wish or need. I also encourage group members to be physically affectionate, demonstrating by being warm myself, often hugging members. Among my college students in encounter groups, especially the Peer Program, one important gain they frequently mentioned in their final evaluations was that they had learned how to express physical affection in nonsexual situations. While they were as sexual as most college students outside the group, they valued the group expression of physical warmth which was nonsexual—at least in terms of action.

Clients are consistent in their expression of feeling that holding helps them be able to experience the fear and pain. Here are some excerpts from typescripts expressing these feelings:

Client: (After having gone through some painful memories and expressing the hurt and anger in an intense way) Oh, Ben. (sigh) I feel so relieved.
Therapist: "It feels *so* good!"
Client: I don't know how I could look at all those things if I couldn't hold on to you. Holding on to you helps so much.
Therapist: "It really helps to hold on."
Client: It really helps to hold on. It really helps. It feels safe and not so terribly alone. I can look at those things and not be so terribly scared.

Another client, working with her fiance, who was being held at the time, started talking about some painful topics and then said:

Client: (Assertively, to the therapist) I want to get held in the *right* way. (Her partner moved over, and I held her, with my arms around her and her head on my shoulder.)

Therapist: Say, "It's my turn to be held."

Client: It's my turn to be held, I *want* to be held!

Therapist: Say "I need to be held."

Client: I need to be held! (Tears) *I need to be held when I feel all that pain!*

Therapist: Say "It's too much pain without being held!"

Client: *It's too much pain to feel all alone!!!!* (Sobbing so hard she cannot talk)

Therapist: "*Too much pain to feel all alone!* TOO MUCH PAIN TO FEEL ALL ALONE!! IT'S SOOO PAINFUL!!! (I continued repeating this with intense feeling about a dozen more times, while she sobbed hard. Gradually the sobbing subsided.)

Client: It's nice being held. I feel better. Now I can go on with that pain. (She continued on, talking about the painful situation, crying and getting subsequent relief. She had previously discussed the same material, but without discharge of emotion, and with much less resolution.)

Another woman client described her feelings in this sequence:

Client: (Sighed) It feels nice to cling without fear that you will trap me.

Therapist: "Without the fear that you will demand that I give up myself."

Client: Yes! But there is something more. It has something to do with body feelings . . . and with almost . . . getting strength from feeling you. As if it is going right from your body to my body.

Therapist: "I get strength from your body." (Softly)

Client: This is the difference. This is the difference. This is the lost piece of my life between sex and being close to somebody.

Therapist: "Between being close and sex."

Client: Being able to hold on and cling and not be pushed away and not be trapped and not be . . . wanted sexually. It was as if I had to give myself sexually to get the holding. It was as if I had to give myself sexually to get the holding. The only other way I got it was to have all those babies—I could hold them. I needed to be held and not be sexual.

(This is a frequent comment by women, who have wanted to be held, but found they had to either avoid being held by a man because of the pressure to be sexual, or have been sexual in order to get the holding. Both men and women comment on the fear of being held by someone of the same sex because of the fear of the homosexual implications, but find it very comforting when they can accept it as the kind of affection they used to get in their family.)

The first part of this chapter describes the techniques which I have found helpful in psychotherapy, and many of them can be useful to therapists with a variety of theoretical viewpoints. But in my work I have developed a theory of what produces therapeutic change, and this guides how I respond and what kind of behaviors I look for and encourage. I would like to share these observations and theories in the hope they will be useful to other therapists. In general I regard myself as eclectic and I have borrowed from all the major schools; I am not going to try to present these ideas as a coherent theory, but simply describe them as I use them in therapy.

First and foremost, I emphasize feeling and emotion; faced with a choice I will always follow a feeling over a thought. I believe in the concept of emotional re-education, and for it to be re-education, it must be emotional. To be emotional it must show the physiological signs of mid-brain activity—tears, trembling, flushing, muscular activity, heart and breathing activity—all the familiar indices of autonomic response, including the facial expressions of the innate type described by Darwin and the primate ethnologists. Furthermore, I think that emotions are the particular domain of the "inner child," and the re-education of the "child" is the goal. All these notions lead to the idea that the goal of therapy is to free up the expressions of feelings—to get the blocks of natural emotional reactions removed; the more intense and prolonged and repeated the discharge of feeling, the better. This is of course catharsis of feeling—where Freud began; I think he left this procedure too soon. My experience has convinced me that when a person is able to experience and discharge in a controlled but intense way all the old hurts and pains and the new ones occurring daily, he will lose the symptoms and anxieties that limit him. I agree with Janov (1970) that insights follow the discharge of feeling; when the conflicts and pain are experienced directly, they cease to be unconscious. In general I find that it is not necessary to go through the symbolic and fantasy expressions; if one can get in touch with the "inner child" he will experience them without distortion. And I find that I can talk directly to the "child," both with the technique described in "Let the Little Child Talk" (see previous chapter) and with Say It Again when I focus on the "child." When one is in touch with the "child" one does not have to go through symbolic or distorted ideation to find out what the childhood feelings and pain are; one can do therapy with the "child" almost as if one had been able to treat him at five or six years old—getting expression of feeling, breaking past the conflicts, correcting misconceptions, and comforting the hurt feelings. While I speak of the "child" I also deal with the "inner parent" and the difficulties between the "child" and the "parent." It is as if one can get in touch with the personality that existed at five, as well as the adolescent and the adult personality. Actually, I think of there being a family "in the head" of the client: father, mother, "good child," "bad child," etc., and we do family therapy with the people that "live in the head." The key is to get each of these "personalities" to express the feelings directly—and then the synthesis into the whole person occurs. An interesting sidelight: for years I have been having students come up after having read about multiple personalities in psychology books and tell me that they felt like that sometimes; I always assured them that multiple personalities were very rare and that wasn't what they were experiencing. Now I think they were right and I wasn't listening; we are all "multiple personalities"—it just doesn't come out that clearly.

The question of the intensity of the expression of feeling is the central issue. My techniques aim at getting "high voltage" discharge, and when I succeed in getting through the resistances to direct expression, it can be very "high voltage" indeed; one difficulty is that people in the next room find the screaming and wailing disturbing. I am not sure whether it is as deep and intense as Janov's primal scream—his description makes it sound even more intense—but it is usually very intense if it gets going full blast—the "square mouth" of the baby cry, cords in the neck strained, abdominal "beats," etc. Other therapists who seem to be working toward this kind of catharsis are Pesso (1969), Bindrim (1969), Zaslow (1969), Perls (1969), Jackins (1965), and Janov (1970). I believe that we are all finding that repeated, intense discharge produces changes beyond the usual "talking cure." There seems to be a learning process that goes on; a person gradually learns to release feelings, and as he does, he goes deeper and deeper and further back into childhood; there is some kind of desensitization process going on that produces central changes.

Of all the feelings which a person may experience I think the most important one is that of crying—the tearful cry of the hurt child. It is interesting that we have given that emotion little attention; we write about sex and hostility and dependency and fear and maternal drives —but the first and most conspicuous childhood emotion—the tearful cry—hasn't gotten much attention. The natural sequence is for the child to be frightened or hurt, to run crying to an adult for comfort, to sob and cry a while, and then to subside and quickly return to his happy, lively state. If the pain or hurt is not too severe, it seems to be "desensitized" by crying and clinging. Harlow's baby monkeys in a frightening environment persist in huddled misery if left alone; with a mother to cling to—even a cloth one—they soon cease being fearful and become bold. I could not tell from his descriptions whether Rhesus infants show a crying response, but it is clear that if their whimpering is "crying," it does not help if they do it alone. Similarly, I think that a child crying alone does not get the relief from the crying; it has to be crying with an adult or at least another child. This crying response seems to be innate among many mammals—the lonely puppy will persist in piteous cries for hours. Lorenz (1953, p. 34) described a "therapeutic cry" in a dog who had "gone bad" when he had left her. When he returned she recognized him and he describes this scene:

Quite suddenly, Stasi scented me and what now took place I shall never forget; in the midst of a heated onrush, she stopped abruptly and stiffened to a statue. Her mane was still ruffled, her tail down and her ears flat, but her nostrils were wide, wide open, inhaling greedily the message carried by the wind. Now the raised crest subsided, a shiver ran through her body and she pricked up her ears. I expected her to throw herself at me in a burst of joy, but she did not. The mental suffering which had been so severe as to alter the dog's whole personality, causing this most tractable of creatures to forget manners, law and order for months, could not fade into nothingness in a second. Her hind legs gave way, her nose was directed skywards, something happened in her throat and then the mental torture of months found outlet in the hair-raising yet beautiful tones of a wolf's howl. For a long time, perhaps half a minute, she howled, and then, like a thunderbolt, she was upon me. . . . Lucky animal, enviable robustness of the nervous system. A mental trauma whose cause is removed leaves in animal no aftereffects which cannot be healed by a howl of thirty seconds duration.

This description of the "wolf howl" and its therapeutic effect sounds very much like what I observe in therapeutic crying of the "child" in therapy.

However, in most children the natural crying response is typically punished and extinguished. I have consistently had clients report not being allowed to cry; sometimes it was done with "Don't cry; it's not all that bad" or "Be a big brave man and don't cry" or "Go to your room if you have to cry" or, worst or all, "If you don't stop crying I'll give you something to cry about." Also, other children will tease and torment a crying child until he learns to control his tears—and to block the natural, healing response to rejection and pain. Sometimes children learn to go off and cry alone—but crying carried on alone has a very different result than crying and being comforted by an adult—or even a friend. Crying alone leads to "feeling sorry for oneself"—somehow when a person tries to comfort himself it does not work well—especially if there is an "inner parent" scolding him for crying. He has to exaggerate the pain to justify the crying, and the pattern of cultivating the pain and misery to justify the crying is set up.

There are a number of complicated cultural responses for suppressing the childhood cry, but the one that I observe most often is that the crying child threatens to set off the crying child in the adult, and the adult stops the child to protect himself. Also, there is probably some deep instinctive response to a crying child—the kind of response that makes it torture to listen to a neighbor's child wailing for a long time when "sent to his room to cry it out"—and adults try to protect themselves from inner distress by stopping the crying.

In groups members will use all kinds of devices to get the other members to stop crying—because the tears threaten their own control since crying is so contagious. On the other hand, tears usually produce a movement toward the person; the crying member is almost always responded to with warmth and compassion. Of course, tears can be manipulative, but then it is usually anger that needs expression.

These theoretical viewpoints lead me to my therapeutic procedures; I try to get the "child" to cry and to cry out all the old pains and hurts—and this is important—while he is being given physical and emotional comfort. Sitting across the room making supportive noises just doesn't produce the resolution in the client—any more than it would with a tearful five-year-old who yearns to be held but is fearful of rejection. But since crying has been made aversive, there is a conflict. The person will cry and then anticipate rejection—or reject himself with his introjected parent. Instead of comforting himself—or accepting my comfort—he rejects himself and produces more misery. The therapeutic task is to get the client to accept the comfort and to keep on crying—to discharge the hurt with tears, wails, and sobs.

The blocks that get in the way of expressing tears are many, and they have to be worked through. Sometimes anger needs to be expressed first, sometimes fear, sometimes love, but there is usually a sequence of emotions and the aversive anxieties attached to them which have to be expressed. I patiently keep on exploring with Say It Again, watching for the feelings of whatever kind, and then trying to amplify them with the techniques I have described. When the blocks are broken through, there is a catharsis of hurt, grief, fear, and pain —and it should be kept going as long as there is any "steam" behind it. Then come the feelings of relief, joy, and most importantly, love.

This is a crucial point. Much has been written about the need to be loved—and this is important. Much less attention has been paid to the need to love and to have that love accepted. And the blocks to the expression of hurt and pain block the expression of love. I find this a central theme in therapy—the blocks in the loving feelings. Sometimes it is because of fear of their own hate, sometimes in retaliation for being rejected, sometimes because their love was exploited, sometimes because they had their love rejected and thought it was "bad," but always there is some block in the giving of love. Often the child makes a conscious decision to stop loving—later forgotten but not given up—and the guilt about this is very crippling. When this decision is re-experienced, and given up, there is relief and joy—and love.

The sequence of finding the feelings, unblocking them, getting catharsis with tears, crying and being comforted, and then feeling relieved and loving is the usual one. The therapist's task is to stay with the client until he finds a way to get to the feelings and to get them expressed—fully, intensely. Often there is a long build-up, minor expressions, backing off, and then the major conflict and impasse—and then the breakthrough into feeling. The process is much like an animal in an approach-avoidance situation—oscillation and ambivalence—but when the goal-area is reached the ambivalence ceases; the breakthrough of feeling is somewhat like this. Once the person is catharting, when the therapist tries to keep him expressing all the pain and anguish, expressing it to the person for whom it was originally intended as if it were a re-living in the "now" of the past.

When the feelings are discharged, there is a surge of love and warmth; the person is able to give and receive love and affection, and there is an expansion of "self." And the response of the group and the therapist is real and warm and appreciative.

Of course, one discharge does not bring about a cure; it is a slow process of going over and over old pains and hurts, and as one set of traumas and conflicts are desensitized, a new set appears which was beneath the other set. It is a re-learning process, with extinction and spontaneous recovery, but gradually the past pains are desensitized and the person is free to deal with the present and not as some old, unresolved situation.

These theories and techniques don't always work, and when they do it is slow and difficult, but when they work they make significant changes, not just "adjustments." A client recently described her feelings about my therapy in a letter:

> Wherever it is I am going I feel I can get there with you. I have never felt that before. Other therapy has left me feeling that I had to live with sort of crippling, emotionally crippling, 'sets' inside myself which I couldn't break through. Just understand and live with. But now I have the feeling of a new way—my right way for me. I feel exhausted and very relieved. But the session was so *good*! And when I get this internalized, I'll leap through life!

DEMONSTRATION SESSION WITH BRENDA

Typescript	Explanatory Remarks
Brenda, you said you would be willing to be a candidate for this; we are going to explore how you are feeling and where you're at today. Would you like to go on down? And can you tell us where you are now? *Brenda:* Yes. Okay.	We had talked about this before and she had said she would like to be a subject for a demonstration. My only concern was that feeling that she might want to "do well" would get in her way and put pressure on her. Lack of pressure is important for SIA to work well.

Finney: Brenda volunteered; she has done this with me before. My only reservations with you are, sometimes when you want to go, you try too hard, and you jam—we stop. I would like to just do a floating one, and see where it goes. (Brenda lies down on the floor, I sit with her head in my lap holding her hand, everyone "plugs in," touches her some way, and communication is established between members of the group, and Brenda.) "Checking out."

The permission to back off if she felt "jammed up" is important. The process of getting the group "plugged in" and for Brenda to check around to see if she is feeling trusting is important. The feelings between her and the group are important and need consideration. Also, it is important for other group members to touch her and to be actively empathetic. When the person "down" gets to childhood pain, it stirs up the "inner child" in other members. If the "child" doesn't get to feel the feelings empathetically, the person often ends up blocked and upset, but to feel "with" the person is releasing.

Finney: Your hand is saying nice warm things.

Brenda: It feels good.

Finney: Say, I trust you.

Brenda: I trust you, Ben.

Finney: I trust you, Ben.

Brenda: I don't know the others around as closely, but I do trust you.

Finney: I don't know other people here really closely, but I do trust you. Say I am willing to kind of go

Her first communication was by touch; I picked it up and translated what I thought I "felt."

This is a prompt; what I felt she was saying with her looks and touch. She accepted it and repeated it.

A repeat of her new addition about the other members, plus a prompt about ahead with you, feeling my trust with you is okay . . .

her willingness to go ahead based on her trust of me.

Brenda: My trust with you is okay . . .

Finney: My trust with you is okay . . . Repeat . . .

Brenda: My trust with you is okay . . . and it's been a long time coming.

Finney: And it's been a long time coming . . . deeper.

A repeat, but with an important addition "it's been a long time coming"; an emotional statement summarizing a lot of therapeutic work.

Brenda: It's been a long time . . .

Finney: A long time to be able to trust this much . . .

Brenda: It's been a long time to be able to trust this much . . . It's been a long time to be able to trust this much . . .

"To trust this much" is a significant addition — bringing it back to "here and now" and a positive feeling. I did not pick this up; better if I had.

Finney: Deeper.

Brenda: It's been really a long time.

Finney: It's been *really* a long time. Say I *like* being able to trust this much.

Now I go back and pick up the "like being able to trust this much."

Brenda: I like being able to trust this much.

Finney: I like being able to trust this much.

Brenda: Feels good . . .

"Feels good" tells me that she is moving; adding new phrases expressing feelings moving.

Finney: Feels good.

Brenda: Yeah . . .

Finney: I like being able to trust this much; it feels good.

Note how I repeat each phrase—sort of give it a push to strengthen the momentum.

Brenda: My trusting goes out from that.

Repeating and letting the feelings build; each repeating lowers the threshold for new feelings.

Finney: My trusting goes out from that.

Brenda: I'm able to trust a lot more things.

Finney: I'm able to trust a *lot* more things.

Note I "amplify" the feeling with my voice underlining the amount.

Brenda: Than I used to be able to do.

Finney: I'm able to trust a lot more things than I used to be able to. And it comes from the trusting.

A repeat that picks up both the old reluctance and the new trusting.

Brenda: Yeah . . .

Finney: Deeper.

Brenda: Trusting . . . It's lonely not trusting.

The word *deeper* is an urging to go further and deeper.

Finney: It's *lonely* not trusting.

Brenda: It's lonely not trusting . . .

Now the new addition—"it's lonely not trusting"; I emphasize the new feeling, "lonely."

Finney: Deeper . . .

Brenda: It's lonely not trusting.

Finney: I've spent a lot of lonely times not trusting . . .

This is a prompt based on my knowledge of her past experience.

Brenda: I've spent a long time lonely . . .

Finney: I've spent a long time lonely and not trusting . . .

Brenda: Lonely inside myself.

Now she moves it to express that the loneliness is *inside* her.

Finney: Lonely inside myself. Keep it going . . .

Brenda: Lonely inside myself and . . .

Finney: Pushing people away . . .

A prompt based on other information.

Brenda: Yeah . . .

Finney: Pushing people away, and . . .

Brenda: Pushing people away, and going away.

Note she adds "going away"; that tells me she made the prompt her own and added to it. An important cue that shows we are working together.

Finney: And, going away . . . deeper . . .

Brenda: Pushing people away and going away. Going away deep inside . . .

Finney: Going away deep inside . . . say deep inside me . . .

Note I move it to "deep" inside *"me"* a bit more personal.

Brenda: Deep inside me where it's lonely.

Finney: Lonely, and it's dark in here . . .

A prompt, "dark in here," that was part intuitive and part based on knowledge that she used to go to her room and cry in the dark.

Brenda: It's lonely, and it's dark in here.

Finney: It's lonely, dark, and there's no one there . . .

Brenda: There's no one there . . .

Finney: And, there's no one there, Ben . . .

An addition that keeps her in touch with the fact she is talking to me; I don't want her "going away and being lonely" in this immediate situation.

Brenda: I don't know where anything is in there . . .

Finney: And I don't know where anything is way in there . . .

Brenda: I'm afraid to breathe . . .

A new introduction of a feeling.

Finney: I'm afraid to breathe? . . .

Brenda: I'm afraid to breathe . . . I wont't breathe.

Finney: I won't breathe . . . Again.

"I won't breathe" says a lot; some a recall of being forced to take ether which we have been through before; some a statement about not letting herself feel.

Brenda: I won't breathe.

Finney: (Hand over mouth) I won't breathe so . . . I won't breathe so . . go on . . . I won't breathe so . . .

Brenda: You can't make me . . .

Now the "little child" is beginning to speak. She moved there spontaneously; but other people will move there if one picks up the statements or feelings of the "child"—often without direct comment.

Finney: You can't make me . . . go on . . . feel a feeling . . .

Finney: I won't, you can't make me . . . you can't make me breathe it . . . Feel it . . . feel a feeling, follow it on down . . . Go on, what's the feeling . . . let it come, let it come, let it come . . .

Now I am urging her to go back and relive the feelings; the "old" feelings are beginning to surface. And "old" feelings can only be changed by present reality if they are vividly experienced simultaneously with the "now" experience.

Brenda: You made me die.

This is the "child" talking; both about the fear of dying she had in her operation for tonsils at seven and the "dying" of her feelings.

Finney: You made me die . . . I won't breathe, you'll make me die. You want to kill me . . . I'll die . . . You're going to kill me I'll die . . . keep it going . . . *Don't*, say DON'T . . . louder. Don't, don't, don't . . .

Now I am pushing hard for the feelings of being afraid of being killed and the protest against it. Note my activity—also trying to get her to say what she didn't then or what was punished then.

Brenda: I won't breathe . . . I won't yell . . .

This is an important "decision" "I won't yell"—one she has kept all her life—holding back her feelings of protest.

Finney: I won't yell . . . I won't yell . . . Say it . . . I promise I won't yell.

Brenda: I won't yell . . . I promise I won't yell.

Finney: Say it with more feeling . . .

Brenda: I promise I won't yell . . . just leave me alone . . . Don't . . . don't leave me alone . . .

Another important "emotional decision"—"just leave me alone." But note the crucial shift "Don't leave me alone"—the child who rejects the love of the adults—and the control—and still doesn't want to be left alone.

Finney: Don't leave me alone. There it is. Don't leave me alone . . . *Please* don't leave me alone . . .

Brenda: It's too scary . . .

Finney: Please don't leave me alone, it's too scary.

I am following and emphasizing these feelings strongly; they are coming clearer in this session than I have heard them before.

Brenda: I don't want to be left alone. If I cry they'll leave me alone, I can't cry . . .

The fear she will be left alone because she cries; coming from her father's criticism of her crying.

Finney: Say it, I can't cry . . . then maybe they won't leave me alone . . . Daddy's going away because I yelled . . . Daddy's going away because I made too much noise . . . Say it . . .

An important prompt; I knew this "event" but what to get it more into feelings.

Brenda: He left me . . .

Finney: He left me because I made too much noise . . .

Brenda: I was too noisy . . .

Finney: They'll never know . . . what I think, and what I die . . . they'll never know and they'll hurt . . . they'll hurt . . .

A prompt moving her toward saying the rejection and anger behind her not crying. Note how she picks it up promptly.

Brenda: And I'll hurt them . . .

Finney: I'll hurt them . . . I'll hurt them and they'll hurt . . .

Brenda: They'll never touch me again.

Note she adds the not touching; a cue that we are moving and developing new material.

Finney: They'll never touch me again . . . I'll never *let* them touch me again . . . Deeper . . .

Brenda: If they can't be there when I need them . . .

The anger and retaliation by pulling back her love; this pattern is an important one.

Finney: If they can't be there when I need them, I'll never let them touch me again . . . Deeper . . .

Brenda: I want to be held . . .

Now the other side; the wish to be held; note how I follow that—shifting with her.

Finney: I want to be held . . .

Brenda: I wanted to be held, but they wouldn't hold me . . .

An important emotional statement; referring to a specific event and also stating a whole lot of events.

Finney: But they wouldn't hold me . . . follow it . . . I wanted to be held . . . Again . . .

Brenda: It's the back seat of the car . . . and I'm back there . . .

Now she makes it specific; a traumatic event of great significance.

Finney: It's the back seat of the car . . . there you are . . . I'm back there and . . . what?

Brenda: Cry . . .

Note I try and get her to re-experience that as if she were there.

Finney: I cry . . .

Brenda: My throat hurts . . . my dad gets mad . . .

Finney: Your dad gets mad . . . What does he say?

Note I keep it, "What does he say?" not, "What did he say?"

Brenda: He says he'll let me out . . .

Finney: He'll let me out . . . he says he'll throw me out of the car . . . If I don't shut up he'll make me get out of the car . . . Is that right?? Keep it going . . .

I keep it going by amplifying and keeping it in "first person"; passive listening would not be enough here.

Brenda: The dog's up there . . .

Finney: The dog's up front . . . Dog's up front . . . but I'm not . . .

The feeling that the dog gets more love; note my addition "but I'm not." It was implicit but I made it explicit.

Brenda: He'll bite me . . .

Finney: He'll bite me if I go up front . . .

Now the fear comes out— and the protective defensiveness.

Brenda: So I'll move all the suitcases and make my own place . . .

Finney: I'll build all these suitcases up, and I'll make my own place . . .

I repeat this important emotional decision—"I'll make my own place."

Brenda: Myself and my doll . . .

Finney: For myself and my doll . . . myself and my doll.

She adds the doll—telling me she is moving; these little additions are important cues.

Brenda: But they took my doll away . . .

Finney: But they took my doll away . . . there it is . . . there it is . . . They took my doll away . . . deeper. They took my doll away! All I had, and they took my doll away . . .

My repeats amplify the anger and anguish.

Brenda: But they didn't take my thumb away . . .

Finney: But they didn't take my thumb away . . . they took my doll away, and the only thing they left me was my thumb . . . and they didn't like that . . .

Brenda: He hit me . . . and tell me I'll die . . .

Finney: He hit me and tell me I'll die if I put my thumb in my mouth.

Brenda: That's all I have.

Finney: That's all I have . . . just my thumb . . .

Brenda: They didn't have to hit me . . .

Finney: They didn't have to hit me . . . they didn't have to take my doll away . . . they didn't have to do those things . . . deeper . . . there's pain there . . . It blocks right there . . . keep at it . . . keep at it . . . they took my doll away. They tell me I can't sit in the front seat, and if I such my thumb . . . I'll get sick.

Brenda: I won't need them anymore . . .

Finney: I won't need them anymore . . . I'll never need them again . . . let your chin say it more . . . Go on . . .

Now the rebellion; "I still have that."

My repeat amplifies that anguish and the feeling of being left with nothing to comfort her.

At this point I personally was feeling her anguish and the tragic misunderstanding going on very strongly; my voice and gestures were sending this strongly.

Repeating and prompting to get her to express this pain with all the intensity it deserves; such a painful situation deserves screaming and yelling. I am keeping it going by prompting and re-running things she has said before.

And now the tragic "decision" she made to cope with her pain and threat: "I'll never need them anymore"—a decision which has caused her much suffering and isolation since then.

Brenda: I won't need them anymore . . . but it hurts . . .

Finney: But it hurts. There it is . . . shake your head and say I won't need them anymore but it hurts . . .

Now she says the pain that goes with the decision "but it hurts." A crucial step for her.

Brenda: That's the hurt . . .

Finney: That's where it hurts . . . There's where the hurt is.

We are working with very central pain here—emotional positions that are gradually shifting for Brenda.

Brenda: I punished them, but I punished me . . .

Finney: I punished them, but I punished me, and that's where the hurt is.

Brenda: I punished them, but I hurt me.

Finney: I punished them, but I hurt me . . . Deeper.

This is the first time I have heard her clearly say and accept her responsibility for her cutting off her feelings. Before it was, "they left me"; now she is accepting "I punished them and it hurt me." A big step.

Brenda: I didn't know how much I'd hurt me . . .

Finney: I didn't know how much I'd hurt me . . .

A recognition of how tragic were the consequences of her decision as a child. And recognizing that she made this decision and that it hurt her.

Brenda: I left me all alone.

Finney: I left me all alone . . .

I "echo" and emphasize that very crucial feeling.

Brenda: All alone and empty inside . . .

Finney: All alone and empty inside . . . Now cry out to them . . . I need you so much . . . I need you so much

Now I am pushing her to break her old resolution—to say and feel the need—

... Break it ... I need you so much ... I know it's hard ... Break it ... I need you so much ... Say it.

Brenda: Mommy, I need you ...

Finney: Mommy, I need you ... deeper ... mommy I want you ...

Brenda: Mommy I want you ...

Finney: Louder ... Mommy I want you ...

Brenda: Where's my mommy?

Finney: Where's my mommy?. . . There it is ... Where's my mommy? I want my mommy ...

Brenda: I want my mommy and my daddy ...

Finney: I want my mommy and my daddy ...

Brenda: Let me have them ...

Finney: Let me have them . . . Please.

Brenda: I don't want to be all alone.

Finney: I don't want to be all alone ... please. I'm lonely and I'm scared ... Your arm says I don't care, don't let it ... hang on tighter.

to give up the "turning away" and to feel and say the need for love and care.

Note the "Mommy"—it says the child is talking; very significantly.

Now she has moved back to the hospital and the loss there.

The poignant pleas of the child left in a strange place, frightened and feeling rejected.

Note that I am reading her body gestures; urging her to hold on to me tighter.

Brenda: When I can't hide, I get scared . . .

Finney: When I can't hide I get scared . . . When I can hide I'm not so scared.

Brenda: When I hide I'm not so scared . . . but I'm lonely . . .

Finney: I want my mommy . . .

Brenda: I want my mommy . . . and then she could put her arms around me and tell me it's OK . . . And I don't have to be scared . . .

The plea for her mommy; now I am holding her, offering some of the care that she didn't get then; comforting the child inside.

Finney: And I don't have to be scared . . .

Brenda: She'll come and put her arms around me . . .

Finney: She'll come and . . .

Brenda: She won't do it!

The ambivalence. The wish and the fear it won't happen. And probably this sequence was repeated many times in her life.

Finney: She won't do it . . . and I need her . . .

Note I pick up the need.

Brenda: I need her . . .

Finney: I need her . . . Mommy I need my mommy . . . Deeper . . .

Brenda: Why did you leave me . . .

Finney: Why did you leave me . . .

Brenda: Why did she leave?

Finney: Why did she leave me . . . Deeper . . . more pain.

Brenda: She doesn't like me . . .

Finney: She doesn't like me . . . I don't know where she is . . .

Brenda: I don't know where she is . . . It's dark here . . . I just want someone to hold me . . .

Finney: (Putting arms around Brenda) You just want someone to hold you . . . You need someone to put their arms around you . . . Does that feel better?

Brenda: I'm scared . . . I won't ask too much . . .

Finney: It's all right to be scared . . . Your mommy and your daddy . . . the hospital told them to go away . . . They're outside waiting . . . the hospital told them . . . They want to come . . . They don't know how scared you are . . . Your mommy and your daddy really do love you . . . They really do love you . . . And when your daddy was upset with you in the back seat of the car, he really didn't mean it . . . He was just upset . . . The hospital didn't know how very scared you were . . . (To Big Brenda) Now wait a minute . . . I don't want you to come back too fast . . . I want you to listen to what I'm saying . . . Did you hear what I said? (Big Brenda has taken over. I'm not

A child needs some explanation. If she doesn't get one from an adult, she makes one up. I'm sure that the hospital told her parents to go away, and that they were concerned. But it didn't get through to her, so she made up the explanation "They didn't love me." Now I help by explaining. This sequence in the face of unexplained loss is very typical: first, "You are bad for leaving me," then, "I will be good; don't leave me," and then the damaging assumption, "They don't love me: I'm no good."

I put my arm around her; giving her some comfort now for the child who is feeling the pain. Then I talk to "Little Brenda," trying to explain to her what should have been explained to her then—or what was unexplainable then but which might be acceptable now with the help of "Big Brenda." This technique of having me— or better "Big Brenda" explain to "Little Brenda" what was happening back then is often very effective.

sure we are finished, but I let her decide.)

Brenda: Yeah ...

Finney: Did Little Brenda hear what I said?

Brenda: Yeah ...

Finney: Did Little Brenda believe in what I'm saying?

Brenda: Yeah ... pause ...

Finney: Little Brenda: do you believe me?

Brenda: Yeah, I guess so ...

Finney: Do you let me comfort you ...

Brenda: Yeah ... It feels good.

Finney: It feels good ... deeper ...

Brenda: It feels really good. It really felt good.

(Note that despite "Little Brenda's reluctance," she is accepting it, and the comforting is getting through, as well as the good feelings of being able to express the pain and anger without being shut off. We will need to go through this again and again, but there were some significant shifts today.)

The "adult" can learn to comfort the "child" and introduce new reality into her fears—including the reality that she did not die and her parents did return. But of course these "events" also express some emotional "realities" a bit differently.

Note the important "decisions" which have appeared and which the "child" has made some steps toward giving up. Since the "child" made the decisions, only the "child" can give them up; as long as these decisions remain unchanged they influence harmfully current adult behavior. The comforting at this point is not disrupting or deflecting; rather it supports and expresses care in a way the child believes— especially Brenda—whose parents "told me they loved me but never showed me by hugging me."

The depth of involvement of the group reflected the power of the emotional feelings being expressed. Checking around the group later was an important step. I find direct physical affection is helpful—just as I would with a real five-year-old. This is child therapy—twenty-five years later—but just as effective now to help "Little Brenda" understand and accept and give up her hurtful decisions.

REFERENCES

Bindrim, P. *Peak-oriented Psychotherapy.* Los Angeles: the author, 1966 (200 Cantata Dr.)

Finney, B. "Let the Little Child Talk: A New Psychotherapeutic Technique," *American Journal of Psychotherapy,* 23 (1969), 230-242.

Gilot, F. and C. Lake. *Life with Picasso.* New York: McGraw-Hill, 1965.

Jackins, H. *Basic Postulates of Re-evaluation Counseling.* Seattle: Rational Island Publishers, 1965. (P.O. Box 2081, Main Office Station, Seattle 98111)

Janov, A. *The Primal Scream.* New York: Putnam's Sons, 1970.

Lorenz, K. *Man Meets Dog.* Baltimore: Penguin Books, 1953.

McCarthy, T. "The Man Who Could Talk to Horses," *American Heritage,* 20 (1969), 3, 58.

Perls, F. S. *Gestalt Therapy Verbatim.* Moab, Utah: Real People Press, 1969.

Pesso, A. *Movement in Psychotherapy.* New York: New York University Press, 1969.

Zaslow, R. "A Theory of Infantile Autism and Its Implications for the Treatment of Behavior Disorders in Children," in L. Breger (ed.), *Cognitive Clinical Psychology.* Englewood Cliffs, N.J.: Prentice Hall, 1969.

CHAPTER 16

THOU ART THAT:
PROJECTION AND PLAY
IN THERAPY AND GROWTH

JOHN B. ENRIGHT, Ph.D.

John B. Enright is in private practice in Corte Madera, California, and is a staff member of the San Francisco Gestalt Institute. Previously he was a psychologist with the Langley Porter Institute in San Francisco, and assistant professor of medical psychology, UCLA Medical School.

Reprinted by permission from John B. Enright, "Thou Art That: Projection and Play in Therapy and Growth," **Psychotherapy: Theory, Research, and Practice**, Vol. 8, 1971, pp. 338-341.

"You're projecting!" is a frequent comment in therapy and encounter groups. Whatever else the response to this ploy, it is usually valid to say, "Of course." The practice of experiencing my own feeling or potential for action as being the property of someone or something "out there" instead of my own is universal. Sick or well, we all do it frequently; the "sick" differ only in doing it more tenaciously.

The purpose of this note is to describe a method of harnessing this basic human process; instead of wasting energy opposing it or criticizing it, to "go with it" as an exercise that can enhance awareness and develop feelings and perceptions more vividly. It is not a new technique. Artists—particularly Japanese sumi painters—have used it for centuries. I have run into it as a parlor game, and even seen it referred to in a *Reader's Digest* article. Fritz Perls developed some variations at some length in *Gestalt Therapy*.[1] Somehow, however, therapists and group leaders have overlooked its simplicity and power. I have used this method perhaps a hundred times in an extensive way, and in a partial way many more, and feel ready to present some concrete instances of its use, and a few of the endless number of possible variations.

In a therapy or encounter group, I usually introduce the exercise during a pause or break by suggesting that each person look around the room and pick an object that stands out vividly for him. Everyone then spends a couple minutes working by himself *identifying* with his object, i.e., making statements as though he *were* the object; describing it, but saying "I" instead of "it." When most seem to have stopped this process I suggest that everyone go back into the exercise and say one or two more things. More often than not, the point of stopping is just when the person is getting close to something particularly interesting. Almost always, a few people in the group get quite excited by what they have run into, and share their projections with the group. Surprisingly strong feeling and involvement is developed within a minute or two by the exercise; this can happen even in first meetings of groups up to 200 in size. A woman, for instance, identifying with a beam in the ceiling, became very distressed as she heard herself say, as the beam, "I'm very old fashioned and uselessly ornate . . . I have a heavy load to bear . . . and I'm not getting very much help; the nearest other beam is a long way away, and I have to carry this part of the load alone." Being close to tears, she asked to stop at that point, but an hour or so later was able to report many important connections with, and some new realizations about, her present life situation. Another woman, identifying with a bright colored section of the wall became quite depressed and cried when she realized that she, as the wall, was unfinished at the top. She had the courage to stay with this painful perception, and within a few minutes was joyful over the fact that this gap actually left her free to grow and be finished in her own way. A man, identifying with a loudspeaker, commented that although he talked a lot, he initiated nothing, but only passed on what other said. I always do the exercise along with the group, frequently with quite involving results for myself. On one occasion, I was not enjoying a group I was working with and rather resented being there. I "happened" to choose a large candleholder, and the following sentences came popping out: "I'm beautiful and sturdy, but have no candle at present; I'm empty. My job is to give light, but I'm not doing it right now." When the group and I stopped laughing, I was freer to get down to work without resentment or distraction.

If the reader has not stopped and tried this experiment already, I suggest doing so; however there is something about the enhancing effect of a group, and seeing someone else use the method well, that makes a group a better setting in which to begin. It is not possible to convey verbally how intense and involving this simple exercise often becomes.

Frequently, when a person begins to "run down" it is possible to manipulate his object or the situation in some way to keep the flow going. One woman, working with a pot with a lid, kept emphasizing how heavy and tightly closed her lid was. I reached over and touched the lid, intending to lift it. In a panic, she leaped on me, and tore my hand off the top; For a moment she really was that pot, and no shrink was going to get *her* lid off! A furled flag can be unfurled, a chair sat upon, a light dimmed or brightened, while a person is identifying with it, and dramatic changes in affect and perception may result.

After a few people have shared their projections, we often begin to run into the "rehearsal" effect: those who have waited too long lose some of the spontaneity of their choice. At this point, I often bring out a box of toy figures and objects, and suggest that people come up one at a time as they feel ready, select one that stands out, and work with it. Since they do not see the objects until after committing themselves to work, rehearsal is not possible. Any toy or object is a candidate for the box[2] I continually have to replenish it, as people frequently ask to keep a figure that was particularly meaningful. Again, the variety of response to these stimulus figures is endless. My favorite is still the sour and self-critical man with a toy buffalo. Suddenly as the buffalo, he was strong, noble and protective of his herd. After a pause he noticed a small bit of plastic sticking to the rear leg and commented, "Even my shit is useful; the Indians dry it and use it for fuel." A woman using a toy gorilla was describing her strength until she noticed a slight defect in the back, and gasped with horror, "I'm wounded!" and went into a very intense death fantasy.

These last examples point up a crucial way in which this method differs from most fantasy and dream techniques. The object provides a recurrent "nudge" into areas that might not emerge in pure fantasy. As person B observes A working with his object, it is obvious to B that A is selecting quite idiosyncratically from the possibilities of the object, missing some "obvious" features, and choosing very peculiar ones that B would never have dreamed of. Person A, however, experiences himself not as choosing, but as being compelled and pulled by what truly seem to him the objective features of the object. He can resist saying what he sees if he feels disturbed or threatened, but he does not feel a choice in seeing it. The subjective experience of doing the identification experiment has been compared with being on a roller coaster; once on it, you go the route, with all its twists and turns and ups and downs. Frequently, after a glance at his object, a person will cease looking at it, and instead work with his fantasy of the object—looking away or closing his eyes as he works. Thus one man, as a toy sports car, was going on about how flashy and elegant he was. Noticing he was looking off into space as he talked, I suggested he get back to simple description. As soon as he again began looking at his toy, he seemed startled, and started talking soberly about all his nicks and scratches, and wondering if he had been in an accident.

When a person begins to slow down in his identification process, there are many ways to renew the flow, usually growing out of the particular way he has talked up to that point. I may suggest he say something to the group as his animal or object, or perhaps wave my magic wand and allow him to make one change for the better in himself as the object. If a person comes to hate the object (himself), I may suggest he choose another, and then create a dialogue between the two. Many times, a person becomes fascinated with another's choice; he may pick up and carry on when the first person has finished. On a few occasions, the whole group has worked in turn with the same object. Very quickly, the group members learn not to speak up when someone else is working, recognizing that their perceptions, completely valid for them, can only be an interruption for someone else. In one group the phrase, "that's *your* gorilla, not mine" became a shorthand term for telling a person not to confuse his process with another's—in the current slang, not to lay his trip on someone else.

Several times, after most people have worked individually, group members have begun to interact from their toy object roles. This has led to very humorous and unlikely but quite productive confrontations. (I was amazed how much a golf ball and a scorpion had to say to each other.) Long standing group problems have been solved in minutes with this exercise. One quite firm, independent woman had stayed on the fringe during all her time in the group, and people had given up pointing this out and trying to reach her. She chose a toy Mack truck, and was very pleased with her strength and ability to carry a heavy load. Then she noticed her cab had room for only one person. Her distress and loneliness stimulated by this perception were so touching that several people in the group opened up to her, and her relation to the group underwent a permanent change. Another time, two alligators had a forty-five minute conversation about life in the swamp. One emphasized how powerful and dangerous she was; the other, how vulnerable—alligator shoes being popular then. The assumptions of these two people about life and themselves became clearer than hours of ordinary conversation could have made them.

The above examples are only a few of the possible ways to develop this method in group work. Others keep spontaneously happening; there seems no limit to a group's creativity. Besides suggesting innovations and variations in this exercise, about all the leader has to do is make sure people stay in the identification mode. Slipping into referring to the toy as "it," or making a statement that assumes a point of view outside of it are resistances that must be pointed out—

or at times, in Gestalt style, accepted as a message from the whole person that he feels threatened and wants to stop working.

The technique is harder to introduce in individual work, but can be equally powerful there. One rigid, compulsive woman with a miserable marriage was once an uncharacteristic five minutes late to a session. She had been so taken by seeing some seals play by the beach that she had stopped to watch. As she described them, I suggested saying "I." Within a minute she was in tears, as she touched the long-buried, thought-to-be-dead, playful part of herself. The seals became a touchstone of therapy for her. Many times as she described some miserable impasse, I had only to ask, "What would a seal do in this situation?" and she knew immediately how to free herself from her self-limitations.

Not surprisingly, some people "click" with this method more than others. Those for whom it works well often begin to use it at home and in the world as a way of tuning in and finding what is going on with them. Thus one chronically depressed lady became aware how frequently she was noticing the lily growing out of her compost heap, as she worked in her garden. Realizing this was a good time for the identification exercise, she began with, "I am a lily growing out of a garbage heap. . . ." The feelings of hope and renewed life she got in touch with heralded a real shift for the better in her mood. I use the technique constantly myself to find out what is going on; and not just for "information," but because the awareness breakthroughs are often intensely pleasurable and rich. As a side effect, I find myself far more responsive to nature and poetry than I was before.

I have at this point no elaborate theory about what happens in this process. In myself I note that what seems to come out when the experiment works well is a feeling-ideation complex that has been developing strength and pressing for awareness. (Often I have been quite restless just before trying the experiment.) The object, the perception "out there," becomes an organizing focus for this complex of feelings. I saw my distressing feelings of deadness and sterility first as a tree branch, broken off in a storm, and another time my feelings of increasing focus and direction as those of the leading goose in a migrating flock overhead. As him, "I always know what direction I have to go in; nothing can turn me the wrong way." The sense of pleasure and relief at this complex emerging into awareness is very strong, even when the feeling is a negative one in some way. Paradoxically, I have found that if people keep "trying" to make connections of self and object as they work, the experiment remains superficial. The more totally I can lose myself in the object, the more deeply I find myself at the end.

In addition to the individual gains in awareness through this method there are some very positive side effects on the quality of group interaction and process. A group that has shared this experience a few times often develops a vivid and metaphoric "in-language." ("There's your damned elephant again.") That is quite expressive and exciting, and even those individuals who don't happen to work well with this technique are affected by this energy. As people get in touch with hitherto dormant and buried parts of themselves they become more vivid and differentiated to others, and less locked into their social roles. Even bitterly antagonistic spouses who are usually far too defensive and frightened to listen to each other in ordinary discourse, find they can hear each other empathically when the partner is deeply into a project. In some groups, that "that's *your* gorilla" experience has generalized. Somehow, as a person works intently with the gorilla it becomes possible for me, the observer, to know deeply that he is *really seeing* what he says, and that it is *really different* from what I see; he is not simply describing ineptly the "objective reality" that I can see so clearly. We really are different, and that is okay. A by-product of this realization has occasionally been the ability to let another person be. Most of us reserve the right to judge another constantly when he is expressing himself in language or social behavior. We feel quite free to say, "What you really mean is . . ." or "You should . . ." When he is deeply involved in expressing himself in the identification exercise, however, it is clearly intrusive and irrelevant for me to say, "But this object is really . . ." or "Your gorilla should . . ." Learning to let him be in this domain sometimes generalizes, and it can give him the ultimate human gift of letting him be, in his uniqueness, in life as well.

For me, however, the greatest effect of this exercise on a group is simply the overall sense of excitement and playfulness the method generates. The realization that fun can be profound, and profundity fun; that we can laugh till we cry and cry till we laugh in the same few minutes; that knowledge of a highly useful sort can be generated by such light-hearted sport helps a group move rapidly away from a heavy, problem-centered orientation toward something much more rich and full. The split between "learning" and "living"—so frequent in life as well as in groups—is well on its way to being healed by this attitude. It hardly matters what else a group does if it can achieve that integration.

NOTES

1. Perls, F. S., R. F. Hefferline, and P. Goodman. *Gestalt Therapy*. New York: Julian Press, 1951.

2. On one occasion, a psychologist became quite excited by this technique when it was presented as a seminar. Having no time to get to a toy store, as his group met in the following hour, he used the objects from a Stanford-Binet kit, with good results.

CHAPTER 17

THE GESTALT APPROACH TO EXPERIENCE, ART, AND ART THERAPY

JANIE RHYNE

Janie Rhyne is presently a faculty member of the Humanistic Psychology Institute, San Francisco, and of the University of California, Santa Cruz. She is also a staff member of the San Francisco Gestalt Institute. She is the pioneer of Gestalt art therapy, developing this approach in work with children and adults in a number of schools and hospitals.

Reprinted from Janie Rhyne, **The Gestalt Art Experience**. Copyright © 1973 by Wadsworth Publishing Company, Inc. Reprinted by permission of Brooks/Cole Publishing Company, Monterey, California.

The word *gestalt* is German and has no exact equivalent in English. *Form, figure, pattern, structure,* and *configuration* are possible translations, but none is quite right, so we have adopted *gestalt* into English and bandy it about quite a bit in various contexts.

I bandy the word about in the context of the art experience. There is gestalt psychology and Gestalt Therapy, and there is the gestaltist's way of perceiving himself and others—a way of being, acting, and integrating experience. The premises of gestalt philosophy most relevant to the art experience seem so natural and so consistent with my attitudes that I find it hard to distinguish between what are gestalt tenets and what are my own personal apprehensions of how we human beings become and are.

Healthy children are naturally gestaltists—they live in the present, give full attention to what they are doing, do what they want to do, trust their own experiential data, and, until they are trained out of it, they know what they know with direct simplicity and accuracy.

Most of us are not allowed to grow up naturally, to learn through experience, to add to our knowledge without losing our naive wisdom: our parents, teachers, and culture coerce us into conforming to the accepted standards of how we should feel, think, and do. With varying degrees of stubbornness we resist and then gradually put away our own individual sensibilities and accept our educators' ideas about what a person ought to be. During this process we are forced to deny much of what we know to be true about our own nature. We want approval and acceptance. Most of us, by the time we are considered adult and mature, have forgotten how to be ourselves. We remember just enough of what being ourselves feels like to be afraid of it. Our fear keeps up in a state of tension or deadness so we spend most of our lifetime performing instead of living and use most of our energy denying our fear of knowing ourselves and each other deeply and wholly.

Gestaltists offer ways to get through this wall of fear—we seek ways to recognize what we have hidden away—and to integrate our disowned parts into our total personality. We work to break through the barriers separating our authentic selves from the artificial roles we play. This isn't easy to do since we assumed these roles (probably during childhood) for defense, praise, attention, avoidance, or power.

Perhaps as children we knew we were only pretending to act in a certain way to get whatever it was we needed or wanted, but when the pretense was successful, we continued to play that game until we fooled even ourselves into believing that our phoniness was genuine.

Now we are adults, supposedly mature and functioning adequately, but with sneaking suspicions that we are not what we seem to be; that if we aren't careful, other people will see through our game—or worse yet, that we ourselves will realize how trite and shoddy is the show we put on.

When some situation in living forces our secret self-doubts out into the open, we have alternatives: we can commit suicide; we can find another self-delusion; we can continue the same boring games, knowing that we are dead; or we can begin the courageous search for finding in ourselves what is genuine. We can learn to give up falseness and grow into realness.

Some people say that change from phony-self to authentic-self can happen quickly and completely in some situations. Maybe, but I am dubious.

For me and for people with whom I share this experience of un-learning and regrowth, I find this a process rather than a happening. We are active in the process, individually responsible for finding our various ways of re-creation of ourselves. No one way is *the* way.

For myself I choose a variety of ways, but the most effective for me is to use art materials to make images that not only allow me to re-discover some of the simple, naive wisdom of the child that I was, but also provide me with a visual imagery that evokes associations, resonances, and insights that are available to me if I just take the time to become aware of them. If I make a drawing of my fantasies, I can see them, I can read my messages, I can learn; I can integrate my past childhood with my present and with visions of my future. I think of my expressive drawings as sources of learning serving me somewhat as my dreams do. These are different from the dreams I experience during sleep but alike in that both kinds of imagery can provide a path not only into the suppressed feelings of me as a child but also into present recognition of what I need and want now. They show how I, as a mature person, can bring all of these realizations together into a pattern of my own gestalt, whose every part is related to the total configuration that is me—past, present, future—and they show that I and my environment are ever-changing and ever-interacting.

DEFINITION OF TERMS

Recently the term *gestalt* has been applied to so many kinds of activities that it seems to have become a sort of mumbo-jumbo magic password to get some people onto a popular bandwagon. I am glad that a gestaltist approach is widely accepted now; I am sorry when it is sold by a traveling medicine man who spiels his formula as a panacea—cheap to buy, easy to take, and guaranteed to cure whatever ails you. I regret this presentation not only because it is false but also because the patented, sold-in-a-bottle, come-on pitch turns many truly thoughtful people away from seeing and knowing for themselves the genuine substance of gestalt psychology and Gestalt Therapy.

Now I must define simply what I mean by the *gestalt art experience*. This combination of words has become meaningful to me; I have chosen the three of them to describe a process that makes sense beyond the boundaries of any verbal definition. But I must use the words to make sense, too; each word is a symbol for many cultural and personal ideas. Too often, when we are communicating verbally, we take for granted that we are each using the same word-symbols to represent exactly the same ideas. Too often we thus miscommunicate and get hopelessly caught in semantic morasses that hide our meanings behind different usages.

Let me define what I mean by the gestalt art experience by discussing each word separately. The last word, *experience*, comes first, just as experience comes first in any self-involving process.

Experience, says Webster's, is "the act of living through an event or events; personal involvement in or observation of events as they occur." Each time you and I draw, paint, or model we are actively living through an event, our own experiential event. Every line you draw is uniquely yours; the ones I draw are individually mine; each of us is involved in a personal happening. As the lines and shapes emerge from our activity, we can observe how we are forming a visible graphic record of some thing or sensation that we perceive. Having recorded that perception we each have a tangible reality to use as we prefer. You can denigrate your drawing with "Oh well, it's not very good. I never could draw, anyway." You can deny your expression with "That drawing doesn't mean anything to me." You can disown the form you've made with "It just came out that way. I didn't have anything to do with it. That's not the way I see and feel."

But your drawing *does* have a lot to do with you—with the way you see and feel and think and with the way you perceive. When you engage in an art activity, you are experiencing yourself; what you produce comes not from a depersonalized "it" but from a very personal you. Your personal art expressions deserve your attention.

Perhaps you've never known an art activity as a real experience— not since you were a child, anyway, and maybe you don't remember scribbling lines and smearing shapes on any handy surface. That was a real experience, but maybe you were punished or persuaded out of that kind of expression. And so you've forgotten that you once knew how to draw freely and experience your delight, anger, and all kinds of living rhythms without self-consciousness. If so, think of the kinds of unself-conscious things you still do—dancing, singing, arranging furniture, choosing your own clothes, and all the other ways your express your personal self. And think of your dreams, both sleep-time and daytime weavings of your fantasies. All of these are events that involve you personally and that you can observe as they occur.

So that's how I use the word *experience*: dreaming, feeling, thinking, acting, expressing, and being aware at the same time that you are the person who is doing all of this.

How am I using the word *art*? I turn to Webster's again and find "human ability to make things; creativity of man as distinguished from the world of nature."

Making things is natural to man; perhaps we became human as we made things. Like our primitive ancestors, we make ourselves shelter, food, clothes, and transportation. Like the cave people, we use a lot of time and energy providing ourselves with more or less of those basics according to our experiences and perceptions of what our basic needs are. How need-satisfactions—physical, cultural, and psychological—evolve from direct survival necessities to luxurious desirables is too complex to discuss here. Very simply, all cultures and the individuals in them have needs beyond survival needs; these additional needs are often called "wants." I make no clear distinction between need and want because when I want something strongly enough, I presume that I need it.

I am presuming, then, that humans both need and want to make things—to engage in art. That desire is an inherent part of our humanity. We use that desire in many different ways, with varying degree of facility and for various ends, but we all do it in one way or another. I believe that we want to and need to if we are seeking our fullest humanity. There are those who disagree; they say, "You are just believing that because you want to. You need some sort of idealism, so you put your faith in man's basic creative urge. You can't prove it!" I hear their arguments—sometimes smugly, thinking I know better, sometimes with sadness, fearing that they are right. However, until some of the "if you can't measure it, you can't believe it" adherents can come up with a better answer, I'll trust my own perceptions and observations. From prehistoric times until today, we have made things that didn't exist before; we have put things and ideas together, presenting a synthesis; we have created symbols and communicated meanings.

I don't know why we do this; I do know that we do. So I start from that assumption and find excitement in exploring how we can perceive and create and communicate better through the media of the forms that we make. So, by *art*, I mean the forms that emerge from our individual creative experiencing.

I originally used the word *gestalt* to relate my orientation in art experience to the assumption of gestalt psychologists.

I discovered gestalt psychology after years of working in art— years that involved much experimenting and exploring and trusting in my own perceptions. My discovery of the theories of gestalt psychology was very exciting because it created a theoretical bridge between what I knew of my processes in art-making and what I perceived in other people's art and life processes.

I had known that various schools of psychotherapy had used art as an auxiliary method for diagnosis, for expression of so-called unconscious material, for emotioanal release, and as occupational therapy. Not until I encountered gestalt psychology did I find support for my belief that the art experience could be a primary, direct, conscious mode of acting out that often integrated fantasy and reality into actuality immediately and constructively.

Basically, "gestalt psychology originated as a theory of perception that included the inter-relationships between the form of the object and the processes of the perceiver. . . . Gestalt thinking emphasized 'leaps' of insight, closure, figure/ground characteristics, fluidity of perceptual processes, and the perceiver as an active participant in his perceptions rather than a passive recipient of the qualities of form."[1]

Not until I met Fritz Perls in 1965 did I learn that he had applied some concepts of gestalt psychology in formulating a practice of Gestalt Therapy in a way that paralleled my own applications of gestalt psychology theories in the kind of art-experience work I was doing. In training and working with Perls and other gestaltists, I learned more about how they did what they did: they were finding ways to facilitate therapeutic growth by showing people how to get out into the open feelings that had been walled off inside themselves, or to make explicit what had been implicit.

I realized that I was doing that, too—using art media as a bridge between inner and outer realities, encouraging people to create their own visual art-forms and to use these as messages they send to themselves. Made visible, the messages can be perceived by their maker; since sender and receiver are the same person, the chances of perceiving a whole pattern—a gestalt—are worth betting on.

The kinship between gestalt theories of perception and their applications in art experience is obvious to me. The psychologist speaks of perceiving whole configurations as being more than the sum of the parts that make up that whole. The artist knows that it is the relationship of the parts within the whole of any art form that creates the meaningful effect; looking at each part separately gives an entirely different impression from perceiving the patterned whole. The gestalt psychologist says that we tend to see similar shapes, lines, and colors as belonging together, so we perceive them as creating a visual group and thus form a figure that stands out in awareness from a less figural background. We tend to perceive continuity in lines and shapes even when there are gaps in the actual visual material that we see; we naturally seek to make wholes out of parts. We feel frustrated when we see things that seem incomplete. When we look at a form that is almost a circle, we tend to perceive a complete circle— that is, our perceptions tend to complete a shape, thus creating closure of that form.

These principles of gestalt perception become easily comprehensible when we experience their application in the process of creating our own art forms. Experientially we can perceive immediately that a number of colored shapes seen as unrelated parts have little effect; if we put them together into an integrated composition, we see a whole that is obviously greater than the sum of the parts. Similarly, when we represent imagery with graphic media, we naturally create figures and backgrounds. In using art media we discover, too, our own tendency toward completing wholes and effecting closure of unfinished parts of wholes. We become aware of the patterns within the configuration, too. We recognize that we are visually selective, since we are more likely to perceive clearly some forms than others. In the art experience, we gain insight into how we perceive generally and how our perceptions are influenced by our individual personalities.

The way we perceive visually is directly related to how we think and feel; the correlation becomes apparent when we represent our perceptions with art materials. The central figures we depict emerge from a diffuse background and give us clues as to what is central in our lives. The way we use lines, shapes, and colors in relationship to each other and to the space we put them in indicates something about how we pattern our lives. The structure or the lack of it in our forms is related to our behavior in living situations.

Realizing how we use our visual perception in creating art forms can give us new insights into how we can use our perceptiveness to create more integrated lives.

So, *gestalt*, as I use it here, means the ability to perceive whole configurations—to perceive your personality as a totality of many parts that together make up the reality of you.

Gestalt art experience, then, is the complex personal you making art forms, being involved in the forms you are creating as events, observing what you do, and, it is to be hoped, perceiving through your graphic productions not only yourself as you are now, but also alternate ways that are available to your for creating yourself as you would like to be.

That's how I describe the work I do now. When I began doing this sort of thing as a child, I didn't call it work, and I gave no name to my activities. I just did what came naturally.

Sharon is living on many levels all at once; I marvel that she can move about in the everyday world practically and effectively while carrying on such a lot of symbolic activity in her inner life. Tiny and delicate physically, she is inclined to be quiet and still. Only her shining, expressive eyes move about quickly, and she tilts her head from side to side as if she wants to see things from many angles. When she feels shy and fearful, Sharon's whole bearing becomes that of a little girl, on the verge of but never quite giving up her held-back tears. When she has that look I see the child who learned to go into her closet and be alone rather than ask for any sort of open emotional expression with her parents. Her mother says that Sharon was an obnoxious child whom she has never understood; her father, a quiet, bookish man, dramatically taught Sharon that the best thing to do with bad feelings was to bury them underground; in a planned ceremony the two went out one evening, dug a hole in the ground, and six-year-old Sharon was told to bury her temper and never let it show again.

Sharon learned her lesson well; her conscious suppression gradually became habitual and her outward behavior fit into the family's pattern of keeping out of sight anything that might be disturbing. In her aloneness, Sharon created a fantasy-companion, as many children do, but Sharon's companion was a machine, about which she writes:

When I was a child I had a machine, smooth, well-honed, slick, and a constant source of a noise in my head. The sound was like grease running through several cylinders of very smooth steel. The noise was high-pitched and relentless. It was a vivid experience for many years. I remember being alone. I felt the aloneness, and the machine would take up all the space in my head, drowning out the everyday sounds, the everyday feelings, providing a transition into unreality as the house got quieter and quieter. The feeling of sliding through all those unending cylinders, being flattened and changing form from bone to liquid, from empty quiet to a roaring silence, from being me to being a substance rolling through a vast process. I would lie on a bed in a room and not recognize my surroundings. A heaviness and flatness would seem to overcome me and everything looked unreal and strange. I would try to break the feeling by getting up and going out of the house. I would see the outside and the trees and I would concentrate on looking at them until I would reach some kind of balance. I would watch the sky and pretend there was a noise coming from the space until I could hear that sound instead of the roaring in my head. As the sky sound would increase I would recognize familiar things, the house and me and where I was sitting and it would all be over.

Sharon went to college, painted, went to a New York art school on a scholarship, and worked for the New York State Council of the Arts. Her inventive techniques for three-dimensional printmaking brought her success but not much happiness. She tried psychotherapy; that didn't seem to help. Her prints were in galleries, and she was in limbo. She took LSD and was shocked out of lethargy; on the drug she felt transported beyond all individuality and felt ecstasy in belonging with all-beingness. She saw joys in non-ego-involvement and envisioned wondrous release in non-being. But she was frightened, too; when she saw herself in a mirror, Sharon saw only translucency. Was that what she wanted—to lose her identity in cosmic unity before she'd ever lived here on this earth? Sharon didn't know. She and a new husband, who was little more than another body in lostness, began wandering. John drove the car; Sharon sat and passively watched the world go by. "It" was "out there, fascinating," but none of "it" was here.

Back in San Francisco, Sharon functioned on a sort of minimal level, limiting herself to superficial involvements. But when her father developed terminal cancer, she chose to be with him during the long months of his dying. At his request, Sharon and her father together did what they could to help him express his buried feelings; he grieved that he had repressed so much of himself and hoped that Sharon would live more freely. After her father died, though, she felt more deadened than ever and could not involve herself deeply in art or anything else.

Sharon realized how much she had cut off her creativity when she saw in a stranger's home a three-dimensional print that she'd made two years before and now could not recognize or remember as her own creation. Shortly afterwards she began coming to art therapy groups and then to weekly private sessions with me.

For the first year, Sharon resisted expressing herself with art forms; given a large sheet of paper, she would draw tiny, delicate decorations in one corner and was inarticulate about them. Six months ago Sharon told me that she was "making little things" at home; she "enjoyed tinkering," she said. She made gifts for people, grew potted plants, decorated her apartment for Christmas—small things, but all of her own creation. She brought small, neat, black and white collages to our sessions, discussing how she was beginning to discover elements in them that related to her individuality. A month ago she brought the four forms shown in Figures 1, 2, 3, and 4.

About six inches high, made from plastic, glass, cotton, and metal, they are very personally Sharon's. At my suggestion, she began expressing her thoughts and feelings by writing. At first this was difficult for her, but now she pours out words, pages and pages of them. In her own way, she describes her self-trait figures:

Aspect I

I am obscure, unclear, non-functional, split, non-directional.
I am soft and dream-like, with sharp tangents of reality and

discomfort. I neither radiate nor direct. I feel helpless and static. My movement is dependent—I can be picked up, placed, and given meaning by an "other." I can also be ignored, passed over, unseen. I can be loved or unloved, unhappy or happy, observant but indecisive, a willing object. I am between a dream and a reality. Life becomes an echo.

Aspect II

I am definite, definitive, directed. My movement starts slowly with a spiraling to conclusions. I am unreasonable, brilliant, angry, rash, permanent, stubborn, and purposeful. I am right, tall, and impenetrable. I have no feeling, but I have logical progressions of a third sense. I reach an end, lose connections with the spiral or process or why, and I become implacable, dreamless, determined, and companionless. I am not here to be loved or loving. I am here to do and to be. There is no echo, I am the voice and the conception. Brittle and breakable.

Aspect III

    I am in balance, shorter but functioning. I can both feel and be at the same time. I combine softness with balance and brittle receptivity. I am open to change that I can maintain in various positions. I can be delighted and graceful, useful and willing. I have a synthesis of dream and reality. I am nonlinear; I can be absurd but not dismissed. I do not alarm, nor do I feel alarmed or vulnerable to breakage. I am perhaps content with the image I am.

Aspect IV

I must combine my dream-observer with real-life situations. Softness can combine with sharpness and still give a pleasing feeling. I can joke about my situation because I am self-willed and not an object of a stranger's needs. I can work with my own needs and experiment with combinations of feelings. I can destroy myself when I feel I need to destroy an unworkable aspect of me. If I do it's okay; I need the time to reach my own conclusions. I can laugh and give my experience to others 'cause I did it myself.

Sharon is now exploring her own experiences through art, with her own intelligence and imagination; recently she wrote: "I don't use my machine any longer, but I have developed a real feel for edges. I

can sense an edge, or a limit, or a closing off of space and time and sound when I am in an uncomfortable situation. . . . I am trying to learn the process of expanding this space without the fear of edges, without the tendency to get lost in another, and without the need to scrap the whole picture if I can't find my place."

Sharon is finding her place: she is working for a public-service agency part time and is also acquiring a clientele for her free-lance services as a designer. She feels that she will have an agency in a few years and is excited about her possibilities. More important, Sharon is increasingly self-determining; she is realistically expanding to fit recognized spaces in her own potential.

This brief vignette is an unenclosed, open-ended image of the here-and-now awareness of a person in process. More eloquent than any words I can say are Sharon's own self-perceptions, both graphic and verbal.

Her story neither begins nor ends. As someone said:

Perhaps all stories should begin with the word *and*. Perhaps they should end with the word *and*, too. It would remind us that no experience ever begins: there was always something that preceded it. What really began, for us, was our awareness of something going on. At the end, the word *and* would remind us that no story ever really ends—something more will happen after. Thus, it may be said that we live in the world of *et cetera*. There is always more to start with than we can take into account. There is always more to say than we can possibly say. There is always more to end with than we can imagine.[2]

NOTES

1 . Joen Fagan and Irma Lee Shepherd (eds.) *Gestalt Therapy Now.* Palo Alto, Calif.: Science and Behavior Books, 1970.

2. "Communications," *Kaiser Aluminum News.* 3, 23 (n.d.) 2.

CHAPTER 18

THE GALLANT STATE TROOPER: A DREAM

JACK DOWNING, M.D. and ROBERT MARMORSTEIN

Jack Downing is in private practice in Palo Alto, California, and is a staff member of the San Francisco Gestalt Institute. He has held positions at the Menninger School of Psychiatry, has been director of San Mateo County, California, Mental Health Services, and president of the First Arica School, in New York City.

Reprinted by permission from J. Downing and R. Marmorstein, **The Gallant State Trooper, Dreams and Nightmares: A Book of Gestalt Therapy Sessions**, New York: Harper and Row, 1973, pp. 30-41.

This is a dream from the Bucks County Seminar Center. I'm enthusiastic about Bucks County. Sadly, it's now closed. This particular morning, first thing, just as the barn furnace rattles and bangs into action, a friendly, quiet, young schoolteacher asks if she can work. I reply ungraciously, "I'm not going to give you permission." She figures out that I mean, "You must decide," gives herself permission, and sits down on the hot seat. A small point, you say? However this establishes who is doing what and for whom. I, Jack, refuse to take responsibility for you, Jean.

Jean: I had a dream last night that I want to work on.
Jack: Fine, hold on a minute. (Starts tape recorder) OK, tell it in the Now, first person, present tense. I am. . . .
Jean: (Voice firm and soft) I am in a car with a girlfriend. She is driving. She has violated some traffic rule and a state trooper saw us. And as she stops I say, "You get into the passenger seat and I'll get in the driver's seat." I don't know why I did that. I felt that I had to do it. The state trooper was coming toward the car. I asked for her driver's license in case he had seen us switch. Then I could show him her driver's license, but she said, "Oh, my license expired last year." So the state trooper came over. He didn't say anything about the switch. He said he'd have to take us in. So we followed him into this building, which was the police station. There was this long table with chairs on either side. On one side there were policemen, on the other, civilians. They were talking back and forth, each with a pile of papers between them. At the end of the table was a place for one more policeman and I thought

that's where we're going to go. But instead he took us—this state trooper was tall and had boots and the whole bit—he took us into this paneled office with a shiny desk and a red carpet and proceeded to seduce both of us. And I thought, I knew that was going to happen. I didn't care, you know. Better than being arrested, and so . . .

Group: (Laughter and a voice says) Just relax. . . .

Jean: (Smiling shyly) That's the end of the dream.

Jack: What aspect of the dream interests you particularly? (I see no obvious split so I throw the ball back to Jean.)

Jean: Why I switched seats with my girlfriend. I don't understand that.

Jack: (Her response suggests a split with her girlfriend. Still, that doesn't feel right to me, so I stall.) All right . . . uh. . . .

Jean: (Half laughing) I feel nervous.

Jack: (Here it is. A more definite clue at the body physical energy level. For "nervous" I translate "excited.") Where do you feel nervous?

Jean: In my legs. (A trembling is visible along the inside of her thighs. She looks down at them as though the trembling is not connected to herself.)

Jack: Stay with your nervousness, just let it . . . exaggerate the trembling. . . . (Pause) What is happening now?

Jean's dream with its open sexual theme is proceeding to work itself out at the body energy or "bioenergetic" level. Words are not important here, only the direct physical experience. My directions are intended to guide Jean in releasing her dammed up energies.

Jean: (Softly) It's stopped. Now it's starting again. I have palpitations.

Her face is blushing. There is a trembling of her thighs and pelvic area accompanied by an irregular tightening and relaxing of her breathing. I recognize the gestalt of orgasm; the sensation of warmth and swelling as blood fills Jean's genitals. All this seems to be coming as a surprise to Jean. She apparently has not let herself be aware of her unsatisfied sexual needs.

Jack: What are you feeling in your genitals?

Jean: Warm. . . .

Jack: All right, be aware of that warmth. (Pause; Jean is looking

down) I want you to put the state trooper in the other chair and
ask him if he knows you had switched seats.

Jean: (Laughing softly) I have no idea where this is going to go and
it's so funny.

Jack: Well, tell that to the state trooper.

Jean: I don't have any idea where you're going to take me, and it
feels really funny. And you're very imposing. And handsome.
And it's warm. (Group laughter)

The group and I are feeling Jean's sexual vibrations very strongly.
We're starting to be turned on. Jean is both a little embarrassed and
encouraged that everyone is laughing in mixed excitement and pleasure.

Jack: Now be the state trooper.

Jean: (In deeper falsetto voice) I know it. (More laughter)

Jack: How do you feel as the state trooper?

Jean: (As state trooper) Very self-assured and confident (Voice
louder and firm) Towering. . . .

Jack: What's happening?

Jean: Palpitations again.

Jack: All right, come back here to your own seat and say to the state
trooper, "You excite me."

Jean: (Moves to first chair, breathlessly) You excite me.

Jack: Ask, "Do you know I traded seats with Mary?"

Jean: Do you know I traded seats with Mary?

Jean: (As state trooper) Doesn't seem to be important whether I
know it or not . . . I don't know what to say to you.

Jack: What's happening?

The Jean-trooper split is not a clear one. Jean has to be returned
over and over again, a clear sign that it is not in the right direction.
In fact, Jean's performance as the trooper tells me that words aren't
the best way for making a breakthrough from her impasse into level
four, the implosive level, and hopefully even further, into the explosive layer. I'm confirmed in my instinct to move her into the bioenergetic area, to help her melt her frozen sexual energy. Physical
expression seems to be the only way through for her. Words will
only interfere.

Jean: (Very confident) I'm not afraid of him!

Jack: Tell that to him.

Jean: (With assurance) I'm not afraid of you.

Jean: (As state trooper) You know I'm not going to hurt you, we're just going to have fun together. No trouble with the law.

Now the split becomes clearer. The trooper is Jean's masculine side of course. Jean has been afraid of her own active maleness and, therefore, of strongly masculine men. Her fear is covered up by the "no's" of society. "Sex is dirty, sex is forbidden, sex is against the law." And here her male side solves the problem. He *is* the law.

Jean: I feel silly.

Jack: Do you like feeling silly?

Jean: My legs are beginning to shake again.

Jack: Lie down on the floor. (General laughter from the group) Or perhaps you'd rather not?

I have decided to use a bioenergetic exercise to release the energy held back in her thigh, belly, and pelvic muscles. As Jean lies on her back, I tell her to bend her knees so that her heels are close to her bottom, and then lift her bottom off the floor an inch or so. This puts a strain on all these muscles which causes them to begin to vibrate strongly after a few minutes.

I become conscious of the group's laughter and suddenly realize that it is directed at me because I am obviously and visibly turned on by the activity on the floor. I become aware of my own voice, which I had not permitted myself to hear before, and realize that my directions to Jean are being given in a sexually seductive manner. I am embarrassed by this for I still retain my share of hangups, one of them being a twinge of guilt at not maintaining the traditional medical taboo against displaying real feeling—especially sexual—toward a patient. To cover my embarrassment, I adopt my most professional voice—bland and neutral—and ask Jean's permission to continue. She's already on the floor and not the slightest concerned about my professional or nonprofessional posture. She doesn't even bother to answer. I place a cushion under her head.

Jack: Bring your knees up comfortably. Now start belly breathing, not with your chest. . . . That's good. (Jean closes her eyes as she relaxes into belly breathing. I see that she is held in by her tight blue jeans.) Undo your waistband and unzip your fly to give more room.

Her hands unclasp the wide belt buckle, unfasten the waistband and unzip the jeans. Breathing becomes deeper and slower, moving down into her lower belly. Still, there is some sense of tightness in her breathing.

Jack: Allow each breath to go deeper until you feel the breathing all through your genitals.

Gradually I note a sense of expansion in Jean's pelvis. Her muscles are beginning to relax and stretch the way nature intended. Her life-long habit of tightness, of pulling in and holding back, of saying, "Stay away; keep out," is giving way to a deep natural flow of breath. Good breathing should be like the tide moving in and out of the river's mouth by natural forces, flooding, nourishing, and cleansing the estuaries of the body. Jean comes to life. Her slender torso stretches, lengthens with each breath. Her breathing becomes increasingly deeper and fuller. Her knees, which were touching each other, holding tightly, protectively to each other, now slowly relax and tilt outward. Her face softens, is younger. A little trembling is seen through her pullover sweater, just above the belly button.

Jack: (Kneeling beside her) Just lift your rear a little higher off the floor. Keep on belly breathing.

Jean now supports her weight on her shoulders and heels which are about six inches from her bottom. The muscles in her thighs tremble under the strain, then the trembling extends up into her belly.

Jack: Good! Exaggerate that trembling!

Jean vibrates more strongly. She moves her pelvis back and forth rhythmically. There is a crescendo of movement—open, direct fucking movement climaxed by a deep pelvic thrust downward and forward with a deep sigh. A ripple of muscle movement spreads down from her chest into her thighs, like a line drawn down her body. Jean opens her eyes and smiles, relaxed. She starts to speak when another violent trembling begins in her thighs.

Jack: Go along with it. Keep belly breathing, deep.

She lifts her bottom from the floor again. Another orgasm follows, freer and more full of movement than the first.

Jack: Make some noise as you breathe.

At first Jean grunts with each breath, then changes to a musical moan as her body and pelvic movements become deeper and spontaneous. Her third and fourth orgasms are deeply sensual, slow, with strong movements through her whole body. Even after five orgasms the uncontrollable trembling continues. Tiny sweat droplets dot her forehead and upper lip, which is also trembling. She is getting very tired.

Jack: (Putting a hand on her shoulder) That's good, real good. Just let your feet slide down and breathe normally. You've done great.

The group is quiet, everyone is feeling drained by Jean's experience. She lies limp, completely unself-conscious. Like five tidal waves her strong orgasms have washed away all taboos and muscle blocks. Jean stretches a nice long stretch and opens her eyes.

Jack: How do you like your dream?
Jean: I see why I wanted to be in the driver's seat when the trooper came.
Jack: What does the trooper say now?
Jean: Well, he's here to help you. (Smiling)
Jack: Let's stop here . . . I'm a little dizzy myself.

Jean has made contact with her frozen sexual assets and has unthawed them. She and I have used our combined awareness to guide her life energy through changes to a healthy release. That's one way to describe Gestalt Therapy. Often I use key words plus body awareness to trigger the emotional reaction that is needed to complete the life pattern, or gestalt.

Key words	+	Awareness of body action	$\rightarrow$	Emotional reaction	=	Completed gestalt
Daddy I hate you	+	Hitting the pillow	$\rightarrow$	Anger	=	I'm not a helpless child. I am a grown man like my father.

Let's work out this illustration. I am uncomfortable around my father. I don't know why I am uptight around him. My therapist tells me to hit a pillow and yell, "Daddy, I hate you." At first this seems silly but suddenly I feel tremendous rage and tear the pillow apart.

The anger was there all the time, tied up in the muscles of my arms and shoulders. The words "I hate you" plus the body movements of hitting, while the therapist takes the blame for what I'm doing, allow me to feel the emotions that have been too dangerous to feel up to now. I break through my fear, get rid of the rage left over from childhood, and take a new look at the old man. As a bonus, I get all that energy that was tied up and frozen in my muscles to use any way I want to.

Some energies, some gestalts, are too deep to be triggered by words alone. Dr. Alexander Lowen developed bioenergetics theory and practice to meet this problem. Although I am not trained in this therapy, I use a few of its tools in my own therapy kit. I notice that I send more and more people to Dr. Lowen as my knowledge of the body increases. Please don't hold him responsible for what I say here, for I've never even read his books. Don't tell him that, or if you do, add I've never read all of Fritz Perls's either. I've read most of *In and Out of the Garbage Pail* by Fritz, which has lots of amusing pictures and reads very easily.

In Gestalt Therapy I am all for the person to have a Now experience of their unfinished personality business, for unfinished gestalts are constantly pushing to be finished. Freud called this the "repetition compulsion." I call it the "merry-go-round principle," but he named it first, so let's settle for "unfinished business." Basically, we're afraid. We're all scared children who can't get close to that horrible unfinished business. The big strong therapist takes our hands and half coaxes us, half drags us up to our fear, and alacazam! The fear turns out to be imaginary!

I learned this principle the first time I took LSD. As I was experiencing an incredible sense of beauty listening to Beethoven's Choral Symphony, a frightening bat-like monster appeared in my mind. I started to run away, panicking. Then I felt love and reassurance from God saying, "Go toward it." I did, despite my fear, and the monster vanished. In its place was an awesomely tender, beautiful triple image: a great Gothic cathedral interior, pillars reaching upward to groined arches; a majestic redwood forest standing free in the wind; and the body of a woman. Approach your fear and it will vanish. You will pass through your frozen implosive self, enter and overcome death, emerge into life and joy.

How are muscle patterns jammed? Imagine you are listening to the radio. Two or three stations are coming over the same channel so you hear the strongest one pretty well and get that message, but the other weak stations interfere so you can't get the whole message.

Similarly, two messages, or three or four, will be in your muscles at once, the strongest coming through but the others interfering. Take another example: the kid who shuffles and drags his feet on the way to grammar school. He kicks trees and curbs and tin cans. His actions are saying, "I have to go to school," next, "I'll plant my feet right here and not go!" last, "I'd like to kick Mother for forcing me to go when I don't want to!" All together, pity Daddy's shoe bill! All these conflicting messages create friction and inefficiency. With start-stop, left-right, up-down, go-don't go, yes-no signals coming in all at once, no wonder a person feels chronic fatigue, malaise, headache, and all the other symptoms the TV medicine man promises to cure. We're all driving with our brakes on!

In your body, the strongest message keeps the other messages from coming through but can't keep them from pushing to be completed. Find out for yourself the next time you need to sneeze. Don't sneeze. Fight the tickle for five minutes as the sneeze impulse fights to be expressed, discharged. Then the next time, go ahead and sneeze a nice big sneeze. AH-CHOOOOO! and it's over with, finished, done for, ready for the next gestalt, for new business.

In Jean's dreamwork, I block her usual muscle patterns by putting her into a position that sets up an unusual strain on her legs and torso, making the muscles get tired. As they tire, they lose the ability to respond to the usual signals in the usual way and begin to let go all the held-back tensions at once. Jean is a well brought up, very decent young woman who learned as she grew up that sexual feelings are to be kept tightly controlled. She does this by holding back, tightening up the muscles in her thighs, vagina, and stomach. This is truly being "uptight." Sure, a lot of people are sexually "liberated" (whatever that means), but a lot more still believe in and live by a more restrained sexual code. Then too, many of us may have "liberated" beliefs, but the old restricting code still hangs on in our bodies. That restraint is *real*, those muscles are straining, working, getting tired, hurting, but managing to keep those sexual feelings from getting through to the head office, to awareness. So Jean can honestly say, "I'm a good woman, I'm faithful to my husband, I don't have sexy feelings. I'm not the kind of woman who wants to be turned on by every good-looking male she meets." And those muscles keep straining away until it all comes out in a dream.

The dream-Jean says, "I need more sexual release; I need to fuck. I need to make fucking movements and feel beautiful, relaxed sexual feelings. I'll dream I meet a gallant, sexy man whom I'll have to obey, so it's all right if we fuck. He makes me obey, so I don't even have to feel guilty." Through the dream-Jean's message, I guide the wake-Jean to muscle release and fuller awareness. Do I hear you say, skeptical reader, "Fine. You had fun and she had herself some fun and the crowd got to see a good show. OK, but where's the psychiatric treatment, what difference will this experience make tomorrow, next week, next year?" Well, for Jean herself I can't speak directly. The next two days of the workshop she was open, happy, social. I haven't worked with her since, so more than that I can't say. Most of the people I encounter after a workshop experience of this intensity tell me they've changed for the better. This much body release unlocks the door which was locked during late childhood and adolescence. It won't be locked again unless the person chooses to do so. Of course, Jean isn't going to become a *belle du jour*, a housewife-prostitute simply because her sexual function is now more fully available to her. She will probably enjoy her husband more and get more of a charge when she sees a well-built man on the beach. She is much less likely to become one of those middle-aged ladies who ban books from libraries because the author spelled fuck, f-u-c-k, rather than f**k. Anything more is up to Jean, who is now *aware* of herself in a way she was not before.

NOTE

1. To my surprise, when she read the dream, Jean told me that her dream about the state trooper had been fused with another dream. However, the resultant synthesis makes the basic bioenergetic point very well.

CHAPTER 19

THE ART OF EMOTIONAL NOURISHMENT: NOURISHING AND TOXIC ENCOUNTER GROUPS

JERRY A. GREENWALD, Ph.D.

An encounter group may vary from a remarkably nourishing, growth-enhancing experience to one that is traumatic, highly toxic and leaves the person fragmented, confused, and frightened. Participants frequently have little idea of what to expect and are easily victimized by toxic attitudes and behavior of the leader, other participants, or by the group process itself.

Labeling a particular group as nourishing or toxic is as unreal as categorizing a person as toxic or nourishing. It is more meaningful to describe an encounter in terms of *what*, in the ongoing group process, is nourishing or toxic in its effect on the participants. The differences in orientation, attitudes, and procedures of the nourishing as compared to the toxic encounter group stand in marked contrast with each other.

In a nourishing group the atmosphere is in itself conducive to a meaningful, discovering experience. It encourages each participant to focus on himself as the center of his personal existence. Unlike much of the experienced world of his past life, his self-centeredness, his prime concern with what *he* is thinking, feeling, experiencing, is valued, appreciated, and encouraged. Usually he experiences new possibilities of discovering more of himself and gaining new vistas of awareness and direction for furthering the development of his own potentials. He may discover more about what he wants and what changes he wishes for his own growth. His experience of openness and sharing with others may reveal new possibilities for relating and intimacy. He begins to see that the masks and facades with which he poisons himself and avoids meaningful interaction may not be as necessary as he imagined.

In the toxic group the emphasis is primarily on catharsis and acting out of pent-up feelings. The possibilities of a growth experience are minimal. The attitude during the encounter group process reflects its orientation as an end-in-itself experience. The emphasis on growth and the discovery of new pathways with which to experiment in changing and varying behavior is lacking. Encouraging the self-initiating potentials of the individual participant is less important than inducing effective "turn ons" by various manipulations. The toxic group does things *to* the participants, who are encouraged, or even pressured into compliance, going along with the group or being passively led through "groovy experiences." The goal is to "turn everybody on." In its most innocuous form the toxic encounter group is like a thrilling roller coaster ride where the person essentially subjects himself passively to an experience, and what happens to him is exciting and stimulating. In more poisonous groups the individual participant may be dominated by the leader of the group. He may be pushed and pressured to "express himself," or "to work," or in some other way to "get with it." He is more likely to be attacked, ridiculed, or judged inferior to the others. The atmosphere of pressure and demands on the participant prevails and with it greater feelings of insecurity and the constant threat of being alienated from the others. There is a lack of warmth and mutual caring. The toxic group remains fragmented within itself throughout the encounter, and the individual participant's feeling of trust toward the group fails to develop.

The most important factor which makes for a nourishing group is the leader. His attitudes of caring and interest in other people, his lack of manipulating others for his own needs, his sensitivity and awareness are critical factors determining the potential nourishing qualities of the encounter group process.

While the nourishing leader does not attempt to control the behavior of the group, he does endeavor to establish the conditions and atmosphere which he believes will most effectively facilitate the functioning of the group. He is open about how he feels he can best contribute to the group in his role as a leader. He does *not* ask that the group agree that his way is the best possible approach. He takes his stand about what he feels is meaningful interaction and what is not. While he may express his boredom or irritation with behavior he feels is overintellectual, bullying, or monopolistic, he does not play policeman or enforcer. When he objects to what is happening in the group, his interest is in minimizing trivial interactions or "game-playing" which deadens the group. He strives for a continuum of alive, meaningful interaction and relating.

The nourishing leader trusts the group and respects the integrity of each member. He trusts the self-regulating potential of others and believes that when they are allowed to move at their own rate and in their own way, the atmosphere is then optimal for openness and growth. He encourages each participant to set his own pace in the risk-taking business of exposing those "unacceptable" parts of his self which generate his fears, anxieties, and inhibitions. The last thing the nourishing leader wishes to do is intrude on the integrity of the participants by using pressure or coercion to "get them to open up."

An effective leader is tuned in to where the person is. He is aware of what the person is doing, how he is striving to accomplish his goal, and how he frustrates himself and gets stuck in his impasses. He is oriented to follow the participant and what he wants rather than lead him where he (the leader) thinks he should go. He shares with the participant how he feels he detours himself away from his goals, blocks his awareness, or in other ways gets himself stuck. The leader is interested in facilitating the struggle of the person toward whatever he needs for himself at the moment.

He is aware that a person often experiences pain in his struggle toward self-discovery and change and that alleviating his suffering may relieve him temporarily and cause more pain in the long run. Allowing him to experience his pain may be the gateway to further growth when it serves to motivate him to mobilize and utilize his own resources. It is in this sense that some leaders consider pain as a necessary prerequisite to growth. Sometimes pain reflects this struggle to break through an impasse and release the bound-up energy for more effective self-nourishment.

At other times pain is the agony of a person wallowing in conflict or confusion. Or it is the rage of frustration when others do not meet his expectations in giving him what he wants (demands). When the nourishing leader senses a futility or uselessness in the person's suffering, he does what he can do to help him get himself unstuck or minimize his futile suffering. But, he is not willing to sacrifice the self-initiating, "standing-on-his-own-two-feet potentials" of the participant in the process. He knows the end does not justify the means. The nourishing leader is aware that he would be contributing to a poisonous experience if he interferes with the participant's self-initiating efforts by attempting to be helpful. He knows he would thereby reinforce existing feelings of incompetency, ineffectiveness and fear of panic that if others will not take care of him he will collapse or perish.

The nourishing leader believes that each individual, at any moment in his existence, cannot be any different than he is at that moment. He leaves the participant free to choose what he will initiate and how he will respond in the group. He accepts the silence of one participant as meeting that person's needs at the moment every bit as much as the "openness" and "willingness-to-encounter" of another. He trusts the inherent potential of each individual to discover for himself what he needs; how to get it, and that he knows better about this for himself than anyone else. He knows that the silent person is often experiencing increasing awareness which will lead to expression and self-initiating behavior at some time other than now. He may, in his silence, begin to melt impasses which have held him frozen for years. When he begins to "open up" or "share himself" (and this may not happen in the course of a particular encounter group), he then has the absolutely irreplaceable experience of self-initiated action which produces growth. No matter how helpful the leader wishes to be, there is no substitute for the self-initiated growth experiences.

The toxic leader rejects or neglects the importance of his role as a major determinant of how the group will function. He may insist that he is simply another member of the group "doing his own thing." This is a favorite copout of toxic leaders which lends itself to rationalizing their own anxieties, feelings of inadequacy, or lack of responsibility when the group is ineffective or a participant is traumatized by some toxic intrusion by the leader himself or the group.

The toxic leader may refuse to set ground rules, to take a stand about what he considers to be meaningful interaction, or to object to any behavior as out of bounds. He thereby invites unnecessary detours which detract from the development of an effective encounter group experience. Participants in an encounter group may not know what to expect or what kind of behavior is appropriate. Without structure they may indulge in, or submit to, a great deal of intellectualizing, psychologizing, and analyzing of each others' behavior. They may use the group as an outlet for their own frustrations or hostilities and adopt a jungle attitude toward each other. They may be victimized by participants who simply want to dominate the group's attention and stay in the limelight by whatever means will achieve this. The toxic leader accepts whatever happens in or to the group.

Other toxic leaders endeavor to manipulate the group to enhance their own egos. A leader has a prime opportunity to use the group as an outlet for his own frustrations or to reassure himself about his own insecurities, or bolster his sagging self-esteem. He may seek submission of the group to his authority. He may give approval to those who are more verbal or encourage competition among those who seek to win his favor. Individual self-expression is apt to be over-shadowed by rivalries, approval-seeking, and other kinds of man-ipulations which arise when hierarchies and levels of status exist within the group. The growth process, which takes place within the self, becomes distorted by contests among the participants.

The toxic leader takes the initiative away from the participant. He contaminates the growth that comes from discovering and experi-encing one's self-supporting capabilities. The toxic effect is often quite subtle, since the participant is usually grateful for the "relief" from his anxiety, chaos, or stalemate. The leader is toxic when he in-sists on "rescuing" the participant.

One of the hallmarks of the toxic leader is his need to produce dramatic results. For example, when the person is experiencing sup-pressed anger the leader may suggest some form of physical ex-plosion for its cathartic value. However, this dissipates the energy which might otherwise have led to a more meaningful growth expe-rience. The participant is robbed of an opportunity to discover what he does to continuously generate his anger and to discover how he frustrates himself. He is deprived of the chance to let go of alien, or obsolete, attitudes or behavior patterns and thereby diminish the continuing source of his frustration and anger.

The nourishing participant hopes the encounter group will facil-itate his endeavors to reach out for growth experiences, find greater meaning in his life, realize more of his potentials, and minimize un-necessary pain. He seeks emotional nourishment and is honest about wanting something for himself. Others attend in bad faith with a variety of ulterior motives and deceptive attitudes. They only mouth "legitimate" reasons for their presence. Their effect on the group is largely toxic. They frequently want to use the group for various purposes: for sexual contacts; to yell and scream; or to act out their impulses in ways which would not be acceptable in their everyday lives. Some come as voyeurists to peek at others while refusing to share themselves. Some come to snicker, scoff and look down on other participants. Others come to put on a performance by what-ever means is effective to get the center of attention and gain brief relief from their chronic fear of isolation. In one way or another, the toxic participant poisons the group process.

The nourishing participant is willing to take responsibility for his actions, his effect on others, and for everything else he does, or allows to happen to him, in the encounter group. He does not give over his power and submit to the leader or group when he honestly objects to what they want from him. The nourishing participant's attitude is that *he* knows best what is valuable and nutritious for him and what is toxic or poisonous. When he errs in his judgment in this respect, he still maintains this responsibility to himself. He decides when he will trust the leader or the group by taking risks in being open. He does this in the hope of experiencing greater awareness and growth. Usually he must struggle to overcome his fears and anxieties so that he can take the risk of exposing his self. But he does not push or force himself to work or be more open when he really doesn't want to.

There are two general attitudes reflected in the behavior of the toxic participant. Sometimes he is a person who is simply so full of poison that he cannot help radiating a toxic effect on others. He comes in good faith. He is aware of the pain and anguish he has experienced in his frustrating efforts to find meaningful relationships. He wants to do something for himself so that his relationships may become more nourishing. The other toxic attitude is found in those who come in bad faith. They come to the group essentially to manipulate. They are less willing to own the suffering and misery they experience. They poison the group with their manipulative roles. Often their participation is largely that of an interrogator who constantly questions the other participants. Or, he may play therapist and interpret other people's behavior. He may act as a saboteur seeking to undercut the leader or render the group ineffective.

The poisoner who comes in bad faith senses that he is increasingly ineffective as the participants move from initial feelings of isolation and aloneness toward greater mutual trust and belongingness. Whatever ground rules are set forth, the poisoner takes exception and argues about how he thinks the group should be run. He may refer to a "really great encounter group" he attended and how it was done there. He may persistently argue or raise questions in the hope of baiting the leader or other participants into bickering or other destructive interaction. He may intimidate those in the group who are more insecure, fearful or uncertain about what will happen.

Other poisoners contaminate the nourishing experiences of other participants. When someone has a meaningful experience, the poisoner comes in with criticism, questions or otherwise distracts the participant from enjoying his new discoveries or assimilating his new awareness.

The poisoner may seek to dominate the group by constantly struggling to gain the center of attention. He may monopolize the interaction by dramatic, explosive reactions which practically force the group to turn its attention to him. Such explosions range from suicidal threats and feelings of going crazy, to threats that he wants to "wreck the place and everybody in it."

The toxic participant frequently "glooms on" to the efforts of others. When someone is endeavoring to work, the toxic participant looks for a free ride from the person who is working. He will express frustration when the other has not worked through his struggle completely: "I was really with you, but dammit, I would have felt so much better if you had really told your mother to go to hell." It is an example of the toxic participant's attitude of insistence that others should live up to his expectations and perform the way he wants them to. This attitude is in contrast to nourishing participants who may also identify with the frustration of another *and* appreciates what the other did which increased his own awareness. He is grateful for the opportunity to have shared the other's struggle but remains responsible for his own struggle to free himself from his own frustrating behavior patterns.

What these and other patterns of the toxic participants have in common is their destructive, disruptive, alienating effects on other group members and the group process as a whole.

GROUP ATTITUDES AND BEHAVIOR

A mutual respect for the integrity of each person is prevalent in the attitude and interaction of the nourishing group. Each person, as an independent agent, chooses what he wants to share of himself and what he is willing to react to or respond to from other members of the group. The nourishing group is marked by an absence of coercive tactics which are used to pressure the person to expose himself or respond. Such endeavors, regardless of the intent ("We're only trying to help you! What did you come here for if you're not willing to participate?"), are attempted intrusions upon the individual. There is an implicit "should" in this kind of manipulation. The group is toxic when it attempts to coerce or pressure a participant and refuses to accept what he wants for himself at that moment, and what he doesn't want. In contrast, the nourishing group's attitude is supportive, but lacks the demand quality so apparent in the toxic group.

Pressure may be a well-meant attempt at helping a person loosen up. With enough pressure from the leader and/or the other participants, the person will frequently open up, and have a genuine cathartic experience. This approach, that the end justifies the means, encourages the person to remain chronically dependent on someone else to "loosen him up." Encounter group experiences then become crutches. He wants to be "turned on" and then he is satisfied. When he isn't, he is frustrated and angry. Either way, his self-reliance as an individual is being crippled.

Another characteristic of toxic groups is an almost phobic attitude toward any procedures which have the slightest hint of restriction on the expression of one's individuality. In some encounter groups this reflects a toxic distortion of the "I do my thing, you do your thing" philosophy. Chaotic and unrestricted behavior is unrealistic. It violates the facts of human existence throughout history. When a nourishing group begins, certain ground rules are assumed to be acceptable to all members of the group. Without this initial understanding, excessive toxic interaction is almost inevitable.

The toxic group frequently fails to take responsibility for how their group functions. The group does not become self-regulating, and the self-initiating potentials of individual members is hampered. They remain dependent on the leader at the expense of their own spontaneity. The leader may become primarily a director who keeps the group moving with a repertoire of techniques, manipulations, and instructions. The passive role of the participants encourages a quick return to their prior state of deadness or dependency when the encounter is over.

When the group proceeds mainly with "turn-on" gimmicks, the encounter may provide an immediate emotional experience, but little possibility for individual growth. Participants of such groups often complain later that they experienced a real high during the encounter group which was short-lived and was followed by an unusually painful low. Turn-ons, of course, do not last. They are experiences *for* the moment and do not provide any breakthrough into greater awareness. Nor do they leave the participant with the momentum of any new discoveries about himself with which to continue a self-initiating attitude after the encounter is over.

An encounter group can easily distort the process by which intimacy develops between people. An attitude that "we are all here to love each other" can have the phoniness of the "Sunday Christian." Openness, straight talk, and honest encountering lead to intimacy and the kind of relating which is mutually nourishing. When this is distorted by assumptions or expectations, the process becomes meaningless or toxic. The group that is programmed to relate or has an expectation of instant intimacy, hampers the likelihood of a real experience.

When the purpose of opening-up techniques are largely used to produce intense emotional reaction, the effect is similar to using penicillin or other powerful antibiotics: repeated usage diminishes their effectiveness. The turn-on power of the technique gradually diminishes. Methods and techniques for *both catharsis and growth* is one of the hallmarks of a nourishing encounter group. The hallmark of the toxic group is its emphasis on the discharge of pent-up emotions as an end in itself. Emotional catharsis per se is endless and is frequently a clear statement of an ongoing toxic behavior pattern which is blocking the person's path toward further growth.

NOURISHING AND TOXIC MANIPULATIONS

The word *manipulation* has a negative connotation with reference to authentic relating between people. Manipulation includes any attitude or behavior initiated by one person toward another for the *primary* purpose of eliciting a particular kind of response from that person. This is in contrast to authentic relating which may be defined as any expression or act by one person toward another *primarily* for the purpose of self-expression. In toxic manipulation, the person's statement to the other has an implicit or explicit demand that the other respond in a certain way. The statement has a "hook" in it. In authentic relating a person may directly ask for something from another, but this request has the flavor of acceptance of the other person's option to respond or not to respond as he chooses.

Many efforts by the leader or the group to help a person express himself, break through an impasse, or give up an obsolete pattern of behavior are manipulative. In nourishing manipulation, the attitude of the leader or group is one of being available. It is left to each participant to say what he wants, share his feelings of being stuck or wanting help, or asking the leader or the group for something. Attempts by the leader or other group members to facilitate his struggle have the flavor of suggestions or invitations. The essential attitude in nourishing manipulation is one of following the person as he struggles to fulfill a need or experience greater awareness. The participant is aware that he is allowing himself to be manipulated for this purpose. He decides what manipulations he will cooperate with and which ones he chooses to reject. He is responsible for rejecting any manipulation when he wants to stop.

When the manipulation is toxic, the initiative is not in the hands of the participant. In various ways he is told (manipulated into) what he should and should not do. Expectations and demands of others are applied against him with an attitude of insistence. His own initiative is being usurped and stifled. He remains dependent on and submissive to his environment. He is led at the instigation of others who persist in directing him until *they* decide to stop.

Anger is a statement of an unfinished situation. It is a manifestation of the tension generated when a person is frustrated in his attempts to satisfy his needs. In the encounter group process catharsis per se is toxic. It focuses only on alleviating a recurring symptom and ignores the message which anger always carries: "I need something for my well-being that I am not getting."

The expression of anger in a toxic group is an end in itself. Whatever the person does to continue to generate his anger remains untouched. The toxic effect persists since chronic anger leads to isolation and makes intimate relationships more difficult. The deprivation which follows creates new frustration which generates new anger, and a vicious cycle ensues. Some people are so consumed by this trap that they literally need to spend a large portion of their time and energy simply to burn off their constantly accumulating anger.

During a toxic encounter group this is often expressed by acting-out through physical release, with the expected reduction in tension for the moment. In the nourishing group, physical expressions of anger are at best a preliminary step. More important is greater awareness of what his anger is all about and how he frustrates himself.

The expression of anger is toxic when it alienates members of the group from each other and only elicits counteranger and counterattack without any attempt at resolution or focusing on the source of the conflict. Some toxic groups are characteristically hostility-oriented. They seem preoccupied with nit-picking, fault-finding, criticizing and challenging one another. Several participants may, for example, unite against a particular member who becomes the group scapegoat. Or, the group may endeavor to coerce one member into doing what they feel he "should" by ridicule, teasing, or other forms of attack. When hostility and the expression of it becomes an end in itself, the group is toxic.

In nourishing groups hostility and aggression are accepted as part of any authentic human interaction. Unresolved hostilities hamper the ability of the group to work more effectively and become more intimate. The expression of anger and hostility, and the release of energy which occurs with this, is seen as an opportunity to gain more awareness of the unfinished situations which continue to generate the person's anger. It is often a situation which is ripe for further integration.

The dramatic effect of the emotional explosion seems to be obviously valuable. While there is important relief in the discharge of pent-up energy, this in itself does not produce growth. It is a sudden vomiting or defecating of accumulated emotional poison which can set the stage for growth but is not in itself an integrating process.

Growth means awareness. In the toxic group the explosion is an end in itself rather than a means to an end. The person feels better; everybody congratulates him on "opening up," and that's all that happens.

In the nourishing group, the person is encouraged to experience his explosion with increasing awareness. He grows in various ways. He learns to take responsibility for this part of himself (his explosiveness). He also learns to maintain his integrity; i.e., to keep his feet on the ground, rather than allow himself to fly into pieces by his explosiveness. Allowing oneself to be overwhelmed by excitement leads to fragmentation, not integration. It is the typical impatient, restless, unable-to-tolerate-frustration attitude of the infant. The more integrated person is able to let go *and* reinstate his controls subsequently. The toxic group encourages turning-on per se, and lends its approval to emotional outbursts. It takes a stand which implies that impulsivity, fragmentation, and chaos are meaningful and desirable.

It is equally cathartic and more realistic to have an intense emotional explosion and still maintain control of oneself. It is a common fear that if a person gives in to his need to cry, scream, or express his anger, some disastrous consequence will occur. When he discovers that he can express intense emotion *and* regain control of himself and that no catastrophe befalls him, he experiences a greater self-trust which in itself is a vital aspect of growth. When the group takes over the responsibility for his "letting it all hang out" or "going berserk," the possibility of a growth experience of greater self-trust is lessened. By turning over his controls to the group the obvious is overlooked: people rarely accept crazy behavior and rarely seek relationships with someone who acts crazy.

There are clearly discernible differences between meaningful, nourishing group interaction and various forms of "rapping" in which huge amounts of verbiage are exchanged with very little meaning for anyone. Since any opportunity to express oneself usually feels good, members often think that they are really encountering and relating to each other on a meaningful level. Toxic interaction often has the flavor of a coffee klatch, a gossiping session, or a psychologizing contest. For example, someone states a problem and what follows is an opinion-giving game in which one is tempted, after the sampling has gone on sufficiently long to become monotonous, to suggest a role call vote on the issue. Other times a person will "share his experience" by referring to an analogous situation and what he did on that occasion. Other participants continuously come up with "helpful suggestions" which usually begin with an expression like, "Why don't you . . .?" Such interaction is superficial, time-wasting, and often serves as a smoke screen to avoid the risks of more meaningful self-expression and openness. It is even more toxic when it encourages a group atmosphere in which verbiage per se is implicitly or explicitly considered to be of value.

The nourishing group has little tolerance for meaningless "head-tripping" and takes its stand against purposeless, time-wasting interaction. It is more interested in meaningful interaction and reacts more quickly with boredom and irritation when such games begin to occur.

The nourishing or toxic atmosphere of a group is often reflected in what happens during periods of silence. The more alienated, isolated, and fragmented the group, the greater the group tension during silence. Any lapse of interaction becomes a threatening possibility. The participants feel greater pressure to say something. In a nourishing group atmosphere, periods of silence are often experienced as a nonverbal kind of sharing. This kind of void during a silent period is more apt to be experienced as a "fertile vacuum." The openness and lack of any demand "to do anything" is often the atmosphere for the birth of creative awareness and puts the person in touch with new dimensions and potentials within himself.

The creative act of self-expression can be distorted in an encounter group and reduce it to a number of isolated "loners" who happen to be "doing their own thing" in the same physical setting. Toxic groups often encourage an attitude which in effect says, "I am doing my thing and if you don't like it drop dead." This kind of toxic game fosters isolation, a lack of caring, and a denial of the reality that many basic human needs can only be satisfied in relationships with others. It is a toxic attitude to imply that being a "mature person" means being an "island unto oneself." There is a difference between individuality and isolation. The toxic groups tend to make the two synonymous. The nourishing group fully appreciates individuality. However, it recognizes that "standing on one's own feet" includes reaching out and initiating relationships with others. A group can "cop out" under the guise of individuality and an "I-am-not-responsible-for-you" attitude. Individual behavior which is isolating or alienating in its effect on others is usually toxic.

Many encounter group "games" and techniques effectively enable a person to regurgitate his poison. He feels relieved, relaxed, even "wonderful." He is grateful to the group and the leader, and feels encounter groups are terrific. Psychological vomiting, like physical vomiting, typically produces a sense of relief. It does not produce growth. What has been vomited up is rejected totally, including what may be potentially nourishing. At best, a psychological stalemate develops in which the person continues to swallow poison and then periodically throws up; i.e., by frequent encounter groups.

A nourishing encounter group emphasizes growth. Rather than settle for the endless poisoning-vomiting cycle, the nourishing encounter group focuses on increasing awareness of the processes by which the person poisons himself. With awareness come the possibilities of experimenting with new behavior patterns and discovering new potential directions for movement. Whenever this occurs, the person has a growth experience. He has broken an impasse and movement is inevitable. He will begin to explore what he is doing. He may be more willing to confront himself with his fear that breaking the stalemate will lead to disastrous consequences. He becomes more aware of his choice between reasonable risk-taking and continuing his chronic process of slowly poisoning himself.

Relating is a process involving mutual feedback. In meaningful interaction each person is sensitized to the other, is aware of how he experiences the other, and responds with statements and reactions reflecting his experience of the other. The sensitivity-awareness-responsiveness cycle is the basic behavior pattern of the nourishing encounter group. It is a way of being which fosters authentic relating.

As the encounter group proceeds, the aliveness of each person grows, the excitement of sharing increases, threat of alienation and rejection diminish, and an attitude of warmth and caring emerges. In the nourishing group this is the dominant attitude within which resentments, hostilities, and anger are expressed, shared, and melted. These "negative" emotions are the most frequent source of fears of alienation and rejection among people. They become a rich source of growth in a nourishing atmosphere. Many of the impasses and obstacles which hamper personal growth and the joy and excitement of being alive are based on unfinished resentment and anger from the past which a person may harbor indefinitely and which block his warmth and openness toward others. One function of the encounter group is alleviating these obsolete hostilities and the countless ways they are expressed; e.g., criticalness, "put-down" attitudes, frozen anger, etc. Unfinished frustrations continue to nurture these tormenting emotions. People who are characteristically angry, irritable, withdrawn, or emotionally lifeless *are* reacting to excessive frustrations from past experiences which they continue to hold onto and which contaminate their ability to nourish themselves and others in the here-and-now.

The accepting climate of a nourishing encounter group is a prime environment for encouraging the participant to risk sharing his vulnerabilities by releasing feelings and emotions which he learned earlier in his life were too dangerous to reveal. The encounter-group process has great potential power to melt these long-standing impasses.

Growth and maturation for the individual mean learning how to stand on his own two feet and develop his own potentials. In this way he increases his ability to satisfy his needs both within himself and in his interaction with others.

The most critical aspect of growth, the process of becoming a person, centers on the risk-taking activities of reaching out for what one needs. As a person discovers his inner strength and potential to reach out effectively for what he wants, he becomes increasingly nourishing to himself and to others. When the group process interferes with this natural ripening of the person's potentials, it is toxic. When it enhances his self-discovery, it is nourishing. All the helpful endeavors to push, cajole, or coerce someone "for his own good" usurp these opportunities and deprive the individual of the chance for a self-initiated growth experience. This most vital issue is often clouded by the obviously valuable catharsis he experiences when he is manipulated into self-expression. The means become the end. The person leans on the group to do his work for him, and regardless of how successful he is in the sense of "feeling better" this process leaves him stuck deeper and deeper in environmental support and reinforces his distrust of his ability to stand on his own two feet.

True growth means the person's attitudes, his way of being in the world, his behavior toward himself and others is evolving. In action and attitude he is always in the process of becoming. Becoming means something new is always emerging.

The nourishing encounter group is characterized as an intense experience in which the person feels a surge of growth as dormant parts of himself become alive and he activates them into his behavior. He experiences greater awareness of new directions in which to focus his attention and energies. Awareness of movement in oneness *is* awareness of the growth process in action and is itself exciting and invigorating. There is no substitute for the self-initiated turn on of being in touch with the inner excitement of one's own aliveness.

CHAPTER 20

TECHNIQUES OF GESTALT SELF-THERAPY

MURIEL SCHIFFMAN

Muriel Schiffman is a lecturer and teacher of self-therapy techniques. She is the author of *Self-Therapy Techniques for Personal Growth* and *Gestalt Self-Therapy: Further Techniques in Personal Growth.*

Reprinted by permission from M. Schiffman, **Gestalt Self-Therapy: Further Techniques for Personal Growth**, Menlo Park, California: Self Therapy Press, 1971, pp. 18-33.

Gestalt Therapy, like psychodrama, is a way of consciously enacting, in concrete form, your unconscious fantasies. When you work with a therapist or Gestalt group leader, he can guide you, give you a push in the direction of solving a neurotic problem. In Gestalt *self-therapy* you are on your own. The purpose, as with any kind of self-therapy, is to *know where you are*.

I want to *know myself*; to be truly aware of the opposing forces within me; to consciously experience the battle raging beneath the surface, that battle whose distant thunder I tend to smother with clenched teeth, headaches, obsessive thinking. When I get down there and plunge into the battle scene, I can experience what Fritz calls the "therapeutic impasse."

Webster defines impasse as "an impassable road or way; a predicament affording no obvious escape." When I try to solve a problem and discover how useless my old neurotic ways are, when I let myself feel the frustration and helplessness, thrashing about desperately for a way out, I am experiencing the therapeutic impasse. Only then, only by hitting rock bottom, do I have a chance to strike out on a new path.

Any time you over-react to another person, no matter how "real" his behavior appears to be, you are projecting something on to him. This is the time to use Gestalt self-therapy to discover something about the hidden side of yourself. As in any kind of self-therapy, once you experience the hidden feeling, the apparent feeling with which you began evaporates. You may come out of self-therapy still disliking the person but the rage or fear or depression is gone.

Nobody ever got better in the psychiatrist's office. Self-therapy, self-awareness, "insights" alone are not enough to change you; nor can pure "will power" (the Parent using brute force to break the Child's spirit) do the trick. Real growth comes as a result of *self-awareness* plus *experiments in new behavior*.

Each time I live through the inner struggle I recognize the terrible chasm between the two sides of myself. After each gestalt experience I find some small area of choice, a compromise between those two opposing forces. Little by little, working over and over again on the same dichotomy, I see the gap narrowing, the difficulty of making choices less desperate. My goal is to integrate the two opposite sides of myself, to end the inner battle.

Gestalt Therapy is a little like psychodrama. In psychodrama, you and other people sometimes reenact actual scenes from your own real or fantasy life. Others take on roles with which you interact. In Gestalt Therapy, you yourself play all the roles. In psychodrama, other people play the different parts of your personality. In Gestalt Therapy you play all the parts yourself.

In Gestalt *self*-therapy you have no outside guidance. You do it all yourself; you are completely responsible for getting the most out of the experience.

In this chapter I will outline three different techniques for Gestalt self-therapy.

1. Exploring a *known fantasy*, one you have already discovered through 1) self-awareness, intellectual observation of irrational patterns of behavior, or 2) experiencing a hidden feeling in self-therapy.
2. Playing all the parts of a recurrent or disturbing *dream*.
3. Playing an imaginary encounter with a *person* who has aroused an inappropriate reaction: irrational feeling, obsessive thinking, anxiety, depression, psychosomatic symptoms.

EXPLORING A KNOWN FANTASY

Many times in self-therapy I have peeled away a layer of an apparent emotion and reached a certain hidden feeling that I knew was also irrational, yet I could not go any deeper. For example, whenever I was taken by surprise by something good coming my way, I would get depressed. Unexpected good luck in landing a job, my students chipping in to buy me a gift, buying a house more elegant than I expected, someone doing me an unexpected favor: any of these could push me into a mild depression. At one time it would take weeks before I got around to doing self-therapy. Nowadays I can feel sadness before depression sets in, and use it for self-therapy. The hidden feeling always is, "I'm not supposed to have bad luck. It was decided long ago that my fate was unhappiness. Somewhere along the line the cards got mixed up and I have somebody else's good luck. That means someone else has my bad luck and it's all wrong. Somebody else is suffering, while I enjoy his good luck, and so I must not enjoy it."

Each time I feel this hidden thing, the apparent emotion, the depression or sadness, disappears and in a few minutes the hidden emotion evaporates, too.

One day I decided to try Gestalt self-therapy on this fantasy. I have described[1] self-therapy techniques that cannot be used unless you are in the midst of an apparent emotion. Gestalt self-therapy is different: you can start in cold blood and gradually work your way into the feelings. My way is to set up a specific date, usually once a week, to do Gestalt self-therapy. During the week I use my old self-therapy techniques to explore any painful problem that crops up and I think about my Gestalt assignment all week. I decide in advance which things I need to work on: uncomfortable situations nagging but not arousing a strong enough feeling for regular self-therapy, obsessive thinking, or hidden feelings which bring relief from the immediate apparent emotion but are obviously covers for something deeper. I use my intellect to plan an attack and to guess about the path I will take, so when I do Gestalt I can plunge right into the dialogue without hesitation.

I expect it to sound and feel wooden at the start, and I always have a great reluctance to get into it. It always feels as if nothing real could possibly happen. But I doggedly plow my way through, saying the words in a matter-of-fact, emotionless way, not faking it, until it comes alive, and in a few minutes it always does. While I am speaking the lines I am also listening to them.

While feeling a strong emotion I ask myself, "What does this remind me of?" "Who did this to whom?" Then I change one or both of the roles and continue with a similar dialogue.

I never forget that my purpose in Gestalt self-therapy is to experience hidden parts of myself. Whenever I hear myself speaking words that apply to some part of myself, I change roles and go on with the inner dialogue, the confrontation between two sides of me.

Here is a condensed version of what happened.

Muriel: I know there is a mistake in the cards. I have to find that other person. How can I find him? (Here I began to cry and continued through most of the experience.) I'm eating up all the food and somewhere a starved person needs me. Where are you? I'm looking for you. Please tell me where you are.

Starved Person: I'm starving. Muriel, where are you? I need you. Save me.

Muriel: I can't find you. I want to feed you, but I can't find you.

Starved Person: Save me, feed me, I'm starving. Give me some, you have so much. (At this point I switched the dialogue to the two parts of myself.)

Muriel 1: I want to save all those deprived people, but I can't. I don't know how.

Muriel 2: You are a rotten, greedy thing. You have no right to all those good things. You have Bernie and work you enjoy, and children you're proud of, and your health. Shame on you for gobbling up all the good things in life.

Muriel 1: I want to share, I want to give. What can I do?

Muriel 2: (Screaming) I hate you, you selfish, greedy thing.

That was as far as I could get then.

The next time I worked on this fantasy, I put my body into it. I began by play-acting. Although I avoided any phoniness, by going through my lines without emotion, I stood up tall with my arms outstretched in an attitude of saintly generosity, the all-giving mother, the Statue of Liberty.

Muriel: Come to me, poor starving people. I will feed you, I have so much and I want to give.

Starved Person: You're a liar. You make promises you can't fulfill. (The whole thing came alive at this point.)

Muriel: (Crying) No, it's true. I want to feed you.

Starved Person: You keep promising, but I'm still starving, and you're gobbling up all the food, you greedy thing. I hate you.

Muriel: I want to, but I don't know how. I don't want all this food. I'm gagging on it. I'm satiated. (Here the starving person became Little Muriel, the child I once was.)

Little Muriel: You promised me when you grew up I'd be happy. You lied. You failed me.

Muriel: I'm sorry. I want to rescue you, but I don't know how.

Little Muriel: You've got everything now, and I'm still back here suffering. Save me, save me.

Muriel: I want to but I can't. I don't know how.

Little Muriel: You promised. You lied to me. You failed me.

Muriel: Forgive me. I can't help it.
Little Muriel: (Screams) Take care of me. Save me, save me.
Muriel: I can't, I can't.

Here I came out of the self-therapy and realized I had been trying to be my own mother ever since she left me when I was five, and I could not do it anymore. I felt I could not feed that emotionally starved Child. I understood now a recurrent dream: I am ready to serve a dinner party. The table is set, I open the oven and discover I have forgotten to buy the roast. I feel frantic with guilt and helplessness.

I also understood my recent aversion to my own food. For the past month I had only been able to enjoy restaurant meals. Nothing I prepared myself seemed appetizing. That food represented the good things in my life, my good luck which the Child within me, stuck in the past, envied and resented.

I had known for some time that my compulsive overworking was irrational. It was hard to find time for recreation when unread students' mail and unfinished household chores loomed up. Often, when I was out to have a good time my mind was so cluttered up with students' problems, lectures, workshops, that I could not have fun. My stepmother was long dead, but I discovered in self-therapy that I was still obeying her.

Muriel: I am so tired.
Stepmother: You're not working hard enough. Come on, stop fooling around. Do those chores, you lazy thing. Don't tell me you're tired. You're just lazy.
Muriel: Oh please, let me play.
Stepmother: Play? What do you mean, play? You have all those things to do. Get to work.
Muriel: You never let me have any fun. I'm so tired of working all the time. I need some fun.
Stepmother: All you care about is fun. Just like your mother. Irresponsible.
Muriel: Oh, no! Please don't tell me I'm like my mother. I don't desert my children. (Here I switched to two sides of Muriel: Parent and Child.)
Parent: Just like your mother, you big phoney. Pretending to love everybody. All you care about is a good time.
Child: It's not true. I do love them. I won't desert them. I just need a little time off.

Parent: I hate you, selfish thing. (Pounding chair) Just like your
  mother.
Child: Stop torturing me. I'm doing the best I can. Let me rest.
Parent: I hate you, hate you.
Child: Please!

Now I understood another meaning of the dream of the missing
roast: my fear of being a depriving mother.

When the Gestalt self-therapy experience is over, when my feelings
have cooled off, my Adult self takes over. I ask myself, "What do I
know about myself now? In terms of my inner conflicts, where am I
at this point?" Then two things happen: (a) the hidden fantasy has a
little less power over my attitudes and behavior because I am more
aware of it; I have less compulsion to act out self-defeating patterns
and (b) the Adult finds some small area of choice, some decision
which is a compromise between the two opposing forces.

I notice that with repeated Gestalt experiences of the same conflicts
over a period of time, my life style is altering. The gap between the
two sides appears to be narrowing. My goal is to close the gap, to
integrate those two opposites so that the inner struggle stops completely and I can function in each of these conflicted areas like Maslow's healthy person; spontaneous, non-blocked, unconflicted.

Fritz believed that modern man is so intellect-oriented, so lacking
in spontaneity, that only in dreams can he be truly genuine. On the
other hand, Harry Stack Sullivan said that by the time we start remembering our dreams we have already distorted them. Research
indicates that patients obligingly produce Freudian dreams, Jungian
dreams, Adlerian dreams, etc. to fit the theories of their therapists.

My own observation is that people who get too absorbed in analyzing their dreams tend to ignore their responsibilities in daily life.
In general, I am against contemplating one's navel at the expense of
real self-awareness. Most of us need encouragement to notice our
self-defeating behavior in everyday life, to explore our mistakes in
problem solving, in our relations with other people, rather than escaping into preoccupation with dreams.

But there are two kinds of dreams I find worth working with: (1) a
recurrent dream and (2) a dream that stays with you the next day,
producing depression, anxiety or obsessive thinking.

Every part of the dream is yourself. Play each role: people and
things. Remember the purpose of Gestalt self-therapy is to experience
all parts of yourself, especially the hidden parts. When you are
playing the dream and have felt some emotions as deeply as possible,

when they have reached a peak and are beginning to cool off, just *before* they disappear, ask yourself, "What does this remind me of?" and change the characters in the dream to parts of yourself.

The Dream

I suddenly remember that I have forgotten to feed and water some white rats in the basement, for whom I am responsible. Filled with fear and remorse, I rush downstairs and find the rats stretched out on the floor, feebly trying to reach a puddle of water nearby. I am overwhelmed with pity and revulsion. I want them to reach the water but can't bear to touch them.

Rat: (Lying on floor) Muriel, save me. I'm dying. (Stretching arms toward water) I can't reach the water.

Muriel: (Crying) Oh, poor little thing. I want to save you but I can't.

Rat: Please, please help me.

Muriel: Try harder, I can't touch you. You're so repulsive. I'm sorry.

Rat: I'm too weak. I can't. Muriel, help me, give me water.

Muriel: You're so pitiful but you make my flesh crawl.

Rat: (Getting weaker) Dying, dying. (At this point, I suddenly saw the rat as part of me.)

Muriel 1: I know who you are. You're that part that's greedy for success. I hate you. You're disgusting.

Muriel 2: I need, I need, give me. Don't let me die.

Muriel 1: You're insatiable, I'm tired of feeding you. Stop blaming me.

Muriel 2: Give me, give me.

Muriel 1: Repulsive little thing, I know you. Whenever I accomplish anything real, help anyone grow, there you are, gloating about your *success*, as if that matters. I can't stand you. I hate you.

Muriel 2: Help, help, please.

Muriel 1: Sick of you. I want to rest. Can't feed you anymore.

Muriel 2: (Feebly gasps) I'm dying.

Muriel 1: THEN DIE, damn you. (Stamps on Muriel 2)

Muriel 2: (Dies)

I was outgrowing an old trait I had long been ashamed of, and had done self-therapy about in past years; the craving for recognition, status, prestige in my work. I don't know when the change occurred because I had not been paying attention to it recently, but after this Gestalt self-therapy experience, I began to notice that I was no longer excited by praise and signs of acceptance from the establishment; it was pleasant, but not thrilling. I realized that at last I was in a place I had wanted to be: that the fascination of my work and my feelings about my students were sufficient incentives for learning and working harder. Popularity, and acceptance by the establishment, no longer preoccupied me.

The Dream

I suddenly remember that I am responsible for a baby and have forgotten all about it. I know the baby has milk, but it is probably very wet and should have been fed additional nourishing foods, especially egg yolk and orange juice. I am overwhelmed with guilt and dash in to find the baby (sometimes in a crib, sometimes in a carriage down in a dark, dank, stray-cat-ridden basement). I am relieved and amazed to see the baby smiling up at me, plump and contented.

I used my old self-therapy techniques a few times and uncovered guilt at being an inadequate mother to my own children.

The first time I tried Gestalt therapy on it was in my first workshop with Fritz Perls.

Muriel: Are you all right? I was so worried about you. I'm sorry I forgot you.
Baby: (Smiling, relaxed) I feel fine. Don't worry about me. I'm happy. (Fritz asks if the baby can get up and walk.)
Baby: I don't want to. I don't even want to sit up. I like it here. Muriel, stop worrying about me.

I was surprised at this, but did not understand the significance of it. After my first Gestalt workshop with Fritz, I began to experiment with Gestalt self-therapy.

Next time I had the same dream, I tried to discover what part of me the baby represented.

Muriel: Thank God, you seem healthy and happy. I was so worried about you. All you've had is milk, and you've been cooped up in that crib with no fresh air.
Baby: You're depriving me. I need eggs and orange juice.
Muriel: But you look so healthy and contented.
Baby: Yes, I can survive on milk but I can't grow. Not without other foods.

(Here I remembered my own psychological test reports: "She is creative, but might be more creative were she not driven to produce . . . she may to some extent be suppressing an underlying need to turn her attention in part away from people and toward her own inner self, e.g., through some artistic pursuit." I changed the baby to Little Muriel.)

Little Muriel: I have lots of milk: books to read and self-esteem from love and success. But you're too busy to feed me real food so I can't grow. I can't be really creative.

Muriel: What do you want, what do you need to grow?

Little Muriel: You know what I need. You've known ever since you took those tests. I need fun and music and dancing and nature.

Muriel: I know, but I don't have time.

Little Muriel: Stop working so hard. Stop *thinking* so much. You're not fair to me. Stop being compulsive. Take care of me, damn you.

Muriel: I did take care of you. Where would you be without me? When you were in those foster homes I grew up fast and learned to figure people out. I was your parent. Don't blame me now. I can't help it if I learned to think too much.

The next time I worked on the dream was in another of Fritz's workshops. This time Fritz told me to talk to the dream.

Muriel: Stop haunting me. Leave me alone.

Baby: You're neglecting me. You don't have time for me.

Muriel: Where would you be without me? I was a father and a mother to you. Oh my God, I sound just like my father (laughing out loud). That's his voice.

Father: I was a father and a mother to you. Be grateful.

Muriel: That's a lie. What did you ever do for me? You boarded me out with strangers. I was alone all those terrible years.

Father: But I always visited you weekends.

Muriel: Big deal! You never gave a damn how I was treated, what happened to me during the week. You conveniently closed your eyes. I managed to survive without you. (I went back to the baby.)

Baby: I managed to survive without you. I don't need you. I'm getting along fine. Don't be such a fool. Stop trying so hard to understand me. I'm healthy and happy.

Fritz: The baby is the healthiest part of you.

Little by little I began to change after that. Some of the changes were deliberate decisions, some came by themselves, I started buying more records, allowing myself time to dance more often. I began to give the baby, the non-thinking part of me, more freedom. In my workshops I became more of a participant on an emotional level, trusting my intuition more, relying less on the computer in my head, and the workshops improved in effectiveness for my students. Evidently, Fritz was right: the baby is the healthiest part of me, my feelings are more useful than my intellect in working with people.

ENCOUNTERS WITH PEOPLE

Most of the Gestalt self-therapy I do is based on irrational or painful feelings about people. This gives me a practical tool for interpersonal relations. Each time I work through an apparent feeling toward someone, it evaporates and I am then able to relate to him in a rational way.

Here are five steps, a loose guideline for Gestalt self-therapy. You may move back and forth from one step to another, but in general it feels like this:

How to Experience an Inner Conflict

I. Notice an intense and/or painful feeling about a person or e-vent: anger, hurt, disapproval, jealousy, envy, dependence, help-lessness, controlling, controlled; or a neurotic symptom aroused by that person: anxiety, depression or obsessive thinking, all three of which are covers for a hidden emotion; or physical symptoms: signs of tension, psychosomatic illness.

II. Have an imaginary confrontation with that person, playing each role alternately. I change seats and bodily stance each time I change roles. Some of my students find this distracting, and do better simply talking in different voices.

Some people feel freer with an audience of self-therapy group members, others can only do it alone in complete privacy. I do best with one person with whom I feel safe; who will not be bored or judgmental.

With a larger audience I am afraid of taking too much time. Alone, I cannot seem to take myself seriously enough to get into it; it feels boring and dead. I always keep my eyes closed to avoid thinking about my audience and to get deeper into my fantasies.

1. Speak aloud the thoughts of both people more frankly than possible in real life.

2. Speak thoughts you imagine the other may be thinking, especially those thoughts which trouble you, even if, *especially* if, the Adult in you says you are being irrational, just projecting. It is the projections we are after.
3. Exaggerate, caricature both sides. I use my whole body to do this, gesticulating, making faces, standing up tall or cringing on the floor.
4. Stay with this encounter until you have felt as deeply as possible. You will reach a peak of emotion and then start cooling off. Just before you cool off, go on to the next step.

III. Ask yourself, "Who did this to whom?" Change one side to a person or persons from (a) your present life, (b) your past. Follow 1, 2, 3, and 4 in step II above. Now play the other person sympathetically. Try to imagine how it feels to be him. Whereas in II you were caricaturing him, now, on the contrary, you are a witness for the defense.

IV. Change both people to two sides of yourself. Follow 2, 3, and 4 as above.

V. "What is my inner conflict?" This is where you are now. Remember to go back and experience this impasse whenever you have an opportunity.

And: "What small compromises can I make between these opposing forces at this stage?"

The following is an example of how I used Gestalt self-therapy to explore an irrational feeling after an encounter with a student.

The Background

In one of my workshops, Jill received valuable negative feedback from the group: She continually frustrated them in three ways: she kept talking compulsively in vague generalities which bored them and never told them how she felt about anything that was happening —the only thing they wanted to hear. She never listened when they tried to tell her their own feelings, and she seemed to be trying to stop them from feeling. True to her pattern, Jill used these same tactics to avoid hearing this feedback.

She was a likeable woman, and the group cared about her. They were frustrated by her refusal to hear them. But I was more frustrated than anyone else. I had known Jill and her husband for some time, and I realized how important this feedback was for her personal life. I had a pretty good idea about the hidden meaning of her pattern, how she got that way, and I was obsessed with the need to make her listen, make her use this experience for growth. I could not stand to see her miss the boat. I had to save her!

So I made time during a break to corner Jill and rapidly diagnose her position, the meaning of her behavior, the value of group feedback, and offer a blueprint for self-therapy. Jill responded to my words just as she had done to the group's comments. She talked compulsively in an effort to drown me out, dealt only with generalities, refused to recognize her feelings and managed to avoid hearing anything of value. My intensity, added to the group's pressure, was evidently more than Jill could bear. She left the workshop a day early. (I later learned that the next week she did self-therapy for the first time, so evidently something important was happening.)

When the workshop was over, I began to think obsessively about Jill, rehearsing over and over again in my mind ways of explaining it all to her, persuading, selling my ideas: this is the form my obsessive thinking usually takes.

When the obsessive thinking became a torment, I tried Gestalt self-therapy. That was Step I, *notice intense or painful feeling* about a person *or a neurotic symptom*: depression, anxiety, obsessive thinking.

Step II. Have an *imaginary confrontation* with that person, playing each role alternately. Speak each person's thoughts aloud. My dialogue with Jill went something like this:

Muriel: Jill, please listen to me. I have such important things to tell you.

Jill: I don't want to hear.

Muriel: Please let me save you. I can't stand to see what you are doing.

Jill: I don't know what you're talking about.

Muriel: Don't you see how you're holding other people at arm's length? That's why you're so lonely.

Jill: I don't know what you're all trying to do to me. Leave me alone.

Muriel: We're trying to get near you. We like you. We want to know you better, but you won't let us. Please listen to me. I want to help you. I understand it all and I can explain it all to you.

Jill: Leave me alone. Go away. I can't hear you.

Muriel: You need this nourishing food I'm trying to feed you. You're starving.

Jill: I can't swallow your food. Stop forcing it down my throat.

Muriel: Please, please don't push me away. Please don't starve yourself.

Step III. Who did this to whom?

Jill: (Shouting) Go away, damn you. You're just like Mrs. L. (The foster mother who force-fed me to the point of vomiting. At this point Jill became Little Muriel and Muriel became Mrs. L.)

Mrs. L: (Standing over Little Muriel, screaming, grimacing) EAT IT! EAT IT, damn you. I'll force it down your throat. (Gesture of forcing food down)

Little Muriel: (Gagging) Please don't. I can't. I would if I could but I can't.

Mrs. L: (Screaming) Eat it, eat it. I'll make you swallow it. I'll beat you if you vomit.

Little Muriel: (On her knees, pleading) Please don't make me. I can't, I can't. Please, please leave me alone.

Step IV. Change both people to sides of yourself.

Muriel 1: Stop forcing people. Let them live. Who the hell do you think you are? Damn you.

Muriel 2: But they're so deprived and I know what they need. I have to save them. I have to help them, poor things.

Muriel 1: You lousy hypocrite! Pretending to be so saintly. You're just power mad, that's all.

Muriel 2: No, it's not true. I have to feed those starving people. I can't stand to see them so deprived when I know what they need.

Muriel 1: Goddamned liar. Rotten phony. I hate you (Pounding chair). I'll kill you if you don't stop. Stop it. Stop forcing people. Let them live.

Muriel 2: I want to stop, I'm so tired, but I can't.

Step V. What is my inner conflict? The struggle between the drive to save people and the wish to give them the freedom to be autonomous, to move at their own pace.

After this experience I was able to be more relaxed with another student whose resistance had been tormenting me for a long time. I could accept on an emotional level what I had known intellectually for a long time: that only she herself could struggle with her resistance, that it was not my battle.

The following are condensed versions of actual experiences in Gestalt self-therapy of five of my students.

The Background

In communication workshop Frieda was told her seven-year-old, Jamie, was too difficult for some people to handle. He kicked them, destroyed their property, and since Frieda would not let anyone lay a hand on him, they were powerless to protect themselves and were beginning to feel hostile toward Jamie. Frieda could not accept their right to handle Jamie themselves with any show of force.

Gestalt Self-Therapy

Frieda: Oh, Jamie, my smallest child! You're such a little, little boy and things have been so rough in the family since you were born. I'll take care of you. I'll protect you. I won't let anyone hurt you.

Jamie: I know. Hardly anything I do bothers you.

Frieda: That's right, my child. I wish you would be nice so people would like you, but I can't get angry with you, I can't let them hurt you. You're so little and I know you try to be good. I'll protect you. You're such a tiny thing, like me, and you're the only one of my children who looks like me. (Here she switches roles. Frieda becomes her grandma, who brought her up, and Jamie becomes Little Frieda.)

Grandma: I'll take care of you, my child. Don't worry about anything.

Little Frieda: But why don't my daddy and mommy live together? Why doesn't my daddy live here?

Grandma: Never mind, my child. Don't bother your head about such things. Your daddy loves you.

Little Frieda: How do you know he loves me? Did he tell you?

Grandma: I know, I know. No, he didn't tell me in those words, but I can tell.

Little Frieda: Then why won't he live with me? And why is Mommy so mean?

Grandma: You're too young to understand. You don't have to think about such things. Don't listen and don't see anything bad. Be happy. A little girl should be happy. I'll protect you. I won't let anything bad happen to you. I love you.

Little Frieda: I know you love me, but you protected me so well I grew up without knowing anything about the real world, and now look at the trouble I'm in. (Back to Frieda and Jamie)

Frieda: Oh, Jamie, I love you so much I'm protecting you from knowing the real world. You're being bad to people and they can't love you and you don't understand. You don't know the only reason they don't hit you is because of me. I'm not being fair to you. You're getting a crazy picture of the world, just like me.

Frieda came out of this experience with a determination to somehow modify her attitude toward her adult friends and their behavior toward Jamie; to give him a chance to know reality.

The Background

Miriam's "friendship" with Ella was a transference relationship in which she felt emotionally dependent on Ella. Miriam's obsessive thinking swung back and forth from intense affection and equally intense resentment against what seemed like Ella's manipulation and teasing.

Gestalt Self-Therapy

Miriam: I'm sick and tired of feeling like this. I want to stop thinking about you. I don't want to have to see you so often. You're driving me crazy.

Ella: I don't know what you mean. I haven't done anything. Come here. Go away.

Miriam: That double-talk of yours, those confused messages are getting me all mixed up. Stop teasing me.

Ella: (Swings an imaginary string back and forth) Here kitty, kitty, kitty! Catch this. Come on, try to catch it. Hah, hah! I won't let you.

Miriam: (On the floor in attitude of kitten, head swinging desperately back and forth, trying to catch imaginary object swinging before her eyes) Damn you, cut it out! Stop it, I say. Leave me alone. Just like my mother.

Mother: Miriam dear, do it my way. I understand you perfectly. Just listen to me. Do this, do that, come on, I'll tell you what to do.

Miriam: Leave me alone. LEAVE ME ALONE, damn it. Get off my back. Let me live my own life. Let me think my own thoughts. (Here she switched to two sides of herself.)

Topdog: Come on now, work hard. Get perfect grades in school. Always be polite and appease people, tell them what they want to hear. Entertain them with jokes. Don't indulge yourself. Don't have any fun. Don't show any feelings. Keep your cool at all times.

Underdog: Get off my back. I'm sick of you. Stop ruining my life. Let me live. Leave me alone! LEAVE ME ALONE! damn you.

After this, Miriam began to wean herself away from her painful dependency on Ella, using Gestalt and other self-therapy techniques whenever she was aware of acting out her irrational cravings. She also began in small ways to modify her perfectionist pattern, experimenting with small doses of anxiety. As she allowed herself more spontaneity, people began to notice that her face became more expressive and attractive, that she was losing a former rigidity and appearance of coldness.

The Background

Sylvia depended on her husband to make decisions for the family's welfare. She acted as if she was incapable of assuming responsibility, waited passively in the hope that he would make wise decisions, complained bitterly and suffered helplessness and anxiety on those occasions when she thought he failed.

Gestalt Self-Therapy

Sylvia: Take care of us. Be responsible. Everything in the family is your responsibility. I can't make these important decisions. Why don't you? Why do you make wrong decisions? It's terrible when you make mistakes. I worry so about the children's welfare and I can't do anything. I'm so helpless. Do it! Do it right! Make things right! I'm so scared. I feel like a helpless child. (Goes back to childhood)

Little Sylvia: Daddy, take care of Momma. Be good to her. She's suffering and I can't take care of her.

Momma: Sylvia, take care of me. I'm dying. Find your Daddy. Make him come home. I'm dying, save me, save me.

Little Sylvia: I can't, I can't. I want to but I'm only a little girl. I tried so hard to save you, to fix things up with you and Daddy, but I can't. Daddy, please take care of Momma. I can't stand to see her suffer and I'm only a little girl. I can't do it. (Here she comes back to her present self.)

Sylvia: I want to save the world. I can't stand all the suffering. Look at the injustice, the cruelty, the deprivation. Change it.

Sylvia: I've been trying all my life, but I can't do it. (Two sides of Sylvia)

Topdog: You are responsible for everybody. Try harder. Be smarter. Study more. Work harder. Don't rest.

Underdog: I can't do it. I'm so exhausted. (Lying down) I just want to rest. I can't carry that burden anymore. So tired, so tired. Just want to lie here and rest, not move.

After this, Sylvia began to assume more responsibility in the family. At times when her attitude differed sharply from her husband's, she was able to assert herself and stand by her convictions. With continued self-therapy she also began to be more realistic about her limitations in saving the world, with less tendency to rush into impulsive, self-defeating action.

The Background

During a Gestalt self-therapy workshop, I cried hard while exploring a problem of my own, acting as a model for the group. When I finished, Sylvia began to work.

Gestalt Self-Therapy

Sylvia: Oh, Muriel, I can't stand to see you cry. It tears me up. Can't stand to see you suffer. I want to say, stop it. Stop suffering. I know this remind me of my mother. Momma, stop crying. Please stop. I can't stand it.

Mother: (Crying) Sylvia, I'm dying. Save me. Take care of me. Tell Poppa to come home. Oh, Sylvia, I'm so unhappy. I'm dying.

Sylvia: Stop it, Momma. I can't stand to hear you. You're disgusting. You repel me—ugh! Can't stand that weakness. (Changes to Strong Sylvia and Weak Sylvia)

Strong Sylvia: I can't stand your weakness. You repel me, disgust me—ecch! You make me sick.

Weak Sylvia: (Crying) I'm so weak and helpless. I can't help it. I want to be strong, but I can't. I'm just like Momma.

Sylvia: Oh, poor Momma. Poor little thing. You can't help it. Poor helpless little thing. (Crying) I'm sorry, Momma. (Cradles Momma in her arms) I love you, poor little thing. I'm sorry you're suffering. I wish I could help you.

This acceptance of her mother's weakness was new for Sylvia and indicated that the gap between her strong and weak sides was narrowing. She now finds herself more open to her true feelings, more capable of experiencing and showing hurt instead of using an old system: covering it up with fake anger.

The Background

Agnes came to a workshop and announced that she didn't feel like working.

Gestalt Self-Therapy

Agnes: I just don't feel like doing the work here. I don't feel like doing anything I'm supposed to do. I'm tired of always being so damned good. I want to quit my job and stop doing all the "nice" things I've done all my life. I'm tired of being the perfect hostess. I could have kicked myself after I offered my home for the last workshop party. I was irritable all week and had a perfectly miserable time at that party. I've never been this way before. I can't imagine what's come over me.

Mother: (In a prissy, indignant voice) I can't imagine what's come over you. Why, you *have* to be hospitable. That's the way we do things in our family. Now you behave yourself and do things properly. I just don't know what you think you're talking about. I don't want to hear any more of that. That's enough!

Agnes: (Boldly) Well, that's where I am now. I'm sick of doing things your way. I don't want to be your good little girl anymore. The hell with that! I'm going to do things my way from now on and if you don't like it you can lump it.

Mother: Now that's enough of that. You'll just have to behave yourself. No more nonsense.

Agnes: I won't obey you anymore. I'm a big girl now. (Begins to tremble) I don't know why I'm shaking like this. I guess I'm scared, but I don't know what I'm afraid of. (Keeps quiet for a while and lets herself shake. The shaking grows more violent. Goes back to the mother of her childhood.)

Mother: (Fiercely) How dare you talk that way! You think you can disobey me? I'll show you, I'll teach you! (Whips Agnes)

Agnes: (Crying) Oh, please don't! I'll be good. I want to be good but I can never please you. Why do you spank me all the time, no matter what I do? Why should you want to hit a little girl?

Mother: (Calmly hitting) That's the only way to bring up a child. How would you know how to behave if I didn't spank you regularly? I have to do it.

Agnes: Somebody help me, save me! Daddy, please help me. Mother spanks me all the time and I'm so afraid of her. You don't know. You're not here when she does it. Please protect me.

Daddy: I don't know what you mean Agnes. How can I help you? I have things to do. You'll have to excuse me now.

Agnes: (Screams) What kind of a father are you? What kind of a man are you? Don't you give a damn about me? I'm your little girl and I'm so scared. (Agnes is still shaking. She lies down on the floor.)

Agnes: (Crying) I'm a little, little girl and I'm lying here on the living room floor crying, hoping someone will hear me and care. I'm so cold here in my nightie. Why won't anyone come and comfort me? Doesn't anyone care? Please, Daddy or Mother, come and put your hand on my cheek and tell me you love me. (Sobbing loudly) Just once tell me you love me. If I could just hear it once it would last me a long time. Nobody hears, nobody cares. It's so cold here. I'd better get up and go back to my bed.

Big Agnes: Get up Agnes. No point waiting for them. Just take care of yourself. Stop all that crying. It won't get you anywhere.

Little Agnes: But I wish they would comfort me.

Big Agnes: Well, they won't, so snap out of it.

Agnes: The shaking stopped. I don't feel scared anymore. Funny, I was so brave and rebellious. I didn't know I was scared underneath. I guess I have to change a little at a time, but I don't want to be her good little girl anymore. Boy, I'd like to shock her. (Laughs out loud) I know what I'd like to do! Go back to that small gossipy town and walk naked down main street. That would give my mother something to think about. She'd hang her head down for the rest of her life.

NOTE: All examples of Gestalt self-therapy in this chapter are condensed. I have indicated change in role and mood but not the length of time required for each stage.

REFERENCES

Schiffman, M., *Self-Therapy Techniques for Personal Growth*, Menlo Park, Calif.: Self Therapy Press, 1971.

CHAPTER 21

WOMEN IN THERAPY: A GESTALT THERAPIST'S VIEW

MIRIAM POLSTER, Ph.D.

Miriam Polster is in private practice in San Diego, California, and is the co-director of the Gestalt Training Center, San Diego. She is also the coauthor of *Gestalt Therapy Integrated*.

Reprinted by permission from M. Polster, "Women in Therapy—A Gestalt Therapist's View, in S. V. Frankl and V. Burtle, eds., **Women in Therapy**, New York: Bruner/Mazel, 1974, pp. 247-262.

Not long ago, in a weekend workshop for couples, we had divided into two groups, husbands and wives. Off by themselves, the women were asked to close their eyes and fantasize what one of their days might be like if they were men instead of women. Afterwards, as we shared our fantasies with each other, one of the women reported how in her fantasy she had started walking through her house from one of the back bedrooms, all the way through the house, and how, as she walked through each of the rooms, she hadn't picked up a single toy or piece of clothing or newspaper, she hadn't closed a single drawer or closet door, she hadn't turned out a single light or mopped up a single spill, and finally she had just walked straight through the house and out the front door, closing the door behind her. After she finished telling us her fantasy, there was a soft crackle of laughter, smiles of recognition and kinship and a chuckle of admiration at her fantasied resolution.

Now I had met the husbands of these women. They were not brutes, bullies or martinets who insisted that household duties be performed with militaristic timeliness and dispatch. But these women didn't seem to need that, anyhow. They had arrived at the point where they felt compelled to do things they didn't really want to do and which they could get out of doing only by special effort, like fantasizing, or under special conditions, like illness. Somehow, they had constructued for themselves standards of behavior that they felt obliged to live up to and which often bore only slight resemblance to the actual pattern of their own personal needs.

A double thread runs through the stories of many of the women I see, married or unmarried. On the one hand, they feel trapped in a round of commitment and activities which keeps them busy but leaves them feeling unsatisfied, frantic and unfulfilled. On the other hand, adding insult to injury, they do not even experience themselves as having a hand in making many of the decisions about how they are to live. They feel locked into a situation—a career decision, a relationship or a life-style—which they didn't elect or which has turned out to have hidden consequences they didn't foresee, but which they feel powerless to change or to abandon. They bottle up the feelings and desires which they believe they can't express, either because expressing them will cause more trouble than they already have or because it won't make any difference anyway and they will only wind up feeling more frustrated and impotent. So they become skillful at learning how to dance when somebody else leads.

The difficulties any person experiences in life will reflect his or her own particular limitations and these, in turn, will relate to the prohibitions and limitations which society imposes on each of us. If a woman is married, societal patterns will have a lot to say about how her husband views the marriage and what expectations he has brought to the relationship. Her own personal bent will, correspondingly, determine how hemmed in she may feel by these expectations and how commited she is to living up to them, whether she finds them compatible or not with her own needs. Single or married, at work she will encounter the expectations her colleagues carry in with their lunch pails or briefcases and her response to built-in expectations also pervades her experiences as a woman at school, within her family and among her friends.

It is a major hunk of work for a woman to integrate all of these inclinations and influences and to come up with a harmonious personal sense of herself where no experience need to be discriminated against as inadmissible or unworthy.

As a child, all of her experience was viewed freshly and uncritically. She made her own standards for what she wanted to do and what she didn't want to do, spinning them out of the shining thread of her own sensations and values. She could play as happily with shit as she could with mud. Only gradually did she begin to learn that some things that made her happy weren't supposed to and some things which weren't so pleasing to her were, nevertheless, better regarded and were to be more highly valued. She began to distrust knowledge based primarily on her own experience and to introject, to swallow whole with the same lack of criticism, the precepts of other stronger and wiser people around her. She began to exchange pure joy for secondhand wisdom. In doing this she had her first exercise in learning how to deny or disapprove of some of the most beautiful parts of her own experience.

But these denied or disowned parts of herself did not just meekly disappear. The imprint of firsthand living is not so easily erased. The taste of honey lingers somewhere in one's insides and sends up vague traces of something better than the present watered-down experience which is only an inadequate substitute. Somewhere underground, her original knowledge of joy sits uneasy and only too ready to contradict or sabotage the surface confluence agreed upon by her shrewder and more politic socialized self which denies the primal zest and richness that she knows can underlie her actions.

Eventually, these antithetical characteristics freeze into postures of mutual alienation and stand-off; this is the genesis of her own personal polarities, those internal contradictions which nourish ambivalence and fatigue. Perls (1969) formulated the concept of polarities into the basic characters of topdog versus underdog, but there is more diversity than this in the cast of polarities making up the composite which is any particular woman. Topdog and underdog imply merely that in these popular struggles one of the opponents appears to be winning or to have the upper hand. However, any characteristic aspect of a woman can spawn its own polar counterpart. So, contests can rage on internally between a woman's ruthlessness and her tenderness, between her conventional self and her rebel, between her meekness and her arrogance. Any woman is a composite of many Dr. Jekylls and Ms. Hydes.

To the extent that a woman keeps herself out of touch with one of the polarities engaged in her personal conflicts, she is ensuring her own immobility and impotence. Rooted in her submerged and disowned underdog are the seeds of change and movement. Like all the disenfranchised, her underdog has little to lose and everything to gain from change. When she remains out of touch with this unacknowledged part of herself, she is, in effect, silencing her own protest against the *status quo*. The parts of herself which she refuses to give ear or voice to remain isolated and unavailable as a support for informed action. They are relegated to underground activities, dissension and sabotage. This is what underlies her sense of being trapped or crammed with unexpressed and inexpressible feelings.

In Gestalt Therapy, a central focus of our work is the individual's responsibility for shaping his or her own existence. In spite of how her environment leans on her, a woman, nevertheless, has to know how to engage with it in ways which will be nourishing and zestful, not just successive acts of self-betrayal. She is creating her own life, bit by bit. She needs all her energy and ingenuity to come up with hours, days and years that she feels she has had a hand in shaping.

To do this she has to be able to integrate her awareness of sensations, actions, wants, values, relationships and all the raw material of her life with her own personal willingness and skill in using this awareness as her basis for action.

When her awareness is unprejudiced and unimpeded, when she has no stake in keeping parts of her experience alien and unknown, her actions can spring expressively from native mobilization. Her sense of her life is that it has flexibility, surprise, enthusiasm and movement. She experiences herself as a free agent, acting from her own needs, making choices from a range of possible alternatives and being free to change whatever she becomes aware of as unsatisfying or toxic.

An example of this is the experience of one woman who came to realize, in her awareness of the tyranny that her family and their rigid upbringing had imposed on her, that she had even furnished her entire house according to their dictates and not at all to her own taste! In addition to standards of interior design, she had also swallowed much of what the family had to say about such virtues as thrift, frugality and conservative behavior. One day we were working with her distaste for her furniture and how angry she was with herself for feeling so stuck with it. She was far from poor and could probably have afforded to chuck it all and simply refurnish. I instructed her to use her anger and give herself a lecture on what she might do with her herd of white elephants. She was a woman of rich imagination and exuberant sense of drama, and she swung into the assignment with energy. Her ideas ranged from burning it and collecting the insurance to giving it all to a charitable organization and claiming it as a tax deduction. But her eventual solution illustrated an important and basic principle in gestalt work with polarities, in this case her esthetic self and her practical self. Resolution of a conflict, in its most effective and enduring form, usually involves respecting both parts of the polarity and merging them into a course of action which represents a synthesis or an alliance of these previously disparate parts. Her solution turned out to be a house sale, leaving her house bare, cannily getting top dollar for her unwanted furniture (even selling some of it to her relatives!), and winding up with a healthy bankroll to finance her refurnishing.

Now all of a woman's actions may not be this exciting or have such a sense of turnaround. Life is not so unstintingly generous. But even when a woman performs humdrum tasks, if she experiences herself as not locked into doing them she is free to recognize that she regards these tasks as necessary and *chooses* to do them rather than delegating them to someone else or letting them go undone. She is also free to stop doing them when she senses that the psychological cost to herself has become more than she is willing to pay.

The experience of being stuck, on the contrary, consists of finding one's present status malnourishing, distasteful or even downright poisonous but feeling unable to do anything but hang on to it. A woman may know exactly what it might take to turn her life around, but such changes may frighten or repel her. On the other hand, she may only vaguely want something more or something different than she has right now, and this amorphous discontent scares her, or results in her feeling guilty, despondent or overly demanding.

What a woman finds unwelcome about making changes in her own life is, at least partly, a projection. That is, what scares her or repels her or makes her feel guilty is the unknown or the unacceptable or the reprehensible *in herself*. What she fears about making changes is primarily the re-awakening of aspects of herself, unpredictable, untried, alien, demanding and leading to consequences she is not sure she is willing to permit. Her self-doubt also has an introjective core. It is the accumulation of the judgments and values of other people which she has taken in and adopted as her own and which she feels uneasy about questioning. Unchallenged, these foreign doctrines govern her actions from a position analogous to that of a distant ruler sending out edicts, which are not to be questioned, to the inhabitants of a territory he has conquered. Instead of viewing herself as a population of potential and unrealized capacities which she might explore, she fears rebellion and the overthrow of her established routine and is immobilized by this fear. She keeps herself in check like an uneasy dictator who fears change. This is how she has arrived at her current impasse—unhappy with her present life, but afraid or unwilling to try new behaviors or adopt new values which might lead to resolution. As a way of relieving herself of the responsibility for this situation, she projects outside of herself her own unwillingness to change and decides that she has no effect on an immutable and intransigent world. She is stuck.

One young married woman deplored the boredom of her life with a husband whom she considered dull, unadventuresome, overweight and her social inferior. Some of these things were true about him, but he was also generous with her, listened to her periodic tirades without getting too angry, and had enough emotional resilience to come out of these combats still loving her and not bearing any grudges. He worked at an unskilled job where he was his own boss and dealt with machinery which he loved. He was not a milktoast; he was an easygoing guy with a good sense of humor and a no-nonsense attitude toward himself and the world around him. He was pretty well informed, had some interest in politics, but mostly he liked his job, his family and his friends.

She was filled with the idea that she was really better than all this, too good for such a husband, and wanted to split. Where she wanted to go and what she planned on doing when she arrived there were inconsequential details that she couldn't be bothered with. She admitted that she very much liked the financial and material comfort she had with him, and he came in very handy when there were practical issues that demanded attention. She had very little tolerance for handling frustration in a creative way, she would get bogged down in emotional upheavals, and his good-humored patience was indispensable at these times. This was not a very good omen for her independent function without him.

During our work together, interestingly enough, she changed very little. He lost weight, became more active in volunteer political organizations, began to read more and talk to her about what he was reading—but she was still not satisfied. She had a great stake in not recognizing change, since she wanted to retain her picture of herself as a woman burdened with an inferior husband. This freed her of the necessity to do anything about making changes in herself that might move her out of her own boredom. Of her shortcomings she remained steadfastly unaware, and when her husband confronted her about them on those occasions when he was moved beyond endurance, her response was tears and hysteria.

This elevated picture of herself had been handed to her by her mother, along with the family recipes. But all she had was a vague sense that she was cut out for better things, and there was very little substance behind these feelings. Her first chore was to learn how to make her own life interesting without blaming her boredom on her husband and expecting him to do something about it. We worked at making her more aware of the specific things she wanted from her husband, and she began to give up expecting him to be a mind reader and divine what she wanted. She began to take a couple of courses at the local university extension program. Not grand actions, surely, but initial steps in shaping her own movement out of boredom.

The need to keep from making changes imposes certain conditions on a woman. She has to keep herself from becoming aware of attractive possibilities for action either within herself or her environment. She has to keep new directions from becoming fascinating or compelling enough to disturb and arouse her. She has to construct and maintain an equilibrium for herself where she can exercise just enough sensitivity to know that she is unhappy, but not enough to discover or invent what she might do about her own unhappiness.

There are several ways she can keep herself in this condition. For the most part, they consist of not allowing her own experience to become sharp enough, figural enough, to articulate clearly what is bothering her. Whenever an individual has a stake in things-as-they-are, she has to do something to obscure the native flux that all living things display. To keep phenomena which *are* changing appearing as if they are not changing at all, she has to prevent herself from seeing them clearly, in rich detail, as well-defined and active figures against the background of her general orientation to her life. In the above example, the young wife had to learn to see change in her husband, as well as work toward changes in herself.

One way of not perceiving clearly is to play dumb or vague by remaining unaware of specifically what she may not like about her present situation. She can't identify what displeases her. Nothing is actually wrong. She has a lovely home, or a good job, or a fine husband, or great kids, or good people to work with, and she can't conceive of how to change anything when nothing is wrong. She blurs her own experience and keeps herself in the dark as a way of short-circuiting the excitement and the arousal to action that awareness brings. Awareness calls for responsive and expressive behavior; it tips the balance against inaction.

Take the example of another married woman, beautiful and intelligent, doing well at a job which she found interesting, loving and being loved by her husband, but still feeling that there was something missing. One day she was recounting her experience with one of the administrators in the agency where she worked. It had been an unsatisfactory interview where she had failed to get her point across to the older woman who had brushed aside her questions, giving her only perfunctory answers and hurrying her out of the office. My patient made excuses for her supervisor, saying she was busy, that she probably had many other things on her mind, and that she had to take other people into consideration and wasn't free to devote herself to just one person's needs. Then she fell silent. I asked her what she was aware of, and she replied that she was holding her breath and she was clenching her teeth. I instructed her to breathe more deeply and regularly and to attend to what happened when she did this. She observed that her teeth remained clenched, but that now she also noticed some tension at the back of her throat. I asked her to make some sound when she exhaled, incorporating the tension in her throat and the clenching of her teeth. What emerged was a somewhat throttled but unmistakable growl. She looked startled at making such a sound. I asked her whom she felt like growling at, and after a pause she said, "You know, I don't really mean what I said about my supervisor. I think she's giving me lousy supervision and I'm angry at her for not giving me the kind of supervision I need." Another moment's pause, "And I'm mad because *I* made it easy for her! *I* let her get away with it!" This led to a chain of memories of instances when she had made it easy for people to ignore her, or not to take her seriously, or not to give her the information she wanted from them. I told her I would play her supervisor and we would start the interview over again and this time to make sure that she got what she needed and didn't let me squirm off the hook. To do this she had to mobilize more of her own aggressive energy, to the point where, when I began to rise out of my chair as if indicating that the interview was over, she put one forefinger against my chest and pushed me back into the chair saying, "I'm not done with you yet!" When we finished she looked lively and vigorous. Subsequently she became more active in getting what she wanted, not only from her supervisor, but also from doctors and salespeople whom she previously allowed to intimidate her.

Another way for a woman to avoid moving directly against her predicament is to retroflect, to direct her disapproval of something back against herself in the form of a blanket condemnation. She condemns herself totally as inadequate or unworthy. Other people are stronger, more capable, more knowledgeable or just plain nicer than she is. Other women manage a home and kids and a job and go to school, and *they* aren't worn to a frazzle and shrewdish like she is. Or they have special talents or ideas and even though they live under some of the same conditions she does, *they* manage to come up with creative and sparkling answers. *They* are more virtuous, less self-centered, less selfish and they never complain about their troubles. Everyone else seems so happy and competent, why is she the only malcontent? All of her troubles exist because she is so incompetent, and she engages in a constant round of self-accusation and blame.

As an example of this, I remember a young woman who was creative, hardworking, generous and loving to her family with these talents. When she was able to do something that made her happy, she was as radiant as a sunrise, and often the things that made her happy were things that made life better for her husband and kids, too. Often—but not always. There were some things she wanted to do for herself; she wanted to paint, and teach practical nursing, in which she was trained, part-time, and more generally to establish an island of personal competence and achievement not rooted in her own home. Her husband gave superficial approval to these ambitions. As long as they didn't interfere with her care of the kids or her maintenance of the house, or her serving as hostess to his family and business associates, and as long as it didn't involve his having to take up the slack in the family living arrangements, it was okay with him.

Her husband was a reliable, conscientious and hard-working young man. He took his responsibilities seriously. He took everything and everyone else seriously too. But what he didn't know about was joy, grace, luminosity and free-flowing love, and he was choking these very qualities right out of his wife. She was ripe for such a bargain, it turned out, because her mother, a conventionally practical woman, had dismissed as trivial her daughter's very real artistic talent and had left her a set-up for anyone who continued the routine. Her husband differed from her mother superficially in that he was indulgent and condescending instead of harsh, but he, too, put her down in his own way. She was so snowed by his good qualities that she believed she was too demanding and he was a saint even to put up with her. He agreed with her and treated her with a tolerant benevolence that bordered on the ludicrous, except that it had such tragic repercussions. I worked with them as a couple on those few occasions when he was willing to come in. Mostly, he thought it was his wife's problem, an effective defense, and he was generously willing to pay for her treatment. So we worked alone, she and I.

Our sessions focused on her becoming aware of what she wanted and how she might get it without needing anything from her husband. If this sounds like a mixture of subversion and autonomy, for many women it boils down to just such a method. She became an expert, using the proceeds from the sale of several of her paintings to hire someone to do some of the work that didn't need her personally. She also got into touch with her own attractiveness, began dressing with more dash and began to hear some of the admiring things that people other than her husband had to say about her. She even considered taking a lover, but decided against it because she really loved her husband, pompous as he was, and reasoned that it would cost her more anguish than she wanted. Her sense of her own worth began to equal her estimate of her husband's worth, and she started to teach him some of the things she needed him to know, like how to make love better. She even realized that in some ways he was more fragile than she, and her loving could more realistically cope with his needs, as well as her own. What she accomplished in therapy was to stop believing exclusively in outside authorities and to look to herself as a person whose experience and authority were at least as valid as theirs. When we terminated, she had a more accurate appraisal of both herself and her husband. She was past idolatrous worship of him that was the obverse of her own self-condemnation.

Another way that some women paralyze themselves is to make their goals so grandiose or drastic that they can't get started on such vast plans. What they conceive it would take for their own personal improvement is a grand societal reformation or family upheaval or graduate degree or administrative position that would give them prestige and clout. Even if this is true, which in some sense it always is, this is not where she can get started. The trouble with these ambitious plans is that they sound so elegant and far-reaching that they become a substitute for action. A woman asserts that she could run her own advertising agency, but she just can't get someone to stay with the kids while she would be away. Another wants a graduate degree, but hates to do required reading. This settling for eternal and obsessive planning with no consummatory action is what Perls called "mind-fucking."

One young woman, lethargic and indolent in her sessions with me, would engage in repetitious denunciations of a society where people didn't care about one another and where women were relegated to subservient roles. But she sat for hours in my office expecting all of the action to come from me, and putting nothing into the pot. I was supposed to lay some kind of therapy on her which would change everything while demanding very little action from her. My aim, whenever she tried to engage me in this way, was to do something which would compel her to take over an active role. So, every time she complained about the evils of the society, I would get her to move out of her usual listless protest by engaging the offenders in an imaginary dialogue or by playing the part of the transgressors defending themselves or by any other means I could come up with to energize her.

One day she began to complain, logically enough, about my not being more active in our sessions. I asked her to scold me and to tell me what she wanted from me. As she berated me, I directed her to listen to what she was saying. Before long, she became aware that she was assuming a subservient role in our work together, perpetuating right in my office what she had ascribed to society's ill will. Our sessions changed after that, with her assumption of more responsibility for the conduct of her own therapy. Her energy was not so devoted anymore to pointless harangues and focused instead on the specifics she wanted to change in her own life; she switched her major at school, selected a new advisor whom she found she could really talk to and joined a couple of activist groups where she began to act on her social grievances in the company of kindred spirits.

In working with a woman who feels stuck, it becomes important to ascertain whether she expends more energy in emphasizing the objections to movement than in supporting her own positive momentum. Many women specialize in throwing roadblocks in their own paths, cluttering up their experience with side issues that obscure and distract from the central concerns, leaving them worn out and with little energy left for the main event. There is usually much for her to be discontented about, but she prevents herself from doing anything about it because she is so hedged in with conditions, precepts, moralisms, projections, contingencies, qualifications, corollaries—*ad infinitum*—all of which must be considered. And considered they are, endlessly, until she begins to sound like a broken record. I recall the fantasy of one woman who was reciting all the contingencies she had to consider before she could do something she wanted to do. I asked her to fantasize that each one of these considerations was a bar in a cage that she was making for herself. As she named each one of the objections she was putting up, she was to picture it as one of the bars. She built a marvelous cage for herself; she had enough objections to ring herself in completely.

Growing up a woman in our society leaves a psychological residue that cripples and deforms all but the most exceptional women. It is no comfort to know that the same distortions also pervade growing up a man with some of the same unhappy consequences. There is also no comfort to be found in the fact that some of the best teachers of these principles are themselves women, who ought to know better from their own experience. Our society reinforces in women dependent, exploitative and defensive behaviors aimed at procuring conventional and stereotyped rewards. For the woman who is disdainful of either the method or the rewards, there is frequently much trouble and meager compensation. No wonder many women give up the fight. For those who persevere in trying to establish an independent sense of their own identity, it is still not without cost in the form of nagging self-doubt, criticism from others and displacement of energy into dealing with side issues and irrelevancies.

For example, one woman was doggedly independent and resented the marginal status of a single woman who couldn't call a man for a date with the same freedom that he could call her. The artifice of sitting at the phone and waiting for him to take the initiative was galling. Many times she just wouldn't wait, but even when she called, knowing it was as much her right as his, she felt precarious and unsure of her welcome. In addition to the universal doubt whether or not someone wants to hear from you when you are the one making the overture, she was worried about the onus of the aggressive female. This kind of defensiveness pervaded many of her actions so that even the simple act of having to put air in her bicycle tires and needing the gas-station attendant to show her how to use the air hose for the first time aroused in her the disgust at looking like another dumb female who didn't understand mechanical contraptions. Our work together was devoted to getting her off the ground and making her strong, assertive energy work for her, rather than against her. She had to learn how to keep her own motor running, how to be as much as she could be and how not to water herself down in order to minimize trouble. She was strong enough to tolerate trouble better than weakness any day. But the fact that she had to work so hard to establish and maintain her own independent function is a black mark against a society that insists on caricatures of women instead of fully dimensional self-portraits.

Even for women who appear to accept the traditional roles and outwardly function well, there is still a hidden personal toll. Physical complaints, boredom, feelings of fatigue, problems about their own sexuality are evidence that all is not well with them either.

One woman came to see me complaining of feeling tired and with head throbbing even when she woke up first thing in the morning. Her doctor had found nothing wrong with her physically and she was desperate. One day, as we worked with her chronic headache, I asked her to attend to her pain and to observe what it felt like. She answered that it felt like a heavy sandbag on top of her, bearing down and oppressing her. I told her to take ownership of the sandbag, to fantasy that *she* was the sandbag and was pressing down on her own throbbing head. She began to speak as the sandbag, "Here I am, right when you wake up and I'm going to stay with you all day, too. I'm going to press down on you and tell you all the things you have to do and I'm going to remind you about all the things you left undone from yesterday. . . ." Tears came to her eyes and she spoke about how she never seemed to let up on herself, even when she was exhausted, always goading herself with lists of chores to be done, always feeling she never did enough." I do this to my husband, too. I ask him to do something and I don't let up on him, I nag at him until he gets it done and I make him miserable and mad, and then I feel like such a bitch!" I remarked that she didn't have to go on sandbagging herself and her husband if she didn't want to, and asked her if she had any ideas about how she might quit this. She continued to talk about how unrealistically high her expectations were from herself and others. As she went on, she evolved a system for herself whereby she would decide which chores she felt were really essential and wanted done right away, and which were less important and could be done whenever someone had the time. She also worked out a motto which she put at the top of her list: "Remember, the sun will rise tomorrow even if I don't pull it up." She was able to stay with this scheme, too, and her headaches went away, along with the discarded sandbag.

Another woman complained that she was overly concerned about her bowel habits, worrying about constipation and drinking prune juice whenever she hadn't had a daily bowel movement. She was constipated, but not seriously, and where she had got the idea that she had to have a daily bowel movement she didn't know. She described how attentive she was to both the quantity and quality of her stool—and was usually not very pleased with what she produced. I asked her to try some homework—not to look at her bowel movements at all, just to shit and then flush the toilet. The very next week she reported that her constipation was gone! Once she stopped evaluating herself and allowed herself just to produce freely, she could just produce shit freely, too. No more prune juice either, nor did the constipation come back for the next year and a half that we saw each other.

I believe that a mode frequently resorted to by women is retroflection, turning back against themselves something they would like to do to someone else or have someone else do to them. It is the recourse of people who have only a minimal expectation of having enough impact on their environment to make it produce what might satisfy them. So they give up their expectation and settle instead for a self-contained action; they do for themselves or to themselves what they would like done for or to them, or what they might like to do to someone else. Often they turn back against themselves their unexpressed feelings of resentment, disappointment, criticism, deprecation and hostility. I remember one woman who, unwilling to criticize her husband who was away a good deal on business trips, made the back of her scalp raw with scabs as she picked at herself instead.

Sexual difficulties in women frequently revolve around a retroflective nucleus of resentment and self-punishment. A fringe benefit, of course, is that in some cases this also permits some punishment of another person as well as herself.

One woman, married for about twelve years, with three children, began suddenly to find intercourse with her husband excruciatingly painful. A gynecological examination revealed no physiological explanation for her discomfort. She was a bright, spunky woman with definite opinions of her own and good insight into the problems of other people, but unable to soften up long enough to see when or how she was defeating herself. We did some work focused on getting her to relax the sphincters of her vagina, moving her pelvis more freely and coordinating her breathing with a feeling of openness throughout her body, not just in her nose and mouth. These exercises were successful in freeing her own feelings of sexual want, but when she got close to her husband she was dismayed to find that she stiffened up and couldn't move softly and loosely into the contact that both he and she wanted. One day she was talking about her father, an overbearing, dictatorial and deeply disrespectful man. Most of her early life had been spent in resisting his insistence that she meekly knuckle under to his orders and opinions. I asked her to fantasy that her father was sitting in the empty chair in my office and to express her feelings directly toward him. She told him of her resentment at his steamroller style, how he just ran over people who opposed him and how the only way she had escaped was by just not taking any crap from him. I asked her what she felt as she said this. She replied that she felt tight and tense all over, just short of trembling. I asked if this was how she felt in her vagina, too. She replied that it was. I directed her to intensify her tightness until she felt she was as tense as she could be, to hold it for a moment longer, and then abruptly let go. There was a moment when she let her breath go after holding it while she had tensed up, and her face softened from its grim expression. She began to yield to crying. She shook her head and said through tears that she remembered how she had hated her father and that she thought she was all through with that, had settled it long ago. I said that it seemed to me that she had stored up all her resentment and centered it in her vagina, where she was still acting as if she wasn't going to take anything from a man, even if she loved him. She closed her eyes for a minute at the sudden rush of self-recognition and wordlessly nodded her head.

A woman in trouble is frequently a woman whose sense of her own boundaries is both rigid and fragile. Her I-boundary (Polster and Polster, 1973), her personal tolerance for permitting awareness to grow and ripen into contactful interaction with her environment, is severely restricted by her inability or reluctace to risk takeover. Her selectivity for contact—which is determined by the I-boundaries she has chosen to maintain for herself—will govern the style of her life, dictating the choice of friends, lovers, husbands, work, geography, fantasy, lovemaking, childbearing and all the other experiences which are psychologically relevant to her life. If she allows herself to become figurally aware of aspects of herself or her life which displease or frustrate her, she risks allowing this growing tide of awareness to surge into a direction which might lead to action. If she is unwilling to risk this, she becomes committed to a policy of un-awareness and inaction.

Awareness is a way of keeping up to date with herself and her current experience. It is a preamble to lively engagement and expressive interaction in the present moment. It is an antidote to remaining fixed in past commitments or outgrown values. The woman who is aware of her wants and can express them experiences herself as being on target and moving toward a sense of completion and release. With the completion of a cycle of awareness-wanting-action, she is free to continue her contemporary interaction with her own experience rather than becoming mired in incomplete and unfulfilled wanting.

Awareness is no guarantee against pain or unhappiness. It means that she may indeed perceive clearly the dead-end quality of a lifeless relationship, she may recognize that a work scene is sterile, she may acknowledge that something she once wanted is, in actuality, no longer what she wants now. It also means that she must take the responsibility for creating and/or perpetuating this unhappy state of affairs.

But until her sense of responsibility and ownership is acknowledged—and eventually welcomed—there is no therapeutic leverage for movement. She has to learn to cherish her awareness because of the information she can glean from it to guide and orient her in making her own decisions and taking subsequent action. She has to want to know herself well so that she can move with grace and spontaneity, confident enough of her own flexibility so that error or second thought needn't scare her. She has to be able to commit herself to a course of action, *not* in perpetuity but in existential enthusiasm. Awareness is a necessary ingredient in this kind of living.

I have found that my own womanhood is a very important factor in my work as a therapist. With some women it adds an expectation of being understood in a way no man could understand them. This leads to a willingness to be open, to discuss things with me that they might "confess" to a man but that they can "tell" me. It leads, also, I believe, to their becoming more confronting, less docile, less cowed by their therapist. Taking me on in argument makes the odds seem a little more in their favor; I swing enough weight as a therapist, at least I am also a woman. It gives me an advantage in working with women because there is a diminished likelihood that they can brush aside my disagreeable comments or observations as less relevant to them because I "don't really know how it is." I *do* know how it is, I have been there and I am still there. This gives a resonance to our relationship that can amplify what I do and say.

My being a woman also enhances my value as a personification of other possibilities of being-a-woman. It is not unusual for a woman to ask me if I juggled the same set of problems she is trying to keep in the air. How did I deal with the conflict between marriage, children, personal and professional needs? Do I ever have trouble with my kids? Do I ever feel rejected or unsure of myself? Have I ever lost a baby? Do I feel the responsibility dumped on me for aging parents? These questions demonstrate an incontrovertible parallel that she is drawing between herself and me. My answers, when I give them, are surely not intended to provide instructions for imitation. When I can, I answer more about *how* I arrived at an answer, about what my contingencies were, than about the actual solution of a particular problem. That way she and I can work toward inventing new answers, personally and uniquely applicable to her.

This is not to be taken as a statement that I believe women should be in therapy with other women and men should seek help only from other men. There are important therapeutic rewards, as I know from personal experience, when women work with a male therapist and men work with a female therapist. The basic human dimension of *personhood* is at stake in therapy—moving beyond stereotypes of man or woman into the full articulation and integration of everything any individual can be when all aspects of one's experience are available.

A good woman has pungency, flexibility, suppleness, energy, responsiveness, tenderness, toughness, grace, depth . . . so does a good man. She doesn't play favorites with these qualities. She needs them all to go about the serious business of creating her own life.

REFERENCES

Perls, F. S. *Gestalt Therapy Verbatim*. Moab, Utah: Real People Press, 1969.
Polster, E. and M. Polster. *Gestalt Therapy Integrated*. New York: Brunner/Mazel, 1973.

CHAPTER 22

THE GESTALT ORIENTATION TO ORGANIZATION DEVELOPMENT

STANLEY M. HERMAN

Stanley M. Herman is a management and organization consultant in Redondo Beach, California. He is also affiliated with TRW Systems in Redondo Beach. A graduate of the Gestalt Institute of Cleveland and the NTL Intern Program, Herman is the author of *The People Specialists*, an examination of organization life.

Reprinted by permission from S. N. Herman, "The Gestalt Orientation to Organization Development," in **Contemporary Organization Development**, Bethel, Maine: National Institute of Applied Behavioral Science, 1972, pp. 69-89.

A few months ago a psychotherapist friend of mine asked me to join him in consulting with one of his patients. The patient, a highly successful general manager of a building supply company, had just been offered the presidency of a very large retail chain organization. Taking over the new assignment would, as he saw it, require drastic changes in the company's way of doing business, and likely the "re-formation" or replacement of several high-level people. That was the dilemma. This energetic, talented and essentially tough-minded general manager had about a year or so before attended a sensitivity training laboratory, had been deeply touched by his experience of warmth, affection and support in the group and had attempted subsequently to expand his knowledge by readings in organizational development. Then, he had tried to apply the principles he had learned to his own and other's relationships in his organization. The results of his attempts had been mixes. Some subordinates had responded well to his openness and participative style. Others had used the greater leeway he gave them as an opportunity to become lax and ineffective. Nevertheless, the general manager stayed devotedly with his perceptions of what good human relations ought to be, and in fact his hesitancy about accepting the new job offer had to do with his doubt that his management approach would work with his new subordinates. And as he put it: "I would rather quit managing altogether than go back to my old authoritarian ways."

After some exploratory discussion it became clear that a certain amount of misinterpretation had occurred in this man's understanding of sound human relations practice (as most experienced O.D. people will have guessed). But in a larger sense a great deal of what was troubling this manager I recognized as a common theme among many people who have been influenced by the sensitivity training theories of O.D. He had come to regard his own power—both his organizational position and his personal force—as something uncomfortable, even bad. And so he worked diligently to restrain that power for the sake of others whom he saw as less powerful. I believe that this discomfort with the overt exercise of directive authority is quite common among many people involved in O.D. theory and practice.

For some time the main thrust of organization development efforts has been directed at changing organization environments in ways that will make them more supportive and facilitative to people. For example, we frequently speak of the requirement to change an organization culture in ways that will support such values as openness, participation, interdependence, etc. I believe that emphasis has been useful but not sufficient. In this chapter I want to suggest an additional approach, one that is largely derived from the theory and practice of Gestalt Therapy.

In the following pages I intend to emphasize the "ungentle" aspects of organizational behavior, those that have generally received less attention and have frequently been regarded with less comfort by many O.D. theoreticians and practitioners. My objective here is not to provide instruction on making the organization culture safer, more pleasant or easier for the individual, but rather to help the individual recognize, develop and experience his own potency and ability to cope with his organization world, whatever its present condition. Further, I would like to encourage him to discover for himself his own unique wants of that environment and his capacity to influence and shape it in ways that get him more of what he wants.

The most formidable barrier to the person and his free expression of himself in the organization setting is probably fear. Fear of others, and how they might affect him and his life, and even more importantly fear of himself and how he might make mistakes, do the wrong thing, and so imperil "his future" and/or his image of himself as a modern manager, specialist, or whatever.

One of the most crucial areas of study in examining organization behavior is the manager-subordinate relationship. In this relationship, probably more than any other, both managers and subordinates frequently constrict the potential range of their interaction (and their potential capacity to enjoy each other). In the sections below I will discuss currently prevalent patterns of relationships and some alternatives, first from the perspective of the manager and the subordinate.

THE MYTH OF OMNIPOTENCE

For many years an important focus for theories of management has been the area of power and control. Even before Douglas McGregor postulated his X and Y theories of management many other theorists advocated caution in the manager's use of power and control. Cases were made for participative, permissive or otherwise moderated styles of supervision. By now it has become clear to almost every manager or supervisor who sees himself as "beyond the dark ages" that bosses are not supposed to be domineering and authoritarian, or, at least if they are, they are not supposed to seem that way to their subordinates. This was a heavy self-imposed requirement of the building supply company general manager in my earlier example.

It is clearly true that a dictatorial or oppressive style of management is no longer generally acceptable in the United States. But I believe that the real basis for this truth is not found in philosophical images of theoretical democracy; rather, it stems from the high probability that most people who work in present-day organizations are unwilling to tolerate oppression. They will find a way of rising up against it, either overtly or covertly, through sabotage.

For many managers though, the image of "democratic leadership" has not served as a useful model. Their attempts to regulate their own behavior to make it "fit the image" have been strained and unnatural, and frequently received with discomfort and suspicion by their subordinates. A man is a man, and if his behavior is authentic it must reflect his own internal personal realities at any given point in time, not a prescribed external ideal. In the Gestalt context, forced or deliberately planned "corrections" in behavior—even when they are ostensibly voluntary—produce exhibitionistic rather than genuine change. Such change is very difficult to sustain and the effort to sustain it is usually at great cost to the individual. *Genuine growth requires that a person first recognize and acknowledge his present qualities before he can proceed with his own natural development.*

Withheld Trust

In the practice of psychotherapy, therapists repeatedly encounter the guilt and anxiety-ridden patient who tortures himself with fantasies of how he has abused or injured others. In this way he brings himself to a state of such self-mistrust or self-hate that he becomes unable to encounter people around him and can only turn inward.

His vitality and excitement are lost as he spends his energy in restraining and punishing himself.

In an organization culture where the exercise of direct authoritarian power is ostensibly disapproved by the established norms of the organization, many people in positions of authority may experience a comparable (though, of course, less extreme) pattern. They may become vaguely uncomfortable or even terribly concerned about the "awesome force" they have over other people. I call this syndrome the myth of omnipotence.

The myth of omnipotence is a specter that can paralyze potency. The manager who believes too much in his own power to harm begins to withhold or divert his energy, his spontaneity and his thrust in order to avoid hurting others. This withheld thrust has adverse affects both on the withholder and on those from whom he withholds. In the course of my organization consulting I have encountered many cases in which the manager of an organization struggles painfully within himself to try to force his behavior to conform to an image of managership in which he is continually benign, non-authoritarian, encouraging and facilitative toward his subordinates. And at the same time within himself he feels but holds back his own wants, convictions, and desires to move things ahead. He also experiences "negative" emotions toward his subordinates, such as irritation, criticism, impatience, and so on and yet withholds these because a "good manager" (like a "good parent") is not supposed to express such things to those who are below him (his children).

Believing the myth of his own omnipotence might have some consolation for a manager if he could, at least subjectively, feel himself stronger and more capable in comparison to his subordinates. But the typical manager seldom enjoys that feeling of superiority even at a subjective level; instead he struggles with intermittent ambivalence and lack of fulfillment.

Perhaps more important, his subordinates may also suffer from the ambiguity of the signals the manager sends out. On the one hand the manager's words are encouraging, patient, and reasonable, but on the other hand the expressions on his face, his tone, his body signs (e.g., fidgeting, tension, etc.) almost invariably also show through, and these too are perceived by his subordinates. The disparities, however, are seldom if ever dealt with.

It would be far healthier for the manager to fully express his feelings, negative as well as positive, and to allow himself fuller expression of his authoritarian-directive impulses as well. With their full expression his subordinates can more completely experience the totality of the manager's reality. Then they can accept or contest it (and him) as they see fit. From this interchange of full expression and full reaction both the manager and his subordinates can grow in a more meaningful way. Their growth follows at least two dimensions. First, in the interpersonal and intrapersonal sense they learn to really know each other more richly and authentically, and through a heightened awareness of their own feelings, they learn to know themselves better as well. Secondly, with repeated practice and greater familiarity between each other, the substance of their ideas can also be more adequately tested and new, more effective ways of working together developed.

In one organization, I worked with the high-level manager of a large staff who had developed a strong, indeed passionate, commitment to "O.D. values." Included in these values, as he saw them, was the requirement for a manager to be fair, rational, and helpful to those who reported to him. Most of the time he conformed to these requirements quite easily and naturally. He was, however, an individual of great personal force, with strong emotions and subject to occasional moodiness. Those who reported to him recognized these qualities and had gradually grown accustomed to them, though as might be expected, comfort with his style differed among them.

Over a considerable period of time this strong, able manager grew increasingly discontented and unhappy in his relationships with several members of his staff, and staff members, in turn, were also troubled. The "problem" can best be illustrated by the patterns of interaction in the manager's staff meetings. These were generally conducted in a fairly free-flowing and participative style with the floor pretty much available to anyone who wanted it. Sometimes the meetings were quite businesslike and at other times they consisted mostly of a series of rambling discourses punctuated occasionally by concise irrelevancies.

For the most part the manager and his staff were fairly satisfied with both the focused and the "non-productive" discussions. From time to time, however, and for no very apparent reason except his mood at the moment, the manager would suddenly jump into the discussion with all the force of a safe dropped from a ten-story window, usually landing on one of about three or four members of his staff. Frequently, though not always, his "attack" was logically sound, it was not so much the substance as the vehemence and unexpectedness that seemed to most affect those who were its targets.

The responses of those who were "attacked" by the boss varied, but few were completely unresponsive. This was clearly not an oppressive environment. Some replied by defending their position with counter-logic. One used humor, including self-deprecating comments to "reduce the tension." Still another acted out and sometimes verbally expressed his feelings of being "punished" by the boss. Whatever the response though, what most frequently seemed to happen was that after a round or two of exchange the boss would cease to respond, frequently settling into a glum, silent posture. When that happened the entire group would experience a long awkward pause, with no explicit resolution of the issue, if indeed an issue was even identifiable from the brief exchange.

After working with the group for some period of time, I found myself face-to-face with their classic syndrome. An important proposal for a change of policy had been made by one of the staff and tentatively supported by two others. The manager's reaction was quick and strongly negative. He accused all the proponents of being panicky, unrealistic, and out of touch with the organization's needs. After the typical pattern of responses from these staff members and another round or two of exchange the manager lapsed into grim silence.

The alternatives for me as a consultant then were: (1) I could intervene in such a way as to focus even more sharply on the disruptive, inhibiting effects on his staff of the manager's outbursts, possibly I could analyze or encourage the group to analyze the reasons for and consequences of the interaction pattern; or (2) I could intervene in a way that *encouraged the fight to continue* (without having any clear idea of what consequences might come out of the other end). With some anxiety I made the latter choice, primarily by allowing my own emotions of resentment and antagonism to come out. I challenged the manager to follow through on his punishing behavior—in fact to really get into it more fully.

After some hesitation the manager began, at first with some awkwardness, but soon with great enthusiasm, to blast a number of his staff. At the same time the people he attacked were encouraged to respond, even counter-attack if they felt like it. Soon other members of the staff also joined the fray, usually on the side of their colleague. This free-for-all style was allowed to develop into a room full of shouting people that more resembled a disorderly convention of longshoremen than a staff meeting of high level managers of a major corporation. And the outcome was marvelous.

As the group re-examined its processes some time later, members recognized that this turbulent meeting (and a few others since) had produced for the entire group a greater sense of vitality, excitement and relatedness than they had felt for many months, and that this feeling had carried over into subsequent staff meetings as well. In addition, the manager reported that their fights had brought him a new sense of respect for the staff members who stood up to him. In subsequent encounters other staff members also began to stand their ground more readily.

What was the theoretical basis for my choice of intervention? First, I need to say that the choice was mostly intuitive rather than theoretical. It came out of my immediate feelings and my willingness to risk making a mistake. (Since I've gotten over my own myth of omnipotence I'm less worried about making *catastrophic* mistakes. As a consultant, I'm just not that crucial to my clients.) Nevertheless, in looking back on the incident for an ex-post-facto theorization I recognize the following:

As I worked with the group over some period of time it became clear to me that the manager was quite aware of the effect of his "attacks" on his staff members, *perhaps too aware*. Why then did he, an enlightened, devoted, "Theory Y" manager, continue this behavior?

The answer is because the feelings behind his behavior were part of him—part of the whole of his humanness, power, and emotionality —those same qualities for which his staff and many others respected and trusted him. What then could be done? To preach self-control or even temperance to this manager hardly seemed worthwhile (whether the preaching was overt and direct or through the more subtle use of group "feedback"). Even if he resolved to stop his verbal interruptions his feelings would still be sensed by others and would float like a pervasive phantom among them all. No, the answer was not for this manager to back away from his impulsive behavior, but rather, again, in the Gestalt framework, *to go further into it*. The point was not to cut himself off with his guilt feelings about abusing his subordinates after an exchange or two and then settle into melancholy self-blame. Rather it was to stay engaged with them in "the battle" until it reached its natural conclusion—until he and they had the opportunity to fully experience and possibly to finish the unfinished business between them.

Over time some major positive effects came from this new style of engagement for the group: The entire staff became more comfortable with the boss and each other, and the manager began to *enjoy* his relations with his people more than he had before. I believe that the experience the manager had in allowing himself to follow through on his aggressive impulse rather than holding back was a significant one in his own growth. He discovered that, lo-and-behold, his "victims" did not perish from his onslaught, but rather seemed to grow stronger. Conversely, I suspect a similar positive effect in the subordinates' discovery that they were able to handle whatever the boss threw at them and to come back swinging.

I have seen several high-level managers, long inhibited by their images of the good "participative manager," finally able to fully and spontaneously release their pent up feelings. When the breakthrough comes out in strong expressions of anger, affection, dislike, or whatever, there may well be an initial shock that is uncomfortable to everyone, including the consultant. But with time and courage to stay engaged, those involved work it through. They are able to deal with each other's strong emotions much better than they can handle the avoidance and phantom expressions, and eventually they may achieve a vital, robust, and mutually satisfying relationship in which both manager and subordinates are far freer and energetic than in the past.

It is of course possible that some managers, if encouraged to fully express themselves, would turn out to be intolerable tyrants. I believe there are few such people. In the context of Gestalt theory the "intolerable tyrant" is likely to ben an individual suffering the myth of his own personal total helplessness. Thus he defends himself by trying to control completely all those around him. In the therapy for such individuals, as they are able to confront their feelings of helplessness and come to recognize for themselves that they are not as totally helpless as they feel, the tyrannical behavior begins to disappear. At any rate I suspect that a straightforward undisguised tyrant is easier and better to deal with than a disguised one.

Consultant's Focus

In most organizations the interaction style just described would not be an easy one for people to initiate and pursue without help. Generally most organizations have too much of an overlay of historical norms and traditions of "appropriate behavior." Here, I believe, is where organization development and the third-party consultant can be of great help. The consultant can concentrate on assisting managers and subordinates to fully experience and express "where they are" both on issues and in relationships with each other. He can highlight their interpersonal process, help them to discover their own vitality, and the satisfaction and excitement of full expression. He can help them to become aware of *how they stop themselves* from completing their experiences. He can help them become aware of their own predictive (and usually catastrophic) fantasies, i.e., the manager imagines: "If I really let myself go I would oppress, over-power, do terrible damage to my subordinates." The subordinate thinks, "I must be very careful because this is a very dangerous en-vironment." And when these murky catastrophic expectations have been surfaced the consultant can help the people explore and test them against reality, and finally work out individual arrangements between people that will allow them greater self-expression and ful-fillment.

While many of the processes I am describing, I'm sure, seem quite similar to typical O.D. consultation theory, in practice there are important differences of execution. "Confrontation," and "owning feelings" are, of course, common concepts in O.D. In my experience, however, many O.D. consultants facilitate confrontation only to the point of emergence of an identifiable problem (e.g., manager A does not listen to subordinate B, or the manager of one organization repeatedly fails to solicit the advice and involvement of other managers with whom he "ought" to be interdependent, etc.). In some organizations the surfacing of such complaints—the fact that they have finally been brought out into the open and acknowledged—can be a major step, but frequently the consultant then moves too rapidly to the task of problem-solving. Thus with the consultant's help, the manager acknowledges his fault and resolves to "listen more carefully" to his subordinate; or action items are prepared and task groups formed to develop new processes to assure better co-ordination between the various organization subunits, etc. The trouble is that this premature movement into problem-solving may be addressing symptoms rather than causes and may produce solu-tions that are superficial and temporary at best.

The Gestalt mode encourages stronger, deeper, and more concrete (as contrasted to abstract or generalized) interactions. Most impor-tantly we emphasize *staying with* the transaction until both parties have *completed* their business with each other. The individual or contesting parties are encouraged to dramatize and even exaggerate their behavior—to become fully aware of what they are doing and how they are doing it (not why). The manager who does not listen is encouraged to go further into his non-listening mode, to discover and be explicit about what he is doing instead of listening, how he keeps himself from listening, and to complete whatever it is he needs to complete before he can give his attention to listening. The sub-ordinate who is not listened to may be encouraged to discover how he keeps himself from being heard (i.e., from talking louder or more forcefully—from *demanding* attention). The managers of the non-interacting organizations are encouraged to state clearly what each wants (or even demands) of the other, with emphasis on meeting his own selfish needs rather than because it would be good organizational practice. And each manager is encouraged to respond "yes" or "no" to each demand. Interdependence is not an automatically presumed virtue in every case (though it may be a real operating requirement) and when consensual decisions cannot be reached within a reasonable time, power-based decisions are not considered disreputable.

THE TYRANNY OF THE UNDERDOG

The other side of the myth of managerial omnipotence is the tyranny of the underdog. O.D. theory has for most of its relatively brief history stressed the support of "the underdog"—the subordinate, the reticent team member, etc.—and the solution of disagreement through rational processes. In the context of our national culture and traditions this is not surprising nor can I object to the general underlying philosophy. Unfortunately, however, some of our approaches have attempted to "help" the underdog by providing an easier world for him through advocating the restraint (usually by "self-control" and under the moral pressure of "human relations rightness") of the powerful manager or team member. I believe this approach is wrong. Not only does it foster the inhibiting omnipotence myth and guilt feelings of the manager discussed earlier, it can also be experienced as a *confirmation of his own inferiority or invalidism by the individual who is granted the so-called benefits of other people holding themselves in for his sake.* Better by far to help the underdog to discover, use and rejoice in his strength and ability to move forward for himself than to have others take turns pushing his wheelchair for him.

Robert W. Resnick (1970), a Gestalt-oriented psychotherapist, makes the point this way in his paper "Chicken Soup Is Poison":

Many therapists see themselves as members of the "helping professions" engaged in the helping relationship. Beware! Such people are dangerous. If successful they kill the humanness in their patients by preventing their growth. This insidious process is somehow worse realizing such therapists typically want the reverse. They want their patients to grow, to live, and to be, and they guarantee the antithesis with their "help." The distinction between true support and "help" is clear: To do for the other what he is capable of doing himself insures his not becoming aware that he can stand on his own two feet. . . .

An important part of Gestalt Therapy is the concept of polarities, the extremes within each of us, i.e., weakness-strength, activism-passivity, etc., that together comprise our full natures. One of the manifestations of polarity is the "top dog" vs. "underdog." The top dog is that part of us that mostly serves the function of director and disciplinarian, that part of our personalities that tell us what we *should do*. The underdog is the resistive part of us, that part that balks at the bossiness of top dog and attempts to subvert or derail his directives.

Our underdog may work at his mission by pleading that we are unable to do what the top dog demands, or he may delay and promise to do it tomorrow, or he may divert the top dog's directions, and so on. Fritz Perls in his development of Gestalt Therapy believed that the underdog in each individual almost always triumphed in the long run over the top dog. This phenomenon, incidentally, may well explain why in organizations as well as elsewhere so many plans and vows to change seem to fare no better than most people's New Year's resolutions.

Great energy is frequently bottled up in the conflict between these two conflicting drives within an individual, energy that is therefore not available for other more satisfying purposes. Further, the conflict between the top dog and the underdog frequently produces unhappiness and a sense of lack of fulfillment for the person.

Relationships between some individuals within organizations have many of the same characteristics as this top dog/underdog conflict. The apparently powerful, assertive person makes demands on the ostensibly weaker underdog, but somehow, the demands are never quite met. And while the top dog's pressure may be great, the underdog's ability to divert, deflect, or delay is often greater. So-called weak parties in a variety of relationships may have very great, though not immediately apparent, advantages in their ability to resist without attacking and to use, like a judo expert, the strong person's own strength against him. I have worked with a number of teams in which one or two members, undoubtedly without conscious intent, skillfully manipulated the apparently stronger members of the group, including the boss into "helping" them. This helping takes many forms. It can be protecting the quiet member, taking his side in a competitive situation, being more sympathetic to his problems and inabilities to meet his commitments than would be the case for other members of the team, etc. One of the most harmful accommodations to the "weak party" involves others holding back their forcefulness and vitality in order to keep from offending or upsetting the underdog.

Ogre Building

A variation of the underdog game is ogre building. Almost all of us in organizations have the capacity to build ogres fearsome enough to scare ourselves half to death. The ogre may be a supervisor, especially one at a higher level than those we are accustomed to dealing with, another organization, or, perhaps most insidious of all, "the system." Ogres can be very useful sometimes in helping us to avoid doing what we don't really want to do anyway. I do not object to the use of the ogre for that purpose if indeed we are conscious of what we are doing and that we *want* to do it. More frequently, however, we are not aware of what we are doing and our ogres are not so clearly useful. They are compounded of some degree of organizational reality plus our own projections and predictions of dire consequences. Organization-development methodology is frequently useful in dealing with ogres, especially the mutual ogres dreamed up by internally competitive organizations for each other. I believe more can be done, especially in working with individuals in helping them discover their courage and capacity to confront and deal with their own ogres.

In the therapeutic process that addresses top dog/underdog conflicts the first step involves heightening polarization. The patient increases his awareness of both forces within himself; especially, he becomes aware of *the power inherent in his underdog position*. With this new awareness grows a sense of excitement, pride, and energy. Later, when he has well experienced his own extremes he may move naturally to an "integration," i.e., he is able to regain his access to those parts of himself he had submerged or renounced and so eventually he becomes able to utilize, as the situation requires, a more complete spectrum of his behavior potential.

In the organization consulting process, especially when dealing with "complaining people"—those who see others and/or their environment as oppressive and preventing them from doing what they want to do—it is a good idea for the consultant to begin working with his client in a way that concentrates on identifying the client's strength. That may not be easy, the complainer's strength is not readily apparent. On the contrary he usually spends much of his time denying he has any strength at all. All power belongs to "the others" —his boss, his more influential, articulate, or aggressive coworkers, or most oppressive of all to "the company."

As a consultant I begin by being suspicious of these complaints. This is not to say that I think the complainer is intentionally deceptive, nor do I doubt that widespread inequalities of power and opportunity for certain classes of organization citizens do exist. Rather, I have found that most people do possess some form of power even if that power is passive, resistive, or a withholding kind that is used to manipulate others, often by triggering feelings of guilt among the more active and assertive people with whom they deal.

A case that illustrates the subtleties of power distribution involved a large government agency I worked with. We began with a team-building session between the top management group (including the chief and his central staff) and about a dozen field supervisors, each of whom headed a local service office. The pattern of complaints, and there were many from each side, were clear and repeated. For the central staff it was that those in the field seldom seemed to be able to respond to the requests for new information that they were asked to provide, nor did they often try out proposed new methods developed by the central staff for use in the field. When they occasionally did try out the recommended procedures, it was in a most cursory way that practically assured failure of the new approach. Finally, after repeated efforts, the central staff people had quietly abandoned their efforts to direct the field supervisors and adopted what they felt to be the more modern management approach of asking the field people to submit their own ideas for innovation and improvement. This approach fared no better.

What I noticed as I heard the presentation of this information from the central staff people was their almost complete lack of emotion. This pattern of relationships which had been going on for about a year must have produced frustration for the agency chief and his staff, yet in listening to the presenters I heard only careful neutrality, infinite patience, and dispassionate though devoted interest in objective "problem-solving."

It took considerably longer for the case of the field supervisors to emerge. Their first responses to the complaints of the central staff were rather desultory and almost apologetic. They had work loads, many new people to train, spent a great deal of time on public relations, and so on. All of which limited their ability to

578   THE HANDBOOK OF GESTALT THERAPY

concentrate on new approaches. Besides, they felt it was quite unlikely that they could develop any new methods that would really
satisfy the central staff, since the central staff people were obviously
so much better informed about the latest trends in their specialized
field. Similarly, the information emerged that in the past year a few
of the field supervisors felt they had attempted to institute some of
the recommended new approaches of the central staff but had not
done well at it. And while they had not been overtly criticized by the
staff they had "felt" disapproved of.

As a consultant here I again experienced myself at a decision point.
I could try to help the field supervisors by encouraging the central
staff to examine their olympian posture and how their cool paternal-
ism put down the supervisors. They could then examine ways they
might change this pattern into a more encouraging one. Secondly, I
could pursue the problem-solving approach by helping the total
group to recognize specific areas of weakness in the supervisors'
skills and then to develop training programs for building those skills.
Thirdly, I could encourage the field supervisors to (in the Gestalt
sense) go even further into their complaints. I chose the third.

I requested that the supervisors (in a "fish-bowl" arrangement)
elaborate further on their grievances against the staff. The result,
after some initial hesitancy, was a veritable river of complaints,
many of which went back for years. In essence, the field supervisors
reported they felt like second-class citizens, without influence or
power in their dealings with the staff. They didn't know what the
staff meant by "innovation," and what's more they didn't much care.
(They did, however, have some good ideas from time-to-time which
they put into effect without fanfare, seldom telling the staff anything
about them.)

When the venting had subsided I asked the field supervisors to talk
about how they characteristically dealt with the staff. After a slow
start the supervisors rolled out a substantial list of "passive-
resistance" and "playing stupid" techniques. In a little while they
were enjoying their catalogue immensely, as were the central staff
people, who prior to this time had perceived themselves in the superior position, and so very much "responsible" for the oppressed feelings of the supervisors.

Sometime later, after the supervisors had become aware of the
way in which they exerted their own resistive power in their dealings
with the staff, we were able to turn successfully to the possibilities of
developing different modes of interaction between the groups. Now,
however, they were able to do so, not as impotent sufferers, but as

equals. Interestingly, one of their demands was that the staff be more clearly demanding. Their experience in the past, they reported, had been confusing. Since the staff (in their efforts to be "understanding") had been so tactful in making requests, it was almost impossible to tell what was really important to them and what wasn't.

Many other aspects of this case emerged and were dealt with in this and subsequent meetings, including our attention to the operating styles of the agency chief and the central staff members, the identification of real developmental needs for both staff and field personnel, and so on. I believe we were able to deal with these other problems better, later on, because we started where we did.

In the model of the consultant's role I advocate the primary step is not to help people embark on self-improvement programs. Rather, it is to encourage them to recognize and appreciate where they are now. Then the consultant may help them find their own unique paths forward to change and growth. It is also important to recognize that this change and growth, at best, will occur naturally rather than being forced either by external pressure or internalized models. Paradoxically, natural change in an individual does not preclude his boss or others from exerting power or expressing their wants strongly and explicitly. *What is explicit and up-front is seldom harmful, though it may be difficult to deal with.* Covert, withheld, or truncated expression is harmful. In most circumstances the consultant will do best to encourage in both individuals and organizations the full recognition and completion of their negative feelings rather than a premature objectivity or problem-solving approach. The consultant will also do best in setting an example through his own clear and explicit statements of what *he* wants and how *he* feels.

We in the field of behavioral science have placed great emphasis on the negative consequences of authoritarian management for both organizations and individuals. In voices sometimes gentle and sometimes determined, we have addressed the power figures in organizations and called upon them to depart from old patterns, to risk a new approach and allow greater and more meaningful participation in the organization's affairs by those below them in the hierarchy. Many of us have made substantial contributions in helping managers to recognize and exercise their responsibilities toward their subordinates. This has in the main been good and worthwhile. The time has come though, I believe, for us to begin to address subordinates as well. We need to help manager and subordinate become aware of alienating and vitality-sapping consequences of both "playing helpless" and "playing helpful." We must question ourselves and encourage others to question unthinking acceptance of and adaptation to someone else's rules of good human relations, without regard to how those feel inside.

I believe it is worthwhile to urge ourselves and others to take new risks—risks of greater self-assertion, more spontaneity, and more willingness to experiment with power and aggression as well as trust and love. If we in O.D. do indeed believe in a wider distribution of power it would be well for us to stop trying to deny power's existence, muffle it, wish it away, or disguise it under velvet wrappings. Rather we encourage as many people as possible at *all* levels of the organization from highest manager to lowest subordinate to discover his own power and use it.

CHAPTER 23

THE SHADOW OF
ORGANIZATION
DEVELOPMENT

STANLEY M. HERMAN

A good deal of current theory and practice in organization development derives from what might be called conventional human relations assumptions. Many organization-development consultants in their work with managers, subordinates, and teams frequently hold powerful, though unexpressed, values that affect their clients as well as themselves. In this chapter, I would like to examine some of these underlying values and to point out that they are primarily derived from a certain set of biases in favor of "positive" emotions and attributes. As a result, some other aspects of human interaction that involve "negative" emotions and attributes have been neglected, given only lip-service attention, or in subtle ways denigrated. I believe this has been the source of a severe limitation of the O.D. field.

In Gestalt Therapy, the theoretical base for the O.D. approach advocated here, the so-called negative emotions are not neglected. Through concepts of polarization and integration the whole range of a person's emotionality is valued. In the Gestalt orientation, for an individual to realize his whole potential, he must be able to get in touch with this continuum. The integrated individual is able to experience both love and hate. He is able to exert dominance, without being or perceiving himself as a tyrant. He is able to experience submission without feeling himself crushed. It is my thesis that both individuals within organizations and organizations themselves, if they are to realize their potential for vitality and growth, need to be in touch with these contrasting aspects of their makeup.[1]

"POSITIVE" AND "NEGATIVE" EMOTIONS

In general, the values of conventional human relations currently prevalent in organization development include:

Logic and rationality
Trust of, and openness toward, others
Collaboration and participation
Affection and responsiveness
Group interest

While these values certainly seem appropriate and important to me in the development of effective and humanistic organizations, I believe we in organization development have neglected values at the other end of the spectrum of human interaction. For example:

Authority and control
Caution and reserve
Autonomy and separateness
Competition and aggressiveness
Dislike and resistance
Self-interest

For many O.D. consultants, the first list represents the healthy and constructive thrust of individuals and organizations, while the second represents harmful, or even neurotic qualities—the "shadow"[2] qualities that the O.D. consultant feels he ought to be trying to change. I believe this (sometimes explicit, sometimes implicit) renunciation of the "negative" has weakened a good deal of organization development effort by depriving it of the vigor and energy that are frequently inherent in the negative thrust. At least equally important, the avoidance and/or disapproval of these aspects of humanness has, I believe, tended to increase clients' discomfort and inability to cope with what might be called the tough parts of their worlds. In a broad sense, the "gentle-reasonable" bias conveyed by conventional human relations has at times fostered discomfort and guilt feelings in managers and executives. I have known several who, after experiencing a sensitivity lab or human relations training session, have returned to their organizations with high resolve to hold back their aggressive impulses and be more considerate to others, with disappointing results.

In a Gestalt approach to organization development, the denial or suppression of so-called negative behavior is discouraged. We encourage the client and those within his system to become fully aware of what they *are* experiencing (rather than what they or the consultant think they *should* experience) and to work out viable relationships based upon their own unique qualities and dynamics instead of the consultant's or anyone else's model of good human relations practice. Thus, in general, we promote full exchanges that acknowledge the reality and health of the so-called negative as well as the positive aspects of the human condition. Further, as I have pointed out in the previous chapter, encouraging genuine behavior change (rather than "acted change") requires that the individual become fully aware of and responsible for his present behavior.

CONVENTIONAL HUMAN RELATIONS AND GESTALT APPROACH CONTRASTS

Following are the major differences, as I see them, between the conventional human relations approach (CHR) and a Gestalt (G) orientation to consulting. Again, the point I make here is not that we ought to throw out the conventional orientation altogether, but rather, that there is a great need for more emphasis on the other end of the spectrum.

CHR	*G*
1. Group-helping/group-building focus	Focus on recognition and mobilization of individual strength and power.

Under conventional human relations theory, the emphasis is on building mutual understanding, mutual adaptation, and cooperative behavior. People are encouraged to help each other and to facilitate each other's efforts. So-called "weaker members" of the team are looked after and encouraged by stronger members. Roles such as "gate keeper" and "summarizer" are encouraged. Dominant members of the group are discouraged from their domination by group pressure, especially when their domination apparently inhibits the less aggressive members. Group members take responsibility for each other's welfare.

In the Gestalt orientation, each individual is encouraged to take responsibility for himself. "Helping weaker members" is not encouraged. The point is for each person to take charge of his own action (or inaction) and to discover his capacity for initiating (and suppressing) behavior. In cases of a relationship problem between a dominant and passive team member, we seldom discourage the dominant member by pressuring or persuading him to hold back his domination. More often, we work with the passive member toward the end of enabling him to interrupt the dominant member and *to get what he wants for himself through his own action*. In a somewhat oversimplified way, it might be said that rather than weakening the "strong" our attempt is to strengthen the "weak" members of the group, thereby strengthening the group as a whole.

An example may serve to clarify the case here. In a typical CHR consulting intervention, when the consultant observes that one member of the group seems to have a difficult time expressing himself, especially in an exchange with a dominant member of the group, the consultant may point out to the dominant member that his style of expression is tending to produce this reluctance and inhibition in the more passive member. Very frequently this intervention, especially when bolstered by other's "feedback," produces a feeling of guilt in the dominant member and he decides to try to hold back his strong, expressive style. This effort takes a great deal of his energy and is frequently unsuccessful over any substantial period of time, since the natural forces within the strongly expressive member are still at work.

A G-oriented consultant would approach the situation differently. He would focus first on the reluctant team member and might ask him whether he has something that he wants to say. If the answer is positive, he might then ask the passive individual how he stops himself from expressing what he wants to express. If the reluctant member responds that he has a difficult time expressing himself in the face of the strong expression of the dominant member, the consultant encourages him to become aware of and explicit about his predictions of the consequences to himself if he were to be more expressive. The consultant does not, however, force the passive member to be more expressive. For example:

Consultant: John, I am concerned that you haven't been saying anything, even though we have been talking about the area you are responsible for.

John: Yes, I know.

Consultant: Is there anything that you want to say on this subject?

John: I guess so, but Dick comes on so strong that I am a little reluctant to talk up.

Consultant: How do you stop yourself from saying what you want to say?

John: Well, I guess I just don't want to interrupt.
Consultant: What's your objection to interrupting?
John: I don't know. I guess maybe it seems impolite to do that.
Consultant: To whom would it be impolite?
John: To Dick, I guess.
Consultant: So you would rather keep yourself from saying what you want to say than be impolite, is that it?
John: Well, I don't know, when I think about it that way maybe not.
Bill (another group member): It doesn't seem to me that Dick holds himself back by being afraid of being impolite.
John: No, that's true. I never thought about it that way.
Consultant: It seems to me that you have to make a choice. You have to take responsibility for yourself and decide whether you are going to say what you want to say or not.
John: Yes, I guess I do. And I guess I will; I do have something to say (Turns to Dick and addresses him).

CHR	G
2. Examination of situational elements of the interaction process and reasons why.	Sharpen awareness of what the individual does and how.

In the CHR approach, the consultant focuses on an examination of the problem situation and the reasons for its existence. The consultant helps those involved in their attempts to explain the situation, and various interpretations are examined, as well as suggestions and proposed solutions. The process proceeds in a sequential, rational way, i.e., data is gathered about the elements of the situation, a diagnosis is made, etc.

In the G-orientation, the consultant focuses on encouraging the parties to become aware of what they are doing and what they are avoiding. An example of this may be taken from the preceding dialogue. A CHR-oriented consultant might have questioned John about organizational considerations that were inhibiting him, such as Dick being in a perceived stronger organizational position, or about his past relationships with Dick and others in the group, or, if the consultant were psychoanalytically oriented, he might have explored past relationships that John had with authority figures.

The G-oriented approach is seldom analytical. It emphasizes the now and the how rather than the historical and the why. The reasons for this is that there are almost invariably multiple explanations for every phenomenon in behavior and, as many of us have learned, an intellectual understanding of why something happened frequently does little to help change perceptions or behavior.

CHR	G
3. Analysis of "problem behavior" and methods for solving or correcting it.	Intensification or dramatization of "problem behavior" until a change in relationship occurs.

In the CHR-oriented group, behavior patterns that are seen as producing problems for an individual in the group or between two or more individuals are spotlighted and identified in explicit ways (usually through feedback). Subsequently proposals are made for the individual to consider changing his behavior. Often these proposals are subtle rather than explicit, i.e., the consultant makes it clear that there is, of course, no compulsion that the group member change his style; however, the disadvantages (sometimes in moral as well as efficiency terms) of continuing the old style are clear. Aside from my objection to the manipulative character of this approach, behavior change that comes from it frequently is acted or forced and requires a great deal of energy on the part of the individual to sustain it. Often the suppressed feeling comes out in other ways, through body tension, restlessness, or other signs and so produces incongruity between words and actions. In fact, as I see it, restrained irritation or affection is seldom healthy for the individual or the group. People sense each other as play-acting and a new sense of "human relations be-nice-to-everybody" (even when you are confronting) principles becomes the norm.

In the G group, members are encouraged to be aware of and acknowledge their feelings and behavior. In working with individuals, the consultant encourages them to be where they are rather than where they "ought to be." They are encouraged to dramatize the polarities in themselves, the forces for and against, toward and away, rather than to analyze and problem solve.

In the Gestalt framework change in interpersonal problem relationships occur in several ways:

• Change in others' reactions to an individual's behavior when they understand his context and purpose more clearly and/or increase their willingness to deal with him in this context.

One example of this, I recall, occurred in a team-building session in which a powerful and vocal manager who had been perceived by many of his subordinates as harshly critical and punitive was encouraged in the group setting to intensify his behavior even further. As he "did his thing" (using a Gestalt exercise) it became clear to all that what was going on involved his very vocal expression of his own frustrations ("keeps me from getting ulcers," he later explained) rather than punishment of his subordinates. In another case a manager who was intensely involved in his own specialty was perceived by his peers to be totally unwilling to listen to their points of view. After their complaints had been expressed fully, they recognized that his intensity was a strength in their team as well as a problem. Ultimately the group agreed that when one or more of them wanted to get a point across to him they might literally have to tell him to "shut up and listen." The intense manager was quite pleased by this proposed remedy and joined me in strongly encouraging it.

- Change in the individual's feeling about himself when he fully experiences and acknowledges his own behavior (e.g., lessening of self-contempt or feelings of failure). Frequently, of course, when a person feels better about himself, others feel better about him too.

  In illustration of this point, I recall an individual organization member who was accused by his peers and manager of being frequently sarcastic and at the same time aloof. His initial response to this criticism was to deny it; however, as we worked together he eventually acknowledged that his sense of humor did run to the ironic, and in fact he tried to control it but sometimes slipped. He disapproved of himself on this score and so "pulled back" whenever he became aware of it. (It was this withdrawal that made him seem aloof to others.) Again, utilizing a Gestalt method, I asked him to dramatize his ironic humor by engaging "ironically" with each member of his group. He did so fully and after some initial sheepishness was delighted with his own performance. The others were too. In later contacts with the group I learned that a positive change in relationships continued long after our session. Though he still made ironic (or sarcastic) comments to others, some of which occasionally stung, he was no longer seen as aloof and most people greatly appreciated his wit.

- Change in actual behavior when the "unfinished business" that stimulates that behavior is completed (e.g., finishing up with past resentments or projections, and so allowing new and clearer perceptions of others to emerge).

One case that illustrates this change involved a long and growing conflict between a department head and his senior subordinate. After working with them for a while the subordinate acknowledged that he resented his manager because he believed he himself should have been promoted to the department head position several years before. In a "two-chair polarization" exercise in which he dialogued with his boss, playing both his own and his manager's parts, he slowly and steadily struggled through his unfinished resentments (of *himself* primarily) and later gradually began to make real contact with his boss.

• Change in the response of the individual to others resulting from clarification of what they want from him (e.g., the person really recognizes for the first time that he is being asked for help and cooperation, rather than being criticized).

• Acceptance of status quo—no substantive change but a reduction of tension as those involved finally accept what is. Interestingly, many times this act of "giving up," in reducing countervailing pressures actually seems to precipitate later substantive change as well.

• A combination of two or more of the above. This, of course, is most frequently the case.

CHR	*G*
4. Aggressiveness and conflict seen as negative forces in system. Bringing conflict to light seen as positive in that it is a sign of openness but something to be resolved as soon as possible.	Aggressiveness and conflict valued as vitalizing forces for contact. Aggressiveness seen as an essential force for periodic breaking of confluence and as a necessary requirement for creativity.

Expressions of aggression or conflict in the CHR-oriented group are generally congratulated in the early stages of the group but primarily as indications that individuals have come to trust each other enough to open up and to express negative feelings toward each other. By and large, conflicts are interrupted relatively quickly in the CHR-oriented group, and efforts are made to analyze the causes of disagreement and to resolve them in a rational "problem-solving" manner. Competitive behavior is not valued except when it is externally focused, that is, in competing with outside organizations. The emphasis within the organization is almost invariably on learning cooperative and collaborative behavior.

In the G-oriented group, aggressiveness and conflict are valued as vitalizing and contact-enhancing forces, not merely as signs of openness. Conflict between individuals and groups is recognized as natural. The manner of working with conflict tends to differ here. Rather than move very quickly into problem-solving (which frequently means premature problem-solving, with the likelihood of later recurrence of the conflict), an effort is made in the G group to polarize and further sharpen the differences and conflict elements in the situation. Individuals are asked to fully expound their complaints against each other even to the point of exaggeration. With a qualified consultant helping to highlight the issues, feelings and beliefs are brought out. Those involved come to recognize that full argument is less embarrassing and "damaging" than they had imagined. Equally important in this process, which is both emotionally and substantively more complete, new perspectives emerge.

In working with the conflict situation, efforts are also made to help individuals to identify their own projections. In working toward this end, the "two-chair" approach mentioned earlier may be used in which the individual conducts a dialogue with himself, portraying both protagonist and antagonist.[3] In this way, he is able to get in touch with his resentments against the alienated parts of himself and thus to eventually re-own those alienated parts. When both parties in the situation have had an opportunity to explore where each stands in the conflict and what parts of the conflict belong to the self, they are then in a better position to deal with each other on an interpersonal basis and to deal with the remaining *real* issues between them. For example, in a conflict situation involving a recently appointed high-level manager, who was black, and two of his peers, who were whites, it was only after the black manager recognized that some part of his antagonism grew out of a feeling of being patronized as a black man that he and his white peers were really able to deal with more substantive issues between them.

CHR	G
5. Emphasis on others' feedback.	Emphasis on individual's own internal feedback.

In the typical CHR-oriented group, the cycle of interaction generally proceeds as follows: the individual acts, he receives feedback from others about his actions and their effect on them, and then has the choice of whether or not to modify his behavior in response to the feedback that he receives—especially if it is negative. This approach to manager development is espoused in a number of training programs throughout the country. For example, as noted in a UCLA brochure on sensitivity training, "the age-old continuing wish of men and women to see themselves as others see them has the most practical basis for those who supervise or serve in key roles in our society. To increase the effectiveness of our relationships with others, we need to know more accurately how they see us—what we do that is useful and what we do that detracts from our usefulness."

Thus in the typical CHR approach, others' feedback may be used as a guide to the individual in modifying his behavior and thereby increasing his effectiveness. As noted earlier when such behavior-modification attempts are made by resolve and the individual is not ready to make them, the changes frequently prove to be forced, temporary, and ineffective, and therefore result in incongruent behavior, which is sensed by others and is frequently disturbing to them. In the G-oriented group, the feedback of others is deemphasized. Rather, through various Gestalt approaches the individual is encouraged to become more aware of what he is doing and how he does it, or what he is avoiding, and how he avoids. In this process, rather than discourage him from behaving in a particular way in the group, the consultant may encourage him to behave in that way even more strongly, so that he can increase his awareness.

For example, while in a CHR group, an individual might get feedback such as "Joe, I feel frustrated. You seem very evasive and that produces a negative reaction in me. I wish you would be more direct." In the G group, Joe could well be encouraged by the consultant to be *more* evasive with others in the group, but in a deliberate way.

One member of a management group whom I worked with recently seemed continually to talk to others haltingly and at an abstract level. Even when he was asked his opinion on specific and immediate issues he would reply hesitantly, with generalizations and theoretical observations. In response to questioning from his peers he indicated that he was not very aware of his own style of communication. Working with him in the group, I asked him if he would be willing to make statements to several members at the most abstract level he could. He consented and began slowly and awkwardly. As he continued with the next person and then others, his voice, manner, and delivery gathered increasing strength and then humor. In increasing his awareness of his present style and in taking charge of what he was doing, he became quite animated and energetic, much to the pleasure of both his peers and himself.

Subsequently, using other Gestalt methods, he was able to become aware of how he used his hesitancy and abstraction to avoid being challenged. Still later he also discovered his own capacity to choose between his present style and a more direct one when he wished to do so.

In the G-oriented group, the consultant observes and encourages movement in harmony with the natural dynamics of individuals according to where they are right now rather than according to an ideal model. He looks at current behavior not to be corrected or changed, but rather as behavior that needs emphasis and increased awareness on the part of each individual. He has confidence that if such behavior is dysfunctional, once there has been a chance to fully experience it, change will occur naturally.

CHR	G
6. Emphasis on interdependence as a goal.	Emphasis on enhancing individual autonomy and competence, and the capacity to choose independent, competitive, or collaborative behavior.

Interdependence may very well be a requirement in some organizations. This is particularly true in organizations responsible for complex technology systems. If subsystems or components of a system are required to interface with each other in order for the total system to work properly, then it is, of course, clear that the people and organizations responsible for producing those components or subsystems must also be able to communicate and deal with one another cooperatively if the products are to be effectively integrated. My contention is, however, that while interdependence may be a requirement, it is not, or ought not to be, a goal. Frequently, CHR-oriented consultants have translated this sometime requirement into a value for work groups.

Often, groups have been exhorted by consultants and CHR-educated managers to work together and to find the synergy in their cooperation. Taken as a moral or ethical or even fashionable imperative, this has sometimes contributed considerable frustration in cases where the actual requirements or the task to be done did not require interdependence or cooperation. In fact, I have worked with groups of managers who had devoted much time and energy in repeated efforts to find ways of being interdependent until they finally came to the realization that neither their functions nor their personal inclinations required interdependence among them, and with a sigh of relief they were able to let go of this artificially imposed demand they had placed on themselves.

In the G-oriented approach, interdependence is recognized when it exists as a requirement of the situation or task to be done, and under these circumstances a competent and well-integrated individual or group is able to work collaboratively with others in order to achieve the purposes that are required. However, when it is not required, the group is not encouraged to strain for interdependence as a mode of operating. A person or group may operate in a solitary and separate manner when that is most appropriate, in a cooperative manner at other times, and competitively at still other times. Important here, as in other cases we have illustrated, is increasing the ability of the individual or the group to operate along a whole spectrum of styles.

CHR	G
7. Values being "open."	Values being "up-front" (even when that means being closed).

In the CHR-oriented group approach, high value is placed on trust and openness, and in fact, quite frequently group pressures are very strong, even to the point of coercion, to encourage individual team members to be open and deal with themselves and each other in intimate, sharing ways. While the G-oriented group does not discourage openness in relationships, neither does it discourage individuals from being closed when that is what they explicitly choose to do. While the group under these circumstances may also apply pressure on the individual to be more sharing, the consultant often will encourage the individual to stand up for his right to remain separate and to restrict his sharing.

In this context, when I work with groups, I place high emphasis, especially early in the group process, on helping individuals to become aware of and more comfortable with their ability to say no both to me and to each other. What I have discovered is that when the individual recognizes his full capacity to say "no" and to choose his own destiny, he can then say "yes" more fully and really share freely when that is what he wants to do.

CHR	G
8. Learning from new concepts and experiments with new behavior.	Emphasis on increasing awareness of present behavior and its completion.

In the CHR-oriented group, members are encouraged to learn, primarily from feedback, and then to try out new methods of behaving and interacting with one another. Attention is focused on such areas as improving communication, actively listening, being nondefensive, etc. There is frequently a search for the "right way" or "most effective way" of interacting. In many cases, the consultant's approach encourages the systemization of behavior in accordance with some prescribed model, such as Theory Y or "the manager's role," etc.

In the G group, as pointed out earlier, the consultant facilitates the client becoming aware of his present behavior and assumes that growth and change occur naturally in the human being, as in other living organisms, through the natural completion of the current set of the individual. The attempt to help a person may well proceed by encouraging him to do the "wrong thing" deliberately within the group so that both he and the other group members can get fully in touch with where he and they are at this moment.

In addition, spontaneous behavior is highly valued, rather than fulfillment of prescribed role behavior. Thus, in allowing himself to be authentic, the individual may well behave from time to time in ways that are less than ideal when measured against a set of guidelines for good human relations practice. The assumption I make is that when there is an authentic exchange between human beings who allow themselves to be as they are, including both the "good" and the "bad" of them, closer, more genuine, and more satisfying relationships come about. And these relationships do not drain energy in "keeping up a front" or doing the "right thing." There is, I believe, room for a great deal of diversity in behavior styles.[4]

CHR	G
9. Consultant role is as neutral observer of process.	Consultant more activist and clearly directive.

The facilitative role of the consultant in a CHR-oriented group frequently is seen by the consultant as demanding of him that he remain somewhat outside the scene of action and apart from the participants. This is especially true in dealing with conflict issues. Some consultants see their proper role as one in which they are objective, fair, noninvolved, and at best, do as little leading of the group as possible. CHR-oriented consultants frequently speak of giving attention to the "group's needs," and believe it is inappropriate to pursue their own needs. Many indicate considerable concern that group members not become dependent upon them.

In the G group the consultant is much more likely to take an active part, to allow himself to act and react impulsively, not merely as a model to others, but also to suit his own needs (which is, after all, the approach he is advocating). His assumption, particularly when working with industrial groups comprised of people with relatively high ego strength, is that group members need not be unduly protected. They will not become dependent upon him if he is freely himself in the group, allowing them to see his own strengths and weaknesses. He has no special image to maintain because of his particular professional function. He may allow himself to experience and express the full range of emotions including anger, affection, confusion, pride, inadequacy, and so on, just as the other members of the group may experience these feelings. Since he makes no assumption about his own omnipotence within the group, he therefore does not convey that impression to others and most often they recognize him for what he is, namely, a human being with a particular set of character traits and skills that he brings to a particular situation.

Another contrast worth noting is that while most CHR-oriented consultants encourage the expression of emotion in sensitivity groups and work groups, they generally treat the expressed feelings as "data" to be considered rationally—a kind of intellectualization of emotion. The G-oriented consultant is more likely to react to the spontaneous expression of a client with a spontaneous expression of his own. He relies less on theoretical construct and more on his and others' intuition, and what I can only describe as his faith in the high value of authenticity even when being authentic is difficult.

CHR	G
10. Focus on changing organization's culture toward increased openness, democratization, etc.	Focus on increasing individual's competence to do what he wants to do, whatever the culture.

A frequent phrase heard among many O.D. consultants has to do with "changing the organization culture." Sending managers off to sensitivity training is not enough, say the consultants; we need to affect the norms and values back at the organization. Usually that means working with managers and their teams within the organization itself, and finding ways to encourage modes similar to those developed in the sensitivity-training group. If patterns are not changed in the "back home" culture, the consultant warns, then the manager returning from his positive experience at a sensitivity lab will run into an inhospitable climate and nonsupport or perhaps even rejection from his fellow managers for his new, more open style. The demise of more than one company's O.D. effort has been attributed to its reliance on sending managers away to training conferences without sufficient concentration being given to changing the company's internal culture.

In the CHR framework certain underlying assumptions are clear. First, the desired and encouraged direction of change is toward what we have been calling the positive emotions, especially group support, collaboration, and participation. Second, it is generally assumed that these values are better for the organization than what we have called the negative emotions—frequently they are assumed to be better both in terms of humanitarian and efficiency criteria. Third, it is also assumed that making these new values operable in the organization requires consensual support by others, i.e., it is too dangerous to be open, sharing, collaborative, etc., if others are not. So, the individual manager can only change if the "system" can be changed to support him.

It will come as no surprise that the G-oriented approach is more individualistically focused, and encompasses the negative as well as positive emotions as sources of human energy and vitality available within the organization. While I have some admitted bias against tyranny, in my experience I have found few business or government organizations that I could seriously categorize under that heading. (It's likely that people who run that kind of organization don't often hire O.D. consultants.) I have, however, worked in a number of organizations where styles of management varied significantly on the dimensions of permissiveness/control, participation/directiveness, etc., and I am far from concluding that one side of the continuum is better than the other, either from the standpoint of effectiveness or humanitarianism.

With this set of assumptions then, the G-oriented consultant is less likely to focus on changing the "culture"[5] and more likely to help his clients identify first: *what they want; how they stop themselves from getting what they want;* and *what alternatives are available to them.* Then, when these questions have been addressed, the client may move forward with greater clarity and vigor to deal with others in the organization, and he may do so in whatever style he finds most promising, given the "culture" as it presently exists, and his own requirements of himself.[6]

One implication of this point is that effective development of team members does not always require that all meet together in dealing with their concerns and conflicts. Rather, an individual team member may meet with a nonfamily group, or even in a private consultation with the consultant and there work toward his own improved effectiveness. Under these circumstances the individual having recognized and mobilized his strength is often able to transfer this mobilization back into his working environment or any other environment that he moves into.

The case I have made in this chapter has been for an active expansion of the organization-development outlook to include the vitality and value of negative as well as positive emotions and attributes. The values of conventional human relations practitioners today derive, I believe, from liberal democratic biases and traditions. In reaction against the mass exploitation and mechanistic outlook of the early days of industrialization, we have fostered, espoused, and found justification for gentility, participation, and rationality. In so doing we have often neglected or denied power, directiveness, and impulse, and these are as vitally important aspects of being a person as their more comfortable counterparts.

NOTES

1. For the sake of clarity and to dramatize the points I wish to make, I intend (in Gestalt fashion) to make my case for the contrast in strong terms. I do recognize that in certain areas the contrast will seem extreme to some readers. Within this field, as in others, there is certainly a range of practice, and there has been some movement toward a broader and more realistic approach to human dynamics on the part of a number of organization-development consultants and practitioners. This is especially notable in the recent focus on the study of power.

2. The concept of the shadow is used in the psychology of C. G. Jung to characterize those aspects of an individual's personality that he has not accepted and integrated into his consciousness and self-image. The shadow thus contains characteristics that often seem negative, alien, and threatening to the individual, and he frequently rejects them. Nonetheless, in denying and disowning them he denies and disowns part of himself and so must be incomplete, uncentered, and unbalanced. He thus uses important life energy in an internal struggle against himself. Since the struggle to repress the shadow can never be completely successful, he is also troubled by its intermittent appearance in his daily life and behavior.

3. For illustrations see F. S. Perls, *Gestalt Therapy Verbatim.* Moab, Utah: Real People Press, 1969.

4. As a personal statement, I ought to say that, at a very basic level, I don't really take most problem behaviors very seriously. People do their things in their own way. Politeness or harshness of style are really not terribly important (though we do make a great deal of the difference). What counts, as the kids say, is whether or not you've got your shit together. And to *that* I do pay a great deal of attention.

5. While I acknowledge that in the O.D. context "culture" may be a useful term to describe rapidly and grossly a general impression of the way a significant number of people tend to interact in a given organization, I also find *culture* and other words like it to be lifeless abstractions that are frequently used in "behavioral science conversations" as substitutes for identifying, focusing in on, and doing something about specific and concrete situations. In the Gestalt framework, abstracting can be a way of avoiding.

6. I believe that for the most effective development of organization relationships as well as for the individual himself it is important for the client to first become aware of his own stance, including his fears, projections, alienations, etc. In working these out he frequently discovers that many of his worries are not real, or are far less terrifying when they are reduced to concrete action possibilities than when they were vague abstractions chasing around his imagination.

CHAPTER 24

CREATIVE BALANCE: AN INTEGRATION OF GESTALT, BIOENERGETICS AND ROLFING

ALLEN DARBONNE, Ph.D.

Allen Darbonne is in private practice in Los Angeles, California. He is president-elect, and a training therapist of the Gestalt Therapy Institute of Los Angeles, and a member of the Institute for Bioenergetic Analysis. His therapeutic work integrates Gestalt, Bioenergetics, and Rolf Structural Integration.

My primary interest is in living fully. Gestalt, bioenergetics, Rolf structural integration, or any therapy, has meaning to me only as it is consistent with, or enhances, living experience and expression of myself and others. Any technique or any therapy that runs counter to that, I'm against. That's my basic operating stance. The most valuable means I've found through experience for getting in touch with the boundaries and the blocks to my, or another person's, living fully is the awareness continuum. By making contact with the boundaries and bringing them into the foreground, we can begin to see where I stop letting my aliveness flow and where you stop letting your aliveness and excitement flow. When I'm working well, the basic question that I'm working with all the time is, "How are you and I interrupting our excitement and our living right now?" When my work goes dead I'm usually somewhere else. And if I come back to that then I'm back in touch with life again. A side question here is, "How do you and I interfere with our basic organismic balancing process or organismic flow?"

There are a handful of basic ideas that underlie the other hundreds of therapeutic concepts. In my experience, unless these basic notions are in the background and frequently brought to foreground, all the other theory, rules, and games of therapy are crap that is at best entertaining. One basic notion for me is that we are our bodies. We know, feel, and exist as our bodies. Our capacity for growth, feeling, and change is limited by our capacity for body awareness. And our capacity for body awareness is limited by our capacity for movement. Without movement I don't believe there is any awareness. Without movement all is the same. And sameness is something we accommodate to and lose contact with. I mean movement in the gross sense and in the minute sense, even down to the capillary level. And where movement is restricted, I believe awareness is restricted. Related to this is an individual's capacity for feeling awareness. Our feelings are emotion, and emotion, if you look at that word, is e-motion: e, which means out, and motion, which means moving. So movement out and the capacity for movement out is the capacity for feeling and living that part of our existence.

Habits limit our movements a tremendous amount, and they also have a great effect on our whole attitude about things. I suggest a simple experiment. I'd like you to fold your hands together. Now notice if you folded your left index finger over your right or vice versa. Now switch that and fold your right over your left or whichever is opposite. And how does that feel? Strange? Awkward? Not right? Annoying? Now go back to the other way again. It's like coming home. We can go so far as to develop supporting theories that there is a right and a wrong way to fold your hands. That's completely absurd, and yet I found myself, when I first did this, thinking, "Well that's not the right way to hold your hands." And that's just a small example of how through our habits we can come to set our attitudes and to repeat what is comfortable. Then the comfortable becomes right, and we get more and more stuck.

The same message about the body comes from people working outside typical gestalt spaces and into expanded consciousness. John Lilly, Oscar Ichazo from Arica, and Carlos Castaneda are examples. Every one of them says first you must tune the body. If you don't do that first, all the other stuff just won't get you anywhere but confused. In terms of awareness, I believe we are most aware at the zero point of creative balance that Fritz Perls talked about. At this point we are balanced and toned optimally. The zero point physically is a point from which we can move with equal ease into flexion or extension. I'll talk a little bit about that last statement in terms of that basic antagonism, that polarity within our bodies. We're at this point on a physical level when we can move with equal ease with both our flexors and our extensors—when we can pull in or reach out with equal ease. I believe this balance is maintained through a full physical, emotional experience of important organismic events. And what's important is whatever emerges as the important foreground for the individual from moment to moment. If he doesn't recognize this importance or if he doesn't allow himself to go fully with that experience, and give expression to his feelings, then he leaves himself unfinished. If he does allow this full response of experiencing and expressing to occur, then integration happens. That event becomes integrated into his existence. Integration isn't something you do, integration is something that happens when you do other things and when you allow yourself to be. Chronic, unfinished business leads to chronic imbalance physically and emotionally, and to disintegration, the alienation of parts, to a loss of sensitivity to ourselves, and then eventually to physical and emotional armoring. This armoring is a rigidifying process. With rigidification we lose awareness because we lose movement. So now the therapist becomes very valuable in terms of focusing our awareness where we no longer are ready to look and experience.

Another thing I'm convinced of is that the degree and the quality of physical-emotional experience and contact is limited by the degree of self-support. This is especially noticeable with our breathing. It also is noticeable in terms of what we do with our legs. What kind of stance do we take for ourselves? How do we muscularly support our other contact apparatus, our eyes, our arms, our genitals, and so on? Related to this is anxiety. As Fritz stated, and I definitely agree, anxiety is an overflow of excitement of living energy that's not supported and not expressed. It spills over into the body in a much more generalized fashion. I believe all emotional dis-ease is a result of some kind of physical/emotional imbalance and self-toxification. One of the major imbalances is the body-mind split that we get into. The body's reflection of this chronic imbalance is what is referred to as body armor. Reading body armor is like being able to read the history of a tree, once you are trained to see structure functionally. You look at the hundred-year-old oak and you can begin to tell some of the stresses it's been through, and some of the structural changes it made to maintain its integrity. These changes are part of its beauty, too.

I want to talk a little about the whole idea of flexion and extension. Part of what happens to build up the body armor is that we overexercise in one direction. Very early in life we may learn through our experience that every time we reach out we don't experience what we expect from reaching. We don't experience comfort or warmth and instead we experience something stressful or painful. So we learn after a number of times reaching out that there's always the stress or the pain and so we pull back. After awhile we start to think of reaching out and we pull back. Eventually, we may develop that as a chronic way of reacting to the world based on that expectation of pain or disappointment. So every time we have the thought of reaching out, the parts of us that become the most active are the muscles involved in pulling in. Even though movement is not obvious on the surface, electromyography shows that the muscle group involved in the thought of pulling in does contract. Thousands of times certain muscles are exercised over others. If we develop a chronic holding-in reaction then the flexors will tend to be exercised more than the extensors. And even after we get into a new situation where we know intellectually we could safely reach out, we can feel in our emotions and musculature that to reach out is much more difficult at that point than to hold back. So we have a stronger tendency to go with what's easier, what seems more consistent with our nature at that point. The process of change and growth, to a great extent, is a relearning through both using the head and integrating head stuff with having some experiences at reaching out and receiving some of the rewards of that kind of experience. It's the same with hitting out or whatever expression we contract against.

I am often asked if rolfing can be of value in the relearning process of such emotionally related imbalance. It can be very valuable. What happens on a physical level is that the body expresses its learning of that event by changing on a tissue level. The fascial sheaths around the muscles that get used more often shorten and thicken in relationship to the ones that are not used so often. One part of rolfing is aimed at stretching and realigning so that the fascial muscles begin to lengthen again. You still have to deal with the memory and you have to deal with whatever experience you have in that musculature, but it's a lot easier if you have flexibility of action. I know from my own experience with crying. I had learned that "big boys don't cry" and for many years I hadn't cried, especially in anyone's presence. What I began to notice when I first got into Gestalt Therapy is that whenever I would start to cry my stomach muscles would tighten tremendously. I had a very hard time letting go even though I wanted desperately to somehow drop into that sadness and release it. In my fifth hour of rolfing there was much work done on my stomach muscles and a lot of release there. The next week I had a Gestalt Therapy working experience and, for the first time, I was able to let go and let my stomach do the kind of abdominal pulsating necessary for the deep sobbing required for releasing deep sadness. I haven't had difficulty that way since. So definitely the two can really add to each other. I suspect that over a long period of time working verbally or using other movement approaches, I could have reached that depth of letting go. Rolfing is very powerful in what it does. I believe that therapy can be shortened a great deal with rolfing.

Mostly, what I see is that muscular armoring functions like a straightjacket, to stop explosions within. An old concept about armoring was that armoring was always there to protect us from outside attack. My experience doesn't fit that. Much more often it is to stop our letting ourselves out to the outside, particularly explosively, whether the explosion is sadness, sexuality, joy, grief, or hate. The way that I use bioenergetics encourages the use of expressive movements along with verbal expression to bring out the real depth of that expression. I call for the expressions that would go along with kicking and hitting, reaching out, biting, disgust, comforting, enticing, or whatever expression seems to want to emerge from the person and is contracted against. This is useful to both assess the capacity for the person to express certain emotions and to begin to extend his boundaries by having new experiences through allowing himself to express feelings and movement patterns that have been held in for possibly years.

The Gestalt framework of polarities is very important with expressive movement. Some bioenergetic work I have seen done falls short whenever a part of the person is somehow alienated in that process, where the bioenergetics focuses so that only one side is identified with and there is hitting and kicking out against the controller to finally get back at mommy or daddy or whoever the controller is. It is valuable to have the person identify with both sides of that polarity so that he is able to experience the controller and also that part of himself that is willing to be controlled or be spiteful. Otherwise, the paranoid thing—that the enemy is always outside—gets perpetuated. What follows is the notion that the only way to deal with the outside is to strike at others. This is related in my mind to the notion about people being toxic. There has been much talk about that recently. This patient is toxic or that person is toxic. I don't put much faith in the idea that the person is toxic and that he toxifies other people. I believe that we toxify ourselves in the way that we don't react to another person. We get into a relationship and at some point we feel annoyed or bitter and, instead of expressing the feeling, we hold it in. This readily happens with us therapists, especially when we are cautious with a new patient. We hold our bitterness in and pretty soon we are tasting our own bile—we are getting a headache, feeling tight, or whatever—and that I believe is a process that we create for ourselves.

Working bioenergetically is simply working with living biological energy, seeing where that energy flows in the person and where the energy is restricted. We see where the person supports the potential expressions of that energy, what feeling expressions the person allows himself and which ones the person does not allow. And in that process, along with becoming aware of where I block or where you block, I then suggest ways of experimenting with your existence to see if you are willing to let go of those blocks. Sometimes I attack the block itself, if the person in getting charged and excited begins to feel immobilizing tension and the muscles begin to knot up. I may go in and massage the tight muscles, putting pressure on an area where the person is already putting pressure on himself and dissolving the block by working directly on it.

Bioenergy is just living energy, and in that sense Gestalt, bioenergetics, and rolfing are all working with and toward the same thing. They are different frameworks. From the way I work and what I am interested in, basically I am looking at the same things. I deal with them maybe verbally one time, or with the third chair one minute, or with the couch the next, and maybe with my elbow next. But they are all energetic approaches, as far as I am concerned.

Rolfing works particularly with gravity, dealing with the energy field of man as related with the energy field of gravity. The work is done through the manipulation of the fascia around the muscular body, the whole myofascial system. We usually see gravity in a negative way, that it is the thing we want to get away from. If we are tired, the first thing we do is to go and try to find a place to lie down. We horizontalize ourselves and minimize gravity's effect on us. And yet gravity really is a very positive and uplifting force that we don't appreciate. Part of the power at this point, the leverage that rolfing has, is that gravity hasn't been considered in that way in terms of human architecture.

We are balanced and aligned physically in one sense, the way that a building is aligned. You can look at the building and understand why that building stands and could withstand even shaking from earthquakes. If we have proper alignment in terms of our bony structure and muscular structure and tendons, then gravity works with us like gravity works with a tent. If you didn't have gravity, you would have a hell of a time getting your tent pitched. But it's the work of that central pole, which is in a sense like the spinal column, that you balance around, that gives you the tent that stands up. In a sense gravity holds your tent up by pulling down when you relate to it in a certain way. The same thing will happen in the physical structure, where, if we get ourselves unbalanced, we begin to get pulled down here and there and have to put a counter pull on our guy ropes in an opposite direction. We end up really tying ourselves up physically with a lot of extra heavy ropes to compensate for our being out of balance. So in rolfing, one of the things you do is to focus on the major segmental blocks of the body, the head, the shoulder girdle, the pelvic girdle, and the legs. You attempt to align those, the centers of gravity of those, in a straight line. And when that happens, the body is in its position of least stress, and actually a person feels a sense of lightness when aligned. He gets a sense of requiring very little energy to move through space. But the minute we begin to push ourselves or to drive ourselves, we begin to get our head forward. Then we've got this big twelve-to-fifteen-pound ball hanging off the top of this building, so we've got to do all kinds of stuff behind it to keep the building from falling on its face. There the big energy expenditure starts to take place.

Another thing that is focused on in rolfing is to get the feet flexibly grounded and to get all the joints moving in correct angles so that the feet can really be on the ground and yet flexibly so, not planted. A big gain for many people in rolfing is that breathing support is increased by loosening up the whole breathing apparatus of the rib cage—and consequently feeling support is increased. A lot of people talk about the pain in rolfing. Much of the body armor—particularly the tensions in the body that develop from emotional experiences—is aimed at avoiding some kind of painful experiences. We tighten, and in a sense hold our breath against experiencing that pain fully, and through a chronic holding, we make that experience isolated from us. The releasing process in rolfing usually puts the person back in touch with some of that pain. With the experience and expression of pain, we allow ourselves to have the full emotional experience with traumatic events that are in the past and that we haven't let be in the past because we still carry them around in our body.
cause we still carry them around in our body.

When I'm working as a therapist, I'll start out verbally with the person and I'll pay attention to what is happening in my body and his body. If something emerges physically, I'll focus on that. Sometimes the person begins to do some verbal work and the words just don't carry the feeling—you know, when you get that disconnected feeling and you say, "I don't know what you are doing, but I just don't trust you." Very often, to me, that is a sign that experientially the cortex is disconnected from the lower nervous system so the two just don't get together. The person does the same work over and over again, verbalizing and verbalizing, and never hooks into the feeling and lets the feeling carry the words. That to me is a time to stop the talk and to begin to work directly with the body and then to bring the two together again. First, I work with movement. I prefer to have the person do as much as he possibly can and to bring awareness to where he is stopping himself. Yet, there are certain points where he "can't." I mean at the moment that is really a "can't" rather than a "won't." Half of therapy is discriminating our true limitations from our fantasied ones. That "can't" moment is when I am willing to bring my energy in, with the person's permission, to do something with my hands to assist them at opening a contraction. If we have gone from words to working bioenergetically and the person is obviously up against his own structure in such a way that he would have to do usual bioenergetic work a thousand times to finish, I will recommend rolfing to him.

I will discuss the process of Rolf structural integration at some length and summarize a number of emotional reaction patterns from my rolfing experience. I believe the value of integrating rolfing and Gestalt Therapy will become apparent.

The process of Rolf structural integration consists of ten hours of manipulation of the muscular fascia toward optimal balance. The rolfer stretches, tones, and repositions the body fascia to establish balance in the total body from right to left, front to back, lower to upper, and inner to outer. In general he words from the surface toward the center of the body.

In the first hour, work is on the superficial fascia and aims at freeing the pelvis from the thorax. Rigidity between the crib cage and pelvis is lessened, as is tension at the hip joint, allowing mobilization of the pelvis toward horizontal alignment. The chest becomes more expansive in all directions and the person begins to sense a new fullness of breath. This deeper breathing is important for future rolf sessions, since the improved metabolism assists the removal of toxins and increases tissue nourishment.

Emotional reactions during the first rolfing session or in shortly subsequent psychotherapy sessions vary with the individual. In my experience some general patterns do emerge. Often fear and sadness related to memories of early expansiveness will come up. Work on tense muscles in the upper chest and shoulder-arm attachments frequently are associated with feelings related to dependency, trust, and reaching out. Here and in all rolf sessions the person's relationship to their pain and their pattern of communication (verbal and non-verbal) with another regarding their pain comes to the foreground. In addition, the person's whole reaction to touch and contact, with or without pain, becomes apparent. He may contract inward and away from the rolfer, puff up or push outward against the rolfer, constantly run away on the couch, space out and appear unreactive, become slippery and sweaty while appearing calm, be openly receptive and communicative, or present many other responses. Usually these responses are consistent with their characteristic contact patterns.

During any actual rolfing session I do not interrupt the rolfing in order to do psychotherapy. While he is open and vulnerable, my experience indicates that interrupting the rolf session does not serve the patient's interest for several reasons. There is so much meaningful structural work to be done in an individual rolf session that prolonged interruption would subtract from the optimal amount of work that can be done with the person. Also the patient is partially imbalanced in the middle of a session by the rolfer's intent. This is not the most effective moment for a lasting balanced-therapy experience leading toward integration. Thirdly, meaningful emotions aroused during rolfing are available for at least a week or so and can be worked through in psychotherapy sessions when time and attention are available for effective focus. During the rolf session I do encourage the person to stay with his feelings and see what is there. I generally interrupt the rolf work only for here-and-now dialogue which enhances openness and participation in the rolfing experience.

The second rolf session aims at placing a footing under the hips and thorax and lengthening the back, which is usually experienced as short relative to the front of the body, which was lengthened in the first hour. Work is done to free the hinge movement of the ankle and knee and to horizontalize their action. Contractions within the foot are also released. Psychologically as well as physically individuals often report a greater sense of contact with the ground. Often individuals begin to be interested in and act in a way which shows they are taking more of a definite stand for themselves after the second hour. Sometimes feelings about running away or having run away will come up at this time. Very frequently, a person's denial of fear will become apparent during this session. He will literally have cold feet with profuse perspiration while he verbally denies any feelings of fear, or allow the upper part of the body to demonstrate fear in any way other than through the holding of his breath.

The third hour is aimed at balancing the forces, anterior and posterior, and lengthening the sides of the body along a lateral line. The body is entered more deeply in this session as a major muscle which connects the twelfth rib to the crest of the pelvis is toned to allow more flexibility and awareness at the body's middle. On an emotional level, the individuals will often begin to become aware of their having attempted to gain self-support by rigidifying their structure. Some sense of vulnerability is often felt by individuals who have thickened and tensed themselves so greatly between the rib cage and pelvis as they are now asked to open themselves to more flexibility here.

Sessions four, five, and six aim at freeing the pelvis from below, above, and posteriorly. Session four work is done to lengthen the medial line between the legs and to tone the musculature of the inner thigh and attachments to the lower pelvis. Most frequent emotional patterns connected to the fourth-hour work have to do with tensions related to sexuality. Feeling and memories about being violated or sexually injured are often mentioned. At times patients will claim they are helpless to make the movements called for by the rolfer at this point and that all they can do is lie there and be done to. Other patients will attempt to be very much in control and to determine how much work is accomplished at this point.

In session five, the abdominal wall is lengthened and toned. Another deep muscle, the psoas, is toned after the outer wall is released. The tone of the psoas muscle is very significant in the overall balancing of the body as well as in sexual movements and graceful walking and running. During and after the fifth session, individuals are often able to soften their bellies in a manner which allows them to feel sadness and sexuality at deeper levels.

Work in the sixth session focuses on freeing the backs of the legs and the muscles of the buttocks and the rotator muscles of the legs, posteriorly, as well as working on the ligaments and tissue around the sacrum and tailbone. Common feelings which emerge around the sixth hour are angry feelings centering about being pushed or controlled. Sometimes embarrassment is expressed about being tight around the ass and about being unable to remain relaxed when that musculature is approached or touched. Recall of memories of having physically or psychologically fallen on one's ass may occur. In men, particularly, anxiety or fantasies about homosexuality come up during the sixth hour. Both men and women will frequently comment on a helpless and vulnerable feeling, of being attacked from the rear. Sometimes the patients will sob deeply and state the physical pain in rolfing was not great but triggered contact with a very painful feeling memory within themselves which they could now give into with deep sobs.

Work in the seventh hour is aimed at allowing the neck to move back so that the head is positioned over the shoulder girdle and remainder of the body. Balance of the right and left side of the neck is also attended to. Tensions in the face musculature are released as well as tensions of the mouth and nose. Tensions of the face and neck are often a nonverbal expression of attitudes which become more vocal during and after the seventh session. Some individuals become aware of feelings in the back of the neck due to looking up to authority. They also become aware of stubbornness and resentment held in their tight jaws as well as all sorts of feelings controlled and withheld by a tight facial mask or a rigidifying of the eyes against expression. Frequently, work in the mouth, particularly under the tongue, will put a person in touch with years of swallowed tears and may lead the person into finishing with grief work that had been swallowed and disconnected from his awareness. Tight muscles at the back of the neck and down toward the shoulders are often related to held-in expressions of anger and rage. Often a person's racing tempo will show a marked slowing down after the seventh session. It was in his seventh session of rolfing that Fritz Perls had one of his most profound physical and emotional experiences, his recall and working through of an experience of having been injured by an anesthetist sometime before. Contacting and working through this unfinished business led to his relief from pain which had plagued him unmercifully.

The eight and ninth rolf sessions are aimed at putting the body together from the center. The large facial planes of the body are integrated so that there is an ease of relationship between the core and sleeve of the body without either dragging on the other. Work in either of these sessions is primarily on the pelvis and lower half of the body or the shoulder girdle and upper half of the body.

In the tenth rolf session every joint is brought to maximal operational mobility from foot to head. The fascial sheets are related in such a way that the joints are free to move. Finishing work is done to maximize reciprocity of extensors and flexors, allowing the person to become the alignment. Emotional reactions to these later sessions are of the type mentioned before, although the reactions and expressions are now often more intense due to greater openness and support for feeling. Individuals also frequently report a sense of more energy, greater body awareness, and a sense of lightness and ease of movement. They also generally have a deeper appreciation of their body and a much more immediate awareness of when they begin to act in a way which is counter to the body's alignment and ease of expression.

A more recent development in the rolfing approach is structural patterning (Rolf-Aston structural patterning in stillness and motion). Structural patterners are specially trained practitioners who guide the individual to greater awareness of both his limitations and possibilities of movement and balance. Often, if rolfing is done without time spent on education, the individual is not fully aware of the new possibilities of his increased range of movement from the rolfing. From my experiences, I believe that patterning both significantly extends the work initiated by rolfing and is a means of recentering after a person has disturbed his alignment by one means or another. After a relatively few patterning sessions during and following the Rolf series, an individual can continue to improve his alignment by taking responsibility and continuing patterns on his own.

Patterning is painless and is sometimes valuable in helping a person assess, before rolfing, what ways rolfing might be of value to them.

In the nature of Gestalt Therapy is its integrative power for the individual. It is an open system encouraging the integration of its theory with meaningful theory from other approaches. My hope is that I have presented a way of working which furthers the living flow of that system.

CHAPTER 25

GESTALT THERAPY AND TRANSACTIONAL ANALYSIS

ROBERT L. GOULDING, M.D.

Robert L. Goulding is the director of the Western Institute for Group and Family Therapy, which has offices in Watsonville, Palo Alto, and Seaside, California. He is a teaching member of the International Transactional Analysis Association, and a Fellow of the American Group Psychotherapy Association. Dr. Goulding is a well-recognized author and teacher of therapies combining Gestalt and Transactional Analysis approaches.

There are as many definitions of Gestalt Therapy as there are Gestalt therapists, and I have great difficulty reading Perls, Shepherd, Fagan, Simkin, Polster, Laura Perls, and others, and coming up with a firm definition. I assume that other authors in this book have also defined Gestalt Therapy, and that another definition from me would be unnecessary. However, in my work using Gestalt techniques in a transactional analysis framework, I need to define what *I* mean by Gestalt. When teaching my trainees, I draw the typical black circle on the poster paper I use, and ask them to describe it. The first one usually gets tricky, and says that he sees a bunch of squiggly lines put together. Finally someone will say he sees a black circle on a white piece of paper on a redwood stand behind which is a wall, a stovepipe, in a barn. For me, it is also necessary to say that the barn is on a ranch on Mt. Madonna near Watsonville, in Santa Cruz County, California, U.S.A., a country on planet Earth, the third planet from the sun, in the Milky Way (or whatever we call this galaxy), in the universe. That, I say, is the Gestalt process, the widening awareness of me, and of you. In order to further use this analogy, if the rest of this world is you, and I am I, then you and I are going to transform that black dot, restricted, contained, and which represents the easily visible you, into a huge flowing picture. I am going to give you the techniques to paint, and you are going to do the painting.

This chapter is about those techniques, and how they fit into the transactional analysis framework. At this point, it is important for me to say something about an essential difference between pure Gestalt, pure transactional analysis, and the combined approach that I, and my wife Mary, have developed. Most Gestalt therapists in the early days, including Fritz Perls, and many of the modern Gestaltists, believed or believe that the patient has the experience in his therapy, that he integrates the experience himself as he breaks through impasses, and that he doesn't need any information from the therapist to integrate. Most pure transactional analysis therapists, including Berne in the early days, and the present remnants of the old San Francisco Social Psychiatry Seminars (excepting me) believe that if the therapist gives the patient enough information about himself, relating to his ego states, transactions, games, and scripts, the patient will use that information to integrate, making decisions from his data processor (Adult Ego State). These purists don't think that the patient needs a "gestalt experience" to integrate and to change, doesn't need to experience himself moving through an impasse.

I was fortunate enough, in the early sixties, to work with both Berne and Perls. I worked under Berne's supervision every Saturday for two years, attended many of the seminars, and thoroughly learned transactional analysis. Fritz came to Esalen, and I was in one workshop with him and Jim, watched him countless times, worked with him a few times, had many experiences with him in my home, and my office, in Carmel. I was also doing co-therapy from time to time with Irma Shepherd and Joen Fagan; did a week's workshop, with Jim leading, at his place, and co-led with him here at our place, as well as having him here many times to teach our trainees his style of Gestalt. We joined forces with Erv and Miriam Polster, who are on our faculty, and have co-led with them, and Mary has been in one of their workshops. We have thus had a large exposure to the leading Gestalt therapists in the area. Everyone knows that Fritz said "lose your head and come to your senses"; most people exposed to Berne knew that he called working with feelings "greenhousing," and worked largely cognitively. Well, I brought Fritz and Eric together at my house in Carmel, and I bring them together in my therapy. I believe, and have a great deal of evidence, that both the Gestalt experience *and* the cognitive material are important and that the individual will do better with both than with either. I will be stressing this point over and over.

The Polsters write about contact as being the first step in Gestalt Therapy; my contact with my patient is my awareness of him, my awareness of me, and what is happening between us. As I watch him, listen to him, I am listening and watching for a series of contacts, of awareness, that are defined in transactional analysis (here after T.A.). I listen for the unpleasant feelings the patient has, and how he gets or maintains these feelings; I listen for the kinds of Games he plays, and find out the kinds of fantasies he has, for it is in the playing of his Games and his fantasy life that he maintains himself in unpleasant feelings. I want to know what he was like when he was a little kid, and how he still behaves like that little kid in all kinds of ways. I want to know what his parents were like, and how he behaves, thinks, feels, and obsesses like they did. I want to know what kind of messages they gave him, and how he reacted to those messages: what he said out loud, what he said inside his head, what he did in response, and what he is still doing, thinking, feeling as he did, mostly outside of his present awareness. I want to find out how he is blocking himself, maintaining himself in impasses, avoiding intimacy, autonomy, creativity, spontaneity, avoiding growing.

Now, I don't want to know all those things in a sterile, history-taking, boring way that most of us learned in graduate school or residency. I want to learn and know about the person in a live, exciting, thrilling process that is part of our engagement, part of our contact. I want him to learn these things about himself, as I learn them; I want him to come up against his impasses, and deal with them; to either admit the impasse, which is dealing with it in one way, or breaking through it, which is dealing with it in another way. It is his choice, not mine, as to whether to maintain the impasse, or go through it. It is also important, in using T.A. as the theoretical tool, that he knows the relevance of his impasse to all the other things I have written about above. His unpleasant feelings or "rackets," his games, his fantasies, his life script, his early original decisions that he made in order to survive in his environment, in response to the overt and covert messages that he received from his parents and other important figures in his life. These messages we categorize in T.A. into injunctions, and counter-injunctions. Impasses can be broken down into first degree, relating to the counter-injunctions, second degree, relating to the injunctions, and third degree, relating to the patient's own awareness of self, what he feels himself to be, what he experiences as being part of him, or him, and not related to the outside messages and pressures. It is our position, and here we differ from many pure Gestalt therapists, that a firm cognitive understanding of the relationship of the impasses to the archaic past, the way in which the patient has not completed old experiences and is still trying to do so through avoidance, blocking, inappropriate thinking, feeling, and behavior, will help him to change.

As we work, then, moving toward impasses we explore his universe, we begin to teach him a method of being autonomous, by asking him to be aware of all the ways he gives away his autonomy. We usually don't listen to him talking *about*, but ask him to talk *to* whomever he is talking about. If he is talking about his wife, we ask him to talk *to* her. If she is not in the room, we ask him to fantasize that she is. If he is talking about his mother, we ask him to bring her into the room, and talk to her as if the event was happening right now, in the room. We know that many Gestalt therapists will only deal with the immediate here and now, asking the patient to work in the here and now without relating to the past. We don't agree with that position, and we ask the patient to be aware of his past as it relates to the here and now, to be aware of his decisions, the injunctions and counterinjunctions, all the related bits.

So, we work with only I-Thou transactions, in the here and now, and not with talking about history. We bring the history into the present, and then the work becomes exciting. The patient, as he relives an old scene in which he is stuck, gets together the memory with the affect, and begins to relive the scene even more. He is overcome by his sadness, or by his anger. He works with the scene until he either completes it, or becomes aware that he is not willing, at this time, to complete it. Completing it means finishing it, not being in the impasse anymore, either in the present or in the original archaic impasse. For example, she may be a little girl of forty, who sounds and looks like she is only ten. She may go back to a scene where she feels as lonely as she confesses to feeling in the present; she may go back to a scene in her childhood, when she is ten years old, when her father is dying. She won't say goodbye to him, because she doesn't want to admit that he is dying; and after he dies, she refuses to mourn, but pretends that he is coming back if she is a good girl and waits for him. She has thus frozen herself into a "Sleeping Beauty" script, in which she stays a little girl, sleeping in the tower waiting for Santa Claus, or the Prince (really father). Until she actually gets back in the scene, and deals with her unfinished business, and says goodbye, and tells fantasized Father that she is not waiting for him anymore, she will stay a little girl. She must go through the scene, sometimes closing the casket, throwing dirt in the grave, saying goodbye. If she backs away from the completion, still holding onto the magic, she is not completing, and she will not let herself grow up, claim her sexuality and sensuality, will stay waiting for someone to find this pure princess and take away her loneliness. The only person that will show up is a burglar.

If she completes the scene, finishes the goodbyes, finishes the mourning, then she frees herself to grow up, and to claim her maturity. In either case, we want her to be sure to understand the nature of the impasses as we see it, what the threads are that bind her to her past, that she uses to block herself, and what she has done, cognitively, to break through if that is what she did. As we connect the affective experience to the cognitive understanding, now we are using T.A. We may draw on the blackboard or poster paper the threads, the connections. We think that is okay to tell the patient something, unlike some Gestalt therapists that say they are insulting the patient if they give him information.

It is necessary for the reader to know something about T.A. to understand completely the connections, and I assume that most readers will know something. Most therapists today know about Ego States, know that Berne postulated that the individual consists of a Parent Ego State, consisting of a collection of parenting experiences; an Adult Ego State, which is primarily a data collector and processor; and a Child Ego State, consisting of all the child experiences. If this is new material for the reader, he/she is referred to the books by Berne. In order to understand my impasse theory, you need to know that there are two kinds of messages, at least, that the child gets from the parents. One, which we call the counter-injunction, comes from the Parent Ego State of the parents, and usually tells the child of the parent's expectations for him—they want him to do things so that they will be proud of themselves for having had him. These messages include work hard, study hard, and many other reasonably rational and appropriate messages about behavior, as well as some rather impossible messages, including "Please me," "Be perfect," "Try hard," "Be careful." The counter-injunction is often a cultural message, passed down from Scotch Presbyterian to Scotch Presbyterian, as "Waste not, want not," or from Hebrew to Hebrew, as "Don't feel too good or something bad will happen," or from Indian to Indian— our friends in Bombay have a sign on their bathroom stating "A penny saved is a penny taxed." The counter-injunction is telling the little kid, over and over again, how to be a good kid—how to please mother, father. The messages are usually straight, overt, such as "work hard," but sometimes they are irrational, as "Be perfect." Many priests received "Be perfect" from their doting mothers, who are trying to get into heaven by becoming the second Mary and giving birth to the second coming of the Lord. Many nuns are trying to be vestal virgins for their fathers, by "being perfect." This is in no way said to be unkind; it just happens to be true, and explains how even the most sincere calling to the religious life may have, also, some strong counter-injunctions as part of the parenting. If this were all, if the counter-injunction was the only message they have to deal with, then the impasse that many religious people have that come here would be easy to deal with. This *first degree* impasse would be easily completed; then the priest or nun would either continue in the

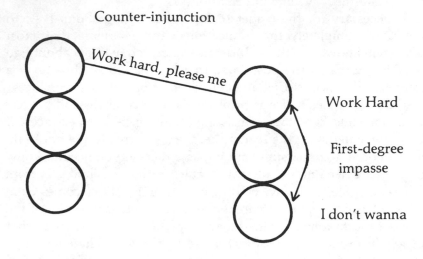

Figure 1

religious life with joy and without ambivalence, or get out of it (as some of them do).

However, in addition to the counterinjunction, the parents give, from their Child Ego State, other irrational messages (called injunctions) which are primarily based on the feelings the parent has about the child, the disappointments, unhappinesses, angers that come from the parents' own Child Ego State. If the parent didn't want the child, and had it anyway, they may say, "If it weren't for you, we could be happy," which is really saying, "I wish you weren't alive," or, "Don't exist." If the Mother at first felt this, and then later decided that she was not nice having such thoughts, she might feel guilty, and then overprotect the child after birth, telling the child "Don't," which means don't do anything that might hurt you—don't walk, run, ride bikes, ride rollers skates, climb trees, etc. If the parent is distant, physically, the injunction is, "Don't be close." If the child is the oldest in the family, she might be told to take care of the others, or, "Don't be a child," while the youngest may be told, "Don't grow up." Other injunctions include don't be you (the sex you are), don't make it, don't be important, don't be well, don't be sane, don't belong, don't think, don't feel, and a few others. There are many suborders of injunctions that fit into one of these. For example, "Don't be sexual" is often a part of the "Don't grow" injunction.

Although Berne wrote about the injunction being like an electrode, that is stuck into the child's head, we take the position that in order for the injunction to have any relevance later in the child's life the child has to buy it, and to make a decision relating to the injunction. For instance, if the injunction is "Don't be," the child in some way has to decide not to be; he is not stuck in such a position simply because the parent gave him the message. I have written about such decisions several times before, but one example relating to the "Don't be" injunction is "If things get too bad I can always kill myself or run away," or "I'll kill myself if you don't change," or "I'll get you even if it kills me," or any of several other decisions. Or, in many cases, he somehow knows that his mother is crazy, and doesn't listen, or his father tells him not to pay any attention, or he finds warm support from grandparents, or uncles, or older siblings, and then doesn't make a suicidal decision.

However, if he does listen, does buy the injunction (and the counterinjunctions), and decides his response, then he has put limits on himself, and has stuck himself in the start of a life script, in which he sets himself up to be depressed, eventually suicidal, and possibly either kill himself or get others to kill him. Now, when he decides to get out of the script, not to listen to the injunction, to redecide whatever it was he decided, or to change that decision to another *new* redecision, he is in an impasse until he actually does such work, and does it while in his Child Ego State. I wrote at some length about impasses in an article in *Voices* (Spring 1974). The first-degree impasse is related to the counterinjunction, as "Work hard." This comes from the Parent of the parent, and is introjected by the patient into his Parent Ego State, which is where he incorporates all the verbal, out-front messages from his parents (Figure 1). When he finally becomes aware that he is working too hard, that he doesn't have to work so hard any more, he is now at an impasse, until he works to get out of it. Such work usually has to be done from both the Adult and the Little Professor (Adult in the Child), while he is in his Child Ego State. His Adult can decide about the facts regarding not working too hard, but usually, until he does some affective work from his Child, he will be uncomfortable in some way. He has not resolved the Parent-Child dialogue until he does the work from his Child.

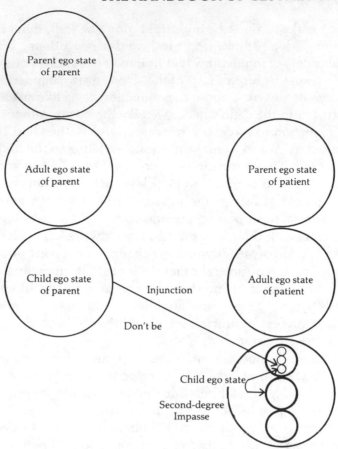

This shows the parent introjected in the parent of the child, so that
the impasse is between parent's Child and
the patient's Little Professor. Figure 2.

Once he has made a firm decision about not working hard, he
begins to set up his life in a different way. He continues to work
through, of course, as there is no magic involved, but he is constantly aware of all the ways in which he sets himself up to work
hard, and even play hard, and slowly stops himself.

The second-degree impasse relates to the injunctions, as for example, "Don't be." If his counter-injunction was "Work hard," and
then the parent said, "or else drop dead," he is now stuck in a "Don't
be" injunction (if he bought it) until he also does some work with
that. This is the danger from many superficial therapists, who do joy
work, or encounter leaders, who promote freedom, or permission
workshops, where the leader is so turned on to rebelling against parents that he forgets that the out-front message, or counter-injunction,

is only one of two messages, and that the often-covert injunction is the one the patient is secretly following. The patient, in the rebel position, says, "Fuck you" to the overt parent, while listening to the covert, and when he no longer gets strokes for "working hard," for instance, he may now feel the full fury of the "Don't be" message: work hard or drop dead. He may get tremendously depressed or suicidal at this time, and it is very dangerous to allow a patient to work out of the first-degree impasse without checking on the injunctions.

The second-degree impasse, then, is of a different kind than the first-degree. In the first degree, dealing with the counter-injunction, the impasse is between the incorporated verbal parent in the Parent Ego State of the patient, and his Child, and more specifically between the little Adult in the Child. The second-degree impasse is between the nonverbal or preverbal Parent in the Child, introjected either before the child had a vocabulary, or introjected in facial expressions, vague shapes, and distortions, without specific words. There may have been words later on, and the patient in dialoguing may use—usually uses—words when taking the part of the parent, but he is also aware of visual impressions. For instance, yesterday when a trainee was working through a second-degree impasse concerning his right to be heard, to be important, he experienced the parent he was talking to to be nine feet tall—which seems to be his memory of his parent when he was an infant (see Figure 2).

The third-degree impasse is between the Child that has survived, that wants freedom, life, spontaneity, and the Child that adapts so early, or so nonverbally, that it experiences self as being this way since birth, and does not experience self as being adapted to the outside environment. The transsexual is a classic example; the men we have seen have always felt themselves to be female since as early as they can remember, and although their mothers may have overtly said "Don't be a man," they feel that this was because their mothers really knew they were girls inside anyway. They experience themselves as females, not just adapting to injunctions. Others state they have always been clumsy, or always been stupid, or always been sickly. Whereas in the first-degree and second-degree work, the dialogue is I-Thou, in the third-degree there isn't a second person, and the patient talks from I about I on both sides. For instance, a formerly depressed and suicidal patient who is no longer depressed, but still feels as worthless as he "always had" says from the worthless side "I don't experience myself as having any value, except when I work." From the free side, he says "Wow, after all the things I have done to myself, I am still alive, I haven't killed myself, I do enjoy much of my life, I do enjoy sex, I do have worth." And so the dialogue goes, the patient now using a better accounting system in totalling up his value.

Often, these dialogues that the patient does, start from body gestures, or from the vocabulary used. For instance, a trainee started yesterday to work on allowing himself more fun, more spontaneity, more fredom, to be what some transactional analysts say is a "natural" or "Free" Child. As he starts, he puts his finger in front of his mouth. "Be your finger," say I, and he says, as his finger, "Shut up. You can't be free." The dialogue that ensues then develops into one between archaic parent, who says, "Don't be childlike. I don't like your noise when you act like that. You make me nervous," and his Child, looking for a way to break through and be more free. He becomes more excited as he responds, and by the time the dialogue is over he is bouncing in his chair, his voice has become louder, firmer, more melodious, zestful, and there is a marked change in his whole body position.

All gestaltists know of the work that I am talking about. Here I am putting the impasse work into a specific framework in which the patient's movements through impasses, or "stuck places" at the impasse, are related to the Injunctions, Decisions, Games, Rackets, Scripts. Even if he doesn't break through them at this time, seeing the relationship helps him to work when not in the session, to come back and work again, to recognize how his behavior defeats him. For example, to join a poker game at night (his response to a "don't have fun; don't be a child" injunction) and his decision to grow before he is ready to, to take care of others (siblings earlier, now psychiatric patients) are decisions designed to inhibit his freedom in the service of pleasing mother or father. Each time he throws off the inhibition, joins in, has fun, he is making a tacit redecision from his Child to ignore the old messages and enjoy himself more, and now his behavior is beginning to reinforce the new position, instead of the old position, as he had formerly been doing. The stroking or recognition he got from others formerly, for doing his old thing, is now changed into stroking from the workshop members for doing the new, and his growth is even more rapid.

I was in a workshop years ago—perhaps ten—with Fritz and Jim Simkin leading. With me were many of the now well-known Gestalt therapists around the country. I did an awareness continuum exercise with Jim, the first day. When I was finished, Jim asked me what I was experiencing. I responded, "It was great," referring to the awareness experience. Jim raised his eyebrows, I caught on, and exclaimed joyously "I am great." I repeated that two or three times, and kept repeating it all week, to the great amusement and support of the rest of the group. That moment marked a change in my life for me. I also used my knowledge of T.A. to put the experience into perspective for me, to see how I had been depriving myself in many ways because I had been taught not to brag, not to claim myself, not to be important, not to be selfish, and all kinds of other *don'ts* that I used to prevent myself from really enjoying me and my life to the fullest.

Here we are back to the statement that I made earlier in this chapter about both the emotionally affective "gestalt" experience and the cognitive level being important in change. I had a good "peak" experience, and I put all my knowledge of T.A. and my own injunctions and early decisions to work for me in making some new redecisions for myself. I especially did this the last day, when Fritz noticed that I was filling my eyes with tears. He asked me if I was all right. I said that I was, that I was experiencing myself as being water boiling in a pot, about ready to blow off my lid. He said, "Be the lid," and I, as the lid, said, "Be careful, Bob, quiet down." Then as Bob, I responded, "I don't need you, lid," and assumed more and more an "ah ha" feeling, as I cognitively and emotionally experienced what I had been doing to myself. I became the hot water, and then the steam, streaming into the air, into space, throughout the universe, and for the first time in my memory was completely in touch with my uniqueness, my power, my ability.

The cognitive information that I already had about myself allowed me to set up all kinds of impasse breakthroughs, so that I freed myself from my former inhibitions. The "working through" that classic group therapists talk about, and that they claim takes place much better as the patient works on and on and on in the group, I did as part of my living experience. I had to change some of my environment, of course, in order to maintain my support system around me, when it was obvious that I would have great difficulty in staying in such a joyous and fulfilling awareness of self, if I remained in the same total environment.

The use of the passive voice and the word *it* instead of *I*, lead to many such awarenesses when the therapist hears them, understands the importance of the injunction-decision complex, and leads the patient to a new discovery of his own importance. Although pure Gestalt work will get him through the immediate impasse, the further use of T.A. to relate the impasse to the archaic impasses enables the patient to make better use of the experience. Also, the patient begins to understand that the original decision to diminish his own importance, to take second fiddle, or a seat in the back of the bus was made because it was the only solution that he could find at that time, in that place, and with those people. It was thus an extremely powerful tool for him. As he works through some of the earlier impasses, he begins to be in touch with the power that he had then, with the power that he used to survive, to stay alive, or sane. As he claims that power for himself, it is much easier for him, in the here and now, to give up one old powerful position, now inappropriate, and to experience a new power with his growth, his broadened awareness. As long as he is down-grading himself for his "faults," he stays in a harassed, inferior position, from which it is difficult to move. When he can say, "Wow, Dad, I beat you after all, and I don't need to do that anymore," he can move from the archaic to the new power position far more easily.

Another helpful way of integrating Gestalt and T.A. is with confrontation of games. A *game* is a series of transactions ending in an unpleasant feeling, which is played outside of the patient's Adult awareness, at the end of which the player says something about himself and/or others, such as "No one loves me," or "I always knew men were no good." A typical example happened in one of the training groups. A therapist from Europe was criticizing my critique of other therapists while working with one of the trainees as therapist. Toward the end of the work she said, "I'm doing something to myself now; I am often very critical of people, of things, and usually I end up feeling bad and someone usually criticizes me for being critical. I don't understand why I do that." I drew the pictures on the board of her ostensibly straight transaction—"You are not honest enough, you stroke for things which are really not good" and the secret message (my Parent)—"please criticize me so that I can feel bad." The response would have been something from me if I had responded harshly (my Child), and the unpleasant feeling at the end. She said, "Sure, and I do that in order to keep feeling bad; it isn't right for me to feel too good, or something bad will happen. If I say something good to somebody, I will in some way harm them. When I was a little child, all I got were criticisms; no one even noticed me when I was a good little girl." She had her hands out, with one hand higher than the other, moving them in the air, and with the higher, left hand making sharp downward motions. I asked her to be her left hand. She said, "This is the part that criticizes, and my right hand is the part that sometimes strokes positively." She then started a dialogue between the two, ending up by stroking her left hand with her right hand; as the day passed she very obviously became less and less critical.

Another trainee recently asked one of his peers if he would take him to Carmel over the weekend. The second trainee, Jim, at first said yes, and then decided he really didn't like Joe, and said no. Joe then pouted, feeling hurt, sad, abandoned. We asked him when he last felt abandoned, and asked him to relate the scene in the present tense. He first talked to the girl with whom he had been living prior to the workshop, and who had split with him after coming to the ranch, expressing his feeling of sadness. Then he talked to his fantasized ex-wife, who had left him a year or two ago, then to a series of girlfriends who had "left" him prior to his marriage. Each time he talked in the present tense. Then he put his mother in the chair in front of him, in fantasy, and talked to her about her abandoning him when he was nine years old, and later killing herself. During this scene (also in the present tense) he was finally able to relive the scene in which she said goodbye to him, to tell her all his resentments, as well as his appreciations, and finally was able to close this old scene satisfactorily. Now he no longer sets himself up to be abandoned, or refused, or rejected, and if he does get turned down, he no longer sits around being depressed and feeling rejected. He is no longer trying to get rid of mother so that he can try to bring her back by letting her know how sad he is. Over and over again he has set up situations in which the only reasonable choice his wife, or girlfriends, or any friend would have would be to leave, or say no.

In each case, the game was obvious. In the game with Jim, he already knew that Jim had asked one of the women to go with him, and had already turned down someone else, so that a part of him had the information that Jim would not be likely to take him. Thus when his ostensibly straight message was, "Take me along," his secret message was, "Turn me down," and the chances were very good that Jim would do just that. When Jim said no, responding to the secret message, Joe then took his payoff in sadness, feeling abandoned, and saying mentally, "No one loves me; they all turn me down"—which was his standard statement about himself and others. By using the feeling he produced at the point of payoff, to take himself back into the past, he completed the archaic "gestalt."

There are some areas of differences between pure Gestaltists and ourselves. I have mentioned some of them. Probably the greatest is our approach to feelings. Most Gestaltists I know encourage people to get into the depth of their feelings, in order to move out of them. We see that people use their fantasies, and their games, to maintain themselves in negative feelings, and that it is not necessary to abreact with greatest zeal. People have been going around from encounter group to marathon to encounter group displaying their wildest rage, or deepest sorrow, for years, and haven't changed a bit. They hold on to their anger and anxiety from the past, in a magical effort to change that past. Our primary therapeutic effort is to encourage patients to be aware of those feelings they are repressing before letting them go, and to let go those feelings they are maintaining within awareness as they recognize how they bring such feelings on themselves. Therapists attending one of my lectures sometimes question my statement that we make ourselves feel bad, that no one but oneself is responsible for his feelings. I then like to ask everyone in the room to close their eyes and remember the last time they felt angry, or anxious, or depressed at or about someone they thought was "making them" feel bad. I ask them to get into the scene, to feel their feelings, and then to conjure another fantasy, in which they are somewhere they most want to be, doing what they most want to do. Almost no one, a minute later, is still in the unpleasant feelings he had given himself.

Doing a regressive scene is often very helpful for patients in letting go. As they remember the scene, and get into a dialogue or even a nonverbal dialogue, and begin to cry, or become angry, I might say, "Will you tell him/her that you are going to stay angry/sad until he/she changes?" This statement usually brings an end to the unpleasant feelings, as the patient has an "ah ha." If he still stays in the feelings, the next line is, "Are you willing to tell him/her that you will stay angry until he/she changes the past?" Then there is almost always an "ah ha." The "ah ha" here comes with the cognitive *and* affective recognition of how ridiculous it is to expect anything to change in the *past* just because one stays angry, that the past can't change, and that all these years the person has been angry at his parents for what they did to him as a little kid, and the past is over. My "ah ha" experience that I described with Fritz, and the "ah ha" experience that a phobic had recently upon recognizing that he had dropped his phobia of heights when his testicles didn't scrunch while on the roller coaster at Santa Cruz, are other examples. "Ah ha," he exclaimed, "even my balls know I'm not scared anymore."

As people make themselves feel bad by going into the past, or the future, or somewhere else (for example obsessing at night about how to pay the bills), they learn to change fantasies. A simple switch is to change from obsessive thinking to sexual fantasy. Another way of moving from unpleasant feelings is first, to evaluate the feeling. What is it, and what is it in response to? Did I really do something, or did someone else really do something, or is it fantasy? If fantasy, change or drop it. If there is a real happening, is there anything I can do? If there is nothing I can do, then the feeling is of no value, and I drop it. If there is something I *can* do, do I want to do it? If I do, then I do it and drop the feeling. If not, the feeling has no further use, and I drop it. For instance, at the moment I am angry at IBM, because my Mag Card 2 Typewriter just ate up the card these words were recorded on, and I am typing them over. When I am through with this page, I will call IBM, express my dissatisfaction, and then go to work, and drop the anger.

One of the most important pieces of therapy that we all learned from Eric Berne is the obtaining of the therapeutic contract, and the awareness of the psychological contract. The therapeutic contract, of course, is what the patient offers to do for himself, to change; the psychological contract is the secret resolve by the Child not to change anything. The latter is usually stated in what I call the first "con," when I first hear the Child's statement that he has no intention of changing. For instance, the statement, "I want to work on my anxiety," sounds great, but in fact if it is taken without confrontation, that is exactly what the patient will do—"work on"—and he will work and work and work, and never change anything. Simkin calls this bear-trapping. It needs to be confronted; for example, "Are you just going to work, or are you changing something?" The therapist's question, "Are you willing to do an experiment, or an exercise?" is often met with "I'll try," and that is exactly what the patient does: try. Do you know the difference between "trying to shit" and "shitting"? I keep a large cowbell by my chair, which I ring vigorously when anyone says "try." This is the best behavior modification that I know; very few people in the workshop say "try" more than once.

There are hundreds of clues to the first con; would like to, perhaps, just, maybe, "you know," can't (usually means won't). *Should,* and other words of a similar nature, usually means that we are about to be offered a Parent contract. "I should quit drinking" means "I don't intend to, but my husband wants me to." We are very wary of Parent contracts, of course, and often ask why when we suspect one. Although *why* is usually a poor word in Gestalt Therapy, sometimes it flushes out the con, in the early work.

We are adamant about getting contracts in most cases, although of course sometimes we settle for exploration for a while. I teach my trainees, in the small-group exercises we do every day, to work no more than twenty minutes, so that they have to sharpen up their ears. If they don't get through an impasse in twenty minutes, they aren't going to get through today, or this time, because they haven't been listening. The Polsters write about not confronting every con, and I understand their intent, but until a therapist knows which one to let by, he had better confront them all. The Polsters are master therapists; not many other people are.

We don't accept "I want to understand myself better," either. Fritz would have called that an "elephant shit contract," and there certainly will be a lot of elephant shit around if we let that one go through. People work for years "trying" to understand themselves better, and nothing ever happens. We want a contract that calls for specific changes—changes in behavior, changes in feelings, changes in thinking, testable. Although certainly we would like the patient to understand—and certainly understanding will help (that is the whole purpose of chapter)—understanding about the self without any connection to symptom change is not a valid contract. At the same time, we do not insist, always, that the patient understand what was going on in the past; sometimes we cure a phobia, for instance, with desensitization, without the patient having any idea why he or she was phobic.

For instance, about a year ago a woman had a cockroach phobia. I usually do some work with second- or third-degree impasses in my phobia work, and in this case I attempted to set up some dialogues, feeling certain that the phobia was displaced from a fear of sex. We went nowhere. I finally stopped, and asked her if she was willing to do some desensitization.

She was, so I asked her to relax in the chair, raise her left forefinger when she became scared and her right forefinger when she was not scared. She agreed, and I proceeded to march a fantasized cockroach in through the door, coming closer to her, until she raised her left finger. I marched that cockroach in and out, in and out, then two cockroaches, then four, then a platoon, then a company, then a batallion, then a regiment, until she finally laughed, got up, picked up an imaginary broom, and swept the imaginary army out. A year later she wrote me, saying that she not only banished her phobia, but also had much better sexual relationships with her husband! My guess was right, I think, but she was not willing to work on that at the time.

Sometimes the patient gets the information in a flash of recognition, an "ah ha" experience, without any reference to his injunctions, decisions, games, script, and makes a redecision, from his Child, in the process. For instance, yesterday a minister here for a workshop said he wanted to do something about his sexual behavior. He offers girls sex, and then somehow secretly says, "Don't take me up on it." He also masturbates and stops himself before he ejaculates. I asked him "Always?" No, he finishes sometimes. Well, obviously if he finishes sometimes he could finish all the time, and he doesn't have to know why in order to change. He stops so as to harass himself, along with other ways of doing so. He also stops because he is "afraid."

I decided that I would go ahead and work with him, even though I could ask him to experiment tonight with masturbating to a conclusion and reporting his experience tomorrow. I asked him to sit in a different chair, and be the adolescent, fantasizing masturbating. In that chair, he stops before ejaculation. Then I asked him what he was feeling. He responded, "Good. I'm a good boy." "What else are you feeling?" I asked. "Irritated that I didn't finish." Now I asked him to sit in the other chair and fantasize finishing. From that chair he reported feeling contented, and scared. I asked him to move back to the first chair, and to say "I'm scared that I will . . ." and to finish the sentence. "I'm scared that I will die," he said. I asked him to sit back in the second chair again, where he had allowed himself to come to orgasm. "How many times have you died?" I asked him. "Ah ha," he exclaimed. "Sit back in the first chair," I said. "Now, say 'I'm scared I'll die' again." "I will not," he exclaimed laughing. "I'm done."

This ah ha experience is like the others I have described. When he drops his fear, when he breaks through the impasse, both cognitively and emotionally, he *suddenly* recognizes that all these years he has been setting up rape games, has been refusing to masturbate to orgasm, because of a very small child fear of dying if he did that. The point is, he could have gone ahead, as he had many times, masturbating without completing the above gestalt. He got in touch with his mother's crazy message, that he would die if he masturbated, which he had so taken in that he had forgotten the message, and only remembered the scared feeling. This certainly was a third-degree impasse, with a memory of a scary face, rather than of actual words, he introjected when a very small child.

Many Gestalt therapists, including Perls and Erv Polster, use themselves a great deal in what I would call setting up transference in the contact with the patient, deliberately. Fritz would do all kinds of maneuvers to frustrate the patient; I remember one well-known Gestalt therapist who hit the patient with a chair. We prefer, usually, not to do this, although of course we do occasionally use ourselves. We are much more likely, however, to endeavor to keep out of the work, and to let the patient do his work against himself, by setting up dialogues, by keeping I-Thou transactions going, by saying "say more" instead of "tell me." Thus we hope that the patient, instead of resisting us, will resist himself, recognize the impasse when he gets to it, and either break through it or stay stuck at the point of impasse. We prefer that he battle against his own internal Parent, instead of with his transferred "parent," us. A clear knowledge from a T.A. standpoint of where the impasse is, is most helpful to the therapist in establishing a useful dialogue.

One more point about T.A. and Gestalt which I think is important. In my experience, the therapist using pure T.A., using only a cognitive approach, with Berne's formula of analyzing Ego States, then Transactions, then Games, and then Scripts, thus ending in the patient's firm cognitive understanding of self, usually develops a patient who changes behavior but often doesn't feel any better. Pure Gestalt, on the other hand, often ends in patients feeling great about themselves but not changing behavior, and often being perfect shits. Our use of both, so that the patient does a great deal of experiential work *and* has a good understanding of his place in his life script, is more likely to change both his behavior and his feelings. Certainly that has been our experience with the hundreds of therapists that we have worked with over the past thirteen years, as we moved more and more into a shotgun approach of T.A., Gestalt, behavior modification, and anything else that we learn or develop that works. Group 8 in the Yalom, Lieberman, and Miles study (Encounter Groups, First Facts) also seems to support this position to some degree.

To sum up, we use all the Gestalt techniques we can muster to allow patients to work through their impasses, and relate the current impasses, almost always, to the archaic ones. We believe—and we have a great deal of experimental evidence for this belief—that the more cognitive information the patient has about his connections from the present to the past, the more he uses his cognitive information to change. If he can connect his earlier scenes to his present feelings, and will make new decisions from his Child Ego State while in the scene, he will then use these redecisions to change his life in the present. Each impasse resolution which solves both present "stucks" and archaic "stucks" brings more freedom, as he spreads and grows, continually expanding his boundaries and his awarenesses.

REFERENCE

Liberman, M. A., I. D. Yalom and M. B. Miles. *Encounter Groups: First Facts.* New York: Basic Books, 1973.

CHAPTER 26

BIOFEEDBACK AND GESTALT THERAPY

CHRIS HATCHER, Ph.D.
MARJORIE TOOMIM, Ph.D.
HERSHEL TOOMIM, B.S.E.E.

Chris Hatcher is coeditor of this volume. Marjorie Toomim is in private practice in Los Angeles, California, and is also director of psychological services for Biofeedback Research Institute. Hershel Toomim is an electronic engineer and president of Biofeedback Research Institute. Actively involved in electromedical instrumentation since 1941, he holds numerous patents in this and related fields.

A major purpose of many psychotherapies is increased awareness for the individual of his behavior. As pointed out by Schwartz (1973), feedback systems have long been employed as a mechanism in increasing awareness. Observation and interpretation by the therapist, video and audio replays, observation and reaction by group therapy members are a few examples of such therapeutic feedback mechanisms.

With regard to feedback in Gestalt Therapy, three important relationships stand out. First, many psychotherapies attempt to work with a psychophysiological system (man) with purely psychological means (verbal interaction). Gestalt ("whole") Therapy by definition is concerned with the total psychophysiological system, utilizing both verbal and physical techniques. Second, Gestalt Therapy is primarily oriented toward intrapersonal processes as contrasted with interpersonal processes. Group and encounter therapies are most interpersonal in that they deal with reactions of participants to each other within the group. Psychodrama is also somewhat interpersonal in that other group members may be called upon to act out the various roles in an individual's conflict. The Gestalt approach is primarily intrapersonal in that it deals with all the life characters (such as top dog, underdog, wife, adult, child, parent) as they exist within the individual. It emphasizes resolution of conflicts and inconsistencies between these characters or forces as they are created and maintained by the individual within himself. Third, although Gestalt therapists have used both verbal and physical techniques, they have relied largely upon the phenomenological report of the individual.

Let us briefly illustrate the way in which feedback systems function in Gestalt. Individuals in Gestalt work are requested to be aware of their verbal behavior (I am aware of the change in my voice), external body activity (limb, facial, or other muscle movement), and their perceptions of internal body processes (I am aware that my hands feel cold, I am aware that my stomach feels tight, etc.). After the individual has gained or increased some basic awareness in these areas, the therapist may request that he be aware of possible inconsistencies within the total gestalt. For example, an individual's verbal behavior (I feel good today, I feel okay now, or I am not bothered by talking about this) may indicate that he is not experiencing any particular discomfort at this time. However, his external body activity may include clenched jaw muscles, or when asked to be aware of internal body processes, the individual may report a tenseness in the chest or stomach. While the therapist may be involved here in directing awareness, the feedback mechanism relies primarily upon the individual's own phenomenological report.

Frequently, the awareness of such an inconsistency is, in itself, sufficient, and the individual will begin to reexamine what is happening in the session. If not, the individual may be requested to choose one of his inconsistent responses and exaggerate it (Tell me how really good and okay you are feeling, and see what happens; decide to tighten or relax the muscles across your stomach, and see what happens). With the verbal exercise, the person may find it difficult to continue, and thereby becomes more open to his not-good or not-okay feelings. With the physical exercise, the person may find he is not successful in relaxing the stomach muscles, and thereby leads to a verbal exploration of this maintained tenseness. Such examples briefly demonstrate the Gestalt therapists' use of feedback that is both verbal and physical, primarily intrapersonal, and phenomenological in report.

Ralph Hefferline, coauthor of the early work, *Gestalt Therapy: Excitement and Growth in the Human Personality* (Perls, Hefferline, and Goodman, 1951), has long been aware of the reliance of the gestaltist upon phenomenological report. He has devoted a good deal of laboratory research to the application of electrophysiological techniques to the study of what he calls "private or intrapersonal events." Hefferline (Hefferline and Bruno, 1972) writing in the *Aldine Annual on Biofeedback and Self-Control*, states that his idea was to make public through instrumentation the private, physiological events that were the focus of self-awareness in his book *Gestalt Therapy* (1951). Researchers, including David Shapiro, Neal Miller, Joe Kamiya, Leo Dicara, Ralph Hefferline, and others have clearly demonstrated (1) that relatively inexpensive instrumentation can be developed to measure autonomic nervous function such as heart rate, blood pressure, brain waves, and galvanic skin response, (2) that individuals can learn to discriminate between different levels, and (3) that individuals can learn to modify these functions to a limited degree.

Clinical applications of this knowledge have been almost totally devoted to cardiac problems, headaches, general pain reduction, relaxation, and systematic desensitization. One exception to this has been the work of Toomim and Toomim (1974) who have employed galvanic skin response (GSR) biofeedback as an integral part of a dynamic psychotherapy process which they describe as eclectic, with emphasis on emotional flooding (Hogan, 1967). Chris Hatcher has given additional exploration and development to this technique within the Gestalt Therapy process.

The following material will briefly review the physiology of skin resistance and the GSR, clinically observed GSR reactivity patterns, the use of GSR biofeedback in the Gestalt Therapy process, and future implications.

PHYSIOLOGY OF SKIN RESISTANCE

In 1880, a French physiologist by the name of Féré found that when a small current was applied to the skin, there were measurable and characteristic changes in the subject's resistance to that current (Lang, 1971). Further work showed these changes to be related to the presence or absence of emotional stimuli. While the exact psychophysiology of this event has not been fully researched, sweat gland activity is accepted as mainly responsible (ibid). Thus sweat gland activity, as determined by changes in the electrical conductivity of the skin, forms part of the emergency reaction to the sympathetic nervous system, and may be employed as a rough measure of an individual's physiological stress pattern. This measure has also been used to indicate general arousal, activation level (Schlosberg, 1954), and energy mobilization (Duffy, 1951).

Several investigators have found various aspects of the GSR within subjects reliable over time. Freeman and Griffin (1939), Lacey and Lacey (1962), and Block (1965) find its magnitude reliable. Bull and Gale (1971) find its latency, magnitude, and recovery reliable. Hughes and Shean (1971) find the interaction of feedback and awareness an effective means of modifying ongoing GSR reactivity in both high and low neurotic subjects.

The GSR has been criticized as a monitor of internal change because it so readily responds to such "psychologically irrelevant" functions as coughing, deep breathing, and body and hand movements. However, the GSR feedback technique described below makes use of these functions, which confound the experimentalist. They are included in determining the individual's "baseline measure." They contribute to an understanding of the general GSR activation pattern of each individual. GSR responses which are defined as psychologically relevant must cause a change in the GSR feedback which is both greater than and more persistent than that created by these extraneous factors. In addition, the psychologically relevant GSR response may be determined by further exploration of the anxiety-provoking or conflictual material which accompanies the skin-conductance change. Thus, if the individual laughs or breathes deeply while talking about, for example, his parents, and the GSR feedback rises (skin conductance increases), it will soon return to baseline if the material is not emotionally arousing. If it is arousing, the GSR will continue to respond at a high level as long as the relevant content is in the foreground and emotionally stimulating.

GSR REACTIVITY PATTERNS

According to pilot clinical observations made by the authors of this chapter and previously reported by Toomim and Toomim (1973), most individuals can be classed into one of three GSR reactivity patterns: overreactors, underreactors, and variable reactors. When attempting to gauge the GSR reactivity pattern, it is, of course, important to make observations under a variety of circumstances. For example, an individual whose GSR freely varies (a variable reactor) in ordinary circumstances may become an overreactor or underreactor when very tired or hungry, or when stressed in a particular manner.

Overreactors are defined as people whose GSR's respond to stimuli with marked deviations from baseline. For example, a deep breath may result in a marked rise in skin conductance which persists for a minute or more. A change from a neutral to an emotionally arousing stimulus results in a sharp rise in skin conductance which persists beyond the time that the subject matter is under consideration. The rise from a baseline of ten micromhos might be three or more micromhos. In addition, the individual may find it difficult or uncomfortable when he attempts to lower his GSR below baseline, through relaxation procedures (attending to breathing, being quiet for a few minutes, etc.). He frequently describes the subjective state which accompanies lowered skin conductance as "a feeling of deadness," or, "This is how I feel when I am depressed."

Underreactors are defined as people whose GSR's respond to stimuli with only minimal changes. A deep breath may result in little more than a rise of one micromho from a baseline of ten micromhos. Even laughter, clapping the hands sharply in front of the individual's face, or the gentle touch of a hand may leave the GSR relatively unaffected. Such individuals tend to report a very narrow range of subjective emotional responses.

Variable reactors are defined as people whose GSR's respond to stimuli in an undulating manner which clearly correlates with observable changes in attention, excitation and emotional involvement. A deep breath results in a marked increase in skin conductance which returns to baseline rather quickly. Changes of two or more micromhos are common. These individuals easily learn to identify which changes in subjective emotional states correlate with a rise or fall in GSR level.

GSR IN THE GESTALT THERAPY PROCESS

In the first section of this chapter, several examples briefly demonstrated the Gestalt therapist's use of feedback that is both verbal and physical, primarily intrapersonal, and phenomenological in report. It should be clear, at this point, that what is being added is feedback that is physiological in report.

The GSR is introduced in the following way. The individual is asked if he wishes to try a different method of increasing self-awareness. One does not label the biofeedback instrument as *the* definition of emotional response. If he indicates that he does, the individual is shown the GSR instrument, and its function as a monitor of nervous system activity is briefly discussed. The instrument is small, portable, relatively inexpensive, readily available commercially, and provides visual and auditory feedback. Electrode cream is placed on the electrodes, and the electrodes are held in contact with the palmar surface of the hand by an adhesive fabric strip. The person is then requested to move his hands. As he moves, he notices a rise in GSR feedback tone which signifies a rise in skin conductance. He is then asked to take a deep breath. Again, there is usually a rise in GSR feedback tone. The intensity of this response as well as the length of time it takes for the GSR to decrease are observed. The individual is requested to be aware of changes in the feedback tone, and is requested to describe any subjective sensations which occur at the same time as a large change in the tone. Readers should be aware that there is a latency of approximately two to three seconds between content and the instrument's audio and visual response.

The reader with some experience in Gestalt Therapy has probably already begun to think of some possible applications of this type of feedback. First, in dealing with the self-awareness exercises described in the first part of this chapter, both the Gestalt therapist and the individual with whom he is working hear the feedback tone. Both the therapist and the individual are free to discount GSR changes, use GSR changes as the guide to areas of focus, or use GSR changes as one of several forms of relevant feedback. Thus, in biofeedback work in Gestalt Therapy, there is a recognition that individuals may choose to accept, reject, or attempt to manipulate any form of feedback. Usually such maneuvers take the form of defensive attempts to avoid dealing with a particular area. Biofeedback has the advantage of being a persistent and consistent source of information on arousal level. Clinical experience has clearly indicated that most individuals find it extremely difficult to reject dealing with such an information source. The Gestalt therapist does not require the individual to accept the validity of GSR changes; instead, he requests that the individual "experiment" with an area consistently identified with GSR changes.

There are two types of GSR changes which appear to be important. First, as we have previously described, a sharp rise in GSR level is indicative of arousal. Second, a paradoxical drop in GSR level appears to be correlated with areas that the individual finds very difficult to deal with. Although further exploration of the drop phenomenon is needed, it is interesting to wonder if individuals have not learned to "physiologically withdraw" from highly conflictual areas.

A second application of GSR biofeedback is in dreamwork. Much of Gestalt dreamwork involves the sharing of a dream, followed by a here and now fantasy exploration of the dream. Again, biofeedback is of much assistance in achieving a more precise focus upon the more arousing material. The authors of this chapter have particularly noted the increased speed of working which this technique appears to provide.

Clearly, there is no single procedure that is *the* technique in psychotherapy. While GSR biofeedback offers a stimulating new source of information, it remains highly dependent upon the sensitivity and skill of the therapist. Thus, a Gestalt session may also include the application of the more classical techniques. For example, GSR monitoring is not used if body work or physical expression is indicated.

The opportunities and necessities for future research are certainly evident. A number of questions need to be answered by collaboration between the physiological psychologist and the clinician. In the therapy setting, can an individual learn to manipulate his GSR level to avoid certain levels? A good deal of previous research does indicate that control of other indices of physiological functioning can be learned. Will changes in GSR levels or patterns produce changes in subjectively reported feelings? Are there contaminating, but unknown artifacts, in these procedures? Do multiple measures offer a preferred area for future efforts? And, importantly, are there other measures, such as heart rate (which is more easily recorded and compared), which might be more effective in looking at Hefferline's "world of private events"?

In summary, stimulating new work is being done in the use of biofeedback to bring increased awareness to the individual of his behavior. Based upon initial work by Toomim and Toomim (1973), this chapter has reported upon the integration of biofeedback techniques and Gestalt Therapy with the goal of stimulating new thought and development.

REFERENCES

Block, J. D. "Stimulus Discrimination Among Automatic Measures: Individual and Group Characteristics," *Psychosomatic Medicine*, 27 (1965), 212-228.

Bull, R. H. C., and A. Gale. "The Relationships Between Some Measures of the Galvanic Skin Response," *Psychonomic Science*, 25 (1971), 293-294.

Darrow, C. W. "Physiological and Clinical Tests of Autonomic Functions and Autonomic Balance," *Physiological Research*, 23 (1943), 1-36.

Duffy, E. "The Concept of Energy Mobilization," *Psychological Review*, 58 (1951), 30-40.

Freeman, G. L., and L. L. Griffin, "The Measurement of General Reactivity Under Basal Conditions," *Journal of General Psychology*, 21 (1939), 63-72.

Hefferline, R. F., and L. J. J. Bruno. "The Psychophysiology of Private Events," in D. Shapiro et al. (eds.). *Aldine Annual on Biofeedback and Self-Control*. Chicago: Aldine, 1972.

Hogan, R. A. "Implosive Therapy in Short Term Treatment of Psychotics," in H. Greenwald (ed.), *Active Psychotherapy*. New York: Lieber-Atherton, 1967.

Hughes, W. G. and G. D. Shean. "Ability to Control GSR Amplitude," *Psychonomic Science*, 23 (1971), 309-311.

Lacey, J. I., and G. C. Lacey. "The Law of Initial Value in Longitudinal Study of Autonomic Constitution: Reproducibility of Autonomic Response Patterns over a Four Year Interval," *Annals of the New York Academy of Science*, 98 (1962), 1257-1290.

Lang, P. J. "The Application of Psychophysiological Methods to the Study of Psychotherapy and Behavior Modification," in A. E. Bergin and S. I. Garfield (eds.), *Handbook of Psychotherapy and Behavior Change*. New York: Wiley, 1971.

Perls, F. S., R. F. Hefferline, and P. Goodman. *Gestalt Therapy: Excitement and Growth in the Human Personality*. New York: Julian Press, 1951.

Schlosberg, H. "Three Dimensions of Emotions," *Psychological Review*, 61 (1954), 81-88.

Schwartz, G. E. "Biofeedback as Therapy: Some Theoretical and Practical Issues," *American Psychologist*, 28 (1973), 666-674.

Toomim, M. K. and H. Toomim. "GSR Biofeedback in Psychotherapy: Some Clinical Observations." Paper presented at California State Psychological Association Convention, Fresno, Calif.: 1974.

CHAPTER 27

CRITICAL INCIDENTS IN THE EMPTY CHAIR

JOEN FAGAN, Ph.D., with David Lauver, Sally Smith, Stan DeLoach, Michael Katz, and Elaine Wood

Joen Fagan, the senior author, is professor of psychology and director of Clinical Training, Georgia State University, Atlanta. Dr. Fagan is a diplomate of the American Board of Examiners in professional psychology. She is also coeditor of *Gestalt Therapy Now*.

Reprinted with permission from Joen Fagan and others, "Critical Incidents in the Empty Chair," **The Counseling Psychologist**, Vol. 4, 1974, pp. 33-42.

The empty chair, probably the best known and most widely used Gestalt technique, is one with tremendous power. In the hands of an expert it looks very simple: the patient is instructed to move back and forth between two seats or positions which represent two different aspects of himself or the relationship between himself and another person and engage in a dialogue. The therapist sometimes simply watches this without comment or indicates that the time has come to change seats. Sometimes he repeats the patient's words or gives him encouragement to continue. Sometimes he asks the patient to repeat his own words or exaggerate what he is saying or doing, calls attention to posture or tone of voice, or suggests sentences to say. These seem to be non-demanding or simple therapeutic tasks, yet extensive skill is required, including sensitivity to non-verbal cues, knowledge of available techniques, ability to deal with resistance and understanding of process. The techniques themselves evoke strong emotion which, when accurately focused, resolves impasses, finishes old business, and heals polarities and splits so that the patient has not just a powerful experience, but a powerfully healing experience. Much of the skill of the expert is in making this very complicated and delicate process appear easy and inevitable.

The varieties of polarities or splits or conflicts that can be adapted to empty chair work are endless. They may appear in a person's body or posture, in discrepancies between his words and non-verbal messages, or be reflected in his descriptions of himself. Splits are often hidden in a self-dissatisfaction or criticism, in boredom and frustration. The first therapeutic task is to hear and see the split and to define it so that the patient has sufficient awareness and interest to begin work. Also essential is sufficient relationship and trust in the potency of the therapist to undertake what initially may seem like a peculiar or self-consciousness-evoking task. For the patient familiar with the empty chair, the knowledge of and experience with the power and unpredictability of direction of this procedure requires possibly even more trust in the competence of the therapist. Setting the stage is the next task, so that the polarities are defined as clearly as possible. Then come many delicate judgments about staying out of the process of intervening at impasses with a large number of different techniques. While many variations are possible, skilled Gestalt therapists will usually follow similar routes—there is an element of clear form or best fit. As impasses and the stuck point that represent the core of the conflict are overcome, then powerful feelings emerge and centering of the conflict begins to occur. (For fuller discussion of impasses see F. Perls, "Four Lectures," in Fagan and Shepherd, 1970.) Basic to the whole procedure is the therapist's knowledge of what is genuine in person and process, and knowledge of Gestalt techniques in no way replaces the main requirement of first being a good therapist.

The problem of conflict is, of course, central to all theories of psychopathology, from Freud's ideas about the individual versus society (or id versus superego); Rogers' real self versus introjected and distorted perceptions; Fromm's needs of the individual versus the pressures of economic and political systems, etc. Perls notes that many polarities can and do occur, this being an inevitable process of differentiation and Gestalt formation and destruction. Problems emerge with this process only when differentiation does not occur or polarities become frozen so that energy remains bound and unavailable for other tasks of living and the individual spends himself reacting to old patterns rather than to the demands and possibilities of the present.

The empty chair serves to make patently available the individual's conflict so that the entire dialogue emerges and is open to resolution. Often the underdog position has not been heard or listened to; the patient is only familiar with the top dog's internal verbal criticisms and directions: "You should . . .," "You never . . .," "Why don't you . . .?" However, giving words to the underdog response in one's head is not enough; the energy for centering, for resolution, becomes available only by mobilizing the full emotion and energy that has been suppressed, and by giving each side in the conflict permission to express and experience both the limitations and the values of its position. The centering process, the resolution of the conflict, is a self-validating process. On-lookers feel highly involved and experience relief and pleasure. The patient looks, moves, acts, sounds different in very positive ways. Internally, he experiences himself as free, energized, clear, joyful, grateful, self-accepting.

The types of conflict dealt with in the empty chair may range from very peripheral to very central, which is to say, easily and even playfully resolved, or involving prolonged and deeply painful struggle. Often neither patient nor the therapist knows at the beginning what will emerge during the process. The need for caution and skill cannot be overemphasized.

Some general principles and bits of advice for therapists directing empty chair work:

1. Don't begin until you have had personal experience as a patient with this procedure.

2. Be ready for explosions or strong emotional responses.

3. Until you are experienced in empty chair work and/or know your patient well, be sure that you can provide adequate follow-up support and that the patient is emotionally solid. Not being able to "turn the corner" and center or resolve the conflict can be damaging, especially to a fragile person, or at least frustrating.

4. As long as the process is moving, keep the therapeutic role to a minimum.

5. Move as gently as possible through impasses. If in doubt, do too little rather than too much. Be satisfied with small steps rather than going for big breakthroughs.

6. If in doubt or confused about what the person is saying or doing, find out before anything else.

7. Given adequate safeguards, experiment and follow your own experience.

The examples which follow were transcribed from the tapes of graduate student psychotherapists, working with each other or with patients. Relatively inexperienced therapists were chosen, so as to accumulate examples of problems with the process of empty chair work.

TRANSCRIPT 1

Therapist 1: What was that: (Patient had closed eyes, gestured.)
Patient 1: Getting into the room. It was like I wanted to get out I guess, so I had to bring myself back in.
Therapist 2: Where do you want to go?
(*Good.* Therapist goes with patient's resistance expressed as leaving and offers a fantasy trip.)

Patient 2: Umm, just away. Out of here. Kind of scares me a little bit. To do this.

Therapist 3: Just go ahead and close your eyes and let yourself be in a place that you want to be.

(*Very good.* The therapist is supporting the patient, moving her gently against resistance onto an appropriate therapeutic task. The alternate choice—finding out about her scare—is a much poorer option because (1) most initial anxiety disappears once into the task anyway, so making much of it represents a waste of time, and (2) opening up quietly stated fear or anger before a base of therapeutic support has been developed is asking for trouble.)

Patient 3: (Pause) Okay.

Therapist 4: Tell me about it.

(Okay. But the therapist runs the risk with this wording that the patient will leave the fantasy, open her eyes and switch her attention to the therapist. Better wording would be "Where are you?" supporting her staying in the fantasy setting.)

Patient 4: Well, let's see. It's a cabin in the forest. It's a log cabin, modern, but very rustic. And it's got a very sloping ceiling, lots of skylights. And I can see the trees. And I'm, uh, lying in bed, in a great big double bed. And with a real thick quilted comforter, like the ones they have in Norway. And I'm naked, and uh, my husband is there. And we're laughing and talking. And we've just made love and we may make love again. And it's very nice.

Therapist 5: What have you got there that you haven't got here now?

(Okay. The therapist is moving to clarify differences and sharpen polarities. But his wording invites a literal answer, "My husband, a bed . . ." Better phrasing would be, "How is it different here?")

Patient 5: I'm sorry?

Therapist 6: What do you have there that you don't have here?

Patient 6: Now that you mention it, right now my husband and I are very unhappy. And, uh, we're in the throes of getting a divorce or a separation. I asked him to move out last night. That's why I'm all spaced out today, and just because I just can't bear a lot of pain that he gives me. And it just makes me so sad. And it's like I'm having to do all this because he's just not a person or something. He just—I don't know—he hurts me all the time. He's just very insensitive. And, uh, I'm having to do all this, but I really love him. But I can't bear all the pain and hurt. So it's kind of like I'm having to do it to defend myself. I'm having to kick him out and ask him to leave. And—but I really love him.

Therapist 7: Okay. Let's say that that's the May—I see a split between the May that loves—what's his name? (Patient: Hank) that loves Hank, and the May that thinks it's the right thing to do to kick him out.

(*Poor.* The therapist's support has helped the patient to bring up clearly painful feelings, and he moves quickly to define the split. However, from a broad therapeutic perspective, a recognition such as "You're really struggling with all kinds of feelings and choices" would be more facilitative. He also hasn't listened too precisely or he would have defined the split as the May that loves Hank and wants him around and the May that hurts so much she has to get out. It's likely that the suddenness with which the patient has brought up a major problem has created some anxiety in the therapist.)

Patient 7: And there's a third May we better make room for, the one who is very much afraid of being hurt again.

Therapist 8: Which one are you closest to right now?

(*Good.* Therapist is setting the stage, starting with where the patient is.)

Patient 8: The hurt one.

Therapist 9: What's the one that's opposite that? What's the one that . . .

Patient 9: The one that's opposite the hurt one?

Therapist 10: The one that wants—yeah.

Patient 10: The angry one.

Therapist 11: Okay.

Patient 11: And that's probably also the one that loves him.

Therapist 12: Okay. Talk to the angry one.

(*Okay.* A little abrupt and impersonal. Better wording, "Okay. Get with the May who's feeling hurt and see what she wants to say.")

Patient 12: Be the hurt one? Be down—I'll be the hurt one.

Therapist 13: Where would you like to be as the hurt one.

Patient 13: This is the angry one, and that's the hurt one. (Indicating a chair)

Hurt May 1: (Switches to "hurting" chair): It's very easy to do. It hurts. I don't like sitting here hurting, but it's almost the easiest thing to do. Because I don't even know what else to do. It's the easiest thing to do. It's the easiest thing to do. So I'm just going to sit here and hurt, even though it hurts. I don't know how to be you. It's been so long.

Therapist 14: Switch.

Angry May 1: (Sighs) I like to see you hurting over there. You know, it really makes me feel good. Because I know that you won't do anything about it. You'll just sit there and hurt and hurt and hurt. And, uh, then you'll just shrivel up and die, and then you'll be gone one day. That makes me feel good. You're afraid to come over here and get angry. And I don't even like people who are afraid of me. And you don't scare me one bit.

Therapist 15: Could you switch again?

(*Okay.* This is a bright, cooperative, motivated patient who as events show can be left on her own and will use this positively, so the therapist's choice of inaction during the next few exchanges is all right. However, a sharper therapeutic response would be to note that the angry May (top-dog) is being critical and sadistic rather than angry and move in the direction of freeing her anger instead of using it to blame herself.)

Hurt May 2: I remember who you are. You know, because I remember I used to be a lot like you and I didn't like you much either, so I adopted this role. And I don't like this role a lot either. It doesn't feel like it's me. I feel a lot more like you. And I'd like to be a lot more like you, the way I used to kind of be.

Therapist 16: What do you like about her?

Hurt May 3: I like about her the fact that she's—

Therapist 17: "I like about *you* . . ."

(*Good.* Therapist keeps the patient in direct contact.)

Hurt May 4: Oh, I like you because, uh, you get it out, and you don't just live with it all the time. You just get it out and get it over with. And, uh, you know where you're at and you express it, and I think that's great. And I like that part of you. And I don't know how to do that. In fact, when you stay over here hurt, all you can do is just be hurt. You don't have a lot of alternatives. You, you just get to throw—you can throw things and slam doors and scream and stomp and rave. And I just have to sit over here and cry, and blow my nose all the time. Makes me quiver just to—I feel my knees shaking and quivering.

Angry May 2: (Switches) Why? Do you want to come over here and be me? I could feel it. I could feel you. You were about to jump up and be me, but you were afraid to do it, weren't you? You were really afraid to come on over here and just let it out. What is it that he's done to you? It's just amazing. You know, you used to be able to—you got mad, you used to get mad. And it was very easy. If you were hurt, you cried, and it was okay. It wasn't a snivelling type of cry, you just cried, a good bellyache cry. And if you were—uh, what's the matter with you? What are you doing over there being so fucking hurt?

Hurt May 5: (Switches) God! You made it sound so easy. It just isn't easy. I guess I've just been doing it for so long. And, you know, he's such a powerful person. And anyway, you know, I know that, uh, well, I know that I hurt him by being so sad. But, ye gods, he really hurts me. And, you know, the anger just isn't there anymore. That would almost be too much of an emotion for him.

Angry May 3: (Switches) What do you mean, too much of an emotion for him? It'd be too much of an emotion for you. I think you're just used to playing that role and you're afraid to come back and be who you are. You're really afraid of me.

Hurt May 6: (Switches) Yeah, that's really an interesting concept. Or an interesting idea. I, uh, thought I just, you know, was hurt. But I've realized that, uh, I was afraid of that, afraid to be angry. Why am I afraid, since you know so much?

Therapist 18: Would it be too much to be angry?
(*Poor.* Patient has moved on these last few exchanges into a clarifying dialogue. However, it has become clear that the two sides of her split are most accurately labeled as between the passive-withdrawing and expressive sides. The therapist probably does best to stay out entirely here, or to relabel her split for her.)

Hurt May 7: It would be a lot to be angry if you're very much afraid to be angry. But there's a lot of anger there. Also I'm a little bit afraid to be angry. It never did anything before. It never did any good before. And so you tried this technique, and it didn't do—this didn't work very well, either.

Angry May 4: (Switches) Well, let's see, you've tried me. But you haven't tried me recently, and I'd really like for you to try me some. And then if it doesn't work, why don't you give up?

Therapist 19: What do you want, Angry May?
(*Okay.* Therapist is trying to help May clarify her anger and fears about expressing it. But his wording is confusing.)

Patient 14: What do I want when I'm May?

Therapist 20: Yeah, what—Angry May, what do you want? What do you want to do?

Angry May 5: I want to come out and be heard. And I want, uh—(Pause)

Therapist 21: What do you want to do to Hank?
(*Poor.* Therapist still hasn't heard the split accurately. Much better would have been "What do you want to *say* (or express) to Hank?")

Angry May 6: I don't want to do anything to him. I just want, uh, I want us to either recognize the fact that we are who we are and we like each other, we love each other, and we're gonna stay together, or we don't and we're gonna split, instead of dragging it all out.

(In his last two remarks the therapist has been heard by May as pushing her too hard toward anger or separateness. She responds with confluence, with "we's" which deny her and Hank's differences.)

Therapist 22: That doesn't sound like Angry May to me saying that.
(*Good.* Therapist has noted May's non-verbal cues changing. While he still is not clear about the split, or the patient's loss of figure in Angry May 6, his calling the patient's attention to her feeling expression is facilitative for her.)

Therapist 23: Did you believe what she said about what she wanted to do to Hank?

Hurt May 8: (Switches) Yeah, but only because I think she's afraid that if she gets angry like she did before nothing's gonna happen again. Because it's not a vindictive anger. Ah, she's you know, defending herself. And she's not doing it to be ugly.
(Therapist's talking to patient and Hurt May (T22-T23) has allowed her to move to self-understanding and away from the denial of Angry May 6.)

Therapist 24: Tell her those things.
(*Good.* Puts patient back into direct contact with her feelings and moves her toward hearing herself and centering.)

Hurt May 9: I know that you're not doing it—I know that you don't want to be angry to be ugly and to hurt Hank. You're just doing it for yourself. You know, I know that you need to come out and speak up. And I know that you are afraid. Because I'm—you're afraid that it won't work. And then it'll all be over with. And you very much fear that. And because you fear that, I sit here and cry. I'm about to cry now. You're about to bring me out again. Your fear always brings me out.

Therapist 25: May, I'm not clear on what's going on.
(*Very poor.* Therapist is probably reacting with anxiety to the patient's approaching tears. While he is also experiencing a lack of clarity, the patient has demonstrated that *she* knows what's going on (Hurt May 7 and 8) and that she can keep moving forward, given any kind of encouragement. The therapist's responses here and in T 26 interrupt her and do to her what she does to herself —suppress feeling expression.)

Patient 25: You're not. Okay. Well, it's all very clear to me. My husband and I are going through a separation-divorce thing. And somehow, I just, you know, I'm not angry. I can't—

Therapist 26: You've made your decision?

Patient 26: No, I haven't. Because I really do love him, but I know that he's—he makes me unhappy in a lot of ways, but then in a lot of ways he doesn't. And he's going to have to change and be more of a person than he is and be more sensitive to me and be more understanding and all that stuff.

Therapist 27: We chose—I chose—we chose the wrong thing to do.

(*Very poor.* Patient has again made an accurate and therapeutically usable statement—moving well toward increased awareness of her need to recognize and express anger as well as her other feelings. Therapist interrupts and shifts attention to himself, almost becoming the patient. Apparently he has gotten into conflict inside his own head either from his own unfinished business with feeling and expressing anger, or with top-dog criticism/underdog fear about not setting the stage correctly, so he stopped listening.)

Patient 27: We did? Why?

Therapist 28: We should have chosen to be your husband and yourself.

(While this is a possible option, the patient makes it clear already that she experienced more of the conflict within herself than between her and her husband, so the therapist in spite of his doubts, chose correctly. Following the preceding response (P26), the therapist could well say, "Say all that to your husband," both bringing Hank into the picture and letting May express herself to solidify her new awareness of the importance of being more open with Hank about her feelings.)

Patient 28: This was a very good one for me just then, because—

Therapist 29: Okay.

Patient 29: I mean, I was working it out for myself regardless of whether you knew it or not. I've been doing this so much anyway. I can't understand why I'm so sad all the time. Like just then, because she's afraid to come out and be angry because if she does she's very much afraid that it's not going to work again and we really are gonna split and so we just—I'm afraid to come out. But, you know, I think I need to get some of that anger out. At least to give it a try.

(The technique provided the patient with more self-understanding and resolution, even with the therapist's uncertainties. Her giving some expression to her hurt and anger will probably facilitate clearer expression of these with her husband. A sharper therapeutic approach would have clarified her retroflection—her holding in expression of many different emotions—followed perhaps by her attempting to say these to Hank in the empty chair to examine and resolve the ways she and he actually block each other's expressiveness and to increase communication potential.)

Overall, the therapist has made good use of Gestalt techniques and kept the interaction moving in a generally forward-going direction, getting considerable help from the patient in this. His main problem was his own internal anxiety, certainly based in part on his limited experience as a therapist, that on occasion interfered with his hearing accurately what the patient was saying. Inexperience also probably accounts for his not seeing the conflict as between suppression and expression of emotion—one of the most common splits. His main technical error was in not continuing or not letting May keep going, even if he was uncertain. Endings are the most important as well as the most skill-demanding part of empty chair, but here, if she had not been interrupted, this patient would have provided her own centering.

TRANSCRIPT 2

This is the second session with the patient (S.), a divorced woman in her late 20s, who is experiencing increased discomfort at the way her mother has assumed direction of her four-year-old daughter (L.) following the accidental death of the mother's youngest son (D.). The patient feels helpless to counter her mother except by leaving the city for a new location.

Therapist 1: So then it was the mouse (patient) and the lion (mother) and now it's the rat against the lion.
(With the support of a therapy session the patient has increased her "under-mouse" to an "under-rat!")
Patient 1: (Laughs) And I am going to leave the lion behind!
Therapist 2: What if the lion follows? What would happen?
Patient 2: She probably will, but she won't find it as easy to come to Alabama to mind my business as she does here.
Therapist 3: How would you handle that, do you think, if she did?
Patient 3: Hmm. I guess I'd have to face it really and true, wouldn't I? (Pause) Well, I think by my making this break . . . See it's—in a way I think I'm going to take some of the responsibility off of her of keeping on trying, when I do this. It's going to be pretty clear to her then that I'm not going to stay right where she tells me to stay. (Pause) I think she's going to be extremely upset.

Therapist 4: Do you hope she is?

Patient 4: No! If I could have what I *really* wanted, she would say to me: "I want you to have the freedom to do what you really want to do." But I mean, that would be just beautiful if she said that.

Therapist 5: Would you like to try that here, sort of in a fantasy way?

(*Okay.* Patient has set up her own dialogue, even if very idealized and unrealistic. Therapist picks up opportunity to use the empty chair. However, starting off with a patient who has never done this can be facilitated by more structure, such as, "I'm hearing many things you'd like to be able to say to her that are difficult when she's really there. Let's try saying them to her here, so you can get clearer what your wishes and feelings are. Would you be willing to try that? Perls' instructions usually included the phrase, "write your own dialogue.")

Patient 5: Yeah.

Therapist 6: Okay. Let's put mother in this chair and let's put you in that chair. And you tell her , first of all, what you'd like her to let you do, what you'd like her to say to you, and how you'd like her to let you live your life.

(*Poor.* Therapist has gotten patient's consent—an obvious if sometimes overlooked requirement, and sets the stage. But he errs in instructing patient to make requests and demands of mother, rather than asking her to describe mother as she sees her, or state what her feelings are. This base of support or self-centering is especially important with a patient who has too little sense of her own position and who feels overwhelmed by the top dog.)

Daughter 1: Oh, okay, Mother, I'd like you to say to me, "I think that you're a human being who has the right, now, to do what you want to do (stated emphatically). And you may make some mistakes, but I probably make some mistakes myself. So, you are L.'s mother. I lost a son, *but* I'm not going to take your daughter to make up for it. So, you're free to live your life and I will cooperate with you" (voice softer here).

(Patient here is not speaking for herself, but for mother. This is a circular dialogue. A valuable technique at impasses where the parent as top dog cannot or will not change is to have patient fantasize her ideal mother and respond as ideal. But this would be inappropriate at this stage. A common error of beginning therapists is to not clearly specify and separate the sides of the conflict, and make certain that patient is in the appropriate chair, so as to provide as clear a figure as possible.)

Therapist 7: Now, I want you to sit over there and be her and answer back to S. How she might answer you back.

Mother 1: (Changes chairs) She would say: Well, (haughtily) I don't know what you're talking about. *I've* made some mistakes? (Laughs) Because I have always bent over backwards and I have always *given* so much to everybody and helped everybody else so much (sighs and then gulps audibly) including you—that you owe me so much now, how could you say this. (Pause) And that's how I see her (almost pleading).

Therapist 8: Okay, go back, and what would you say to that?

(*Poor.* Therapist is making two subtle but important errors. His not getting patient to switch chairs when she paused let her move back into herself instead of staying in role. This same switch out of role occurs in several other places (Daughter 1, Daughter 2, Mother 5, etc.) This exchange is the specific place where therapist needs to say, "Switch chairs as soon as you've finished making a statement," and to follow this up verbally or with hand signals as often as necessary. The second error is in the use of the conditional *would* (which is repeated (Th 14, Th 15, P 24) several other times. Both the dropping of role and the conditional are distancing devices. Therapist, out of inexperience, lack of knowledge of ground rules and personal insecurity, is not pushing the patient's full involvement, and hence is setting up probably failure.)

Daughter 2: (Changes chairs) Well, that's when I'd say: Well, I'm going to Alabama and I'll let you know where I am, and perhaps we both, *in time*, will be able to discuss this with each other better. And if you want to see L. you can *see* her. I would really prefer that you come down there to see her, for a while. So that you saw her on *my* terms. Because I'm not going to let her *live* with you and I'm not going to send her up here for a weekend and find out that you plan for her to stay for the rest of the year. (Voice very controlled, firm)

Therapist 9: Can you tell her how you feel about what she's done?

Daughter 3: I feel that you are taking over *my* daughter and saying, like you've said about so many different things, like that I haven't got enough, uh, I'm not (pause) *capable* of doing things like you are (sounds like hostility beginning to surface) and, therefore, you will do it for me. But *I'm* going to raise my daughter.

Therapist 10: Can you tell her that you feel capable to raise your daughter?

(*Good.* Therapist's responses are supporting patient's getting in touch with her anger and power. However, his "can you's" of Th 9 and 10 imply possible weakness. Statements are always better: "Tell her how you feel.")

Daughter 4: Yes. I do feel capable to raise my daughter (laughs). As a matter of fact, I can tell you that *I* think that you *did* make some mistakes (talking fast, energetic), and that I probably won't make any more than you did.

Therapist 11: Okay. Answer for her.

(*Poor.* "Answer for her" also implies lack of role differentiation. Better is simply "Answer.")

Patient 11: (Changes chairs) Well, at this point she's crying.

Therapist 12: Okay. Be her. She doesn't say anything when she's crying?

(*Poor.* When one participant in the dialogue resists by refusing to speak, Therapist must use one of several options to reopen the communication. Refusals often represent precisely those places where underdog gets defeated or impasses occur. Here therapist could ask, "Mother, what are your tears saying?")

Patient 12: No. She's probably left the room.

Therapist 13: Okay. What do you do when she cries and leaves the room?

Patient 13: Well, I give in.

Therapist 14: And what would you say to her?

(*Poor.* Therapist's responses here leave patient feeling helpless and unsupported. When power imbalances occur so that the underdog is about to be "wiped out," a variety of therapeutic responses are possible and needed. Generally, these can involve a gentle questioning of mother's motivation or procedures. ["Do you really want to leave now?"], or supports for patient's strength and alternate responses ["What would you *like* to say to her?"]. The conditional *would* here serves only as a bridge to a new kind of response, which Therapist can then support unconditionally, possibly, "I don't like you to leave.")

Daughter 5: (Changes chairs) Well, (softly) I'm sorry I hurt you.

Mother 5: She'd say (changes chairs), "Well, quit! And just leave me alone!"

Patient 14: But I don't know (voice quivering a bit) it's like a fantasy. It wouldn't be like this. I never know exactly how it's going to be.

Therapist 15: But this is maybe sort of like it might be?

(*Poor.* Therapist is also feeling inadequate and uncertain, and needs a stronger statement to reset the stage. "Let's go back and make it different.")

Patient 15: Yes. (Pause) We've never been able to have a discussion and it is not . . . and it goes very far without it ending up . . .

Therapist 16: Like this? Like it did here?

Patient 16: Yeah. Without her crying or leaving or . . .

Therapist 17: Mother, why don't you come back and tell S. how you feel about her going to Alabama and taking L. with her?

Patient 17: (Changes chairs; sighs)

Therapist 18: Tell S. how that makes you feel when she just said, "Now I'm going to go to Alabama."

Mother 6: Oh well, L. is all I have now. So I need her. (Pause)

Therapist 19: How are you going to feel when she goes to Alabama? (*Good.* Therapist in Th 17, Th 18 and Th 19 is reopening the dialogue by directly questioning mother.)

Mother 7: Well, I'm going to feel that I have nothing to live for (piously).

Therapist 20: Okay. Go back and say how you feel when she says that. (*Poor.* Patient got wiped-out last time mother responded with self-pity and hurt. Therapist needs to clarify what is going on with mother, so that patient can get out of her impasse. One form of clarification is for Therapist to recognize top dog's underlying feelings, to accept these as reasonable, but to suggest that the accompanying behavior is inappropriate and self-defeating and that top dog has other options. ["You've been hurt by your son's death, and that makes you feel alone and scared. (Pause) But the only way you know to make up for that loss is holding on—by using being hurt to hang onto your granddaughter and control your daughter. (Pause) I wonder if that's what you really want to do."] A more classical Gestalt procedure would be to ask mother to amplify or exaggerate her self-pity, to "ham it up," anticipating that either mother or daughter would then recognize the weakness and dead-endedness of this position.)

Daughter 7: (Pause) Well, let's see. This is . . . I can feel all these things I dread, 'cause this is when I start weakening (Voice catching). Uh, I feel that you have everything to live for. You have got probably more than I have. You've been settled in this community. You've got a lot of family. (Pause) And I don't see how you can say that, and even if it's true, it doesn't change things. L. is still my daughter, and she's not your daughter! And as sorry as I am I still can't bring D. back.

(Daughter again goes out of role and speaks for mother rather than herself. However during the pause, she is able to get back some self-support.)

Therapist 21: (Pause) Tell her about how you don't think you can keep up this constant hitting against the wall over L.
(*Okay.* Better would be: ". . . how you don't *want to* or *won't* keep up . . .")

Daughter 8: Well, what I think is that you tend to tell people you're helping them until you help them to be nothing. I think you did it with your own son and I think you do it with me. And you keep on doing it. You don't give up. If you don't keep L. this week you'll try something again next week. And you're liable to say you're helping me but you're *not* helping me. (Pause) I think you should know better. I think that you do this to a lot of people. You sure did it to me.

Therapist 22: Tell her how it makes you feel when she does that to you.

Daughter 9: It makes me feel very weak and very incapable (pause) and I think you could keep on doing it until you made me really wonder if I should raise my own daughter or let you.

Therapist 23: (Pause) Come back and be her. Respond to that.
(*Poor.* Therapist apparently was hoping in Th 22 that patient would continue her assertive anger. He could have supported this with, "You're saying you don't like . . ." When she collapses back into weakness he apparently is unsure how to proceed. It is a truism that beginning therapists suggest switching chair when they don't know what else to do. Fortunately, this often works. Here it doesn't. The general principle is that each exchange should serve to deepen feelings, increase the sharpness of perception, or move toward centering. Here underdog has simply fallen back into her assumed vulnerability and the re-emergence of mother can only reinforce that.)

Patient 23: (Changes chairs) Well it's hard for me to do that because, like I said, she and I have never talked things through. At this point she would be crying.

Therapist 24: And at this point when she cries you would do that?
(*Poor.* Therapist repeats the pattern established earlier—Th 13, P 13, Th 14—without any evidence that patient can respond differently.)

Patient 24: (Pause) I would leave it alone. And it would go on the way it was, probably.

Therapist 25: So you'd sort of step back from the wall for a while.

Patient 25: Yeah. (Pause) It has never gone this far. There has never been a discussion. Mother has never said to me that . . . admitted anything about herself. She never let me close to her and her feelings, inside. I'm sure she has a lot of them. I feel for her. It's like she can say at least she has no regrets and this, that and the other. And yet I'm sure that she does and just won't face them.

Therapist 26: Why don't you say that now, sitting in her place? Why don't you tell S. about how you have lots of problems, lots of feelings and you just may not be willing to face them.

(*Good.* A belated effort to clarify mother's underlying motives and turn gossip into confrontation.)

Mother 8: (Pause) Well, I guess, really I probably need L. so much (continues) because I'm so insecure and I probably have done a lot of things I've done so much for show, because I *need* people's approval so much.

Patient 26: (Pause) You see, I'm interjecting my thoughts into her. She doesn't see that at all. But I do.

(Patient at least has a somewhat clearer idea of mother's motivations. It is rare that we *don't* have an accurate perception of the motivations of persons we're close to. Often the simple act of being the other person opens up this awareness with a surprising degree of accuracy. But even this knowledge can feel self-defeating to patient without a sense of her own power and ability to resist her mother's manipulations.)

Therapist 27: So you sort of need her approval then?

Patient 27: No, I'm saying she does this.

Therapist 28: Oh, you're saying she needs the approval?

(*Poor.* Therapist in Th 27 and Th 28 is not listening, probably mostly aware of his inability to "turn the corner" and effect a centering and closing, and abandons any efforts at empty chair work. Patient again begins gossiping, and her unrecognized anger gets expressed as snideness.)

Patient 28: Yeah. Of course part of this is, you see D. . . . D. and Mother were not really that close at all. D. talked about her terribly most of the time. She is bearing up wonderfully well under the loss of D., but nobody's ever going to forget it. It's just there every minute. They're just going to have to notice how wonderful . . . She's a martyr. (Pause) She probably even, this is terrible to say (Laughs), but this will give her something else when I go. I'm sure she'll cry around for days. (Begins to talk about past experiences with mother.)

This therapist apparently asks questions when he is uncertain what to do or say (fifteen questions in twenty-eight responses), possibly providing mild verbal support, but on a deeper level, this makes him oddly invisible, in that he neither confronts nor supports. (Contrast a possible Th 2 response of "Doing something to protect yourself sure feels good.")

In contrast to the patient in the previous example, this patient feels very weak as the underdog—given conflict with another person, both she and her mother rely on leaving the field. The therapeutic task here is to support the underdog position in any of several ways suggested in the transcript so that the underdog can get a clearer experience of her own strength and of the underlying and unexpressed needs and fears of top dog. The patient did decide to move, and left the following week. It seems highly likely that if the therapist had been able to put her in touch with some strength and assertiveness in the empty chair dialogue that she could have remained in touch and in therapy, and that her failure in the empty chair attempt to resolve some of the issues with her mother solidified her decision to leave. This example illustrates the importance of beginning practicing Gestalt techniques with patients who have access to self-support.

TRANSCRIPT 3

Therapist 1: Will you take a moment to see how you feel? (Pause)

Therapist 2: When you're ready, will you start off saying things like "I'm aware . . ."

Patient 2: I'm aware of the way that I'm sitting, and that I (stuttering) I'm not feeling very well supported, even though I've crossed my legs. I feel like I'm sliding forward. I'm aware that I feel like I'm sliding forward onto the floor.

Therapist 3: Can you exaggerate that a little more?

(*Good.* Therapist starts off with a patient who is not offering an immediate problem. As often occurs, the simple process of staying with awareness and exaggerating body perceptions quickly leads to a split worth pursuing.)

Patient 3: Well, you mean with my body? I feel like I'm going down this way (Patient sliding forward) and that by crossing my legs, you know, I'm giving myself more support, stopping that "falling feeling." (Pause)

Therapist 4: Would you come close to the edge of the couch? (Patient moves) Keep your legs crossed, just come a little closer. Get in touch with the feeling of falling, or like you're about to fall. Then start telling me that "I'm aware of—I'm aware that I'm about to fall."

(*Poor*. Therapist would do better here to get patient's permission and commitment, ["Do you want to explore this falling feeling?"] and then ask patient whether she's more in touch with her need for support or for falling. After these, then Th 4 as a response would be appropriate. What happens here is that therapist compounds patient's lack of support by his not giving enough.)

Patient 4: Yeah, I'm aware that this is not comfortable for me (voice still fairly low). I'm aware that I *know* I'm not going to fall off the edge of the sofa, but I'm also aware that I feel like I'm on the edge of a (stuttering) a sort of a precipice—that it's deeper than it really is from here to the floor.

Therapist 5: What's in the precipice?

Patient 5: (Slightly laughing sigh) As I look at the rug I can remember the feeling of being in the top of a stadium with—and looking very far down onto the—onto the people in the very bottom.

Therapist 6: What's it like to be at the very top of the stadium and look way down?

(*Poor*. Both Th 5 and Th 6 are too quick and too concrete. Both times, either silence or "stay with that feeling" are better.)

Patient 6: I don't like it (unemphatically but very finally).

Therapist 7: Can you tell me more? "I'm aware of feeling . . ."

(*Okay*. Better to echo the more specific feeling, "*I don't like . . .*" with emphasis.)

Patient 7: I'm aware that I feel . . . I (stuttering) I've been there before, and I'm aware that I feel dizzy, (slight pause) and if I think about it hard, that feeling comes back to me of—kind of vertigo, when I'm at the very top.

Therapist 8: "I'm at the very top . . ."

(*Okay*. It's hard to tell without hearing voice tone or tempo whether patient is delaying or therapist is pressuring. Again here, therapist chooses the less focusing description rather than feeling or body state. "I'm feeling dizzy . . .")

Patient 8: And I'm aware of wanting to move back to the wall (voice slightly lower and words more slurred)—to come off the edge of the couch. And I'm aware that I wish people were around me that I could reach out for them (gesturing out in either direction) so that I wouldn't fall—so I couldn't fall.

Therapist 9: What would happen if you fall right now? (Pause)

(*Poor*. Therapist isn't paying enough attention to patient's several-times stated need for support which she has communicated by specific verbal statements, by body sensations, by image metaphor and by pausing in ways which evoke therapist's response. A summary and stage setting here would be valuable. "So part of you feels like falling and part wants to move back and hold on to people and get support.") (Continuing) "I'm afraid that . . ."

(*Good.* Focusing on patient's specific feelings intensifies her response and moves her forward into her "falling.")

Patient 9: Well . . . ahh . . . ohh . . . (Pausing) . . . If I think about it too hard I can get very dizzy. I can feel myself falling over and over.

Therapist 10: Okay. What's that like? "I'm falling . . ." Can you describe that for me? (Slight pause) "I'm falling . . .? I'm turning . . .?"

Patient 10: I'm falling, and I'm turning in circles (slowly) . . . and it makes my head feel peculiar . . . I haven't any . . . I haven't any balance. It's . . . I'm completely dizzy. (Words low and almost slurred) And I'm not aware of the impact of the ground or the people below. I'm only aware of the sensation of falling—the vertigo or dizziness; and the feeling of kind of being suspended in this space, (slight pause) without any support. (Longer pause) Now . . . now my fingers are tingling (moving fingers on both hands). (Pause)

Therapist 11: Both hands? (Patient nods in agreement) What do they want to do?

(*Poor.* Therapist has abandoned the falling-dizzy-fear figure which patient has gotten with in a fairly powerful way and followed her into a less immediately affectful place. The clue is patient's ". . . without any support," followed by the long pause. Best therapist response here is probably to echo "without any support . . .")

Patient 11: (Delaying a moment) They're just . . . throbbing and tingling . . .

Therapist 12: Okay, will you shake them, then? (Pause as patient shakes hands in air) Is there one hand that is a little more alive and tingling than the other?

(*Poor.* Two errors. Therapist assumed that tingling means "alive" rather than asking patient what tingling means. [Probably patient's dizziness and discomfort have been focused in her hands— and the experience is much more negative than implied by "alive."] Also, asking patient to shake her hands is moving toward reducing or draining off her experience rather than intensifying it [In Th 11-P 11 she has just turned down encouragement to "do something" in favor of experiencing her sensation.].)

Patient 12: Yes . . . the right hand.

Therapist 13: How does your left hand feel?

Patient 13: It's quit tingling.

Therapist 14: Which one are you most with right now?

Patient 14: This one (gesturing with right hand).

Therapist 15: The tingling one? Can you tell me . . . okay "I'm aware that my right hand is tingling." Can you describe that? Awareness?

Patient 15: I'm aware that my right hand is still tingling, and my fingers feel like they want to play (last word said almost childishly) they want to go out and play (voice takes on more affect, voice gets slightly higher and seems pleasurable).

Therapist 16: *Let* them play . . . let them do what they wish.

(*Poor.* Again moving patient into action too quickly. No response by therapist is probably most appropriate here.)

Patient 16: And they want to wave (patient quite involved as fingers on right hand are moved about), and they want to play. And they feel very little and sort of, uhm, loose. (Voice still higher than initially and somewhat child-like) (Pause)

Therapist 17: How does it feel? To play . . . to play . . .?

Patient 17: (Still low, but somewhat less childishly) It's fun. I, I like it.

Therapist 18: Yeah.

Patient 18: But I—I'm also aware that something tells me I shouldn't —I shouldn't be doing that, you know?

Therapist 19: Who's telling you you shouldn't be doing it?

(*Poor.* "Who" is premature. Best therapist response is to repeat the words, "You *shouldn't* be playing . . .")

Patient 19: Uh (pause). (Sigh) . . .

Therapist 20: Something stopped you there—what is it?

Patient 20: This hand (gesturing with left) felt like it wanted to reach over and slap that one (slightly laughing), you know? Tell it to stop playing.

Therapist 21: Okay . . . Become your left hand. Let your left hand talk to your right hand right now. Let your left hand say what it needs to say. "Stop playing! . . ."

(*Okay.* By moving patient into enacting her split, therapist is now supporting her much more clearly. The immediate result is that she is able to go back and re-open her "dizziness" as well as state that her hands-play theme is an avoidance of the deeper anxiety-producing figure of having no support.)

Left: Stop playing . . . (rushing on) you're just—you're just running away from things by playing. Whenever you get to feeling anxious, you want to go play; and you know that's not—that's just an *escape* in this case. You felt dizzy and so you wanted to go wave at the people and play and dance and get on that stage; but that—but that wasn't because you were *really* playing—that was because you were *running*. (Pause)

Therapist 22: Now let your right hand answer that to your left hand. Move over. Move over to your left (getting confused on directions as he sits facing patient) a little bit (as patient moves to left). Now you're right hand—move to your right. Now you are your right hand. Answer that . . .

(*Poor.* Patient has summarized her conflict as running-avoidance-play versus anxiety and confrontation. This is not a top dog criticism representing a polarity, but a clear existential statement in need of support and exploration. Therapist's best response here, in either event, is "You were running from . . .")

Patient 22: Okay, my right hand says (pause) . . .

Therapist 23: "You always run away." Your left hand says "You always run away . . . you always run out and play when things get tough."

Patient 23: My right hand says "I can do anything I want to" (not very definite).

Therapist 24: Say that again.

Right: (Much more emphatically) I can do anything I *want* to.

Therapist 25: I still hear a question.

Right: I'm tired of you telling me when I can play and when I can't. Way I look at it, I'm just making up for lost time, when you never *let* me out.

Therapist 26: Say that again.

Right: I'm only making up for lost time when you never let me out and if I'm appropriate now—inappropriate now—it's your own fault.

Therapist 27: Say that again. "It's your own fault."

Right: It's your *own* fault if I play when you think I should be working, or if I run from things 'cause I don't feel like facing them right then, it's your *own fault* (still not sounding very certain).

Therapist 28: Say that again. "I don't feel like facing things right now."

Right: I—I don't feel like facing things right now (voice dropping off). I don't feel like falling right now. I'd rather *play*.

Therapist 29: Okay. Move back over to your—and become your right hand—left hand (again confused on directions).

(On this whole series of instructions Th 22 to 29), therapist is going through the motions of directing empty chair work in a Gestalt style. However, this is effort expended on a side issue. Almost everyone has a split between the sides that argue "play," "No, work," so there's no great harm done in getting patient to explore this some. However, this issue, as patient has already stated in P 21, is a "running away," and her "popping out" in P 30 represents not so much resistance as an expression of the fact that her main energy and conflict is in another place.)

Left: Well, that's your business, but as long as you sit around playing like that you're never going to get anywhere, and you know *exactly* what I mean. Falling's not the last thing—not the *worst* thing you have to worry about (said without much emotion and somewhat "tiredly"). (Pause)

Therapist 30: Where are you right now? What's happening?

Patient 30: *I'm* right here. *I'm* in the middle (moving over to center of couch). In the middle, and my left hand and my right hand are fighting it out, and I think it's funny (not laughing). Really, I think it *is* . . .

Therapist 31: Can you say that again . . .

Patient 31: (Interrupting) (Laughing) I think it's *funny* . . .

Therapist 32: Say it to your hands . . .

Patient 32: . . . because they've done it before . . .

Therapist 33: (Interrupting) Say it to your—say "I think you're funny . . ."

Patient 33: (Hurrying on and with more resolution) I think you're both ridiculous (slight laugh). You are really wasting time; because I know everything that both of you are doing (still smiling and slightly laughing), and as long as I do, you are just making fools of yourselves. (Slight pause) Now, you (pausing and turning to look at right hand)—I have a lot of confidence in you, that you can play when you need to and you know how to take care of yourself, and I have a lot of confidence in *you* (turning attention to left hand) that you've got the strength to keep . . . that playing . . . under control when you need it. Why do you sit around and bicker with each other? It's just an unnecessary drain on my energy (voice dropping off somewhat).

(Therapist and patient continue for forty more exchanges along this same line with patient telling her two hands, representing top dog and underdog, that she doesn't like their bickering and each responding in style. She is correct in her final statement in P 33— trying to resolve this particular split is an energy drain.)

Patient 101: (More firmly) I can't get you out—both of you are *there*. I can't pretend they're *there* (gesturing to the floor). (Pausing) This is my right hand (gesturing with hand) and this is my left hand, and they're there, they're not out there. They're in here. (Pause)

Therapist 101: I experience you as not wanting to go on with this anymore, which is fine with me. Uh, are you okay with you? That was a pretty frustrating thing in the sense that I don't feel like I made *much* contact with, uh, any part of any one of the three, and I don't like finishing up when the three parts of you are fighting with one another.

(Therapist feeling stymied, drops his role. In any type of therapy, one of the strongest cues inside the therapist is a feeling of being in contact with the patient and his/her conflict so that the figure is very sharp and powerful. When therapist gets out of contact, his basic task is to get back in.)

Patient 102: They're *not* (mildly insistent).

Therapist 102: Well, you're not—*they're* fighting with each other and you're kind of absorbing them, but that doesn't sound like you made peace with them.

Patient 103: I'm not fighting with them—the part of me that's in the middle—the Adult—isn't fighting with them. What I told them— what I felt like at the end is that—I said to them, "Look, you can't talk to each other—you're only going to fight." Well, one's like my Child and the other's like the Critical Parent—and I don't like T.A. terms too much, but—they *fight*, they can't get along. They can't talk to each other and make friends. But they can talk to *me*, because the me that was up here was the Adult and either one of them can come to me. And what I felt at the end was that I had told them to stop fighting with each other over my head—you know—stop fighting each other, don't talk to each other, just come to me and we'll work it out because I can listen to both of you, and I can work it out.

(Several exchanges follow with therapist and patient each giving their view of what occurred.)

Therapist: Feel finished?

Patient: . . . yeah, I do, I.—I feel better, because, uh, so often they carry on their little battles so subtly, so (slight laugh), you know, so much inside, that to let 'em out and do it—to let them let it out and do it in public—it's—it seemed more releasing. And you forced—you forced the whole thing through, too. You forced them to finish with each other or come to a conclusion, whereas

usually it'll just keep going on and on in my head without the Adult stepping in and saying "Look . . .!"
(Patient does believe that something was gained on her play-self-critical split.)

The therapist in this excerpt apparently felt a strong need for something to happen, and, aware of the patient's resistiveness, over-used Gestalt techniques in a pressuring way. He "tracked" too closely, responding on a number of occasions (Th 5, Th 6, Th 8, Th 11, Th 16, etc.) to the last sentence given by the patient rather than to the crux of her message. Close tracking to the naive therapist, patient, or observer may look like something is happening, and that the therapist is in charge or supporting the process, but more often he is actually floundering after an evasive patient who can then subtly direct the process since she knows what the therapist's response will be. Two basic skills for all therapists, but especially necessary for directing empty chair work, are the ability to listen clearly and openly with Zen-like naiveness to what the patient is saying without the intrusion of therapist wishes and expectations, and the instinct or intuitive awareness that moves toward the area of greatest intensity or affect in the patient.

A second issue raised in this transcript is the extent to which resistance comes from within the patient or is produced by the therapist. Superficially, the patient looks resistant—she pauses, she evades, she argues with the therapist, she only partially complies with directions. However, her very quickly stated problem was committing herself to her own anxiety, to space, to falling without support. This kind of "letting go" can be done only with firm therapeutic assistance; and the therapist's inability to offer this degree of support made the patient's resistiveness appropriate.

REFERENCE

Fagan, Joen and Irma L. Shepherd (eds.) *Gestalt Therapy Now*, Palo Alto, Calif.: Science and Behavior Books (1970).

CHAPTER 28

THREE SESSIONS WITH IRIS

JOEN FAGAN, Ph.D.

Reprinted with permission from Joen Fagan, "Three Sessions with Iris," **The Counseling Psychologist**, Vol. 4, 1974, pp. 42-60.

In learning about approaches to therapy, I have been grateful to the books by Haley and Hoffman (1967) and Ellis (1971) for providing a look into the heads of therapists as they make decisions during therapy sessions. These transcripts of Iris are presented to allow a similar detailing of choice of procedures and goals within a Gestalt framework.

The sessions with Iris were chosen for several reasons:

1. They have already been analyzed by an "outside" observer. I saw Iris for these sessions at the request of Fleischer, who wished to study Gestalt techniques for his dissertation (Fleischer, 1973). He had raters examine a number of variables, including patterns of interaction between patient and therapist and trends in language usage over the three sessions. Thus an objective research-oriented view of this material is available.

2. While a number of tapes, films and transcripts of recognized Gestalt therapists are available, almost none of these are representative of typical ongoing therapy:[1] most were made in workshop settings; sessions have usually been selected *post hoc* and illustrate therapeutic peak experiences with deep emotional rebirth, and patients have either been well-trained to cooperate with Gestalt techniques or have been "naturals." Iris, then, represents a balance to these, having started "cold" with the therapist, demonstrating resistance to some Gestalt procedures and having to be "trained into" them, being chosen *pre hoc* to serve as an example of a therapist's Gestalt work, and having the ongoing therapeutic flavor of three consecutive sessions.

3. Tapes of the sessions can be obtained[2] making accessible voice tone and timing, both of considerable importance in Gestalt Therapy.

An obvious question which arises is the extent to which these sessions are typical of Gestalt Therapy and Gestalt therapists. Fleischer, having summarized those therapist behaviors which he thought were distinctive to the Gestalt approach, made a number of hypotheses, some of which were supported by ratings of the sessions with Iris and some not. Concerning the latter, he wondered about the representatives of this particular therapist and patient, noting, ". . . the conspicuous lack [of direct encountering], or even the absence of direct interpersonal involvement of the patient and therapist. . . . This gives Dr. Fagan's approach a more analytic flavor" (Fleischer, 1973, p. 97). Latner (1973) notes that there are regional styles in Gestalt Therapy and that methodology differs of necessity when applied to individuals, groups, etc. He also points out that the workshop format poses its own demands, and while this setting was congruent with Perls' style and personality, it does present many limitations. With respect to those behaviors which characterize Gestalt therapists, he suggests, "Awareness, contact, support, encounter, experimentation, and the concept of incremental changes are the basic tools" (Latner, 1973, p. 184). Kogan (1974) lists twenty-four methods and techniques employed in therapy, defines each, and compares Gestalt, psychoanalysis and behavior therapy on the relative frequency of their use. His work offers a good base for comparative studies, within and between therapeutic approaches.

Compared to many Gestalt therapists, I do think I push and tie ideas together more often. My main goal is to help this patient as much as I can, and for me this takes precedence over purity of approach or putting on a good demonstration. Some Gestalt concepts: giving responsibility to the patient for change and "I do my thing; you do yours" are too often made into excuses for therapist irresponsibility or carelessness and represent one of the main misuses of the Gestalt approach (see the interviews with Simkin and Enright reported in Kogan in chapter 30 of this book). I also find it easier to be more classically Gestalt in a workshop setting where participants are lifted out of time and context so that encountering in the present becomes inevitable. I see Iris as being an example of good, hard, routine work with a resistant patient in individual therapy in a heavily Gestalt style.

The main reason Iris was chosen for Fleischer's study was that she was available. Her therapist—a graduate student in psychology—had left a few weeks earlier to go on internship and another therapist would not be available for a month. A second requirement was that she had no experience with Gestalt Therapy. Finally, she was willing to participate under the conditions of the study, which included being videotaped through a one-way observation mirror and being interviewed by the experimenter after each session. My contact with Iris before the first session was limited to a fifteen minute meeting with Fleischer and his research assistant to get acquainted and clarify procedures. I did not examine any previous therapeutic notes or test material.

Following these three sessions, Iris was in group therapy for several months, but participated minimally. I had no contact with her until a chance meeting on the street during the preparation of this article. She looked good and greeted me warmly. She reported that she was still in school, had a part-time job and had gotten married. She said in summary, "I'm feeling really good."

SESSION 1

Patient 1: Would you rather I sat there?

Therapist 1: Take your choice.

Patient 2: Well, I kind of don't want to watch the camera. (Takes seat facing away from one-way window)

Therapist 2: Okay. So we've got forty-five minutes today, tomorrow and Friday a week. I'd like to know what you want for you and what you would like me to work on with you.

Patient 3: (Laughs) I never can remember . . . Oh, hell! . . . I don't know just, ah . . . I really can't think of it.

(A response of mild dismay in the therapist at this point. This degree of blankness looks like a powerfully resistive patient, and working with her is probably going to be hard going. I decide to get more information, both to give myself some support as well as to let Iris have something specific to do to "feel into" the therapy context and to get to know me.)

Therapist 3: Well, let me ask you a little bit more about you, so I know you a little bit better.

Patient 4: Yeah, maybe I'll remember then.

Therapist 4: Okay. Ah, how long have you been coming here?

Patient 5: About a year.

Therapist 5: Why did you first come?

Patient 6: I was quite depressed and I was starting to break inhibitions that I've had all my life. Such as, I started taking dope. I was extremely lonely, and I started drinking and that scared me. You know, I was real lonely and I was starting to do dope.

Therapist 6: Okay. So you were feeling lonely and depressed and the way you were using to try to handle those was by using chemicals. And that scared you. (Patient: Yes) What have you found out in the last year about your depression and your loneliness?

Patient 7: Um, I can do something about my loneliness. Ah, when I, say, lose a boyfriend, it takes a while before I can get on my feet again, but I, I know if I hang on long enough to feel good and go outside, I'll be okay. It just depends. I just stay depressed until I find someone that I care about and I don't do much of anything. And, ah, sometimes I go to sleep, and I'm afraid of that. And sometimes I stay away from other people, withdraw, and invariably I don't want too much of anything. I cry but I don't want to. I don't know whether to go to sleep or drink or cry or what.

Therapist 7: And then what happens when you do find your way out of it?

Patient 8: Then I feel good; I eventually perk up. I can do my art ·work. (Therapist: Um hmm) Um, I don't get bored, hardly at all. I can just sit around and not feel bad, not too bad. Ah, I just feel better. I don't do things to hurt myself.

Therapist 8: Ah. So, when you first came in the main thing you knew, you used to do about being depressed generally was chemical. And where you are now with that is knowing that if you take a deep breath and hang on for a while you would find somebody else and feel better with what you get from them. But I'm getting the idea that you'd still like to be able to do this on your own, without having to hang onto anybody else.

(The last three therapeutic responses (Th 6, 7, and 8) are worded carefully so as to reflect Iris's responsibility and self-support, all implying that she can do something about her problems and what she has done has been deliberate rather than unthinking. This is a mild effort at countering her initial helplessness.)

Patient 9: Yeah! There you are! Yeah, that's a good think to work on (laughs). Have you got a Kleenex, by the way?

Therapist 9: We ought to, shouldn't we?

Patient 10: Yeah, thank you. Well, that's a good enough thing to work on. I just can't ever remember things like that though, really. Somebody else asks me and my mind just goes blank trying to think of things like that.

(In P 9, Iris responds to my proposal of self-support with both confirmation and a warning that tears and depression will be involved. In P 10 she says she blanks herself and becomes helpless when she's involved in responding to someone else's questions about what she wants.)

Therapist 10: Okay. So here again, now, you're saying, "My mind goes blank. I can't take care of me by remembering things." Then I can say, "Hey, how about, ah, trying this?" You say, "Hey, yeah, that's good." (Patient: Laughs) (Pause) Okay. Let me ask you to try something then. Would you try getting in touch with or feeling into the Iris who goes blank and ask her where somebody else can find her? See if you can get in touch with her. (Long pause) It looks like your lips are squeezing.

(Here I am trying to connect up what was said in Th 8—the idea that outside in the real world, Iris can get help with self-support —to what has just gone on between her and me in the present. Basically I am trying to give the message, "I will help you work on your self-support by telling you what you can say to yourself or do at those times of blankness so you need not feel wiped out by them." Iris's laugh, and her responsiveness in P 9, encourage me to tackle blankness and resistance, trying to set this up as an empty chair dialogue with a top dog who says "Don't know" and an underdog who disappears. The long pause immediately afterward suggests that I have moved too quickly and/or that Iris has no contact with the underdog, that she really is silent and invisible. I then become aware that Iris is squeezing her lips, and by calling attention to this hope that either Iris will release her mouth and let some words out that might be meaningful, or else will get more in touch with her retroflected "Don't talk" message.)

Patient 11: (Looks down at hands.) Oh, yeah. That is just something to fill time. I wasn't where that girl would be.

Therapist 11: Try letting it out. It looks like you're putting your lips together.

Patient 12: I keep doing them anyway. (Pause)

Therapist 12: What are your lips saying when you squeeze them?

Patient 13: I don't really know. I was having a rough time getting back to where that girl was. (Therapist: Um hmmm)

Therapist 13: So, one thing your lip squeeze is, is to try to help you get in touch with your insides. (Patient: Uh hmm) (Therapist is squeezing her lips together, so Iris can see her.) What my mouth says when I squeeze it together is, um, from deep down inside me is, "Let me out."

(My hope at Th 10 has not worked out. Iris can't get in touch with her underdog, and she denies that there is any meaning in her lip movement. In working with patients' symptoms, I often have the analogy of digging in a garden and running into a rock. In trying to remove the rock, I shake it a little to see if it gives and if it doesn't, I dig around it some more and deeper, stopping to shake it again and re-dig. It's becoming obvious that Iris's resistance or blankness is a deeply embedded part of her and to get around and underneath it, to lift it out, is going to take trying many different approaches. In Th 13, I'm hoping that if I suggest to her the motive of using her mouth to get in touch with her feelings, that this may help her to do this rather than feeling her closed-in-ness as being resistance.

Patient 14: That's a thought.

Therapist 14: So, ah, squeeze your lips together again. See what happens.

Patient 15: Not much of anything, to be quite honest.

Therapist 15: Okay. . . . Let me ask you a specific question then. How old do you feel being this Iris, the one holding in?

(Having tried in Th 13 to tie together movement and words in a modeling way and gotten some mild response from Iris, I try again in Th 14 to see if she can make any connection. Again, she doesn't, so I dig under the rock again, trying to now set this up so as to tap into some specific childhood memory that will give her a concrete person to refer back to rather than a vague underdog.)

Patient 16: Um. You mean in the amounts of time. (Therapist: Yeah. Um-hmm) Well, sometimes I feel, well I guess you could say, I feel rather—I don't know. Sometimes I feel old, now that I think about it. I feel like . . . but no, I don't. I don't know, damn it. I don't know what to say.

Therapist 16: Okay. Simply take your best guess.

Patient 17: I keep wanting to say I feel old. I've outgrown everybody. And sometimes that's true. At other times, I feel very young, like they've all left me. I think that's a little truer. I feel like I've been left behind.

Therapist 17: Um hmm. And about how old would you be when you were left behind?

Patient 18: About ten.

Therapist 18: Let's go a little bit further with this then. Okay? (Patient: Okay) Okay. Would you put ten-year-old Iris over here. And now just, just put her here. (Patient: All right) And would you take a look at her? And would you tell me first about, ah, how she looked when she was ten, or how she is looking?

(The rock has finally moved. Iris comes out with some feelings and is willing to put forth a ten-year-old. Th 18 is an effort to set up the tasks as concretely as possible so that Iris does have a very definite, clear image to respond to.)

Patient 19: Well of course, she's smaller than I am now. (Therapist: Um-hmm) Her hair is shorter. She's, ah, she's wearing a blue dress and she's got on white ankle socks and little black shoes. She's been to a funeral. She looks sad.

(Considerable relief on my part. We've gotten to some material that sounds very important and Iris is now responding in a "workable" way.)

Therapist 19: Whose funeral?

Patient 20: Her grandfather's.

Therapist 20: So she's been to Grandfather's funeral and she looks sad. (Patient: Um hmm) How are you feeling toward her?

Patient 21: Oh, that's too bad.

Therapist 21: Okay. Would you say that to her?

Patient 22: Iris, that's too bad. Everybody dies. That's too bad. You better get used to it. I'm sorry.

Therapist 22: Okay. Would you come over here and be her? (Patient moves to other chair.) Okay. You've just come from your grandfather's funeral. You're wearing a blue dress.

(Anticipating that Iris will have difficulty in getting with or feeling into her child or underdog, I try to set this up very concretely by repeating her description. Her next response confirms the difficulty she has in letting her child have feelings.)

Patient 23: I felt sadder sitting there looking at her than I do here. Maybe it was just getting up for a minute.

Therapist 23: Okay. Are you then saying, "I guess I'm really not feeling very sad?"

Patient 24: Not as much as I was sitting over there. It's there, yeah, but . . .

Therapist 24: Could you tell big Iris what you're feeling? She's feeling very sad for you and she'd like you to know that.

Ten-year-old 25: Oh, I feel pretty bad too but I don't feel all alone. Now I'm beginning to feel sad. Oh, . . .

Therapist 25: Okay. Would you stick right now with that ten-year-old whose grandfather has died. (Patient: Okay) What he meant to her, and what his dying meant to her?

(Getting Iris in touch with her feelings involves a delicate back and forth, in-and-out-of role. Usually, therapist's efforts should be directed at keeping someone in an empty chair position in role, but Iris's inability to maintain clear feeling contact with the ten-year-old requires considerable coaching.)

Ten-year-old 26: Um. He, in a way, meant everything. I mean, you know, I had somebody to run around with. I don't know, he was like a parent. (She begins quietly crying.)

(Iris is getting closer to being able to feel her way back into the ten-year-old. I don't have any clear idea of where this is going, but in a patient who presents initially feelings of depression centering around other people's leaving her and being unable to support herself, this loss of the grandfather must be extremely important. I want to move in the direction of uncovering that denied early sadness as thoroughly as possible. I anticipate that Iris's inability to grieve for her grandfather, possibly because no one in her family could support her sadness, constitutes a very important piece of unfinished business. If this is so, then I would expect her to move in the direction of fully expressing her grieving and having Grandfather express the feelings toward her that the ten-year-old child was unaware of, so that this energy can be released and free present on-going relationships so that they will not end in abandonment and grief.)

Therapist 26: You are feeling some sadness now.

Patient 27: Yeah, now I am.

Therapist 27: So he meant a great deal to you.

Patient 28: Yeah, and that's the ten-year-old, the child. I'm not really so used to his death yet, not that much. It's terrible, but it hasn't been around very long, you know.

Therapist 28: Like you don't know yet what you should do? (Patient: Um hmm) As a child were you able to tell him what he meant to you?

Patient 29: Uh, I, I didn't tell him verbally. I don't know, I might have said something. I didn't actually come right out and say, "I love you, Pop." I never said that.

Therapist 29: Would you be willing to talk to him now? (Patient: I guess.) Okay. Would you put him over there and describe him?
(Iris in the earlier exchange responded very well to the concrete visual image of herself as a ten-year-old, so I am trying to use this again in setting up her exchange with grandfather.

Ten-year-old 30: Hm. He's got on an old dingy sort of turned-up overalls, Lee overalls. And a blue work shirt. And his shoes are old and muddy. One of them is a little torn and he can pick up with his toe and stick his toe out and tease us with it. (Therapist: Uh hmm) And he's pretty much bald-headed except for a little thing of hair around here. And he wears rims and, uh, he's got a square chin, something like mine, only square. (Therapist: Uh hmm) He's an old man. When he works, he's always in the field. He has this, he's got on a safari hat when he works, and when he doesn't work he's sitting on the sofa, like he's doing now. And either watching TV or just sitting on the sofa, like he's doing now. And either watching TV or just sitting there, not saying much. Um, sometimes, he has a little can of beer, not very often, just once or twice. And he just sits there, and rests.

Therapist 30: As you see him, how are you feeling toward him?

Patient 30: I miss him, actually.

Therapist 31: Would you say that to him now?

Ten-year-old 32: I miss you.

Therapist 32: Go ahead and say some more about missing him and about what he meant to you.

Ten-year-old 32: I miss sitting on your lap. (Patient begins crying more heavily.) And sitting out on the well with you, and you used to talk to Minnie Pearl, that was one of the chickens, she was crippled. (Therapist: Um hmm) Um, I don't know . . . just sitting in the rocking chair, just, just following you around really, that's really about all I ever did, but I miss that.

Therapist 33: So, there was a lot of warmth, ah, you're appreciating him as you watch him—what you got from him. Would you say to him what watching him and feeling that meant to you? Tell him that.

Patient 33: Well, I felt like I had me a buddy. Somebody that wanted me around, really, which he did. He did. I was his favorite grandchild.

Therapist 34: Somebody that really liked you.

Patient 34: Yeah. And I always preferred men to women, somehow. I don't know. Now I feel more comfortable around women as such, but I still try to be around men.

Therapist 35: I hear you, almost as if you're trying to back off from your feeling right now?

Patient 35: Yeah, I guess I am.

Therapist 36: I think what you had going was mighty important and I'd like to see you get to it a little bit more . . . Are you saying to him, "I don't want to say good-bye to you?" (Patient: Yeah, I reckon.) Would you say that and see what happens?

(Iris has been getting in touch with some of her feelings and memories and then in P 34 backs off from these. In Th 36, I'm trying to give her enough support to get back with her ten-year-old and her sadness.)

Ten-year-old 36: I don't want to say good-bye to you.

Therapist 37: Would you tell him what you would like to do, what you got from him?

Patient 37: I'm trying to figure, well, I've got the memory, I guess that's not good enough, though, or I wouldn't be doing this.

Therapist 38: Tell him what your tears are saying.

Ten-year-old 38: Well, I, I feel lonely really.

Therapist 39: Okay. Say that to him then. "In comparison to you
. . . now that you're gone . . ."

Patient 39: Um, I never really felt quite like anybody else wanted
me around that much. You know, I mean . . . (crying)

Therapist 40: You're saying, "You wanted me around more than
anybody I've ever felt."

Patient 40: Yeah. Far as I could tell. I really don't feel that comfortable around other people anymore. Well, maybe for a while,
not *that* comfortable, no. I start feeling like, "Well, I'd better leave
them," or "Frankly they'd . . ." I think most people I don't want to
be around too long. Some of 'em I do, and they don't want me, or
I don't think they do.

Therapist 41: Some of your tears are saying that other people aren't
as good as he is. In the past, too. So to get away from dealing with
him, thinking that other people aren't as good. Iris, did you make
that commitment to him at his funeral?

(In the last five exchanges, Iris has been unable to stay in the ten-
year-old role and in touch with her sadness except very briefly,
even with much support. I'm thinking here that Iris may be having
difficulty in getting with her grief as a first step to giving Grandfather up because she has nobody to replace him with and because,
in a transactional analysis sense, she has made a decision not to
let go of him. The rock's not going to move yet, so dealing with
the resentful part of Iris represents another effort at unblocking
some of her feelings.)

Patient 41: I don't remember that . . . (Long pause) I don't know if
I made it to him so much. I must have made it though. I don't
know if this is necessarily so or not. Um . . . 'cause I can remember
now, just vaguely, standing in front of the coffin, not very well,
you know 'cause I've been to, God, over ten funerals. I remember,
though, standing next to Mother and she was crying like all hell.
If I made it to anybody, I probably made a promise to her, at least
as well. I just . . .

Therapist 42: What was that promise?

Patient 42: I guess it would be that I would go along with her, which
I . . . I did love Pop as much as I said, but I always went along with
Mother's sympathy, or whatever, up until last year when I started
cracking, as I called it at the time. It was one of the best things I
ever did, I think. I was leaving her, finally.

Therapist 43: I don't know what you meant by, "I will go along
with Mother's sympathy."

(Mother now comes along as a significant figure who, by crying and needing herself, makes it hard for Iris's child to experience her sadness.)

Patient 43: Okay. Um, well, I'm going to, uh, to, you know, if a person feels bad and they're with me I feel like I have to, you know, rub my nose in the dirt too, and I was always that way around Mother.

Therapist 44: Okay. So your mother spent a lot of time feeling unhappy or depressed or grieving. And you had to be there to take care of her.

Patient 44: Sure, of course, when Pop died, I really did feel that bad, but other times she has grieved, I didn't, but I just went along with her.

Therapist 45: So what you're remembering now, then, is at his funeral, making something like a promise to her that in her grief you were going to be there and take care of her.

Patient 45: I guess I did. I didn't promise Pop anything. I don't even remember doing that. I don't think I really looked that much. I don't even, I must have walked up to the coffin, but I don't know. I do remember Mother always being all broken up about things. She's so emotional.

Therapist 46: Okay. Let me ask you to say two sentences to him and see how correct or incorrect each of these feels. I want you to see him and say, "I felt so good and close to you that nobody else can ever measure up to that."

(In P 44 and 45, Iris twice starts talking about Pop and switches to having to take care of Mother. I still want her to go back and be able to express some of her grieving with him before tackling Mother, and am hoping that our clarifying Mother's saying to her, "Don't you grieve, take care of me," will now let her go back and be with grandfather.)

Ten-year-old 46: Right. I felt so good and close to you that nobody else can ever measure up to that . . .

Therapist 47: Okay. How does that feel?

Patient 47: It feels kind of automatic, though.

Therapist 48: Okay. Like that's almost what you had been saying?

Patient 48: Yeah, I guess so. I mean that I said that kind of straightly.

Therapist 49: Um hmm. Would you be him and see what he answers to that? (Patient switches chairs.)

Grandfather 49: Ah . . . No, I'm not all that good, really, I appreciate it though just the same, but, ah, but you've got your mother and your daddy and your sister and you've got a lot of people yourself (fades out).

Therapist 50: Would you listen to your tone of voice as you say that, Grandfather?

Patient 50: It sounds kind of whiney.

(Iris, as is apparent both before and after this, has learned well from her family the right words to say to cover up her thoughts and feelings, but often her voice tone makes what she really wants to say clear and she can often hear that.)

Therapist 51: Would you put some words on your voice tone? What is your voice really saying?

Grandfather 51: And I'm going to miss you too.

Therapist 52: Yeah. Go on and say more about that. What do you feel for that gal?

Patient 52: About the same thing she felt for me, or feels, or whatever.

Therapist 53: Would you tell her that? "You're awfully important to me . . ."? Whatever your words would be . . .

Grandfather 53: Um . . . I don't know . . . I miss you, kid, I really do . . . I mean it was nice having a granddaughter to care about her grandpa. Your sister didn't, really. Hell, I don't know. I don't sound right exactly. It really doesn't.

Therapist 54: What's happening with your right now?

Grandfather 54: Hell, it sounds like rhetoric to me. Um. You're cute kid, right? I love you and I loved having you around. But I was old and I had to die. And I'm glad I did, frankly, because I was tired of it all.

Therapist 55: What would you like to leave her with, with respect to your feeling about her and her feeling about you? How do you want her to be with other people?

Grandfather 55: Well, I want you to love them as you love me. I don't believe that somehow.

Therapist 56: Okay. What was your head shaking?

Patient 56: He didn't really say that. I was getting kind of misty again. Yeah, I guess it was true because I, I don't want to believe. I can't believe that Pop would just be stuck in a hole. You know, I don't buy that exactly. Maybe because I bought that already. I don't know! I'm just confused. I mean that seems like what I'm supposed to say and I'm not supposed to say anything. But, it seems like a conclusion I am being led to, either by you or by myself. If it's by myself, of course, I don't want to believe it. I guess.

(Iris is correct in that I have been pushing her to explore her and her grandfather's feelings about each other. There are still too many blocks and resistances to allow her to get to this on a deep level, so what has occurred is mostly rhetoric.)

Therapist 57: I hear you saying what you heard then, the words when you were saying, "You've got a lot of other people." But the tone of voice may be saying something different.

Patient 57: I, Mama thought he didn't want to go, really. When I said, "I'd like to go," I sounded more like me than I did him, tell you the truth. I don't really want to, but I, between the two of us, I've been more or less wanting to run away more than he did. So when I said I was old and ready to die I didn't sound like I was hearing Papa sound.

Therapist 58: You said a while ago that sometime when you felt blank and depressed that you felt older than other people.

Patient 58: Yeah. I did. Now I guess that's how I would. (sigh) Because a little kid needs love. That would sound like I didn't love Pop and I did and I do. That isn't right. But as a little kid I was loved. Oh, I probably still am now, I just don't feel I am though. Not all the time, not usually though. I guess that's where it comes from.

Therapist 59: "As a little kid I was loved." (Patient: Yeah) How old a kid are you talking about now? I hear you talking about Iris.

Patient 59: Well, now I'm just talking about me. When I was younger, maybe six, seven, like that.

Therapist 60: Okay. You're saying then that when you were six or seven you were feeling loved by your family, your mother and father.

Patient 60: Yeah, I guess I was. I didn't really notice them too much because I had Pop. Yeah, yeah, I did sometimes. When like I'd go to see Mama and Pop on the weekends, then I'd come home. And I wanted to go there on weekends and then I wanted to come home afterwards. I guess I was, yeah.

Therapist 61: Okay. Let me get . . . I'm not quite clear. What do you call your father?

Patient 61: Daddy.

Therapist 62: Daddy. And Pop is your grandfather?

Patient 62: And Mama was my grandmother. Then there's Mother and Daddy.

Therapist 63: Okay. Mother and Daddy and Mama and Pop. Is that right?

Patient 63: Yeah. (Therapist: Okay) Yes. I guess you didn't know that. That's what Mother called them, so we did too . . . (long pause) Oh, I know Mother loves me now. At least she says she does. But I don't feel it too much.

Therapist 64: Okay. Let me go back and get you to remember your tone of voice just then.

(Again Iris's tone of voice contradicts her words. She's beginning to hear this clearly.)

Patient 64: Sounded kind of resigned, I think. I guess, sort of . . . hm, I don't know. I didn't sound too happy. Sounded like I was . . .

Therapist 65: It didn't sound too believable, did it?

Patient 65: No. No, that's a good one. Um . . . well, I mean I couldn't sit here and say my mother loves me. Because I don't, I don't believe it fully. I mean, I feel like she must, but then I don't really. I mean, you know, I couldn't tell you either, because I don't believe either one.

Therapist 66: What I'm hearing is a lot of words in your family that were the right words—"Your mother does love you" and so forth, but often the feeling and the tone of voice that went with them didn't match 'em.

Patient 66: Yeah, and sometimes, no. Well, I would say she does because the other day we both had an argument and it ruined both of our days. It ruined my day that I'd gotten her mad at me. And it ruined her day that she got me mad at her. But in those arguments I remember just really being pissed off at her for nothing really. I was just in a bad mood and I lashed out. It was, you know, worrying the hell out of me. And she got just as mad at me as I did at her. And, you know, a lot of times I don't think I love her. And so, I don't guess she loves me. At least not at some of the time I know she doesn't 'cause I don't love her some of the time.

Therapist 67: Okay. It's like loving means you got to like and feel good toward somebody all the time?

Patient 67: Well, yeah, it sounds like that. That's the way I see it.

Therapist 68: Okay. What I'm hearing you say so far today is that there are at least two kinds of people in your life. There was your grandfather and boyfriends now, who come and go and make you feel good while they're there. But they go too. (Patient: Yeah, Huh) And then you feel depressed again. (Patient: Um) And there's your mother who stays around, but that you have . . . You keep trying to get away from, but that you keep coming back to her, in brief arguments or in longer ones. (Patient: Yeah) So that I'm hearing you say with men you clump all the good feeling together for a while; these really, you feel very good. They make you feel good, and then you're really going to feel bad when they disappear and go. (Patient: Uh huh) And your mother, and maybe some other women, I don't know, you sort of feel mixed good and bad about more. It is more of a mixed up . . .

Patient 68: Yeah. Especially with women it sounds realer. More real.

Therapist 69: Uh huh. And what makes sense to me, to sort of focus on, is getting clearer on where some of the bad feeling part gets going (Patient: uh huh) and I think what we may need to do is go back and do a chunk more talking with both your grandfather and your mother and some other people in your family. (Patient: laugh) It really sounds like you've got two sets of parents.

Patient 69: Yeah. Yeah, it seems like I do.

Therapist 70: Uh hmm. One is confusing enough. (Patient: Yeah (laugh) So, um, anyway, that's what I'm thinking then. Ah, trying to get closer on what they were actually saying to you and what you're actually answering. Below the words, because everybody knows the words, "Sure I love you," and "Yeah, I miss you." What's really being said, too, underneath that.

Patient 70: Okay. You're looking at me like you expect something.

Therapist 71: Well, I wasn't sure if you were doing some thinking or what.

(This section is a good argument for a fairly pure Gestalt approach. I have unloaded several of my best interpretations, all probably quite accurate, and the patient has responded with six or eight agreeing noises, and then absolutely nothing.)

Patient 71: Well, both thinking and then wondering, you know, if I'm supposed to do that now or later. It seems like later, maybe next time or something.

Therapist 72: Well, we have about ten minutes today.

Patient 72: Well, I don't know.

Therapist 73: Would you do a check on your insides now. Your hands are doing something with the Kleenex.

Patient 73: I'm nervous. I'm always nervous about thinkg like this.

(What has happened is that Iris becomes anxious when she is "talked at" rather than being helped to hear her own talking, either through images, or getting in touch with her body. She told me that clearly earlier, in P 10, but I suppose I'm hoping that we've made enough contact for her to now hear me.)

Therapist 74: Okay. Where's your nervousness coming from right now? Do a check in your body and see if you can find out where it is.

(Body messages seem to be one way to loosen the rock some. If I can't easer her tenseness by words and ideas—and indeed, even increase it this way—then helping her become aware of body sensations and relaxing these is a route worth trying.)

Patient 74: It's tight in there. In my stomach. (Therapist: Okay.) Now I, now I know how I remember it. I relax my stomach, but see . . . it doesn't stay that way at all. It's tense again and then I just relaxed it. (Therapist: Uh hmm) It doesn't stay that way.

Therapist 75: So you can tell your stomach to relax and obey you temporarily. And then when you're not looking, as soon as you stop looking, it's back tense again.

Patient 75: Yeah, that's right (laugh). I just did it again. It does that. If I'm alone I can relax and then pretty much stay that way sometimes. (Therapist: Um hmm) It's just when I'm around other people I start getting nervous. I just can't sit still.

Therapist 76: Okay. It's when you're with other people, then, that your stomach is tense. And a chunk of you then is uncomfortable. (Patient: Uh huh) By yourself . . .

Patient 76: It's not so bad . . .

Therapist 77: You have . . . Check with your stomach then. Is your stomach being a kind of armor in the same way your mouth was?

Patient 77: (Laughs) It makes sense that way. I guess it would be, 'cause it's, you know . . . Hmm.

Therapist 78: Yeah. Let's try a brief dialogue then. Could you say to your stomach, "Hey. Hey, relax. Stop all this." Whatever you have to tell it.

Patient 78: Ah, it's like I tell it in my head, "Loosen up! Relax. Just be flexible. Don't tense again either."

Therapist 79: What does your stomach answer you?

Patient 79: It tenses back up.

Therapist 80: Then you can say, "Ah, I'm getting tense again."

Patient 80: Uh huh. It says, "Uh, . . ."

Therapist 81: Now would you say that directly. Give your stomach words. Be your stomach.

Stomach 81: It says . . . um . . . well, I can't relax because I'm nervous and if I relax then you might be nervous elsewhere.

Therapist 82: Okay. Stomach is saying, "I'm carrying your nervousness for you. I'm taking it." (Patient: Yeah [sigh]) Was that sigh from you or your stomach?

Patient 82: Ah, I don't know. I do it so much I don't know. I never give it any thought.

Therapist 83: How do you feel about loading your tension into your stomach? Would you tell her?

Patient 83: Well, I don't notice it, I don't notice your being tense. When I do, sometimes it bothers me. Sometimes I feel a little sickish. But, ah, if I don't notice it, it doesn't bother me. I don't always go around noticing it. It's mostly when I'm in a situation like this, when somebody's talking to me and digging things . . . I wonder if that's where it all is. That's what you said though. That's . . . I don't know. Like I wouldn't want to do this after a heavy meal.

Therapist 84: What are your feelings right now toward your stomach?

Patient 84: Ah, I don't know . . . I was feeling like it was my friend. That's kind of bad though because if it's my friend it's helping me hide things. Because I'm quite devious that way. I really like the little fella (laughs) (Therapist: laughs) I don't know . . . I'm afraid I do feel like he's my friend.

Therapist 85: Okay. You say, "Thank you, buddy."

Patient 85: Yeah, I know I am. That's bad, but I'm doing it just the same.

Therapist 86: Okay. Be your stomach and answer. (Patient: Hhmm??) Be your stomach and answer.

Stomach 86: Well, you're welcome (laughs). Oh, oh . . . you can't relax too much, bit by bit by . . . Well, if I relax too much then, then you'll look more pot-bellied too.

Therapist 87: But your stomach's also helping you to look good.

Patient 87: Oh, yeah. It helps, but it doesn't do much, but it helps.

Therapist 88: Okay. Question: Who was that a minute ago that told you you shouldn't, it was bad to . . .

Patient 88: My head. Well what? that it was bad to be friends with my stomach? (Therapist: Um hmm) My head. My head was. Well it's, you know, reasonable.

Therapist 89: What's reasonable?

Patient 89: Well, it figures out logic, that's kind of reasonable.

Therapist 90: What figures out logic?

Patient 90: My head does. I mean like, okay, my stomach and I are friends. And my stomach's tense and holding things back that I should be letting go. My head has learned that that's not good in a situation like this. So it says, No. You see?

Therapist 91: Uh hmm. There's somebody up there that says, "But you shouldn't take care of you, and you should't defend you, and you shouldn't be tense, and you ought to be able to walk right into any situation and handle it and um."

(Iris's head is such a mass of critical top-dog messages that almost anything she says or does is immediately and negatively commented on. This is so pervasive with her that she doesn't begin to have any idea other messages inside her head are possible. It is hardly surprising that she would try to drown or fog some of this out with drugs and alcohol. It is also not surprising that she would feel frequently called on to defend herself from someone else's observations, and to be very wary about putting her thoughts and feelings out on the line. While it is certainly true all through these sessions that Iris time after time displays much resistance, it is also not hard to see between the lines the amount of self-protection that is involved in this. It is also clear that when she hears me supporting her in a way that filters through the haze of expectations of criticisms that she is genuinely grateful and responsive.)

Patient 91: Well, that sounds like logic to me.

Therapist 92: It sounds like criticism to me.

Patient 92: Oh, critical logic (laughs). It still sounds like it comes from my head. Well, of course, it's criticism, yeah . . . like criticism for being a goof, or criticism for not cooperating as I should and I say "should" because it's going through my head again.

Therapist 93: Uh hmm . . . Your head is telling you then that anybody else, anything anybody else wants you to do for your good . . . . (Patient: Um hmm) You certainly should go with . . .

Patient 93: Yeah (laughs), that's what it says. And then, of course, my stomach doesn't feel like that.

Therapist 94: Um hmm . . . Okay. So your head and your stomach are in an argument.

Patient 94: Um hmm. This is kind of amusing, but it's true, yeah. When I said that "This is kind of amusing," I felt like that was my stomach. Then when I said, "Yeah, but it's true," that was my head. (Therapist: Um hmm) Gosh, what a split (Therapist: Yeah)

Therapist 95: I've got no doubt but what there are a great many lectures you give yourself. (Patient: Umm) And I think this is something that we also can well do some listening to . . . (Patient: Okay. . . . is that I think you have a very critical Parent in your head, that's all the time gently and helpfully shouting you orders. And somebody down there apparently resists, I think for good reason, and she is going to take some listening to. (Patient: Yeah) Okay. Anything else, ah, you need to say today or want to say before we leave? (Patient: No) Okay. I'll see you tomorrow then. We've done some fairly heavy work today.

Patient 95: Yeah. I hope I don't fall in two pieces though (laughs). Well, thank you. (Therapist: Okay)

(She's beginning to hear her under-dog! My last comment came from a recognition that [probably from being on display] I had pushed

Iris hard to "get somewhere." Iris's last comment seems to also partially reflect that. Iris did forget at the end of the session that she was to stay afterward for the post-session interview and left the waiting room very quickly.

Iris's reaction to the first session was elicited in an interview by Fleischer.

> The first post-session interview was held immediately before the second session, as Iris left the building, "forgetting" about the post-session interview, right after the first therapy session. The interviewer had her close her eyes, in essence, take a fantasy trip back to immediately after the first session. The patient remembered that she felt older than other people and recalled that she felt loved as a child during the session. Iris experienced some sadness and "grieving" when she dealt with her grandfather's death (when the patient was ten years old) during the session, but seemed unsure as to how she really felt about him. During the post-session interview she expressed ambivalence; wanting to leave her grandfather along with new awareness that she really did not want to let him go. She became aware of this when Dr. Fagan had her remember his funeral, and in the dialogue with him during the session Iris realized she had a "real split" between her head and her stomach. Iris experienced this dialogue as "weird." Iris recalled blanking out at several points and she remembered that Dr. Fagan attended to her lip movement at one of these blank points.
>
> The patient reported that she liked the therapist and felt that the therapist was competent, sensitive, perceptive and very bright. She said that she felt more comfortable with her and trusted her more than in the pre-study meeting. Iris appreciated what she perceived as Dr. Fagan's sympathy and understanding, especially when Iris cried during the session. She felt Dr. Fagan really listened to her and was really "with me." Iris pinpointed Dr. Fagan's moving up on the edge of her chair as having communicated this to her. She also appreciated Dr. Fagan's structuring the session during Iris' very first blank out by asking Iris why she came for therapy to begin with. Iris felt a "little nervous" at first, but felt "Okay," "better" when she left; she could not pinpoint when the change occurred. She reported that she disliked switching roles and chairs, but that she would do it anyway. "She didn't resent or dislike anything else about the session." (Fleischer, 1973, pp. 56-57)

SESSION 2

Patient 1: I ran away yesterday (laugh) . . . I'm going to take my shoes off the floor (takes shoes off).

Therapist 1: Okay. When you said you ran away yesterday, I'm not sure if you're saying from me or what.

Patient 2: Oh, after you let me go, I disappeared. I forgot to stay (laughs).

Therapist 2: What kind of responses did you have yesterday to what we did?

Patient 3: Ah, I figured it was a pretty good session really. Uh, I got something out of it.

Therapist 3: Okay. Any other thoughts about anything else come to you?

Patient 4: Hm, you mean, like anything I learned new or anything like that.

Therapist 4: Or anything that popped up in your head after you left between then and now.

Patient 5: Uh . . . nothing in particular. Um, I don't know if I mentioned it or not, but, you know, when I was Pop and I was talking to me, um . . . (Therapist: Um hmm) I, you know, how it was occurring to me that, instead, maybe he wasn't, you know, wouldn't, didn't want to let me go. I don't know if I mentioned it or not, but, you know, I don't want to let him go. It occurred to me that way. Ah, it wouldn't surprise me too much.

(Even though I'm pushing for her thoughts, she doesn't "blank out" and comes back with some awareness.)

Therapist 5: Talk about that a little bit more.

Patient 6: Okay. Well, if I did, you know, just want to dismiss the whole thing. I would do it. But since I don't, I don't.

Therapist 6: Dismiss the whole thing?

Patient 7: Yeah, his death and his being gone, and not, not clinging onto it and the memory of it. I mean, "I should forget it," my head says. It says, "It's been eleven years." Um . . . for some reason I don't. Maybe I like to feel sorry for myself. "Poor lonely thing," you know.

(She's gotten clearer about the self-critical messages coming from her head (top dog) and that she has "some reason" for not dismissing her grandfather. However, she still doesn't hear her underdog response or have any belief or expectation that there are positive rather than negative "reasons.")

Therapist 7: Okay. I think you've got good reasons for not finishing up with that yet. I think there's a lot more in there to say. But before we get back to that, let me check out one thing with you. When you say, "Maybe I just keep hanging onto it so I can feel sorry for myself," in the inside of your head, look around behind you and see if anyone else in your family is listening to that and nodding as you say it.

(Iris, of course, can't let her grandfather go until she has finished her grieving and found more about the meaning he and she had for each other. First, though, I see a need to help her identify more clearly here where much of the initial criticism came from, so that some of the internal static can be reduced, then we can go back and get in deeper and more genuine touch with her feelings. Her mother's overdone asking for sympathy has contributed specifically to Iris's difficulty in grieving.)

Patient 8: I said, "I do that to feel sorry for myself." (Long pause) Oh hell, I see mother again! I always put her back there though and I don't know if that's true or not. It's just . . .

Therapist 8: That's what you told me yesterday.

Patient 9: Yeah, I'm always blaming her for things.

Therapist 9: Too, you told me in part that your mother hangs on to you by always hurting.

Patient 10: Yes, she does. But as far as this, I feel like I answered too quickly. I'm always seeing her back there somewhere.

Therapist 10: Okay. Maybe she belongs back there.

Patient 11: Okay. Maybe she does. (Laughs) But she thinks she doesn't. She's always the first one back there. (Therapist: Uh huh) Usually.

Therapist 11: Okay, you see the odds are, that for any female that has a mother, is that that's where she got most of her messages from.

Patient 12: Yeah (laughs), I guess so (laughs). You know, well, Daddy never gets back there so . . .

Therapist 12: Okay. What often happens is you have to clean your mother's messages out first before you start hearing his because often they weren't as constant, and involving you, and so on . . . um . . . Okay, going back to what I said a few minutes ago, I think your answer, "Maybe I'm holding on so that I can get sympathy," is not your real answer. I think you got a lot better reasons than that. It may be that, ah, you got more genuine affection from him than from anybody else when you were growing up within a certain time period. Ah, and saying "Goodbye" to him gets kind of scary, because there may not be anybody there. But we don't know that yet. (Patient: Yeah) Um. What I'd like to suggest then is let's continue some of the talking with your grandfather and see what else we can find out about what you were saying. And I'd like you to start with the two of you talking about it being hard to let go of each other. (Patient: Okay) Let me say this before you begin. Getting some of this clear doesn't really mean you're going to finish up and dismiss him. It means you're going to get clearer on some of the stuff left over that has caused some difficulties. Not that you are totally wiping him out of your life forever, you can't do this. What we're trying to do is let you keep the good stuff without having a load of some things that are not helpful to you, in addition to that. Patients often fear that saying goodbye to past relationships will involve a loss of meaning. Since this is compounded by what Iris is struggling with, I want to remove this fear as another possible source of resistance.

Patient 13: So I've forgot what you want me to do (laughs) talk between . . .

Therapist 13: Talk between you and him about how hard it is to let go of each other.

Iris 14: All right, let's see . . . well . . . it's like hard to say "Goodbye" to you, Pop, because, ah, well, ah, I mean, one day you were there and next day you weren't. Only physically I remembered I dreamed about you not long after you died, and it was kind of a spooky dream because, because you were dead, sort of, but then you weren't. And I don't think I've ever really caught, caught hold of the fact that you weren't around. It's, ah, it's like I keep it in my head that you're somewhere around, sometimes, not always. But I don't think of you as, I don't think of you as something lying in the ground. That's your body. But you're not there. No, you're not dead really. You're just, I just can't see you anymore. It's pretty damn true.

Therapist 14: Okay. When you come to what feels like a natural pause, and you just did that, go and move over yourself.

Pop 15: Okay. (Moves over) This is Pop now. Let's see now . . . Well, I am around. Not all the time, not as much now that Mama died. But I'm still around. We're both around sometimes. Um, you know, It just depends . . . it's only if you need me or not, or whatever.

Therapist 15: Pop, are you saying that, um, the main reason you're around is in case or when Iris might need you?

Pop 16: Sounds like it. Yeah.

Therapist 16: Uh huh. Okay. So you're saying to her you really can't let her go.

Pop 17: Yeah, I guess I am.

Therapist 17: All right. How come?

Pop 18: 'Cause I love her.

Therapist 18: Yeah. Let's see what else comes to you . . . If you don't have her to watch over, does it mean that you disappear? That you get your existence from . . .

(I'm trying to both focus Pop's feelings and thoughts and give support in Th 16, 17 and 18. In empty chair work, saying goodbye to an important person who has died, almost inevitably leads toward the dead figure saying the equivalent of "I release you—to go find others." But Iris-Pop is a long way from recognizing this, and, so that "I love her" (Pop 18), a cliche rather than real response won't block the process, I put in my best guess as to what lies underneath the holding on.)

Pop 19: I'm sure I get most of it, or a lot, from my mother, too. (Mother's name) But . . . I feel like, you know, I get more of it from Iris. I don't think I'd disappear entirely, no. I would start fading, yeah.

Therapist 19: You get some of your enjoyment in living from having her around (Pop: Um hmm) So you can hold on then and not really be gone, by sort of staying around for the women in your family.

Pop 20: But is that so wrong?

(Here again as I try to clarify or give some ideas, Iris hears this as critical of her.)

Therapist 20: Is part of you saying it's wrong?

Patient 21: No . . . I don't know. I'm just confused about that. I don't really see how it is wrong, but if it's hurting somebody, I guess it is. I didn't mean for that . . .

Therapist 21: What's coming to you? What's happening?

Patient 21: I noticed I've got my foot on the chair (Therapist: Um hmm), and I was rubbing my foot up and down.

Therapist 22: Uh hmm. What was your foot saying? Do it again.

Patient 22: Kind of a . . . well, I was doing that because it feels good to my foot.

Therapist 23: Um hmm . . . so that your foot was being, um, in touch or comforted somehow? (Patient: Uh huh) Do it again. See if your foot's saying anything to the chair.

Patient 23: Uh, no. I'm afraid I'm just noticing the contours of the leg of the chair. (Therapist: Um Hmm) And it scratches my foot and feels good to my arch.

Therapist 24: Okay. I'm wondering if there's something in there like, said to the chair, "I'm glad you're there to comfort me even if you can't, ah . . ."

Patient 24: God! Oh wow! (Laughs)

(Again Iris responds very positively to the combination of putting her in touch with her body and giving her some support by way of positive reasons for what she's doing.)

Therapist 25: Uh, to rub against.

Patient 25: Boy, it sort of sounds possible, doesn't it? Um, well, then that makes me, uh, sound like a martyr, huh? Or is that Iris? I'm Pop in this chair. It makes me sound something like a martyr.

Pop 25: I'm just sticking around to help you.

Therapist 26: Uh hmm, yeah. Feel that out carefully . . . When you want, switch over to Iris and see her response.

Patient 26: I guess. I don't know. I'll try. (Switches chairs) Kind of a lot to grasp. Okay. (sighs) Um, I put myself in the same way. (Therapist: Um hmm) (laughs slightly) I'm not wishing to be selfish, um . . . Pop leans on me and I lean on him. Perhaps, or vice versa. I really don't think he ever leaned on me as much as I did on him . . . Okay. I'm the martyr. Well, I don't think he ever, you know, leaned on me, I'm trying to say, quite as much as I leaned on him. He had a wife and two kids of his own and his children. (Therapist: Um hmm) And, um, I didn't have very many, much of anybody else but him. I didn't have many friends and, I had, you know, lots of cousins. But now and then we'd fight and I'd fight with my sister. So I was the martyr. I'm the one that, well, I'll lean on you. And I'll give you support, too. And if you lean on somebody, you're not necessarily giving them support. But then you are. Oh God! I'm getting all tangled up now (sighs).

Therapist 27: I think it is clear now, Iris, that Pop and you got something very positive from each other. Ah. Given that he had more age, more experience, more people resources, maybe it still did not mean that he couldn't thoroughly enjoy you and appreciate very much your loving him. It may have seemed like a love with less entanglements than you got from some of the other people.

Patient 27: Maybe. It was mostly I just kinda like followed him around, and all like that.

Therapist 28: What I'm hearing, though, it's as if a part of you is still trying to follow him around. (Patient: Um hmm) And that part then isn't available for what may be here and now in your life as it goes on.

Patient 28: No, ah, you better run that by me again.

Therapist 29: Okay. That there's a part of you that's still saying, "I'm going to get my nurturing from Pop." (Patient: Um hmm)

Ah, then, that says, "I'm not going to get it from Bill or Susie or real live people who happen to be here."

Patient 29: (Laughs) I see. Yeah. All right then, let me pose a question. What if I seek this nurturing from someone else and then I don't get it? Then it's natural to go back to Pop. Wouldn't it be?

Therapist 30: Let that, put that in your own head and see what kind of an answer you get.

(The last few exchanges—P 26 to P 29—have felt like good cooperative endeavor: Iris has been listening and thinking without much defensiveness or internal criticism. Her head seems to be working well, so I want to switch her into a recognition of that and a position of self-support.)

Patient 30: Okay. (Long puase) It would seem natural to me. If I was going to someone else and I wasn't, see, if I wasn't getting from the relationship what I wanted, . . . then I would eventually go somewhere, and . . . I guess I'd more or less keep running home. I don't know, but that's what I've been doing, whether going there, or well, I don't get stoned anymore when I'm depressed because that's bad, but I will drink a little. Just beer, but it's something I know I'm doing to hurt myself and I don't do it. And when at times like that it's just a kind of demonstration. (Sighs) I don't know. I'm trying to say that if, if a relationship with someone else doesn't go right, it, perhaps it's because I'm not putting the right things into it, but I don't know. Sometimes I think I've put in more than I should, quite honestly I do, sometimes, think that. (Therapist: Uh hmm) You know, maybe I don't and I only think I do . . . No, I don't really believe that.

Therapist 31: Um. Let me see if this helps any . . . um, from what you said yesterday, it sounds like . . . your relationship with Pop there was a little bit more coming from him to you. (Patient: Uh huh) In your relationship with your mother, there was more going from you to her. (Patient: Or I think so.) Yeah. She was the one feeling bad and you were the one that was trying to comfort her or make her feel better. (Patient: Uh hmm) Um, it sure is true in all human relationships, sometimes it goes one way and sometimes it goes the other. And sometimes it gets messed up in between. (Patient(laughs) What I'm hearing you say, or what I'm wondering is, to what extent you superimpose over most, if not all, people you're wanting something from . . . a kind of cut-out ghostly image of Pop, and you then check them out to see if they're as good as he is or if they can do things the way he did. And if and when they don't, because they can't, they're not him, you say, "Well, you won't do. It's never going to work out, I can't get it," and feel miserable. So that in a way this blurs your seeing other people.

Patient 31: I guess I usually do that.

Therapist 32: And I'm guessing the opposite when you see somebody that wants something from you, you simply impose a kind of image of your mother.

Patient 32: And then I can't give enough. Oh, wait . . . if they want something from me, I can't give enough . . . That's probably it, really. I guess it'd be best not to expect too much from everybody, or expect nothing.

(This feels like progress—Iris listens to a long string of therapist thoughts, hangs in there and adds something herself. This time instead of criticism, however, she expresses hopelessness. Even knowing about what she does doesn't make any difference, because there's nothing much she can do or expect by way of response from others. I am trying next to get her to hear this as ideas put into her, rather than any real reflection of how things are in reality.)

Therapist 33: Okay. Who are you hearing there?

Patient 33: My head (laughs).

Therapist 34: It sounds like your mother when she's really wanting something and doesn't suppose anybody will ever . . .

Patient 34: Yeah, oh yeah, I, that does. "Well, I just won't, I won't ask you. Just never mind." Yeah, that's her. Yeah, that's my head though, that's the Parent.

Therapist 35: Okay . . . and what we're trying to find in her is your own voice. (Pàtient: Um hmm) With what you want to ask from and give to the real people in your life, as you meet them, as you get involved with them . . . (Patient: Yeah) What's your hand doing with that one right now?

Patient 35: This one was rubbing that one. (Therapist: Um hmm) It's sort of a gesture of comforting, maybe?

Therapist 36: How does that feel?

Patient 36: Well, it feels good (laughs).

Therapist 37: Can your hands right now then give you any information about taking care of and being cared for? One hand was rubbing the other and it felt good.

Patient 37: Okay, well it was the right hand was working for the left . . . hmm . . . Well, I'm right-handed.

Therapist 38: Just listen to what your hands are saying. (Patient: Okay.) What's your right hand saying?

Right 38: It's saying, "I want to make you feel good, left hand."
(Laughs)
(In this sequence, Iris is now much more able to attribute meaning
to her gestures and to spell these out in a positive way.)
Therapist 39: Okay. And left hand says . . .
Left 39: Thanks a bunch (laughs). Really. (Therapist: Okay.) The
left one's doing most of the work. I don't know, that's just what
they're doing . . . Do you know the answer to this riddle or are you
just wanting to see what I'd say?
Therapist 40: The answer to what riddle?
Patient 40: I feel like, I feel like that you know what I'm doing, you
know, more than I do right here like . . . Okay, I'm comforting my
left hand with my right one, but I feel like you're leading to something, and I'm not sure what. Unless maybe it's the relationship
between me and my mother or perhaps Pop and me. I guess that,
ah . . . Pop, me; me rather (looks alternately at right and left
hands).
Therapist 41: I didn't know a few minutes ago anything specific or
have anything specific in mind. I was simply aware of your hands
doing something together in a way that caught my attention. And
wondered to what extent they might parallel what we were talking
about. It looked as if one hand was sort of taking care of the other,
but I don't know that until I ask you to say it.
(Again, Iris's critical top dog intervenes, and for the second time in
these sessions she expresses some suspiciousness of what I am putting in her head. This seems like reasonable self-preservation considering everything her mother has put in her head. At this point
then, it seems important that I level with her as a kind of reality
check.)
Patient 41: Oh, yeah, Okay. (Laughs) It, it does amaze me how y'all
pick out things like that. I do fidget them a lot. I get nervous and
all. Feel self-conscious and fidget a lot.
Therapist 42: And then what do you hear your fidgeting say as we're
talking about it today?
Patient 42: Fidgeting in general?
Therapist 43: Well, well earlier your foot rubbing against the chair
and then your hands rubbing.
Patient 43: Frankly, in general, it means I wish I could get the hell
out of an uncomfortable situation that I'm in. Um, because the
more I fidget, the more I'd like to run. But that's only in general.
Therapist 44: You know, that's not quite what I heard your hands
and feet saying though; I heard them both sort of reaching out for
contact or for ease or comforting.

Patient 44: It doesn't sound like running, does it? (Therapist: No, it doesn't.) Maybe I've been wrong . . . Yeah, I guess you could take it both ways, too. If, if I'm uncomfortable, I want to run to a better situation and I'm comforting myself or trying to if I can't get up and go.

(P 41 is again self-critical name calling. It looks like a chance to call out some self-support and get a recognition of a positive rather than a negative reason for her behavior. In P 44, she's able to do both.)

Therapist 45: Well, let me say it another way, since, both those times, I, another person, was actually present, and maybe those are the points, with somebody, either somebody present or potentially present, you were sitting there thinking, your hand or your foot is saying, "I'm in need of some kind of contact or comforting." (Patient: Uh huh) And you've got three choices. (Patient: laughs) You can do it for yourself, or get something sort of inanimate like a teddy bear or whatever else that doesn't demand anything (Patient: laughs) or you can take off completely, you can leave. Or you can approach the person and say to them specifically, 'I'm bothered right now, pat my back, or whatever." I've heard you a little bit more in your life taking a possibility, you're beginning more to explore than you have been in the last year and you're increasing to do more. (Patient: Uh huh) But, I think some of the business with Pop is, you're saying, someway or another that ten-year-old is saying, "Now that he's gone, I don't have anybody, now it's up to me to take care of Mother and everyone else. There goes my chance."

Patient 45: Uh hmm. It's a lot for one person to do, too. (Therapist: Yeah) Now I feel like I'm being watched. Like when I was fidgeting around I felt like, "Don't do that!"

(Again, Iris expresses discomfort or even a mild paranoia at being observed. There is a therapeutic tightrope here; if not watched and pushed, Iris feels detached and hopeless; if pushed too hard, she feels criticized and self-conscious and resistant. Again she responds well when I point out the self-criticism messages and suggest some of where this comes from.)

Therapist 46: Uh huh, you sure do have something in your head that says, "If you're doing it, don't." (Patient: [laughs] Yeah, I do.) As if once you know what you're up to, you're supposed to stop it instead of, ah . . .

Patient 46: Yeah, because I've tried not to. Remember yesterday the way I was doing my mouth when you asked me something?

(Therapist: Uh huh) I was trying not to, I was sure I was doing it
. . . I guess it's like getting caught at something and trying to find
something else (Laughs) It's rough.

Therapist 47: What that says to me is something like this: that when
somebody in your immediate family calls your attention to something, he wants to tell you to stop it.

Patient 47: Yeah . . . well, yeah. I think either to stop or watch them
do something or something like that . . . There a long time ago . . .

Therapist 48: (Interrupts) Let me, let me give you a sentence and ask
you to try saying it. Would you say this to your mother, which is
my best guess as to where you got most of that from, ah, "Mother,
when I'm watching myself I'm learning something and hearing
something about me, and that's good."

(It now feels like time to go more directly after her mother as a
source of much of her self-criticism, since several times in this session what might otherwise be forward moving steps are bogged
down in her own criticism, or criticism is projected onto me. I
want to start with giving her some power to use back against her
mother, some support for examining herself and letting another
person watch her.)

Patient 48: "Mother, when I'm watching myself I'm learning and
hearing something about me. That's good." Would I actually say
that to her?

Therapist 49: No, I'm just asking you to try it now.

Patient 49: Okay. Mother, when I'm watching myself I'm learning
things about me and that's good (laughs).

Therapist 50: Okay. What does she answer?

Mother 50: Um. (Switches chair) Ah, did you take your vitamins
today? She's on a vitamin kick. (Therapist: Um hmm) You know,
like she doesn't really care. I mean I know that.

(Mother's response can be loosely translated as "What I am giving
you is good for you, so you better swallow it.")

Therapist 51: Okay. When she says, "Have you taken your vitamins?" what do you answer?

Patient 51: I took one this morning.

Therapist 52: What's your tone of voice saying to her?

Patient 52: It's saying, "Fuck off!"

Therapist 53: Would you say that straighter then, as to what you're
mad about in response to her.

Patient 53: Fuck off, Mother. I'm really getting tired of it, I am. I
mean, take your own vitamins, I'll take mine. I'll be more inclined
to, if you'll leave me alone. I'm sorry, but just don't bother me

anymore about them, all right? I'm tired of ya. I feel good when I say that, I really do.

Therapist 54: Uh hmm . . . Okay, so you were saying to her, "I don't want you standing over me all the time saying 'Have you done this, are you doing this, did you do right?' "

Patient 54: Yeah . . . God. Okay, here comes the protective part. I feel like she hasn't got anybody else.

Therapist 55: To stand over them and tell them how to run their life?

Patient 55: Really, yeah, Daddy quit listening to her years ago, and she never has any control over Abby and I was the only one left. I will admit I do feel sorry for her, but I torment her, though, and then I get mad at myself for doing it. (Therapist: Um hmm) Shit.

Therapist 56: So it's as if she really has to be telling somebody what to do. This is how she stays involved with somebody? (Patient: Um hmm) At this point, for various reasons, you are more "it" than anybody else.

(Again, I let Iris slide off to the direct empty chair confrontation into a "talking about." Under most circumstances this is bad form and to be clearly avoided. With Iris, however, I am having to coach and shape her into being able to contact the roles and her feelings. Her ability to do this does show an improvement not only between sessions but within them.)

Patient 56: Yeah . . . it really, you know, it gets to me. (Therapist: Uh huh) Because ah, well, she's always trying to get us all on diets for instance. Well, I could lose some weight, but frankly I'm down to a fairly good weight. I mean according to the scales. (Therapist: Um hmm) I don't feel bad. (Therapist: Uh huh) I don't want to go on a diet and so, you know, she eats all these icky-tasting diet foods. And frankly, I just like a good glass of plain milk. She gets powdered milk. It's cheaper and also nonfat. (Therapist: Uh hmm) I'm tired of that.

(It is certainly one of the curses of the middle class that parents frequently feel they have to keep after and keep after their children to do better, or else they are not doing a good job as parents. This also hides the parents' need to be needed. And, as far as the child is concerned, a critical parent is still better than no parent at all.)

Patient 57: (Laughs) Oh, she tried to improve herself all the time, or so she thinks.

Therapist 58: Until she or you are good enough for what?

Patient 58: Good enough for, I know, until she's good enough for herself. I guess 'til I'm good enough for her, too.

Therapist 59: And then what?

Patient 59: Nothing?

Therapist 60: Um hmm. So one day you're all improved. You've taken all the vitamins you can hold. You've lost weight down to some swell size eight or something. (Patient: laughs) Then what? Then when you're good enough, then what?

Patient 60: Then I'm not good enough. I'm never good enough.

Therapist 61: Okay, I guess what I think of is, so then what do you talk about? If you finally run out of ways for her to improve you and for you to be improved, what do you talk about?

(I'm really loading some messages in here: criticism doesn't help much with changing behavior, criticism substitutes for more genuine relating; you'll never please Mother; don't take her so seriously.)

Patient 61: Nothing, I guess. (Therapist: Yeah) Hell!

Therapist 62: So this is . . .

Patient 62: That keeps us together, sort of. (Therapist: Yeah) Like we haven't got anything else in common but hassling each other at this point. (Therapist: Yeah) Hardly, that is . . . yeah, I do parent her because I do perceive her as a child. I don't know.

Therapist 63: Let me give you something to think about a little bit. Um, are there any things the two of you have in common that you can enjoy? (Patient: Um) As opposed to those times when things are stickiest. So that you know automatically that if you come in wearing sloppy clothes or something, that she's going to fuss and you're going to fuss back and you know, there you go. So that (Patient: laughs) you can predict with certainty that if you bring up certain topics or look certain ways or you do certain things, you're in for it.

(This is me pushing again, possibly aware of the three session limitation and how much support rather than criticism this girl needs. Iris gets some criticism of Mother out along the way, but it ends up nowhere and deservedly so.)

Patient 63: That's pleasing to me and her.

Therapist 64: Yeah, versus those things that both of you, ah, get along pretty well in.

Patient 64: Let's see, anything I would do that I like and she likes, right? (Therapist: Uh hmm) Hmm . . . I can think of, you know, like hobbies we have in common, but that's about as far as it goes. (Therapist: Um hmm) I can't think of a single thing really. Nothing . . . because every time we're in a situation, I feel like she's pushing me. (Therapist: Um hmm) Either into or out of it.

Therapist 65: Part of what you're saying then is that there might be some things that would be okay and that you would enjoy with her except for her having to push as much as she does. (Patient: Yeah) Or to use every occasion to improve you or tell you how to do it . . .

Patient 65: She really does. She always is. (Therapist: Yeah) No, nothing, I'd just as soon be with somebody else. Oh, I don't I don't completely mean that. I have the feeling . . .

Therapist 66: Okay. Let's see if this is a more accurate statement: "Most of the time there are other people I have a lot more in common with, enjoy more. There are sometimes when it would be very nice if we could have a peaceable evening, dinner, or something . . ." (Patient: Yeah) And make contact, huh?

Patient 66: Yeah. Talk on the same level on the same subject. Oh, that sounds like I'm an intellectual snob. Frankly, against her I feel like one. I don't feel that is terrible to say. I really, I feel like one against her.

Therapist 67: Okay. "In some things I know more and . . ." (Patient: I do.) Okay.

Patient 67: Come to think of it, I do. Um . . . yeah, she has a tendency to agree with my sister on things. She won't ever agree with me.

Therapist 68: So she would not recognize your brightness.

Patient 68: No, she doesn't. That always bothers me. She seemed to prefer Abby to me. I don't resent Abby, I don't. I think she's about the best friend I've got. But, I don't know, it just makes me resent Mother more.

Therapist 69: Can you tell her you're bright, there are some things you know a lot about?

(Again I'm feeling it important to help her assert herself and her positive characteristics against the massive critical top dog, both inside her head and a little bit in reality with her mother. She has many resentments we could explore, but with the limited time we have, supporting her self-assertiveness and positive self-concept takes precedence.)

Patient 69: Yeah, I'm, I'm intelligent, Mother, I'm bright and I do know some stuff that you don't know . . . depending on what the subject is (laughs) especially. (Therapist: Yep) Um, and, I'm, I know enough to eat enough of the right foods and where I'm not going to drop dead next week. I know how to ride a horse and you can't tell me I don't, because I do, Goddamn it! (Sighs) Um, if I don't want to go to the "Y," I don't want to go to the "Y." You go ahead, but I don't want to do it. Don't try to drag me into it. And if I don't want to go to Dagmar's and play music, quit trying to push me.

Therapist 70: Okay. That tone of voice sounded straighter to me, as if that's a straighter message to her than what you were saying a while ago. "Yeah, I took my vitamins." (Patient: Yeah [laughs]) One thing I'm aware of, and we're about out of time today, is that I wanted to give you something to take away, and I think it makes some sense . . . Ah, as you were talking to your mother, and about her, that some of the main things she does to improve you or make you healthy, wealthy and wise, to say, if you swallow things, vitamins, food, or don't swallow things, vitamins, food, this can do the trick; and I'm wondering if that's where you thought of drugs and alcohol. This is Mother one step removed; "By just taking the right things, it's going to make you feel good."

Patient 70: Ah, I think I really did that out of spite, because, um, I know, she doesn't like it . . .

Therapist 71: But she's saying certain things you jolly well better take, like vitamins and other things.

Patient 71: That's what I was thinking, 'cause it was bad for me. (Therapist: Yeah) But that's a thought, I guess, as to why I did that.

Therapist 72: It's one way of saying, "Fuck you, Mother." But it's also saying a little bit too much, "Fuck you, Iris," at the same time. (Iris has said earlier that she's reduced the amount of drugs and alcohol she uses, but since this was one of her original big problems, I'm glad to have a chance to put in some reasons for her not to overdo them. Implying that she's pleasing Mother when she does is both accurate and, I hope, blocking of such behavior. It's also gratifying that Iris is now responding with insight to my connecting bits and pieces, rather than seeing me as being critical.)

Patient 72: (Laughs) Oh God! Yeah, I guess it is. I didn't think of it . . . hmm, she gets in every time, doesn't she! Oh, well.

Therapist 73: So she's a pretty smart woman, so you've got to be smart too.

Patient 73: (Laughs) Yeah. I still know more about dope than she does. I just can't tell her so, or how I know. Oh wow, yeah!

Therapist 74: Okay. Any other thing before you go? (Patient: No. Nothing.) Okay. See you next week.

Patient 74: Okay. Do I just sit in here and wait for Jerry?

Therapist 75: Ah, I think go on out there, I think he'll see you in another room. I like your, ah, pants patches.

(While I doubt that I had this in mind at the time, in retrospect it appears that I am supporting Iris's mild rebelliousness while at the same time indicating that I have observed her and like what I see.)

After the second session Iris reported that some new "things" occurred to her. She remembered that Dr. Fagan pointed out to her that she was rubbing the grandfather's chair with her foot while in a dialogue with him. This seemed to make her aware that she was uncomfortable and her grandfather was comforting her. Iris was aware of not wanting to let go of her grandfather and she reported that she expressed her hostile feelings toward her mother during the session and, as a result, felt relieved, calmer and "taller" at the end of the session. She remembered talking about how her mother is "always trying to improve me," and the relationship of this to her taking things orally, and, in turn, to her use of drugs to avoid depression. Iris felt "more aware of my stomach and my head . . . of my bodily actions," in this session. She gave the chair rubbing episode as an example of this, along with the dialogue with her mother. When talking with her mother she felt "more and more anger and joy when I felt like I hurt her," that she was "getting back at her." Iris related that she felt better toward herself mostly resulting from her catharsis with her mother, but that she had not really changed significantly in other ways. She again said she liked Dr. Fagan and that she felt more "used to her," even though she still felt self-conscious with her. Iris mentioned that she liked Dr. Fagan's smiles and Dr. Fagan's observations, interpretations or explanations; she reported viewing Dr. Fagan as "sort of omnipotent." Recalling the therapist's intervention, "What are you doing with your hands now?" Iris felt that whatever she answered would make sense and "fit right into the context." She appreciated that the therapist took her "seriously," meaning that Dr. Fagan accepted her feelings. Again Iris remarked that she disliked switching chairs and being two different people. However, she did feel that this was beneficial for her, and she felt that she "got into it fairly good" during the session. Dr. Fagan's feeding words to her and actually talking to her as if she were Grandfather seemed to help her "get into it," Iris said. (Fleischer, 1973, pp. 57-58)

SESSION 3

Therapist 1: (Who is fifteen minutes late) I managed to miss the time or put the time down wrong today, so . . .

Patient 1: Oh. That's all right. I was sitting there reading, so . . . it doesn't matter.

Therapist 2: So, good morning.

Patient 2: Good morning.

Therapist 3: You're looking quite cheery today.

Patient 3: Yeah, I'm a little sleepy. But I had a real good time last night. I just feel good. I feel about to fall asleep, too. (Laughs)

Therapist 4: Looks like something is going on in your head.

Patient 4: (Pause) Yeah . . . I, I always feel uncomfortable in these silences, you know. Like if the therapist doesn't ask a question, I've got to think of something. I always feel uncomfortable until something gets going.

Therapist 5: Ah, I guess I was assuming that I had very quietly put a question on the floor in the middle of us which was—wondering what's been going on in your head since last week and what would you like to do today?

Patient 5: Oh, I don't know. It's hard to think. I don't know, not that much has been going on in my head really. If I wasn't so sleepy it would be all right. I don't know what I want to do. I guess I'm not much help . . . I don't know.

Therapist 6: Are you sort of blanking yourself out again?

Patient 6: I don't know if I'm really doing that. I just get different things on my mind, and that does push other things out. I mean, I can't think of things that bother me until they're bothering me. And right now, the only thing that's bothering me is that I can't think of anything. So . . .

(Back to blankness in starting a session. This time, however, we have a relationship and a past base of support so that tackling this might be more successful. Since Iris has several times before responded to my being humorous, I decided to try to exaggerate her being bothered about not being bothered.)

Therapist 7: Okay. Would you try to be *very* bothered about it . . . ?

Patient 7: Very bothered about . . .

Therapist 8: See how much bother you can accumulate.

Patient: (Laughs) Well, yeah, I don't want to waste your time, you know, or their time, or like that.

(It looks like part of Iris's blankness is the same kind of phenomenon that creates blocking on exams; becoming so aware of the process of thinking or trying to remember that the brain simply cannot go about its business of actually remembering. Another part of this is being aware of the expectations of the critical top dog observers, and being able to defeat them passively-aggressively by blanking herself out.)

Therapist 9: That would be terrible, wouldn't it? (Patient: Right.) All these big, important people around, and waiting for you to do something.

Patient 9: Oh, wow! . . . Yeah, well, I guess I like it that way. I don't know, when you say stuff like, "That would be terrible." I know it's ridiculous, too, but . . . I just get nervous about it.

Therapist 10: I keep getting the idea from what you're saying that there is a standard of behavior that other people have in mind for you. "I'm expecting you to act in a certain way. Act right!" And you sort of come in here, you know, several feet down, and you sort of wait to see what I'm going to tell you to do. And I've got all the important words, and all the ones you've got the squatty, weak, little, short words.

Patient 10: That sounds about right. (Laughs)

Therapist 11: Would you be willing to do something on that?

Patient 11: I guess so.

Therapist 12: Ah, would you be willing to try exaggerating that even more? (Patient: Ah, yeah, ah . . .) Okay. I have a specific suggestion. Okay . . . if you'll get up . . . Would you get down on the floor? Okay. Look way up. (Patient: All right.) Okay. And I think your words start off something like, "I don't know what in the world to do."

Tiny Patient 12: Okay. I don't know what in the world to do. I'm so small. My God, what am I going to do? All these people. They all expect me to be something that I'm not.

(The underdog finally shows up! After being invisible in the first session, she now exists, though in a very puny, tiny state.)

Therapist 13: All right. If this feels right to you, "Please tell me what to do. I haven't any idea."

Tiny Patient 13: Please tell me what to do. I don't have any idea. (Therapist: Um hmm) There you are. (Laughs, points up) I can't be me. I have to do what you say, or nothing. Therapist: Um hmm) Oh God, I feel puny.

Therapist 14: My guess is that you have a crick in your neck, that should hurt somewhat.

Patient 14: Oh, I don't notice it so much. I just feel like, "Pshew!" small.

Therapist 15: Um hmm. Okay, would you be the other part of this now. (Patient: Augh!) That's a kind of wobbly chair to stand on, so just, ah . . .

Patient 15: I'd rather not stand on a chair really. I get shaky. (Therapist: Okay.) Ah . . .

Therapist 16: "You down there!"

Giant Patient 16: I can't find me. Oh, Okay. (Laughs) Um, let me think. Get out of my way! There's no one, um . . . You're so insignificant I can't even see you. You know, you look about like an English pea down there, and if you don't get out of my way, I'm liable to trip and step on you. I mean, my God, I can't look out for you. I can hardly see you as it is.

Therapist 17: "You're not even worth my time" or . . .

Giant Patient 17: Yeah, I mean, you know, I'm sorry, but . . .

Therapist 18: "nothing personal . . ."

Giant Patient 18: Yeah, that's right, but hell! You're so little I can't even find you hardly, let alone look out for you. I don't know what you want. How can anybody know what an English pea wanted anyway? (Laughs) You're somewhere in that little patch right there. I'm sorry, I mean, I'd help you if I could see you, but hell, you're so little.

Therapist 19: Okay. Would you see what the English pea has to say?

Pea 19: (Laughs) Go to hell! Got a mouth on her, all right, that English pea.

(The underdog not only exists, it is apparent she also has access to some feelings and can assert herself feeling-wise, even when she is about to be squashed. This feels like an indication of real progress.)

Therapist 20: Um hmm. Okay. The English pea doesn't like being genteelly brushed aside. Anything else to say?

Pea 20: Yeah. I'll sit here if I want to. If I don't want to roll away, you'll just have to step over me . . . If you don't want to do that, that's too damn bad. You know, you're so tall I can't find your head either. Being one, then the other makes me wonder which one's Iris. When I'm this little I can't see the top of the other one's head and when I'm that one, I can't see me down here, so . . .

Therapist 21: So it's almost like you're not seeing each other at all.

Patient 21: Yeah. Okay. That's it. That's a nice one.

Therapist 22: Anything else you want to say to her?

Patient 22: No, not really. (Therapist: Okay.) It's not worth my time either.

Therapist 23: Okay. Anything you want to say to her? (Referring to reversed position)

Patient 23: Um . . . No, still can't see her. Yeah, that's it. I don't have anything else to say. (Therapist: Okay.) That's strange.

Therapist 24: Um hmm. You were grinning through a lot of that like you were enjoying it . . .

Patient 24: Oh, I enjoyed it, really! I mean, when I was standing right here I could picture me down there; when I was down there I was having a little trouble, but I felt better. It's really neat. (Laughs)

Therapist 25: Um hmm. Anything you want to say to me now?
(While the top dog and underdog are not centered, Iris clearly says she's gotten something and has been able to assert herself.)

Patient 25: No, not in particular. Just it . . . no, it just seemed like there was a lot of distance between the two.

Therapist 26: It sure seemed like the big one had all the power. She could move around and get things done. (Patient: Um) And the little one didn't like it (Patient: Um) How much of your power to get things done, then, do you want to give to me or other people? How much do you want to keep?
(In Th 26, I come back to where we started at the beginning of the first session; that Iris does not have access to her power or responsibility.)

Patient 26: Um . . . I don't really know. 'Cause if I say I'd like to be able to do it all myself, I start thinking about that's a lot to have to do and I don't know if I want to do all that. (Therapist: Um hmm) So, I don't know. It'll probably be safe to say fifty-fifty, at this point. (Therapist: Um hmm) That probably would be what it would even out to be.
(I really miss here. In Th 26 I ask Iris about giving power to other people, and she answers directly, opening a big door. I can't think of any good reason for not following this up.)

Therapist 27: I'm hearing your head saying that, though, more than your insides, because these two ended up without doing much reconciling. They just sort of agreed they'd ignore each other.

Patient 27: Yeah. (Laughs) I guess they did. Um. (Long pause) It wasn't that uncomfortable being the tall one. I guess it was because, because I didn't have to squinch up.

Therapist 28: Um hmm. You're saying you feel good but you also have to ignore part of you. (Patient: Um) "I can't really see you from here."

Patient 28: Ah. I don't want to answer too quickly. I'm not sure. (Therapist: Um) Maybe I'm just looking for a way to agree. I don't know. But yes, when I feel good I do try to ignore that which makes me feel bad. (Therapist: Um hmm) I don't see what's wrong with that, but . . .

Therapist 29: It's sort of like what you were saying earlier, um, "I can't remember about feeling bad unless I'm feeling bad."

Patient 29: Yeah. That's true. (Long pause)

Therapist 30: What's happening?

Patient 30: Oh, I was thinking about the class I was going to take this fall, and about in the group therapy how lucky it was my class is over at 3:30, 'cause our therapy was changed to start at 3:30 instead of 3:00. So . . .

Therapist 31: So that part of your life is meshing nicely?

Patient 31: Yeah, it seems to be now.

(Following TH 29 and my side trip, Iris doesn't make much use of this observation. This time, in her retreat into her head, she is thinking about something that is happening good for her rather than being self-critical. This feels like a considerable achievement. There are no particular clues as to where to go next so I make an observation from her gestures. She responds with a description with no discernable self-criticism!)

Therapist 32: (Pause) You're playing with your shirttail, now.

Patient 32: Um. Yes. It's a little frayed right there. I keep rolling it under and I find a place where some of the stitches are starting to come loose.

Therapist 33: Um hmm. As you do, would you be describing your shirt, and would you describe it in the first person? Um, "I've got some places I'm coming loose here." Try it. Describe it.

Shirt 33: Yeah, I'm loose right here at the corners where it feels sewn, I can't feel some of my stitches. Yeah, I can. Some of my stitches are all pulled out. Um, some of me isn't holding myself together.

Therapist 34: Um hmm. "And if I tuck me under, maybe I won't show."

Patient 34: Yeah. Of course, it doesn't ever look right exactly. It always unrolls, but it's fun to do, too. Tuck it under like that neatly and hold it a while. Seems like maybe it would stay.

Therapist 35: "Seems like I'd stay"?

Shirt 35: Seems like I'd stay. Yeah, and I let it go and it starts . . . (Therapist: Um hmm) undoing again. And then here's a part I found that, of me, that I don't want to say, is, "that isn't well put together at all." Well, it's not fixed the way it once was. Which I didn't notice at first, but there it is. It's that one little part right here that seems to be holding it together. I don't know how or for how long. It looks kind of weird.

Therapist 36: Say that about you now and see if it makes any sense to you.

Patient 36: Okay. There is a part of me in the middle that seems to be holding together, but it looks weak and I don't know for how long it'll be that way, it'll be strong . . . Because it looks weak. I look weak. (Therapist: Uh huh) I was thinking of that the first time I said it . . . Ah, I don't know why I won't keep those as it's my head and my stomach over here. (Therapist: Uh huh) But it just seems natural . . . Maybe because I don't notice my stomach as easily as I do my head.

Therapist 37: What would you call the part of you that's staying well sewed together?

Patient 37: I was just thinking of that and I decided I'd call it my throat. (Therapist: Um hmm) I mean it came to my head and I thought about it and it made sense that way. Like I don't a lot of time, most of the time, I have trouble crying when I need to if I'm around somebody. I don't as much in front of you as, say, any other woman therapist. Although I feel at ease with one, I do have trouble with her. I have to stay calm in here, I guess, so these two won't show (pointing to throat, then stomach and head), and hold them together.

(While Iris "blanked out" and changed the subject in P 30, following opening up in P 28 the possibility of feeling bad, she now comes back via speaking for her shirt. Finding an object for protection, describing it objectively, then reassimilating the projection is often a valuable way of getting in touch with oneself. In Th 33 through 37 I have no idea of where any of this is heading, but simply encourage her to move through the process.)

Therapist 38: As long as . . . that stays stitched up, then these won't come apart.

Patient 38: Mercy, what a shirt. (Laughs) Yeah! (Therapist: laughs)

Therapist 39: What does crying or not crying mean to you?

(Again a closing of the circle as to where we started with the first session and Iris's depression. Her tears and her sadness re-emerge.)

Patient 39: Um, well in front of someone, I hate to admit that crying still makes me feel I'm weak in front of them, like I'm vulnerable and I'm easily embarrassed and . . . (Therapist: Um hmm) I just, I hate to be that way, but I still am.

Patient 40: Yeah, yeah, like . . . I don't know how else to explain it but to me it's a sign of weakness for *me* to cry. I don't mind if other people do it, usually.

Therapist 40: But you shouldn't be weak or vulnerable. (Patient: Yeah) Or said another way, letting your feelings or hurting show, this would make you vulnerable.

Patient 41: Uh huh, and I also did that since realizing it. And crying, while I'm doing it, I feel . . . I feel small. (Therapist: Um hmm)

And I feel like somebody's laughing at me too, and I don't like that at all.

Therapist 41: So it's not only small, but it's put down (Patient: Um). Humiliated.

Patient 42: Yeah . . . So a lot of times it's hard for me to cry in front of anyone. I usually go off by myself.

Therapist 42: So you are then trying to take care of your feelings of hurt by yourself. (Patient: Uh huh) Away from everyone else. (Patient: Uh huh) I'm hearing you say then that you've got some tears in you that make you aware periodically of either feeling like crying or of wanting to. (Patient: Ah, yeah) Where did this message come from about not crying? And about being ridiculed?

Patient 43: Well, again, just before you brought that up, it was just a few minutes ago, I was remembering about, see, this is hard to explain, recently my sister got mad at me for something. I mentioned her paranoia to someone. And she told, just blessed me out. She said, "I'm tired of all your God-damned manias and everything!" which I pretty well . . .

Therapist 43: I didn't hear you. All your God-damn what??

Patient 44: Manias. And I didn't want to say too much to her because I don't know what she'd do. She can hit me or something, and make me feel worse or something like that. And do I just because, you know, like don't mention anything like that around her anymore. And that's happened on several different occasions over the years, so that simply came to mind. I can't dwell on things that I'm talking about due to crying. I don't know if I'd run away from that or not. I think I did.

Therapist 44: I'm, I'm not clear on what you were telling me about the argument with your sister. Somewhere in it you said to her, "You're being paranoid"? (Patient: Yeah) and she said, "I'm tired of you calling me fancy names"?

Patient 45: Well, I, I was telling her that I was feeling that way. And she said, I'm tired of hearing that . . ." Really, she said, "I'm tired of hearing about your problems." That's it. (Therapist: Um hmm) But I forgot what you asked me. Would you repeat it? Or can you remember now?

(It's hard to tell here whether Iris is having a really powerful blanking out, or whether she's reaching back to Th 43 where I raised the question about her "Don't cry" injunction.)

Therapist 45: Okay. Let me try to do a little thinking out loud. Um, sister was then saying to you, "If you've got problems, don't tell me about them. (Patient: Yeah) I'm tired of putting up with you."

(Patient: Yeah) Um, and she was also then saying, "If you're hurting, don't come around until it disappears."

Patient 46: Uh huh. Okay. That's what you asked me about, yeah. I've gotten that message a lot.

Therapist 46: So that part of you is often told to disappear as far as your family is concerned.

Patient 47: Ah, at least as far as she is concerned. I'm trying to remember the other two.

Therapist 47: (Pause) Is there a kind of family motto that says, um, "When we hurt we keep to ourselves and don't show it"?

Patient 48: Oh, no. Because when my mother hurts, she lets everybody know. And she can get hurt over the silliest things; well, to me they're silly.

Therapist 48: Okay. She, then overdoes this to the extent that it gets kind of embarrassing or feels goopy?

Patient 49: Yeah. Well like, ah, when my sister got married for the first time, I came home from school and Mother said, "Abbey's married!" And she looked at me just like, "Oh, isn't that terrible! You better cry too." And I didn't care really. I sat down with her, but I couldn't work up any emotion. I was tired . . . (Therapist: Yeah) And I wanted something to eat. And so in that respect I get a little sick of it myself.

Therapist 49: Um hmm. So then there are two things your family does. If they're hurt they either make a big display of it, or, not willing to do that, they don't mention it.

Patient 50: Yeah. And now Daddy, ah, he, he doesn't mention it that much to anybody. I don't see him that much, 'cause he works all the time, you know. Say, like his taxes are, you know, getting real bad or something, he needs more money or something like that. He's bothered. He just more or less whines about all this, he whines to me sometimes, and I feel sorry for the man. I want to help him and, I, I can't really. (Therapist: Um hmm) And so that's another one, um.

Therapist 50: So you don't like whining either as a way of expressing being hurt.

Patient 51: No, I don't know what to do. It makes me feel bad. I'm sorry it's that way. But I can't help it, that's the way . . . He should have planned for that earlier.

Therapist 51: His whining makes you feel helpless.

Patient 52: Yeah, it does. There you are.

Therapist 52: I'm hearing you saying, then, when it comes to expressing your hurting, you don't want to make other people feel helpless or overloaded in such a way that they, "Augh."

Patient 53: I want them to cheer me up, and if I bring them down, they can't. (Therapist: Um humm) And so I feel like I'm bothering them. So, I'd rather just go off by myself and get it out of my system, not to be embarrassed by the display of it or not bother them in any way. And not have them to tell me just to shape up. Yeah, that's it. So, I'd rather be by myself than do that.

Therapist 53: Um hmm. Of all the responses other people can make when I'm feeling bad, most of them are bad. Most of them make you feel worse.

Patient 54: Yeah. One time, one time I got the right response. It was from Noel, who's my boyfriend, and I was telling him I didn't pass the review in art. It's something you go through. And I'm still in the program and I just didn't pass yet. And I was feeling bad about that. He didn't say a single thing, he just listened. (Therapist: Um hmm) And after I finished there was a bit of a pause and he said, "Yeah, the music department's pretty rough to get through, too." That's all he said, and that felt good. Nobody does that, so I must do something wrong.

Therapist 54: So, ah, putting your feelings out then involves almost no chance of getting a response back that you like.

Patient 55: Yeah, that's true, but . . .

Therapist 55: At least by putting your feelings out in any way that your family showed you. (Patient: I know.) Okay. (overlapping) Excuse me. Go on with your . . .

Patient 56: No, I just said it's terrific, I mean this whole little sequence worked out so well. I mean, like I got my head cleared up as far as this goes, and I feel like I found out something I didn't know before.

Therapist 56: What is that?

Patient 57: About crying, why I won't do it in front of anyone. I often wondered exactly what it was myself. And it's all three things.

(This feels like a real important knowing and a kind of victory. It is clearer as to why the expression of sadness is so difficult for Iris and why she has not been able to let herself grieve. The support from her boyfriend feels poignant in that this minimal support is the one time she says she got some kind of genuine response. This sequence illustrates the depressive paradox: people become depressed from experiencing too little of their genuine sadness, not from being enmeshed in too much.)

Patient 58: Yeah, Mother, Abby, Daddy . . . I just . . . that's terrific. (Laughs) (Therapist: Good) You were starting to say something.

Therapist 57: Okay. Nothing that I don't think that wasn't simply repeating what you were just saying.

Patient 59: (Long pause) I wish I wasn't so sleepy. I feel like I have a head full of hot cotton. I got stoned last night. It took a while before I could get to bed.

Therapist 58: Was it a good stoned?

(Another piece of Iris's blankness is coming up, tied in with her use of drugs and possibly overextending herself slightly physically.)

Patient 60: It was, I enjoyed it . . . Only had three hits. That's all I needed.

Therapist 59: Sounds like it was good stuff.

Patient 61: It was. I was at the concert at the auditorium and it was real nice with all the music and everything. (Therapist: Um hmm) Of course, by the time we left I could walk, so it was all right. I'm often rather tired the next day from staying up so late.

Therapist 60: Um hmm. Kind of before that you were feeling like your head had cotton in it. And I'm thinking it sure feels like a big chunk of stuff that needs wrestling with, or how often your head does seem to feel blank or cottony or not much in there. And it's sort of like, at a lot of times, some of which may be important, some not, something comes in there and says, "Don't think too clearly. Don't remember very well." And I'm thinking, getting rid of that message and that set of instructions is something which will probably take some good wrestling with. I don't think we can do much more today other than saying that it's important to give your head back to you.

Patient 62: When nobody's talking to me or anything, my thoughts just run on and on and on and on. And those people I only talk with, I guess superficially is the right word, I don't know, but small talk like what you think of them and so, actually I thought it was not that. But when they start asking things about me, well, it gets to be such a muddle. There's so much in me and so little I want to say. Lots of times, yeah, I do get really spacy and I don't really say much that really makes sense to anybody, really. Just . . . I don't know. Too much to explain that they don't understand it at all. Lot of times I just don't want to, and it does get rather blank in there.

Therapist 61: Sounds like you're saying two things. Both that your head gets blank and somehow, even though your words kind of follow, the way you put 'em out are such that a lot of people are not going to understand very well anyway. (Patient: Um hmm) So, if you've got words people can easily misunderstand 'em. If you don't . . . what follows often . . . (Lost)

Patient 63: Yeah. Well, lot of times people I've found are not even listening. And I'm like that. I mean . . .

(Another part of the blankness has to do with not really believing people will listen to her anyway.)

Therapist 62: You don't say, "Hey listen!"

Patient 64: I'm sure I have. I don't make a rule of it, no. They don't listen a lot and I feel like I'm just babbling on, so I either do just babble on until I get tired or I don't say anything at all. People have told me I'm a good listener. Really, I'm not. If I'm feeling good, I have my mind on something else and I can handle the comments along sort of halfway listening, and that makes them happy. And . . .

Therapist 63: That's the way people are hearing you when you talk?

Patient 65: I think they do, really. And so . . . (Therapist: Okay) So, I really don't listen to them.

Therapist 64: So it's both, then, how to make words available in your head. (Patient: Um hmm) And how to choose your words in such a way that you are saying something which you want to to other people. (Patient: Yeah) Sort of like taming words in a way and having them available to you. (Patient: Um hmm) And I heard then a lot of the words that you didn't get taught about too well are those having to do with you and your own feelings, especially hurting ones. So it's almost at times like you can't remember or you can't think about it. And I expect the words you have most trouble with, with other people are words that try to say some of those things. "This is how I'm feeling." Ah, "This is me" and especially those words that tell, "I'm not feeling so good."

Patient 66: Yeah. Well, you know, that's right. That makes it sound like there's either so much or so little there I really don't know at times how I'm feeling. I start thinking well, maybe I don't feel that way and I just think I feel that way maybe. So I just don't fool around with things like that that much. But like I say, I really don't think they care. 'Cause, well, okay, quite frankly. I don't care what they're doing either, and that's the truth, I don't. Abby said I was conceited and she's right. I am. I figure as long as a person thinks I care and I'm happy knowing I don't, then it's all right. 'Cause it's usually not a crisis for them anyway. If I was in need too much, I'd try to find somebody who does care.

Therapist 65: Would you listen to your voice as you remember it in your head right now? What is it saying?

(I'm hearing several things here: Iris's passivity and lack of power and responsibility and her not expressing her feelings. She has been successful before in hearing her voice tone as saying, something more real than her words and she responds with awareness.)

Patient 67: I know that I can't express this. It's like . . . like I'm giving up so easily.

Therapist 66: Um hmm. I was hearing a real flat deadish sort of quality. Something like, "This is the way it is. There's nothing to be done. And what the hell." (Patient: Um hmm) I think what I'm hearing you talk about is the degree to which at times you really feel very separate from and out of reach of other people, out of reach from yourself and partially this is okay, you can take care of yourself and not disappear, or hurt yourself or whatever, but still there's a big gap there. And I'm hearing in part to cover that gap you are saying, "Well, it really doesn't matter" and "Not much to be done about it anyway."

Patient 68: Yeah, that, ah, sounds like what I said.

Therapist 67: I guess I'm hearing some sadness there.

Patient 69: I can't believe my mind's going blank again.

Therapist 68: Something I've found in myself and in other people, that sometimes when I fog out is when something is right there. (Patient: Um hmm) And I can almost feel just like a fog descends. (Patient: Exactly.) And at that point, the words are lost and I can't remember anything and I have to say, "That felt like it was very important; say it again very slowly in words of one syllable; let me repeat it after you."

Patient 70: Um hmm. That's exactly the way it goes.

Therapist 69: So that may be a very good clue. A friend of mine calls this a "truth signal." And different people have different truth signals. Some people's stomach may start hurting suddenly. Somebody else may have trouble swallowing, or whatever else. But it says, "At this particular point something important is going on. It's a true, important thing." So when you feel that happening to you, you can say, "Aha! Something important is going on."

Patient 71: And then when I run after it and it's lost . . . That's the trouble.

Therapist 70: If you run after it on your own, frequently, it is impossible.

Patient 72: Yeah, I think, boy, that's lost. I still have some vague notion of it.

Therapist 71: At that point, what it does take is asking me to repeat it.

Patient 73: Yeah, that's true . . . At that time I was starting to feel a little sadness too. (Therapist: Um hmm) There's still some of it around. Not much, but it came on about when that blank . . . I'm thinking about gaps.

(This series beginning with Th 67 feels very important. I begin by going back to her sadness and this emerges as the possible final condition for blankness. I now define her blankness as saying something important or signaling something important and positive going on with her, and at P 73 she is able to furnish her own support after I say it's okay to ask for mine, undo the blankness and recall what was happening that led up to it.)

Therapist 72: What was that?

Patient 74: (Gestures—draws a gap) "Pssht!" And you have to stoop under it. That kind of gap.

Therapist 73: So, therefore you are having a real clear kind of image feeling.

Patient 75: That I can do. (Therapist: Um hmm) That I can do. (Therapist: Um hmm) Like the sea and the sod or whatever.

Therapist 74: Along with that image, then, a feeling of what a big gap that was.

Patient 76: Yeah, it's like I mean if I move an inch or two backwards or forwards too far, I know it isn't that.

(Iris is giving herself credit for what she does well here.)

Therapist 75: Okay. We've got about five minutes. And I'm wondering since this is the last time, uh, anything you need to finish up or that you'd like to say to me about what we've been doing.

Patient 77: I don't know. I kind of like this sort of stuff really. Honestly, I've gotten more out of these three sessions than I have certainly with equal time in with any other therapy. I've been in three different ones already before this one. And . . . I feel like I got a lot out of today. I just . . . it's pretty nifty. I'm always off playing with my shirt or a piece of the rug or something.

Therapist 76: Uh huh. So these are some ways then that let you hear you better (Patient: Yes). And something I think you are struggling with are ways of getting you clearly into view, of hearing you better and taking care of the blank periods. (Patient: Um hmm) And, ah, these are sure procedures you can use for yourself. When you say, "Gee I gone blank right now," you can simply be aware of what you're doing and try to see what kinds of words would go with that. And what you hear you say, in words, is one way of getting words back into you even when you're not expecting to.

Patient 78: Okay. It is really nice, now that I know. It's not so hard.

Therapist 77: I sure have appreciated your willingness to do this.

Patient 79: No trouble at all.

Therapist 78: Now I want to say something positive to you, so don't cut out too soon. (Patient: Laughs) I sure feel you looking very hard to get something out of you. Working very hard at it. And, um . . . it's as if there are lots of hurdles and blocks and obstacles and your kind of blank-outs, and in trying to avoid them 'cause I sure know there's a lot of them there. And I can appreciate how hard it is to get into it. Just forcing won't do. I sure feel you pushing ahead over those obstacles.

(I leave Iris with a very genuine appreciation of her willingness to work, of the difficulty of the internal struggle she is having and of liking for her. I find my words here don't communicate this as well as I would liked to, but I also have no doubt but what she has heard this. I am very pleased with what, to me, feels like real progress in these three sessions. I note on review that we have touched on all of the issues she gave as her original presenting problem.)

Patient 80: Well, thank you.

Therapist 79: Okay, then. Good luck to you.

Patient 81: Thank you. Nice knowing you.

Therapist 80: Goodbye.

Iris felt that she experienced "a couple of revelations about myself," during the third and final session. She became very aware of how she blanks her thoughts out and "why" she does not cry in front of others. She became aware of why she does not cry in public when Dr. Fagan asked her from whom she got the message about crying and pursued this until the patient recalled her parents' messages about showing sadness and hurting. Iris recalled the dialogue between her "big" and "small" internal persons, and how Dr. Fagan attended to her small voice, reflecting this.

With regard to the dialogue involving her shirt, the patient recalled being requested to carry out the dialogue in the first person, and finally experiencing herself as a "rather frayed person," and as "being split into three parts." She experienced the therapist as competent and she explained this in terms of the therapist having allowed her to deal with whatever she wandered off to and "that brings me back to whatever we're discussing, which was me," as Iris stated. She reported no particular changes in her experiencing of the therapist. She appreciated Dr. Fagan's acceptance of her feelings, and cited an example of another therapist who considered her "ridiculous" when she cried with him. No resentments of the therapist were reported.

Iris felt that her Gestalt Therapy experience as a whole was "better" than any other therapy she had experienced.[3] She seemed most impressed with Dr. Fagan's use of her "wanderings" so that she felt she could stop "blaming myself for wasting time" in therapy. The patient felt that in other therapies it took her quite a while to "get down to anything," while such was not the case in this particular therapy experience. Stating that "a week is a pretty short time to say that I've grown," Iris nevertheless felt she had gained some new learnings in the therapy. As far as her behavior outside therapy, she said there had been no changes, and she felt that it was too early to tell if her feelings about herself had changed.

Iris never felt domineered or controlled by the therapist, nor did she ever feel that there was not enough concern or direction by the therapist. Iris felt that the post-session interview had affected her behavior slightly. She felt that she had not adequately answered the questions specifically referring to Dr. Fagan, and so she tried to attend more to what the therapist was doing in the last session. She said this change was small, however. Like the therapist, Iris had difficulty selecting what she felt was the most productive session. She chose the second session, specifically remembering her dialogue with her grandfather. She felt she chose that session because "it stayed with me," but she also felt that the third session was quite productive for her (Fleischer, 1973, pp. 58-59).

NOTES

1. The main exception being family sessions in Gestalt-experiential style as presented by Kempler (1973).

2. Tapes of the three sessions are available for $15.00 from the writer (Department of Psychology, Georgia State University, 33 Gilmer St. SE, Atlanta, Georgia 30303).

3. Her previous therapy had been with psychology graduate students who were relatively inexperienced.

REFERENCES

Ellis, A. *Growth Through Reason.* Palo Alto, Calif.: Science and Behavior Books, 1971.

Fleischer, J. A. *An Observational-Descriptive Case Study in Gestalt Therapy.* Unpublished doctoral dissertation, University of Tennessee, 1973.

Haley, J., and L. Hoffman. *Techniques of Family Therapy.* New York: Basic Books, 1967.

Kempler, W. "Gestalt Therapy," in R. Corsini (ed.) *Current Psychotherapies.* Itasca, Ill.: Peacock, 1973, 251-286.

Kogan, G. *The History, Philosophy and Practice of Gestalt Therapy.* (Doctoral dissertation, University of California, Berkeley.) Ann Arbor, Mich.: University Microfilms, 1974. No. 74-1329.

Latner, J. *The Gestalt Therapy Book.* New York: Julian Press, 1973.

Part IV

PERSPECTIVES AND RESOURCES

CHAPTER 29

LIMITATIONS AND CAUTIONS IN THE GESTALT APPROACH

IRMA LEE SHEPHERD, Ph.D.

Irma Lee Shepherd is professor of psychology and director of postgraduate training at the Institute for Psychological Services, Inc., Georgia State University, Atlanta. Dr. Shepherd is a diplomate of the American Board of Examiners of Professional Psychology, and a member of the executive council of the American Academy of Psychotherapists. She is also coeditor of *Gestalt Therapy Now*.

Reprinted with permission from I. L. Shepherd, "Limitations and Cautions in the Gestalt Approach," in J. Fagan and I. L. Shepherd, eds., **Gestalt Therapy Now**, Palo Alto, California: Science and Behavior Books, 1970.

New approaches and innovations, often welcomed by jaded professionals, may stir up both enthusiasm and skepticism. The skeptic may avoid discovering and utilizing valuable insights and skills; the enthusiast may overextend the usefulness into indiscriminate application, with glowing promises that cannot be fulfilled. It is to the latter that this article is directed. Gestalt Therapy offers powerful techniques for intervention into neurotic and self-defeating behaviors, and for mobilizing and redirecting human energy into self-supporting and creating development. The work of Perls, Simkin, and others, as reported in articles and shown in films, tapes, and demonstrations, attests to this. Rarely in the literature of Gestalt Therapy, however, is there reference to the limitations and contra-indications essential to effective practice.

The most immediate limitation of Gestalt or any other therapy is the skill, training, experience, and judgment of the therapist. Since Gestalt techniques facilitate access to and release of intense affect, a therapist using this approach must neither be afraid nor inept in allowing the patient to follow through and finish the experience of grief, rage, fear, or joy. The capacity to live in the present and to offer solid presence standing by are essential. Without such presence and skill the therapist may leave the patient aborted, unfinished, opened, and vulnerable—out of touch with any base of support, either in himself or available from the therapist. The therapist's capacity for I-thou, here-and-now relationships is a basic requisite and is developed through extensive integration of learning and experience. Probably the most effective application of Gestalt techniques (or any other therapeutic techniques) comes with personal therapeutic experiences gained in professional training workshops and work with competent therapists and supervisors.

Beyond the basic issue of therapist competence, the use of appropriate application of Gestalt techniques hinges on questions of *when*, *with whom*, and *in what situation*. In general, Gestalt Therapy is most effective with overly socialized, restrained, constricted individuals—often described as neurotic, phobic, perfectionistic, ineffective, depressed, etc.—whose functioning is limited or inconsistent, primarily due to their internal restrictions, and whose enjoyment of living is minimal. Most efforts of Gestalt Therapy have therefore been directed toward persons with these characteristics.

Work with less organized, more severely disturbed or psychotic individuals is more problematic and requires caution, sensitivity, and patience. Such work should not be undertaken where long-term commitment to the patient is not feasible. The patient needs considerable support from the therapist and beginning faith in his own self-healing process before he can undertake to experience in depth and intensity the overwhelming pain, hurt, rage, and despair underlying most psychotic processes. It is preferable, then, in the initial stages of therapy with a severely disturbed patient to limit therapeutic activity to procedures that strengthen the patient's contact with reality, his confidence in his own organism, and the good will and competence of the therapist, rather than involving him in role-playing or reenactment of past experiences of pain or conflict. In short, with the deeper struggles the therapist postpones those techniques that release the most intense affect, although these must be dealt with later in time to reduce major aspects of unfinished business and develop freedom to move on. It is helpful to use techniques to facilitate the patient's reclaiming freedom to use eyes, hands, ears, body; in general, to increase sensory, perceptual, and motor capacities toward self-support and mastery of his environment.

The therapist's willingness to encounter the patient with his honest and immediate responses and his ability to challenge the patient's manipulative use of his symptoms without rejecting him are crucial. It is important for the therapist to listen to the patient's refusal to undertake experiments, at times exploring his catastrophic expectations, at times simply accepting his judgment that he does not have access to sufficient support in himself or from the therapist to risk open confrontation with the terrors within. The challenge to the therapist lies in discerning the fine line between overprotection and genuine acceptance of the patient's final wisdom in the moment. In some instances, the acceptance of the patient's appraisal of the situation is sufficient support for the patient to undertake spontaneously that which he avoided only moments before.

Individuals whose problems center in lack of impulse control—acting out, delinquency, sociopathy—require a different approach. Obviously, techniques that are useful in freeing expression imply this as a desired goal and may be used by the patient for rationalization of his actions with disregard for consequences and responsibility. Carelessly used, such techniques further arm the patient to continue avoiding the deeper levels of pain that he early learned to avoid through acting rather than experiencing. Here the therapist needs to be able to determine genuine from manipulative expressions of affect, to confront without rejecting, and to support without being exploited. Gestalt exercises in "taking responsibility for" are often useful. So is the therapist's willingness to confront patient responses or behavior not experienced as genuine with, "I don't believe you," or, "I don't believe you are finished now," or similar reports of the therapist's own response and perception. At the same time, the therapist needs to be aware of the patient's severely damaged sense of trust and the despair and hopelessness that he wards off by his aggressiveness, manipulativeness, and acting-out.

A skillful Gestalt therapist will design experiments to facilitate the patient's working within the therapy session, thus reducing his need to act outside. However, work with acting-out individuals, as with psychotics, cannot be considered without commitment to a longer, and often slower, process than many Gestalt therapists are willing to undertake.

Because Gestalt techniques, in general, facilitate the discovering, facing, and resolution of the patient's major conflicts in often dramatically short time, the inexperienced therapist-observer or patient may assume that Gestalt Therapy offers "instant cure." Even in experienced Gestalt therapists, the temptation to direct or push the patient to a stance of full self-support too fast, too soon, may result in pseudointegration and subsequent disappointment. In many patients, the task of relinquishing their immaturities is a tedious and long-term process filled with tentative risking and retreating, requiring the steadfast presence and support of the therapist. He constantly asks the patient to face his responsibility and at the same time encourages him to take risks in order to find his own support, thus reducing the likelihood of the pathological dependencies potential in any therapeutic endeavor. In an effort to reduce or eliminate transferences, it is easy for the Gestalt therapist to reject the patient along with rejecting his manipulative efforts at avoiding self-support. While the patient is to be encouraged to discover his own values and identity, it is absurd to disclaim the influence of the therapist as model; in many instances, he is a good model of a parenting adult who values the growth and freedom of his "children" (patients or students). Sometimes, however, the therapist's goal of patient self-support may be short-circuited by his own impatience in much the same way that parents restrict their child's development by demanding adult behaviors prematurely.

The use of Gestalt Therapy with groups is common, but frequently this amounts to individual therapy in a group setting rather than the usual group approach of extensive interaction and "group process." While there is often a high degree of involvement on the part of the group participants, at times with considerable affect and self-insight as they watch one patient working with the therapist, this approach inevitably reduces time for potentially useful spontaneous group interaction. A skillful therapist may reduce this limitation by directing the individual to confront the group as individuals, to use them for trying out new perceptions or communication skills, or to deal with his projections with them and to get their feedback in return. The degree of individual growth and development in such groups may well compensate for the loss of more traditional group experiences.

A major hazard, however, is the therapist's assuming excessive responsibility for the direction of the group by too much activity, thus fostering patient passivity and defeating his own goal of patient self-support. In this case, the group, too, responds passively, regarding the therapist as an expert or magician and themselves as having little to contribute without his special techniques and skill. Certainly, this is not inevitable, but it can be decreased and modified by therapist judgment and action.

One of Perls' most valuable contributions is his approach to projections as the patient's disowned attributes that he has failed to assimilate in the process of growing up. The technique of "playing" the projections (the disowned roles or characteristics) has proven valuable in helping the patient regain and integrate much lost power, energy, and self-support. However since any statement that a patient makes about another person can, within this system, be described as a projection, caution should be exerted before denying the reality factors in the perception. When one patient confronts another with his dislike or other strong response, the therapist will have to make a decision as to whether to deal with this in terms of the interaction and relationship between the people—whether to encourage the object of attack to explore his stimulus value—or whether to deal with it as a projection of the attacker. The distinction is especially important in patient evaluations of or confrontations with the therapist. A defensive therapist holds a powerful weapon if he labels all statements about himself as projections and fails to differentiate accurately. If honest encountering is valued, it must be a two-way process. The therapist needs to listen carefully and admit, "What you say is true of me" if it fits, rather than dealing with this as the patient's fantasy and implying inaccuracy or distortion of perception. The exercise of taking both sides—that is, "This is true of me," or, "This is not true"—may provide the most comfortable solution for both therapist and patient. In any case, personal openness and reappraisal is essential.

The theoretical emphasis in Gestalt Therapy on awareness, self-support, etc., tends to magnify the role of the individual as individual, master of his own fate, separate and distinct from other people, often with little emphasis on his important ongoing relationships and the effects of the vocational, institutional, and cultural systems of which he is a part. This may mean that relationships may too often be viewed as projections and as clearly secondary in importance to the internal pressures, and difficulties may be ignored. The emphasis on the patient himself as being solely in possession of the key to his own destiny and happiness can distort the realities of everyday existence. There is a risk in the temptation to make a valid growing and emerging process into a dictum, a *should*, and thus substitute a new tyranny for the old. Full functioning, integration, and actualization, unless experienced in the moment rather than viewed as end states, can become as cruel an expectation and requirement as salvation. Gestalt Therapy's focus on a Zen-like dilemma, both experiencing the value of this process, yet finding little in the environment that supports this way of life. Gestalt Therapy may often offer a promise of integration, freedom, and satori that is very difficult to achieve in this culture.

The consequences of successful Gestalt Therapy may be that by teaching the patient to be more genuinely in touch with himself, he will experience more dissatisfaction with conventional goals and relationships, with the hypocrisy and pretense of much social interaction, and may experience the pain of seeing the deficiencies and destructiveness of many social and cultural forces and institutions. Simply stated, extensive experience with Gestalt Therapy will likely make patients more unfit for or unadjusted to contemporary society. However, at the same time, they may hopefully be more motivated to work toward changing the world into a more compassionate and productive milieu in which human beings can develop, work, and enjoy their full humanness.

CHAPTER 30

PERSPECTIVES: INTERVIEWS WITH JAMES SIMKIN AND JOHN ENRIGHT

JERRY KOGAN, Ph. D.

The two interviews which follow have been excerpted from a longer study [1] which concerns attitudes, practices, and philosophies of a selected group of Gestalt therapists and trainees. As a matter of identification and contrast, interviewees were assigned the designation of first-, second-, or third-generation gestaltists according to their distance from Fritz or Laura Perls. For purposes of this publication only two interviews (which have been slightly shortened) have been included from the original study. These interviews were held in March 1973, with Jim Simkin, an early student of Fritz and Laura Perls, and with John Enright, a later student of Fritz. While space does not permit inclusion of the analysis of these interviews from the longer study, the two interviews in themselves have interest in that they reflect some quite personal attitudes and beliefs of practicing gestaltists. However, in no way are these first-generation therapists representational of a larger set of Gestalt therapists, despite some important similarities in position. Differences between Simkin and Enright are also apparent. As you will note, Simkin, with little modification, continues to identify with the practice and philosophy of Gestalt Therapy according to Perls. Enright, on the other hand, incorporates or integrates Gestalt Therapy into an eclectic perspective that is uniquely his own. Overall, however, both Simkin and Enright look to Fritz Perls as a creative and even brilliant therapist and innovator.

JIM SIMKIN: FIRST GENERATION INTERVIEW
MARCH 11, 1973

Kogan: What was your earliest contact with Gestalt Therapy?
Simkin: (Microphone trouble) . . . then there was a group . . . like

Fritz and Paul Weiss and myself and a few others who were really the professional group, and there was a split . . . and again, I have some interesting historical material, some of the minutes of the meetings that sound very much like the San Francisco Gestalt Institute.

Kogan: (Laughs)

Simkin: (Too low) . . . (laughs) . . . which phase . . . There was never any real agreement as to the value of training non-therapists, and that was always where the group got hung up. It's happening now in Cleveland. It happened in '53-'54 in New York. It probably will happen . . . I'm not sure. It may happen in Los Angeles. I think that Los Angeles is a little bit . . . has an advantage . . . in that regard, and it'll tear San Francisco apart.

Kogan: (Comments on San Francisco Institute briefly)

Simkin: The problem is that some people are unwilling to crawl before they walk and unwilling to do what's necessary and . . . unfortunately Gestalt Therapy attracts thousands . . . and . . . some of Fritz's own psychopathy was very . . . (not clear) . . .

Kogan: Okay. Would you describe the nature and the extent of your own training in Gestalt Therapy?

Simkin: Yeah. When I first started with Fritz, he recommended that I have a two-hour therapy group, and there was a post-group session . . . (not clear). I stayed in the training group for two sessions and dropped out of that because real high-powered people, Paul Goodman and Elliott Shapiro, and some of the others . . . I couldn't keep up with the bullshit and the elephant shit and . . . that was not what I was looking for. So, I instead had an hour-and-a-half, in those days an hour-and-a-half was ninety minutes, of therapy with Fritz. So, on Tuesday, I'd have ninety minutes of therapy . . . I had two hours of group, two hours of post-group, home . . . and would be impossible to live with till Sunday. Then come back on Tuesday for another week of that. Saturdays were seminars in which principles and techniques . . . theory of . . . that sort of thing. Sometimes it would be on Wednesday evening. And what I did was I took some of the courses that were offered and had one-and-a-half hours of individual treatment, two hours of group . . . for about . . . a little over a year and a half. Then I cut down to one hour of individual . . . and continued the group, and I dropped the group after two years and finished after another half or so . . . (unclear) . . . two-and-a-half years . . . and during that time I had three, four, maybe five, courses, seminars, workshops . . . whatever you want to call them . . . plus occasional real workshops, I also joined that theory thing again . . . that administrative thing where we wrestled with things like . . . (unclear) . . . criteria and that sort of thing. So most of my training was in the actual group . . . and therapy. Some of it was in these courses and some courses I started and didn't like and dropped out . . . attempts made to systematize and to have courses which would lead to advanced courses, etc. . . . (too low) . . .

Kogan: When did you come out to the West Coast?

Simkin: I came out in '58, July '58. I finished my formal training in '55. I was concurrently chief clinical psychologist at the V.A. . . . Mental Hygiene Clinic and would occasionally have Fritz come in or somebody else . . . do some training with my staff, etc., and I think one or two of my staff got interested in Gestalt and went into treatment or some training in New York. Then Fritz came out to the West Coast in '60. He'd gone up to Mendocino. He was invited to consult with the fellow there that was the chief psychologist . . .

Kogan: Wilson Van Dusen?

Simkin: Wilson Van Dusen . . . and . . . Fritz did not have enough work there so he came down to San Francisco and started doing something . . . it wasn't enough for him either (chuckle), so he came down to Los Angeles, and we organized a study group (1960). There's where the big names come in . . . the study group met in my office and we had a second one . . . people like Walt Kempler, Stu Shapiro, Bob Girard, Ev Shostrom, etc., etc. These are well-known names now, and each pretty well known on their own. And this was a very successful ten-person . . . oh . . . Gene Sagan used to come down from the Bay Area.

Kogan: Oh . . . Gene comes in there?

Simkin: Yeah. He had started with Fritz up north.

Kogan: Those were the circuses . . .

Simkin: And he followed Fritz. He'd fly down or he'd drive down and back . . . Once we presented the study group—how it functions—at a meeting of the Los Angeles Society of Clinical Psychologists, and . . . very well received and there was immediate sign-up for another group; a second group got started. I dropped out after a year of this, discovered that what I wanted were friends and I found my friends. And I wasn't using it for therapy or training. And then . . . and Walt and I split up his two routes. He had a Santa Ana Freeway route and he had a Santa . . . (laughter—hard to hear) . . . and Walt took the San Bernadino Freeway route and I took the Santa Ana route. Fritz would actually do that . . . he had stops along the way. Like the Metropolitan State Hospital on the way . . . Ev Shostrom's place in Santa Ana.

Kogan: That answers the training question. Have you had any subsequent training?

Simkin: Subsequent to . . .

Kogan: These initial experiences.

Simkin: Nothing I'd define as my own training.

Kogan: Okay. That takes care of the background information. When you think of Gestalt Therapy, what's the first thing you want to tell me?

Simkin: First thing that I think of is a philosophy of life. A . . . at this point for me, a very cogent, fairly cohesive body of theory . . . a way of living life in a very simple, direct, and easier way, much less complicated. I think of the psychology of the obvious and how much easier it is for me to live life.

Kogan: When you think of Fritz Perls, what's the first thing you want to tell me?

Simkin: Oh, I think of (hah) a wide range of contradictions, a shy, flamboyant person, a soft-warm generous, stingy guy . . . a genius, an idiot, a guy who put Gestalt Therapy on the map, and a guy who almost took Gestalt Therapy off the map (chuckles) . . . contradictions . . . of polarities . . . come to mind.

Kogan: Have you modified the theory of Gestalt Therapy?

Simkin: Well . . . in a number of ways, I have . . . a series of what are called mini-lectures, and these mini-lectures are constantly evolving. And I've been comparing some that I've made, and what I do. I mini-lecture after I work. And what I'm becoming aware of is the evolvement is moving in a certain direction and becoming fairly consistent to a point now where I'm ready to publish some of this . . . and . . .

Kogan: What is an example of one of the mini-lectures—a topic?

Simkin: Yeah. It's like some of the constructs . . . concepts of support, or contact-withdrawal or confluence . . .

Kogan: Any issue of the technology or philosophy . . .

Simkin: Right. For example, I believe that there's intrapsychic contact. I don't consider all withdrawal as . . . in terms of contact-withdrawal, in terms of interpersonal contact-withdrawal . . . intrapsychic contact-withdrawal . . . That's an example of adding to the theory.

Kogan: Have you written on this?

Simkin: I may have . . . (laughs) . . .

Kogan: How is that intrapsychic contact-withdrawal manifest?

Simkin: . . . Look . . . when I am aware that I am in touch with what I'm thinking-feeling inside. To you I may look as if I'm withdrawn.

To me, I don't feel withdrawn. I feel in touch with what I'm doing. I consider withdrawal when I retrospectively become aware that I don't know where I was. And when you see me as having been withdrawn, and I see me as not having any contact on the world . . . so I make the distinction—I find it a useful distinction—especially when people have the erroneous idea that awareness is a "should." To me Gestalt Therapy is without "should" . . . you should be aware . . . so they don't understand how it's possible to live in a "should-less" type of world . . . and that's how they get into an impasse and get hooked—get stuck. That's one example of adding to the theory or modifying the theory.

Kogan: Have you extended your modification of Gestalt Therapy to a new content area?

Simkin: I don't know what you mean by a new content area.

Kogan: A new physical or geographical location, for example.

Simkin: Oh . . . oh . . . oh . . . I'm one of the most hidebound traditionalists around now, and I have changed my approach in terms of who to train and who to accept the training etc., etc. . . . In that sense I'm biased and I still insist that having a background in Gestalt Therapy—that is, having a background in psychotherapy. Being a licensed . . . psychotherapist. I will not train or apply this to educators or to . . . Some of the people that I've trained may be . . . . who don't have my hideboundedness . . . unwilling as I am to use my time and effort outside of training psychotherapists . . . maybe fine, I don't know.

Kogan: Okay. Then the next question. How do you see Gestalt Therapy in relation to the Human Potential Movement, and do you see any trends as a consequence of that relationship?

Simkin: The Human Potential Movement is a . . . for me, a big disappointment. It was something that I saw as potentially a very exciting advent in the early sixties. I'm remembering that Fritz and Walt and I did the first training thing at Esalen in '64. It was alive, a beautiful place. . . . The problem is this, the Human Potential Movement has attracted . . . a large number of operators . . . a large number of entrepreneurs, people who mouth—pay lip service to human potential, and who are primarily interested in some kind of enterprise—or the enterprise is encounter groups . . . or the enterprise is starting a growth center, or the enterprise is . . . having a string of women they can fuck . . . a setting which is conducive to that . . . and I'm very disappointed with what the Human Potential Movement has turned out to be. What it has done is attract and select out people who are dissatisfied with their own field, and instead of the promise . . . the promise was the people from architecture to come to the Human Potential Movement and see all the marvelous ways to reach architecture and then go back and do something with architecture . . . and go back to the community development program and . . . do something with the community and do something with whatever they were into. It's gone the other way. The people who are dissatisfied drop out of architecture, or community development or medicine . . . and they become stuck, in a sense, like that. And what's happened then is that there are little enclaves of not really human potential-creative movement, but little enclaves of bitter, disappointed people who are (laughs) . . . I look at that with a lot of regret, and I saw something that was potentially beautiful . . . just . . . ripped off . . . ripped off badly. Now Gestalt Therapy in relation to this is unfortunately very attractive to rip-off artists and people running around who call themselves Gestaltists and . . . who do bioenergetics, massage, meditation, and Gestalt. Really . . . appalling thing. And Gestalt becomes a technique that's used by people in the so-called Human Potential Movement. I'm disrespectful of the people who function this way.

Kogan: Do you have some attitude toward Esalen?

Simkin: Oh, yeah. I have disassociated completely. I won't have anything to do with them . . . the past year-and-a-half now . . . and that place is just poison. Just recently, Esalen purportedly has been offering a three-month training program in Gestalt Therapy. Then these . . . (not clear) . . . a number of people who have no training in Gestalt Therapy as offering training . . . and they have two or three people who are legitimate, who have training. They apparently got ten to twelve people involved in this. I've just finished working with two of those people this past week. Two young psychiatrists in Chile, and they haven't had any training at all, with the exception of the one week Bob Martin of the Los Angeles Institute was out there. They have people who are going way beyond their competence. They mislead, they misrepresent. And what I see is that, if anything, if people imagine, if that is what Gestalt Therapy training is, it'll detract from the growth of Gestalt Therapy. I don't think that can happen anymore. I don't think that Fritz can get in the way of Gestalt Therapy anymore. I don't think that Esalen can get in the way of Gestalt Therapy anymore. I don't think that operators can interfere. Gestalt Therapy is much too substantial, and it's got such integrity as a system, as a philosophy, as a therapy and as a broad-base approach that . . . that can't happen anymore.

I'm very much in touch with what's happening with Gestalt Therapy around the country and some parts of the world, and some very good, substantial foundations have been made and I see some . . . that you'd call . . . second-generation Gestalt therapists who are beautiful . . . really solid. If you have any opportunity to interview a first-generation Gestalt therapist, get Erv Polster. He'll be coming to San Diego in August. He does gorgeous work. Some of the second-generation people . . . well you have . . . with Cindy . . . and then you have a first-generation person like Elaine (Kepner)—very solid, substantial people. Los Angeles, then in Cleveland, and a few people around like Vince O'Connell, or Jim Simkin or people who aren't affiliated with an institute.

Kogan: Thank you. Has your practice and/or study of Gestalt Therapy affected your own life-style or philosophy of life?

Simkin: (Smiling) I believe that since 19 . . . I started in training in 1952. I consider that I completed my training in '60. And a lot of . . . in between . . . a lot of experimenting with my own life-style. I think I . . . around 1962; and became very alive when I started to risk training others around '64, '65, and the way I conduct my life . . . my own contact with, and taking seriously what I do, and living this way . . . an enormous change. It's no longer an introject for me . . .

Kogan: Can you say something more specific about your own life philosophy?

Simkin: Yeah. I . . . am appalled at what a liar I was . . . and how I perpetuate the lie in my . . . and telling my kids stories and not being straight with them. Instead of saying, "I don't approve," "I don't like this" . . . taking a stand . . . to drag in others—"society doesn't approve" or "that's not right" . . . I look back and I'm appalled, amazed and grateful that I don't do this. I don't lie as much. And I'm willing to say what I am, what I believe, and I don't attempt to rationalize. In terms of my own philosophy and life-style . . . people call me very honest. They call me very hard . . . that I make harsh judgments . . . that I . . . arbitrary, and that's the truth. I like that about me. And instead of playing games and playing flexible . . . I'm not . . . I'm arbitrary and I like my arbitrariness. I'm also much more critical . . . (not clear) . . . a lot of changes . . . Every opportunity I get to undercut the so-called educational philosophy I do. The whole business of teaching fraudulence and pretense . . .

Kogan: Can you think of any question I could have developed more fully with you?

Simkin: Yeah. It's in terms of my own interests. My own interests are in terms of training Gestalt therapists . . . in terms of selection of Gestalt Therapy trainees—of what constitutes adequate training. What goes into my curriculum of training. I had some stuff missing in my own training, of course. I want this . . . for my trainees. So I'm much more systematic and make sure people are exposed to a wide variety of styles. I want people to have more understanding of the theory and the philosophy and I like the experience of teaching. And the Los Angeles Institute is my baby. And that could be an example of what I think is a worthwhile investment of time and energy.

Also—would like to counteract two things that have a prevalence. One is Gestalt Therapy is something that you have a session or do a weekend and cured or very dramatic . . . I think that's a misrepresentation . . . (not clear) . . . What I would develop as questions which would be answers—things I'm interested in . . . How long does it take on the average to work through problems by Gestalt Therapy? What's an average length of Gestalt Therapy? What typically happens during Gestalt Therapy sessions? And I'd like much more emphasis on the non-dramatic and cut down the expectations . . . my bias is to balance out what I think needs some balancing.

Kogan: How does your training differ from that of Los Angeles?

Simkin: What I've been experimenting with is condensed style. I call it massed versus spaced learning. In the L.A. Institute, people will be in a group for six weeks or two months or three months . . . whatever . . . they go to another . . . after a period of time they can petition to go into an advanced group, demonstrate before a committee, and if the trainers agree, they go into an advanced group. In an advanced group they have the right to select their own trainers. They no longer are rotated through the trainers that are available. My style is that I will not take people who I'm unwilling to train. So I spend some time on selection. I had eleven applicants. Of those I was willing to consider seriously nine. I selected six. The style of working is very different. Instead of working mostly in groups, or exclusively in groups, I do a lot of individual work. People have an individual hour every day over a period of three months—that's a lot of individual work. It's massive dosing as opposed to the spaced practice. It's an experiment to see whether I can dose massively, train massively, and people can assimilate. Fritz and I got into a big hassle about this. He said no. I said yes. I have some data I've collected. The clinical evidence I have so far is that it's possible. Two of these people I would refer to without any question. I consider them peers. All of them now I will refer to. So my clinical impression is yes, it's possible to train people in a three-month format. And in addition to that, six different Gestalt therapists with six different approaches came . . . Laura Perls came . . . she has beautiful eyes. So massed versus spaced, more individual work—there's an ever-present accent on experimenting, checking out—on feedback, a lot of emphasis on the I-Thou. I think that goes on a lot in Los Angeles too.

Kogan: Great. Thank you.

JOHN ENRIGHT: FIRST GENERATION INTERVIEW
MARCH 14, 1973

Kogan: What was your earliest contact with Gestalt Therapy?

Enright: I was taking informal training in psychodrama and every now and then the guy would do something really elegant—it would stand out from everything else, like a diamond in the gravel. And every time that happened I had this perception of beauty. I'd ask, "Where did you get *that?*" He always mentioned this guy Perls. The third or fourth time that happened I sensed there was something going on that was particularly interesting, so I'd ask this fellow about Perls. He said he was off in Japan at the time and he'd call him when he came back. Fortunately he was a man of his word, and a few months later he called and I joined an ongoing group—weekly group in L.A. That's where I was at the time.

Kogan: I see. Was this about 19 . . .

Enright: '63. This was almost exactly ten years ago. Fritz reappeared from wherever he had been. I was never very clear on that. And I joined the group. Ongoing group of ten professionals. Nine of 'em were in this one hospital, and I was a visitor. [Up to this point in time, 1963, Enright had never read anything of G.T.] I went to that group and within five minutes I knew I had found something I'd wanted. This was early '63.

Kogan: Do you recall the first thing you read in Gestalt Therapy?

Enright: After some months, I read the book *Gestalt Therapy.*

Kogan: What was your impression of that book?

Enright: The very first thing was a flash of disappointment. It looked like a lot of work instead of just easy swallowing. Followed by intrigue and fairly systematic working through the book, the first half. About a year or so later . . . about two years later . . .

after I had some practice in Gestalt, I then read the second half and wrote my first chapter on Gestalt. I was ready for the intellectual half of the book after a couple of years. I found the exercises useful . . . doubtful that I would have, had I not had the contact with Fritz.

Kogan: How would you describe your orientation before Gestalt?

Enright: Mushy eclectic.

Kogan: Was there any particular emphasis in this eclecticism?

Enright: A negative one. I knew that psychoanalysis and its close relatives were not my dish of tea, and I was, I was hoping that something would appear someday that would fit me. I dropped out of being a therapist for some years, and I just couldn't handle the existing theories of Rogers and Freud . . . were meaningless to me. Essentially I was a diagnostician and researcher for several years. Just got back into doing group therapy. In Hawaii. And I finally realized that even without knowing anything about it, the group was useful in a hospital setting, and I wanted to come back to the mainland to get more training. I was looking very, very, almost desperately for an approach that would make sense to me. Psychodrama . . . was the closest I'd found . . . I liked it but it wasn't really clicking. The first five minutes with Fritz, I knew I'd found . . . profoundly.

Standard Ph.D. psychology training. A year's internship at a mental hospital, Langley Porter. Supervisors were Rogerian, Freudian, and another bunch of eclectics. I had no sense at all of what therapy was about. I just stumbled and struggled and mostly had done work at hospitals . . . adminstration . . .

Kogan: What school did you go to?

Enright: U.C., Berkeley. I got my Ph.D. in '59.

Kogan: Would you describe the nature and extent of your training in Gestalt Therapy?

Enright: The Group was a very powerful part of my training. The next day I started doing Gestalt. That was it. That was my orientation from then on. I took A.B.E.P. exams, and the clinical material I used for that examination was essentially a Gestalt Therapy session. Which was considered pretty radical by then, but they took it. That was my orientation for the next three years or so. I . . . nine months and a weekly group with Fritz. Several weeks at Esalen. Everytime he appeared in Northern California, I'd moved up here, I showed up in the group. I was his chauffer and chess partner part of the time, and drive him from . . . (not clear) . . .

managed to spend quite a bit of time with him in a quasi-student, quasi-group member . . . sometimes I was sort of his assistant, y'know that phrase. I was sort of his unofficial apprentice for a while. Up here. After about three or three-and-a-half years, I really got scared that I was learning too much from him. I was afraid I was learning to be a lonely, dirty old man along with learning his skill, and I practically stopped working with him. And ceased functioning as a Gestaltist primarily . . . for sometime when I joined Synanon. In 1966. Phased out of Gestalt for about three years. Still in my clinical work, which was very skimpy at the time. I did Gestalt-like things . . . I don't know what I was. I was confused. I was sitting between two chairs. When I dropped out of Synanon in '69 and joined the Gestalt Institute, I plunged back in a hurry. My skills had not rusted too badly. My goal was to be with Fritz whatever capacity I could. He didn't ask me to shine his shoes, but I would have . . . I'd estimate that it was around three hundred hours with Fritz. Within less than one year I would say I was probably really thoroughly skilled as a Gestalt therapist. By the end of the second year, I had a really thorough cognitive grasp. I had already written my first paper . . . by the end of the second year. In the first year, just very soon I had a grasp of what it was all about. Very quickly I was presenting it to students up here. I had a Gestalt group at Langley Porter. '65. I wrote that first paper that was later published in Fagan and Shepherd.

Kogan: Okay. What has been your subsequent professional training?

Enright: (Laughs) . . . Very, very intensely and deeply into Synanon for three-and-a-half years. Two years of bioenergetic therapy . . . primal therapy and some more training since then in bioenergetics. Some work in psychodrama. I just never stop. I'm always . . . EST . . . Ehrhardt . . . very consistent with Gestalt. I'd say somewhere around two years ago I turned some corner and became primarily myself rather than a Gestaltist or . . . Since then, one to three years, I became an integrating source myself and . . . (unclear) . . . unique and identifiable.

Kogan: Another kind of eclecticism—a new synthesis . . .

Enright: Yeah. A real solid, not a mushy eclecticism. More than eclectic. Everything I do has the stamp of me—no matter where it came from. So it's no longer eclecticism.

Kogan: You spent some time with Naranjo . . .

Enright: Yeah. Thank you . . . that's another one . . . six months with Claudio.

Kogan: Okay. That takes care of the background material . . .

Enright: Wanna know if I'm . . . I'm French-Irish . . . (laughs) . . . born in Washington State . . . I'm one of the few non-Jewish Gestalt therapists around . . . (chuckles) . . .

Kogan: Uh . . . what do you make of that point? That's an interesting anecdote.

Enright: Much more than an anecdote. It's the background of the fact I'm going in the next few years to be in a very different place, have a very different place in the profession, in the world, than most any other psychologist. I'm going to get out in the next few months, totally out of the therapy point of view, and become a social revolutionary. I'm . . . (not clear) . . . it's going to be heavily influenced by Gestalt. I'll no longer be a therapist.

Kogan: What do you mean by "social revolutionary"?

Enright: I'm going to create . . . new social forms . . . combining, using the Synanon idea of making the vehicle for personal growth action in the world, and no one else has quite gotten that together as well as Synanon and EST has to some extent, and I . . . I feel like the physicist looking at matter and anti-matter floating around the universe, and I'm . . . get that together. I see a kind of center that I'm going to start that will be very, very aggressively growth-oriented and at the same time be attacking real problems in the world. A Center for Action on . . . I think that something about my background ultimately. I came into psychology and identified with the intellectual . . . the Jewish point of view . . . almost totally and now I'm moving away from that, away toward more of an action-oriented point of view. Like Chuck Diedrich is a German, uh, doing German, and Synanon is full of doing too much. That's its problem. Somehow I'm getting the doing and being together, and what most of the growth movement lacks is the capacity to do . . . anything . . . kind of ability to press into the physical universe and achieve results in a consistent basis. The ultimate test of knowing is doing. You consider "I'll be a writer" all your life, and when you have written something you are a writer. Ultimately doing is the test of being. For me. I think it has to be transcended and passed through so you don't have to do any more. For most of us intellectuals in this society, until we have done in the world, we can't be sure we are. I'm not saying that doing is being . . . that doing . . . for us, the way we started in life is an essential test. The essential space to go through to be, and then we can let go of it again. Also . . . will involve physical fitness . . . very extensive exercise program . . . a whole body trip.

Kogan: There are six content questions . . . When you think of Gestalt Therapy, what's the first thing you want to tell me?

Enright: Awareness . . . the core of it is awareness. Recently I have seen that that's not *quite* complete. The goal of Gestalt is to get the right and left hand knowing what the other is doing. To enhance awareness, bring things together, bring things under the same light that have been operating out of contact.

Kogan: Okay. When you think of Fritz Perls, what's the first thing you want to tell me?

Enright: Smoke. Relaxation . . . uh . . . wise . . . enigmatic look. I'd stay with enigmatic . . . wise is a projection. Sitting slumped somewhat, leaning back in a slightly broken down easy chair at the old house in Esalen.

Kogan: Okay. Have you modified the theory of Gestalt Therapy?

Enright: Yes. I've looked at the essence of it and in my emphasis . . . I will emphasize certain things more than what Fritz did. Two basic ways. One is he almost totally lost touch with the fact that most people out in the world don't have all that much free energy or excitement available. He worked in a situation that almost completely guaranteed that by the time they got into the hot seat their excitement or energy level would be very high. And he gradually dropped out of his thinking or awareness that that's an absolutely necessary condition for Gestalt work. So in the last few years his theory became one-sided—became incomplete. He stopped paying enough attention to the need for developing energy. So to practice Gestalt Therapy out in the ordinary world, if your name is Joe Schlack and they haven't paid two hundred bucks and gone to Big Sur, uh, you gotta remind yourself something that Fritz had forgotten about, developing energy, making sure the energy is there before you work. So I'm saying that in my training I've brought that back in. Fritz forgot that he had this tiny specialized environment that produced automatically that which most of us Gestalt therapists cannot hope to have.

What I have brought back is this fact, plus techniques for mobilizing . . . in ordinary therapy experiences. See, Fritz knew that . . . if he were here . . . I'm not telling anything new. He just kind of forgot that as he worked and thought . . . his awareness. When he worked at Mendocino State Hospital, Wilson [Van Dusen] got him a job there, he didn't like to work with psychotics, basically because they didn't have free energy. He knew this fact, but he lost sight of it because of the special situation in which he was and so the people who learned in the last few years of his life, primarily when he was at Esalen, didn't realize this and they'd go out and try to do what he does out in the world and it doesn't work, and so some of my writing . . . a lot of my training is filling in that neglected gap.

Kogan: How?

Enright: The most important thing is to get people to know that it's there. Have you ever seen that triangle that I have . . .

Kogan: Yes.

Enright: At the bottom of that triangle is my extra emphasis. Fritz taught almost exclusively about awareness and some about responsibility. Rarely . . . of course the title of his second book did have that title in it . . . but rarely after that did he say much about excitement. So that I have brought that awareness—that focus—back in. So that when one of our trainees sits down, looks around, doesn't start doing awareness stuff until the energy is high. And the specific techniques are unimportant. Focusing on that is what I've brought back. There's to be no awareness work until the level of excitement has been reach . . . unbound excitement.

Kogan: Okay.

Enright: The second thing . . . although Fritz was clear himself and always taught responsibility, a lotta people got the idea that expression is enough or experience is enough, and it's not enough! Experience has to be from cause position rather than victim position. That if I'm experiencing my loneliness and all the time I'm experiencing that loneliness . . . I'm also thinking "God, my Goddamn parents left me . . . and my wife's leaving me . . ." I'm not experiencing it out. I'm not finishing the business. I'm not getting through the impasse. I'm just circling very close around it. To experience something from the victim position is not to finish it. And to finish it experience has to be from the responsible position. That I colluded in this. That I went along with it. I ultimately am cause. Fritz knew that. You can see it in his work. But somehow a lot of people that worked with him didn't quite get that and a lot of the promiscuous pillow-pounding that goes on in Gestalt groups and wild flailings around and hysterias and so forth don't lead to any kind of change. The experiencing is done without full responsibility. When most people say Perls, they mean awareness . . . he was that center. That triangle was just solidly filled in with Fritz. He was just beautiful there. Most of the top part of responsibility too is pretty well taken care of there too. A few holes there, and in the bottom part he began to leave out in his later years. He knew it all. It came less clear in his teaching in the last . . .

Kogan: Okay. The second part of this question is, have you extended this modification to a content area in which it has not been previously applied?

Enright: No. I would say I have defined the limits of pure Gestalt and shown how it integrates with other points of view and when to transit from one to the other. I think the Gestalt contract is limited . . .

Kogan: For example?

Enright: The Gestalt contract . . . as a total contract . . . as Fritz used to say: "You wanna go kill yourself . . . get turned on or not turned on . . . that's your trip. I take no responsibility whatsoever, and I'm here, I'm available." That's not a sufficient contract or suitable contract . . . the methods can be used with anybody. But the basic Gestalt contract of ultraresponsibility . . . that one is not suitable for most people.

Kogan: What inclusions have you made?

Enright: Rather than including it, I take it as one piece of a jigsaw puzzle and found the other pieces around it. The piece labeled Gestalt I can show where, with certain people, you need to add. With Synanon you need to add this . . . I put it as one piece in a larger theory. My theory is more comprehensive. I'm not trying to get elegant as a theory, but it's what I know. It's a very crude beginning. It's very practical. It's very brief.

Kogan: Besides Gestalt, what are some of the other elements in your theory?

Enright: Personal construct theory—George Kelly—semantics. I spent a week with Korzybski years ago. That's had an influence on me all along. Bioenergetics. Lots I had stolen from Scientology, Claudio. Synanon is the other major source. Ralph Waldo Emerson. My earlier contributions were particularly in polishing and sharpening and developing new group-structured exercise. Suitable for very large groups suitable for training other than therapy. I guess my major contribution was to drop the word *therapy* and substitute *training*. That was my choice, and Esalen took it over and Fritz bought it. And I get away from therapy and recognize this applies to all of life. I don't do a demonstration with one person, everybody does something.

Kogan: Then the next question is, how do you see Gestalt Therapy in relation to the Human Potential Movement, and do you perceive any emergent trends as a consequence of that relationship?

Enright: I'll answer the second part. It's been rather badly misunderstood and misused by the Human Potential Movement. To do your own thing aspect of it is, I consider, quite destructive. The Human Potential Movement has lifted some of the worst aspects of Gestalt. The lack of responsibility of one human for another— you do your thing, I do mine. Lack of caring. Fritz, when he said I don't care whether you commit suicide or not was saying that from a position of years and years of skill and highly unlikely that anyone would do that . . . a couple did anyway. But when some asshole with a year's experience says that, he's being irresponsible. So, I would say that some of the worst aspects of Gestalt were picked up by the Human Potential Movement and blown up. One key incident of that is leaving off in that picture, y'know, "You do your thing, I do mine," leaving off the last line, "If not, it can't be helped," bowdlerized, castrated it, made it kind of sloppy and sentimental and made it kind of hippie irresponsibility instead of Gestalt. Leaving that in, it seems to me, really says to the person, "Okay, you do your thing and I do mine," and the possibility is that we won't be together. That faces it . . . with the last line in. With the last line out, it doesn't face that. That's my sense of how Gestalt has been misused by the Human Potential Movement.

Fritz was incapable himself of a close, enduring human relationship, and that flaw runs through all his . . . manifesting the theory . . . the theory is pure. All his manifesting of it is swagged by that, and secondly it's swagged by his need always to be on center stage. Y'know, it's possible to do Gestalt Therapy from the back of the room. Except Fritz couldn't do that. So those are the two flaws in the way that Fritz manifested Gestalt, and both of those are in the process of being redeemed now. But a lot of people picked up both of those. Picked up the showmanship. Dependence is a fact of human life, and the massive putdown of that by gestaltists is a perversion. Too much of a good thing. They were certainly right in questioning the extent and the unnecessary prolonging of dependence, but they often get too harsh with it.

Kogan: In relation to the Human Potential movement then, how do you see Gestalt Therapy?

Enright: Obviously an important contributor to it. Very, very heavy influence on . . . if you think of it as a tapestry, it's one of the main threads.

Kogan: And the second part of this question, do you see any emergent trends?

Enright: I'd say that has been a trend in the past that may be less of a problem now. Gestalt is not standing up quite so much. Five years ago it was *the* dominant force. I would say it's still important but not *as* dominant . . . other . . . psychosyntheses. Other threads have been woven in. Gestalt doesn't always stand out quite so much. It's becoming somewhat more background.

Kogan: What do you base this observation on?

Enright: Just count the number of lines in the Esalen Catalog of pure Gestalt and notice the number of integrations—the Browns, Gestalt Plus, a workshop on Gestounter—Gestalt is being woven in all over the place and losing its clear identity and not losing its importance. It's losing its identifiability. It's becoming woven into the background. That's a favorable comment on it not standing out quite so much as a figure.

Kogan: You don't see Gestalt, like psychoanalysis, being easily identifiable over a long period of time . . . in a continuous way?

Enright: Gestalt will not . . .

Kogan: Why is that?

Enright: It's not sufficiently complete to be the synthesis and there *will be* a new synthesis. This is the decade of synthesis we're entering now. The last decade was the decade of innovation and of parts; and now, like EST is one of the first . . . and there will be good syntheses around. This is the decade of synthesis, and Gestalt is not complete enough to do that one. It's already failed to be that one, and there will be one.

Kogan: Obviously you are one of the people that . . . indicating what you've done by making this point. So you are one of the people that have developed a new synthesis.

Okay. Then the next question is, has your own practice of Gestalt Therapy affected your own life style or philosophy of life?

Enright: (Long laughing) Slightly. Total revolution. I was started . . . almost too late. I was a very rigid, uptight intellectual, cold, aloof, frightened . . . all kinds of things . . . all of which I still am, but I know it and it's not in the same way or same degree. If you want (laughs) evidence of that, talk to Hilde Burton who knew me in '59 (laughs).

Kogan: What about your own philosophy of life?

Enright: That . . . I feel now more on course in my life now than I had been for years, and I find that some of my oldest and deepest fantasies of around when I was in high school are still around and are being manifested, and that Gestalt has helped me get on or stay on the track of my deepest being instead of getting caught up in surface bullshit laid on me by others. So rather than a change, it's helped me return me more to source—not changed my direction, but helped me get back on track.

Kogan: What you're now saying suggests something I'd thought of earlier in relation to your statements about eclecticism, which I considered was something more like synthesis . . . that you've come to that eclectic path again.

Enright: Yeah. That's true.

Kogan: Now, with what you've said of your philosophy . . . you're more or less confirmed that . . .

Enright: Uh huh . . .

Kogan: Would it be fair to say some sort of quality of independence and doing your own thing . . . is very close to your own philosophy of life.

Enright: Yes. That may be the . . . two things . . . the thing that Synanon and Gestalt have—in many ways they are opposite—but that one thing they share, that "speak the utmost soul with real conviction." Emerson said that; maybe that's why those two are so . . . most important to me. They both help me to stay on my own path instead of getting sucked off by the attractions and the immediate rewards of doing the socially acceptable thing.

Kogan: So you've taken a path of less immediate rewards.

Enright: Oh, definitely . . . and now the rewards are really rolling in . . . (unclear) . . .

Kogan: Okay. Then the last question. Can you think of anything else I might have asked you that would explicate any point about Gestalt Therapy?

Enright: No. The integration of personal and professional . . . like we already touched on . . . that was . . . (unclear) . . .

Kogan: Okay. Then the last question. Did you learn anything?

Enright: It's nice to review where I'm at. I learned something about my own . . . I'm right in the process of making a life's choice. It's just about made, and talking today is confirming that I'm going in a direction that's right for me.

Kogan: Sort of clarification.

Enright: Definitely.

Kogan: Hearing your own commitments out loud . . . that's very nice . . . thank you very much.

Enright: I really enjoyed your interview.

REFERENCE

1. *The History, Philosophy, and Practice of Gestalt Therapy: Theory of Human Conduct* in Frederick Perls' Psychology. Doctoral dissertation, Univ. of California, Berkeley, 1973. Ann Arbor, Mich.; University Microfilms, 1974. No. 74-1329. © Gerald Kogan, 1973.

CHAPTER 31

A PSYCHOANALYST LOOKS AT GESTALT THERAPY

STEPHEN A. APPELBAUM, Ph.D.

Stephen A. Appelbaum is a psychologist in the Adult Psychotherapy Department and a Fellow in Advanced Study, Department of Education, The Menninger Foundation; an editor of the *International Journal of Psychoanalytic Psychotherapy*, associate editor of the *Bulletin of the Menninger Clinic* and the *Interamerican Journal of Psychology*. He is a faculty member of the Topeka Institute for Psychoanalysis, and practices adult and child psychoanalysis and psychotherapy at the Menninger Foundation. He has published widely on research in psychotherapy, the psychoanalytic and psychotherapeutic process, on diagnostic psychological testing, the psychology of groups, and has recently been studying the relationship between psychoanalysis and other therapies and human-potential activities.

As a psychoanalyst writing about Gestalt Therapy, I am almost sure to write something that either a psychoanalyst or a Gestalt therapist will disclaim as being not the way he does or understands his work. Individual practitioners behave and believe differently from one another, although they nominally practice the same theory and technique. We shall have to allow as best we can for such individual differences and acknowledge that we are to make do with generalizations.

Another difficulty in discussing psychoanalysis and Gestalt Therapy is the socio-psychological nature of our times. The field of psychotherapy has recently become a highly competitive marketplace for men's minds and dollars. In such an atmosphere people tend to lose their identities and become fantasies in the eyes of others; ideas tend to be used as justifications or weapons rather than to be reflected upon. Psychoanalysis, because of its first and formidable claim to the field, its exclusive training practices, and its identification with the doctor-patient model tends to be seen as the establishment authority against which new ideas must be measured, if not rebelled against. The comparable fantasy about Gestalt therapists is that they are an errant younger brother scrambling for a place in the sun, reckless of the damage done to older institutions and bolstering their shaky conviction with contempt for orthodoxy. Finally, I as an individual must be included in this list of difficulties. My Gestalt experience consists of the reading of some basic texts, discussions with Gestalt therapists, observation and participation in a dozen or so Gestalt Therapy groups in Los Angeles, Esalen, and Topeka. I have not practiced Gestalt Therapy except for using some of its techniques and emphases within the context and structure of

psychoanalytic therapy. I run the risk, therefore, of misrepresenting
and inadequately understanding Gestalt. But if we wait for people to
be fully trained and experienced in both psychoanalysis and Gestalt,
the task of comparing the two will be greatly delayed. [1]

INTERPRETATION

The delivery of insight by way of interpretation is probably the
most crucial distinction between Gestalt Therapy and psychoanalysis. The extreme Gestalt position would be that no interpretations are made in Gestalt work, indeed no active attempt is made to
convey insight. The extreme psychoanalytic position might be that
the major technique of analysis is to convey insight by way of
properly-timed and accurate interpretations. Both of these extreme
positions collapse when one thinks of interpretation as a process of
communication, the goal of which is to enlarge awareness or consciousness. Such a process may include *an* interpretation, that is, an
explicit statement of meaning. It also may include any expressive behavior on the therapist's part which, because of its timing and the
interpersonal and intellectual context in which it is inserted, can convey emotional and cognitive understanding. Such sources of insight
are silence, the reactions of others, matter-of-factness or emotional
responsiveness, suppression or encouragement. All can be cues as to
what meanings the patient can ascribe to his productions. On the
basis of my experience, Gestalt Therapy will have to stand up and be
counted as a highly effective purveyor of insight, however much
gestaltists may dislike being characterized in this way. They cannot
have it both ways: to encourage full awareness on the one hand and
claim not to deal in insight on the other. It is true, however, that
Gestalt therapists minimize and some no doubt abstain completely
from explicitly interpretive or "explaining" remarks. Thus, they try
not to tell the patient in so many words about himself (although I
have seen this done by some esteemed Gestalt therapists along with
hortatory, educative, inspirational, and summing-up comments).
They do make highly educated guesses about what to emphasize,
what roles should be played out in dialogue, what should be repeated
louder, what elements in a dream should be attended to—all under a
guiding clinical sophistication, reflecting *their* insight or awareness
and encouraging the same in the patient.

I think a better distinction than insight and interpretation versus
no insight and interpretation would be that Gestalt therapists are

hypersensitive to the invasion of the interpretive process by emotionally isolated cognition, and have designed their techniques accordingly. In Gestalt Therapy the patient quickly learns to make the discrimination between ideas and ideation, between well-worn obsessional pathways and new thoughts, between a statement of experience and a statement of a statement. The Gestalt goal of pursuing experience and not explanations, based on the belief that insight which emerges as the gestalt emerges is more potent than insight given by the therapist, does help the patient and therapist draw and maintain these important distinctions. Psychoanalysts and their patients, on the other hand, have to struggle harder with what seems at times a contradictory attitude with respect to the pursuit of insight in psychoanalysis, e.g., it is said that those insights are best which come from the patient himself, and yet much of psychoanalytic technique has to do with the analyst's making interpretations; insights are held to be most useful when they are accompanied by affect, but interpretations of meaning are not infrequently made with widely varying degrees of emotional involvement.

CAUSE AND CHOICE

Gestalt therapists regularly instruct their patients to substitute "I won't" for "I can't." This little but powerful device is an entry into what in psychoanalysis would be called character analysis. With it the Gestalt therapist implies that he knows that the patient is inclined to minimize his ability and to see his difficulties as external and therefore apart from his control. Thus the Gestalt therapist counters any of the patient's inclinations to be stubborn, petulant, or self-defeating. He implies that the patient has the capacity to solve problems, and that if he doesn't it may well be because he does not want to, all things considered. Such a point of view is in the traditions of psychoanalytic ego psychology, which posits a capacity for problem-solving that is partly independent of and partly an outgrowth of drives, a function of consciousness, will, judgment, decision-making, mastery, and self-determination. This view contrasts with the simplistic understanding of behavior as being solely determined by the id, instincts, or unconscious drives and wishes. A person without choice, driven solely by instincts, could never have been intended by Freud. The essence of psychoanalysis is internal conflict; the id is opposed by the ego, and wishes contend with fears, to say nothing of the competition between impulses themselves. To argue against a conflictual view of human nature is to have misunderstood early psychoanalysis and to be oblivious of later psychoanalysis. Such an error is in a sense understandable, however; some psychoanalysts sound as if they too believe that drive, wish, and symbolism are all that is important in any given bit of behavior.

Psychoanalysis has had difficulty moving from the discovery and drama of unconscious motives and symbolic meanings to the general psychology intended by Freud. It has remained for systematic innovators, such as Roy Schafer (1968a, 1968b, 1973a, 1973b, 1973c), Allen Wheelis (1950, 1956, 1973), and others to make systematically explicit within psychoanalysis the place of action, reason, will, and the making of decisions as these take place with greater or lesser degrees of insight, awareness, and consciousness. Determination in psychoanalysis is actually multi-determination. Saying that a behavior is unconsciously determined is not the same as saying that it is fully and inexorably determined that way. It merely asserts that unconscious motivation is an influence. In this sense gestaltists, as they help people see and experience early relationships which are influential in the present, are no less deterministic than are psychoanalysts. [2] They are, however, more explicit, forceful, and perhaps more confident of people's conscious capacities to deal adequately with their troublesomely determined natures.

MEMORY AND THE HERE-AND-NOW

"Talk to your long-dead relative now," "say how you feel now," "act it, be it now," "use the present tense," say the Gestalt therapists in their pursuit of the here-and-now of experience. Their zeal for phenomenology often results in wild-swinging accusations which make it sound as if psychoanalytic work consists solely of the reconstruction of a figurative past on the assumption that this alone will bring about change. This is at best a half-truth, as discussed by Appelbaum in a review of McGuire, *Reconstruction In Psychoanalysis* (1972). Psychoanalysts and gestaltists essentially agree that the most mutative experiences are those which involve the whole person, are most fully experienced, and take place in the present. In psychoanalysis the most powerful tool for achieving these experiences is the transference, which by definition is seen most clearly by the patient in the here-and-now of the psychoanalytic hour. Transference duplicates past relationships. Indeed Freud described transference as a way of remembering. Recalling an event from the past while leaving it localized there is very different from experiencing the past in the present by way of the transference. (Even recall, however, can be experienced with its associated feelings, in the present. For example, patients will comment that they had often thought of such and such past event, but never "saw" it in the same way as they did when it was recalled during the psychoanalytic hour.) Indeed, a past re-created in the transference may have a greater claim to being in the here-and-now than a past imaginarily re-created in Gestalt role-playing and dialogues.

Finally, much of the here-and-now of group behavior and of the relationship with the therapist is ignored by gestaltists. Gestalt therapists are far less innocent about the past and its uses than one might gather from some of their comments. For example, a Gestalt therapist might say to a patient, "get into your time machine," as an invitation to remember the past. Their patients do, in fact, usually tell of past experiences which have seemingly played a major determining role in the difficulties which they focus on in the Gestalt sessions. Such devices as forcing the patient to use the present do underline the importance of the past as it is presently experienced, and thus guard against allowing abstraction and intellectualization to dessicate experience. For reasons discussed below Gestalt techniques powerfully evoke emotional awareness of the past as it is experienced in the present.

THE BODY

The importance of the body to personality has as its antecedent in psychoanalysis Freud's understanding that the sense of self is first experienced in bodily terms, which he called the body ego. His theory had its beginning in the borderland between psychological and physical processes where he was led by his early patients who had bodily symptoms for which no physical cause could be found. He attempted to spell out psychological processes neurologically in *The Project For A Scientific Psychology* (1966 [1895]); and although he gave up this model, he hoped that physico-chemical processes underlying psychological events would eventually be specifiable. Wilhelm Reich (1949), writing as a traditional though innovative psychoanalyst, suggested that the body not only could express conflict in symptom formation but that the whole configuration of a person's drives and defenses could be inferred by observing him physically. Ella Freeman Sharpe (1938) suggested that the body was a carrier of explicit memories localized in its various parts, and that dream imagery often referred to specific bodily experiences of early childhood.

Psychoanalysts have always considered bodily symptoms, posture, gait, and inadvertent movements to be expressive of personality. Typically, however, these observations in the psychoanalytic are limited to the way the patient enters the office, his movements on the couch (as these may be observed by the analyst behind the patient), and the way he leaves. Even since the brief period when Freud attempted to stimulate reverie by putting his hands on the patient's forehead, direct use of the body has been eschewed in psychoanalysis, consistent with Freud's settling on psychophysical parallelism as his solution to the mind-body problem. By contrast, Gestalt Therapy emphasizes the opportunities for observing the body, exaggerating its expressiveness, and for explicit manipulations of it. Observations are often abetted, especially in Gestalt group sessions, by the opportunity people have for walking around and finding different positions on the floor. Assuming that the body is a carrier of memory and experience often outside of awareness, gestaltists attempt to release such experience through the direct interventions of urging the patient to concentrate on his body, to express himself with it, to change his breathing and body posture, and they often use bioenergetic exercises for these purposes as well.

In summary, psychoanalysis and Gestalt Therapy share similar assumptions about the relationship of body to personality, but psychoanalytic technique, through its emphasis on insight, its adoption of psycho-physical parallelism, and its standardized physical arrangements, has allowed such ideas to atrophy through limited use of them, while Gestalt Therapy has exploited them.

ACCEPTANCE

Both psychoanalysts and Gestalt therapists assert their non-judgmental acceptance of the patient. Therefore, they both struggle with the paradox that even while claiming acceptance, they are nonetheless engaged in a procedure which is designed to facilitate change. The way this paradox is usually solved by both of them is to say that they merely offer the conditions for change, and it is up to the patient to decide what, when, and how changes should occur. For practical reasons, this is probably a serviceable point of view, but it ought not to obscure the recognition that the therapist knows full well that when one goes to a therapist one wants to change something felt to be inimical to his well-being. (If the patient were fully accepted by himself and the therapist, there would hardly be any motivation on the part of anyone to work; putative patients would just be dilettantes, "groupies," whom no therapy would benefit.) The Gestalt therapists, despite the fact that they often claim the title "therapist," may assert that they are not interested in symptoms and cure, in any goals for the patient except that of increasing awareness, raising consciousness, encouraging a sense of whole from parts. In contrast, psychoanalytic patients are inclined to present specific symptoms or complaints to the analyst. If they do not do so, most analysts consider it helpful to work toward the patient's recognition of what is alien and unwanted by himself. However, the psychoanalyst might similarly say he was interested only in making the unconscious conscious, in strengthening the ego, in the patient's integrating felt disparate parts of himself. One must distinguish between an atmosphere of nonjudgmental acceptance of the patient and his productions within the context of the treatment and the overall expectation of something better coming of this work which determines whether to embark on it and when to end it as a socio-professional enterprise. Gestalt therapists seem unnecessarily exercised about acknowledging change as a goal, as if such acknowledgment leads necessarily to a lack of acceptance of the patient's production and where he "is" at any given moment during the treatment. Some psychoanalysts, because of their medical training and the medical role which they assume politically, socially, and administratively, may have to struggle even more than Gestalt therapists with maintaining this distinction between acceptance in the therapeutic hour and the unacceptability of symptoms and symptomatic behavior. Other psychoanalysts may fall into a routinized, timeless, passive position vis à vis purposes, life behavior outside treatment, and termination, which are dangers inherent in long-term treatment (see Appelbaum a).

RESISTANCE

The issue of acceptance probably comes up most pointedly around the concept of resistance. Gestalt therapists at times seem to declare resistance out of court with their exquisite attention to, and premium placed upon, where the patient "is" at the moment. If that "is" does not include an openness to feelings and thoughts and a wish to exploit these, then the patient, at least in group situations has the option of not "working." He stays off the "hot seat" and may or may not relate himself to others in the group. Indeed, he may wander entirely out of the situation without his behavior being an object of particular therapeutic interest to anybody. Instead of analyzing resistance Gestalt therapists assert that the patient needs his resistances, but as a conscious option rather than an unconscious

compulsion. Nonetheless, Gestalt therapists do work with the patient's struggle to be in touch with his thoughts and feelings. Often,
they use bodily tonus and stimulation to overcome what a psychoanalyst might call a condition of resistance. For example, they may
have the patient attend to his body, breathe deeply, do exercises, get
in touch with the lower levels of his mind by acting the part of primitive people or animals. The Gestalt therapist's seeming desirelessness
about resistance makes for an effective way of dealing with resistances. For example, he may ask the patient to notice how he is resisting experience and to exaggerate such behavior until the patient feels
tired, rueful, found out, or ridiculous at so defeating himself. If the
patient expresses resistance by waking up before the dream is ended,
the therapist may ask, "If you had not awakened, how would the
dream have ended?" If the resistance is in the form of not remembering dreams, the therapist may ask, "If you had not forgotten it, what
would the dream have been?"

"Going with" the resistance in such ways is a powerful technique.
At one stroke the therapist may achieve all or some of the following:
neutralize the patient's stubbornness and negativism by offering him
the feeling of independence and control which oppositional people
usually crave; recognize with the patient his need for resistances,
thus underlining the therapist's human understanding and acceptance; stay out of the potential "countertransference bind" of wanting
the patient to go at his own pace but also wanting to move the therapy along; stay out of the potential transference position of judging
some behavior as having to be gotten rid of as if it were by nature
bad; avoid acting in the paradigm of therapist activity, i.e., getting
rid of the resistance, and in the paradigm of patient passivity, i.e.,
allowing the resistance to be taken away, which may be felt by the
patient as a deprivation, attack, or loss.

I have been particularly impressed by the degree to which many
patients take the analyst's interventions as prohibitions and criticisms, no matter how neutrally and nonjudgmentally expressed and
felt by the analyst. The analyst may know that his interventions are
functional rather than moral, but the distinction seems difficult for
many patients to maintain, and it may not always be easy for the
analyst either. After all, he *does* value an intrapsychic situation
which is relatively unimpeded by resistances, and he *is* inclined to
describe a patient who can overcome his resistances as a "good" patient, and he *does* usually select for analysis only those patients who
give evidence of capacities favorable to analytic success. The Gestalt
point of view and consequent feeling about resistances, even apart

from the particular techniques used, helps minimize any such tendencies toward being judgmental in other than functional ways.

Psychoanalysts usually make resistance the figure without self-consciously attending to the ground of the open, "working" state of consciousness as such; Gestalt therapists make the working state of consciousness the figure, with what are in effect resistant states of mind and consciousness unlabeled and undesignated as such, though very much attended to. They agree on the nature of resistance, however. The Gestalt emphasis on helping the patient discover "the mechanism by which he alienates part of his self-processes and thereby avoids awareness of himself and environment" is a serviceable definition of resistance (Yontef, 1969).

DREAMS

In psychoanalysis the dream is the guardian of sleep in that it allows partial expression of impulses by symbolically fulfilling the wishes which are psychological expressions of such dammed-up impulses. In Gestalt Therapy a dream is described as an existential message from one part of the self to another part of the self. On the surface these viewpoints might seem quite different, but in point of face the differences are more apparent than real. Even as stated there is nothing necessarily contradictory about these formulations. After all, unfulfilled wishes and their consequences are most of what existence is about. And there is at least a bit of psychoanalytic lore to the effect that if one traced all the possible associations to any one dream the whole personality would be revealed.

Any seeming differences are even less apparent when one moves from metapsychology to the way psychoanalysts use dreams in practice. The dream is not always taken as an actual event of the night, but rather a communication from the patient to the analyst in the here-and-now of the psychoanalytic hour. Thus patient and analyst may learn from when the dream was mentioned, how it was told, and what the patient does with it once it is told. The analyst may understand the introduction or report of a dream at a particular moment as an avoidance of the here-and-now, he may call attention to that, or simply ignore the dream. Or he may react to it as an existential message which the patient, for defensive reasons or through lack of conscious awareness, is unable to express in less coded ways. Rather than offering an explanation (which many Gestalt therapists seem to think he would invariably do), the psychoanalyst would likely encourage the patient not only to associate to elements in the dream but to come up with his own understanding. Just as a Gestalt therapist might do, the psychoanalyst might remind *his* patient that the dream was a creation of the dreamer's mind rather than a representation of people or events apart from himself.

While both kinds of therapies are likely to collect associations to dream elements, no matter how seemingly irrelevant or unimportant, Gestalt therapists do employ a technique not ordinarily employed by psychoanalysts—a kind of guided imagery-associative process. This technique is to have the patient *be* a person or element in the dream, and say, in effect, what comes to mind as this person or element. Proceeding on the belief that everything in the dream reflects aspects of the person, gestaltists assume that a spoon, window, or coffin, can be learned from just as can such more obvious self-representations as people or animals.

In recent years, the importance of the dream in psychoanalytic technique has diminished to the point that some analysts claim to ignore dreams entirely. It may be that these analysts have learned that at least their way of using dreams has led to dreams being used more as resistance than as a useful point of entry into the inner life. It seems to me worth the while of psychoanalysts to explore the Gestalt techniques of role-playing with elements in the dream. By observation and experience I have been impressed that they lead quickly and usefully to emotional experience and insight.

OBJECT RELATIONS VIA DIALOGUE

Constructing a monologue or dialogue based on dream parts is only a variation of the major Gestalt Therapy technique of having the patient "play the parts" of himself and people significant in his life. This technique, too, is foreign to psychoanalysis, and might well be investigated for its possible effectiveness. Such a procedure, among other things, dramatizes what the psychoanalyst informed by object relations theory might label as the "inner world of objects." It provides dramatic illustrations of the relationships between self and others as these are carried out within the mind of the patient. It demonstrates the interchangeability and empathy that one can have with the people who comprise one's self. Improved self-awareness, and by implication greater tranquility and effectiveness, come about by owning up to rather than disowning these "introjects," as one forgives, adjusts to, or otherwise integrates them into a workable, less conflict-laden whole. Gestaltists work, first, toward recognition of the separateness of introjects, visible by way of their being projected, then toward a reintrojection of them into the self. Such a formulation and way of working would be compatible to many psychoanalysts particularly those of Kleinian or other object-relations persuasion.

FREE ASSOCIATION AND "WORKING"

Initially I was surprised at how articulate Gestalt Therapy patients were in talking about their personal problems and difficulties in front of a group. I wondered whether I would be able to "work" adequately on the hot seat at all. Such fears were unfounded. In a short time I was able to shift gears into a state of consciousness not unlike what one experiences on the psychoanalytic couch which facilitates free association, openness to experience and reverie. Maybe the inhibiting effect of a face-to-face confrontation is diminished by there being many faces; maybe the atmosphere of acceptance so prevalent in Gestalt work helps one overcome inhibitions; maybe observing others doing the same thing allows a sense of community that helps allay fear and embarrassment; maybe impeding the development of a transference relationship is helpful in this regard (see below).

Articulateness and verbal productivity in the Gestalt session seem to stem in large measure from the free associative process. Some Gestalt therapists may be surprised at my applying such a term to the flow of ideas when a patient is "working," but I think that might be due to a common misunderstanding of the term and phenomena of free association. "Free association" is a misnomer. Associations, by definition, follow rules if not laws. Psychoanalysis posits that associations are determined by motives or impulses and are therefore meaningful. What is "free" about the phenomenon is a state of mind that allows thoughts to come, unhampered by judgments as to whether they are moral, intelligent, or important. Freed of such strictures, the patient is helped to allow the rules of determination to operate "freely." Psychoanalysts make these conditions formal with the basic rule—tell whatever comes to mind—which in large part is only a formality. The atmosphere provided by analysis is enough to encourage the associative process without the rule, just as seems to occur in Gestalt Therapy sessions. However, the expliciteness of the task denoted by the basic rule is a powerful adjunct to the basic free-associative process, making for wider-ranging associations and for the emergence of resistances whose analysis becomes central to the understanding of the personality. By contrast a somewhat more narrative framework, adopted by "working" Gestalt patients, may go deeper and faster, though less broadly. Essentially, however, "working" comes about by letting one thought lead to another, i.e., free associations.

PSYCHOSEXUAL STAGES

Frequently during Gestalt work I found myself translating back and forth between the language of the Gestalt session and the language of psychoanalysis. At times this procedure served as a resistance; my psychoanalytic self felt slightly guilty and resolved to get back to work. This contrasts with the Gestalt view that such wavering attention indicates a natural wisdom as to how much can be integrated. A particular example occurred when the issue of intimacy was discussed in a group which I attended. (This was an example of a more didactic and explanatory comment than one might surmise, from Gestalt writing, would often be made. It was done with a lightness of touch and humanism which I thought increased its intellectual cogency and probably usefulness.) As discussed, the problem of intimacy was to find a comfortable and effective point between the extremes of confluence, characterized by lack of discrimination between people out of a clinging need for others (which might be labeled grossly as orality) and excessive distance, a hyperdiscrimination between self and others with rigidly prescribed means of interpersonal contact (which might be labeled grossly, anal). The comfortable and effective midpoint between these extremes allows an integration of both of them, in the service of discharging effectively the task of intimacy, getting the most from and giving the most to relationships (which might be labeled phallic-genital).

The Fritz Perls model (1969) of taking in through the mouth what is compatible and spitting out what is not seems identical with the oral-dependent-oral-aggressive paradigm in psychoanalysis. Thus, Gestalt workers observe and work clinically with the experiences and behaviors which psychoanalysts work with, though psychoanalysts relate these constellations of behavior theoretically to psychosexual stages and modes.

CHANGE AND TIME

Gestalt therapists often use what could be labeled corrective emotional experience. They encourage their patients to try out thoughts, expressions, and behaviors to see what feels right for them. They depend on the non-occurrence of the unconsciously expected consequences as being reassuring to the patient, thereby encouraging him to use these new behaviors and be emboldened to try out still more new ones. This idea seems to underlie "risk-taking": "Sure you feel anxious," the Gestalt therapist says, "but don't let that hold you back, try it out, go ahead and see what happens." Gestaltists do this to increase awareness rather than simply to encourage mindless new behavior as some therapists do out of a belief that behaving differently in and of itself is sufficient. The traditional though not exclusive psychoanalytic approach would be to try to help the patient understand what was making him anxious. With the consequent diminution of anxiety, the patient can proceed with the behavior which had been inhibited by fear. Some psychoanalysts probably are convinced that in all instances insight precedes change and consider the taking of action and the assertion of will by the patient as outside the range of psychoanalytic work. In my opinion the roles of will, action, decision-making, and an openness to the possibility that changed behavior can precede and bring about insight are inherent in psychoanalytic thinking, though perhaps they are only recently becoming fully recognized. The use of understanding, insight, the psychoanalysis itself as a possible defense against the anxiety of changing one's behavior is, or should be, well-recognized; as Freud said, sooner or later a phobic patient must face, rather than merely talk about, his phobias (1955 [1919]). Some psychoanalysts may encourage understanding beyond a point where taking on extra-analytic challenges should be encouraged (such encouragement can be done analytically, through interpretation, as well as through exhortation). Gestalt therapists probably avoid this kind of error with their de-emphasis on insight as an explicit goal and their emphasis upon the immediate taking of risks, if only in speech during the Gestalt sessions. The danger is that they merely inspire the patient to behave differently, based essentially on suggestion and borrowing the strength of the therapist. Away from the therapeutic influence the changed behavior might well collapse, or the patient may be unable to deal with the consequences of the new behavior.

The Gestalt Therapy attitude toward time is flexible, soft, and maternal: There need never be endings, Gestalt patients may continue attending group or individual sessions indefinitely, and these sessions themselves may go on until their idiosyncratic conclusion. How one feels at the particular moment is all-important, with the understanding that this feeling may change in an instant. The demands of continuity, predictability, beginnings, middles, and ends which are identified with the masculine elements in personality are relatively unattended to (Mann, 1973). Some patients may experience such a point of view as reassuring. It lightens the burden of commitments; it relieves the need for promising and being responsible in the future. Yet the relatively brief time usually allotted to the therapy puts a premium on solving problems quickly.

By contrast, psychoanalysts are rigid about the time boundaries of each session, often make gross predictions of the length of treatment, and are attuned to the psychologies of beginnings, middles, and ends. This scrupulousness about time lies in uneasy apposition with the implicit timelessness within the treatment period—what isn't dealt with today can be dealt with tomorrow, the wheel comes around again, themes will recur, and four or five years of four or five times a week treatment is unremarkable. For some patients the stipulation of a period of time of treatment may imply that they cannot change their behavior until the treatment has been concluded or has taken effect. The analyst has to alert himself and the patient to the immanence of now, the capacities for self-help which can in principle operate at any given moment. He and the patient must overcome the passivity implicit in waiting and must come to terms with the illusion that a period of time and treatment, even when it is a long period of time, can in and of itself result in an improved life ever after.

SELF-SELECTION OF GESTALTISTS AND PSYCHOANALYSTS

There seems no reason to exempt the choice of Gestalt Therapy or psychoanalysis by practitioners or patients from the participation of unconscious motives. Even granting that there was no Gestalt Therapy for middle-aged and older psychoanalysts to choose, the life styles typically practiced by the two groups suggest fundamental differences in their personalities. Gestalt therapists are more informal than psychoanalysts, less inner- and goal-directed, more direct in their interpersonal relationships, more responsive to the primitive and romantic in man, more optimistic, hedonistic, and socialistic. Aggression seems less central in their personalities and even in the group atmosphere. The defensive purposes served by contrasting life styles of psychoanalysts and gestaltists probably interfere with their attempts to understand one another's theories and practices for their intrinsic worth. Instead, both groups tend to see in each other caricatures of the warded-off parts of themselves: the uptight, rigid, button-down, hyperintellectual, unfeeling, materialistic, hidebound psychoanalyst; the sloppy, childlike, fuzzy-faced, fuzzy-minded Gestalt therapist. It is a sad commentary on people who espouse wholeness to split off and project aspects of themselves—sad, but all too understandably human. In principle at least, an integrated psychotherapist could adopt insights, techniques, emphases, and values from wherever they might arise toward increasing his effectiveness. He could do the same with himself as a person. The alternative position would be to be convinced that the way one works achieves the best results possible for all patients, under all circumstances, at the least expense of time and money, and with the least risk—a breathtakingly bold and self-confident position. That he could not improve himself or his life would be, if anything, even more breathtakingly bold and self-confident.

CLOSURE

Both Gestalt therapists and psychoanalysts sound at times as if they have closure as a realizable goal. In Gestalt Therapy lack of closure is "unfinished business," an unexpressed and unintegrated feeling relative to a person or situation, which by implication at least can be finished. Psychoanalysts set forth goals such as the resolution of the transference, resolution of conflicts, and a full and complete psychoanalysis. Yet, at the same time both gestaltists and psychoanalysts also hold as a goal the patient's developing tools with which he can help himself in the future, through self-analysis or through the capacity to make himself increasingly aware. This suggests that neither field considers that its formal treatment efforts provide an absolute solution to the patient's problems. In one systematic research of psychoanalytically oriented psychotherapy and psychoanalysis little conflict resolution was found to have occurred, at least as judged from psychological tests. Other changes in conflicts such as awareness of them in consciousness occurred more frequently (see Appelbaum b). Reanalysis or further brief analytic work is not uncommon (although Freud's dictum that every person should have further analytic work every five years is honored more in the breach than in the observance). Gestalt patients often attend continued workshops where they are reminded that what is true for one moment need not be true for the next moment and that determination or ambition for too much change over too long a period of time is inimical to awareness and change ("trying is lying").

"Closure" or "resolution" are most clearly applicable to those moments during the therapeutic work when something is integrated, usually signaled by a feeling of liberation and relief, and the patient is released toward new challenges. It is paradoxical to apply the language of closure—termination, ending, and completion—to the treatment as a whole while at the same time believing that the patient should deal with continuing conflicts in new, perhaps ever-changing ways. This is a particular issue for psychoanalysts, who posit comprehensiveness, if not completion, as a purpose and justification for the considerable time and expense of analysis. Such an implication is made concrete by the work's having a fixed ending and being offered in the social context of the health-sickness model (inapplicable as that model is to psychoanalysis). In that model, with a prescribed treatment one hopes to cure a sickness definitely.

Gestalt therapists are more easy-going in this respect. They are satisfied with fragmentary interventions with respect to the personality and to the structure of the treatment. While some gestaltists may use a regular schedule of appointments with a fixed ending, others give patients the option of coming or not coming and when there working or not working. This may open the way for patients' resistances. They may either keep attending Gestalt workshops, and in that way appear to be trying to improve themselves even though not achieving greater awareness; or they may in response to the anxiety of emerging, unintegrated awareness, simply stop attending.

All those who work toward human change might benefit from asking themselves whether "closure," "resolution," "completion" are satisfactory words and concepts at all, whether the human condition permits or admits of them. Rather than achieving enduring solutions or lasting joy, the patient, as does any person, has to learn to live with the quest for awareness itself, with recognition of the mystery, profundity, and ambiguity of human life and its ultimately unsatisfactory, and in many ways incomplete, ending.

RELATIONSHIP WITH THE THERAPIST-ANALYST

The following experience is consonant with the Gestalt therapist's attitude toward differentiated interpersonal relationships between patient and therapist:

I had to be late to a Gestalt workshop, and therefore missed the new therapist's self-introduction and preliminary work. Feeling the need to "work," however, I took the hot seat as soon as I could and achieved intensely experienced new insights. I left the workshop not yet knowing the name of the therapist who asked me the right questions, told me the right things to associate to in dreams, interrupted a defensive tangent, made an aspect of my inner world live, and found ways to encourage its intense emotional expression.

Insofar as the temporary Gestalt experience may be concerned, the lack of a differentiated sense of the therapist could be helpful. In the example just cited, I was absorbed with an internal puzzle and in a low-key, unself-conscious way was sufficiently satisfied with what I had seen of the therapist's working with others to be content with knowing what was expected of me and what was to be forthcoming from him. Transference characteristics of the therapist, even a "real" relationship with him, could conceivably at that moment have been an impediment. If, however, having an extended individual relationship with a benevolent other is in and of itself important to enduring change, then its absence from Gestalt Therapy may be an important loss for some patients. Some psychoanalysts—such as the so-called interpersonal school of Sullivan, Will, and Fromm-Reichmann—are much more convinced and explicit about the curative effects of such relationships than are other psychoanalysts. Whatever the curative effects of the relationship, psychoanalysts focus upon the relationship between patient and analyst not for purposes of practicing interpersonal relationships or to provide corrective emotional experience, but as a powerful aid to learning about internal relationships. A transference relationship as a way of learning about one's self is mostly lost to Gestalt patients.

All psychoanalysts are aware that the presence or absence of relationship phenomena can be helpful or harmful, depending upon the situation at the time and the nature and goals of the treatment. It is not a question to be satisfactorily answered for everybody in the abstract. It does, however, define a psychoanalysis; without a transference relationship the therapy would not be psychoanalysis. This is a major difference between psychoanalysis and Gestalt Therapy.

The psychoanalyst is often caricatured as a passive, inscrutable, stone-faced figure sitting in interminable silence. Psychoanalysts employ relative passivity, inactivity, and the "active" use of silence so that associations can range widely and deeply. They offer as much neutrality as possible so that the patient can see how he transfers upon the analyst other and past relationships. When the Gestalt patient falls into a free-associative state of consciousness, the therapist is highly directive as he circumscribes the general area of association. In place of the patient's relative freedom to let any associations come to mind, the Gestalt therapist stimulates the patient's productions in limited directions to some extent. In so doing he decreases the patient's opportunities to react to the therapist in idiosyncratic ways.

Also militating against the growth of the relationship between therapist and patient are some Gestaltists' somewhat hit-and-miss attitudes toward schedules and toward extended work with only a single
therapist.

Gestaltists might profitably ask themselves whether on balance
they gain or lose more from minimizing the transference and in being
so active. Psychoanalysts might ask themselves if they have perhaps
overestimated the amount of injury to the transference and working
relationship likely should they be more active. Neutrality, after all, is
in itself only relatively neutral; the patient gains a great amount of
information from the way the analyst conducts himself, as well as
from what he learns of the analyst outside the hour. If the baseline
includes increased activity and the use of various active techniques,
such behavior may not unmanageably influence the transference,
and may provide as revealing and useful a baseline as the "neutral"
traditional one does.

CORRECTIONS FOR PSYCHOANALYSTS AND OTHERS WHOM IT MAY CONCERN

The Gestalt emphasis upon the immediacy of experience, self-
responsibility, and mind-body holism could provide a correction for
possible errors in psychoanalytic technique. The danger of such
technical errors is part of the cost which psychoanalysis pays for its
elaborate theory whose avowed purpose is to understand all human
behavior, motives, adaptations, morals, art, and social groupings. It
is a price, too, that psychoanalysis pays for being comprised of
several theories (metapsychological, clinical, experiential, and
empirical) which were set forth over a period of three-quarters of a
century, each generation of analysts learning somewhat different
versions. That is a lot of theory to keep in mind, sort out, and pick
from when working with patients. Gestalt practitioners have no such
ambitious goals as formulating a science, and their theory is by comparison compact and homogeneous. I do not think that there is anything in Gestalt which is essentially contradictory to the psychoanalytic understanding of personality; with translation, Gestalt
would fit comfortably into the commodious psychoanalytic super-
structure. That Gestalt techniques differ from those of psychoanalysis, however, gives one pause. People change beneficially as a result
of treatment by both kinds of practitioners (and many other kinds of
practitioners as well). Such an observation suggests that there are
common elements in all these interventions, which patients respond

to regardless of the language and concepts and techniques of the practitioners. This is not to say that all interventions do equally well with all kinds of patients and with all kinds of objectives. That involves empirical questions which no one has decisively and definitively answered as yet.

Gestalt techniques were in part designed to counter alleged errors in psychoanalytic technique and theory. Gestalt criticisms can join with such revisionist trends within psychoanalysis as dropping the structural and economic points of view, and emphasizing phenomenology, process, and experience, all of which have implications for changes in technique. The Gestalt challenge may serve as a helpful stimulus in reraising, in novel ways, issues of flexibility, empathy, concreteness, present-past emphasis, and the capacity and autonomy of the patient, in addition to its offering new techniques in psychoanalysis.

CORRECTIONS FOR GESTALTISTS AND OTHERS WHOM IT MAY CONCERN

One way psychoanalysts can contribute to Gestalt Therapy is to assert the need for an encompassing, differentiated theory of personality on which clinical sophistication and flexibility for differing clinical emergencies can be based. While for the most part I found Gestalt therapists remarkably sensitive, selecting patient material and techniques which to my mind were responsive to the patient's needs, I have seen instances where I thought a better overall clinical understanding of patients based in theory would have increased the Gestalt therapist's helpfulness to them.

In one such instance a patient seemed to be smugly complacent about a way of life and kind of self which made others responsible for him, and in which aggression was masochistically bound rather than constructively available. In my opinion the therapeutic task and ethical responsibility were to test the limits of his apparent contentment. If he really was without workable or usable conflict, then the therapist should not interfere with his chosen way of life, and in fact could not make any headway toward changing it anyway. Yet patients may present themselves as satisfied only to respond to probing diagnostic interventions by becoming anxious and aware that they wish they could live and feel differently. In this instance one such intervention could have been to confront the patient with why he was participating in the Gestalt workshop. But such an intervention could not be made when a perfectly acceptable reason for being there was simply to "enlarge awareness" or to "raise consciousness." As with any jargon, such phrases can obscure motives and deflect potentially unsettling intrusions. Moreover, as I found out, such confrontations were alien to the spirit of the therapy group, and fell on unreceptive ears. This patient may go from one Gestalt Therapy group to another, increasing his awareness and raising his consciousness without ever coming to terms with the conflicts which I suspect are depriving him of choice as to his way of life.

In another example, a woman portrayed herself as not being able to find a man who could provide her with as much joy as did her lover in the occasional moment when he had time for her. The therapist seemed to accept at face-value that no other man in the world could satisfy her, ignoring the information that when she was not available, her lover's interest in her increased. In my opinion her need for such a sadomasochistic relationship is preventing her from finding other kinds of gratification. To suggest, as was done, that for her the task was simply to decide whether the joy she was able to get from this relationship was sufficient or not, and to proceed accordingly, could help spell the end to her stated hopes for marriage and motherhood.

Even if my judgments in these examples are correct, they hardly prove anything. A Gestalt therapist, indeed another psychoanalytic clinician, could find in the caseloads of any psychoanalyst "mistakes" of one kind or another. I cite the examples only to illustrate how training rooted in an understanding of psychopathology is necessary to guide clinical actions and decisions.

I am concerned, also, about the casual attitude on the part of some Gestalt workers toward shaky ego functioning—the potentiality for injuring the patient through encouraging more psychological work than he can master. Their attitude may stem from an inability to assess such dangers, often a difficult task for anyone no matter how well trained, which sometimes requires hours of psychological testing. It is often explained by them as being based on the belief that the patient should be given credit for the ability to maintain himself. I think it is likely that there is a range of instances in which psychoanalytic clinicians might step in with support too soon, minimizing the patient's capacity to help himself. I think it just as likely that there is a range of instances in which the patients cannot sufficiently help themselves, and, if unsupported, needlessly develop symptoms, act on the environment in harmful ways, commit suicide, or become psychotic. I saw no such instances myself; indeed, I saw a Gestalt therapist deal effectively with one such danger by unwinding the patient from an emotional pitch which threatened to get out of hand, primarily through helping the patient anchor himself in his bodily experiences. I do think, however, that some patients, if subjected to Gestalt work without interpersonal or environmental supportive measures being available, would risk being harmed. Deciding if, when, and how such measures should be used seems to me to require a comprehensively trained clinician with a wide range of interpersonal or environmental options available.

Such clinical mistakes as I have suggested occurred should hardly be surprising. Gestalt therapists say, on paper, that they are in favor of systematic training of practitioners, and compared to some new brands of psychotherapy they do have extensive training and high standards. However, compared to that of psychoanalysts, the training of Gestalt therapists is limited, being shorter, less systematic, and providing less wide-ranging clinical experience. The surprising thing to me is not that there were occasional errors (or at least times when I felt at odds with the strategy and conclusions) but that I saw so few. Without adequate comparative studies, we are left with the questions about the usefulness, for the treatment of patients, of the therapist's knowing developmental theory, general psychology, the differing psychologies of men and women, psychopathology, and other aspects of psychoanalytic training. But the training issue cannot be solved without at the same time resolving questions of differing goals of the treater, and with respect to different capacities and wishes of the patient. Training has to be commensurate with task, although to ascertain what a particular therapeutic task should be itself, requires considerable expertise.

A VIEW FROM ABOVE

We may ask ourselves in what way the overall system, the culture, our world is being served by the emergence of Gestalt Therapy and the many other therapies that have developed in recent years. We are encouraged to take this perspective by the fact that these therapies seem part of a cultural revolution; they are not just technical or scientific emendations and discoveries. One not only practices Gestalt Therapy instead of psychoanalysis, but often does it without shoes, using first names, with psychedelically inspired pillows, while being casual toward time boundaries, nourished by organic food, hostile toward material possessions and Western culture, and admiring abstemiousness and Eastern philosophy. In short, Gestalt Therapy is cresting a wave of frustration and revolt, of regret for the past, distrust of the present, and pessimism about the future, while at the same time formulating an optimistic response with ancient antecedents. The present generation of world citizens is the first to have been born into a world in which death to the whole community, from nuclear destruction, is always a hairbreadth away. Rather than being unduly fanciful, it seems parsimonious and hardheaded to me to understand current resentment of how we got here, and determination that the future will be different, with reference to this atmosphere of imminent extinction.

Psychoanalysis began as an intellectual rebellion, as a decisive new chapter in Western man's thoughts about his nature and the world in which he lives. But through its association with science and materialism and emphasis upon reason, psychoanalysis is seen as a social and administrative arm of Western establishment; it is legally and socially sanctioned by it. As such many people feel it is something to be rebelled against. In principle, this should not matter. The substance of psychoanalysis still remains a powerful means of systematically understanding all of human nature. Psychoanalysis still offers the ultimate freedom which lies in being able to think all of one's thoughts and liberate all of one's behavior from constraints unknown to the person. Psychoanalysis is itself always in rebellion against much of what is wrong in our culture. Unfortunately, many workers in the field of human change have only a smattering of knowledge about psychoanalysis, and they condense its social and legal position with its substance. In large part psychoanalysis has only itself to blame for this. Its exclusive training practices have made it impossible for many people interested in and capable of working with the human condition to learn psychoanalysis. That such people should find a new path, perhaps in part founded upon resentment at being excluded, is hardly surprising.

From a general systems point of view Gestalt and the other new therapies have been used by the overall system to bring about corrections, additions, and emphases beneficial to the whole of the science of human improvement and change. The human mind, scientific or otherwise, works in dialectical ways, polarizing, going from one extreme to the other. In sharp contrast to the "activity" of a traditional medical practitioner at the turn of the century, Freud discovered that "passivity" allowed the emergence of information about the mind. Psychoanalysis is now identified with being passive, and may in some ways indeed be too much so. The same criticism of overemphasis could be leveled against such psychoanalytic discoveries as the importance of unconscious motivation and the influence of the past on the present. Within psychoanalysis the dialectical pendulum has been making its way back toward a more balanced view as analysts become more active, as they take multidetermination more seriously, and through their increased recognition of the implications of autonomous ego functions, neutralized drives, manifest dream content, and the power of consciousness. Further rethinking and corrections are implicitly being offered by Gestalt Therapy, among others, as part of the overall scientific system which embraces and is responsible for the development of all thought. If any of us are to benefit from the ideas and experiences of others, then the whole has to be defined not as psychoanalysis alone, nor Gestalt Therapy alone, but as knowledge. Only knowledge can unite disparate schools, techniques, and views of man and change. Only knowledge is boundaryless and infinite.

NOTES

1. I have had my comments about Gestalt reviewed by Gestalt workers Jerome Fleischer, John Heider, and Philip Himelstein. I am most grateful to them.
2. People often sound as if they subscribe to single causes or determinants when they know better. Ambiguity, choice, weighting, and unsureness are all difficult to deal with, especially in the face of the anxiety generated by intensive work with patients. Sounding as if one believes in unidetermination is sometimes caused by one's difficulty in thinking and speaking of more than one thing at a time.

REFERENCES

Appelbaum, Stephen A. "Did It Really Happen?" *Psychotherapy and Social Science Review*, 7 (1972): 24-27.
———"Parkinson's Law in Psychotherapy." *International Journal of Psychoanalytic Psychology*, 4: 272-302, 1975.
———"Psychotherapy Before and After." In Press.
Freud, Sigmund. "The Project for a Scientific Psychology." *Standard Edition*, Vol. 1, 283-397. London: Hogarth Press, 1966.
———"Lines of Advance in Psycho-analytic Therapy." *Standard Edition*, Vol. 17, 157-168. London: Hogarth Press, 1955.
Mann, James. *Time-Limited Psychotherapy*. Cambridge: Harvard University Press, 1973.
Perls, Fritz S. *Ego, Hunger, and Aggression*. New York: Vintage Books, 1969.
Reich, Wilhelm. *Character Analysis*. Third enlarged edition. New York: Orgone Institute Press, 1949.
Schafer, Roy. "The Mechanisms of Defence." *The International Journal of Psycho-Analysis*, 49 (1968) (1), 49-62.
———"On the Theoretical and Technical Conceptualization of Activity and Passivity." *The Psychoanalytic Quarterly*, 37 (1968): 173-198.
———"Action: Its Place in Psychoanalytic Interpretation and Theory." *The Annual of Psychoanalysis*, 1 (1973): 159-196.
———"Concepts of Self and Identity and the Experience of Separation-Individuation in Adolescence." *The Psychoanalytic Quarterly*, 42 (January, 1973) (1), 42-59.

————"The Idea of Resistance." *The International Journal of Psycho-Analysis*, 54 (1973), Part 3, 259-285.

Sharpe, Ella Freeman. *Dream Analysis: A Practical Handbook for Psychoanalysis*. New York: Norton, 1938.

Wheelis, Allen. "The Place of Action in Personality Change." *Psychiatry*, 13 (1950): 135-148.

————"Will and Psychoanalysis." *Journal American Psychoanalytic Association*, 4 (1956): 285-303.

————*How People Change*. New York: Harper & Row, 1973.

Yontef, Gary M. *A Review of the Practice of Gestalt Therapy*. Los Angeles: Trident, California State College, 1971.

CHAPTER 32

GESTALT THERAPY RESOURCES

JERRY KOGAN, Ph.D. and PHIL HIMELSTEIN, Ph.D.

Phil Himelstein, a coeditor of this volume, is Professor of Psychology, University of Texas, El Paso, Texas.

Books

Barnett, M. *People, Not Psychiatry*. London: Allen & Unwin, 1973.

Brown, G. I. *Human Teaching for Human Learning: An Introduction to Confluent Education*. New York: Viking, 1971.

Downing, J., and Marmorstein, R. *Dreams and Nightmares: A Book for Gestalt Therapy Dream Seminars*. New York: Perennial Library, 1973.

Dye, H. A. *Gestalt Approaches to Counseling*. New York: Houghton Mifflin, 1975.

Fagan, J. and Shepherd, I. L., eds. *Gestalt Therapy Now*. Palo Alto, Calif.: Science and Behavior Books, 1970 (Harper Colophon, 1971).

Fagan, J., and Shepherd, I. L., eds. *What is Gestalt Therapy?* New York: Perennial Library, 1973 (reprint of selections from *Gestalt Therapy Now*).

Fagan, J., and Shepherd, I. L., eds. *Life Techniques in Gestalt Therapy*. New York: Perennial Library, 1973 (reprint of selections from *Gestalt Therapy Now*).

Faraday, A. *Dream Power*. New York: Coward, McCann & Geoghegan, 1972 (Berkeley Medallion, 1973).

Greenwald, J. A. *Be the Person You Were Meant to Be: Antidotes to Toxic Living*. New York: Simon & Schuster, 1974.

Kempler, W. *Principles of Gestalt Family Therapy*. Costa Mesa, Calif.: Kempler Institute, 1974.

Latner, J. *The Gestalt Therapy Book*. New York: Julian, 1973 (Bantam, 1974).

Lederman, J. *Anger and the Rocking Chair: Gestalt Awareness with Children*. New York: McGraw-Hill, 1969.

Levy, R. *I Can Only Touch You Now*. Englewood Cliffs, N.J.: Prentice-Hall, 1973.

Lewis, H. R., and Streitfeld, H. S. *Growth Games*. New York: Harcourt Brace Jovanovich, 1971 (Bantam, 1972).

Loew, C. A.; Grayson, H.; and Loew, G. H., eds. *Three Psychotherapies: A Clinical Comparison.* New York: Brunner/Mazel, 1975.

Lyons, Joseph. *Experience: An Introduction to a Personal Psychology.* New York: Harper & Row, 1973 (esp. ch. 10).

Naranjo, C. *The Techniques of Gestalt Therapy.* Berkeley, Calif.: SAT Press, 1973.

Passons, W. R. *Gestalt Approaches in Counseling.* New York: Holt, Rinehart and Winston, 1975.

Perls, F. S. *Ego, Hunger and Aggression.* London: Allen & Unwin, 1947 (Random House, 1969).

Perls, F. S. *Gestalt Therapy Verbatim.* Moab, Utah: Real People Press, 1969.

Perls, F. S. *In and Out of the Garbage Pail.* Moab, Utah: Real People Press, 1969 (Bantam, 1971).

Perls, F. S. *The Gestalt Approach and Eye Witness to Therapy.* Palo Alto, Calif.: Science & Behavior, 1973.

Perls, F. S.; Hefferline, R. F.; and Goodman, P. *Gestalt Therapy.* New York: Julian Press, 1951 (Dell, 1965).

Polster, E. and Polster, M. *Gestalt Therapy Integrated.* New York: Brunner/Mazel, 1973.

Pursglove, P. D. *Recognition in Gestalt Therapy.* New York: Funk & Wagnalls, 1968.

Rhyne, J. *The Gestalt Art Experience.* Monterey, Calif.: Brooks/Cole, 1973.

Rosenblatt, D. *Gestalt Therapy Primer.* New York: Harper & Row, 1975.

Rosenblatt, D. *Opening Doors: What Happens in Gestalt Therapy.* New York: Harper & Row, 1975.

Schiffman, M. *Gestalt Self Therapy.* Menlo Park, Calif.: Self Therapy Press, 1971.

Shepherd, M. *Fritz: An Intimate Portrait of Fritz Perls and Gestalt Therapy.* New York: Saturday Review Press, 1975 (Bantam, 1976).

Shostrom, E. L. *Man, the Manipulator.* Nashville: Abingdon Press, 1967, (Bantam, 1968).

Simkin, J. S. *Mini-Lectures in Gestalt Therapy.* Albany, Calif.: Wordpress, 1974.

Stephenson, F. D., ed. *Gestalt Therapy Primer: Introductory Readings in Gestalt Therapy.* Springfield, Ill.: Charles C Thomas, 1975.

Stevens, B. *Don't Push the River.* Moab, Utah: Real People Press, 1969.

Stevens, J. O. *Awareness: Exploring, Experimenting, Experiencing.* Moab, Utah: Real People Press, 1971.

Stevens, J. O., ed. *Gestalt Is.* Moab, Utah: Real People Press, 1975.

Walkenstein, E. *Beyond the Couch.* New York: Crown, 1972.

Walker, J. L. *Body and Soul: Gestalt Therapy and Religious Experience.* Nashville: Abingdon Press, 1971.

Yontef, G. M. *A Review of the Practice of Gestalt Therapy*. Los Angeles: Trident Shop, California State University, 1971 (also in *Gestalt Therapy Primer*, edited by F. D. Stephenson).

Chapters

Beisser, A. R. "The Paradoxical Theory of Change." In *Gestalt Therapy Now*. Edited by J. Fagan and I. L. Shepherd. Palo Alto, Calif.: Science and Behavior, 1970, 77-80.

Close, H. T. "Gross Exaggeration with a Schizophrenic Patient." In *Gestalt Therapy Now*. Edited by J. Fagan and I. L. Shepherd. Palo Alto, Calif.: Science and Behavior, 1970, 194-196.

Cohn, R. C. "Therapy in Groups: Psychoanalytic, Experiential, and Gestalt." In *Gestalt Therapy Now*. Edited by J. Fagan and I. L. Shepherd. Science and Behavior, 1970, 130-139.

Cohn, R. C. "A Child with a Stomachache: Fusion of Psychoanalytic Concepts and Gestalt Techniques." In *Gestalt Therapy Now*. Edited by J. Fagan and I. L. Shepherd. Palo Alto, Calif.: Science and Behavior, 1970, 197-203.

Denes-Radomisli, M. "The Context of Therapeutic Innovations: A Gestalt Therapist's View." *Innovation in Psychotherapy*. Edited by G. D. Goldman and D. S. Milman, 104-117.

Ennis, K. and Mitchell, S. "Staff Training For a Day Care Center." In *Gestalt Therapy Now*. Edited by J. Fagan and I. L. Shepherd. Palo Alto, Calif.: Science and Behavior, 1970, 295-300.

Enright, J. B. "An Introduction to Gestalt Therapy." In *Gestalt Therapy Now*. Edited by J. Fagan and I. L. Shepherd. Palo Alto, Calif.: Science and Behavior, 1970, 140-219 (also in *Gestalt Therapy Primer*. Edited by F. D. Stephenson).

Enright, J. B. "Awareness Training in the Mental Health Professions." In *Gestalt Therapy Now*. Edited by J. Fagan and I. L. Shepherd. Palo Alto, Calif.: Science and Behavior, 1970, 263-273.

Enright, J. B. "Gestalt Therapy in Interactive Groups." In *Gestalt Therapy Now*. Edited by J. Fagan and I. L. Shepherd. Springfield, Ill.: Charles C Thomas, 1975, 127-141.

Fagan, J. "The Tasks of the Therapist." In *Gestalt Therapy Now*. Edited by J. Fagan and I. L. Shepherd. Palo Alto, Calif.: Science and Behavior, 1970, 88-106.

Fagan, J. "Gestalt Techniques with a Woman with Expressive Difficulties." In *Gestalt Therapy Now*. Edited by J. Fagan and I. L. Shepherd. Palo Alto, Calif.: Science and Behavior, 1970, 1969-1993.

Fantz, R. "Fragments of Gestalt Theory." In *Gestalt Therapy Now*. Edited by J. Fagan and I. L. Shepherd. Springfield, Ill.: Charles C Thomas, 1975, 80-86.

Fantz, R. "Polarities: Differentiation and Integration." In *Gestalt Therapy Now*. Edited by J. Fagan and I. L. Shepherd. Springfield, Ill. Charles C Thomas, 1975, 87-96.

Greenwald, J. A. "The Art of Emotional Nourishment: Self-Induced Nourishment and Toxicity." In *Gestalt Therapy Now*. Edited by J. Fagan and I. L. Shepherd. Springfield, Ill.: Charles C Thomas, 1975, 113-126.

Hall, R. K. "My Life Measured Out in Abandoned Words." In *Gestalt Is*. Edited by J. O. Stevens. Moab, Utah: Real People Press, 1975, 201-222.

Havens, J. "Gestalt, Bioenergetics, and Encounter: New Wine Without Skins." In *Religious Systems and Psychotherapy*. Edited by R. H. Cox. Springfield, Ill.: Charles C Thomas, 1973, 268-283.

Joslyn, M. "Figure/Ground: Gestalt/Zen." In *Gestalt Is*. Edited by J. O. Stevens. Moab, Utah: Real People Press, 1975, 229-246.

Kempler, W. "Gestalt Therapy." In *Current Psychotherapies*. Edited by R. J. Corsini. Itasca, Ill.: F. E. Peacock, 1973, 251-286.

Kepner, E. and Brien, L. "Gestalt Therapy and Behavioristic Phenomenology." In *Gestalt Therapy Now*. Edited by J. Fagan and I. L. Shepherd. Palo Alto, Calif.: Science and Behavior, 1970, 39-46.

Lederman, J. "Anger and the Rocking Chair." In *Gestalt Therapy Now*. Edited by J. Fagan and I. L. Shepherd. Palo Alto, Calif.: Science and Behavior, 1970, 285-294.

Levitsky, A. and Perls, F. S. "The Rules and Games of Gestalt Therapy." In *Group Therapy Today: Styles, Methods and Techniques*. Edited by H. M. Ruitenbeek. New York: Atherton, 1969, 221-230 (also in *Gestalt Therapy Now*. Edited by J. Fagan and I. L. Shepherd, 140-149; *Contemporary Readings in Psychopathology*. Edited by G. Davidson and K. P. Price. New York: John Wiley, 1974, 271-277).

Levitsky, A. and Simkin, J. S. "Gestalt Therapy." In *New Perspectives on Encounter Groups*. Edited by L. N. Solomon and B. Berzon. San Francisco: Jossey-Bass, 1972, 245-254.

Marcus, E. H. "Gestalt Therapy." In *Current Psychiatric Therapies* (Vol. II). Edited by J. H. Masserman. New York: Grune & Stratton, 1971, 45-51.

Naranjo, C. "Contributions of Gestalt Therapy." In *Ways of Growth: Approaches to Expanding Awareness*. Edited by H. A. Otto and J. Mann. New York: Grossman, 1968 (Pocket Book, 1971, 135-154).

Naranjo, C. "Present-Centeredness in Gestalt Therapy." In *The Nature of Human Consciousness: A Book of Readings*. Edited by R. E. Ornstein. New York: Viking, 1974, 343-354 (also in *Gestalt Therapy Now*. Edited by J. Fagan and I. L. Shepherd).

Naranjo, C. "I and Thou, Here and Now: Contributions of Gestalt Therapy." In *Gestalt Therapy Now*. Edited by J. Fagan and I. L. Shepherd. Springfield, Ill. Charles C Thomas, 1975, 34-53.

Naranjo, C. "Present-Centeredness: Technique, Prescription, and Ideal." In *Gestalt Therapy Now*. Edited by J. Fagan and I. L. Shepherd. Palo Alto, Calif.: Science and Behavior, 1970, 47-69.

O'Connell, V. F. "Crisis Psychotherapy: Person Dialogue, and the Organismic Approach." In *Gestalt Therapy Now*. Edited by J. Fagan and I. L. Shepherd. Palo Alto, Calif.: Science and Behavior, 1970, 243-256.

Patterson, C. H. "Gestalt Therapy." *Theories of Counseling and Psychotherapy* (2nd ed.). New York: Harper & Row, 1973 (Ch. 15).

Perls, F. S. "Gestalt Therapy and Human Potentialities." In *Explorations in Human Potentialities*. Edited by H. A. Otto. Springfield, Ill.: Charles C Thomas, 1966 (also in *Gestalt Therapy Primer*. Edited by F. D. Stephenson, 1-7).

Perls, F. S. "Four lectures." In *Gestalt Therapy Now*. Edited by J. Fagan and I. L. Shepherd. Palo Alto, Calif.: Science and Behavior, 1970; 14-38.

Perls, F. S. "Dream Seminars." In *Gestalt Therapy Now*. Edited by J. Fagan and I. L. Shepherd. Palo Alto, Calif.: Science and Behavior, 1970, 204-233.

Perls, F. S. "Gestalt Therapy." In *Inside Psychotherapy*. Edited by A. Bray. New York: Basic Books, 1972, 57-70.

Perls, F. S. "Gestalt Therapy Verbatim." In *Human Development: Selected Readings*. Edited by M. L. Haimowitz and R. N. Haimowitz. New York: Thomas Y. Crowell, 1973, 426-442.

Perls, F. S. "Morality, Ego Boundary, and Aggression." In *Gestalt Is*. Edited by J. O. Stevens. Moab, Utah: Real People Press, 1975, 27-37.

Perls, F. S. "Resolution." In *Gestalt Is*. Edited by J. O. Stevens. Moab, Utah: Real People Press, 1975, 69-73.

Perls, F. S. and Goodman, P. "The Theory of The Removal of Inner Conflict." In *Gestalt Is*. Edited by J. O. Stevens. Moab, Utah: Real People Press, 1975, 39-43.

Perls, F. S., Hefferline, R. F., and Goodman, P. "Gestalt Therapy." In *Psychotherapy and Counseling Studies in Technique*. Edited by W. S. Sanakian. Chicago: Rand McNally, 1969, 520-553.

Perls, F. S. "One Gestalt Therapist's Approach." In *Gestalt Therapy Now*. Edited by J. Fagan and I. L. Shepherd. Palo Alto, Calif.: Science and Behavior, 1970, 125-129.

Polster, E. "Sensory Functioning in Psychotherapy." In *Gestalt Therapy Now*. Edited by J. Fagan and I. L. Shepherd. Palo Alto, California: Science and Behavior, 1970, 70-76.

Polster, E. "Stolen by Gypsies." In *Twelve Therapists*. Edited by A. Burton. San Francisco: Jossey-Bass, 1972, 143-161.

Polster, E. "Techniques and Experience in Gestalt Therapy." In *Gestalt Therapy Primer*. Edited by F. D. Stephenson. Springfield, Ill.: Charles C Thomas, 1975, 147-150.

Polster, E. "Trends in Gestalt Therapy." In *Gestalt Therapy Primer*. Edited by F. D. Stephenson. Springfield, Ill.: Charles C Thomas, 1975, 151-160.

Polster, M. "Women in Therapy—A Gestalt Therapist's View." *In Women in Therapy: New Perspectives for a Changing Society*. Edited by V. Franks and V. Burtle. New York: Brunner/Mazel, 1974, 247-262.

Rosanes-Berrett, M. B. "Gestalt Therapy as an Adjunct Treatment for Some Visual Problems." In *Gestalt Therapy Now*. Edited by J. Fagan and I. L. Shepherd. Palo Alto, Calif.: Science and Behavior, 1970, 257-262.

Rhyne, J. "The Gestalt Art Experience." In *Gestalt Therapy Now*. Edited by J. Fagan and I. L. Shepherd. Palo Alto, Calif., 1970, 274-284.

Shaffer, J. E., and Galinsky, M. D. "The Gestalt Therapy Workshop." In *Models of Group Therapy and Sensitivity Training*. Englewood Cliffs, N.J.: Prentice-Hall, 1974, (Ch. 7).

Shepherd, I. L. "Limitations and Cautions in the Gestalt Approach." In *Gestalt Therapy Now*. Edited by J. Fagan and I. L. Shepherd. Palo Alto, Calif.: Science and Behavior, 1970, 234-238.

Simkin, J. Mary. "A Session with a Passive Patient." In *Gestalt Therapy Now*. Edited by J. Fagan and I. L. Shepherd. Palo Alto, Calif.: Science and Behavior, 1970, 162-168.

Simkin, J. S. "The Use of Dreams in Gestalt Therapy." In *Progress in Group and Family Therapy*. Edited by C. J. Sager and H. S. Kaplan. New York: Brunner/Mazel, 1972, 95-104.

Simkin, J. S. "An Introduction to Gestalt Therapy." In *Direct Psychotherapy: 28 American Originals* (Vol. 1). Coral Gables, Fla.: University of Miami, 1973, 423-432 (also in *Gestalt Therapy Primer*. Edited by F. D. Stephenson. Springfield, Ill.: Charles C Thomas, 1975, 3-12).

Simkin, J. S. "Gestalt Therapy." In *Issues and Approaches in the Psychological Therapies*. London: John Wiley, 1975, 147-161.

Snyder, J. Jackie. "An Experience in Self-Applied Gestalt Therapy." In *Gestalt Therapy Primer*. Edited by F. D. Stephenson. Springfield, Ill.: Charles C Thomas, 1975, 97-112.

Stevens, B. "Body Work." In *Gestalt Is*. Edited by J. O. Stevens. Moab, Utah: Real People Press, 1975, 157-184.

Stevens, B. "Voids, Voids, Voids—Noddings!" In *Gestalt Is*. Edited by J. O. Stevens. Moab, Utah: Real People Press, 1975, 185-200.

Stevens, J. O. "Hypnosis, Intention, and Wake-fulness." In *Gestalt Is*. Edited by J. O. Stevens. Moab, Utah: Real People Press, 1975, 247-257.

Stevens. J. O. "Engagement and Attachment." In *Gestalt Is*. Edited by J. O. Stevens. Moab, Utah: Real People Press, 1975, 259-269.

Stevens, J. O. "Support and Balance." In *Gestalt Is*. Edited by J. O. Stevens. Moab, Utah: Real People Press, 1975, 271-274.

Van Dusen, W. "The Perspective of an Old Hand." In *Gestalt Is*. Edited by J. O. Stevens. Moab, Utah: Real People Press, 1975, 111-115.

Wallen, R. "Gestalt Therapy and Gestalt Psychology." In *Gestalt Therapy Now*. Edited by J. Fagan and I. L. Shepherd. Palo Alto, Calif.: Science and Behavior, 1970, 8-13.

Zinker, J. C. "On Loving Encounters: A Phenomenological View." In *Gestalt Therapy Primer*. Edited by F. D. Stephenson. Springfield, Ill.: Charles C Thomas, 1975, 54-72.

Journal Articles

Anderson, W. Fritz Perls revisited. *Human Behavior*, 2 (4) (1973): 16-23.

Beahrs, J. O. and Humiston, K. E. Dynamics of experiential therapy. *American Journal of Clinical Hypnosis*, 17 (1974): 1-14.

Binderman, R. M. The issue of responsibility in Gestalt therapy. *Psychotherapy: Theory, Research and Practice*, 11 (1974): 287-288.

Bricklin, B. A role-playing Rorschach procedure. *Journal of Personality Assessment*, 39 (1975): 453-461.

Brown, G. I. Awareness training and creativity based on Gestalt therapy. *Journal of Contemporary Psychotherapy*, 2 (1969): 25-32.

Brown, G. I. Teaching creativity to teachers and others. *Journal of Teacher Education*, 21 (1970): 210-216.

Brown, G. I. "Beyond" Gestalt therapy. *Journal of Contemporary Psychotherapy*, 5 (1973): 129-133.

Brown, M. The new body psychotherapies. *Psychotherapy: Theory, Research and Practice*, 10 (1973): 98-116.

Carmer, J. C. and Rouzer, D. L. Healthy functioning from the Gestalt perspective. *The Counseling Psychologist*, 4 (4) (1974): 20-23.

Denner, B. Deception, decision-making, and Gestalt therapy. *Journal of Consulting and Clinical Psychology*, 32 (1968): 527-531 (also in *Gestalt Therapy Now*. Edited by J. Fagan and I. L. Shepherd, 301-309.)

Dublin, J. E. Gestalting psychotic persons. *Psychotherapy: Theory, Research and Practice*, 10 (1973): 149-152.

Emerson, P. and Smith, E. W. L. Contributions of Gestalt psychology to Gestalt therapy. *The Counseling Psychologist*, 4 (4) (1974): 8-12.

Enright, J. B. Thou art that: projection and play in therapy and growth. *Psychotherapy: Theory, Research and Practice*, 9 (1972): 153-156 (also in *Gestalt Is*. Edited by J. O. Stevens, 149-155).

Fagan, J. and others. Critical incidents in the empty chair. *The Counseling Psychologist*, 4 (4) (1974): 33-42.

Fagan, J. Three sessions with Iris. *The Counseling Psychologist*, 4 (4) (1974): 42-59.

Finney, B. C. Say it again: an active therapy technique. *Psychotherapy: Theory, Research and Practice*, 9 (1972): 157-165.

Foulds, M. L. Measuring changes in self-actualization as a result of growth group experience. *Psychotherapy: Theory, Research, and Practice*, 8 (1971): 338-341.

Foulds, M. L. The experiential-Gestalt growth group experience. *Journal of College Student Personnel*, 13 (1972): 48-52 (also in *The Innovative Psychological Therapies: Critical and Creative Contributions*. Edited by R. M. Suinn and R. G. Weigel. New York: Harper & Row, 1975, 90-95.)

Greenwald, J. A. An introduction to the philosophy and techniques of Gestalt therapy. *Bulletin of Structural Integration*, 1 (3) (1969): 9-12.

Greenwald, J. A. Structural integration and Gestalt therapy. *Bulletin of Structural Integration*, 1 (3) (1969): 19-20.

Greenwald, J. A. The ground rules in Gestalt therapy. *Journal of Contemporary Psychotherapy*, 5 (1972): 3-12 (also in *Gestalt Therapy Primer*. Edited by F. D. Stephenson, 100-112).

Harman, R. L. Goals of Gestalt therapy. *Professional Psychology*, 5 (1974): 178-184.

Harman, R. L. Techniques of Gestalt therapy. *Professional Psychology*, 5 (1974): 257-263.

Horne, D. Response to Tubbs' "Beyond Perls." *Journal of Humanistic Psychology*, 14 (1974): 73-75.

Kempler, W. Experiential family therapy. *International Journal of Group Psychotherapy*, 15 (1965): 57-71 (also in *Recognitions in Gestalt Therapy*. Edited by P. D. Purseglove, 84-106; *Changing Families: A Family Therapy Reader*. Edited by J. Haley. New York: Grune & Stratton, 1971, 133-145).

Kempler, W. The moving finger writes. *Voices*, 2 (1) (1966): 166-172.

Kempler, W. The experiential therapeutic encounter. *Psychotherapy: Theory, Research and Practice*, 4 (1967): 166-172.

Kempler, W. Experiential psychotherapy with families. *Family Process*, 7 (1968): 88-89 (also in *Gestalt Therapy Now*. Edited by J. Fagan and I. L. Shepherd, 150-161).

Knight, W. A. Gestalt therapy and pastoral counseling. *Pastoral Counselor*, 5 (1) (1967): 16-21.

Lamper, N. The healing hands of Cowichan. *Psychotherapy: Theory, Research and Practice*, 8 (1971): 310-314.

Levin, L. S. and Shepherd, I. L. The role of the therapist in Gestalt therapy. *The Counseling Psychologist*, 4 (4) (1974): 27-30.

Lieberman, A. and Hoagland, A. J. Gestalt techniques and other new innovations for use in a family agency. *Professional Papers from the Desert: FACS*, July 1970, 52-56.

Mermin, D. The Gestalt theory of emotion. *The Counseling Psychologist*, 4 (4) (1974): 15-20.

Miller, R. and Bloomberg, L. Breaking through the process impasse. *Voices*, 4 (3) (1968): 33-36.

Nelson, W. M. III, and Gorman, W. D. Neurotic verbalizations: an exploration of a Gestalt therapy assumption. *Journal of Clinical Psychology* 31 (1975): 732-737.

O'Connell, V. F. Until the world becomes a human event. *Voices*, 3 (1967): 75-80.

Passons, W. R. Gestalt therapy interventions for group counseling. *Personnel and Guidance Journal*, 51 (1972): 183-189.

Perls, F. S. Theory and technique of personality integration. *American Journal of Psychotherapy*, 2 (1948): 565-586 (also in *Gestalt Is*. Edited by J. O. Stevens, 45-68).

Perls, F. S. Group vs. individual therapy. *ETC*, 24 (1967): 306-312 (also in *Gestalt Is*. Edited by J. O. Stevens, 9-15).

Perls, F. S., and Clements, C. C. Acting out vs. acting through. *Voices*, 4 (4) (1968): 66-73 (also in *Gestalt Is*. Edited by J. O. Stevens, 7-26).

Perls. L. Notes on the psychology of give and take. *Complex*, 9 (1953): 24-30 (also in *Recognitions in Gestalt Therapy*. Edited by P. D. Purseglove).

Perls, L. Two instances of Gestalt therapy. *Case Reports in Clinical Psychology*, Kings County Hospital, Brooklyn, N.Y., 1956 (also in *Recognitions in Gestalt Therapy*. Edited by P. D. Purseglove).

Polsky, H. W. Consider starting a well-being institute. *Social Work*, 18 (1973): 13-19.

Polster, E. A. A contemporary psychotherapy. *Psychotherapy: Theory, Research and Practice*, 3 (1966): 1-6 (also in *Recognitions in Gestalt Therapy*. Edited by P. D. Purseglove, 3-19).

Purinton, M.; Healy, J.; and Whitney, B. Layers of self—a group fantasy technique. *Psychotherapy: Theory, Research and Practice*, 11 (1974): 83-86.

Resnick, R. W. Chicken soup is poison. *Voices*, 6 (2) (1970): 75-78 (also in *Psychotherapy Bulletin*, 3 (2) (1970): 14-16; *Gestalt Therapy Primer*. Edited by F. D. Stephenson, 142-146).

Resnick, S. Gestalt therapy: the hot seat of personal responsibility. *Psychology Today*, 8 (6) (1974): 111-117.

Resnick, S. Gestalt therapy as a meditative practice. In *Gestalt Is*. Edited by J. O. Stevens. Moab, Utah: Real People Press, 1975, 223-228.

Rosen, S., and Kassan, M. Recent experiments with Gestalt encounter, and hypnotic techniques. *American Journal of Psychoanalysis*, 32 (1972): 90-105.

Rhyne, J. The Gestalt approach to experience, art, and art therapy. *American Journal of Art Therapy*, 12 (1973): 237-248).

Rhyne, J., and Vlich, M. A. Psychological growth and the use of art materials: small group experiments with adults. *Journal of Humanistic*

Psychology, 7 (1967): 163-170 (also in *Readings in Humanistic Psychology.* Edited by A. J. Sutich and M. A. Vlich. New York: Free Press, 1969, 336-346).

Roth, M. C. Why I like Gestalt therapy, as a hole. *Personnel and Guidance Journal,* 51 (1973): 336-339.

Smith, E. W. L. Altered states of consciousness in Gestalt therapy. *Journal of Contemporary Psychotherapy,* 7 (1975): 35-40.

Stewart, R. D. The philosophical background of Gestalt therapy. *The Counseling Psychologist,* 4 (4) (1974): 13-15.

Stone, A. A. Play: the "now" therapy. *Psychotherapy and Social Science Review,* 5 (2) (1971): 12-16.

Thorne, S. Translation of Gestalt theory into technique: polarities and centering. *The Counseling Psychologist,* 4 (4) (1974): 31-32.

Tobin, S. A. Self-support, wholeness, and Gestalt therapy. *Voices,* 5 (4) (1969): 5-12 (also in *Behavior Disorders.* Edited by O. Milton and R. G. Wahler. Philadelphia: J. B. Lippincott, 1973, 279-290; *Gestalt Is.* Edited by J. O. Stevens, 129-147).

Tobin, S. A. Saying goodbye in Gestalt therapy. *Psychotherapy: Theory, Research and Practice,* 8 (1971): 150-155 (also in *Gestalt Is.* Edited by J. O. Stevens, 117-128).

Tubbs, W. Beyond Perls. *Journal of Humanistic Psychology,* 12 (1972): 5.

Van Dusen, W. Wu wei, no-mind, and the fertile void. *Psychologia,* 1 (1958): 253-256 (also in *Gestalt Is.* Edited by J. O. Stevens, 87-94).

Van Dusen, W. Existential analytic psychotherapy. *American Journal of Psychoanalysis,* 20 (1960): 35-40 (also in *Recognitions in Gestalt Therapy.* Edited by P. D. Purseglove, 29-41).

Van Dusen, W. The phenomenology of a schizophrenic existence. *Journal of Individual Psychology,* 17 (1961): 80-92 (also in *Gestalt Is.* Edited by J. O. Stevens, 95-116).

Van Dusen, W. Invoking the actual in psychotherapy. *Journal of Individual Psychology,* 21 (1965): 66-76 (also in *Gestalt Is.* Edited by J. O. Stevens, 75-86).

Walker, A. R. The issue of "authenticity" for psychotherapists treating children and adolescents. Paper read at the 19th annual meeting of the American Academy of Child Psychiatry, New Orleans, La., October, 1972; reported in *Sandoz Psychiatric Reporter,* 8 (10) (1973): 18-20.

Ward, P. and Rouzer, D. L. The nature of pathological functioning from a Gestalt perspective. *The Counseling Psychologist,* 4 (4) (1974): 24-27.

Zinker, J. C. Note on the phenomenology of the loving encounter. *Explorations,* 10 (1966): 3-7.

Zinker, J. C., and Fink, S. L. The possibility for psychological growth in a dying person. *Journal of General Psychology,* 74 (1966): 185-189.

Zweben, J. E. and Hammann, K. Prescribed games: a theoretical perspective on the use of group techniques. *Psychotherapy: Theory, Research and Practice,* 2 (1970): 22-27.

Unpublished Papers

Bloomberg, L. and P. Bloomberg. "Using Intensive Groups for Developing Community." Gestalt Institute of San Francisco, 1968.

Blumenstein, S. "Sense and Non-sense: The New Gestalt." Georgia State University, 1969.

Gladstone, A. "The Put-down Society, or, How I Became a Middle-aged Drop-out." Gestalt Institute of San Francisco, 1969.

Foulds, M. L. "Ways of Growth: Approaches to Expanding Human Awareness." Bowling Green State University (paper read at American Psychological Association convention, 1974).

Greenwald, J. A. "An Introduction to the Philosophy and Techniques of Gestalt Therapy." 1029 Second Street, Santa Monica, Calif., n.d.

Greenwald, J. A. "The Art of Emotional Nourishment." 1029 Second Street, Santa Monica, Calif., 1969.

Greenwald, J. A. "The Art of Emotional Nourishment: Self-induced Nourishment and Toxicity." 1029 Second Street, Santa Monica, Calif., 1969.

Greenwald, J. A. "The Art of Emotional Nourishment: Organismic Flow and the 'Yes-No' Process." 1029 Second Street, Santa Monica, Calif., 1969.

Greenwald, J. A. "The Art of Emotional Nourishment: Self-induced Loneliness." 1029 Second Street, Santa Monica, Calif., 1970.

Grodner, B. "Gestalt Therapy: A Study Guide and Annotated Bibliography." Veterans Administration Hospital, Albuquerque, New Mexico, 1974.

Kepner, E. F. "Gestalt Training Methods as Consciousness-raising Tools." Gestalt Institute of Cleveland (paper read at American Psychological Association convention, 1974).

Miller, R. "A Note on Creative Withholding." Gestalt Institute for Multiple Psychotherapy, San Francisco, n.d.

Naranjo, C. "The Unfolding of Man." Research Note EPRC 66-47-3, Menlo Park, Calif.: Educational Policy Research Center, Stanford Research Institute, 1969.

Nevis, E. C. "Beyond Mental Health." Paper No. 2, Gestalt Institute of Cleveland, 1968.

Polster, E. "Techniques and Experiences in Gestalt Therapy." Paper No. 4, Gestalt Institute of Cleveland.

Polster, E. "Trends in Gestalt Therapy." Paper No. 11, Gestalt Institute of Cleveland.

Polster, E. "Structured Training Programs." Gestalt Institute of San Diego (paper read at American Psychological Association convention, 1974).

Resnick, R. "The Sorcerer's Apprentice and a School for Sorcerers." Gestalt Associates, Santa Monica, Calif. (paper read at American Psychological Association convention, 1974).

Shepherd, I. L. "Actualization of the Gestalt Approach in a Graduate Clinical Training Program." Georgia State University (paper read at American Psychological Association convention, 1974).

Sheldon, C. "Origins and Current Methods of Training in the Gestalt Institute of San Francisco." Gestalt Institute of San Francisco (paper read at American Psychological Association convention, 1974).

Simkin, J. S. "An Introduction to Gestalt Therapy." Paper No. 6, Gestalt Institute of Cleveland.

Tobin, S. A. "Philosophical Foundations of a Gestalt Therapist." Gestalt Therapy Center of San Fernando Valley, Encino, Calif., n.d.

Tobin, S. A. "Gestalt Therapy with Frustrating Patients." Gestalt Therapy Center of San Fernando Valley, Encino, Calif., 1972.

Films

Films, Incorporated, 1144 Wilmette Avenue, Wilmette, Ill. 60091:

What is Gestalt (24 min.)
Awareness (27 min.)
The Philosophy of the Obvious (25 min.)
Madeline's Dream (20 min.)
Memory and Pride (24 min.)
Marriage (25 min.)
The Gestalt Prayer (Couples) (24 min.)
Everything is Aware Process (28 min.)

The Media-Psych Corporation, P. O. Box 7707, San Diego, Calif. 92107.

Birth of a Composer (24 min.)
The Case of Mary Kay (15 min.)
The Death of Martha (40 min.)
Demon (14 min.)
Grief and Pseudo-Grief (33 min.)
The Impasse (22 min.)
The Mini-Satori (14 min.)
Resurrection (14 min.)
Relentless Greed and Obesity (16 min.)
Self-Sabotage (27 min.)
A Session With College Students (50 min.)
Stuttering (12 min.)

Psychological Films, Inc., 189 N. Wheeler Street, Orange, Calif. 92669.

Actualization Therapy: An Integration of Rogers, Perls and Ellis (27 min.)
James S. Simkin: In The Now (45 min.)
Frederick Perls: A Session With College Students (1 hr.)
Frederick Perls and Gestalt Therapy (Film 1, 39 min., Film 2, 36 min.)
Three Approaches to Psychotherapy: Rogers, Perls, Ellis (Perls Segment, 32 min.)

Tapes

American Academy of Psychotherapists A.A.P. Tape Library, 1040 Woodcock Road, Orlando, Fla. 32803:

Marjorie Creelman. "Elizabeth: Termination Dream" (#73, 2 hours)
Eric Marcus. "Introduction to Gestalt Approaches" (#82, 31 min.)
Frederick S. Perls. "Gestalt Therapy Seminar" (#16, 2 hours)
Eugene Sagan. "Gestalt Expressive Therapy" (#18, 44 min.)
James Simkin. "Individual Gestalt Therapy, Interview with Dr. Frederick Perls" (#31, 1 hour)
Harold Streitfeld. "The New Body Therapies" (#67, 1 hour)

Big Sur Recordings, 2015 Bridgeway, Sausalito, Calif. 94965.

Claudio Naranjo. "On Being Oneself Among Others" (#2520, 3 hours)
Claudio Naranjo. "Working Through Feelings of Disgust" (#2600, 1½ hours)
Fritz Perls. "Dream Theory and Demonstration" (2140, 1 hour)
Fritz Perls. "Fritz Perls Reads From 'In and Out of the Garbage Pail' " (#2300, 1 hour)
Fritz Perls. "Gestalt Therapy and How It Works" (#2910, 1 hour)
Fritz Perls. "Neurosis, Psychosis and Dreams" (#2310, 2 hours)
Fritz Perls. "The Perls Encounter" (#3060, 9 hours)
Fritz Perls. "Working With Dreams" (#3070, 4 hours)
James Simkin. "Gestalt Therapy: Lecture-Demonstration" (#4800, 1½ hours)

Gestalt Institutes

Gestalt institutes provide training for professionals, growth groups, and referral services. The following is not designed to be an exhaustive listing nor an endorsement of any program. Institutes are proliferating rapidly, and there is, as yet, no procedure for the evaluation of professional staff and program. The first four listed institutes provide the most extensive training available in Gestalt Therapy in the United States.

New York Institute for Gestalt Therapy, 7 West 96th Street, New York, New York 10025. The first Gestalt institute in America, begun by Fritz and Laura Perls, and Paul Goodman, now directed by Laura Perls. The New York Institute does not have a published curriculum.

Gestalt Institute of Cleveland, 12911 Euclid Avenue, Cleveland, Ohio 44112. This institute was established by Fritz Perls and some of his Cleveland students. Next to the New York Institute, Cleveland has the longest training history in the United States. This institute has the most comprehensive training, public service, workshop, and publications program.

Gestalt Therapy Institute of Los Angeles, 337 South Beverly Drive, Suite 206, Beverly Hills, California 90212. Fritz and a group of his students started this institute in the early 1960s. Like the Cleveland and San Francisco institutes, this group offers extensive training in Gestalt Therapy, with emphasis on didactic and experiential learning.

Gestalt Institute of San Francisco, 1719 Union Street, San Francisco, California 94123. Again, Fritz and a group of his students were responsible for beginning this institute in 1968. The training program consists of a two-year curriculum which also emphasizes personal therapy.

More recently, additional institutes have been established. These include:

Gestalt Training Center—San Diego
7255 Gerard Avenue
La Jolla, California 92037.

Gestalt Therapy Institute of Canada
Lake Cowichan
Box 39
Vancouver, British Columbia, Canada

Gestalt Institute of Chicago
c/o Bob Shapiro
Oasis Midwest Center for Human Potential
Chicago, Illinois

Gestalt Institute of the Southwest
7700 Alabama Street
El Paso, Texas 79904

Additionally, there are now Gestalt Institutes in Denver, Colorado, Miami, Florida, and Hawaii, for which complete addresses were not available.

Name Index

Subject Index